Contemporary Issues in International Law

Contemporary Issues in International Law

Phani Dascalopoulou-Livada

eleven
international publishing

Published, sold and distributed by Eleven International Publishing
P.O. Box 85576
2508 CG The Hague
The Netherlands
Tel.: +31 70 33 070 33
Fax: +31 70 33 070 30
e-mail: sales@elevenpub.nl
www.elevenpub.com

Sold and distributed in USA and Canada
Independent Publishers Group
814 N. Franklin Street
Chicago, IL 60610
USA
Order Placement: (800) 888-4741
Fax: (312) 337-5985
orders@ipgbook.com
www.ipgbook.com

Eleven International Publishing is an imprint of Boom uitgevers Den Haag.

ISBN 978-94-6236-947-4
ISBN 978-94-6274-510-0 (E-book)

For Christopher, Danaë and Max

Table of Contents

Foreword

The aim of this book is to provide the reader with overviews and at the same time with insights into four major contemporary issues of international law. These issues are: a) The Rise of International Criminal Law and the creation of the International Criminal Court; b) Human Rights Law and International Humanitarian Law in the Face of Terrorism; c) Aspects of International Law of the Sea; and d) Water in International Law, which are examined in four parts of the book.

It can of course be argued that these four issues do not represent a full list of 'contemporary' or 'major' issues of international law and that there are, perhaps, more 'topical' ones which are not being addressed. While these arguments are valid, there is also no doubt, at least in the writer's view, that these particular topics are at the core of any list of such major contemporary issues of international law, or, to put it in more practical terms, that they are certain to be of relevance with regard to many and various specific problems and questions arising on the international scene on an almost daily basis. These problems and questions are, in their turn, bound to be examined, analysed, commented upon and dealt with in Ministries of Foreign Affairs and their Legal Departments as well in International Organizations and international meetings and are going to preoccupy, more often than not with pressing urgency, anyone who deals with international law matters on a professional basis, such as diplomats, international lawyers and legal advisers. Students of international law may also benefit, the writer believes, from the succinct presentation of these issues, particularly since it is combined with extensive references and bibliography for further study.

A variety of angles is used to examine each one of the abovementioned issues. Their historical background and their development over time is one of them. This is particularly so in connection with Part I on 'The rise of International Criminal Law and the Creation of the International Criminal Court' where the precedents of the post-World War II Nuremberg and Tokyo Tribunals are laid out, as are those of the 1990s *ad hoc* Tribunals for the Former Yugoslavia and for Rwanda. Another angle is the exploration of real-life examples of the issues examined, such as, in Part IV on 'Water in International Law', the case of the Nile and of the Euphrates and Tigris Rivers, both emblematic of the kind of problems having to be faced and resolved by international water law. Similarly, in Part III on 'Aspects of International Law of the Sea', two of the most discussed disputes in recent years – concerning the East China Sea and the South China Sea islands respectively – are being reviewed. In all cases, jurisprudence is followed closely, while doctrinal theories, legal literature and other writings are also referred to and commented upon.

Finally, in all four parts, some conclusions are drawn, identifying, as the case may be, the points of concern and merit in each particular issue, as well as the possibility for solutions or the mitigation of difficulties.

Part I

The Rise of International Criminal Law and the Creation of the International Criminal Court

1 Present and Past[1]

1.1 From the 1990s Onwards

International criminal law has seen spectacular development since the early 1990s. The catalyst was the establishment of the two *ad hoc* Tribunals for the crimes committed in former Yugoslavia and in Rwanda, in 1993 and 1994 respectively. The creation of these tribunals emboldened those who believed in the idea of a global and effective international criminal justice system to revive the plan for the establishment of an international criminal court which had long been abandoned. Indeed, after the creation, at the end of World War II, of the Nuremberg and Tokyo tribunals which tried the German and Japanese perpetrators of the abhorrent crimes committed during the course of that war, it

---

1 On the International Criminal Court and on International Criminal Law generally, *see* Otto Triffterer (ed) *Commentary on the Rome Statute of the International Criminal Court: Observers' Notes*, Baden-Baden, 2nd edn., 1999 and 2008; Antonio Cassese, Paola Gaeta and John R.W.D. Jones (eds), *The Rome Statute of the International Criminal Court: A Commentary* (Oxford, 2002); Roy Lee *et al.* (eds), *The International Criminal Court – The making of the Rome Statute: Issues, Negotiations, Results*, the Hague, 1999; Roy Lee *et al.* (eds), *International Criminal Court – Elements of Crimes and Rules of Procedure and Evidence*, N. York, 2001; William A. Schabas, *The International Criminal Court, A Commentary on the Rome Statute*, Oxford Commentaries on International Law, 2010; William A. Schabas, *An Introduction to the International Criminal Court*, Cambridge University Press, 5th edn., 2016; Cherif Bassiouni (ed), *International Criminal Law*, 2nd edn., New York, 1999; Robert Cryer, Häkan Friman, Darryl Robinson, Elizabeth Wilmshurst, *An Introduction to International Criminal law and Procedure*, 3rd edn., 2014; Gerhard Werle, *Principles of International Criminal Law*, 2nd edn., 2009 and 3rd edn. by Gerhard Werle and Florian Jessberger, 2014; Bruce Broomhall, *International Justice and the International Criminal Court: Between Sovereignty and the Rule of Law*, Oxford, 2003; St. Perrakis (ed), *International Criminal Court, A New Dimension in International Justice, Questions and Prospects for a New Humanitarian Order*, Proceedings of the Santorini Colloquium, 2002; Ramesh Thakur & Peter Malcontent (eds), *From Sovereign Impunity to International Accountability, The Search of Justice in a World of States*, United Nations University, 2004; Antonio Cassese, *International Criminal Law*, Oxford, 2003; Kriangsak Kittichaisaree, *International Criminal Law*, Oxford 2001; Roberto Belleli, (ed), *International Criminal Justice, Law and Practice from the Rome Statute to its Review*, 2010; Philippe Sands, *From Nuremberg to the Hague: The Future of International Criminal Justice*, Cambridge, 2003; Leila Sadat, *The International Criminal Court and the Transformation of International Law*, New York, 2002; Antonio Cassese, Guido Acquaviva, Mary Fan, and Alex Whiting, *International Criminal Law, Cases and Commentary*, Oxford, 2011; Herman A.M. von Hebel, Johan G. Lammers, Jolien Schukking, *Reflections on the International Criminal Court*, T.M.C. Asser Press, The Hague, 1999; Carsten Stahn (ed), *The Law and Practice of the International Criminal Court*, Oxford University Press, 2014; Gideon Boas & Pascale Chifflet, *International Criminal Justice, Principles of International Law Series*, Edward Elgar Publishing, 2017; Philipp Castner (ed), *International Criminal Law in Context*, Routledge, 2018; Phani Dascalopoulou-Livada, *International Criminal Court, From Nuremberg to the Hague*, Athens, Nomiki Vivliothiki, 2013 (in Greek); Roger O'Keefe, *International Criminal Law*, Oxford University Press, 2016; Sarah Babaian, *The International Criminal Court – An International Criminal World Court?* Springer, 2018; Hervé Ascensio, Emmanuel Decaux, Alain Pellet (eds), *Droit International Pénal*, Pedone, 2018; Julian Fernandez, Xavier Pacreau, Lola Maze (eds), *Statut de Rome de la Cour pénale internationale: commentaire article par article*, Pedone, two vols., 2012.

would have been logical to expect the establishment of a permanent court to prosecute and punish the perpetrators of grave international crimes. The permanent character of such a court would have also responded to the criticism that the Nuremberg and Tokyo tribunals had been applying 'victor's justice'.

In fact, the U.N. General Assembly (UNGA, GA) had invited, in 1951, the International Law Commission (ILC), to study

> the desirability and possibility of establishing an international judicial organ for the trial of persons charged with genocide or other crimes over which jurisdiction will be conferred upon that organ by international conventions.[2]

Although the Commission expressed the opinion that this was indeed desirable and possible and some steps were taken to pursue the matter further,[3] the ensuing cold war which prevailed between the two superpowers and their respective allies for more than four decades, prevented progress on this question – like on so many other – which, as a consequence, remained in deep hypnosis during that time.

It took the sweeping changes in the Soviet Union and in the Eastern bloc in the early 1990s and the radically different political climate thereafter, to bring the matter of international criminal justice to the fore again. This new environment became clearly visible with the establishment of the two *ad hoc* criminal tribunals for the former Yugoslavia[4] and for Rwanda[5] mentioned above.

As a result of this development, the idea for a permanent Criminal Court was invigorated. It was made clear, first of all, that creating such an institution was possible. If indeed it had been feasible to muster the political will required to create the *ad hoc* tribunals, it should also be possible to find such a will in order to establish a court which would try similar crimes at all times and, hopefully, wherever they were committed. A permanent court would secure legal certainty and uniformity, considerations of paramount importance for the establishment of a sense of international criminal justice working equally for all.

Within this atmosphere and with these considerations in mind, the G.A. requested the ILC in 1992 to draw up the draft Statute for an International Criminal Court,[6] a task which the Commission finalized, with remarkable celerity, in 1994.[7]

---

2 Resolution 260 B (III) of 9 December 1948.

3 *See Summaries of the Work of the International Law Commission, Question of International Criminal Jurisdiction*, available at: http://legal.un.org/ilc/summaries/7_2.shtml, last accessed on 2 April 2018.

4 S/RES 827(1993) of 25 May 1993.

5 S/RES 955(1994) of 8 November 1994.

6 A/RES/47/33 of 25 November 1992.

7 ILC Final Draft Statute, Report of the International Law Commission on the work of its forty-sixth session, 2 May-22 July 1994, *Official Records of the General Assembly, Forty-ninth session, Supplement No. 10* A/49/10 and *Yearbook of the International Law Commission 1994*, Vol. II, Part II.

An originally *ad hoc* and then Preparatory Committee was then mandated by the G.A. to negotiate, on the basis of the ILC text, a draft Statute which could gather the support of the largest possible number of states, with a view to its ultimate submission to an International Conference for consideration and, possibly, adoption. The Committee did so in successive meetings held in the course of almost four years and the product of its work formed the text which would be subsequently submitted to the Conference as its basic working document.[8]

Once the Preparatory Commission had concluded its task, the Conference was convened in Rome in 1998.[9] The negotiations, although difficult, were brought to a successful conclusion with the adoption of the Statute by a vote in which 120 states voted in its favour, 21 abstained and 7 voted against.[10]

Just four years later, the sixty ratifications required for the entry of the Statute into force had been assembled, and the International Criminal Court was constituted in 1 July 2002.[11]

1.2 Historical Notes

Traces of ideas or even action for the establishment of institutions which could be considered as forerunners of 'an international criminal court' can be located at various times and places. Among those of the past century, it is worth mentioning the Versailles Peace Treaty of 1919 which, following the recommendations of the fifteen-member Commission on 'Responsibilities and Penalties'[12] provided for the punishment of war criminals, including *Kaiser Wilhelm II* of the Hohenzollern, who was to be surrendered by the German *Reich* to the military tribunals of the Allied Powers.[13] However, these provisions were never applied.[14]

8 A/CONF.183/2/Add.1, 14 April 1998.

9 From 15 June to 17 July 1998.

10 Among the latter, the U.S., Israel and China. The vote was not officially registered by country (roll call). As a consequence, the vote of each particular country cannot be absolutely certain unless it made a statement in the Plenary following the vote (the three states mentioned here did make such a statement confirming that they cast a negative vote).

11 For an historical survey of the efforts to establish an International Criminal Court from 1919 onwards, *see* M. Cherif Bassiouni, Historical Survey: 1919–1998, in The Statute of the International Criminal Court: A Documentary History (compiled by M. Cherif Bassiouni, 1999).

12 The "Commission on the Responsibility of the Authors of the War and on Enforcement of Penalties" ("*Commission des Responsabilités des Auteurs de la Guerre et Sanctions*") also known as Peace Conference Commission or 1919 Commission, was tasked to investigate the responsibility for the initiation of World War I and the crimes connected to it, and to indicate a competent court to try those accused of them (*See* Report of the Commission to the Preliminary Conference of 29.3. March 1919, reproduced in 14 AJIL (1920) 95).

13 Art. 227.

14 *See infra*, 4.2.3.2 an 4.2.5.2.

Undoubtedly, the precedents which were of direct and particular relevance for the development of international criminal law as well as for the establishment of international criminal tribunals after 1990, were the Nuremberg and Tokyo tribunals which were set up after World War II and the trials conducted by them.

1.2.1 The International Military Tribunal at Nuremberg (IMT)

The Nuremberg Tribunal was established by agreement between the four victorious powers of World War II (U.S., France, U.K. and the USSR) to prosecute and punish the major war criminals of the European Axis (London Agreement of 8 August 1945),[15] which was ratified by another nineteen countries.[16] Attached to the Agreement was the Charter of the International Military Tribunal (London or Nuremberg Charter) on the basis of which the trial was conducted in the city of Nürnberg (Nuremberg) in Bavaria, Germany.

The decision to punish the perpetrators of crimes committed during the war had, however, been articulated earlier, in the Moscow Declaration of 30 October 1943 which contained a 'Statement on atrocities' signed by U.S. President *Franklin D. Roosevelt*, British Prime Minister *Winston Churchill* and Soviet Union Premier *Josef Stalin*. In the Declaration, these Powers pledged that when the war would be over, those responsible for war crimes would be sent back to the countries where they had committed them to be tried according to the laws of these countries, while those 'whose offenses have no particular geographical localization will be punished by joint decision of the governments of the Allies'.

The Nuremberg trial opened on 20 November 1945, little more than six months after the surrender of Germany. The Tribunal consisted of eight judges, four main and four alternate, who were appointed by the four core allied countries. The President of the Court was the British Lord Justice *Geoffrey Lawrence* and Chief Prosecutor the American *Robert Jackson*.

The Tribunal indicted[17] twenty-four persons[18] who represented the political, military, diplomatic and economic leadership of Nazi Germany.[19] However, only twenty-one were to stand trial, since the industrialist *Gustav Krupp* was found unfit for that purpose, *Martin Bormann*, Secretary of the Nazi Party, was tried and convicted *in absentia* and

15 82 UNTS 279, 59 Stat. 1544, and the Annexed Charter of the International Military Tribunal.

16 Australia, Belgium, Czechoslovakia, Denmark, Ethiopia, Greece, Haiti, Honduras, India, Luxembourg, Netherlands, New Zealand, Norway, Panama, Paraguay, Poland, Uruguay, Venezuela, Yugoslavia.

17 The Indictment was submitted to the Tribunal on 10 October 1945.

18 *See infra*, fns. 26-29.

19 *Adolf Hitler, Heinrich Himmler* and *Joseph Goebbels* had already committed suicide and the IMT decided not to try them posthumously.

Robert Ley, Head of the German Labour Front, committed suicide before the trial started. Six organizations were also indicted.[20]

The charges were: a) common plan or conspiracy to commit crimes against peace, war crimes and crimes against humanity; b) planning, preparation, initiation and waging of wars of aggression, which were also wars in violation of international treaties, agreements and assurances[21]; c) war crimes as defined in Article 6(b) of the Charter[22]; and d) crimes against humanity as defined in Article 6(c) of the Charter.[23]

It may seem surprising that genocide did not appear in the list of crimes under the jurisdiction of the IMT, as the crimes of Germany, particularly against the Jews, would undoubtedly be considered as genocide today; however, genocide was practically unknown as a legal notion at the time and in any event the crimes concerned were covered by the notion of crimes against humanity, which were already a novelty adopted by the IMT Statute.[24]

The rules of procedure were an amalgam of Anglo-American common law and continental European civil law rules, the former being preponderant.

The trial lasted ten months. The judgment, issued on 1 October 1946,[25] sentenced twelve of the twenty-four indicted persons to death,[26] three to life imprisonment,[27] four

---

20 These were: a) The Reich Cabinet (*Die Reichsregierung*); b) The Leadership Corps of the Nazi Party (*Des Korps der Politischen Leiter der Nationalsozialistischen Deutschen Arbeiterpartei*); c) The Elite Guard-SS (*Die Schutzstaffeln der Nationalsozialistische Deutsche Arbeiterpartei*), including the Security Service-SD (*Sicherheitsdienst*); d)The Secret State Police (*Die Geheime Staatspolizei* – known as the *Gestapo*); e) The Stormtroopers (*Die Sturmabteilungen der Nationalsozialistischen Deutschen Arbeiterpartei* – known as the SA); and f) The General Staff and High Command of the German *Wehrmacht* (the German armed forces of the years prior to and during World War II).

21 "Initiation of invasions of other countries and wars of aggression in violation of international laws and treaties, including but not limited to planning, preparation, initiation or waging a war of aggression, or a war in violation of international treaties, agreements, or assurances, or participation in a common plan or conspiracy for the accomplishment of any of the foregoing."

22 "Namely, violations of the laws or customs of war. Such violations shall include, but not be limited to, murder, ill-treatment or deportation to slave labour or for any other purpose of civilian population of or in occupied territory, murder or ill-treatment of prisoners of war or persons on the seas, killing of hostages, plunder of public or private property, wanton destruction of cities, towns or villages, or devastation not justified by military necessity."

23 "Murder, extermination, enslavement, deportation, and other inhumane acts committed against any civilian population, before or during the war; or persecutions on political, racial or religious grounds in execution of or – in connection with any crime within the jurisdiction of the Tribunal, whether or not in violation of the domestic law of the country where perpetrated."

24 *See infra*, section 1.2.5.

25 *See* "Trial of the Major War Criminals, before the International Military Tribunal, Nuremberg, 14 November 1945-1 October 1946," Published at Nuremberg, Germany, 1947, Vol. 1, "in accordance with the direction of the International Military Tribunal by the Secretariat of the Tribunal, under the jurisdiction of the Allied Control Authority for Germany," Official text in the English language. Judgment on pp. 171-341.

26 *Martin Bormann, Hans Frank, Wilhelm Frick, Hermann Göring, Alfred Jodl, Ernst Kaltenbrunner, Wilhelm Keitel, Joachim von Ribbentrop, Alfred Rosenberg, Fritz Sauckel, Arthur Seyss-Inquart and Julius Streicher.*

27 *Walther Funk, Rudolf Hess and Erich Raeder. Hermann Göring* committed suicide while awaiting his execution.

to shorter sentences,[28] while three were acquitted.[29] Four of the indicted organizations were found to be criminal.[30]

1.2.2 Subsequent Nuremberg Trials[31]

Despite the successful conclusion of the trial of major war criminals, no further trial was conducted by the IMT, due to mounting tensions between the Allies, particularly between the U.S. and the Soviet Union. As a result, the trials that followed were held under the authority of Allied Control Council Law No. 10 issued on 20 December 1945[32] in order to allow the prosecution, on the basis of uniform rules, of criminals other than those referred to the IMT. National military tribunals were thus established by the Americans, the French, the British and the Soviets in their respective Zones in occupied Germany. The crimes under Law No. 10 were: a) crimes against peace; b) war crimes; c) crimes against humanity; and d) membership in categories of criminal group or organization which were declared criminal by the IMT.[33]

On the basis of Law No. 10 and Ordinance No. 7, the Americans carried out twelve trials in Nuremberg between October 1946 and April 1949 (subsequent Nuremberg trials).[34] The defendants in those proceedings were high-ranking members of the Hitlerite regime, such as diplomats, politicians,[35] cabinet ministers, military leaders,[36] SS leaders,[37] as well as industrialists[38] and distinguished doctors. The judges were American as was the Chief Prosecutor, Brigadier General *Telford Taylor*.[39]

Although less known than the Nuremberg trial of major war criminals, these trials were from a legal point of view of equal if not of more significance than the former, marking a most important milestone in the development of contemporary international

28 *Karl Dönitz, Konstantin von Neurath, Baldur von Schirach* and *Albert Speer.*

29 *Hans Fritzsche, Franz von Papen* and *Dr. Hjalmar Schacht.*

30 The leadership Corps of the Nazi Party, the Gestapo and SD, and the SS.

31 Kim C. Priemel & Alexa Stiller (eds), *Unearthing the Subsequent Nuremberg Trials. Transitional Justice, Trial Narratives, and Historiography*, 2012.

32 Control Council Law No. 10, Punishment of Persons Guilty of War Crimes, Crimes Against Peace and Against Humanity, December 20, 1945, 3 Official Gazette Control Council for Germany 50-55 (1946).

33 Crimes against humanity under Law No. 10 included, apart from the crimes against humanity under the Nuremberg Charter, those of imprisonment, torture and rape.

34 These were: The *Ministries Case*, the *High Command Case,* the *Doctors' Case* (it concerned mainly the medical 'experiments' conducted by the Nazis on prisoners), the *Judges' Case*, the *Milch Case*, the *Hostages' Case*, the *Pohl Case*, the *Flick Case*, the *IG Farben Case, the RuSHA, Case*, the *Einsatzgruppen Case* and the *Krupp Case.*

35 Such as the State Secretary of the Foreign Office *von Weizsaecker*, and cabinet ministers *von Krosigk and Lammers.*

36 Such as Field Marshals *von Leeb, List*, and *von Kuechler.*

37 Such as *Ohlendorf, Pohl, and Hildebrandt.*

38 Such as *Flick, Alfried Krupp*, and the directors of *IG Farben.*

39 In all, prosecution was exercised against 182 persons.

criminal law. Especially noteworthy among them were the *IG Farben, Einsatzgruppen* and *Krupp* trials.

The Americans also held trials elsewhere in Germany, as did the British, the French and the Soviets. Such trials were also carried out in Austria and Italy. National trials of German war criminals and their collaborators in occupied countries were, furthermore, conducted in many countries.[40]

1.2.3 *The International Military Tribunal for the Far East (IMTFE) - Tokyo Military Tribunal*

In the Potsdam Declaration of 26 July 1945, the Allies who had fought in the war against Japan stated that the punishment of the Japanese war criminals was among the terms for the acceptance of the surrender of Japan. The term was accepted in Japan's Document of Surrender of 2 September 1945. Following these events, the Tokyo Tribunal was created on 19 January 1946 by Special Proclamation of the American General *Douglas MacArthur*, Supreme Allied Commander in the Southeastern Pacific Area.[41] General *MacArthur* also approved the Charter (Statute) of the Tokyo Tribunal attached to the Declaration.

The jurisdiction of the IMTFE under the Statute included a) crimes against peace; b) conventional war crimes; and c) crimes against humanity.[42]

The Tribunal was composed of eleven judges, and its judgment was issued in November 1948.[43]

Six of the accused were sentenced to death[44] and sixteen to life imprisonment.[45] Shorter sentences were imposed on two.[46]

40 The most well-known was that of *Adolf Eichmann* which was held in Jerusalem in 1961. *Eichmann* was the principal organizer of the expulsion of the Jews of Europe, and he was transferred to Israel following a spectacular abduction operation in Argentina where *Eichmann* lived, by the Israeli *Mossad* (*Eichmann*, Israel, District Court of Jerusalem, Judgment of 12 December 1961, Translation into English in 36 ILR 5-276; Also, *Eichmann*, Israel, Supreme Court, Judgment of 29 May 1962, Translation into English in 36 ILR, 277-342).

41 Special Proclamation, Establishment of an International Military Tribunal for the Far East, 19 January 1946, TIAS No. 1589, 3.

42 Art. 5, first para.

43 4 November-12 November 1948.

44 *Dohihara, Hirota, Itagaki, Kimura, Muto, Tojo.*

45 *Araki, Hashimoto, Hata, Hiranuma, Hoshino, Kaya, Kido, Koiso, Minami, Oka, Oshima, Sato, Shimada, Shiratori, Suzuki, Umezu.*

46 *Togo* and *Shigemitsu.*

Trials of Japanese war criminals were also conducted by the U.S., U.K., the Netherlands, Australia, the Philippines and China. Most widely known trials are those of General *Tomoyuki Yamashita*[47] before the U.S. Supreme Court, and of Admiral *Soemu Toyoda* before a mixed Allied Court.[48]

1.2.4 *Effect of the Cold War*

Very soon after the end of the war, however, the emergence of the cold war and the fierce military antagonism between the U.S. and the Soviet Union took a heavy toll on the efforts to restore justice for the atrocities committed during World War II. The new political situation, already exemplified by the Korean War, imposed the need for a speedy normalization of relations with both, Germany and Japan. In that context, *John J. McCloy*, American former Deputy Minister of Defence and High Commissioner of the U.S. in Germany in 1949, promoted the so-called Clemency Act of January 1951, by which many of the sentences imposed on convicted war criminals were commuted to more lenient ones. By 1958, almost all convicted Nazis had been released from prison.[49] In Japan, from the sixteen sentenced to life imprisonment by the Tokyo Tribunal, thirteen were released between 1954 and 1956[50] with the consent of the Americans whose priorities had now changed due to the cold war. Indeed, they now believed that their release would be conducive to political stability in Japan.

1.2.5 *Legacy of the MIT and the IMTFE*

Two major advancements were brought to international criminal law by these post-war Tribunals. The first was the internationalization of grave crimes (such as those provided for in their Statutes) which up to then belonged to the exclusive jurisdiction of national courts. The second was the recognition of the international responsibility of individuals for crimes which until then were considered as 'acts of a state' to which no individual criminal responsibility was attached (a remnant of the perception that waging war was a right afforded to a sovereign). The Nuremberg judgment put this new legal reality in very

---

47 *Yamashita v. Styer*, U.S. Supreme Court, 317 U.S. 1; 66 S 340, Judgment, 4 February 1946. *Tomoyuki Yamashita*, Commanding General of the Japanese Army in the Philippines, surrendered in 1945 to the U.S. Army in the Philippines. He was then tried by a U.S. Military Commission in Manila and sentenced to death for the atrocities committed by Japanese Army members during the Japanese occupation of the Philippines. *Yamashita* finally addressed to the U.S. Supreme Court a petition for *habeas corpus*. The Supreme Court confirmed his conviction and *Yamashita* was executed by hanging.

48 *US v. Toyoda*, War Crimes Tribunal Courthouse, Tokyo, Japan, 6 September 1949, 161-162. *Toyoda* was acquitted.

49 Kevin Jon Heller, *The Nuremberg Military Tribunals and the Origins of International Criminal Law*, Oxford, 2011, pp. 345 *et seq.*

50 The remaining three had already died in prison.

clear terms: "Crimes against international law are committed by men, not by abstract entities, and only by punishing individuals who commit such crimes can the provisions of international law be enforced."[51]

On the other hand, the Nuremberg and, even more so, the Tokyo tribunal, were criticized for having rendered 'victor's justice', i.e. that the law they applied was biased and tailored to their own wishes and objectives as winners of the war. The critics pointed out, for example, that no German and no Japanese judge sat at the bench of the Nuremberg and the Tokyo Tribunal respectively, and that there had been several procedural defects, such as extensive reliance on affidavit evidence.[52] However, the most important substantive defect that has been consistently put forward is the non-respect of the legality principle, as encapsulated in the maxim '*nullum crimen nulla poena sine lege*'. This was particularly true in connection with crimes against humanity and crimes against peace which were new categories of crimes. By contrast, war crimes, as identified in the 1907 Hague Convention and its Regulations[53] as well as in the 1929 Geneva Convention,[54] had been, by 1939, "recognized by all civilized nations and were regarded as being declaratory of the laws and customs of war."[55] Violations of these provisions could therefore be qualified as war crimes entailing individual criminal responsibility, while the Nuremberg Charter did not constitute, with regard to them, new law which ran contrary to the *nullum crimen* principle.[56]

Crimes against humanity, on the other hand, were introduced to fill an existing legal gap deriving from the fact that a great number of Nazi crimes could not be qualified as war crimes because they were committed against German nationals, i.e. mainly the Jews. As such, crimes against humanity could hardly be considered as punishable under pre-existing law. It was in fact on this point that the question concerning the ambit of the *nullum crimen* maxim acquired its real dimensions, i.e. whether it was to be construed in terms of strict law, in other words that it should be contained in a formal legal rule prohibiting the particular conduct or in terms of a more 'loose' rule, such as a 'legal principle' or a 'principle of justice'. The IMT followed the latter course, accepting that it was sufficient that the perpetrators of heinous crimes were aware of the wrongfulness of

51 IMT at Nuremberg, Case of the Major War Criminals, Judgment, *supra*, section 1.2.1, fn. 25, p. 223.

52 Cryer, Hakan Friman *et al.*, *op. cit.*, p. 95. *See also* p. 96 and pp. 99-100.

53 Hague Convention (IV) Respecting the Laws and Customs of War on Land and its annex: Regulations concerning the Laws and Customs of War on Land, 18 October 1907.

54 Convention relative to the Treatment of Prisoners of War, Geneva, 27 July 1929.

55 IMT Judgment, (*supra*, fn. 25), p. 254.

56 On this issue from a contemporary judicial perspective, *see* the EctHR Grand Chamber Judgment in *Kononov v. Latvia*, (Application No. 36376/04) of 17 May 2010 which found that war crimes were recognized as such by international law prior to the Nuremberg Charter (*i.e.* in 1944 when the crimes at issue were committed).

their actions.[57] Today this problem has been resolved, as international criminal law has already elevated crimes against humanity to the highest rank of criminal offences with an international character; at the time, however, it would perhaps have been excessive to require a stronger link between the criminal conduct concerned and the then existing legal rules, in the face of the indisputably egregious character of these crimes and the risk of letting them go unpunished.

For the crime of aggression, the IMT invoked the 1929 *Kellog-Briand* Pact – to which Germany was a party – as proof that aggression was already recognized as a crime when it was included as such in the London Charter. Again, the impact of aggression, which was at the root of all the evils brought about by World War II could not, reasonably, have been ignored because of lack of express international criminal law rules regarding its recognition or punishment as an international crime, although this continues to be a controversial matter.[58]

On the other hand, post-war international criminal justice was not completely rid of bias insofar as the Allies, although the primary victims of the crimes committed in the war, they had themselves committed grave crimes in its final phase, such as the bombardment of Dresden and Hamburg and the use of the atomic bomb on Hiroshima and Nagasaki, for which they were never called to justice.[59] Allegedly, this is the reason why certain German crimes went, correspondingly, unpunished or were punished with rather lenient sentences.[60] Indicative of selectivity and political expediency was also the fact that the Japanese royal family remained immune to the allied justice, while its involvement in the planning of the war was not in doubt. Even more, thanks to the American intervention, Emperor Hirohito retained his position.[61]

Despite their flaws, it is undeniable that the Nuremberg and Tokyo trials had a catalytic effect on the development of international criminal law and on its perception by the international community. Indeed, in a huge stride, these trials transformed international criminal justice from an opaque idea entangled in legal complexity to a palpably clear reality emerging out of the ruins of war. At the same time, they created a solid precedent

57 Its statements have not always been entirely unambiguous, however, as it has stated both, that the Charter '*is the expression of international law existing at the time of its creation,*' (IMT Judgment, *supra,* fn. 25, p. 218, and that *nullum crimen* was a '*principle of justice*' that was satisfied merely because the defendants knew that what that they were doing was wrong – *Ibid.*, p. 219.

58 *See, e.g.*, Christian Tomuschat, "The Legacy of Nuremberg," 4 *J. Int'l Crim. Just.* 830 (2006), p. 833.

59 In an extreme expression of his belief in the Allied one-sidedness in this respect, IMTFE Judge *Pal* of India claimed, in his dissenting opinion, that the actions of Japan were but a reaction to Western provocation and that the trial was unfair because of the colonialist character of the countries which conducted the prosecution and their use of the atom bomb on Hiroshima and Nagasaki.

60 *See* Cryer, Hakan Friman *et al., op. cit.,* p. 96, where are mentioned as examples of the non-exercise of prosecution against Germany for the air raids on London and other Nazi crimes, in order to avoid opening the question of the British air raids on Germany and of similar conduct of other allies elsewhere (*e.g.*, by the Soviet Union in Poland and Germany).

61 *See* Herbert P. Bix, *Hirohito and the Making of Modern Japan*, Harper Collins, 2009.

for later time, when circumstances would be ripe for its use; this happened four decades later.

2 The Ad Hoc Tribunals for the Crimes Committed in Former Yugoslavia and in Rwanda[1]

As already noted, the end of the cold war in the beginning of the 1990s liberated many ideas which had been imprisoned within the constrictions and inertia of that war, among which the idea for a functional international criminal justice system such as that which had been successfully tested almost half a century earlier in the Nuremberg and Tokyo trials. It was that radically new climate which allowed the establishment, by Resolutions taken by the S.C. on the basis of Chapter VII, in 1993 and 1994 respectively, of the two *ad hoc* Tribunals for the crimes committed in the former Yugoslavia and in Rwanda during the armed conflicts that took place there.[2]

2.1 The International Criminal Tribunal for Former Yugoslavia (ICTY)

The war in Yugoslavia during the 1990s[3] had a devastating effect on a large part of the population, particularly in Bosnia, where the atrocities committed, culminating in the Srebrenica (Сребреница) massacre in July 1995, had not been experienced in the European continent since World War II. In the spring of 1992, the Security Council issued Resolution 757[4] which imposed severe sanctions against the FRY[5] (Serbia and Montenegro). Further deterioration of the situation led to the adoption of Resolution 808 (1993)[6] which announced the establishment of the Tribunal as a subsidiary organ of the S.C. under Chapter VII of the U.N. Charter and then of Resolution 827 (1993) by which the Statute of the *ad hoc* Tribunal for the crimes committed in the former Yugoslavia was

1 *See* Guénaël Mettraux, *International Crimes and the Ad Hoc Tribunals*, Oxford University Press, 2005; Stuart Ford, *The Impact of the Ad Hoc Tribunals on the International Criminal Court*, 2018, available at: SSRN-id3128531.pdf, last accessed 6 April 2018.

2 *See* United Nations, International Criminal Tribunal for the Former Yugoslavia, 1993-2017; United Nations, Legacy website of the International Criminal Tribunal for Rwanda.

3 1992-1995 (War in Bosnia) and 1995-1999 (War in Kosovo).

4 On 30 May 1992, following Resolutions 713(1991) of 25 September 1991 and 724 (1991) of 15 December 1991.

5 Federal Republic of Yugoslavia.

6 S/RES/808 of 22 February 1993.

adopted,[7] despite certain doubts expressed at the time regarding the legality of such action being taken by the Security Council.[8]

The question of legality was later put before the tribunal itself in the *Tadić Case* trial and, rather predictably, the tribunal found that the establishment of ICTY had been lawful.[9] Despite such initial doubts, however, it has been generally recognized that ICTY, just like ICTR, the other *ad hoc* Tribunal set up by the S.C.,[10] produced a *corpus* of jurisprudence of undeniable value for the development of international criminal law.[11]

Indeed, prior to the establishment of the *ad hoc* Tribunals, the application of international humanitarian law had not been tested judicially, as there had been no specific international judicial mechanism to do so since World War II. When, however, the *ad hoc* Tribunals were created for that purpose, they found themselves in a very different position from that which had confronted those of Nuremberg and Tokyo. In fact, the latter had to apply legal rules which left numerous gaps in a less than coherent whole, while the *ad hoc* Tribunals were called to enforce a much more solid body of humanitarian customary and treaty law as well as other pertinent rules of international law which had developed significantly during the decades following World War II.

2.1.1 Jurisdiction of ICTY

According to its Statute, the personal jurisdiction of ICTY (jurisdiction *ratione personae*) extended over natural persons allegedly responsible for serious violations of international humanitarian law committed in the territory of the former Yugoslavia since 1 January 1991. Its subject-matter jurisdiction (jurisdiction *ratione materiae*) included a) grave breaches of the Geneva Conventions of 1949 (Art. 2)[12] b) violations of the laws or cus-

7 S/RES 827(1993) of 25 May 1993.

8 Alain Pellet, *Le Tribunal Criminel International pour l' Ex-Yougoslavie, Poudre aux yeux ou avancée decisive? See also* the intervention of the Permanent Representative of Brazil in the Council meeting where Resolution 827 was adopted. There was also criticism as regards the substance of the Statute provisions (*see, e.g.*, Michael P. Scharf, A Critique of the Yugoslavia War Crimes Tribunal, Denver Journal of International Law and Policy/Wintr. 1997).

9 ICTY, *Duško Tadić* (IT-94-1-AR72), Decision on the defence motion for interlocutory appeal on jurisdiction, 2 October 1995, paras. 20-22.

10 S/RES 955(1994) of 8 November 1994. On ICTR *see infra*, at 2.2.

11 Fausto Pocar, *The International Criminal Tribunal for the Former Yugoslavia*, στο International Criminal Justice, Law and Practice from the Rome Statute to its Review, Roberto Belleli (ed), 2010, p. 67-77.

12 According to Art. 2 of the ICTY Statute: "The International Tribunal shall have the power to prosecute persons committing or ordering to be committed grave breaches of the Geneva Conventions of 12 August 1949, namely the following acts against persons or property protected under the provisions of the relevant Geneva Convention: (a) wilful killing; (b) torture or inhuman treatment, including biological experiments; (c) wilfully causing great suffering or serious injury to body or health; (d) extensive destruction and appropriation of property, not justified by military necessity and carried out unlawfully and wantonly; (e) compelling a prisoner of war or a civilian to serve in the forces of a hostile power; (f) wilfully depriving a prisoner of war or a civilian of the rights of fair and regular trial; (g) unlawful deportation or transfer or unlawful confinement of a civilian; (h) taking civilians as hostages."

toms of war (Art. 3)[13] c) genocide (Art. 4)[14] and d) crimes against humanity (Art. 5).[15] Although the jurisdiction of ICTY and that of domestic courts was concurrent, the former was given primacy over the latter.[16]

2.1.1.1 Grave Breaches

ICTY was the first international judicial institution to apply the provisions on grave breaches of the 1949 Geneva Conventions. According to these Conventions[17] and their Additional Protocol I,[18] grave breaches may be committed only in international armed conflict. However, by adopting the test of 'overall control' (which is exercised by another state over forces operating in the state where the conflict is taking place) in order to determine whether an armed conflict is international, ICTY widened the definition of international conflict, therefore also extending the ambit of application of the grave breaches regime.[19]

At the same time, the Tribunal narrowed down the differences between the law applicable in international and in non-international conflicts, strengthening, by the same to-

13 According to Art. 3: "The International Tribunal shall have the power to prosecute persons violating the laws or customs of war. Such violations shall include, but not be limited to: (a) employment of poisonous weapons or other weapons calculated to cause unnecessary suffering; (b) wanton destruction of cities, towns or villages, or devastation not justified by military necessity; (c) attack, or bombardment, by whatever means, of undefended towns, villages, dwellings, or buildings; (d) seizure of, destruction or wilful damage done to institutions dedicated to religion, charity and education, the arts and sciences, historic monuments and works of art and Science; (e) plunder of public or private property."

14 According to Art. 4: "1. The International Tribunal shall have the power to prosecute persons committing genocide as defined in paragraph 2 of this article or of committing any of the other acts enumerated in paragraph 3 of this article. 2. Genocide means any of the following acts committed with intent to destroy, in whole or in part, a national, ethnical, racial or religious group, as such: 5 (a) killing members of the group; (b) causing serious bodily or mental harm to members of the group; (c) deliberately inflicting on the group conditions of life calculated to bring about its physical destruction in whole or in part; (d) imposing measures intended to prevent births within the group; (e) forcibly transferring children of the group to another group. 3. The following acts shall be punishable: (a) genocide; (b) conspiracy to commit genocide; (c) direct and public incitement to commit genocide; (d) attempt to commit genocide; (e) complicity in genocide."

15 According to Art. 5: "The International Tribunal shall have the power to prosecute persons responsible for the following crimes when committed in armed conflict, whether international or internal in character, and directed against any civilian population: (a) murder; (b) extermination; (c) enslavement; (d) deportation; (e) imprisonment; (f) torture; (g) rape; (h) persecutions on political, racial and religious grounds; (i) other inhumane acts."

16 Art. 9 of the ICTY Statute.

17 Convention (I) for the Amelioration of the Condition of the Wounded and Sick in Armed Forces in the Field, Geneva 12 August 1949, ('Geneva Convention I'), Art. 50; Convention (II) for the Amelioration of the Condition of the Wounded, Sick and Shipwrecked Members of Armed Forces at Sea, Geneva 12 August 1949, ('Geneva Convention II'), Art. 51; Convention (III) Relative to the Treatment of Prisoners of War, Geneva, 12 August 1949, ('Geneva Convention III'), Art. 130; Convention (IV) Relative to the Protection of Civilian Persons in Time of War, Geneva, 12 August 1949, ('Geneva Convention IV'), Art. 147.

18 Protocol Additional to the Geneva Conventions of 12 August 1949, and Relating to the Protection of Victims of International Armed Conflicts (Protocol I), 8 June 1977 ('Additional Protocol I'), Art. 85.

19 Concerning the way in which this test differs from that employed by the ICJ in the Nicaragua Case, *see infra*, p. 70.

ken, the protection of persons in the latter type of conflict.[20] Explaining its position on the matter, the ICTY Appeals Chamber stated in *Čelebići* (Delalić et al.), that to maintain a distinction between the two legal regimes and their criminal consequences in respect of similarly egregious acts because of the difference in nature of the conflicts would ignore the very purpose of the Geneva Conventions, which is to protect the dignity of the human person.[21] Going even further, the Appeals Chamber put forward, in connection with the definition of 'protected persons', the notion of ethnicity rather than nationality which 'may become determinative of national allegiance' drawing the conclusion that "under these conditions, the requirement of nationality is even less adequate to define protected persons."[22]

Despite their good intentions, these jurisprudential innovations have been, however, the object of severe criticism for going further than they should have, breaking away from the jurisprudence of the International Court of Justice (ICJ) (as far as the test for the distinction between international and non-international conflict is concerned) or by resorting to non-objective criteria (such as that of 'allegiance').[23]

2.1.1.2 Genocide

The *Krstić Case*,[24] was the first one on genocide to be tried by ICTY. Having found that the Srebrenica massacre constituted genocide,[25] the Tribunal went on to clarify the elements of the crime, including that of *dolus specialis* (special intent).[26] On appeal, however, *Krstić* was not found to have that particular intent and was convicted, *inter alia*, for aiding and abetting genocide.[27] Convictions for genocide were entered in the cases of *Vujadin Popović* and *Ljubiša Beara*.[28, 29]

---

20 The ICTY Statute neither excludes nor provides for the criminalization of serious violations of the laws or customs of war committed in the context of internal armed conflict.

21 *Delalić et al.*, Case No. IT-96-21-A, Appeals Chamber Judgment, 20 February 2001, para. 172.

22 ICTY, *Dusko Tadic*, Case No. IT-94-1-A, ICTY Appeals Chamber Judgment, 15 July 1999, paras. 163-169.

23 *See, e.g.*, for example, Marco Sassóli and& Laura M. Olson, *The Judgment of the ICTY Appeals Chamber on the merits in the Tadic Case*, 30.9. September 2000 Article, International Review of the Red Cross, No. 839.

24 ICTY, *Radislav Krstić*, Case No. IT-98-33-T, 2 August 2001, Trial Judgment, and IT-98-33-A, 19 April 2004, Appeal Judgment. *Radislav Krstić* was a General-Major in the "Vojska Republike Srpske" (VRS) and Commander of the Drina Corps.

25 *See* William Schabas, *Genocide in International Law: The Crimes of Crimes*, 2000.

26 For an analysis of the *Krstić* Case, *see* Mark Drumbl, Melb. J. Int'l. Law, vol. 5, no. 2, Case Notes, *Radislav Krstić:* ICTY authenticates genocide at Srebrenica and convicts for aiding and abetting, 2004.

27 ICTY, *Radislav Krstić*, Appeal Judgment, paras. 8, 9, 12. The Appeals Chamber reversed the genocide conviction because of insufficient evidence that *Krstić* had the specific intent which was required for him to be convicted as a direct perpetrator of genocide on the basis of joint criminal enterprise (JCE). Instead, the Appeals Chamber found *Krstić* guilty of aiding and abetting genocide and confirmed his guilt for aiding and abetting extermination and persecution (crimes against humanity) and murder (war crime).

28 ICTY, *Popović et al. (Vujadin Popovid, Ljubiša Beara, Drago Nikolid, Radivoje Miletid, Vinko Pandurevid, Ljubomir Borovčanin and Milan Gvero)*, Case No. IT-05-88-T, 10 June 2010, Trial Judgment and IT-05-88-A, 30 January 2015, Appeals Judgment.

29 On genocide generally, *see also infra*, section 4.2.1 and 4.2.1.1.

2.1.1.3 Violation of the Laws or Customs of War (War Crimes)

The list of war crimes appearing in Article 3 of the Statute finds its main origin in the Hague Regulations annexed to Hague Convention IV, Respecting the Laws and Customs of War.[30] Already the Nuremberg Military Tribunal had found that the Regulations reflected customary international law. In the 1995 *Tadić Case* the ICTY found that Article 3 of the Statute of that Tribunal included: a) violations of the Hague Law on international conflicts; b) violations of provisions of the Geneva Conventions other than those qualified as 'grave breaches'; c) violations of common Article 3 of these conventions and other customary rules on non-international conflicts; and d) violations of agreements which are binding on the parties to the conflict which constitute 'conventional law', i.e. they are not customary law.[31]

As the list of crimes in Article 3 of the ICTY Statute is illustrative, not exhaustive, other crimes may, as a consequence, be considered to fall within the scope of application of the article in question. As regards the conditions which have to be fulfilled for a crime to fall within the ambit of Article 3, ICTY has answered as follows: a) the violation must constitute an infringement of a rule of international humanitarian law; b) the rule must be customary in nature or, if it belongs to treaty law, the conditions required by the treaty must be met; c) the violation must be serious, i.e. it must constitute a breach of a rule protecting important values and the breach must involve grave consequences for the victim; and d) the violation of the rule must entail, under customary or conventional law, the individual criminal responsibility of the person breaching the rule.[32]

The Tribunal finally adds that:

> It follows that it does not matter whether the 'serious violation' has occurred within the context of an international or an internal armed conflict, as long as the requirements set out above are met.[33]

2.1.1.4 Definitions of Gender Crimes

Particularly important are the definitions and clarifications of the Tribunal concerning gender crimes.[34, 35] In the *Kunarac Case*, the first trial based solely on charges of sexual violence, the Tribunal found the accused guilty of rape, enslavement and outrages on

---

30 On war crimes generally, *see infra*, section 4.2.3.

31 *Duško Tadić*, Decision on the defence motion for interlocutory appeal on jurisdiction, 2 October 1995, para. 89.

32 *Ibid.*, para. 94.

33 *Ibid.*, para, 94 *in fine*. Also, ICTY, *Kunarac et al.*, Case No. IT-96-23/1-A, 12 June 2002, para. 66.

34 *See, e.g., Kunarac, Kovač and Vuković*, IT-96-23-T & IT-96-23/1-T of 22 February 2001, para. 460 (definition of rape), paras. 539-540 (definition of enslavement), para. 497 (definition of torture) as crimes against humanity.

35 The Tribunal clarified that the crime of rape could also constitute the crime of torture and the crime of genocide (*see infra*).

personal dignity, as war crimes and crimes against humanity. Going further than previous judgments which focus on the elements of coercion, force or threat of force in rape, the *Kunarac* Trial Chamber held that the use or threat of force is just one factor, among other, to indicate the absence of consent on the part of the victim. Furthermore, the Tribunal held that in time of armed conflict no consent could be inferred from lack of evidence of resistance to a sexual crime and that even the uncorroborated evidence of a single witness, if reliable and credible, could support a conviction for rape.

2.1.1.5 Torture

The Tribunal has also contributed to the legal analysis of the crime of torture, the prohibition of which, it stated *obiter*, constitutes a norm of a *jus cogens* character. ICTY identified a general prohibition of torture in international law that cannot be derogated from by treaty, national law or any other instruments. In the *Furundžija* case, the Trial Chamber declares that "the prohibition of torture imposes upon States obligations *erga omnes*, that is, obligations owed towards all the other members of the international community, each of which then has a correlative right."[36] Torture is therefore a crime subject to universal jurisdiction and its *jus cogens* status under international law has been consolidated. Furthermore, the Tribunal gradually abandoned the requirement provided for in the Torture Convention[37] that the individual committing this crime must act in an official capacity.[38, 39]

2.1.1.6 Crimes Against Humanity

The ICTY Statute follows the IMT Charter requiring, unlike the Statute of the ICTR, that crimes against humanity be connected with armed conflict, which may be either international or non-international. It has not, therefore, followed the growing tendency towards delinking crimes against humanity from the state of war and of admitting the possibility of their commission in peacetime. The Appeals Chamber held, nonetheless, that "the existence of an armed conflict is not a constitutive element of the definition of crimes against humanity, but only a jurisdictional prerequisite."[40]

36 ICTY, *Anto Furundžija,* Trial Chamber, Judgment, IT-95-17/1-T, 10 December 1998, para. 151.

37 Convention against Torture and Other Cruel, Inhuman or Degrading Treatment or Punishment of 10 December 1984, entry into force 26 June 1987.

38 ICTY, *Kunarac* Appeal Judgment, para.148; ICTY, *Kvočka* Appeals Judgement, para. 284; ICTY, *Limaj et al.*, Trial Chamber, Judgment, IT-03-66-T, 30 November 2005, para. 240.

39 Further information and analysis of ICTY jurisprudence on war crimes is also made in connection with the analysis of war crimes under the ICC Statute.

40 ICTY, *Šešelj,* Decision on Motion for Reconsideration of the 'Decision on the Interlocutory Appeal Concerning Jurisdiction,' IT-03-67-AR72.1, 15 June 2006, para. 21.

2.1.2 *Modes of Liability and Participation*[41]

The Tribunal has expanded on the issue of modes of liability (joint criminal enterprise (JCE), aiding and abetting, command responsibility). These modes were not sufficiently elaborated in the Nuremberg or the Tokyo Trials. The *ad hoc* Tribunals worked out the constituent elements of each form of participation, on the basis of customary international law, as their Statutes were not particularly expansive in setting out the jurisdictional framework within which the Tribunals were called to operate.

2.1.2.1 Joint Criminal Enterprise (JCE)

According to Article 7(1) of the ICTY Statute and Article 6(1) of the ICTR Statute:

> A person who planned, instigated, ordered, committed or otherwise aided and abetted in the planning, preparation or execution of a crime referred to in [...] the present Statute, shall be individually responsible for the crime.

JCE is therefore characterized by the existence of a common criminal plan or purpose pursued by many persons, all contributing to the carrying out of crimes in execution of a common purpose. All participants are guilty irrespective of the part they carried out. In *Tadić*, the Appeals Chamber opined that the notion of common design as a form of accomplice liability is 'firmly established in customary international law' and is upheld, albeit implicitly, by the Statute of the International Tribunal.[42] JCE therefore allows the attribution of criminal responsibility for such criminal group activities to the mastermind of the plan who will usually operate behind the scenes, and who may be a high-level leader or military commander using his/her subordinates to carry out their criminal objectives.

2.1.2.2 Extension of Commission

According to the *Tadić* Appeal Judgment, 'committing' refers to a) "the physical perpetration of a crime by the offender himself, or the culpable omission of an act that was mandated by a rule of criminal law"; or b) "participation in the realization of a common design or purpose" (or participation in a JCE).[43] It is to be noted that the ICTR Appeals Chamber in the *Gacumbitsi* case expanded the definition of commission by stating that in the context of genocide, "'direct and physical perpetration' need not mean physical kill-

41 *See* Morten Bergsmo, Cheah Wui Ling, Song Tianying and Yi Ping (eds), *Contribution of the United Nations Ad Hoc Tribunals to the Development of International Criminal Law*, Historical Origins of International Criminal Law: Volume 4, Cambridge University Press, 2018, pp. 125-159.

42 ICTY, *Dusko Tadić et al.*, Appeals Chamber, Judgment, ICTR-2001-64A, para. 220.

43 *Ibid.*, para. 188.

ing."[44] This extended form of commission did not, however, meet with general agreement, as it was found to go far beyond the jurisprudence of the Tribunals and customary law. At the same time, the ICTY Appeals Chamber rejected, in the *Stakić* case, the notion of co-perpetratorship which had been adopted by the Trial Chamber judgment, returning, instead, to the notion of JCE.[45]

2.1.2.3 Aiding and Abetting

This is the form of accessory liability[46] which is most commonly known in criminal law jurisdictions all over the world. It consists in the act of rendering practical assistance, encouragement or moral support, which has "a substantial effect on the perpetration of a certain crime."[47] ICTY has maintained a wavering jurisprudence in connection with the element of 'specific direction' as a required element of the *actus reus* of the aiding and abetting liability.[48]

2.1.2.4 Command Responsibility

The ICTY Statute adopts the doctrine of command or superior responsibility (criminal responsibility of superiors) in its Article 7(3).[49] The first time where ICTY dealt with command responsibility was in the *Čelebići* case. In its judgment which has been seminal on this question, the Trial Chamber found that the doctrine, as formulated in Article 7(3), consists of three elements:

a. the existence of a superior-subordinate relationship;
b. the superior knew or had reason to know that the criminal act was about to be or had been committed and

---

44 ICTR, *Sylvestre Gacumbitsi*, Appeals Chamber, Judgment, ICTR-2001-64A, 7 July 2006, para. 60.

45 ICTY, *Milomir Stakić*, Appeals Chamber, Judgment, IT-97-24-A, 22 March 2006, para. 62.

46 ICTY, Dusko Tadić *et al.*, Trial Chamber, Judgment, IT-94-1-T, 7 May 1997, para. 666.

47 ICTY, *Kunarac* Appeal Judgment, para. 516.

48 The 'specific direction' requirement as an element of the *actus reus* of aiding and abetting liability was first mentioned in the *Tadić* Appeal Judgment rendered in 1999 (*Tadić* Appeal Judgment, para. 229). In the same vein was the ICTY Appeal Judgment in *Momcilo Perišić* (IT-04-81-A, 28 February 2013, paras. 25–36); In the *Mrkšić and Šljivančanin* case, the Appeals Chamber clarified, however, *"that 'specific direction' is not an essential ingredient of the actus reus of aiding and abetting"* (54 ICTY, *Mrkšić et al.*, Appeals Chamber, Judgment, IT-95-13/1-A, 5 May 2009, para. 159), a position also taken by the Appeals Chamber in ICTY, *Vidoje Blagojević et al.*, Appeal Judgment (IT-02-60-A, 9 May 2007, para. 189). This decision was upheld by the ICTY Appeals Chamber in *Lukić and Lukić* (IT-98-32/1-A, 4 December 2012, para. 424) and confirmed in *Šainović et al.*, Appeal Judgment (IT-05-87-A, 23 January 2014, paras. 1621 and 1650). For a full analysis of the matter *see* Liu Daqun, in Morten Bergsmo et al. (eds), Contribution of the United Nations Ad Hoc Tribunals to the Development of International Criminal Law, Historical Origins of International Criminal Law: Volume 4, pp. 142-145.

49 Which reads: "The fact that any of the acts referred to in articles 2 to 5 of the present Statute was committed by a subordinate does not relieve his superior of criminal responsibility if he knew or had reason to know that the subordinate was about to commit such acts or had done so and the superior failed to take the necessary and reasonable measures to prevent such acts or to punish the perpetrators thereof."

c. the superior failed to take necessary and reasonable measures to prevent the criminal act or punish the perpetrator.[50]

Further on, the Chamber observes that for superior responsibility to be established a *de jure* superior-subordinate relationship does not suffice; it is necessary for the superior to have 'effective control' over the subordinate who committed the crime.[51]

In *Aleksovski*, the Trial Chamber identified the distinction between Articles 7(1) and 7 (3) of the ICTY Statute. It held that a superior is responsible not for his acts sanctioned by Article 7(1) of the Statute but for his failure to act. It notes that "a superior is held responsible for the acts of his subordinates if he did not prevent the perpetration of the crimes of his subordinates or punish them for the crimes."[52] In the same vein, the Trial Chamber found, in *Halilović*, that command responsibility is a "sui generis responsibility for dereliction of duty,"[53] while the Appeals Chamber observed, in *Krnojelac*, that

> it cannot be overemphasized that, where superior responsibility is concerned, an accused is not charged with the crimes of his subordinates but with his failure to carry out his duty as a superior to exercise control.[54]

The conclusion which can be derived from the above is that the doctrine of command responsibility has developed significantly since the trials of war criminals of World War II, where the U.S. Military Commission in Manila had found that Yamashita, commander of the Japanese armed forces in the Philippines during the war

> failed to discharge his duty as commander to control the operations of the members of his command, permitting them to commit brutal atrocities … and that he had therefore violated the laws of war.[55]

The Commission had therefore applied the principle of objective liability for command responsibility, as neither the 'effective control' of the commander over his subordinates nor his knowledge of their criminal conduct was required for him to be considered equally responsible for the crimes materially committed by them,[56] the 'should have known' standard sufficed for this purpose.

---

50 ICTY, *Delalić et al.*, Trial Chamber, Judgment, IT-96-21-T, 16 November 1998, para. 346 (*Čelebići* Trial Judgment').

51 *Ibid.*, para. 378.

52 ICTY, *Zlatko Aleksovski*, Trial Chamber, Judgment, IT-95-14/1-T, 25 June 1999, para. 67.

53 ICTY, *Sefer Halilović*, Trial Chamber, Judgment, IT-01-48-T, 16 November 2005, para. 42.

54 ICTY, *Milorad Krnojelac*, Appeals Chamber, Judgment, IT-97-25-A, 17 September 2003, para. 171.

55 *See also supra*, section 1.2.5, fn 47.

56 Liu Daqun, *Contribution of the United Nations Ad Hoc Tribunals to the Development of International Criminal Law, loc. cit.*, p. 145.

2.1.3 Prosecutions and Judgments

ICTY prosecuted 161 persons and conducted 126 trials.[57] The most well-known cases were that of the former President of Serbia Slobodan Milosević, who died during the trial,[58] and of the Bosnian Serb former President of the Republika Srpska and commander-in-chief of Serb forces in Bosnia, Radovan Karadžić.[59] The arrest of Bosnian-Serb General Ratko Mladić[60] and former President of the 'Republic of Serbian Crajna' in Croatia, *Goran Hadžić*,[61] marked the end of the ICTY investigations.

2.2 The International Criminal Tribunal for Rwanda (ICTR)[62]

This *ad hoc* Tribunal was also established by the Security Council as its subsidiary organ, under Chapter VII of the U.N. Charter, to try those accused of the crimes committed in the Rwanda civil war in 1994 where an estimated 800,000 people found death in genocide.[63]

In July 1994, the U.N. Security Council (UNSC) had established an Expert Commission to investigate the situation. Following the Report of the Commission and while it was clear from journalistic reports that a full-blown genocide had been taking place there, the S.C. passed Resolution 955[64] under Chapter VII of the U.N. Charter, by which an *ad hoc* Tribunal to prosecute "persons responsible for genocide and other serious violations of international humanitarian law committed in the territory of Rwanda … between 1 Jan-

57 Of whom 99 were sentenced, 19 acquitted and 13 referred to domestic courts. The United Nations International Criminal Tribunal for Rwanda, during its period of activity, indicted 96 individuals of whom 62 were sentenced, 14 acquitted and 10 referred to domestic courts.

58 ICTY, *Slobodan Milosević* (IT-02-54). The indictment against *Slobodan Milosevic* – confirmed on 22 November 2001 – included 29 counts among which genocide and conspiracy to commit genocide, committed between 1992 and 1995 in Bosnia-Herzegovina. The indictment was submitted to the tribunal by the then ICTY Prosecutor *Carla Del Ponte* on 12 November 2001.

59 ICTY, Radovan Karadžić (IT-95-5/18-1). On first instance (Judgment of 24 March 2016), Karadžić was found guilty, as a member of joint criminal enterprises, of genocide in the area of Srebrenica in 1995, crimes against humanity and war crimes committed by Serb forces during the armed conflict in Bosnia and Herzegovina (BiH) from 1992 to 1995 while he was acquitted of genocide in other municipalities in BiH in 1992. He was sentenced to forty years of imprisonment. He appealed against his conviction before the Mechanism for International Criminal Tribunals (MICT, *see infra*, p.), in 2016 (MICT 13-55). The appeals judgment extended his conviction to life imprisonment on 20 March 2019.

60 ICTY, *Ratko Mladić* (IT-09-92). On first instance *Mladić* was found guilty, as a member of various joint criminal enterprises, of genocide, crimes against humanity and war crimes and was convicted to life imprisonment (ICTY Judgment of 22 November 2017). In March 2018 he appealed his conviction before the MICT.

61 ICTY, *Goran Hadžić* (IT-04-75). Proceedings against *Hadžić* were terminated due to his death in July 2016.

62 *See* Alison Des Forges, *"Leave None to Tell the Story": Genocide in Rwanda* (New York: Human Rights Watch, 1999), pp. 1, 6, 15-16; I. Carlsson, "The U.N. Inadequacies," 4 *J. Int'l Crim. Just.* 837 (2005), p. 841.

63 The *Interahamwe*, ("Hutu Power") movement and the interim government of Rwanda massacred, maimed and raped an estimated 500,000 to 800,000 Tutsi and moderate Hutu.

64 On 8 November 1994.

uary 1994 and 31 December 1994" was established.[65] The Statute of the Tribunal was annexed to the Resolution. The Tribunal had its seat in Arusha, Tanzania. It also had offices in Kigali, Rwanda, while its Appeals Chamber was seated in The Hague. The subject-matter jurisdiction of the tribunal covered genocide,[66] crimes against humanity[67] and violations of common Article 3 of the Geneva Conventions as well as violations of the second Additional Protocol of 1977 to these Conventions.[68] The nature of the conflict in Rwanda being non-international – between the *Hutu* and the *Tutsi* – it was necessary to attribute to this Tribunal jurisdiction over crimes committed in conflicts of this type which were provided for in common Article 3 of the Geneva Conventions and in the 1977 Additional Protocol II. As a result, the contribution of ICTR in the development of the rules of international humanitarian law applicable in non-international armed conflict and in the recognition of the customary character of the provisions of Additional Protocol II has been significant.[69]

Individual criminal responsibility could be attributed, under the ICTR Statute, to any defendant who "planned, instigated, ordered, committed, or otherwise aided and abetted

---

65 It is noteworthy that Rwanda, which at the time held one of the non-permanent seats on the Security Council, voted against the establishment of ICTR mainly because this Tribunal would not impose the death penalty, a sentence which was provided for under Rwandan legislation.

66 Art. 2 of the ICTR Statute which provides: "2. Genocide means any of the following acts committed with intent to destroy, in whole or in part, a national, ethnical, racial or religious group, as such: a) Killing members of the group; b) Causing serious bodily or mental harm to members of the group; c) Deliberately inflicting on the group conditions of life calculated to bring about its physical destruction in whole or in part; d) Imposing measures intended to prevent births within the group; e) Forcibly transferring children of the group to another group. 3. The following acts shall be punishable: a) Genocide; b) Conspiracy to commit genocide; c) Direct and public incitement to commit genocide; d) Attempt to commit genocide; e) Complicity in genocide."

67 Art. 3 of the ICTR Statute which provides: "The International Tribunal for Rwanda shall have the power to prosecute persons responsible for the following crimes when committed as part of a widespread or systematic attack against any civilian population on national, political, ethnic, racial or religious grounds: a) Murder; b) Extermination; c) Enslavement; d) Deportation; e) Imprisonment; f) Torture; g) Rape; h) Persecutions on political, racial and religious grounds; i) Other inhumane acts."

68 Art. 4 of the ICTR Statute which provides: "The International Tribunal for Rwanda shall have the power to prosecute persons committing or ordering to be committed serious violations of Article 3 common to the Geneva Conventions of 12 August 1949 for the Protection of War Victims, and of Additional Protocol II thereto of 8 June 1977. These violations shall include, but shall not be limited to: a) Violence to life, health and physical or mental well-being of persons, in particular murder as well as cruel treatment such as torture, mutilation or any form of corporal punishment; b) Collective punishments; c) Taking of hostages; d) Acts of terrorism; e) Outrages upon personal dignity, in particular humiliating and degrading treatment, rape, enforced prostitution and any form of indecent assault; f) Pillage; g) The passing of sentences and the carrying out of executions without previous judgement pronounced by a regularly constituted court, affording all the judicial guarantees which are recognized as indispensable by civilized peoples; h) Threats to commit any of the foregoing acts."

69 It was an early decision of ICTR to concentrate on the major criminals in the Rwanda civil war rather than in the thousands of perpetrators who did not participate in the decision-making process. Competence on the latter would be assumed by the national courts of the country or by the traditional Rwandan dispute-resolution process known as *gacaca* (on the latter *see* William A. Schabas, "Genocide Trials and Gacaca Courts," 3 *J. Int'l Crim. Just.* 87, 2005).

in the planning, preparation or execution of a crime."[70] No immunities which might otherwise be applicable, could attach to governmental officials[71]; furthermore, command (superior) responsibility applied on the basis that the defendant

> knew or had reason to know that the subordinate was about to commit such acts or had done so and the superior failed to take the necessary and reasonable measures to prevent such acts or to punish the perpetrators thereof.[72]

Finally, superior orders did not relieve an accused subordinate of criminal responsibility, although this was a factor which might be taken into account in sentencing.[73]

2.2.1 *Jurisdiction of ICTR*

The personal jurisdiction of the Tribunal (jurisdiction *ratione personae*) covered both, to those allegedly having committed any of the crimes within the subject-matter jurisdiction of the Tribunal in Rwanda, as well as to Rwandan citizens who allegedly committed such crimes in the territory of neighbouring States in the course of 1994. The ICTR exercised concurrent jurisdiction with national courts; however, the Tribunal had supremacy over them.[74]

2.2.2 *Genocide*[75]

The ICTR was the first of the *ad hoc* Tribunals to try a genocide case, that of *Jean-Paul Akayesu*,[76] and the first to try such a case since the Genocide Convention entered into force in 1951.[77] Equally noteworthy is that another indictee by the ICTR, *Jean Kamban-*

70 Art. 6(1).
71 Art. 6(2).
72 Art. 6(3).
73 Art. 6(4).
74 Art. 8(2) of the Statute.
75 Payam Akhavan, "The Crime of Genocide in the ICTR Jurisprudence," 3 *J. Int'l Crim. Just.* 989 (2005), p. 1001. *See also* Paul Behrens, The Criminal Law of Genocide, in Ralph Henham and Paul Behrens, (eds), *International, Comparative and Contextual Aspects*, 2006.
76 ICTR, *Jean-Paul Akayesu*, Case No. 96-4-T, 2 September 1998 and 96-4-A, 1 June 2001. *Akayesu* was bourgmestre of the *Taba* commune in Rwanda from April 1993 to June 1994. He was accused of not trying to stop the killing of about 200,660 Tutsis by Hutu *génocidaires* in *Taba*, and of, instead, facilitating and encouraging the latter. He was convicted of genocide and crimes against humanity, in particular extermination, murder, torture, and rape.
77 The Genocide Convention was adopted on 9 December 1948 and entered into force on 12 January 1951.

da, became the first head of government to be ever convicted of genocide by an international court.[78, 79]

Genocide presupposes the existence of specific intent (*dolus specialis*), which, according to Article 2 of the ICTR Statute, is "the intent to destroy, in whole or in part, a national, ethnical, racial or religious group, as such …"

In *Akayesu* the Trial Chamber dealt, *inter alia*, with the complex issue which is central to genocide, i.e. what constitutes an ethnic group (or any of the other groups protected under Art. 2). More particularly it examined whether an 'ethnic group' must be objectively considered as such, or if it is enough that the victimizer subjectively considered it to be so.

In its judgment, the Trial Chamber defined all four categories of protected groups.[80] Thus, it defined 'ethnic group' as "a group whose members share a common language or culture."[81] However, the application of these criteria resulted in the *Tutsi* and the *Hutu* not belonging to distinct ethnic groups, as they share the same language, *Kinyarwanda*, and have common cultural traits. In fact, traditionally the *Hutu* and the *Tutsi* were identifiable on the basis of 'lineage rather than ethnicity' and on other factors, mainly social and economic, which could be subject to change, e.g. by marriage.[82]

The Trial Chamber also decided that any group similar in terms of stability and permanence with those four mentioned in the Genocide Convention should also be included in the list of protected groups.[83] It claimed that, by 1994, Rwandans considered the *Tutsi* a distinct 'ethnic' group. As a result, the Chamber found the *Tutsi* to be a 'stable and permanent group' falling within the scope of the definition of genocide. In the *Kayishema and Ruzindana* case,[84] the Trial Chamber came to the same conclusion by broadening the definition of 'ethnic groups' so as to include not only groups sharing a common language and culture but also those which are self-identified as ethnic groups or are so identified by others, including the perpetrators of the crimes.[85] In *Rutaganda*,[86] the Trial Chamber followed a differentiated approach, maintaining that the identity of the groups in ques-

78 ICTR, *Jean Kambanda*, Case No. 97-23-S, 4 September 1998 (Trial Judgment and Sentence), and 97-23-A, 19 October 2000 (Appeal Judgment).

79 As already noted, the Nuremberg trials had not adjudicated on genocide since the crime did not exist as such at the time. It is worth noting that even the charges against *Adolf Eichmann* were for an offence against the Jewish people.

80 *Akayesu*, Trial Judgment, *supra*, paras. 512-515.

81 *Ibid.*, para. 513.

82 *Ibid.*, para. 81. *See also* Robert D. Sloane, The International Criminal Tribunal for Rwanda in Chiara Giorgetti (ed), *The Rules, Practice, and Jurisprudence of International Courts and Tribunals*, 2012, pp. 261-282.

83 *Akayesu (supra)* paras. 516 and 701-702. This was claimed to be based on the *travaux préparatoires* of the Genocide Convention. Contra: Payam Akhavan, "The Crime of Genocide in the ICTR Jurisprudence," 3 *J. Int'l Crim. Just.* 989, 2005, p. 1001.

84 *Kayishema and Ruzindana*, Case No. ICTR-95-1-T, Judgment, 21 May 1999.

85 *Ibid.*, para. 98.

86 *Georges Rutaganda*, Case No. ICTR 96-3-T, Judgment, 6 December 1999.

tion should be based on subjective rather than objective criteria, i.e. that the victim must be perceived by the perpetrator of genocide as belonging to a group "slated for destruction."[87] This perception may also be held by the victim.[88]

Thus, the ICTR retained the principle that self-identification or identification by others of an ethnic group may suffice to satisfy the requirement of Article 2 of the Tribunal's Statute in this regard – even though this may be scientifically unsound (as is the case with the *Hutu* and *Tutsi*).

2.2.2.1 Rape as Genocide

In *Akayesu*, the ICTR found that rape could be part of genocide. While rape is a crime against humanity and a war crime under the ICTR Statute (Arts. 3(g) and 4(e) respectively),[89] it is particularly noteworthy that the Trial Chamber found that rape and sexual violence could

> constitute genocide in the same way as any other act as long as they were committed with the specific intent to destroy, in whole or in part, a particular group, targeted as such.[90]

2.2.2.2 Incitement to Genocide – The Media Case[91]

The case involved three media executives (*Nahimana, Barayagwiza* and *Ngeze*), accused, *inter alia*, for direct and public incitement to genocide through the use of hate speech. The defendants used such speech against the *Tutsi*, writing for *Kangura*, a newspaper of wide circulation, and in the broadcasts of *Radio Télévision Libre des Mille Collines (RTLM)*. All three defendants were convicted by the Trial Chamber under Article 6(1) of the ICTR Statute because they employed media in essence as a weapon, with intent to kill. The Trial Chamber held them responsible not only for the content of what they published but also for the consequences resulting therefrom. However, the Appeals Chamber reversed on several points the judgment of the Trial Chamber, finding that the longer the lapse of time between the hate speech and the result (killing), the more difficult it is to infer causation.[92] Thus, according to the Appeals Chamber, the earlier broadcasts or publications which were read or heard later could, at most, constitute in-

---

87 *Ibid.*, para. 56.

88 *Ibid.* However, the Trial Chamber invokes the *travaux préparatoires* of the Genocide Convention to exclude political and economic groups from the ambit of the Convention's definition. It describes such groups as "mobile" which "one joins through individual, political commitment," while the Convention purported to cover "relatively stable and permanent groups" (para. 57).

89 In the case of Art. 4(e) as an outrage upon personal dignity.

90 *Akayesu, supra*, para. 731.

91 *Ferdinand Nahimana, Jean-Bosco Barayagwiza and Hassan Ngeze*, Case No. ICTR-99-52-T of 3 December 2003 and Case No. ICTR-99-52-A of 27 November 2007.

92 *Nahimana et al.*, Appeal Judgment, *supra*, para. 513.

direct incitement to genocide. The Appeals Chamber clarified, however, that while hate speech does not, *ipso facto*, constitute persecution, the encouragement of or calls for violence, combined with hate speech by the RTLM, could constitute a crime against humanity and be qualified as acts of persecution and incitement of others to persecute.[93]

2.2.3 Crimes Against Humanity

The Nuremberg and Tokyo Charters required that crimes against humanity be committed before or during the war. The Statute of the ICTR delinked crimes against humanity from war, i.e. they might have been committed at any time. According to the definition set out in Article 3 of the ICTR Statute, crimes against humanity presuppose 'a widespread or systematic attack against any civilian population on national, political, ethnic, racial or religious grounds'. However, the ICTR jurisprudence, following that of ICTY on the matter, has dispensed with the requirement for 'discriminatory intent' for crimes against humanity, on the basis that crimes against humanity are in any event committed against civilian populations which have been specifically targeted for national, political, ethnic, racial or religious reasons.[94] It is furthermore asserted that a "discriminatory intent is not required by international humanitarian law as a legal ingredient for all crimes against humanity."[95] The Appeals Chamber concluded that the only crime which required a discriminatory intent was the crime of persecution.[96]

2.2.3.1 Rape as a Crime Against Humanity

In connection with the definition of rape, the Trial Chamber in *Akayesu*, noting firstly that rape "cannot be captured in a mechanical description of objects and body parts," went on to set it out as "a physical invasion of a sexual nature, committed on a person under circumstances which are coercive."[97] By the use of the phrase 'physical invasion', the judgment allowed an interpretation which did not require the exercise of direct physical force on the victim of the sexual assault. Indeed, the judgment expressly and convincingly states that "threats, intimidation, extortion and other forms of duress which prey on fear or desperation may constitute coercion."[98] The ICTR has, therefore, defined rape more widely than ICTY and the ICC, thus facilitating the prosecution of acts of sexual violence.[99] As a crime against humanity, rape must, according to Article 3 of the ICTR

93 *Ibid.*, paras. 1033-1036.
94 *Akayesu* Appeal Judgment, Case No. ICTR-96-4-A, 1 June 2001, para. 464, quoting *Tadic* Appeal Judgment (para. 297).
95 *Ibid.*, paras. 464 (referring to the *Tadic* Appeal Judgment, para. 288) and 466.
96 *Ibid.*, para. 467.
97 *Akayesu,* Trial Judgment, *supra,* paras. 598, 688.
98 *Ibid.*, para. 688.
99 *See* Robert D. Sloane, *loc. cit.*, p. 275.

Statute, also be part of a widespread or systematic attack against a civilian population. As already mentioned, the requirement for discriminatory grounds, although included in the definition, would not be applicable according to the jurisprudence of both the *ad hoc* Tribunals.[100]

The ICTR Chamber also found in *Akayesu* that rape "in fact constitutes torture when inflicted by or at the instigation of or with the consent or acquiescence of a public official or other person acting in an official capacity."[101]

Sexual violence according to the Tribunal includes rape. The Chamber has also found that sexual violence

> falls within the scope of "other inhumane acts," "outrages upon personal dignity" and "serious bodily or mental harm,"[102] the latter including without being limited to "acts of bodily or mental torture, inhumane or degrading treatment, rape, sexual violence, and persecution."[103]

The Chamber was of the opinion that "'serious harm' need not entail permanent or irremediable harm."[104]

2.2.4 War Crimes

2.2.4.1 Elements to Be Ascertained

In the *Kayishema and Ruzindana* case,[105] the Trial Chamber identified the elements for a violation of common Article 3 of the 1949 Geneva Conventions or of the provisions of Additional Protocol II to be established.[106] These are: a) existence of an armed conflict 'not of an international character' at the time of the violation; b) existence of a 'link between the accused and the armed forces' of one party to the conflict; c) the crimes must have been committed *ratione personae* and *ratione loci*, i.e. against victims qualifying as civilians or civilian population relative to the particular armed conflict and within the place in which the conflict occurs[107]; and d) there must be a *nexus* between the crime and the conflict.[108] More particularly in connection with each one of these elements:

100 *See supra,* section 2.2.3.
101 *Akayesu,* Trial Judgment, *supra,* para. 597.
102 *Ibid.*
103 ICTR, *Musema,* Trial Chamber, Judgment, ICTR-96-13-T, 27 January 2000, para. 156.
104 *Ibid.*
105 *Clément Kayishema and Obed Ruzindana,* Trial Judgment, Case No. ICTR-95-1-T, 21 May 1999.
106 In addition to the required *actus reus* and *mens rea* of a particular crime.
107 *Kayishema, supra,* para. 169.
108 *Ibid.*

i. *Definition of non-international armed conflict.* The ICTR defined this type of conflict as an armed conflict which takes place in the territory of a High Contracting Party between its armed forces and dissident armed forces or other organized armed groups, in accordance with Protocol II.[109]
It should be noted in this regard that the scope of application of common Article 3 is not identical with that of Additional Protocol II,[110] it being generally accepted that the scope of the former is wider than that of the latter. In fact, while common Article 3 of the Geneva Conventions requires only an "armed conflict not of an international character occurring in the territory of one of the High Contracting Parties,"[111] Protocol II adds that the conflict must be between the armed forces of a High Contracting Party and dissident armed forces or other organized armed groups which, under responsible command, exercise such control over a part of its territory as to enable them to carry out sustained and concerted military operations and to implement the Protocol.
However,[112] in the case of the Rwanda civil war, the distinction between the abovementioned provisions was immaterial as both of them were satisfied in fact (it is nonetheless noticeable that the judgment endorsed rather unquestionably their simultaneous application, i.e. in essence Protocol II).[113]
ii. *Link between the accused and the armed forces.* The ICTR furthermore found that if the defendants do not belong to the armed forces of one of the parties to the conflict, the Prosecutor must at least establish "a link between them and the armed forces."[114] As a result, the Tribunal stated, quoting *Akayesu,*[115] that Additional Protocol II also applies to individuals who were legitimately mandated and expected as public officials or agents or persons otherwise holding public authority or de facto representing the Government to support or fulfil the war efforts.[116]
This means that not only members of an armed force, but also civilians may be held accountable for violations of common Article 3 and Additional Protocol II.
iii. *Definition of 'civilians' and location of the commission of the crime(s).* The Trial Chamber concluded on this matter that, for purposes of protection of the victims of an armed conflict, 'civilian' and 'civilian population' must be defined in the negative, i.e. as all persons 'who are not members of the armed forces'. Along the same lines, the Chamber decided that, taking into account that the acts referred to in common

109 *Ibid.*, para. 170.
110 Despite the fact that Protocol II states in its Art. 1(1) that it "develops and supplements Article 3 common to the Geneva Conventions."
111 *Kayishema, supra,* para. 170.
112 Art. 1(1).
113 *Ibid.*, para. 171.
114 *Ibid.*, para. 175.
115 *Akayesu,* Trial Judgment, *supra,* para. 631.
116 *Kayishema, supra,* para. 175.

Article 3 are prohibited whenever and wherever committed, the relevant war crimes need not be committed in 'the actual theatre of operations'.[117]

iv. *Nexus requirement.* Finally, the Tribunal held that a nexus, i.e. a 'direct link' between the offences and the conflict, must be established. This is a factual matter which has to be decided on a case-by-case basis. In *Kayishema and Ruzindana*, it was found that while 'the armed conflict had been used as a pretext to unleash an official policy of genocide', this did not constitute evidence of a 'direct link between the alleged crimes and the armed conflict'.[118] Indeed, the 'nexus' requirement does not seem to be easily attainable. Thus, it was not established in the case of *Akayesu*, whose crimes were found not to be sufficiently related to the civil war. Conversely, in *Rutaganda* the Appeals Chamber found a sufficient link (i.e. beyond reasonable doubt) between the actions of *Rutaganda* and the armed conflict in Rwanda.[119] It thus allowed the Prosecutor's appeal, reversed the findings of the Trial Chamber and convicted *Rutaganda* for war crimes, the first such conviction entered by the ICTR.

2.2.4.2 Command Responsibility

A case relating to this issue is that of *Baglishema*,[120] who was *bourgmestre* of the *Mabanza* commune at the time of the Rwandan genocide. Although indicted on the basis of command responsibility for his alleged failure to prevent, suppress or punish crimes committed by his non-military subordinates, the Trial Chamber found the evidence insufficient to sustain a conviction, a verdict which was upheld on appeal. However, the Appeal Judgment found that the Trial Judgment had erred "to the extent that it suggested that the control exercised by a civilian superior must be of the same nature as that exercised by a military commander."[121] Indeed, the Appeals Chamber held that "it is sufficient that, for one reason or another, the accused exercises the 'required degree of control' over his subordinates, namely, that of effective control." This error did not, however, have any consequence on the verdict.[122]

---

117 *Ibid.*, para. 176.

118 *Ibid.*, para. 603.

119 *Rutaganda*, Appeals Judgment, Case No. ICTR-96-3-A, 26 May 2003, paras. 580-581.

120 *Ignace Bagilishema*, Appeals Judgment, Case No. ICTR-95-1A, 3 July 2002.

121 *Ibid.*, para. 55.

122 *Ibid.*

2.2.5 *Prosecutions and Judgments*

After 96 indictments and 62 convictions,[123] the ICTR terminated its functions on 31 December 2012, having delivered its last trial judgment on the *Ngirabatware* case on 20 December 2012.

2.3 Mechanism for International Criminal Tribunals (MICT)

This mechanism was established by S.C. Resolution 1966 (2010) and has been entrusted with the continuation of essential functions of the ICTY and the ICTR and the preservation of their legacy. Essential functions include, *inter alia*, the enforcement of sentences, administrative review, appeal proceedings, contempt, requests for the revocation of the referral of cases to national jurisdictions, access to materials, disclosure, changes in the classification of documents, and requests for compensation and assignment of counsel.

In January 2015 began the transfer of judicial records of ICTY to the MICT. The residual functions of ICTR were also transferred to the Mechanism, which started assuming its functions as from 1 July 2017.

Among the several cases pending before the MICT at the time of writing[124] is the appeal of *Ratko Mladić*, while the Trial Chamber's judgment on the case of *Vojislav Šešelj* (acquittal) was recently partly reversed following an appeal by the Prosecution.[125] The 2019 appeal judgment concerning *Radovan Karadžić* increased the appellant's sentence to life imprisonment.[126]

123 While 14 of the accused were acquitted and 10 referred to domestic courts. For further data *see* The ICTR in Brief, Legacy Website of the ICTR, http://unictr.unmict.org/ and http://cld.unmict.org/?q=en/cases/ictr-icty-case-law-database.

124 2018-mid 2019.

125 For ongoing cases before the MICT and other related information, *see* its website www.unmict.org/en.

126 *See supra*, section 2.1.3, fn. 59.

3 Other Courts: Mixed or Hybrid Tribunals

3.1 Introduction

Mixed or hybrid tribunals, so qualified because they are composed of both national and international judges, is a more recent phenomenon. Sharing this general characteristic, they are however differentiated from one another in their special features, such as their relationship with the U.N., the degree of their autonomy within the country they operate, their subject-matter or personal jurisdiction, etc. Such tribunals are the Special Court for Sierra Leone, the Extraordinary Chambers in the Courts of Cambodia, the War Crimes Chamber in the Court of Bosnia and Herzegovina, the East Timor Special Panels, and the Kosovo Regulations 34 and 64 Panels. Here we will deal with the Special Court for Sierra Leone, the Extraordinary Chambers in the Courts of Cambodia and the Special Tribunal for the Lebanon.

3.2 The Special Court for Sierra Leone (SCSL)[1]

Chronologically the first of mixed courts, the Special Court for Sierra Leone was established in 2002 by agreement between the U.N. and the Government of Sierra Leone, in application of Security Council Resolution 1315/2000.[2] It sat in Freetown and was composed of Sierra Leone and independent judges, the latter being the majority.[3] The Court's subject-matter jurisdiction included crimes against humanity, violations of Article 3 common to the Geneva Conventions and of Additional Protocol II, other serious violations of international humanitarian law, as well as crimes under the law of Sierra Leone.[4] Persons who could be prosecuted were those 'bearing the greatest responsibility'[5] for these crimes which were committed during the eleven-year long civil war in Sierra Leone (1991-2002), in which 150,000 people found violent death and hundreds of thousands others suffered atrocities of every kind.

1 On this Court *see* Charles Chernor Jalloh & Simon Meisenberg, *The Law Reports of the Special Court for Sierra Leone*, two vols. 2014, and vol. III, 2015. Also, Charles C. Jalloh (ed), *The Sierra Leone Special Court and its Legacy: The Impact for Africa and the International Criminal Court*, 2013.

2 S/RES/1315 of 14 August 2000.

3 According to Art. 12 of the Statute, in each one of the two Trial Chambers which could be formed, two judges would be independent and one from Sierra Leone. In the Appeals Chamber there were five independent judges and three from Sierra Leone.

4 Arts. 2-5 of the Statute.

5 *Ibid.*, Art. 1(1).

3.2.1 The Cases

The SCSL tried and imposed sentences on nine persons in four trials.[6] In three of them the defendants were military commanders. These trials were: a) the Revolutionary United Front (RUF) Trial,[7] b) the Armed Forces Revolutionary Council (AFRC)[8] Trial and c) the Civil Defense Force (CDF) Trial.[9]

However, the most well-known trial of the SCSL is that of *Charles Taylor*,[10] sitting President of Liberia at the time of his indictment, who had a direct involvement in the Sierra Leone civil war.[11] The judgment on Taylor was issued in 2012, finding him guilty of "some of the most heinous and brutal crimes recorded in human history."[12] He was convicted of aiding and abetting as well as of planning acts of terrorism, murder, rape, sexual slavery, cruel treatment, recruitment of child soldiers, enslavement and pillage. The judgment was upheld by the Court of Appeal with certain limited exceptions.[13]

Particularly noteworthy is that the SCSL was the first to recognize, in the AFRC Trial, that recruiting and using child soldiers was a war crime not under its own Statute alone,[14] but also under customary international law. It was also the first international Court to recognize in the RUF trial that 'forced marriage' constituted a crime against humanity[15] under the 'other inhumane acts' category of crimes provided for in its Statute.[16] It was

6 On the SCSL sentencing judgments, *see* Shahram Dana, The Sentencing Legacy of the Special Court for Sierra Leone, *Ga. J. Int'l. & Comp. L.*, vol. 42, no. 3, pp. 615-686.

7 The RUF rebel army was formed in Sierra Leone in the late 1980s aiming to overthrow the government of the country which it claimed to be corrupt. The RUF trial involved the RUF members *Issa Hassan Sesay, Morris Kallon* and *Augustine Gbao*, Case No. SCSL-4-15-T of 2 March 2009) and Case No. SCSL-04-15-A of 26 October 2009).

8 The AFRC was a group of rebel soldiers of Sierra Leone which in the late 1990s formed an alliance with the RUF *(supra).* The AFRC trial involved the AFRC members *Alex Tamba Brima, Brima Bazzy Kamara* and *Santigie Borbor Kanu*, Case No. SCSL-04-16-T of 20 June 2007 and Case No. SCSL-04-16-A of 22 February 2008.

9 The CDF was a fighting force which was loyal to the legitimate government ousted in 1997. The CDF trial involved the CDF members *Moinina Fofana* and *Allieu Kondewa,* Case No. SCSL-04-14-T of 2 August 2007 and Case No. SCSL-04-14-A of 28 May 2008.

10 Case No. SCSL-03-01-T of 30 May 2012 and SCSL-03-01-A of 26 September 2013. The trial was conducted in The Hague for security reasons.

11 Mainly through the AFRC and RUF rebel forces operating in Sierra Leone, which joined forces with the National Patriotic Front of Liberia (NPFL) which was led by *Charles Taylor.*

12 Trial Judgment, para. 70

13 Thus, with regard to "aiding and abetting," the SCSL Court of Appeal rejected the "specific direction" standard adopted by ICTY in the *Perišić* case (*see* para. 486 of the SCSL Appeal Judgment), attributing a wider interpretation to "aiding and abetting."

14 Art. 4(c).

15 *See* Jennifer Gong-Gershowitz, Forced Marriage: A "New" Crime Against Humanity? *Northwestern Journal of Human Rights*, Vol. 8, Issue I, Fall 2009.

16 Art. 2(i) of the SCSL Statute. The AFRC Appeal Judgment, although recognizing forced marriage as a crime, it did not enter any new conviction for it because the evidence which was relied on for forced marriage was used in connection with the count of outrages upon personal dignity.

furthermore the first to impose sentences, in the RUF trial, for attacks directed against United Nations peacekeepers (UNAMSIL).[17]

The Court completed its mandate in 2013 and transferred the functions which have to continue (preservation of archives, etc.) to the 'Residual Special Court for Sierra Leone' (RSCSL) established pursuant to an agreement concluded between the U.N. and the Government of Sierra Leone in 2010.

3.3 The Extraordinary Chambers in the Courts of Cambodia (ECCC)[18, 19]

In 1997, Cambodia requested the assistance of the U.N. to set up a Tribunal in order to try those responsible for the horrific crimes committed by the *Khmer Rouge* during the period of Democratic Kampuchea (1975-1979). That regime had caused the death of an estimated 1,700,000 to two million people, i.e. one quarter of the population of the country at the time, through executions, torture, starvation, forced labour and the forcible evacuation of cities. In 2001, the Cambodian National Assembly passed a Law "on the establishment of extraordinary chambers in the courts of Cambodia for the prosecution of crimes committed during the period of Democratic Kampuchea" (ECCC Statute) which caused concerns to the U.N., as it settled many questions on the basis of Cambodian law alone. After tortuous negotiations between the U.N. and the Cambodian government, an agreement on the matter was finally concluded between them in 2003.

The purpose of the Agreement, as proclaimed in Article 1, was to regulate cooperation between the U.N. and Cambodia and to bring to trial

> senior leaders of Democratic Kampuchea and those who were most responsible for the crimes and serious violations of Cambodian Penal Code, international humanitarian law and custom, and international conventions recognized by Cambodia committed from 17 April 1975 to 6 January 1979.[20]

The aforementioned Cambodian Law is recognized as valid and applicable by the Agreement.[21] However, the latter – which was ratified by Cambodia – has precedence over

---

17 As provided in Art. 4(b) of the SCSL Statute.

18 អង្គជំនុំជម្រះវិសាមញ្ញក្នុង តុលាការកម្ពុជា in Khmer, Chambres extraordinaires au sein des tribunaux cambodgiens (CETC). Website: www.eccc.gov.kh/en.

19 Simon M. Meisenberg & Ignaz Stegmiller (eds) *The Extraordinary Chambers in the Courts of Cambodia*, Asser, Springer, 2016; Nina H.B. Jørgensen, *The Elgar Companion to the Extraordinary Chambers in the Courts of Cambodia*; Rebecca Gidley, *Illiberal Transitional Justice and the Extraordinary Chambers in the Courts of Cambodia*, 2019.

20 *I.e.*, the date that the *Khmer Rouge* came to power and the date that their regime was toppled by Vietnamese forces.

21 Art. 2(1) of the Agreement.

national law, by express reference to Articles 26 and 27 of the 1969 Vienna Convention on the Law of Treaties.[22]

The Tribunal (Extraordinary Chambers), which started its operations in 2006, consists of the Trial Chamber, composed of three Cambodian and two international judges, and the Supreme Court Chamber, which serves as both appellate chamber and final instance, and is composed of four Cambodian and three international judges.[23] The Office of the Prosecutor is composed of one national and one international judge.

The subject-matter jurisdiction of the ECCC extends over the crime of genocide as defined in the U.N. 1948 Genocide Convention,[24] on crimes against humanity as defined in the ICC Statute, on serious violations of the Geneva Conventions of 1949 and on other crimes provided for in the abovementioned national Cambodian law.

The court was as from the beginning beset with problems of political interference and economic mismanagement. As difficulties and delays persisted, many of those mainly responsible for the crimes committed under the Democratic Kampuchea regime died or grew very old – *Pol Pot* ('Brother Number One') leader of the *Khmer Rouge*, had already died in 1998 – as a result of which there was a clear risk that the crimes would go unpunished.

3.3.1 The Cases

Finally, the ECCC made its first indictments in 2007 and the first trial, in regard to *Kaing Guek Eav*, known as '*Duch*' (Case 001) started in 2009. *Duch* had been Commander of the *Khmer Rouge* 'S-21 Security Centre' (which was, in reality, a prison and interrogation centre) in Phnom Penh, where about fifteen thousand people had found death. On 26 July 2010, the court convicted '*Duch*' of crimes against humanity[25] and grave breaches of the Geneva Conventions of 1949.[26] The Court sentenced him to thirty-five years of imprisonment. On appeal,[27] the Supreme Court Chamber extended the sentence to life

22 Art. 2(2) of the Agreement. The drafting is nonetheless revelatory of the effort to strike a difficult balance between the two applicable texts.

23 The concurrence of five judges is required for a decision to be taken.

24 It is perhaps a paradox that, contrary to popular belief, events in Cambodia between1975 and 1979 did not in fact constitute genocide under the 1948 Genocide Convention, which covers only "national, ethnical, racial or religious group[s]" (Art. 1) but not political ones, nor situations where a government exterminates its political or perceived political opponents, which was what happened in Cambodia at the time. That is why genocide charges have been brought only with regard to crimes against the Cham and the Khmer Krom minorities which qualify as national or ethnical groups (*infra*, fns. 41 and 44).

25 Namely, of persecution on political grounds, subsuming the crimes against humanity of extermination (encompassing murder), enslavement, imprisonment, torture (including one instance of rape), and other inhumane acts.

26 Namely, of wilful killing, torture and inhumane treatment, wilfully causing great suffering or serious injury to body or health, wilfully depriving a prisoner of war or civilian of the rights of fair and regular trial, and unlawful confinement of a civilian.

27 Appeal judgment of 3 February 2012.

imprisonment. For the rest, it mainly modified the legal qualification or the categorization of certain crimes.[28]

Case 002 which was subsequently taken up, involved four senior *Khmer Rouge* leaders, *Ieng Sary*,[29] *Nuon Chea*,[30] *Ieng Thirith* and *Khieu Samphan*.[31] However, only *Nuon Chea* and *Khieu Samphan*, both in their eighties, remained on trial,[32] since *Ieng Sary* died in 2013 and his wife, *Ieng Thirith*, was released in 2012 as she was found mentally unfit to stand trial.

Because of the extraordinary volume of the case, it was decided to divide it into smaller trials (phases).[33] In the judgment on the first phase (Case 002/01), issued on 7 August 2014, the Court found both defendants (*Nuon Chea* and *Khieu Samphan*) guilty of the crimes of humanity of extermination (encompassing murder), political persecution on political grounds and 'other inhumane acts' (comprising forced transfer,[34] enforced disappearances and attacks against human dignity).[35] The judgment found *Nuon Chea* ('Brother Number Two') to have been 'directly responsible and responsible as a superior' for the commission of the crimes referred to above.[36] Both were found to have been part of a 'joint criminal enterprise' (JCE)[37] to commit the crimes. The sentence imposed on both was life imprisonment. On appeal, the Supreme Chamber affirmed, on 23 November 2016,[38] the convictions for the crimes against humanity of murder, persecution on political grounds and other inhumane acts in relation to the evacuation of Phnom Penh immediately after the fall of the city on 17 April 1975. It also affirmed the conviction for the crime against humanity of other inhumane acts, and entered a conviction for the crime against humanity of murder in relation to the second phase of population transfers (between 1975 and 1977). However, the appellate judgment reversed the convictions entered by the Trial Chamber for the crime against humanity of extermination in relation

28 Thus, it quashed the Trial Chamber's decision to subsume under the crime against humanity of persecution the other crimes against humanity for which it found the defendant responsible; it affirmed the defendant's conviction for the crime against humanity of persecution and it entered additional convictions for the crimes against humanity of extermination (encompassing murder), enslavement, imprisonment, torture, and other inhumane acts.

29 Foreign minister of the *Khmer Rouge* regime.

30 Chief ideologue of the *Khmer Rouge* regime.

31 Former Head of State.

32 Born in 1926 and 1931 respectively, they were remitted to trial in 2011.

33 The decision concerning the scope was taken by the Court of First Instance on 4 April 2014. On 29 July 2014, the Supreme Court Chamber decided in favour of the severance of the case following an appeal by the defendants; after many delays, trial hearings resumed on 21 January 2015.

34 The evacuation of cities undertaken by the *Khmer Rouge* in their "quest of an agrarian Marxist utopia" (The Telegraph, AFP, 3 March 2015) caused untold suffering to and had a devastating effect on the evacuees.

35 Judgment, Disposition, p. 622.

36 The judgment clarifies that where an accused is found to be both directly responsible and responsible as a superior in relation to the same conduct, the Chamber will convict on the basis of the former and consider the superior position of the accused as an aggravating factor in sentencing (para. 688).

37 *See* Trial Chamber Judgment on Case File No. 002/19-09-2007/ECCC of 7 August 2014, paras. 392-396.

38 The judgment comprised 520 pages.

to the evacuation of Phnom Penh and the second phase of population transfers, as it found the evidence produced insufficient for that purpose. In connection with the second phase of population transfers, the appellate judgment quashed the convictions for the crime against humanity of persecution on political grounds, again for reasons of lack of relevant evidence. The convictions for the crimes against humanity of extermination, murder and persecution on political grounds at the *Tuol Po Chrey* execution site in North-western Cambodia were also reversed as the Court found that the relevant events could not be attributed to the accused.

Finally, the judgment stated that the sentence of life imprisonment was appropriate in view of the gravity and massive scale of the crimes and the complete lack of consideration on the part of the defendants for the fate of the Cambodian population.

Almost 4,000 civil parties participated in the proceedings to whom the ECCC awarded moral and collective reparations, endorsing 11 projects relating, *inter alia*, to the remembrance of the victims, therapy, psychological assistance and education.[39]

The second phase of the trial against the same defendants (Case 002/02), which started in October 2014,[40] concerned for the first time charges of genocide (against the *Cham* Muslim minority),[41] as well as, *inter alia*, charges of forced marriage, rape and internal purges.[42] On 16 November 2018, the Trial Chamber convicted *Nuon Chea* and *Khieu Samphan* of genocide, crimes against humanity and grave breaches of the Geneva Conventions of 1949, committed at various locations in the country from April 1975 to January 1979.

Case 003 concerns former naval commander and holder of other official positions, *Meas Muth*, charged *in absentia* in March 2015, who appeared before the international co-investigating judge later in the same year. He was accused of genocide, crimes against humanity (among which murder, extermination, enslavement, imprisonment, torture, persecution and other inhumane acts), war crimes (grave breaches of the Geneva Conventions of 1949), as well as of premeditated homicide in violation of the 1956 Cambodian Penal Code. The crimes were committed at various security centres, among them the S-21 Security Centre (*Tuol Sleng*). The investigation by the international co-investigating judge was concluded in January 2017, eight years after its initiation. In November 2017,

---

39 Judgment, Disposition, p. 622.

40 In April 2014 the Trial Chamber decided to proceed to an "additional severance of Case 002."

41 The *Cham* population in Cambodia, most of whom are Muslim, was estimated to be between 150,000 and 250,000 before 1975. Living peacefully until then, they subsequently suffered severe persecution under the *Khmer Rouge* regime. In fact, one-third of Cambodia's *Chams* were murdered between 1975 and 1979. With the defeat of the Khmer Rouge, the *Cham* were able to return to their traditional ways of life and practice their religion (Source: World Directory of Minorities and Indigenous Peoples, available at: http://minorityrights.org/minorities/cham/).

42 The relevant evidentiary hearings concluded in January 2017 and closing statements were made in June 2017. In December 2017 the Trial Chamber ordered an expert medical and psychiatric evaluation of the accused to verify that they remained fit to stand trial for the purposes of delivery of the judgment in Case 002/02.

the international and national co-prosecutors filed their final submissions. One year later, the co-investigating judges (national and international) issued two separate and contradicting Closing Orders, due to disagreement between them about whether *Meas Muth* is subject to the ECCC's personal jurisdiction as a 'senior leader' or one of the persons 'most responsible' for crimes committed during the Democratic Kampuchea period. The investigation conducted in the context of the same case with regard to the suspect *Sou Met*, was terminated following his death in 2014.

Case 004 which originally concerned three suspects, *Im Chaem, Ao An* and *Yim Tith*, was subsequently separated into three case files. In case 004/1, *Im Chaem* was charged with crimes against humanity and homicide as a violation of the 1956 Cambodian Penal Code. The case was, however, dismissed in February 2017 because the accused was found not to be subject to the personal jurisdiction of the ECCC as she was neither a senior leader nor among those most responsible among *Khmer Rouge* officials. The international co-prosecutor filed an appeal against the co-investigating judges' closing order to the Pre-Trial Chamber. The five Judges came to different conclusions regarding the merits of the appeal. Three judges concluded that there was no personal jurisdiction of the ECCC over *Im Chaem* while the other two found that the evidence provided sufficient grounds to consider that the defendant was among those most responsible and that the ECCC could therefore exercise jurisdiction on the case. As four out of five votes are required to overturn a decision of the co-investigating judges, the decision means that the ECCC has no jurisdiction over *Im Chaem*.

Ao An (Case 004/2) was accused of genocide of the *Cham*, crimes against humanity (including, *inter alia*, forced marriage, rape, enforced disappearances, physical abuse, forced labour and inhumane conditions of detention), as well as of violations of the 1956 Cambodian Penal Code. The crimes had been committed in numerous locations, mainly in forced labour and execution sites.[43]

In December 2016, the co-investigating judges concluded their investigation regarding *Ao An*. On 16 August 2018, they issued two separate Closing Orders in the case, due to disagreement whether the accused was subject to the personal jurisdiction of the ECCC. According to the international co-investigating judge, *Ao An* was indeed so, while the national co-investigating Judge maintained that he was not, as the accused was not a 'senior leader' in the *Khmer Rouge* regime.

43 *See* Statement of the International Co-investigating Judge regarding Case 004, of 14 March 2016 (ECCC site).

Although the submission of separate Closing Orders creates a unique procedural situation which, however, the co-investigating judges consider permissible under the law governing the ECCC, the matter will probably be resolved by the Pre-Trial Chamber.

In December 2015, *Yim Tith* was charged by the international co-investigating judge with genocide of the *Khmer Krom*,[44] crimes against humanity, grave breaches of the Geneva Conventions committed as part of an international armed conflict between Cambodia (then Democratic Kampuchea) and Vietnam, and with violations of the 1956 Cambodian Penal Code. The offences were committed in a variety of locations, mainly in security centres, worksites and execution sites. After many years of investigation, in 2017 the co-investigating judges concluded the investigation in *Yim Tith*'s regard. In 2018, the national and international co-prosecutors filed separate final submissions for the case, the national co-prosecutor concluding that it should be dismissed because the accused was not among the senior leaders of the regime or among the most responsible for the crimes committed, and the international co-prosecutor that the trial should go ahead.

Although the process continues, an eventual dismissal of the case is highly probable.[45]

3.3.2 Concluding Remarks

Two main, non-legal problems can be identified in the creation and functioning of the ECCC. The first is that the trials came too late, as a result of which many of the perpetrators had already died or were not in a position to stand trial while those still alive were simply too old and too few to allow the trials to acquire their full paradigmatic character and effect. The second problem is connected with the fact that the Extraordinary Chambers operated within a highly politicized and controversial atmosphere, as exemplified by the repeated instances of diametrically opposed positions taken by the national and international judges and by the national and the international prosecutor respectively. This is a clear indication of the ambivalence, if not mistrust, prevalent in the country and certainly in the government, as to the role of the Extraordinary Chambers. As a consequence, the main message of these trials, which should be that atrocities such as those

---

44 The *Khmer Krom,* meaning the 'Khmer from Below' *i.e.,* from the Mekong Delta region, live in the southwest of today's Vietnam, their presence there preceding that of the Vietnamese. In the 1970s about 200,000 *Khmer Krom* lived in Cambodia, their number increasing as border clashes broke out between Cambodia under the *Khmer Rouge* regime and Vietnam. However, the *Khmer Rouge* viewed them with suspicion as spies and allies of the Vietnamese, as a result of which many of these *Khmer Krom* were murdered by the regime. (Source: Minorities Rights Organization, http://mirocambodia.org/?page_id=11).

45 Briefing Paper of Open Society Justice Initiative, Recent Developments at the Extraordinary Chambers in the Courts of Cambodia: Threat to Permanently Stay Cases 003, 004 and 004/2A (Executive Summary), June 2017. *See also* their Briefing Papers of September 2018 and January 2019.

suffered by the Cambodian people in the period of 'Democratic Kampuchea' should in no way go unpunished or left to be forgotten, has been blunted.[46]

3.4 THE SPECIAL TRIBUNAL FOR LEBANON (STL)[47]

A special case within the context of mixed courts is the Special Tribunal for Lebanon. The Tribunal was established by Security Council Resolution 1757 (2007), to try those accused for the assassination, on 14 February 2014, of the Lebanese former President *Rafiq Hariri* and of twenty-two other persons as well as for injuries caused to hundreds more.[48] The process for the creation of STL had, however, started two years before, with a request of the Lebanese Prime Minister *Fuad Siniora* to the U.N. Secretary General for the establishment of such a Court.[49] Following difficult negotiations between the U.N. and the Lebanese Government, an agreement was reached between them. Having, however, been impossible for the Lebanese Parliament to ratify it, due to internal political strife,[50] the S.C. was obliged to adopt the Agreement and the Statute attached to it, through the above-mentioned resolution 1757 (2007).[51] It is, however, noteworthy that although the Resolution was taken under Chapter VII of the U.N. Charter,[52] the STL, unlike the *ad hoc* Tribunals, was not made a subsidiary organ of the Security Council.

The STL and the national courts of Lebanon have concurrent jurisdiction, but the Tribunal has primacy over national courts (Art. 4 of the Statute).

The eleven judges and prosecutors are Lebanese and international and are appointed by the UNSG. For reasons of security, the seat of the Tribunal is in The Hague.

---

46 *See, e.g.*, the article "ECCC Great Cambodian Achievement," Khmer Times, November 19, 2018.

47 On the Special Tribunal on the Lebanon, *see* Amal Alamuddin, Nidal Nabil Jurdi, David Tolbert (eds) *The Special Tribunal for Lebanon: Law and Practice* (Oxford Monographs in International and Humanitarian and Criminal Law), 2014; Nadim Shehadi & Elizabeth Wilmshurst, *Chatham House, The Special Tribunal for Lebanon: The U.N. on Trial?* (2007), available at www.chathamhouse.org.uk/files/9408_bp0707lebanon.pdf; Marko MilanoviĆ, 'An Odd Couple: Domestic Crimes and International Responsibility in the Special Tribunal for Lebanon, 2007 5 JICJ 1139, p. 1140; Marko MilanoviĆ, *The Oddity that is the Hariri Tribunal, 5 September 2007, available at SSRN: https://ssrn.com/abstract=1014906 or http://dx.doi.org/10.2139/ssrn.1014906; Antonios Tzanakopoulos, ASIL Insight, 7 August 2009, Vol. 13, Issue 11; Nidal Nabil Jurdi, The Subject-Matter Jurisdiction of the Special Tribunal for Lebanon, J Int Criminal Justice (2007) 5 (5): 1125-1138.*

48 By way of a massive blast which shook downtown Beirut. To investigate the incident, the U.N. initially set up the U.N. International Independent Investigation Commission (UNIIIC).

49 UN Doc. S/2005/783, 13 December 2005.

50 Opposition to ratification was expressed by the Lebanese President, the Speaker of the Parliament and a number of parliamentarians.

51 Russia, China, Qatar, Indonesia and South Africa abstained. The Agreement, to which the Statute is attached, appears as an Annex to the Resolution.

52 Among the several resolutions issued on the *Hariri* assassination prior to Resolution S/RES/1757(2007), the S.C. had also issued Resolution S/RES/1664(2006) which requested the SG to negotiate an agreement with the Lebanese Government with a view to the creation of an international tribunal for Lebanon in connection with this particular crime and the crimes committed against other persons simultaneously with it.

The STL started its operations in March 2009. With regard to its subject-matter jurisdiction, STL finds itself in sharp differentiation to the other mixed or *ad hoc* tribunals which were or have been endowed with wide jurisdiction over a variety of grave international crimes. Indeed, the jurisdiction of the STL is monothematic, encompassing essentially only one crime, i.e. the *Hariri* assassination,[53] although it is provided that it may be extended if the Tribunal finds that other attacks which occurred in Lebanon between 1 October 2004 and 12 December 2005 are connected with, and are of a nature and gravity similar to the 2005 attack.[54] Crimes committed after 12 December 2005 may also be included in STL's jurisdiction provided that the same criteria are fulfilled and it is so decided by the Lebanon and the U.N. with the consent of the Security Council.[55] The narrowness of STL's jurisdiction is particularly noteworthy in a country which has been ravaged by grave crimes of international concern which were committed all along its troubled recent history, i.e. in the civil war from 1975 to 1990, as well as during the other conflicts which took place in the country in recent decades[56] and for which there has been no accountability.[57] Questions of selectivity, indeed an 'extreme form' of it[58] are, therefore, inevitably raised and are only enhanced by the fact that Syria has been considered *ab initio* the main suspect for the commission of these crimes, giving the impression that the focus of interest on the matter stems from political rather than humanitarian or legal considerations.

The Tribunal applies solely Lebanese law, i.e. the Lebanese Criminal Code.[59] Despite efforts to include crimes under international criminal law,[60] particularly crimes against humanity,[61] in the jurisdiction of the Tribunal, the effort failed as did the suggestion to also apply the 1998 Arab Convention on the Suppression of Terrorism to which Lebanon is a party. Thus, according to Article 2(a) of its Statute, the Tribunal has mainly jurisdic-

53 Art. 1 (1) of the Agreement.

54 *Ibid.*

55 *Ibid.*

56 In particular during the 22-year Israeli occupation of Southern Lebanon until 2000, the Syrian domination over the country from 1976 to 2005 and the Israeli attack on *Hezbollah* in the Lebanon in 2006.

57 Many crimes were amnestied on the basis of the Lebanese General Amnesty Law of 26 August 1991.

58 *See* Chatham House, International Law Middle East and North Africa Programmes: Meeting Report, The Special Tribunal for Lebanon and the Quest for Truth, Justice and Stability, December 2010, p. 6, available at: www.chathamhouse.org.uk, last accessed 30 June 2017. The Report notes, however, that selectivity is "unfortunately endemic in international criminal justice, and can be ameliorated only with an increase in the universality of accountability mechanisms."

59 The imposition of the capital punishment and forced labour, which are provided for in Lebanese law, were excluded.

60 Nonetheless, Resolution 1757/2007 qualifies the *Hariri* assassination as a "terrorist act," the "implications" of which "constitute a threat to international peace and security."

61 There is, however, legal difficulty in qualifying the Hariri assassination as a crime against humanity. For argumentation in favour of such qualification, *see* Nidal Nabil Jurdi, The Subject-Matter Jurisdiction of the Special Tribunal for Lebanon, *supra*, fn. 47.

tion over acts of 'terrorism, crimes and offences against life and personal integrity',[62] as provided in Lebanese law. The crimes under the jurisdiction of the Tribunal therefore pertain to domestic rather than to international criminal law,[63] and this is another important divergence from legal regime governing the *ad hoc* or the other hybrid, mixed or internationalized tribunals.

In 2011, the pre-trial judge of STL posed a number of questions 'on the applicable law' to the Appeals Chamber of the Tribunal pursuant to Rule 68(G) of the Rules of Procedure and Evidence.[64] In response to these questions, three of which concerned the relationship between the crime of terrorism as provided for by Lebanese law and the relevant international law,[65] the Appeals Chamber issued an important interlocutory decision.[66] The Chamber notes first that although Lebanese criminal law is the substantive applicable law, international law may be taken into account as an interpretative aid for that law under certain conditions. These conditions arise when the interpretation or application of Lebanese law "appears to be unreasonable, or may result in a manifest injustice, or is not consonant with international principles and rules binding upon Lebanon."[67] The Appeals Chamber goes on to accept that, apart from its corrective function, international law may also play the role of a general interpretative aid.[68]

With regard to the questions on terrorism,[69] the Appeals Chamber held that the Tribunal "must apply the provisions of the Lebanese Criminal Code, and not those of inter-

62 Art. 2 of the STL Statute (Applicable Criminal Law) provides that:
The following shall be applicable to the prosecution and punishment of the crimes referred to in Art. 1, subject to the provisions of this Statute:
a. "The provisions of the Lebanese Criminal Code relating to the prosecution and punishment of acts of terrorism, crimes and offences against life and personal integrity, illicit associations and failure to report crimes and offences, including the rules regarding the material elements of a crime, criminal participation and conspiracy; and
b. Articles 6 and 7 of the Lebanese law of 11 January 1958 on "Increasing the penalties for sedition, civil war and interfaith struggle".

63 Resolution 1757/2007 qualifies the *Hariri* assassination as a "terrorist act," the "implications" of which *"constitute a threat to international peace and security."*

64 According to this Rule, "The Pre-Trial Judge may submit to the Appeals Chamber any preliminary question, the interpretation of the Agreement, Statute and Rules regarding the applicable law, that he deems necessary in order to examine and rule on the indictment."

65 These questions were: "(i) Should the Tribunal take into account international notions on terrorism even though Article 2 of the Statute only refers to the Lebanese Criminal Code ('LCC')? (ii) If so, is there an international definition of 'terrorism' and how should it be applied? (iii) If not, how is the Lebanese definition of 'terrorism' to be interpreted by the Chamber?"

66 Case STL 11-01/I, STL, Appeals Chamber, Interlocutory Decision on the applicable law: Terrorism, Conspiracy, Homicide, Perpetration, Cumulative Charging, issued on 16 February 2011 *See* www.stl-tsl.org/sid/55.

67 *Ibid.*, para. 39.

68 Thus, it held that "[W]e must [...] interpret provisions of the Lebanese Criminal Code as they would be interpreted by Lebanese courts and thus for this purpose we take into account international law that is binding on Lebanon" (*Ibid.*, para. 41).

69 *Ibid.*, paras. 42-148.

national treaties ratified by Lebanon or customary international law to define the crime of terrorism."[70] It then accepts, however, "that international conventional and customary law can provide guidance to the Tribunal's interpretation of the Lebanese Criminal Code."[71]

As Article 314 of the Lebanese Criminal Code defines terrorist acts as

> acts intended to cause a state of terror and committed by means liable to create a public danger such as explosive devices, inflammable materials, toxic or corrosive products and infectious or microbial agents

the Appeals Chamber found, on the basis of the abovementioned rationale, that the definition of terrorism under Lebanese law had to be given a wider interpretation in accordance with the relevant rules of international law. Making reference to the jurisprudence of ICTY and the ECtHR, the Chamber argued that the application of the law may be subject to development as social conditions change.[72] This should, however, be foreseeable so as not to run contrary to the *nullum crimen* principle.[73]

On the status of the crime of terrorism, the Chamber argues that it constitutes a crime under international law, at least in time of peace. It asserts that several treaties and U.N. Resolutions as well as state practice indicate that a customary rule of international law on the crime of terrorism has emerged.[74] Furthermore, the Chamber identifies three elements of the definition of the crime of terrorism: a) perpetration or threatening of a criminal act; b) intent to spread fear among the population or coerce a national or international authority to take some action or to refrain from taking it; and c) a transnational element as part of the act.[75]

The findings of the Appeals Chamber were not endorsed by the international academic community which rejected both its assertions, i.e. that the prohibition of terrorism by international treaties and other instruments has allowed the emergence of a crime of terrorism under international law and that there is a universally accepted definition of the crime.[76]

---

70 *Ibid.*, para. 44.
71 *Ibid.*, para. 45.
72 Para. 135.
73 Paras. 136-138.
74 Paras. 83 *et seq.*
75 Para. 85.
76 *See* Kai Ambos, Judicial Creativity at the Special Court for Lebanon: Is There a Crime of Terrorism under International Law?, *Leiden Journal of International Law*, 24 (2011), pp. 655-675. According to Ambos "at this juncture, one may consider terrorism, at best, as a particularly serious transnational, treaty-based crime that is – probably comparable to torture – on the brink of becoming a true international crime"; Ben Saul, *Legislating from a Radical Hague: The United Nations Special Tribunal for Lebanon Invents an International Crime of Transnational Terrorism* 677ff; For another perspective, *see* Alexander Grabert, *Dynamic Interpretation in International Criminal Law: Striking a Balance between Stability and Change*, 2015.

3.4.1 *Trials In Absentia*[77]

Concerns have also been raised by the fact that the STL Statute allows trials *in absentia* (Art. 22), i.e. without the presence of the accused, provided that the latter

> (a) has expressly and in writing waived his/her right to be present; or (b) the state in which he/she is located refuses to surrender him/her to the Tribunal; or (c) if he/she has absconded or otherwise cannot be found, despite all reasonable attempts to secure his/her presence.

If a trial *in absentia* is to be held before the STL, the accused may be represented by counsel of his own choosing or one appointed by the Tribunal. Article 22(3) mitigates the effect of these provisions by providing that

> [i]n case of conviction in absentia, the accused, if he or she had not designated a defence counsel of his or her choosing, has the right to be retried in his or her presence, unless he or she accepts the judgement.

Trials *in absentia*, known to civil law systems, have gradually receded due to the advancement of human rights, particularly the right to a fair trial as established in human rights universal or regional treaties.[78] Thus, the possibility for such trials has all but disappeared from the Statutes of international tribunals.[79] In the case of STL it reappeared, not so much because trials *in absentia* are recognized under Lebanese law, but because the countries involved, Lebanon and particularly Syria, were not likely to hand over the accused found on their territory. The STL Appeals Chamber addressed the issue of trials *in absentia* when dealing with a related challenge brought by the defence in the *Ayyash et al. Case*,[80] finding that the Trial Chamber which had issued the impugned decision[81] had

77 Moha Hadi Zakerhossein & Anne-Marie de Brouwer, Diverse approaches to total and partial *in absentia* trials by international criminal tribunals, 2015; Amal Alamuddin, Nidal Nabil Jurdi, David Tolbert (eds), *op. cit.*, pp. 229 *et seq.*; Maggie Gardner, Reconsidering Trials *In Absentia* at the Special Tribunal for Lebanon: An Application of the Tribunal's Early Jurisprudence (2011) 43 *Geo Wash Int'l L Rev* 91; William Schabas, 'In Absentia Proceedings before International Criminal Courts', in Göran Sluiter and Sergey Vasiliev, *International Criminal Procedure: Towards a Coherent Body of Law*, London: Cameron May, 2009, pp. 335-380.

78 *See* in particular Art. 14(3)(d) of the ICCPR.

79 ICTY Statute, Art. 21(4)(d); ICTR Statute, Art. 20(4)(d); ICC Statute, Arts. 63 and 60(1). By contrast, trials *in absentia* were provided for in Art. 12 the Charter of the International Military Tribunal at Nuremberg.

80 *Ayyash et al.*, Appeals Chamber, Decision on Defence Appeals Against Trial Chamber's Decision on Reconsideration of the Trial In Absentia Decision Case No.: STL-11-01/PT/AC/AR126.1; 1 November 2012 (In Absentia Reconsideration AC).

81 *Ayyash et al.*, Trial Chamber, Decision on Reconsideration of the In Absentia Decision, Case No.: STL-11-01/PT/TC; 11 July 2012 (In Absentia Reconsideration TC).

not erred in refusing to reconsider its finding that the trial could be held *in absentia*, since it (the Trial Chamber)

> applied the highest evidentiary standards in establishing that the Accused were informed of the charges against them, of their right to participate in the proceedings and of the consequences if they did not appear.[82]

3.4.2 *The Cases*

Ayyash et al.[83] is the first case to open before the Tribunal. The accused are *Salim Jamil Ayyash, Hassan Habib Merhi, Hussein Hassan Oneissi* and *Assad Hassan Sabra*, all allegedly *Hezbollah* members. The indictment was issued in 2011 and has been modified several times to take into account relevant developments. However, as the warrants issued for their arrest remain outstanding, the trial, which started on 16 January 2014, is being conducted *in absentia*. In February 2018, the presentation of the Prosecutor's case was completed and the trial entered its final phase with the presentation of the Defence case.[84]

A connected case concerns the attacks against the Lebanese politicians *Marwan Hamadeh, George Hawi* and *Elias El-Murr*[85] and it is still in the phase of investigation.[86]

82 *Ayyash et al.*, Appeals Chamber, *supra*, fn. 264, para. 46.

83 STL-11-01.

84 However, the only Defence case presented is by the Counsel of the defendant *Oneissi*, the other defendants having apparently decided not to do so.

85 STL-11-02.

86 The STL has jurisdiction to impose criminal penalties for conduct interfering with the administration of justice or threatening the integrity of the judicial proceedings, including interference with witnesses. On 31 January 2014, two individuals and two media companies were charged with contempt and obstruction of justice in relation to media reports containing information about alleged confidential STL witnesses. Two of them were acquitted (STL-14-05) while the other two, *Ibrahim Mohamed Ali Al Amin* and *Akhbar Beirut S.A.L.* (STL-14-06) were found guilty and have been fined.

4 The International Criminal Court (ICC)[1]

4.1 Scope

In connection with the International Criminal Court, we will examine the Court's subject-matter jurisdiction, which extends over a) genocide, b) crimes against humanity, c) war crimes and d) the crime of aggression.[2] This will include, apart from the description and analysis of the substantive content of these crimes, some brief historical notes as well as references to relevant jurisprudence of the ICC and other international tribunals.[3]

4.2 Crimes Under the Jurisdiction of the ICC

The ICC Statute entered into force on 1 July 2002.[4] Since then, the Court may prosecute persons for the commission of crimes under its jurisdiction, provided that all the other applicable conditions formal and substantive prescribed by the Statute, are fulfilled.

Each of the categories of crimes mentioned above is defined in the Statute. Nevertheless, for further assistance to the judge, the Assembly of States Parties (ASP) has also produced, as mandated by Article 30 of the Statute, 'Elements of Crimes' which "shall assist the Court in the interpretation and application of Articles 6, 7, 8 and 8 bis."[5]

4.2.1 Genocide

Genocide is rightfully considered the gravest of all international crimes ('crime of crimes'). It has nonetheless never ceased to be committed, under various denominations, all along the course of human history. The twentieth century has seen two major, well-known genocides, that of Armenians by Turkey and Jews by Nazi Germany, while other

1 For bibliography on the ICC see *supra*, fn. 1.

2 The jurisdiction of the Court over the crime of aggression which remained inoperative until at least thirty states had ratified the Kampala amendments with regard to this crime and all other relevant requirements had been fulfilled, will be activated as of 17 July 2018, following a Resolution of the Assembly of States Parties to the ICC Statute of December 2017 (see *infra*, pp. 101-103).

3 Other relevant topics may also be mentioned or covered briefly.

4 For an historical survey of the efforts to establish an International Criminal Court from 1919 onwards *see* M. Cherif Bassiouni, Historical Survey: 1919-1998 in The Statute of the International Criminal Court, A Documentary History, Compilation by Cherif Bassiouni, pp. 1-35.

5 Their adoption required, according to Art. 30, a majority of two thirds of the ASP.

ethnic and similar groups such as the Pontian or Pontic Greeks[6] and the Roma[7] have suffered less known genocides by the same regimes respectively. The genocides in Cambodia[8] and in Rwanda are more recent examples of this crime in the twentieth century, while the *Yazidis* of Northern Iraq suffered the same fate when under ISIS control from 2014 to 2016 and beyond.[9]

4.2.1.1 Historical Notes

Despite its gravity, genocide was late to be recognized as a crime on its own. Thus, it did not appear in the Nuremberg and Tokyo judgments (although it did appear in the indictments) as it was covered, for the purposes of the relevant trials, by 'crimes against humanity', another novel term at the time. The term 'genocide' was coined by *Raphaël Lemkin*, a Polish-Jewish lawyer who had been himself a victim of Nazi persecution in Germany.[10]

The conceptual and legal autonomy of genocide as a crime was, however, recognized shortly after World War II. In its very first session in 1946, the United Nations General Assembly adopted a Resolution declaring that genocide constitutes a crime under international law.[11] The Genocide Convention which was adopted in 1948 asserts that genocide is a crime under international customary law whether committed in time of peace or in time of war.[12] Indeed, the reason why genocide needed to be a separate crime at the time was that crimes against humanity, which could also cover it in substance, were linked with war, thus excluding the possibility of their commission in time of peace. Today, the fact that crimes against humanity have been disassociated from war makes the legal need for the existence of the crime of genocide less obvious.

Genocide is also a crime under the Statutes of the *ad hoc* Tribunals for the crimes committed in the former Yugoslavia and in Rwanda respectively[13] and both have issued

6 350,000 Greeks of the Pondos (Black Sea) were massacred by Turkey between 1914 and 1923. For a brief account, *see* Jeff Benvenuto and John Lim, *The Genocide of Ottoman Greeks, 1914-1923*, Rutgers University, http://www.ncas.rutgers.edu/center-study-genocide-conflict-resolution-and-human-rights/genocide-ottoman-greeks-1914-1923.

7 258,000 gypsies are estimated to have been exterminated by the Nazi regime. *See, e.g.*, Genocide of European Roma (Gypsies), 1939-1945, The Holocaust Encyclopedia, The United States Holocaust Memorial Museum. (www.ushmm.org/wlc/en/article.php?Moduled=10005143), accessed on 9 June 2017.

8 On this issue *see infra, 4.2.1.2.*

9 The Independent International Commission of Inquiry on the Syrian Arab Republic established on 22 August 2011 by Resolution S-17/1 of the Human Rights Council, has recognized in its Report A/HRC/32/CRP.2 (Advance Version) of 15 June 2016 that "ISIS has committed the crime of genocide as well as multiple crimes against humanity and war crimes against the Yazidis, thousands of whom are held captive in the Syrian Arab Republic where they are subjected to almost unimaginable horrors." (p. 1. Summary).

10 The term appeared in his book: Axis rule in occupied Europe: Laws of occupation, analysis of government, proposals for redress, Washington DC: Carnegie Endowment for World Peace, 1944. Raphaël Lemkin is also the author of the book "Genocide as a crime in international law," 1947.

11 Res. 96(1) of 11 December 1946.

12 Art. 1.

13 *See supra*, sections 2.1.1 and 2.2.1.

judgments sentencing a considerable number of individuals for genocide.[14] Pivotal among them are the *Akayesu*[15] and *Kambanda*[16] judgments of the Rwanda Tribunal.

4.2.1.2 Genocide Under Article 6 of the ICC Statute

Under this article, genocide is defined as in the 1948 Genocide Convention, i.e. as

> any of the following acts committed with intent to destroy, in whole or in part, a national, ethnical, racial or religious group, as such: (a) Killing members of the group; (b) Causing serious bodily or mental harm to members of the group; (c) Deliberately inflicting on the group conditions of life calculated to bring about its physical destruction in whole or in part; (d) Imposing measures intended to prevent births within the group; (e) Forcibly transferring children of the group to another group.[17]

The five acts described in Article 6 constitute the *actus reus* of the crime. The distinguishing characteristic of genocide which sets it apart from the other crimes, is, however, that the relevant acts must be committed not only with the corresponding mental element (*mens rea*)[18] but also with a 'special or specific intent' (*dolus specialis*) which is to 'destroy' the members of the groups concerned (genocidal intent).

However, which exactly must be the quantitative or qualitative content of such destruction or of each one of the acts mentioned in Article 6 of the Statute is a matter of considerable discussion or even disagreement between scholars which is ultimately being left to the courts to decide upon.[19] In any case, jurisprudence has answered these questions with significant variability.[20]

The groups targeted for genocide may be, according to the definition, national, ethnic, racial or religious. The enumeration has been considered overly restrictive, particularly as it does not include political, social or cultural groups. The omission of political groups, for example, would not allow the qualification of the extermination of political opponents of the *Khmer Rouge* regime in Cambodia in the 1970s as genocide.

Even more restrictive on the matter has been considered the aforementioned *Akayesu* judgment issued by the Rwanda Tribunal which found that: "...a national group is de-

---

14 *See supra*, section 2.2.2.

15 ICTR, *Jean Paul Akayesu*, ICTR Case No. 96-4, Ch. 1, 2 September 998.

16 ICTR, *Jean Kambanda*, ICTR Case No. 97-23-S, 4 September 1998.

17 It is worth noting that the Statute does not specify further the defining characteristics of the groups which may be the victims of genocide nor is this done in the "Elements of Crimes."

18 As defined in Art. 30 of the ICC Statute.

19 This of course includes the jurisprudence produced by the *ad hoc* tribunals and other criminal courts whether international or national.

20 On this issue *see* William Schabas, *An Introduction to the International Criminal Court*, 3rd edn., Cambridge, 2010, pp. 93-96.

fined as a collection of people who are perceived to share a legal bond based on common citizenship, coupled with reciprocity of rights and duties" and that an ethnic group is "generally defined as a group whose members share a common language or culture." According to the same judgment, the definition of a racial group "...is based on the hereditary physical traits often identified with a geographical region, irrespective of linguistic, cultural, national or religious factors" and a "religious group is one whose members share the same religion, denomination or mode of worship."[21] This narrow interpretation has not, however, been sustained by later judgments of the *ad hoc* Tribunals.[22]

4.2.2 *Crimes Against Humanity*

Like genocide, crimes which are recognized today as crimes against humanity have never stopped been committed all along human history. They had not, however, been the object of legal analysis, at least not as much as war crimes, until about the middle of the past century, mainly because war crimes seemed to cover them insofar as crimes against humanity were committed in war time.

4.2.2.1 Historical Notes

The first international text which recognized that the use of certain weapons would be 'contrary to the laws of humanity' was the Declaration of Saint Petersburg of 1868 'Renouncing the Use, in Time of War, of Explosive Projectiles under 400 grammes Weight'.[23] Three decades later, in the Preamble of the 'Hague Convention with Respect to the Laws and Customs of War on Land' adopted by the Hague Conference in 1899, the laws of humanity were mentioned in the context of the *Martens clause.*[24] The clause was repeated in the Hague Conference of 1907 as well as in most of the other international instruments on humanitarian law, among which are the 1949 Geneva Conventions and their 1977 two Additional Protocols.

Crimes against humanity were also mentioned in the 1915 Common Declaration of Britain, France and Russia, which condemned the massacre of 1,500,000 Armenians by

21 *Akayesu, supra,* paras. 512-515.

22 *See, e.g., ICTR, Clément Kayishema and Obed Ruzíndana,* (ICTR-95-1-T), Judgment, 21 May 1999, para. 98; ICTR, *Rutaganda* (ICTR-96-3-T), Judgment, 6 December 1999; ICTY paras. 56-58, *Goran Jelisić,* (IT-95-10), Judgment, 14 December 1999 paras. 70-72. On more cases *see* Agnieszka Szpak National, Ethnic, Racial, and Religious Groups Protected against Genocide in the Jurisprudence of the ad hoc International Criminal Tribunals, *European Journal of International Law,* 2012.

23 29.11 November/11.12 December 1868.

24 The purpose of the *Martens* clause is defined in its text as follows: "Until a more complete code of the laws of war is issued, the High Contracting Parties think it right to declare that in cases not included in the Regulations adopted by them, populations and belligerents remain under the protection and empire of the principles of international law, as they result from the usages established between civilized nations, from the laws of humanity and the requirements of the public conscience" (www.icrc.org/eng/resources/documents/article/other/57jnhy.htm).

Turkey in that year. In the Declaration, the crimes committed then were qualified as crimes against humanity and civilization (it is indicative of the proximity of concepts of genocide and crimes against humanity that since then these crimes have been qualified as genocide) for which responsibility was attributed to all the members of the Turkish government and its organs involved in the massacres. Nonetheless, certain trials which commenced in accordance with Ottoman law and resulted in the execution of a few convicts in 1919 were interrupted with the ascendance of the 'Young Turks' in power. The Treaty of Sèvres of 10 August 1920, which provided for the creation of a court to try those responsible for the crimes against the Armenians committed after the beginning of World War I, never entered into force.[25] Finally, the Lausanne Peace Treaty of 24 July 1923, which replaced the Treaty of Sèvres, provided amnesty for all the crimes committed between 1914 and 1922.

Following World War I, a special War Crimes Commission set up by the 1919 Versailles Peace Conference, proposed, in its Report to the Conference, the creation of an international criminal court to try the crimes committed during 'the Great War'. The Court should also have jurisdiction over crimes against humanity (violations against the laws of humanity). However, the proposal did not have any follow-up.

The fact that some of the most egregious Nazi crimes before and during World War II remained outside the category of war crimes for various reasons, among which because they were committed against German nationals, particularly Jews, prompted the allies to include in the Nuremberg Charter the 'new' category of crimes against humanity. These crimes included

> murder, extermination, enslavement, deportation, and other inhumane acts committed against any civilian population, before or during the war, or persecutions on political, racial or religious grounds in execution or in connection with any crime within the jurisdiction of the Tribunal, whether or not in violation of the law of the country where perpetrated.[26]

The 1944 Law No. 10 issued by the Allied Control Council[27, 28] allowed the arrest by the Allied Powers of persons accused of war crimes and other crimes of similar nature who were not among those brought before the Nuremberg International Military Tribunal,

25 *See* Rodney Dixon, *Crimes Against Humanity*, Otto Triffterer, *Commentary on the International Criminal Court, op. cit.*, para. 1 chapeau, pp. 121-129.

26 Art. 6(c).

27 The U.S., the Soviet Union, Great Britain and France.

28 See *also supra*, pp. 7-8.

and the establishment of tribunals elsewhere in occupied Germany where the accused would stand trial. Law No. 10 added to the list of crimes against humanity of the Nuremberg Charter those of imprisonment, torture and rape.[29] The list contained in Law No. 10 stated expressly that it was indicative, which differentiated it from the Nuremberg Charter, but only partly so, since the Nuremberg Charter provided also for the jurisdiction of the Tribunal over 'other inhumane acts'. Furthermore, the jurisdiction of these tribunals over crimes against humanity was not constrained by a requirement that the latter should have been committed 'in execution or in connection with any crime within their jurisdiction'. That meant that such crimes could have been committed even outside an armed conflict.

The Tokyo Charter of 1946 also provided for the jurisdiction of the Tokyo Tribunal over crimes against humanity, repeating almost entirely on this matter the Nuremberg Charter, one difference being that persecution for religious reasons was not included, since such reasons had played no part in persecutions in the Far East. Another element of differentiation was that, like for any other crime under the Tokyo Charter, also for the exercise for prosecution for a crime against humanity, it was necessary to establish its linkage with the crime against peace (aggression).

In the following decades, the cold war did not allow for any major development in connection with the prosecution and punishment of crimes against humanity on an international level. On a national level, some well-known trials involving the commission of war crimes and crimes against humanity during World War II were held, particularly that of *Adolf Eichmann* in Israel, and *Maurice Papon* and *'Klaus' Barbie* in France. There was also the adoption, in the context of the U.N., of several declaratory and normative instruments in connection with crimes against humanity. The first in time was the 1946 UNGA Resolution which recognized the 'concept' of these crimes.[30] Relevant normative texts were the Convention on the Non-applicability of Statutory Limitations to War Crimes and Crimes against Humanity of 1968,[31] the Convention on the Suppression and Punishment of the Crime of Apartheid of 1973[32] and the Convention for the Protection of all Persons from Enforced Disappearance of 2006.[33]

As noted above, the lists of crimes against humanity in the ICTY and ICTR Statutes were based on that of the Allied Council Law No. 10. However, the jurisdiction of ICTY was restricted to crimes committed in the context of armed conflict, whether internal or international, while the jurisdiction of the ICTR contained no similar restriction.

---

29 According to Art. II.1(c) of the Law, crimes against humanity were: "Atrocities and offences, including but not limited to murder, extermination, enslavement, deportation, imprisonment, torture, rape, or other inhumane acts committed against any civilian population, or persecutions on political, racial or religious grounds whether or not in violation of the domestic laws of the country where perpetrated."

30 Res. 95(1), U.N. Doc A/64/Add. 1(1946).

31 26 November 1968. Adopted by G.A. Resolution 2391.

32 30 November 1993. Adopted by G.A. Resolution 3068.

33 20 December 2006. Adopted by G.A. Resolution 177.

4.2.2.2 Crimes Against Humanity Under Article 7 of the ICC Statute

The Statute adopts an extended list of crimes against humanity[34] which are enumerated in Article 7(1). Most of them are provided with legal definitions; this was done for the first time by the Statute of an international criminal tribunal,[35] which constitutes a major achievement of the Rome Conference which will certainly have a resonance beyond the ICC Statute and the Court's jurisprudence, influencing domestic legislations and developments in international humanitarian and criminal law in general.

A development of great significance is that, under the ICC Statute, crimes against humanity are not required to be connected with an armed conflict. This had been a major issue during the negotiations on the Statute where, despite the efforts of a significant number of states to have such a linkage with armed conflict, the opposite view finally prevailed, thus extending the scope of application of the Statute over criminal practices which are very often carried out in time of peace as well.

Some of the crimes are novel to the category of crimes against humanity, as is the case with the crimes of forced pregnancy and enforced prostitution, as well as with the crimes of apartheid and enforced disappearance of persons. All crimes listed in Article 7 are subject to several conditions which are mentioned in the *Chapeau* of that article.

Of particular importance for the interpretation of the general provisions of the Statute with regard to crimes against humanity (in connection with both, *actus reus* and *mens rea*) is the Introduction to the Elements of these crimes which clarifies various relevant issues, including some which had remained pending in the Rome Conference in view of the elaboration of the Elements of Crimes by the Assembly of States Parties.[36] Thus, the Introduction to the Elements states, *inter alia*, that the provisions of Article 7 must be strictly construed consistent with their appurtenance to international criminal law and the application of the legality principle.[37] It also explains that the reprehensible conduct described in Article 7 is required to be 'impermissible under generally applicable international law, as recognized by the principal legal systems of the world'. The last phrase represents a compromise attained with a significant number of countries, which believed

34 These are: Murder; Extermination; Enslavement; Deportation or forcible transfer of population; Imprisonment or other severe deprivation of physical liberty in violation of fundamental rules of international law; Torture; Rape; Sexual slavery; Enforced prostitution; Forced pregnancy, enforced sterilization or any other form of sexual violence of comparable gravity; Persecution against any identifiable group or collectivity on political, racial, national, ethnic, cultural, religious, gender as defined in para. 3, or other grounds that are universally recognized as impermissible under international law, in connection with any act referred to in this paragraph or any crime within the jurisdiction of the Court; Enforced disappearance of persons; The crime of apartheid; Other inhumane acts of a similar character intentionally causing great suffering, or serious injury to body or to mental or physical health.

35 Art. 7(2).

36 On this matter *see* Göran Sluiter, "Chapeau Elements" of Crimes against humanity in the Jurisprudence of the U.N. Ad Hoc Tribunals, in Leila Nadya Sadat (ed), *Forging a Convention on Crimes Against Humanity*, Cambridge University Press, 2011.

37 Art. 22 of the Rome Statute.

that the criminalization of certain conduct could include practices which were permissible under their own legal customs (e.g. the *Shariah*).

According to the Chapeau of Article 7, all the crimes must be committed 'as part of a widespread or systematic attack directed against any civilian population, with knowledge of the attack'. These, as indicated in the Introduction to the Elements of Crimes, are the contextual elements within which crimes against humanity must be committed.[38] As a consequence of the language used by the Statute, the attack need not be cumulatively widespread *and* systematic: either of the two would suffice on its own. The use of the phrase 'any civilian population' is meant to include within the victims of crimes against humanity not only persons with the nationality of the enemy but also persons who are nationals of the state which commits the attack against them. The Introduction to the Elements of Crimes[39] provides that such an attack, which need not have a military character,

> is understood to mean a course of conduct involving the multiple commission of acts referred to in article 7, paragraph 1, of the Statute against any civilian population, pursuant to or in furtherance of a State or organizational policy to commit such attack.[40]

Such policy 'requires that the State or organization actively promote or encourage such an attack against a civilian population'.

As already noted, Article 7 of the ICC Statute contains the requirement for 'knowledge of the attack' which is repeated in the elements of individual crimes against humanity. This constitutes an additional mental element which is not identified with the *mens rea* requirements of Article 30 which are applicable to all crimes under ICC jurisdiction.[41] 'Knowledge of the attack' does not require proof that the perpetrator had knowledge of all the details of the attack or of the plan or policy it served.[42]

4.2.3 War Crimes

These are serious violations of the rules of international humanitarian law (IHL) which entail individual criminal responsibility. IHL is the law applicable in armed conflict and

---

38 Para. 2 of the Introduction to the Elements of Crimes.

39 *Ibid.*, para. 3.

40 On the problems created by the phrase "multiple commission" in combination with "pursuant to or in furtherance of a State or organizational policy to commit such attack" regarding, *inter alia,* the alternative application in "widespread or systematic attack", *see* Kai Ambos, Crimes against Humanity in the Statute of the International Criminal Court, in Leila Nadya Sadat (ed), *op. cit.*, p. 285.

41 *Ibid.*, p. 288.

42 Introduction to the Elements of crimes against humanity. From the ICTY jurisprudence *see* Kunarac *et al.*, Appeals judgment, para. 98.

enemy occupation, formerly known as law of war (*jus in bello*). The rules of IHL derive either from international customary law or from international treaties. However, as happens with other rules of international law, it is not always clear or there is not always general agreement on whether a particular rule of IHL has reached the status of international customary law.[43, 44]

As a matter of tradition, IHL is composed of the 'Hague Law' and the 'Geneva Law'. The former comprises the Conventions produced by the two Hague Conferences of 1899[45] and 1907[46] which regulate the means and methods of warfare for the purpose of alleviating suffering and preventing or reducing destruction. Most important among these conventional texts are the 'Regulations respecting the Laws and Customs of War on Land' annexed to Convention IV of the 1907 Hague Conference. 'Geneva Law', on the other hand, primarily concerns the protection of civilians and persons who no longer participate in hostilities. It consists of the four Geneva Conventions of 12 August 1949 which are: a) Convention for the Amelioration of the Condition of the Wounded and

43 *E.g.*, it is contested by a number of states and scholars whether the rules contained in Additional Protocol II to the Geneva Conventions reflect customary international law.

44 In 2005, the ICRC published a Report containing 160 rules of customary international humanitarian law which, as such, are binding on all states. Several states contested whether some of these rules form indeed part of customary international law, mainly arguing that their application has not been confirmed by state practice.

45 The 1899 Conference adopted three Conventions and three Declarations, comprised in its Final Act: I. Convention for the Peaceful Settlement of International Disputes; II. Convention regarding the Laws and Customs of War on Land and Regulations respecting the Laws and Customs of War on Land annexed thereto; III. Convention for the Adaptation to Maritime Warfare of the Principles of the Geneva Convention of 22 August 1864. The Conference also adopted three Declarations: I. Declaration concerning the Prohibition of the Discharge of Projectiles and Explosives from Balloons or by Other New Analogous Methods; II. Declaration concerning the Prohibition of the Use of Projectiles with the Sole Object to Spread Asphyxiating Poisonous Gases; III. Declaration concerning the Prohibition of the Use of Bullets which can easily Expand or Change their Form inside the Human Body such as Bullets with a Hard Covering which does not Completely Cover the Core, or Containing Indentations.

46 The 1907 Conference adopted thirteen Conventions and one Declaration comprised in its Final Act. These were: I. Convention for the Pacific Settlement of International Disputes (which expands the 1899 Convention I); II. Convention respecting the Limitation of the Employment of Force for Recovery of Contract Debts; III. Convention relative to the Opening of Hostilities; IV. Convention respecting the Laws and Customs of War on Land and Regulations respecting the Laws and Customs of War on Land annexed thereto; (confirms, with slight modifications, the Convention of 1899 and its attached Regulations); V. Convention relative to the Rights and Duties of Neutral Powers and Persons in case of War on Land; VI): Convention relative to the Legal Position of Enemy Merchant Ships at the Start of Hostilities; VII. Convention relative to the Conversion of Merchant Ships into War-ships; VIII. Convention relative to the Laying of Automatic Submarine Contact Mines; IX. Convention concerning Bombardment by Naval Forces in Time of War; X. Convention for the Adaptation to Maritime Warfare of the Principles of the Geneva Convention of 6 July 1906; XI. Convention relative to Certain Restrictions with regard to the Exercise of the Right of Capture in Naval War; XII. Convention relative to the Establishment of an International Prize Court (it did not enter into force); XIII. Convention concerning the Rights and Duties of Neutral Powers in Naval War; Declaration Prohibiting the Discharge of Projectiles and Explosives from Balloons (which extended the validity of the related Declaration of 1899 to the close of Third Peace Conference, which, however, never took place due to the outbreak of WWI). The Conference did not reaffirm the Declarations Prohibiting Asphyxiating Gas and Expanding Bullets.

Sick in Armed Forces in the Field (GC I); b) Convention for the Amelioration of the Condition of Wounded, Sick and Shipwrecked Members of Armed Forces at Sea (GC II); c) Convention relative to the Treatment of Prisoners of War (GC III); and d) Convention relative to the Protection of Civilian Persons in Time of War (GC IV). The Conventions are complemented by two Protocols Additional to them, adopted on 8 June 1977: Additional Protocol I (AP I) relating to the Protection of Victims of International Armed Conflicts, and Additional Protocol II (AP II), relating to the Protection of Victims of Non-International Armed Conflicts.[47]

4.2.3.1 Historical Notes

Rules on the conduct of armed conflict go back thousands of years and they have not been the product of either a single geographical area or of a single civilization. Thus, in ancient Greece, there were rules which were applicable in time of war for the purpose of alleviating suffering and establishing a measure of mercy. Temples and priests were inviolable as were, generally, envoys of the enemy, while the right of sanctuary was respected. *Coleman Phillipson* notes that prisoners were 'ransomed and exchanged' while safe-conducts, truces and armistices were granted and respected.[48] The use of poisoned weapons and treacherous means was prohibited.[49] Philosophers, poets, artists, and, generally, 'men of intellectual distinction' were spared out of respect even if belonging to the side of the enemy.[50]

In Rome, *jus belli* imposed restrictions on the way warfare was conducted, and condemned barbaric practices and treachery.[51] Established proceedings prior to formal proclamation of war were adhered to by the Romans, who also regularly granted and observed truces. In general, they accepted numerous rules for the mitigation of warfare including those introduced by the Greeks.[52]

In India, the ancient Hindu epic *Mahabharata* referred to rules on the conduct of warfare which provided for the humane treatment of civilians and prisoners. The ninth-century Islamic law contained rules prohibiting the killing of women, children and the elderly as well as of the blind, the crippled or the 'helpless insane'.[53]

---

47 There is also Additional Protocol III of 8 December 2005 relating to the Adoption of an Additional Distinctive Emblem. The Protocol introduced a third emblem, the Red Crystal, which does not have any religious connotation in order to facilitate the work of medical and humanitarian aid personnel operating in war zones.

48 Coleman Phillipson, The International Law and Customs of Greece and Rome, MacMillan, 1911, vol. 2, p. 221.

49 *Ibid.*

50 *Ibid.*

51 *Ibid.*, pp. 223 *et seq.*

52 *Ibid.*, p. 233.

53 *See* Leslie Green, The contemporary Law of Armed Conflict, 1993, p. 20, referring to The Islamic Law of Nations, (Shaybani's Siyar), circa the beginning of the ninth century, translated by Khadduri (1966), s. 29-31, 47, 81, 110-111.

In the Middle Ages, prohibitions of certain means of war are found in the *Corpus Juris Canonici* (1500 A.D.). Thus, the Church forbade Christians from using darts or catapults in their wars (in order to reduce as far as possible the number of 'the engines of destruction and death'),[54] under threat of anathema. Adherence to this rule was, however, doubtful.[55]

In 1863, during the American civil war, the *Lieber Code*[56] became law by President *Abraham Lincoln*. The Code, although domestic legislation of the U.S., reflected the generally recognized customary law on armed conflict at the time. A salient example of the humanitarian provisions of the Code is Article 16 according to which:

> [M]ilitary necessity does not admit of cruelty – that is, the infliction of suffering for the sake of suffering or for revenge, nor of maiming or wounding except in fight, nor of torture to extort confessions. It does not admit of the use of poison in any way, nor of the wanton devastation of a district. It admits of deception, but disclaims acts of perfidy; and, in general, military necessity does not include any act of hostility which makes the return to peace unnecessarily difficult.[57]

In 1864, the Geneva Convention for the Amelioration of the Condition of the Wounded in Armies in the Field was adopted. The Convention was amended, revised and complemented by the subsequent Geneva Conventions of 1906 and 1929.

In 1868, at the initiative of Russia, a Conference was convened in Saint Petersburg, where the abovementioned Declaration of 11 December 1868 was adopted. This was a conventional instrument which prohibited the use of certain projectiles weighing less than 400 g which exploded upon contact with the human body. The Declaration applied in both, war on land and at sea.

There followed the 1874 Brussels Conference and in 1899 and 1907 the two Hague Conferences referred to above. Although the advent of World War I caused the postponement of the Third Conference, it led, in reaction to the use of poisonous and similar gases in its course, to the adoption by the League of Nations, in 1925, of the Protocol for the Prohibition of the Use of Asphyxiating, Poisonous or Other Gases, and of Bacteriological Methods of Warfare.[58]

54 *Ibid.*, p. 21 and fn. 26.

55 *Ibid.*, p. 21 and fn. 27.

56 From the name of Professor Francis Lieber who wrote it. The Code is also known as "Instructions for the Government of Armies in the Field," AJIL, Volume 1.

57 *See also* Arts. 37, 44, 47.

58 Of 17 June 1925.

Following the adoption of the 1949 Geneva Conventions and their two 1977 Additional Protocols, a series of conventional instruments considerably extended and reinforced 'Hague Law'.[59]

4.2.3.2 Criminalization of Violations of International Humanitarian Law

The first well-known attempt to prosecute individuals responsible for war crimes on an international level was made, as already mentioned, by the Versailles Peace Treaty, immediately after World War I. The Treaty furthermore provided for the establishment of an international tribunal to bring the *Kaiser* to justice, while the Allied could try those accused for war crimes before their own national courts.

The ground for these provisions had been prepared by the Commission on Responsibilities and Sanctions against those Responsible for the War. The Commission had established four groups of crimes for which the accused would be tried: a) crimes against the sanctity of treaties' b) crimes against international morality' c) violations against the laws of humanity' and d) 'genuine' war crimes, i.e. violations of the Hague Regulations, the Treaty of the Red Cross of 1864 and of recognized rules of naval warfare.

However, the plans of the Allied did not come to fruition. The Netherlands, where the Kaiser had taken refuge, declined to surrender him (so did Germany with regard to all the accused for war crimes). Finally, the international tribunal was not set up, while very poor results were produced by the trials held in Germany before the German Supreme Court (*Reichsgericht*) in Leipzig.[60] The only legal heritage left by the Commission was the list of violations of humanitarian law it drew up, which was later taken up by the Nuremberg Charter.

The Charter defined war crimes as 'violations of the laws or customs of war' which included but were not limited to

59 These are: The 1954 Convention for the Protection of Cultural Property in the Event of Armed Conflict with Regulations for the execution of the Convention, together with a First Protocol thereto. A Second Protocol was elaborated in 1999; The 1972 London, Moscow and Washington Convention on the Prohibition of the Development, Production and Stockpiling of Bacteriological (biological) and Toxin weapons and on their Destruction (BTWC); the 1980 Convention on Prohibitions or Restrictions on the Use of Certain Conventional Weapons which may be Deemed to be Excessively Injurious or to have Indiscriminate Effects (CCW), with its accompanying Protocols on Non-Detectable Fragments (Protocol I), on Prohibitions or Restrictions on the Use of Mines, Booby-Traps and Other Devices (Protocol II) and on Prohibitions or Restrictions on the Use of Incendiary Weapons (Protocol III), as well as the Protocol on Blinding Laser Weapons of 1995 (Protocol IV), and the Protocol on Explosive Remnant of War of 2003 (Protocol V); The1993 Convention on the Prohibition of the Development, Production, Stockpiling and Use of Chemical Weapons and on their Destruction; the 1997 Convention on the Prohibition of the Use, Stockpiling, Production and Transfer of Anti-Personnel Mines and on their Destruction; The 2008 Convention on Cluster Munitions (CCM); The 2013 Arms Trade Treaty (This list does not include treaties relating to nuclear weapons).

60 Characterized as "show trials" (*See* Gerhard Werle, Principles of International Criminal Law, *op. cit.*, pp. 4-5).

> murder, ill-treatment or deportation to slave labour or for any other purpose of civilian population of or in occupied territory, murder or ill-treatment of prisoners of war or persons on the seas, killing of hostages, plunder of public or private property, wanton destruction of cities, towns or villages, or devastation not justified by military necessity.[61]

The jurisprudence produced by the IMT on the basis of these provisions – as well as, of course, on the basis of those regarding the other crimes provided for in the Nuremberg Charter – constitute, together with the jurisprudence of the Tribunals under the regime of Control Council Law No. 10, their lasting legacy on international criminal law.

Less influential, on the other hand, was the Tokyo Charter, which simply stated that the Tokyo Tribunal would exercise jurisdiction over 'conventional war crimes', i.e. over 'violations of the laws and customs of war'.[62]

The four 1949 Geneva Conventions – the major conventional texts produced in the wake of World War II on IHL – provide for the obligation of states to criminalize only the 'grave breaches' mentioned in each one of them.[63]

War crimes were, obviously, within the jurisdiction of the *ad hoc* Tribunals established by the UNSC in the 1990s. Two categories of such crimes were included in the Statute of ICTY: a) grave breaches of the 1949 Geneva Conventions[64] and b) serious violations of the laws and customs of war.[65]

Two categories of war crimes – although different from the above because of the nature of the conflict in Rwanda as non-international – were also included in the Statute of the ICTR: a) violations of common Article 3 of the 1949 Geneva Conventions and b) violations of Additional Protocol II to these Conventions.

4.2.3.3 Basic Principles of IHL

These principles underpin the fundamental rules of IHL at its current stage of development. In accordance with these principles: a) Only combatants can undertake military action (combatant's privilege) and they cannot be held responsible for their participation in the armed conflict; b) There must be always be a distinction between combatants who may be the object of attack, and non-combatants, i.e. civilians and former combatants

61 Art. 6(2).

62 Art. 5(b).

63 GC I Art. 49, GC II Art. 51, GC III Art. 130, GC IV Art. 147.

64 Art. 2.

65 The (indicative) list of serious violations enumerated in Art. 3 of the ICTY Statute is as follows: "employment of poisonous weapons or other weapons calculated to cause unnecessary suffering; (b) wanton destruction of cities, towns or villages, or devastation not justified by military necessity; (c) attack, or bombardment, by whatever means, of undefended towns, villages, dwellings, or buildings; (d) seizure of, destruction or wilful damage done to institutions dedicated to religion, charity and education, the arts and sciences, historic monuments and works of art and science; (e) plunder of public or private property."

(prisoners of war and combatants who have been placed *hors de combat* due to injury, sickness or shipwreck) who must be protected (principle of distinction). The same principle applies in connection with military objectives which may be attacked and civilian objects which must be protected; c) Attacks which would cause excessive collateral civilian damage must not be undertaken (principle of proportionality); d) Measures permitted in armed conflict are those which are necessary to accomplish a legitimate military purpose and are not otherwise prohibited by IHL (principle of necessity); e) The methods and means of armed conflict which cause unnecessary suffering and excessive human pain are prohibited (principle of humanity).[66]

4.2.3.4 War Crimes Under Article 8 of the ICC Statute

War crimes lie at the heart of the jurisdiction of the International Criminal Court, as evidenced by the long list of such crimes appearing in Article 8 of the Statute, a list which keeps being added to, as will be seen below.

According to Article 8, the ICC has jurisdiction over war crimes "in particular when committed as part of a plan or policy or as part of a large-scale commission of such crimes."[67]

The categories of crimes under the jurisdiction of the ICC in the case of an international armed conflict are: a) Grave breaches of the Geneva Conventions[68] and b) Other serious violations of the laws and customs applicable in international armed conflict, within the established framework of international law.[69]

In the case of an armed conflict not of an international character, the crimes under the jurisdiction of the Court are: a) serious violations of Article 3 common to the four 1949 Geneva Conventions[70] and b) other serious violations of the laws and customs applicable in such conflicts within the established framework of international law.[71, 72]

66 *See* R. Cryer, H. Friman, D. Robinson, E. Wilmshurst, An Introduction to International Criminal Law and Procedure, 2007, *op. cit.*, p. 223, under the title: Key principles of humanitarian law (12.1.3); *See also* www.diakonia.se/en/ihl/the-law/international-humanitarian-law-1/introduction-to-ihl/principles-of-international-law/ last accessed 11 April 2018; Chatham House, The Law of Armed Conflict: Problems and Prospects, 18-19April 2005, available at: www.chathamhouse.org/sites/files/chathamhouse/public/Research/International%20Law/ilparmedconflict.pdf, last accessed 11 April 2018.

67 ICC Statute, Art. 8, Chapeau.

68 Art. 8(2)(a) of the Statute.

69 Art. 8 (2)(b) of the Statute.

70 Art. 8(2)(c) of the Statute.

71 Art. 8(2)(e) of the Statute.

72 As stated by the Court, Art. 8(2) applies to both international and non-international conflicts, with 8(2)(a) and (b) applying to international conflicts and 8(2)(c) and (e) applying to non-international ones (*Bemba*, Pre-Trial Ch. II, Decision Pursuant to Art. 61(7)(a) and (b) of the Rome Statute on the Charges of the Prosecutor against *Jean-Pierre Bemba Gombo*, ICC-01/05-01/08-424, 15 June 2009, para. 216).

4.2.4 *Issues Related to War Crimes Under the ICC Statute*

4.2.4.1 Nexus With Armed Conflict

War crimes are obviously committed in the context of an armed conflict the existence of which is a condition *sine qua non* for the prosecution of those responsible for their commission. The context of armed conflict consists of a time and a location element, i.e. the crime must have been committed during the war and on the territory where such war is being conducted. This, however, does not suffice; there must also be a substantive nexus with the armed conflict in question. For example, a crime of passion or a murder due to a land dispute which was committed in a country involved in an armed conflict at the time of its commission is not substantively connected with the armed conflict in question and remains a common crime to be punished according to the national criminal legislation of the state involved in the conflict. This becomes clear in the Elements of War Crimes which repeat, in every particular crime, that this must have been committed 'in the context of and (be) associated with an armed conflict'. Particularly important in setting out a test for the existence of the requisite nexus has been the jurisprudence of the ICTY in the *Kunarac* case.[73] Nexus with an armed conflict does not mean, insofar as the location element is concerned, that the crime must have been committed in the very theatre of the war or within the hostilities themselves.[74] It is enough for it to be associated with the hostilities.[75] Similarly, it is not required that the time of the commission of the crime coincide with the time of conduct of hostilities.[76]

4.2.4.2 Persons Responsible for the Commission of War Crimes

War crimes may be committed by members of the armed forces or other armed groups who may be of any rank from the highest to that of foot soldier. They may also be committed by any non-combatant[77] provided that the condition of the association of the crime with the armed conflict is satisfied.[78]

It may be asked whether the perpetrator must be aware of the existence of an armed conflict. The Elements of War Crimes answer this question in the affirmative requiring that the perpetrator must indeed be 'aware of the factual circumstances that established

73 ICTY, *Kunarac* (IT-96-23 & IT-96-23/1-A), Appeals Ch. 12 June 2002, paras. 57-59. *See also* ICTY, Limaj *et al.* (IT-03-66-T), Judgment, 30 November 2005, para. 84; ICTR, *Rutaganda*, Appeals Ch., 26 May 2003, paras. 569-570; SCSL, *Sesay et al.* (SCSL-04-15-T), Judgment, 2 March 2009, para. 99.

74 *Lubanga* (ICC-01/04-01/06), Decision on the confirmation of charges, 29 January 2007, para. 288.

75 *Katanga et al.* (ICC-01/04-01/07), Decision of the Pre-Trial Chamber on the confirmation of charges, 29 January 2008, para. 381. ICTY has also issued many judgments to the same effect.

76 ICTR *Bagilishema* (ICTR-95-1-A-T), Trial Chamber, Judgment, 7 June 2001, para. 105.

77 *See* A. Cassese, G. Aquaviva, M. Fan, A. Whiting, International Criminal Law, *op. cit.*, pp. 122-132, the analysis of the relevant cases of *Rohling et al.*, Superior Military Government Court of the French Occupation Zone in Germany, Judgment of 25 January 1949. Also *Enigster*, Israel, Tel-Aviv Court, Judgment of 4 January 1952.

78 K. Kittichaisaree, International Criminal Law, *op. cit.*, pp. 133-134.

the existence of an armed conflict ...' The Introduction to the Elements clarifies and to a certain degree lowers the level of this requirement by providing that the perpetrator's awareness need not be 'a legal evaluation as to the existence of an armed conflict ...'[79] Nonetheless, further on, the Introduction links the awareness requirement, in a rather unclear fashion, with the 'awareness of factual circumstances that established the existence of an armed conflict that is implicit in the terms 'took place in the context of and was associated with'. By referring back to the nexus of 'context' and 'association', this provision seems to nullify the efforts made by the Elements to clarify or somehow lower the level of the perpetrator's 'awareness'.

4.2.4.3 Victims of War Crimes

Such victims are specifically identified in several provisions of the ICC Statute on individual war crimes, for the purposes of the particular provision. The provisions regarding the most important war crimes, i.e. the 'grave breaches' of the Geneva Conventions to which the ICC Statute refers in Article 8(2)(a),[80] identify as victims those who are 'protected persons' under the Geneva Conventions. There is, in fact, a number of GC provisions which refer to various protected persons: civilians, the wounded and the sick of the armed forces on land, the wounded, the sick and the shipwrecked of the armed forces at sea and prisoners of war.[81]

Article 8(2)(c) of the ICC Statute which deals with serious violations of common Article 3 of the Geneva Conventions, i.e. crimes committed in an armed conflict not of an international character, identifies as 'protected persons' (without, however, mentioning the term) those no longer taking active part in hostilities including members of armed forces who have laid down their arms and those placed *hors de combat* by sickness, wounds, detention or other cause. Non-combatants, as are all those falling under the above categories, are further defined by Geneva Convention IV as

> ... those who at a given moment and in any manner whatsoever, find themselves, in case of a conflict or occupation, in the hands of a Party to the conflict or Occupying Power of which they are not nationals.[82]

The nationality criterion, which is established by Geneva Convention IV, has been replaced by a considerably wider one in the Elements of Crimes of the ICC Statute accord-

79 The same awareness of the perpetrator and the same limitation in connection with its "legal evaluation" are also required as regards the character of the armed conflict as international or non-international (Elements of Crimes, Introduction to war crimes, (a) and (b), *in fine*).

80 "Grave breaches" are those enumerated in Arts. 50 GC I, 51 GC II, 130 GC III and 147 GC IV.

81 Arts. 13, 24, 25, 26 of GC I, Arts. 13, 36, 37 GC II, Art. 4 GC III, Arts. 4, 13, 20 GC IV.

82 Art. 4 of Geneva Convention IV.

ing to which "the perpetrator needs only to know that the victim belonged to an adverse party to the conflict."[83]

As already mentioned above, other provisions of the Statute protect specific categories of persons, such as the 'civilian population'[84] and personnel involved in humanitarian assistance or in peacekeeping missions.[85] The Elements of Crimes clarify that the list of persons who may be victims of war crimes includes civilians as well as medical or religious personnel.[86]

Civilian objects, defined as 'objects which are not military objectives'[87] are also protected according to several provisions of the ICC Statute. Thus, attacks against buildings dedicated to religion, education, art, science or charitable purposes, historic monuments, hospitals and places where the sick and wounded are collected, are war crimes[88] as are attacks against towns, villages, dwellings or buildings which are undefended.[89] Furthermore, the extensive destruction and appropriation of property, if not justified by military necessity and carried out unlawfully and wantonly, constitutes a grave breach under GC I.

4.2.4.4 International and Non-International Armed Conflicts

While IHL deals with both international and non-international conflicts, the four Geneva Conventions predominantly deal with the former type of conflicts, containing, in common Article 3, only a minimal number of rules applicable to non-international ones. About thirty years later, almost the same pattern is repeated in the case of the 1977 Additional Protocols I and II to the Geneva Conventions, with AP II, which deals with non-international conflicts, containing far fewer rules than AP I which deals with international conflicts, a testimony to the persisting resistance of states, at the time of the adoption of the Protocols, to accepting the application of a full spectrum of IHL rules on their territory in the case of non-international (civil) war. Forty years on, AP I is generally accepted as constituting customary international law, while AP II is not.

Nonetheless, there is now a discernible tendency to bring the treatment of the two types of conflict much closer; it is even proposed that all differences between them should be completely eliminated. This is due mostly to the realization that the majority of conflicts worldwide are now internal, which means that IHL would gradually lose much of its

---

83 Elements, Art. 8(2)(a)(i), fn. 33, applying to the corresponding element in each crime under Art. 8(2)(a). The ICTY jurisprudence had already expanded the criterion to "genuine ties of faith and allegiance" (ICTY, *Tadić* (IT-94-A) Appeals Chamber, Judgment, 15 July 1999, para. 166).

84 Art. 8(2)(b)(i).

85 Art. 8(2(b)(iii).

86 The latter term (religious personnel) including those non-confessional non-combatant military personnel carrying out a similar function (fn. 56 in Art. 8(2)(c)(i)-1).

87 Art. 8(2)(b)(ii).

88 Art. 8(2)(b)(ix) and 8(2)(e)(iv).

89 Art. 8(2)(b)(v).

relevance if left to apply only to international armed conflicts.[90] At the same time, the belief that civil wars are a question to be dealt with internally by the state concerned and only of marginal interest to the world at large (otherwise it would be an involvement to that state's affairs) is becoming increasingly obsolete.

A major step towards the criminalization of war crimes in non-international armed conflicts was the adoption of the ICTR Statute and the subsequent establishment of the *ad hoc* Tribunal by the Security Council in 1994. The Tribunal had jurisdiction over serious violations of common Article 3 of the Geneva Conventions and over other violations which are contained in Article 4(2) of AP II. These violations were therefore recognized as war crimes by the ICTR Statute.[91]

At the same time, the ICTY jurisprudence gave considerable assistance to the criminalization of violations of IHL in internal conflicts. Thus, in the 1995 judgment of the Appeals Chamber of ICTY on the *Tadić Case*,[92] the Tribunal, although not considering violations of common Article 3 of the Geneva Conventions as grave breaches,[93] qualified them as violations of the laws and customs of war which were, as such, subject to its jurisdiction.[94] The Tribunal also found that many IHL provisions which apply in international armed conflicts are equally applicable in non-international ones.[95, 96] Such provisions are, for example, those which prohibit attacks against non-combatants as well as the use of certain weapons.[97] Furthermore, ICTY set out a number of criteria or 'factors' in order to determine whether a rule would also be applicable in non-international armed conflict.[98] It also held that many IHL provisions which are applicable in non-international armed conflicts have a customary law character.[99]

Regarding the ICC Statute, although it would have been desirable that it completely set aside the distinction between international and non-international conflicts and to provide for the punishment of the same crimes in both cases, this would have been extremely difficult, if not impossible, in the Rome Conference. It is, however, indisputable that the Statute has marked an important milestone on this matter, as it has included a significant number of crimes committed in the context of non-international conflicts – about half of those committed in international ones – in the Court's jurisdiction. Further improvements became possible in the Kampala Review Conference in 2010 as well in the 2017 ASP in New York.

---

90 *See* R. Cryer, H. Friman, D. Robinson, E. Wilmshurst, An Introduction to International Criminal Law and Procedure, 2007, *op. cit.*, pp. 229-232.
91 *Supra*, pp. 31 *et seq.*
92 ICTY, *Tadić* (IT-94-1-AR72), Appeal on Jurisdiction – *Tadić* Interlocutory Appeal, 2 October 1995.
93 *Ibid.*, paras. 79-85.
94 *Ibid.*, paras. 86-137.
95 *Ibid.*, paras. 96-137.
96 *Ibid.*, paras. 126, 127.
97 *Ibid.*, paras. 120 *et seq.*
98 *Ibid.*, paras. 128, 129 *et seq.*
99 *Ibid.*, paras. 128 *et seq.*

An internal armed conflict may be transformed to international if another state participates in it, while an international armed conflict may coexist with an internal one. Complex questions arise when forces which participate in a presumably internal conflict act in favour of a foreign Power. The specific question raised in such a case is the threshold over which the particular internal armed conflict is transformed into international due to the participation of these forces.[100] ICTY confronted this question in the *Tadić Case* where it found that the applicable test should be that of the 'overall control' of the foreign Power on these armed actors (paramilitaries, insurgents, etc.). This test is less strict than that adopted by the ICJ in the Case of 'Military and Paramilitary Activities in Nicaragua' according to which, for the emergence of the responsibility of the foreign state, the actors in question must be under the 'effective control' of that state, i.e. not only be paid or financed or controlled by it, but receive concrete instructions for the conduct of specific operations.[101] The ICJ confirmed its support for the 'effective control' test in the *Bosnian Genocide Case*.[102]

The ICTY judgment, on the other hand, was strongly criticized for its softening of the ICJ criteria.[103] Nonetheless, the 'overall control' criterion appears to have found the support of the ICC.[104]

Finally, in order to consider that there is an internal armed conflict, the ICC Statute, following the ICTY jurisprudence in this respect,[105] provides that an internal armed conflict may also exist where only armed groups are involved in it,[106] in contrast to AP II, under the regime of which an internal armed conflict requires the participation of government forces.[107]

---

100 Concerning the interpretation of common Art. 2(1) of the Geneva Conventions, *see* ICC Bemba (ICC-01/05), Decision Pursuant to Art. 61(7)(a) and (b) of the Rome Statute on the Charges of the Prosecutor against *Jean Pierre Bemba Gombo*, 15 June 2009, para. 223.

101 ICJ, *Military and Paramilitary Activities in and Against Nicaragua (Nicaragua v. USA) (Merits) 1986, ICJ Rep. 14* para. 115.

102 ICJ, *Application of the Convention on the Prevention and Punishment of the Crime of Genocide (Bosnia and Herzegovina v. Serbia and Montenegro), Judgment, I.C.J. Reports 2007, p. 43*, paras. 396-406.

103 *See, e.g.*, Stefan Salmon, The Various Control Tests in the Law of State Responsibility and the Responsibility of Outside Powers for Acts of Secessionist Entities, *International and Comparative Law Quarterly*, Vol. 58, 2009.

104 ICC, *Lubanga, supra*, fn. 344, para. 211; ICC, *Katanga, supra*, fn. 345, para. 220.

105 *ICTY, Tadić* (IT-94-1), Decision on the Defence Motion for Interlocutory Appeal on Jurisdiction, 2 October 1995, para. 70. The Tribunal held that "... an armed conflict exists whenever there is a resort to armed force between States or protracted armed violence between governmental authorities and organized armed groups or between such groups within a State. International humanitarian law applies from the initiation of such armed conflicts and extends beyond the cessation of hostilities until a general conclusion of peace is reached; or, in the case of internal conflicts, a peaceful settlement is achieved. Until that moment, international humanitarian law continues to apply in the whole territory of the warring States or, in the case of internal conflicts, the whole territory under the control of a party, whether or not actual combat takes place there..."

106 Art. 8(2)(f) *in fine*.

107 Art. 1(1).

Internal Riots

The Statute clarifies that Paragraph 2(c) of Article 8 which deals with internal conflicts does not apply "to situations of internal disturbances and tensions, such as riots, isolated and sporadic acts of violence or other acts of a similar nature."[108]

This provision, which echoes that contained in AP II,[109] draws attention to an important distinction between an internal armed conflict in the course of which crimes (which may fall within the jurisdiction of the ICC) are being committed, and internal riots and similar situations (which remain within the exclusive jurisdiction of the internal legal order of the state where they have taken place). The ICTY Appeals Chamber has formulated a test to distinguish between the two situations, by setting out two criteria, i.e. the intensity of the conflict and the organizational level of the parties involved.[110] To have a situation of internal conflict, both these elements must attain a higher level than that occurring in riots or 'internal disturbances'.

Threshold for the Exercise of Jurisdiction

The Court has jurisdiction over war crimes 'in particular when committed as part of a plan or policy or as part of a large-scale commission of such crimes'. It is obvious that while the provision aims at establishing a threshold over which it will be possible for the ICC to exercise jurisdiction with regard to war crimes, this purpose remains unfulfilled since the words 'in particular' allow the exercise of ICC jurisdiction even below that level.

---

108 Art. 8(2)(d).

109 Art. 1(2).

110 ICTY, *Tadić* (IT-94-1), Decision on the Defence Motion for Interlocutory Appeal on Jurisdiction, 2 October 1995, para. 70.

4.2.4.5 Crimes Committed in International Armed Conflict

1. Grave breaches (Art. 8(2)(a)): The Geneva Conventions of 12 August 1949 create a special 'grave breaches' regime[111] in connection with particularly serious violations of their provisions.[112] Thus, they recognize them as crimes under universal jurisdiction, imposing on all states the obligation to prosecute those accused for their commission, unless they decide to extradite them.[113] As the Geneva Conventions enjoy general acceptance, the rules on grave breaches have attained the status of customary international law. AP II Article 85 has added further grave breaches to those of the Geneva Conventions. However, these were not included in Article 8(2)(a) of the ICC Statute as not all of them were considered to reflect customary international law. Interestingly, Paragraph 5 of the same Article 85 of Additional Protocol I stipulates that all grave breaches of the 1949 Geneva Conventions and of the Protocol constitute war crimes.[114]

   Grave breaches must be committed in the context of an international armed conflict and be directed against persons or property which are protected under the Geneva Conventions.
2. Other serious violations of the laws and customs applicable in international armed conflict (Art. 8(2)(b)): According to this provision of the ICC Statute, the Court has jurisdiction over 'other serious violations of the laws and customs applicable in international armed conflict, within the established framework of international law', which

111 Geneva Convention I, Arts. 49-51, Geneva Convention II, Arts. 50-52, Geneva Convention III, Arts. 129-131, Geneva Convention IV, Arts. 146-148.

112 Namely, "any of the following acts against persons or property protected under the provisions of the relevant Geneva Convention: (i) Wilful killing; (ii) Torture or inhuman treatment, including biological experiments; (iii) Wilfully causing great suffering, or serious injury to body or health; (iv) Extensive destruction and appropriation of property, not justified by military necessity and carried out unlawfully and wantonly; (v) Compelling a prisoner of war or other protected person to serve in the forces of a hostile Power; (vi) Wilfully depriving a prisoner of war or other protected person of the rights of fair and regular trial; (vii) Unlawful deportation or transfer or unlawful confinement; (viii) Taking of hostages" (Art. 50 of Geneva Convention I, Art. 51 of Geneva Convention II, Art. 130 of Geneva Convention III, Art. 149 of Geneva Convention IV).

113 In accordance with the principle *aut dedere aut judicare* applicable in the case of international crimes. In order to be able to prosecute, on the other hand, states must have enacted the requisite domestic legislation.

114 "Without prejudice to the application of the Conventions and of this Protocol, grave breaches of these instruments shall be regarded as war crimes." This provision has generated a discussion whether grave breaches have been absorbed by war crimes or retain their autonomy, (Marko Divac Ōberg, The absorption of grave breaches into war crimes law, International Law Review of the Red Cross, vol. 91 Number 873, March 2009, available at: www.icrc.org/en/author/marko-divac-oberg, last accessed 21 February 2018).

it goes on to enumerate.[115] The phrase 'within the established framework of international law' is repeated in the Introduction of the Elements of War Crimes in connection with all the crimes contained in Article 8(2) (grave breaches and serious violations in both international and non-international conflicts). The phrase creates serious interpretation problems and is certain to owe its existence to a rather unfor-

115 These are: (i) Intentionally directing attacks against the civilian population as such or against individual civilians not taking direct part in hostilities; (ii) Intentionally directing attacks against civilian objects, that is, objects which are not military objectives; (iii) Intentionally directing attacks against personnel, installations, material, units or vehicles involved in a humanitarian assistance or peacekeeping mission in accordance with the Charter of the United Nations, as long as they are entitled to the protection given to civilians or civilian objects under the international law of armed conflict; (iv) Intentionally launching an attack in the knowledge that such attack will cause incidental loss of life or injury to civilians or damage to civilian objects or widespread, long-term and severe damage to the natural environment which would be clearly excessive in relation to the concrete and direct overall military advantage anticipated; (v) Attacking or bombarding, by whatever means, towns, villages, dwellings or buildings which are undefended and which are not military objectives; (vi) Killing or wounding a combatant who, having laid down his arms or having no longer means of defence, has surrendered at discretion; (vii) Making improper use of a flag of truce, of the flag or of the military insignia and uniform of the enemy or of the United Nations, as well as of the distinctive emblems of the Geneva Conventions, resulting in death or serious personal injury; (viii) The transfer, directly or indirectly, by the Occupying Power of parts of its own civilian population into the territory it occupies, or the deportation or transfer of all or parts of the population of the occupied territory within or outside this territory; (ix) Intentionally directing attacks against buildings dedicated to religion, education, art, science or charitable purposes, historic monuments, hospitals and places where the sick and wounded are collected, provided they are not military objectives; (x) Subjecting persons who are in the power of an adverse party to physical mutilation or to medical or scientific experiments of any kind which are neither justified by the medical, dental or hospital treatment of the person concerned nor carried out in his or her interest, and which cause death to or seriously endanger the health of such person or persons; (xi) Killing or wounding treacherously individuals belonging to the hostile nation or army; (xii) Declaring that no quarter will be given; (xiii) Destroying or seizing the enemy's property unless such destruction or seizure be imperatively demanded by the necessities of war; (xiv) Declaring abolished, suspended or inadmissible in a court of law the rights and actions of the nationals of the hostile party; (xv) Compelling the nationals of the hostile party to take part in the operations of war directed against their own country, even if they were in the belligerent's service before the commencement of the war; (xvi) Pillaging a town or place, even when taken by assault; (xvii) Employing poison or poisoned weapons; (xviii) Employing asphyxiating, poisonous or other gases, and all analogous liquids, materials or devices; (xix) Employing bullets which expand or flatten easily in the human body, such as bullets with a hard envelope which does not entirely cover the core or is pierced with incisions;(xx) Employing weapons, projectiles and material and methods of warfare which are of a nature to cause superfluous injury or unnecessary suffering or which are inherently indiscriminate in violation of the international law of armed conflict, provided that such weapons, projectiles and material and methods of warfare are the subject of a comprehensive prohibition and are included in an annex to this Statute, by an amendment in accordance with the relevant provisions set forth in Arts. 121 and 123; (xxi) Committing outrages upon personal dignity, in particular humiliating and degrading treatment; (xxii) Committing rape, sexual slavery, enforced prostitution, forced pregnancy, as defined in Art. 7, para. 2(f), enforced sterilization, or any other form of sexual violence also constituting a grave breach of the Geneva Conventions; (xxiii) Utilizing the presence of a civilian or other protected person to render certain points, areas or military forces immune from military operations; (xxiv) Intentionally directing attacks against buildings, material, medical units and transport, and personnel using the distinctive emblems of the Geneva Conventions in conformity with international law; (xxv) Intentionally using starvation of civilians as a method of warfare by depriving them of objects indispensable to their survival, including wilfully impeding relief supplies as provided for under the Geneva Conventions; (xxvi) Conscripting or enlisting children under the age of fifteen years into the national armed forces.

tunate compromise with a view to allay the concerns of those who had difficulties accepting the criminalization of 'new crimes', such as those referring to gender.[116]
The list of crimes contained in the category of 'other serious violations of laws and customs applicable in international armed conflict' is impressively long but exhaustive, which means that the addition of further crimes may be done only by way of amendment in a special and strictly prescribed manner.[117] This differentiates the ICC Statute from that of ICTY where the short list of acts which are criminalized by Article 3 is open-ended ('including but not limited to').[118]
The main source of the crimes included in Article 8(2)(b) are The Hague Law and AP I to the Geneva Conventions. Some provisions which provide for the criminalization of the use of certain weapons find their origin in the Regulations attached to the Hague Convention No. IV (Respecting the Laws and Customs of War on Land), in the 1925 Geneva Protocol[119] and in the 1899 Declaration on Exploding Bullets.
There are, however, also novel provisions which do not derive from either The Hague or the Geneva Law and are mainly those criminalizing attacks against personnel participating in humanitarian assistance and U.N. peacekeeping missions, as well as against their installations and material.[120] Although less novel, other crimes in the ICC Statute are however explicitly spelled out, identified and criminalized. Such is the case of sexual crimes,[121, 122] i.e. rape, sexual slavery, enforced prostitution, forced

116 On this question see William A. Schabas, An Introduction to the International Criminal Court, *op. cit.*, pp. 123-124. According to Theodor Meron, however, the provision aims to safeguard the future development of customary international law (*War Crimes Law Comes of Age, Essays*, Clarendon Press, Oxford, 1998). *See also* the Declaration made by the U.K. in connection with this phrase.

117 Art. 121(5) of the ICC Statute.

118 *See also* the *Tadić* Case which confirms that the list in Art. 3 is indicative. Nonetheless there would most probably be a risk of collision with the legality principle if a 'new crime' were added in such a list.

119 On the Prohibition of the Use of Asphyxiating, Poisonous or Other Gases, and of Bacteriological Methods of Warfare.

120 Art. 8(2)(b)(iii). This crime is also among those punished when committed in non-international armed conflicts (Art. 8(2)(e)(iii)). On this crime *see* Christiane Bourloyannis-Vrailas, Crimes against United Nations Personnel in Gabrielle Kirk McDonald & Olivia Swaak-Goldman (eds), *Substantive and Procedural Aspects of International Criminal Law, The Experience of International and National Courts*, Kluwer Law International, 2000, pp. 337-365.

121 Indeed, in many IHL instruments (*e.g.*, in the Geneva Conventions) gender or sexual crimes are restricted to "violence to life and person" or to "outrages upon personal dignity." Under GC IV, enforced prostitution is an "attack upon a woman's honour." However, Art. 75 of AP I clarifies that "outrages upon personal dignity" cover in particular "humiliating and degrading treatment, enforced prostitution and any form of indecent assault," to which AP II adds rape. The ICC Statute, on its part, has done away with linkage to "honour," which does not relate to the contemporary perception of rape and other sexual crimes (either as crimes against humanity or as war crimes). It must also be reminded, in this connection, that rape, enforced prostitution and any form of indecent assault are criminalized (as crimes against humanity or war crimes) under the Statutes of ICTY, ICTR and SCSL.

122 Art. 8(2)(b)(xxii) of the ICC Statute.

pregnancy and enforced sterilization,[123] as well as the crimes of the use of child soldiers[124] and of the use of starvation of civilians as a method of warfare.[125] According to the ICC Statute, the sexual crimes mentioned above as well as 'other forms of sexual violence also constituting a grave breach of the Geneva Conventions or a serious violation of Common Article 3 of the Geneva Conventions' constitute war crimes in both international and non-international[126] armed conflicts. Furthermore, 'rape, sexual slavery, enforced prostitution, forced pregnancy, enforced sterilization, or any other form of sexual violence of comparable gravity' constitutes a crime against humanity under the ICC Statute. On the other hand, not all the serious violations of IHL provided for by The Hague or the Geneva Law are criminalized, since some of them were not considered to reach the requisite level of gravity for purposes of criminalization. A typical example is the grave breach of unjustified delay in the repatriation of war captives or non-combatants provided for by Protocol I which is not criminalized either by Paragraph 2(a) or Paragraph 2(b) of Article 8 of the Statute. Much more importantly, the use of chemical and biological weapons, which is prohibited under customary international law, was not initially criminalized by the Rome Statute.[127] However, the amendments adopted by the Assembly of States Parties (ASP) of December 2017 corrected this omission.[128]

From a drafting point of view, the list of crimes constituting 'other violations of the laws and customs of war' suffers from extensive overlapping and has been criticized for it. However, this has been largely the result of the wish of the wide majority to remain with the phraseology of generally accepted conventional texts in connection with each crime, even at the cost of creating overlaps.

The common Elements for all the crimes in this category are: a) that the conduct took place in the context of and was associated with an international armed conflict and b)

123 Art. 8(2)(b)(xxii). This crime is among those also punished when committed in non-international armed conflicts (Art. 8(2)(e)(vi)).

124 Art. 8(2)(b)(xxvi) This crime is among those also punished when committed in non-international armed conflicts (Art. 8(2)(e)(vii)).

125 Art. 8(2)(b)(xxv).

126 Art. 8(2)(e)(vi).

127 For the reasons of the omission *see* R. Cryer *et al.*, An Introduction to International Criminal Law and Procedure, *op. cit.*, p. 255.

128 *See infra*, at 4.2.4.6.

that the perpetrator was aware of factual circumstances that established the existence of an armed conflict.

4.2.4.6 Crimes Committed in Non-International Conflicts (Art. 8(2)(c) and (e))

The crimes committed in non-international conflicts on which the ICC may exercise jurisdiction are: a) Serious violations of Article 3 common to the four Geneva Conventions of 12 August 1949[129]; b) Other serious violations of the laws and customs applicable in armed conflicts not of an international character, within the established framework of international law.[130]

It has been said that the ICC Statute widens the criminalization of IHL violations to include those committed in internal armed conflicts to a degree unknown before in international criminal law. This becomes clear when taking into account that the IHL rules applicable in such armed conflicts today, i.e. common Article 3 of the four GCs and AP II to them, do not include most of the rules applicable in international armed conflicts and

---

129 These are, as reminded by Art. 8(2)(c) of the ICC Statute: "any of the following acts committed against persons taking no active part in the hostilities, including members of armed forces who have laid down their arms and those placed hors de combat by sickness, wounds, detention or any other cause: (i) Violence to life and person, in particular murder of all kinds, mutilation, cruel treatment and torture; (ii) Committing outrages upon personal dignity, in particular humiliating and degrading treatment; (iii) Taking of hostages; (iv) The passing of sentences and the carrying out of executions without previous judgement pronounced by a regularly constituted court, affording all judicial guarantees which are generally recognized as indispensable."

130 According to Art. 8(2)(e), these are: "(i) Intentionally directing attacks against the civilian population as such or against individual civilians not taking direct part in hostilities; (ii) Intentionally directing attacks against buildings, material, medical units and transport, and personnel using the distinctive emblems of the Geneva Conventions in conformity with international law; (iii) Intentionally directing attacks against personnel, installations, material, units or vehicles involved in a humanitarian assistance or peacekeeping mission in accordance with the Charter of the United Nations, as long as they are entitled to the protection given to civilians or civilian objects under the international law of armed conflict; (iv) Intentionally directing attacks against buildings dedicated to religion, education, art, science or charitable purposes, historic monuments, hospitals and places where the sick and wounded are collected, provided they are not military objectives; (v) Pillaging a town or place, even when taken by assault; (vi) Committing rape, sexual slavery, enforced prostitution, forced pregnancy, as defined in article 7, paragraph 2 (f), enforced sterilization, and any other form of sexual violence also constituting a serious violation of article 3 common to the four Geneva Conventions; (vii) Conscripting or enlisting children under the age of fifteen years into armed forces or groups or using them to participate actively in hostilities; (viii) Ordering the displacement of the civilian population for reasons related to the conflict, unless the security of the civilians involved or imperative military reasons so demand; (ix) Killing or wounding treacherously a combatant adversary; (x) Declaring that no quarter will be given; (xi) Subjecting persons who are in the power of another party to the conflict to physical mutilation or to medical or scientific experiments of any kind which are neither justified by the medical, dental or hospital treatment of the person concerned nor carried out in his or her interest, and which cause death to or seriously endanger the health of such person or persons; (xii) Destroying or seizing the property of an adversary unless such destruction or seizure be imperatively demanded by the necessities of the conflict; (xiii) Employing poison or poisoned weapons; (xiv) Employing asphyxiating, poisonous or other gases, and all analogous liquids, materials or devices; (xv) Employing bullets which expand or flatten easily in the human body, such as bullets with a hard envelope which does not entirely cover the core or is pierced with incisions."

to the extent that they do, they do not qualify them as grave breaches, as a result of which their criminalization is not provided for, despite improvements brought about by the ICTR and ICTY jurisprudence mentioned above. It is therefore indisputable that one of the big successes of the Rome Conference was the criminalization by the ICC Statute of a considerable number of IHL violations committed in non-international armed conflicts. The Kampala Review Conference, on its part, added to this list three more crimes which are committed in non-international conflicts, namely a) 'employing poison or poisoned weapons'; b) 'employing asphyxiating, poisonous or other gases and all analogous liquids, materials or devices'; and c) 'employing bullets which expand or flatten easily in the human body, such as bullets with a hard envelope which does not entirely cover the core or is pierced with incisions'.[131] The addition brings therefore in line, as far as these three crimes are concerned, the list of crimes committed in international conflicts with that of crimes committed in non-international ones.

Furthermore, the ASP of December 2017 added the crimes of a) employing weapons, which use microbial or other biological agents, or toxins, whatever their origin or method of production; b) employing weapons, the primary effect of which is to injure by fragments which in the human body escape detection by X-rays; and c) employing laser weapons specifically designed, as their sole combat function or as one of their combat functions, to cause permanent blindness to unenhanced vision, that is to the naked eye or to the eye with corrective eyesight devices. All three crimes are punishable whether committed in international or in non-international conflicts.

The amendments to the Statute so as to include more war crimes were made pursuant to Article 121(5), which is applicable in the case of amendment to Articles 6, 7 and 8 of the Statute. This means that these amendments have to be ratified by the states parties to the Statute willing to undertake this obligation, whereupon the amendments will enter into force for them one year following ratification.[132] States which do not ratify will not be bound by the amendments, and the ICC will not therefore be able to exercise its jurisdiction with regard to these crimes when committed on the territory of those states or by their nationals.

131 Amendments to Article. 8, additions xiii, xiv and xv to para. 2(e) thereof.
132 Art. 121(5).

4.2.5 *The Crime of Aggression*

The fourth of the crimes within the jurisdiction of the ICC, aggression,[133] is radically differentiated from the other three. It concerns and is connected to *jus ad bellum*, and

---

133 *See* Benjamin B. Ferenz, A Proposed Definition of Aggression: by Compromise and Consensus, 22 *ICLQ*, 1973, pp. 407-433; Benjamin B. Ferenz, *Defining International Aggression – The Search for World Peace: A Documentary History and Analysis* (two vols.), 1975; Benjamin B. Ferenz, Ending Impunity for the Crime of Aggression, *Case Western Reserve Journal Int'l. L.* 41 (2009) 281; Benjamin B. Ferenz, A World of Peace under the Rule of Law: The View from America, in *Washington University Global Studies Law Review*, Vol. 6, Art. 3, 2007, pp. 663-674; Oscar Solera, *Defining the Crime of Aggression* (2007), Cherif Bassiouni & Benjamin B. Ferenz, The Crime against Peace in Cherif Bassiouni (ed), *International Criminal Law*, 2nd edn., New York, 1999; Gerhard Werle, *Principles of International Criminal Law*, 2nd edn., 2009, 1312 *et seq.;* Elizabeth Wilmshurst, Aggression, in Robert Cryer/Häkan Friman/Darryl Robinson/ Elizabeth Wilmshurst, *An Introduction to International Criminal Law and Procedure*, 2nd edn., 2010, pp. 312 *et seq.;* Giorgio Gaja, The Long Journey Towards Repressing Aggression, in Antonio Cassese, Paola Gaeta, John Jones (eds), *The Rome Statute of the International Criminal Court: A Commentary*, vol. I, 2002, pp. 427 *et seq.;* Roger Clark, Nuremberg and the Crime against Peace, 6 *Washington University Global Studies Law Review* 527, 533, 2007; Roger Clark, Negotiating Provisions Defining the Crime of Aggression, its Elements and the Conditions for ICC Exercise of Jurisdiction, *EJIL* 20, 2009 1103, pp.1104-05, Carrie McDougall, When Law and Reality Clash – The Imperative of Compromise in the Context of the Accumulated evil of the Whole: Conditions for the exercise of the ICC's jurisdiction over the crime of aggression, *ICLR* 7 (2007) 277, pp. 281 *et seq.*; Bengt Broms, The Definition of Aggression, *Recueil des Cours*, vol. 154 (I), 1977, p. 348; Robert Schaeffer, The Audacity of Compromise: The U.N. Security Council and the Pre-Conditions to the Exercise of Jurisdiction by the ICC with Regard to the Crime of Aggression, *ICLR* 9 (2009) 411; Mohammed Gomaa, The Definition of the crime of aggression and the ICC Jurisdiction over that crime, 56, in M. Politi and G. Nesi (eds), *The International Criminal Court and the Crime of Aggression*, Aldershot, Ashgate, 2004; Paula Escarameia, The ICC and the Security Council on Aggression: Overlapping Competencies? in M. Politi and G. Nesi (eds), *supra,* pp. 133-143; Phani Dascalopoulou-Livada, Aggression and the ICC: Views on Certain Ideas and their Potential for a Solution, in M. Politi and G. Nesi (eds), *supra,* pp. 79-85; Theodor Meron, Defining Aggression for the ICC, *Suffolk Transnational Law Review* 13, 2001, 1; Andreas Zimmermann, "Article 5" in Otto Triffterer, ed., *Commentary on the Rome Statute of the International Criminal Court: Observers' Notes, Article by Article*, 2nd edn., Baden-Baden: Nomos; Oxford: Hart Publishing, 2008); Kai Ambos, The Crime of Aggression after Kampala, 53 *German Yearbook of International Law*, 2010; Maurice Kamto, *L' aggression en droit international*, Paris, A. Pedone, 2010; Herman A.M. von Hebel, Johan G. Lammers, Jolien Schukking, *Reflections on the International Criminal Court*, 1999; Phani Dascalopoulou-Livada, Aggression, Actual State of Play-the Greek/Portuguese proposal in S. Perrakis (ed), *International Criminal Court, A New Dimension in International Justice. Questions and Prospects for a New Humanitarian Order*, Proceedings of the Santorini Colloquium, 2002, pp. 127-133; Muhammad Aziz Shukri, J.S.D., The Crime of Aggression, Problems in the Negotiation in the Preparatory Commission, in S. Perrakis (ed), *supra,* pp. 113-121; M. Dumée, Le crime d' aggression, in Ascensio, Decaux, Pellet (eds), *Droit international pénal*, 2000, pp. 251-264, Yoram Dinstein, *War, Aggression and Self-Defence*, 4th edn., Cambridge, 2005, Christine Gray, *International Law and the Use of Force*, 2nd edn., Oxford, 2004; Phani Dascalopoulou-Livada, *The crime of aggression: Making operative the jurisdiction of the ICC – Tendencies in the Prep Com*, Proceedings of the 96th Annual Meeting of the American Society of International Law, 13-16 March 2002, pp. 185-190; A. Rifaat, *International Aggression, Almqvist and Wiksell International*, Stockholm, 1979, *Historical Review of Developments Relating to Aggression*, United Nations, New York, 2003, W. Daspenckgruber, St. Barriga, Ch. Wenaweser (eds) *The Princeton Process on the Crime of Aggression*, 2003-2009, Ramesh Thakur and Peter Malcontent (eds), *From Sovereign Impunity to International Accountability*, U.N. University, 2004, Anthony Clark Arend and Robert Beck, *International Law and the Use of Force*, 1993, Stefan Barriga and Claus Kress (eds), *The travaux préparatoires of the crime of aggression*, Crime of Aggression Library, Cambridge, 2012; Claus Cress, Stefan Barriga (eds), *The crime of Aggression: A Commentary*, Vols. 1 and 2, Oxford University Press, 2016; Symposium: The crime of aggression before the International Criminal Court, *European Journal of International Law*, Vol. 29, Issue 3, 9 November 2018.

not to *jus in bello* as is the case with war crimes or may be the case with genocide and crimes against humanity. Indeed, the commission of the crime of aggression depends on the occurrence of an act or acts of aggression performed by a state against another state. Thus, individual criminal responsibility for this crime presupposes and coexists with the international responsibility of a state for aggression.

It is contested whether the prohibition of aggression constituted, until World War II, customary international law which could attribute international responsibility to the aggressor state. Even more contested is whether the 'mother of all crimes' or, to use the phraseology of the Nuremberg Tribunal, "the supreme international crime,"[134] could, at the time preceding that war, attribute individual criminal responsibility to the person or persons who planned or executed aggression, despite certain efforts made after the Great War (World War I). In the aftermath of World War II, however, the Statutes of the Nuremberg and Tokyo Tribunals elevated the 'crime of aggression' to the principal crime within the jurisdiction of both.[135]

Soon thereafter, the Charter of the United Nations placed unique emphasis on the prohibition of the use of force (aggression) and of the threat to use force as state conduct,[136] making such prohibition one of the three basic pillars of the post-war world order together with settlement of international disputes and collective security. However, enthusiasm for the prohibition of aggression and the punishment of the relevant crime was not destined to last long, as the cold war set in. Thus, it was only in 1974 that the U.N. General Assembly was finally in a position to adopt a definition of aggression (by a state against another state) by Resolution XXIX (3314). Today, the customary character of the prohibition of aggression and of its G.A. definition has acquired general acceptance.[137]

On the other hand, the recognition of individual criminal responsibility for the crime of aggression did not follow a course as direct as that which the torrential developments in the international political scene opened up for the crimes of genocide, war crimes and crimes against humanity since 1990, which led to the establishment of several international criminal tribunals such as, primarily, those for the crimes committed in the Former Yugoslavia and in Rwanda. Nonetheless, the start of the negotiations in 1994 for the elaboration of the ICC Statute also signalled the beginning of discussions for the recogni-

134 *Nuremberg Judgment*, p. 186.

135 Primarily on the basis of the Kellogg-Briand Pact. On this *see* Robert Cryer *et al. op. cit.*, p. 263, Cassese, *op. cit.*, p. 111, Gerhard Werle, *op. cit.*, pp. 478-479.

136 In Art. 2(4), which provides: "All members shall refrain in their international relations from the threat or use of force against the territorial integrity or political independence of any State, or in any other manner inconsistent with the purposes of the United Nations."

137 *See, e.g.*, ICJ, *Military and Paramilitary Activities in and against Nicaragua (Nicaragua* v. *United States of America)*, Judgement of 27 June 1986, *I.C.J. Reports* 14, para. 195. Also, ICJ, *Armed Activities on the Territory of the Congo (Democratic Republic of the Congo v. Uganda)*, Judgement of 19 December 2005, *I.C.J. Reports*, para. 146. A view in favour of the customary character of the G.A. Resolution 3314 was taken in the U.K. in the *Case of R v. Jones and Others* (2006) 2 All ER 741 (House of Lords).

tion of individual criminal responsibility also for the crime of aggression. In the case of this crime, however, the discussions were particularly difficult because the issues dealt with were not only legal or technical but predominantly and unavoidably political, since they involved several extremely delicate questions of that order.

Indeed, the main problems concerned on the one hand the definition of the crime of aggression as committed by an individual and on the other the linkage (if one was to be recognized) between the ICC and the Security Council, the latter being, according to the U.N. Charter,[138] the organ with the power to decide whether a (state) act constitutes aggression. But while on the first question there was, at least, the 'compass' of the 1974 G.A. Resolution – although, of course, relevant only to state aggression – the second had to find its solution on the basis not of legal considerations alone but also taking into account political realities, such as the opposition, primarily by the permanent members of the S.C., to the ICC deciding on its own on the crime of aggression as this, they maintained, clashed with the 'exclusive' powers bestowed on the S.C. by the U.N. Charter on this question.

The quest for a solution to both the above problems – as well as to a host of other ones – proved to be a long and uncertain journey which started from the first sessions of the Preparatory Committee for the elaboration of the ICC Statute on the basis of a Draft Statute prepared by the ILC,[139] and went on to the 1998 Rome Conference, the 2010 Kampala Review Conference, each one of them making a stride towards a settlement, to be finally achieved in the 2017 Assembly of States Parties to the Statute (ASP) in New York.

4.2.5.1 Aggression as Illegal State Action

According to the Covenant of Paris of 1928 (*Kellogg-Briand*),[140] aggression was an internationally illegal act which generated the international responsibility of the aggressor state. Similar provisions were contained in older, bilateral or multilateral agreements. Among those was the 1907 Hague Convention which provided for the limitation of force employed by states for the recovery of conventional debts. This Agreement, known as *Drago-Porter* Agreement, was concluded at the initiative of the U.S. and Venezuela, as a reaction to the blockade and bombardment of Venezuelan ports by British, German and Italian warships in 1920-1923 for debts of that country. The avoidance of use of force and recourse to arbitration was also provided by the *Bryan* Agreements[141] concluded by the U.S. and its neighbouring countries in 1913-1914. Similar provisions were contained in

138 Art. 39 thereof.

139 *See Yearbook of the International Law Commission 1994*, Vol. II, Part II, fn. 7, *supra*. The mandate was given by the Sixth (Legal) Committee of the GA

140 "General Treaty for the Renunciation of War," called *Kellog-Briand Pact* after the names of the U.S. Secretary of State and the French Minister of Foreign Affairs (*Frank B Kellog* and *Aristide Briand* respectively) who drafted the text. Although adhered to by 65 states, the Pact failed to stop the outbreak of World War II.

141 From the name of *William Jennings Bryan*, then U.S. Secretary of State who promoted them.

the Pact of the League of Nations of 1919 as well as in the Geneva Protocol of 1924 for the Peaceful Settlement of Disputes.

These texts, the most important of which was the *Kellogg-Briand* Pact, did not, however, avert World War II. After the end of that war, the U.N. Charter solemnly confirmed, in Article 2(4), that aggression was illegal under international law. States would therefore bear international responsibility if engaged in aggression. It had not, however, been possible to define aggression, mainly because of the negative attitude of powerful states which clearly sought freedom in their own appreciation of different situations and in acting accordingly. Finally, this was made possible in 1974, when the G.A. adopted its well-known Resolution XXIX (3314) on aggression which, as already noted, is now recognized to constitute international customary law. Many other G.A. resolutions refer to specific cases of aggression, condemning the aggressive action undertaken by various states.[142] The same is not true with regard to the Security Council, which has very rarely issued resolutions qualifying action of this kind as aggression.[143] This stance of the S.C. is obviously due to lack of the required consensus between all its five permanent members, a lack which is often expressed by the use of the veto power by one of them.[144]

The International Court of Justice (ICJ), on its part, has dealt with the matter in several cases, issuing important advisory opinions and judgments concerning aggression as state action and other connected issues. Thus, in its advisory opinion concerning 'Certain expenses of the United Nations', the Court stated that the responsibility which is attributed to the S.C. by virtue of Article 24 of the U.N. Charter is primary but not exclusive.[145] Other judgments which concern aspects of the question of aggression are those on the 'Case of Military and Paramilitary Activities' (*Nicaragua v. the U.S.A*)[146] and on the 'Case of the Diplomatic and Consular Staff of the U.S.A in Tehran' (*USA v. Iran*).[147] The ICJ also decided on the concept of aggression under international law in

142 *See, e.g.*, G.A. Res. 498(V), on the intervention of China in Korea in 1951; Res. S-9/2 of 1978 on the occupation of Namibia by South Africa and its use of Namibian territory to attack independent African states (Angola, Zambia); Res. 1954 (XVIII) of 1963 on the attack of South Africa against Angola, Botswana, the Seychelles, Lesotho, Mozambique, Swaziland, Zambia, Zimbabwe; Res. 36/27 of 1981 on the attack of Israel against the nuclear installations of Iraq, and series of Resolutions from 1981 to 1990 on the Israeli attacks against the Palestinian people in the occupied Palestinian territories and outside those territories in the refugee camps in the Lebanon.

143 Thus, the Council condemned the aggressive acts of South Rhodesia against Zambia, Mozambique and Botswana, as well as the aggressive acts of South Africa against Angola, Botswana, Lesotho, the Seychelles and other South-African countries. The S.C. qualified as "illegal aggressive acts" two Israeli raids against Tunisia because it hosted the headquarters of the Organization of Liberation of Palestine (PLO).

144 It is indicative of this state of affairs that the aggression of Iraq against Kuwait in 1990 was not qualified as such in Resolution 660 (1990), nor in subsequent resolutions of the S.C. on the same issue.

145 *ICJ, Certain Expenses of the United Nations*, Opinion, *I.C.J. Reports* 151, p. 16.

146 *ICJ, Military and Paramilitary Activities in and against Nicaragua Case (Nicaragua v. United States of America)* Judgment 27 June 1986, *I.C.J. Reports,* 14, para. 195.

147 ICJ, *United States Diplomatic and Consular Staff in Tehran,* Judgment of 24 May 1980, paras. 40-43.

the 'Case of Armed Activities on the Territory of the Congo'[148] as well as, again, in the 'Case of Military and Paramilitary Activities' (*Nicaragua v. the U.S.A*).[149]

4.2.5.2 Aggression as a Crime Entailing Individual Criminal Responsibility

Until World War II, there were very few cases of individuals who had faced criminal prosecution and had been sentenced for this crime. Indeed, although some isolated cases may be traced in different periods in history, they constitute, as aptly described by distinguished scholars,[150] 'historical curiosities' rather than a real attempt to impose individual criminal responsibility for aggression. The case of Kaiser Wilhelm II, repeatedly mentioned above, who was accused after World War I for 'supreme violation of international morality and the sanctity of treaties', remained without trial since the international court which was supposed to be established for this purpose, never saw the light of day.

I The Crime of Aggression in the International Military Tribunal of Nuremberg (IMT)

The London Charter[151] which embodied the Statute of the Nuremberg Tribunal[152] was practically the first international legal text to recognize aggression as a crime which entails individual criminal responsibility. Article 6(a) of the Charter provided that:

> The following acts, or any of them, are crimes coming within the jurisdiction of the Tribunal for which there shall be individual responsibility: (a) crimes against peace: namely planning, preparation, initiation or waging of a war of aggression, or a war in violation of international treaties, agreements or assurances, or participation in a common plan or conspiracy for the accomplishment of any of the foregoing.

It is to be noted that 'crimes against peace' is an older denomination for the crime of aggression which was slightly wider than the latter, as it also included war in violation of treaties, agreements and guarantees. However, once the Nuremberg Tribunal decided on the existence of aggressive war,[153] it did not consider it necessary to examine in detail whether this war also violated treaties, agreements or guarantees. Indeed, both the Nuremberg and Tokyo Tribunals gave a central place to the crime of aggression. Indicative of this is the well-known phrase of the Nuremberg Trial Prosecutor, *Robert Jackson*,

148 ICJ, *Armed Activities on the Territory of the Congo (Democratic Republic of the Congo v. Uganda)*, Judgment 19 December.12. 2005, ICJ Rep., para. 146.

149 *ICJ, Military and Paramilitary Activities in and against Nicaragua Case (supra)*, 14, paras. 106 *et seq.*

150 *See* R. Cryer *et al. op. cit.*, p. 262, fn. 2, where the trial of *Conradin von Hofenstafen* in 1268 for engaging in aggressive war is referred to as an example of such "*historical curiosities.*"

151 Which was annexed to the London Agreement.

152 G. Ginsburgs and V. N. Kudriatsev (eds), *The Nuremberg Trial and International Law* (Dordrecht: Nijhoff), 1990.

153 Sheldon Glueck, *The Nuremberg Trial and Aggressive War*, A.A. Knopf, 1946.

from his inaugural speech in the Tribunal (which he qualified as 'The greatest tribute ever paid by power to reason)' that

> The ultimate step in avoiding periodic wars, which are inevitable in a system of international lawlessness, is to make statesmen responsible to law. And let me make clear that while this is first applied against German aggressors, the law includes, and if it is to serve a useful purpose it must condemn, aggression by any other nations, including those which sit here in judgment[154]

thus also responding to the claim that the Nuremberg Trial was an expression of 'victor's justice'.

On the basis of Article 6, the indictment contained two counts in connection with aggression out of a total of four. Count one consisted of 'the common plan or conspiracy to commit crimes against peace'[155] and count two of 'the planning, preparing, initiating and waging war as crimes against peace'[156] (count three concerned war crimes and count four crimes against humanity).

The Nuremberg judgment.[157] In its judgment, the Nuremberg Tribunal referred, firstly, to the factual background, i.e. the events that prepared and carried out the plans of Germany against a number of states. It then found that the seizure of Austria and Czechoslovakia, the invasion of Poland, Denmark, Norway, Yugoslavia, Greece and the Soviet Union as well as the declaration of war against the U.S.A. constituted aggressive wars. Of the twenty-four persons accused for the crime of aggression, eleven were sentenced to death or to long sentences of imprisonment.[158]

---

154 Opening speech of the Chief Prosecutor for the United States, reprinted in Trial of German Major War Criminals by the International Military Tribunal Sitting at Nuremberg Germany (2001), 45.

155 Count one described the acts of aggression between 1936 and 1941 against 12 countries which were: Austria and Czechoslovakia (1936-1939), Poland (1939), Denmark and Norway, Belgium, the Netherlands and Luxemburg, Yugoslavia and Greece (1939-1941), the Soviet Union (1941) and the U.S.A., in collaboration with Japan (1941).

156 Count two described the acts connected with the planning, preparation, initiation and engaging in aggressive wars against 12 countries which were: Poland (1939), Great Britain and France (1939), Denmark and Norway, (1940), Belgium, the Netherlands and Luxemburg (1940), Yugoslavia and Greece (1941), the Soviet Union (1941) and the USA (1941).

157 Trial of the Major War Criminals before the International Military Tribunal, Nuremberg, 14 November 1945-1 October 1946, Library of Congress (42 volumes); On the judgment *see* Hans Kelsen, Will the Judgment in the Nuremberg Trial Constitute a Precedent in International Law? 1947, *International Law Quarterly* 153; Matthew Lipmann, Nuremberg Forty-Five Years Later, 1991, 7, *Connecticut Journal of International Law* 1; Telford Taylor, The Anatomy of the Nuremberg Trial, London, 1993.

158 *See* Historical Review of Developments relating to aggression, United Nations, New York, 2003.

II The Crime of Aggression in the International Military Tribunal for the Far East (IMTFE)[159]

The Charter of the Tokyo Tribunal was very similar to the Nuremberg Charter also in connection with crimes against peace, one difference being the addition, by the former, that 'aggressive war' might be 'declared or undeclared'. This difference was considered by the U.N. War Crimes Commission as simply one of 'drafting'.[160]

The indictment contained three clusters of crimes and fifty-five counts against twenty-eight accused.[161] Fifty-two of the counts referred to or concerned crimes against peace.[162]

III The Crime of Aggression in the Tribunals Under Allied Control Council Law No. 10

Law No. 10 of the Allied Control Council[163] – of which the Nuremberg Charter constituted an integral part – contained a definition of crimes against peace which was practically the same with that of the IMT Charter with two differences: a) that Law No 10 expressly included invasion as a crime against peace and b) it left open the enumeration of ways in which those accused of aggressive war had participated in it.[164] In any event, the tribunals constituted under Law No. 10 considered the Nuremberg judgment to be binding on them.

Four of the cases brought before the American courts in Germany pursuant to Allied Control Council Law No. 10 concerned crimes against peace. These were the *High Command,*[165] *I.G. Farben,*[166] *Krupp*[167] and *Ministries* cases.[168]

---

159 *International Military Tribunal for the Far East (IMTFE).* In connection with that trial *see* N. Boister and R. Cryer, *The Tokyo International Military Tribunal*, 2008, P.R. Picigallo, *The Japanese on Trial*, 1979, B.V.A Röling και A. Cassese, *The Tokyo Trial and Beyond*, 1993.

160 United Nations War Crimes Commission, History of the United Nations War Crimes Commission and the Development of the Laws of War, 1948, p. 259.

161 The first cluster (counts 1-36) concerned crimes against peace, the second (counts 37-52) murders, and the third (counts 53-55) conventional war crimes and crimes against humanity.

162 Given that according to the indictment the crimes included in the second cluster (see fn. 432) which concerned "murders" were also crimes against peace (like ordinary war crimes and crimes against humanity).

163 Control Council Law No. 10, Punishment of Persons Guilty of War Crimes, Crimes Against Peace and Against Humanity, 20 December 1945, Official Gazette of the Control Council for Germany, No. 3, 3 November 1946, pp. 50-55.

164 Art. II of the Law which provides: "1. Each of the following acts is recognized as a crime: a) Crimes against peace: Initiation of invasions of other countries and wars of aggression in violation of international laws and treaties, including but not limited to planning, preparation, initiation or waging of a war of aggression, or a war in violation of international treaties, agreements or assurances, or participation in a common plan or conspiracy for the accomplishment of any of the foregoing."

165 *United States of America v. Wilhelm von Leeb et al.* 14 persons were convicted for crimes against peace.

166 *United States of America v. Carl Krauch et al.* The case concluded by the conviction of 23 persons for crimes against peace.

167 *United States of America v. Alfred Felix Alwyn Krupp von Bohlen und Halbach.* The Tribunal convicted 12 persons for crimes against peace.

168 *United States of America v. Ernst von Weizsäcker et al.* 3 persons were convicted for crimes against peace.

In its own Zone, France established the General Tribunal of the Military Government which tried the *Roechling Case*[169] involving several counts for the commission of crimes against peace.[170]

Under Law No. 10, it was a prerequisite in connection with crimes against peace that the person accused

> ... held a high political, civil or military (including General Staff) position in Germany or in one of its Allies, co-belligerents or satellites or held high position in the financial, industrial or economic life of any such country.[171]

It is therefore no novelty that the same prerequisite (*leadership crime*) is being adopted, as will be seen below, for the crime of aggression under the ICC Statute.

IV After the Nuremberg and Tokyo Tribunals

In 1946, the U.N. General Assembly unanimously adopted the 'Principles of International Law Recognized by the Charter of the Nuremberg Tribunal and the Judgment of the Tribunal'.[172] While the question of the definition of aggression as an illegal act of state

169 The Government Commissioner of the General Tribunal of the Military Government of the French Zone of Occupation in *Germany v. Hermann Roechling*. *Roechling* was finally acquitted for the commission of crimes against peace since, as the Supreme Military Government Court (Court of Appeal) found, his activities did not reach the very high standard required by the International Military Tribunal of Nuremberg (IMT) for crimes against peace (pp. 1109-1110).

170 *Indictment, Trials of War Criminals before the Nuremberg Military Tribunals*, United States Printing Office, vol. XIV, pp. 1061, 1072-1074.

171 Art. II, para. 2 (f) of Law No. 10.

172 By Resolution 95(1) of 14 December 1946.

was resolved by GA Resolution 3314[173] of 1974,[174] the question of aggression as a crime committed by an individual remained unresolved, although closely connected to it. Fi-

---

173 A/RES/29/3314, Annex, U.N. GAOR 29th Sess., Supp. No. 31, 142, U.N. Doc. A/9631(1974). *See also* the Report of the Special Committee on the question of the Definition of Aggression, 11 March-12 April 1974, *Official Records of the General Assembly, Twenty-Ninth Session, Supplement No. 19* (A/9619 and Corr. l).

174 The Definition is as follows:

"Article 1. Aggression is the use of armed force by a State against the sovereignty, territorial integrity or political independence of another State, or in any other manner inconsistent with the Charter of the United Nations, as set out in this Definition.

Article 2. The First use of armed force by a State in contravention of the Charter shall constitute prima facie evidence of an act of aggression although the Security Council may, in conformity with the Charter, conclude that a determination that an act of aggression has been committed would not be justified in the light of other relevant circumstances, including the fact that the acts concerned or their consequences are not of sufficient gravity.

Article 3. Any of the following acts, regardless of a declaration of war, shall, subject to and in accordance with the provisions of article 2, qualify as an act of aggression:

a. The invasion or attack by the armed forces of a State of the territory of another State, or any military occupation, however temporary, resulting from such invasion or attack, or any annexation by the use of force of the territory of another State or part thereof,
b. Bombardment by the armed forces of a State against the territory of another State or the use of any weapons by a State against the territory of another State;
c. The blockade of the ports or coasts of a State by the armed forces of another State;
d. An attack by the armed forces of a State on the land, sea or air forces, or marine and air fleets of another State;
e. The use of armed forces of one State which are within the territory of another State with the agreement of the receiving State, in contravention of the conditions provided for in the agreement or any extension of their presence in such territory beyond the termination of the agreement;
f. The action of a State in allowing its territory, which it has placed at the disposal of another State, to be used by that other State for perpetrating an act of aggression against a third State;
g. The sending by or on behalf of a State of armed bands, groups, irregulars or mercenaries, which carry out acts of armed force against another State of such gravity as to amount to the acts listed above, or its substantial involvement therein.

Article 4. The acts enumerated above are not exhaustive and the Security Council may determine that other acts constitute aggression under the provisions of the Charter.

Article 5.

1. No consideration of whatever nature, whether political, economic, military or otherwise, may serve as a justification for aggression.
2. A war of aggression is a crime against international peace. Aggression gives rise to international responsibility.
3. No territorial acquisition or special advantage resulting from aggression is or shall be recognized as lawful.

Article 6 Nothing in this Definition shall be construed as in any way enlarging or diminishing the scope of the Charter, including its provisions concerning cases in which the use of force is lawful.

Article 7 Nothing in this Definition, and in particular article 3, could in any way prejudice the right to self-determination, freedom and independence, as derived from the Charter, of peoples forcibly deprived of that right and referred to in the Declaration on Principles of International Law concerning Friendly Relations and Cooperation among States in accordance with the Charter of the United Nations, particularly peoples under colonial and racist regimes or other forms of alien domination: nor the right of these peoples to struggle to that end and to seek and receive support, in accordance with the principles of the Charter and in conformity with the above-mentioned Declaration.

Article 8 In their interpretation and application the above provisions are interrelated and each provision should be construed in the context of the other provisions."

nally, the Draft Code of Crimes against Peace and Security of Mankind,[175] adopted by the International Law Commission in 1996,[176] included aggression in the list of these crimes, providing that:

> An individual who, as leader or organizer, actively participates in or orders the planning, preparation initiation or waging of aggression committed by a state, shall be responsible for a crime of aggression.[177]

By that time, however, the discussions on the crime of aggression were taking place in the context of the negotiations for the establishment of the International Criminal Court.

V From 1948 to 1998

In the context of the *ad hoc* Committee constituted in 1994 to elaborate the Statute of the International Criminal Court, there were, initially, many hesitations if not overt hostility towards including aggression as a crime in the Statute, mostly because it was considered 'too political' to be dealt with as a matter of law. It was furthermore considered by many including, in particular, the five permanent members of the S.C., that the extension of the Court's jurisdiction over this crime would intervene with the powers of the Security Council.[178] Conversely, the main argument of those in favour of including aggression in the Court's jurisdiction was that this crime had been included (in the form of 'crimes against peace') in the jurisdiction of the Nuremberg and Tokyo Tribunals and several defendants had been convicted for it. The omission, therefore, of aggression as a crime, fifty and more (at the time) years later, would send a very negative signal to the international community, encouraging potential aggressors to believe that they could commit this crime with impunity. It was, furthermore, an undeniable fact that aggression constituted the root cause for the commission of war crimes and crimes against humanity, and it would be unproductive, inconsequential, and indeed an oxymoron, to punish those while letting aggression go unpunished. Such arguments finally convinced the *ad hoc* Committee to retain the crime of aggression for consideration by the Rome Conference.

175 *Yearbook of the International Law Commission 1951*, vol. II, pp. 43-69 (A/CN.4/44), Second Report for a Draft "Code of Crimes against the Peace and Security of Mankind" by the Special Rapporteur I. Spyropoulos.
176 UN Doc. A/51/332.
177 Art. 16.
178 On the basis mainly of Art. 39 of the U.N. Charter.

VI The 1998 Rome Conference and Subsequent Developments (1998-2010)

In Rome, it was finally agreed that aggression would be included in the list of crimes within the jurisdiction of the ICC; such jurisdiction would, however, remain inoperative for the time being. The suspension would last until a definition of the crime of aggression had been formulated and the conditions for the exercise of the Court's jurisdiction over this crime had been set out (Art. 5(2) of the Rome Statute).[179] The second prerequisite was a clear reminder that before the ICC could exercise jurisdiction over the crime of aggression, the question of the eventual involvement of the Security Council should have been resolved. If an agreement on these elements were reached, the crime would be introduced in the Statute in accordance with the procedure for amendments. The task to seek an agreement on the abovementioned elements was assigned – this was part of the compromise achieved – to a Preparatory Commission (*Prep Com*) to be set up after the Rome Conference in order to deal with various pending issues until the Court was established.[180]

The two questions left open by the Rome Conference were promptly taken up by the 'Working Group on the Crime of Aggression' (1999-2002) of the Preparatory Commission and then – after the establishment of the Court – by the 'Special Working Group on the Crime of Aggression' (2003-2009). Concerning the definition, the main issue was whether a generic formula, i.e. one which would describe the crime of aggression in general terms would be enough or a 'specific' one with reference to the acts of aggression mentioned in Resolution 3314 should be preferred. A combination of the two approaches was the compromise reached which, after being adopted by the Assembly of States Parties (ASP) to the Rome Statute, was submitted to the Kampala Review Conference in 2010 for its consideration.

The second question was more complicated as it involved an eminently political issue, i.e. that of the relationship between the ICC and the S.C. regarding the crime of aggression. In practical terms, what was basically asked was whether the ICC could proceed with the prosecution of a person accused of having committed the crime of aggression without a prior S.C. Resolution that there had been aggression on a state level.

As already noted, the prior involvement of the S.C. was claimed to be based on Article 39 of the U.N. Charter, which empowers the S.C. to '[d]etermine the existence of any

179 Which provided that: "[T]he Court shall exercise jurisdiction over the crime of aggression once a provision is adopted.... setting out the conditions under which the Court shall exercise jurisdiction with respect to this crime. Such a provision shall be consistent with the relevant provisions of the Charter of the United Nations."

180 Final Act, Annex I, Resolution F. The relevant part of this Resolution is as follows: "..7. The Commission shall prepare proposals for a provision on aggression, including the definition and Elements of Crimes of aggression and the conditions under which the International Criminal Court shall exercise its jurisdiction with regard to this crime. The Commission shall submit such proposals to the Assembly of States Parties at a Review Conference, with a view to arriving at an acceptable provision on the crime of aggression for inclusion in this Statute. The provisions relating to the crime of aggression shall enter into force for the States Parties in accordance with the relevant provisions of this Statute;"

threat to the peace, breach of the peace, or act of aggression ...' and which, if ignored, there would be, allegedly, a violation of the 'exclusive' rights of the S.C. in connection with aggression. In reply, it was observed, *inter alia*, that as provided by Article 24 of the U.N. Charter and held by the ICJ, the powers conferred on the S.C. for the maintenance of international peace and security are primary, not exclusive,[181] and that, as a consequence, the ICC could not be impeded from being seized of a crime of aggression case if the S.C. had not previously determined that an act of aggression on a state level had taken place.[182]

A further practical consideration of crucial relevance was, furthermore, that in reality the S.C. had very rarely acted on its powers to qualify the action of a state against another as aggression,[183] thus potentially creating a *quasi*-impossibility for the ICC to exercise its jurisdiction on this crime if a prior determination by the S.C. were to be required.

Irrespective, however, of the existence of valid arguments in favour of the freedom of the ICC to try cases of aggression without prior involvement of the S.C., the fact remained that it would be difficult to have a solution which would not limit that freedom to some extent. What was sought, in the end, was finding a viable compromise to satisfy the greatest number of states participating in the negotiations and address as many of the problems, questions and hesitations as possible.[184] That was done in Kampala.

---

181 ICJ Advisory Opinion on *Certain Expenses of the United Nations*, I.C.J. Reports 1962, p. I51, where the Court found that, in accordance with Art. 24 of the U.N. Charter, the responsibility of the S.C. on this issue is "primary" but not "exclusive" (p. 16).

182 For other relevant arguments, *see* Phani Dascalopoulou-Livada, The crime of aggression: Making operative the jurisdiction of the ICC—Tendencies in the Prep Com, Proceedings of the 96th Annual Meeting of the American Society of International Law, 13-16 March 2002, *supra*, pp. 185-190.

183 The term "acts of aggression" has been used in the case of the raids of the then racist regime of South Africa against other African states (*See, e.g.*, Resolutions S/RES 567(1985), S/RES 572 (1985), S/RES 574 (1985), S/RES 577(1985) and in few other cases (*see supra*, p. 419).

184 The preparatory work for this purpose was undertaken by the "Princeton Process." This was the name used for the negotiations on this matter that took place in meetings organized by Princeton University at the initiative of the *Liechtenstein Institute on Self-Determination* of the University. The aim was to find a point of balance between two requirements, *i.e.*: the preservation of the integrity of the Statute, while respecting the powers of the Security Council. On these there were two fundamental points of disagreement: a) the character of the S.C. powers as exclusive, as claimed mainly by the permanent members of S.C., or as (only) primary, as maintained by most states, and b) the related issue of the role of the S.C., which the majority of states connected, on the basis of the wording of Art. 39 of the U.N. Charter, with international peace and security alone, a view not shared particularly by the permanent members of the S.C. which attributed a much larger meaning to that role. Despite the fact that two of the five permanent members of the S.C. were parties to the ICC Statute (U.K. and France), there was no differentiation between all five regarding these points. The issue of the involvement of the S.C. remained therefore pending to be resolved by the Review Conference as did the question of the applicable amendment procedure. By contrast, all the questions regarding the definition of the crime of aggression were resolved by the *Princeton Process* and its conclusions were adopted in 2009 by the Working Group on the crime of aggression set up by the Assembly of States parties to the ICC Statute, thus forming the main negotiating text put before the 2010 Review Conference in Kampala, Uganda.

4.2.5.3 The 2010 Kampala Review Conference[185] and the Adoption of Amendments to the Rome Statute Regarding Aggression

The 2010 Review Conference was convened in Kampala, Uganda, and adopted, by consensus, six amendments to the Rome Statute regarding aggression, the most important of which were:

1. the addition of Article 8(bis) containing the definition of the crime of aggression;[186, 187]

---

185 *See* Christian Wenaweser, Reaching the Kampala Compromise on Aggression: The Chair's Perspective, 23 *Leiden J. Int'l. L.* 883(2010); Stefan Barriga/Leena Grover, A historic breakthrough on the crime of aggression, *AJIL*, 2011, vol. 105:477, pp. 531-533; Jennifer Trahan, The Rome Statute's amendment on the crime of aggression: Negotiations at the Kampala Review Conference, *ICLR* 11 (2011); Claus Kreß/Leonie von Holtzendorff, The Kampala Compromise on the Crime of Aggression, *Journal of International Criminal Justice*, 8 (2010), 1179-1217; Niels Blokker/Claus Kreß, A Consensus Agreement on the Crime of Aggression – Impressions from Kampala, *LJIL* 23 (2010) 889, 890-891; Robert L. Manson, Identifying the rough edges of the Kampala compromise, *CLF* 21 (2010), 417, 425; Hans-Peter Kaul, Kampala 2010 – A first review of the ICC Review Conference, *Goettingen Journal of International Law* 2 (2010), pp. 649-667.

186 Contained in RC/Res. 6, Annex I.

187 Which reads as follows:

1. "For the purpose of this Statute, "crime of aggression" means the planning, preparation, initiation or execution, by a person in a position effectively to exercise control over or to direct the political or military action of a State, of an act of aggression which, by its character, gravity and scale, constitutes a manifest violation of the Charter of the United Nations.
2. For the purpose of paragraph 1, "act of aggression" means the use of armed force by a State against the sovereignty, territorial integrity or political independence of another State, or in any other manner inconsistent with the Charter of the United Nations. Any of the following acts, regardless of a declaration of war, shall, in accordance with United Nations General Assembly resolution 3314 (XXIX) of 14 December 1974, qualify as an act of aggression:
   a. The invasion or attack by the armed forces of a State of the territory of another State, or any military occupation, however temporary, resulting from such invasion or attack, or any annexation by the use of force of the territory of another State or part thereof;
   b. Bombardment by the armed forces of a State against the territory of another State or the use of any weapons by a State against the territory of another State;
   c. The blockade of the ports or coasts of a State by the armed forces of another State;
   d. An attack by the armed forces of a State on the land, sea or air forces, or marine and air fleets of another State;
   e. The use of armed forces of one State which are within the territory of another State with the agreement of the receiving State, in contravention of the conditions provided for in the agreement or any extension of their presence in such territory beyond the termination of the agreement;
   f. The action of a State in allowing its territory, which it has placed at the disposal of another State, to be used by that other State for perpetrating an act of aggression against a third State;
   g. The sending by or on behalf of a State of armed bands, groups, irregulars or mercenaries, which carry out acts of armed force against another State of such gravity as to amount to the acts listed above, or its substantial involvement therein."

2. The addition, in connection with the exercise of jurisdiction by the ICC over this crime, of Article 15(bis) on state referrals or *proprio motu* investigations by the Prosecutor[188] and Article 15(ter) on referrals by the Security Council.[189] In all cases, the ICC would be able to exercise its jurisdiction only over crimes of aggression committed one year after the ratification or acceptance of the amendments by thirty states parties to the Statute. Furthermore, and once these thirty ratifications had been gathered, a decision had to be taken, after 1 January 2017, by the Assembly of States Parties by the same majority as required for the adoption of amendments (i.e. two-thirds).[190]

---

188 Which reads as follows:

1. "The Court may exercise jurisdiction over the crime of aggression in accordance with article 13, paragraphs (a) and (c), subject to the provisions of this article.
2. The Court may exercise jurisdiction only with respect to crimes of aggression committed one year after the ratification or acceptance of the amendments by thirty States Parties.
3. The Court shall exercise jurisdiction over the crime of aggression in accordance with this article, subject to a decision to be taken after 1 January 2017 by the same majority of States Parties as is required for the adoption of an amendment to the Statute.
4. The Court may, in accordance with article 12, exercise jurisdiction over a crime of aggression, arising from an act of aggression committed by a State Party, unless that State Party has previously declared that it does not accept such jurisdiction by lodging a declaration with the Registrar. The withdrawal of such a declaration may be effected at any time and shall be considered by the State Party within three years.
5. In respect of a State that is not a party to this Statute, the Court shall not exercise its jurisdiction over the crime of aggression when committed by that State's nationals or on its territory.
6. Where the Prosecutor concludes that there is a reasonable basis to proceed with an investigation in respect of a crime of aggression, he or she shall first ascertain whether the Security Council has made a determination of an act of aggression committed by the State concerned. The Prosecutor shall notify the Secretary-General of the United Nations of the situation before the Court, including any relevant information and documents.
7. Where the Security Council has made such a determination, the Prosecutor may proceed with the investigation in respect of a crime of aggression.
8. Where no such determination is made within six months after the date of notification, the Prosecutor may proceed with the investigation in respect of a crime of aggression, provided that the Pre-Trial Division has authorized the commencement of the investigation in respect of a crime of aggression in accordance with the procedure contained in article 15, and the Security Council has not decided otherwise in accordance with article 16.
9. A determination of an act of aggression by an organ outside the Court shall be without prejudice to the Court's own findings under this Statute.
10. This article is without prejudice to the provisions relating to the exercise of jurisdiction with respect to other crimes referred to in article 5."

189 Which reads as follows:

1. "The Court may exercise jurisdiction over the crime of aggression in accordance with article 13, paragraph (b), subject to the provisions of this article.
2. The Court may exercise jurisdiction only with respect to crimes of aggression committed one year after the ratification or acceptance of the amendments by thirty States Parties.
3. The Court shall exercise jurisdiction over the crime of aggression in accordance with this article, subject to a decision to be taken after 1 January 2017 by the same majority of States Parties as is required for the adoption of an amendment to the Statute.
4. A determination of an act of aggression by an organ outside the Court shall be without prejudice to the Court's own findings under this Statute. 5. This article is without prejudice to the provisions relating to the exercise of jurisdiction with respect to other crimes referred to in article 5."

190 Art. 121(3) of the ICC Statute.

Several other amendments, mostly of a consequential nature, were made, such as the addition of Article 25(3)(bis), which qualifies the crime of aggression as leadership crime and of Article 20(3) concerning the application of principle *ne bis in idem* in its regard. Furthermore, the Elements of the crime of aggression were elaborated and inserted in the text of the 'Elements of Crimes',[191] while a number of 'Understandings' which refer to the amendments themselves and to the definition of aggression were also adopted,[192] following a U.S. proposal. More particularly on the amendments concerning the crime of aggression as well as on the procedure which was followed in their regard:

I The Definition of the Crime of Aggression

The definition of the crime of aggression was submitted to the Kampala Conference for its consideration practically in its final form. It consists of a 'Chapeau' and a main text.

In the Chapeau, the definition deals with two parameters: aggression as the act of an individual, i.e. the crime of aggression, and aggression as an act of a state (collective act). In connection with the crime, the main question which the definition clarifies is that it may only be attributed to individuals with a leading role (leadership crime). In connec-

191 RC/Res. 6, Annex II, amending Art. 9(1) of the Statute.

192 RC/Res. 6, Annex III. The "Understandings regarding the amendments to the Rome Statute of the International Criminal Court on the Crime of Aggression" are as follows: "Referrals by the Security Council

1. It is understood that the Court may exercise jurisdiction on the basis of a Security Council referral in accordance with article 13, paragraph (b), of the Statute only with respect to crimes of aggression committed after a decision in accordance with article 15 ter, paragraph 3, is taken, and one year after the ratification or acceptance of the amendments by thirty States Parties, whichever is later.
2. It is understood that the Court shall exercise jurisdiction over the crime of aggression on the basis of a Security Council referral in accordance with article 13, paragraph (b), of the Statute irrespective of whether the State concerned has accepted the Court's jurisdiction in this regard.
   Jurisdiction ratione temporis
3. It is understood that in case of article 13, paragraph (a) or (c), the Court may exercise its jurisdiction only with respect to crimes of aggression committed after a decision in accordance with article 15 bis, paragraph 3, is taken, and one year after the ratification or acceptance of the amendments by thirty States Parties, whichever is later.
   Domestic jurisdiction over the crime of aggression
4. It is understood that the amendments that address the definition of the act of aggression and the crime of aggression do so for the purpose of this Statute only. The amendments shall, in accordance with article 10 of the Rome Statute, not be interpreted as limiting or prejudicing in any way existing or developing rules of international law for purposes other than this Statute.
5. It is understood that the amendments shall not be interpreted as creating the right or obligation to exercise domestic jurisdiction with respect to an act of aggression committed by another State.
   Other understandings
6. It is understood that aggression is the most serious and dangerous form of the illegal use of force; and that a determination whether an act of aggression has been committed requires consideration of all the circumstances of each particular case, including the gravity of the acts concerned and their consequences, in accordance with the Charter of the United Nations.
7. It is understood that in establishing whether an act of aggression constitutes a manifest violation of the Charter of the United Nations, the three components of character, gravity and scale must be sufficient to justify a "manifest" determination. No one component can be significant enough to satisfy the manifest standard by itself."

tion with the state act, the Chapeau sets out its general features and establishes a threshold that such an act must 'by its character, gravity and scale' constitute 'a manifest violation of the U.N. Charter'.[193] In the series of understandings adopted by the Conference, there are two which concern the definition of aggression.[194] One of them, which is relevant in this context, states that the elements on the basis of which the manifest character of the violation of the U.N. Charter will have to be ascertained (i.e. character, gravity and scale of the act), must occur cumulatively, while according to a further clarification – which may not be particularly useful given the generality of the terms used – none of these elements can satisfy the requirement for 'manifest violation' on its own.

The list of actions constituting aggression appears in the main body of the definition and reproduces that of G.A. Resolution 3314 of 1974. The question of whether such list is 'open' or 'closed' is avoided since the definition does not mention anything expressly. However, it is reasonable to assess that it is closed and that the addition of further cases must be made through amendment.

II Actus Reus and Mens Rea of the Crime of Aggression

A Actus Reus

It has been noted several times that aggression is a leadership crime. This means that, as rule, it may be committed only by persons holding a leadership position in the state hierarchy either as politicians or as military leaders. Such persons must also be in a position to exercise effective control or to direct the political or military action of the aggressor state.

Perpetrator of the crime of aggression is whoever plans, prepares, initiates or executes an act of aggression. However, in order to establish criminal responsibility in connection with the acts of planning and preparation (the two notions are rather hard to distinguish in practice), the act of aggression must at least have begun.[195] Threat of use of force (aggression) is not enough to establish individual criminal responsibility for aggression under the Kampala amendment on aggression, in the same way as it was not under the Nuremberg and Tokyo Charters as well as under Law No. 10 of the Allied Control Council.

The amendment refers to aggression and not to aggressive war or war of aggression as a collective act of the state in which the accused has participated under the terms mentioned above. The obviously restrictive notion of aggressive war had been used by both

193 Report of the Special Working Group on the Crime of Aggression, ICC Doc. ICC-ASP/7/20/Add. 1, Annex II, App. 1 (2009) (*See also supra*, fn. 78).

194 *Ibid.*, paras. 6 and 7.

195 *See* Element 3 of the Elements of the crime of aggression (Kampala Amendment).

the Nuremberg[196] and the Tokyo Charters[197] while it was also mentioned in Law No. 10 of the Allied Control Council. However, the definition of aggression adopted in Kampala followed the pattern of the 1974 GA Resolution 3314 which uses predominantly the wider terms 'aggression' and 'use of force'.[198]

The act of aggression of a state must reach a certain level of gravity. Pursuant to the amendment, it must constitute 'on the basis of its character, gravity and scale, a manifest violation of the U.N. Charter'. Border skirmishes and isolated episodes would not, therefore, qualify as acts of aggression.

The definition of aggression according to the Statute remains within the bounds of the classic state action against another state. This corresponds to international customary law in force. It does not, therefore, cover activities engaged in by mercenaries or other groups of individuals (e.g. terrorists) which are not connected with another state.

B Mens Rea

According to the fundamental rule contained in Article 30 of the Rome Statute, the constituent elements of *mens rea* are intent and knowledge. In the case of the crime of aggression this means that the planning, preparation the initiation and/or the execution must be committed with the intention to proceed to or participate in an aggressive act (*animus aggressionis*). If the accused has knowledge of the collective intent and continues to participate in the preparation, initiation and/or the execution of an act of aggression, this constitutes a reasonable ground for prosecution.[199] Examples of the required intent and knowledge are provided in the cases of *Schacht, Bormann* and *von Schirach* who were tried by the Nuremberg Tribunal.[200]

Furthermore, the accused must have two more kinds of 'knowledge' which are specified in the Elements of this crime. Thus, he/she must have knowledge of the real circum-

196 Art. 6(a) of the Nuremberg Charter.

197 Art. 5(a) of the Tokyo Charter.

198 Resolution 3314 uses interchangeably the terms "aggression" and "use of force" and once, in Art. 5(2), the term "aggressive war." Apparently, however, the Resolution did not attribute particular importance to the distinction between these terms, as it was a text of political rather than legal nature (*see also* Principle 1(2) of the U.N. 1970 Declaration on the "Friendly Relations of States" which qualifies aggressive war as a "crime against international peace").

199 R. Cryer *et al.*, An Introduction to International Criminal Law and Procedure, *op. cit.*, p. 274.

200 *Hjalmar Schacht*, who was responsible for the rearmament program of Germany, was acquitted because the rearmament did not constitute a criminal act in accordance with the Nuremberg Charter and it had not been proved that the accused proceeded to the rearmament as part of waging aggressive war (Nuremberg Judgment, 1 October 1946, in (1947) 41 *AJIL* 172, p. 300). The Court followed the same line as in the case of *Martin Bormanm* who was acquitted from the accusation for crimes against peace because it had not been proved that he knew, despite being close to Hitler, of the latter's aggressive plans (*Ibid*, p. 329). It was for the same reason that *Baldur von Schirach*, Leader of Hitler's Youth was acquitted from accusations for crimes against peace. General *Wilhelm Keitel* (Nuremberg Judgment, 1 October 1946, The Trial of the German Major War Criminals, Proceedings of the international Military Tribunal Sitting at Nuremberg, Germany, Part 22 (1950), p. 491 *et seq.*) and Admiral *Karl Dönitz* (*Ibid.*, p. 507) on the other hand, were convicted for such crimes because the required intent and knowledge was proved to exist.

stances which affirm that the use of armed force in which the accused participated – in ways which constitute the *actus reus* of the crime – was inconsistent with the U.N. Charter, i.e. that it violated the Charter. These 'real circumstances' must also affirm that the violation has been 'manifest'.

III Conditions for the Exercise of Jurisdiction by the ICC on the Crime of Aggression[201]

The question of the conditions for the exercise of jurisdiction by the ICC on cases involving the crime of aggression was, as repeatedly noted above, of critical importance. In Kampala, a decision was finally reached[202] according to which the Prosecutor may proceed either with state requests or *proprio motu* investigations provided that a) there is already a determination by the S.C. that an act of aggression has been committed by the state concerned and b) in case no such determination exists, the Prosecutor will notify the S.C. about the case and if the latter does not make such a determination within six months, he/she may proceed with the investigation if this is authorized by the Pre-Trial Division.[203]

It is furthermore provided that the Court may, in accordance with Article 12, exercise jurisdiction over a crime of aggression, arising from an act of aggression committed by a state party, unless the latter 'has previously declared that it does not accept such jurisdiction by lodging a declaration with the Registrar', the withdrawal of which may be effected at any time.[204] This provision is combined with an assertion that the Court cannot exercise jurisdiction over the crime of aggression when it has been committed by a national of a state non-party to the ICC Statute or on the territory of a non-party.[205] In this way, the rule enshrined in Article 12(2) which provides for the extension of the applicability of the Statute to states which are not party thereto under specific conditions[206] – a rule which had always been objected to by a number of states – was overturned in the case of the crime of aggression as part of the compromise attained in the Review Conference, a conclusion which, although vigorously rejected by many, was confirmed by the 2017 ASP, as will be seen below.

Finally, concerning S.C. referrals, the Council may, as in the case of the other crimes, refer a 'situation' of aggression to the Court under Chapter VII of the U.N. Charter. The prior issuance of a resolution confirming that an act of aggression has indeed taken place would not be necessary in such a case. Furthermore, it is significant that 'the determina-

201 The provisions on aggression agreed upon in Kampala were inserted in the Rome Statute by Resolution RC/Res. 6 of 11 June 2010 of the Kampala Review Conference.

202 Art. 15 bis (6-8) of the Statute, as amended by Resolution 6 of the Conference (*see supra*, fn. 454).

203 Art. 15 bis (8) of the Statute, as amended. In the case of the other crimes it is the Pre-Trial Chamber which authorizes the commencement of the investigation.

204 Art. 15 bis (4) of the Statute, as amended.

205 Art. 15 bis (5) of the Statute, as amended. On the combination of provisions 15 bis (4) and 15 bis (5) of the Statute.

206 According to Art. 12(2) of the Statute, the Court's jurisdiction may be activated even when only the state where the crime was committed is party to the Statute while the state of the perpetrator's nationality is not.

tion of an act of aggression by an organ outside the Court', including, therefore, the S.C., is without prejudice to the Court's own findings under the Statute.[207]

There were also some procedural conditions, i.e.: a) that the Court would exercise jurisdiction only with respect to crimes of aggression committed one year after the ratification or acceptance of the amendments by thirty state parties; b) that a decision would be taken after 1 January 2017 by the ASP; and c) such decision would be taken by the same majority of states parties as is required for the adoption of an amendment to the Statute, i.e. two-thirds.

IV Procedure of Amendment

A question which greatly preoccupied discussions on the aggression amendments during the Review Conference, and subsequently to it, was whether, how and to what extent states parties to the Rome Statute would be obligated to accept the amendments on aggression, a question also connected with that of the conditions for the exercise of ICC jurisdiction over the same crime.

The decision finally taken in Kampala was to apply the amendment procedure prescribed in Article 121(5) of the Rome Statute,[208] as opposed to that of Article 121(4).[209] Indeed, despite the wish of a large part of states that the amendments should be binding on all states which were already parties to the Statute as provided in Article 121(4), on the basis on the fact that aggression as a crime was included in the Court's jurisdiction from the very beginning,[210] this had met with insurmountable resistance, which led to the decision to opt for the application of Article 121(5), requiring states parties to the Statute to accept the amendments so that they may be binding on them. In other words, states

207 Art. 15 bis (9) of the Statute, as amended.

208 Which provides: "Any amendment to articles 5, 6, 7 and 8 of this Statute shall enter into force for those States Parties which have accepted the amendment one year after the deposit of their instruments of ratification or acceptance. In respect of a State Party which has not accepted the amendment, the Court shall not exercise its jurisdiction regarding a crime covered by the amendment when committed by that State Party's nationals or on its territory."

209 Which provides: "Except as provided in paragraph 5, an amendment shall enter into force for all States Parties one year after instruments of ratification or acceptance have been deposited with the Secretary-General of the United Nations by seven-eighths of them."

210 *See* Arts. 5 (Crimes within the jurisdiction of the Court) and 12 (Preconditions to the exercise of jurisdiction) of the Rome Statute. According to Art. 5: "The jurisdiction of the Court shall be limited to the most serious crimes of concern to the international community as a whole. The Court has jurisdiction in accordance with this Statute with respect to the following crimes: (a) The crime of genocide; (b) Crimes against humanity; (c) War crimes; (d) The crime of aggression. According to art. 12(1): A State which becomes a Party to this Statute thereby accepts the jurisdiction of the Court with respect to the crimes referred to in article 5."

failing to ratify the amendments would not be bound. However, the unrelenting effort to find a compromise capable of rallying consensus led to the addition of the possibility for states parties to deposit an opt-out declaration,[211] which rather confused than clarified the issue. As a result, the relationship between ratification of the amendments (or not) and the submission of an opt-out declaration (or not) and its consequences remained unclear at best, which, in its turn, led to two opposing interpretations, a broad and a restrictive one, by two groups of states in the period leading up to the 2017 Assembly of States Parties and during the latter's course. The particular issue at stake was whether the ICC would have jurisdiction, in connection with the crime of aggression, over nationals of states parties to the Rome Statute which had neither ratified the relevant amendments nor opted out from them.[212] Those taking the broad view on the matter argued that in the case of state referrals or *proprio motu* investigations, the Court would have jurisdiction over such nationals when the crime of aggression had been committed in a state that had ratified the Kampala amendments. Under the opposite (restrictive) view, the ICC would not have jurisdiction in such cases (state referrals, *proprio motu* investigations) when the crime of aggression was committed by nationals or on the territory of states that had not ratified the amendments and had not made an opt-out declaration.

It is of course true that Article 121(5) does not sit well with the 'broad view' and it may even be argued that such view 'trespasses' over conventional normality as expressed in the 1969 Vienna Convention on the Law of Treaties. However, it can be observed in this respect that even if this were true, this is no threshold that had not already been 'trespassed' by the Statute as it emerged from Rome, since the ICC may, according to Article 12(2), exercise jurisdiction over nationals of a non-party to the Statute for crimes committed on the territory of a party thereto. In any event, the matter was finally resolved by the 2017 Assembly of States Parties.

4.2.5.4 The 2017 Assembly of States Parties (ASP)

The Assembly was convened in New York, in December 2017. At that time, the conditions required for considering the activation of the jurisdiction of the ICC over the crime of aggression had been fulfilled since the required period of seven years from the Kam-

211 Art. 15(bis)(4) of the Statute, as amended by Kampala Review Conference Resolution RC/Res.6, Annex I, which provides: "The Court may, in accordance with article 12, exercise jurisdiction over a crime of aggression, arising from an act of aggression committed by a State Party, unless that State Party has previously declared that it does not accept such jurisdiction by lodging a declaration with the Registrar. The withdrawal of such a declaration may be effected at any time and shall be considered by the State Party within three years."

212 For an account of the relevant issues and the negotiations held in New York in December 2017, *see* Claus Kreβ, On the Activation of ICC Jurisdiction over the Crime of Aggression, *Journal of International Criminal Justice*, Volume 16, Issue 1, 8 March 2018, pages 1-17, https://doi.org/10.1093/jicj/mqy007, Oxford Academic.

pala amendments had elapsed and the required thirty ratifications had been attained. As regards the major issue which confronted this particular ASP, i.e. the activation of the Court's jurisdiction over the crime of aggression, the Assembly did indeed decide favourably, by consensus.[213] Regrettably, however, it refrained from taking the bold step of adopting the broader view described above under iv. Indeed, while recognizing the importance of the Kampala amendments, the Assembly decided that

> … in the case of a State referral or *propio motu* investigation the Court shall not exercise its jurisdiction regarding a crime of aggression when committed by a national or on the territory of a State Party that has not ratified or accepted these amendments.[214]

It has been suggested, in connection with this decision, that the mention in the next paragraph of the Resolution of Articles 40(1) and 119(1) dealing with judicial independence and the Court's competence to settle disputes concerning its own judicial functions respectively,[215] is an attempt to 'leave the door open' for a re-examination, by the ICC, of the 'broad' and 'restrictive' positions referred to above. Even if this assessment were correct, however, in our opinion Paragraph 3 of the Resolution would be doing nothing more than 'stating the obvious', i.e. the Court's 'competenz-competenz'.

The activation was put into effect as of 17 July 2018, which marked twenty years from the adoption of the Rome Statute.

4.2.5.5 Assessment of the Aggression Amendments

The Kampala Review Conference dealt with the crime of aggression in a way which differed from that applied to the other crimes, which is not surprising taking into account its special nature and the political connotations this particular crime carries. Thus, many procedural steps were added before the amendments adopted at Kampala could be applicable, aiming at ensuring that the will that appeared at the time to have aggression as a crime in the Statute remained undiminished. Furthermore, an opt-out system specific to this crime was established which allows the non-applicability of jurisdictional rules which are applicable to other crimes, while a stronger jurisdictional filter (in the form of a decision of the Pre-Trial Division) has been added before the Prosecutor may proceed to the investigation of a case involving the crime of aggression.[216]

---

213 In addition to the activation of the jurisdiction of the Court over the crime of aggression, the ASP also dealt with the amendments to Art. 8 of the Rome Statute.

214 Para. 2 of Resolution ICC-ASP/16/Res. 5 of 24 December 2017 on the "activation of the jurisdiction of the Court over the crime of aggression."

215 Para. 3 of ICC-ASP/16/Res. 5 "on activation of the jurisdiction of the Court over the crime of aggression" which reaffirms the application of Art. 40(1) and, more importantly for this purpose, of para. 1 of Art. 119 (1) of the Rome Statute.

216 In case there has not been a prior Resolution of the S.C. concerning the occurrence of an act of aggression.

Despite all these checks and 'precautions', the fact nevertheless remained that the Kampala amendments awakened the dormant jurisdictional possibilities of the ICC on the crime of aggression. This became possible primarily by setting aside the widespread perception that the ICC should be barred from deciding on its own in cases against individuals for committing the crime of aggression (a perception based on the argument that this would bring the Court in collision course with the powers of the S.C. concerning state aggression). Eliminating this perception has indeed been a remarkable achievement of the Kampala Review Conference. On the other hand, a situation involving the crime of aggression can always be referred to the ICC by the S.C.; this, although desirable in principle, may nonetheless appear less so if the fact is taken into account that those S.C. members that are not parties to the Rome Statute may do so (refer a situation involving aggression to the ICC) while remaining themselves safely beyond any similar risk. A response to this certainly correct observation could be that this is a reality which also applies with regard to the other crimes under the Court's jurisdiction, while the involvement of the S.C. may be the only possibility to engage the ICC if the latter's jurisdiction is impeded for any legal reason. In any event, the involvement of the S.C. can be expected to be rather limited, taking into account the difficulty this body has always had in finding that state aggression has occurred.[217]

The 'crime of aggression saga' has therefore reached the end of its negotiating course which led it through the discussions for the creation of the ICC in the mid-nineties and continued unabated until the 1998 Rome Conference and from then on into the first decade of the century, through the Princeton Process and the Kampala Review Conference to find its conclusion in the 2017 ASP in New York where the discussions on the ICC Statute had started twenty-three years earlier. The outcome is certainly not entirely the one which many would have wished for, but it is equally certain that it is now a reality which appeared all but unattainable at the time this remarkable endeavour started.

In the last analysis, in spite of any second thoughts and complaints one may have – with good reason – on certain issues, it cannot be denied that the Kampala Review Conference, together with the 2017 ASP which decided on the activation of the Kampala amendments on aggression, signalled the opening of a new page in international criminal law and justice. As such, these developments have the potential to bring about significant changes in the international legal order to the benefit, ultimately, of the international community, parts of which continue to suffer from the brutal violation of the most fundamental rule of international law established by the U.N. Charter, i.e. the prohibition of aggression.

217 As shown by the Council's practice thus far. According to this pattern, it will be rather rare that the S.C. will proceed to a determination on aggression, either with or without a request by the ICC.

4.3 Cases, Situations, Prosecutions, Judgments

Up to the time of writing, twenty-eight cases have been brought before the ICC, eleven of which have been tried (at first instance or also on appeal), convicting or acquitting the defendants, or declared closed.[218] The rest are pending.[219] At the same time, several situations are under investigation by the ICC Prosecutor[220] or under preliminary examination.[221] Two situations have been referred to the Court by the S.C. (Sudan in connection with Darfur,[222] Libya[223]), while state referrals so far concern situations existing on the territories of the referring states themselves (self-referrals) (Uganda, DRC Congo, Central African Republic (CAR-two cases), Mali). Finally, four cases (situations) have been opened by the Prosecutor *proprio motu* (Côte d'Ivoire, Kenya, Georgia, Burundi).

Concerning the situation in Uganda, the trial of *Dominic Ongwen* opened in 2016,[224] while the leader of the *Lord's Resistance Army (LRA), Joseph Kony*, remains at large. Three other cases have been closed.[225]

In connection with the situation in the DRC, the ICC has sentenced two defendants, *Thomas Lubanga Dyilo*[226] and *Germain Katanga*,[227] the former for the war crime of conscripting children aged under fifteen years and for using them to actively participate in military activities in the context of a non-international conflict, and the latter as an accessory to the crime against humanity of murder and for various war crimes (murder, attacking a civilian population, destruction of property and pillaging).[228] In March 2017, the Court awarded collective and individual reparations to 297 victims of the crimes committed by *Katanga* amounting to $1 million and ordered that small amounts of cash be paid to them; the Decision also awarded collective reparations in the form, *inter alia*, of support for housing and education.[229] It was a landmark decision, as it was the first time that a convicted person has been ordered by the ICC to pay reparations to

218 For a variety of reasons, *e.g.*, because the defendants passed away or the charges against them were not confirmed or were withdrawn. As closed may also appear those cases for which a conviction/sentence or an acquittal has become final (*see* ICC website: www.icc-cpi.int/).

219 Among them are those remaining at the pre-trial stage because the defendant is at large, as trials *in absentia* are prohibited.

220 Uganda, Sudan, CAR I, Kenya, Libya, Côte d'Ivoire, Mali, CAR II, Georgia, Burundi.

221 Afghanistan, Bangladesh/Myanmar, Colombia, Guinea, Iraq/UK, Nigeria, Palestine, the Philippines, Venezuela, Ukraine (for details and updates *see* the ICC website, *supra).*

222 By S/RES/1593 (2005).

223 By S/RES/1970 (2011).

224 ICC-02/04-01/15.

225 Due to the death of the accused *Vincent Otti, Raska Lukwiya* and *Okot Odhiambo.*

226 ICC-01/04-01/06, Judgment of 14 March 2012.

227 ICC-01/04-01/07, Judgment of 7 March 2014.

228 The crimes were committed in 2003 during the attack on the village of *Bogoro,* in the district of *Ituri,* DRC.

229 Decision on Reparations pursuant to Art. 75 of the Statute, 24 March 2017. Nonetheless, as *Katanga* was not in a financial position to pay the sum ordered by the Court (which included 250 dollars for each one of the victims), the Court ordered for the payments to be made by the Trust Fund for Victims.

individual victims.[230] It also settled several practical issues, such as the identification of victims, the losses incurred and the amounts to be paid. Lastly, apart from the didactic importance it carries, it is significant that the Court considered the judgment as an important step towards achieving reconciliation.

One more case is in process in relation to the situation in the DRC,[231] while two others were closed,[232] and one suspect against whom a warrant of arrest has been issued remains at large.[233]

With regard to the situation in the Central African Republic (CAR), *Jean-Pierre Bemba Gombo*, Military Commander of the MLC,[234] was unanimously found guilty by the Trial Chamber in 2016 of two counts of crimes against humanity (murder and rape) and three counts of war crimes (murder, rape and pillaging)[235] committed by his troops in CAR from 2002 to 2003, on the basis of command (superior) responsibility.[236] The Court sentenced him to eighteen years of imprisonment. However, on appeal, *Bemba* was acquitted, by majority, of all charges[237] on the basis of a restrictive interpretation of Article 18 of the ICC Statute which is far more lenient as regards the obligation of military commanders to prevent and repress crimes committed by their subordinates. Thus, the judgment recognizes that commanders are allowed to 'make a cost/benefit analysis when deciding which measures to take, bearing in mind their overall responsibility to prevent and repress' such crimes,[238] while it arguably indicates that the 'remoteness' of the

230 It is also noteworthy that the Decision substantiates G.A. Resolution of 2005 on "Basic Principles and Guidelines on the Right to a Remedy and Reparation for Victims of Gross Violations of International Human Rights Law and Serious Violations of International Humanitarian Law."

231 *Bosco Ntaganda* (ICC-01/04-02/06), whose trial opened in 2015.

232 *Mathieu Ngudjolo Chui* was acquitted of the charges of war crimes and crimes against humanity, while the charges against *Callixte Mbarushimana* were not confirmed.

233 *Sylvestre Mudacumura* (ICC-01/04-01/12).

234 *Mouvement de Libération du Congo.*

235 *Jean-Pierre Bemba Gombo*, ICC-01/05-01/08, Trial Chamber Judgment, 21 March 2016.

236 It was the first time that the ICC entered a conviction under Art. 28 on command responsibility, as well as its first conviction involving sexual violence. On the conviction on command responsibility *see* Chantal Meloni, Command responsibility, joint commission and "control over the crime" approach in the first ICC jurisprudence, www.academia.edu.

237 On 8 June 2018. For an analysis *see* Leila N. Sadat, Fiddling while Rome Burns? The Appeal Chamber's Curious Decision in *Prosecutor v. Jean-Pierre Bemba Gombo*, EJIL Talk, 12 June 2018.

238 Para. 170 of the Judgment.

commander may also be a determining factor for the non-attribution of responsibility to him/her.[239]

In connection with the situation in Mali, in a ground-breaking judgment issued in 2016, the Court found *Al Mahdi* guilty, under Article 8(2)(e)(iv) of the Rome Statute, for the war crime of intentionally directing attacks against religious and historic buildings[240] and convicted him to nine years of imprisonment. The case concerned the destruction of the *Timbuktu Mausoleums* in Mali in 2012, during the occupation of the city by jihadi forces. The ICC Prosecutor noted that these issues will become increasingly relevant to ICC practice, reminding the repeated destruction of cultural heritage in the context of armed conflict by groups like ISIS.[241] In 2017, the Trial Chamber issued a Reparations Order, declaring *Al Mahdi* liable for 2.7 million euros for individual and collective reparations for the community of Timbuktu. In view of *Al Mahdi*'s indigence, however, the Trust Fund for Victims was encouraged to complement the reparations Award. In 2018, the Appeals Chamber confirmed most of the Reparations Order.

Also in connection with Mali, The Prosecutor issued an arrest warrant against *Al Hassan Ag Abdoul Aziz Ag Mohamed Ag Mahmoud* in March 2018 on charges of crimes against humanity and war crimes committed in Timbuktu.[242] *Al Hassan* was then surrendered to the ICC and the process for the confirmation of the charges has been initiated.

As already mentioned, the ICC Prosecutor noted, in connection with the *Al Mahdi* case, the repeated destruction by ISIS of cultural heritage monuments in Iraq and Syria. It is indeed clear that monuments such as the Palmyra *Tetrapylon* in Syria and the ancient city of *Nimrud* in Iraq are of great importance not only for the people living in the areas, states or regions where the destruction took place but also for the world at large. From a legal perspective, these acts constitute violations of international law, in particular huma-

239 In a connected case involving *Bemba* and members of his legal team (Gombo *et al.* Aimé Kilolo Musamba, Jean-Jacques Mangenda Kabongo, Fidèle Babala Wandu and Narcisse Arido) (ICC-01/05-01/13), the Trial Chamber found, on 19 October 2016, the defendants guilty of offences against the administration of justice, in relation to the presentation of false testimonial evidence by defence witnesses in the first (main) case against *Jean-Pierre Bemba Gombo.* A Decision of 22 March 2017 imposed sentences and fines for these offences. On 8 March 2018, the Appeals Chamber reversed some findings of the Trial Chamber but confirmed most convictions for giving false testimony and corruptly influencing witnesses. Following *Jean-Pierre Bemba's* acquittal in the main Case in June 2018, it is uncertain whether reparations to victims may be issued, since no reparations order can be issued when there is no conviction. It seems, however, that "alternative" solutions are being sought through the Trust Fund for Victims (TFV).

240 *Ahmad Al Faqi Al Mahdi*, ICC-01/12-01/15-171, Trial Chamber Judgment, 27 September 2016.

241 *Prosecutor v. Ahmad Al Faqi Al Mahdi*: Cultural Property and World Heritage in International Criminal Law, Conclusions, pp. 34-35.

242 ICC-01/12-01/18 *("Al Hassan case").*

nitarian and human rights law as well as crimes against humanity or war crimes under international criminal law.[243, 244] It is therefore imperative that such cases are ultimately submitted to justice, whether national or international.[245]

From the angle of ICC jurisdiction, given that Syria and Iraq[246] are not parties to the ICC Statute, the prosecution of those responsible for the destruction and looting of cultural monuments and related objects of cultural importance can be carried out only to the extent that such persons are nationals of countries which are parties to the Statute, unless, of course, there has been a S.C. Resolution to this effect on the basis of Article 13(b) of the Statute.[247]

In connection with the situation in the Darfur province of Sudan, cases are pending against the (now former) Sudanese President *Omar Hassan Ahmad Al Bashir*[248] and other officials of his government.[249] The fact that *Al Bashir* has been able to travel to other African states parties to the ICC Statute which have failed to live up to their obligation to arrest him has been one of the major causes of friction between the ICC and these countries.[250]

---

243 *See* Alexandros Kolliopoulos, Destruction ciblée des monuments et sites archeoloqiques en periode de conflit arme et la dimension culturelle de la paix internationale, Annuaire Francais de Droit Internationale, LXI – 2015 – CNRS Éditions, Paris, pp. 119-143; Caroline Ehlert, Prosecuting the Destruction of Cultural Property in International Criminal Law (With a Case Study on the Khmer Rouge's Destruction of Cambodia' Heritage), Martinus Nijhoff, 2014.

244 The destruction of important monuments is, however, only one side of the coin, the other being the pillaging of cultural property and its illegal sale on the international market. It is worth noting in this respect that of the several resolutions issued by the S.C. on ISIS (ISIL), the *Al Nusra Front* (ANF) and similar entities (among which Resolutions 2161 (2014), 2178 (2014), 2199 (2015) and 2253 (2015)), Resolution 2199 (2015) specifically prohibits trade, including cross-border trade, in Iraqi and Syrian cultural property and other items of archaeological, historical, cultural, rare scientific, and religious importance which were illegally removed from Iraq since 6 August 1990 and from Syria since 15 March 2011, with a view to their eventual return to the Iraqi and Syrian people (para. 17).

245 On the issue of ISIS crimes, see also *infra*, section 8.4.1.

246 Furthermore, neither of these countries is party to the 1999 Second Protocol to the Hague Convention of 1954, for the Protection of Cultural Property in the Event of Armed Conflict which establishes universal criminal jurisdiction (Art. 16(1)(c)) in respect of acts of destruction of cultural objects on a large scale provided for in Art. 15(1)(c) of the Protocol.

247 Phani Dascalopoulou-Livada, The CAHDI and the implementation of the International Criminal Court Statute: Issues and Challenges, Past and Present, in *The CAHDI Contribution to the Development of Public International Law, Achievements and Future Challenges*, Council of Europe (ed), *Brill/Nijhoff*, 2016, pp. 45-51.

248 ICC-02/05-01/09.

249 Like *Bashir, Ahmad Muhammad Harun ("Ahmad Harun"), Ali Muhammad Ali Abd-Al-Rahman ("Ali Kushayb")* (Case for both ICC-02/05-01/07) and *Nourain-Abdel Raheem Muhammad Hussein* (ICC-02/05-01/12) remain at large. The charges against *Bahr Idriss Abu Garda* were not confirmed. Two Sudanese rebel leaders, *Abdallah Banda Abakaer Nourain* and *Saleh Mohammed Jerbo Jamus* (Case for both ICC-02/05-03/09) who were charged with the war crime of killing twelve African Union peacekeepers in 2007 appeared voluntarily at the pre-trial stage. Proceedings with regard to the latter were terminated due to his death while the former is now at large.

250 Al Bashir was deposed from his presidential office in April 2019, following intense demonstrations and riots in Sudan against his rule.

The Security Council also referred the situation in Libya to the ICC.[251] Following the death of the former President of Libya *Muammar Abu Minyar Gaddafi*, the ICC has charged four persons[252] with war crimes and crimes against humanity.[253]

The Prosecutor exercised *proprio motu* prosecution for the first time in the case of the situation in Côte d'Ivoire (Ivory Coast) following the acceptance of the jurisdiction of the ICC by the country in 2003, in accordance with Article 12(3) of the Rome Statute[254] (Côte d'Ivoire became party to the ICC Statute in 2013). The investigation related to the post-electoral violence which erupted in the country in 2010 and 2011[255] and led to the indictment of *Laurent Gbagbo*, former President of Côte d'Ivoire who was arrested in 2011. The charges against him for crimes against humanity were confirmed in 2014. *Gbagbo* was the first head of state to be arrested and face trial before the ICC. In 2015, the case was joined with that of *Charles Blé Goudé*, a close associate of *Gbagbo* and Youth Minister at the time.[256] A warrant of arrest was also issued for *Simone Gbagbo*, the former president's spouse,[257] but the government of Côte d'Ivoire refused to surrender her to the Court.[258] The trial started in 2016 and on 15 January 2019, the Trial Chamber acquitted both, *Gbagbo* and *Blé Goudé*, from all charges for crimes against humanity, on the basis of insufficient evidence. The Prosecutor has, however, expressed her intention to appeal the decision.

Proprio motu prosecutorial powers were also exercised in the case of the situation in Kenya where six persons were accused, including the then Deputy Prime-Minister and later (having won the 2013 elections) President *Uhuru Muigai Kenyatta* for crimes committed during post-election violence in the country in 2007-2008.[259] However, all six

---

251 S/RES/1970 of 26 February 2011.

252 Of whom *Muammar Gaddafi*'s son *Saif Al-Islam Gaddafi* remains at large, as do *Al-Tuhamy Mohamed Khaled*, former Lieutenant General of the Libyan army and former head of the Libyan Internal Security Agency (ISA) and *Mahmoud Mustafa Busayf al-Werfalli*, Major in the *Al-Saiqa* Brigade. The case against Muammar *Gaddafi*'s son *Abdullah Al-Senussi* was declared inadmissible.

253 ICC-01/11-01/11 and ICC-01/11-01/17.

254 By a statement of 18 April 2003, confirmed in 2010 and 2011.

255 The Prosecutor started an investigation into the situation in Côte d'Ivoire in 2011 for crimes committed in that country from 19 September 2010 to 28 November 2010.

256 ICC-02/11-01/15.

257 ICC-02/11-01/12.

258 *Simone Gbagbo* was in the meantime convicted in 2015 by a Court in Côte d'Ivoire to twenty years imprisonment for offences against the security of the state. She was however acquitted in March 2017 for crimes against humanity and war crimes (The New York Times, 28 March 2017).

259 The case involved *Uhuru Muigai Kenyatta, Francis Kirimi Muthaura*, and *Mohammed Hussein Ali* (ICC-01/09-02/11) and *William Samoei Ruto, Joshua Arap Sang* and *Henry Kiprono Kosgey* (ICC-01/09-01/11). However, in 2012 the Court declined to confirm the charges against *Henry Kiprono Kosgey*. In the same year, charges against *Francis Kirimi Muthaura* and *Mohammed Hussein Ali* were also withdrawn for insufficient evidence. Charges against *Uhuru Kenyatta* were withdrawn in 2014 and proceedings terminated in 2015 while those concerning *William Samoei Ruto* and *Joshua Arap Sang* were terminated in 2016. *Uhuru Kenyatta* was re-elected President of Kenya in 2017.

cases were terminated in 2015 due to lack of evidence.[260] In sum, the cases related to Kenya marked a serious setback for the Court, which has not been able to provide adequate witness protection and, in the last analysis, to overcome the refusal of Kenya to cooperate in bringing the suspects at the highest echelons of power to justice. Although this was, perhaps, an unfair battle, it nonetheless clearly demonstrates the difficulties the ICC has to face in high-profile cases and the hurdles it has to overcome in dealing with a culture of 'entrenched impunity'.[261] The case has also highlighted the lack of determined support by the international community. It is obvious that the Court has to address all these issues in order to maintain its credibility and play the role that is expected of it.

260 The only cases which remain in connection with the situation in Kenya, are those against *Walter Osapiri Barasa* (ICC 01/09-01/13), *Paul Gicheru* and *Philip Kipkoech Bett* (ICC-01/09-01/15) for obstructing justice by tampering with prosecution witnesses. Arrest warrants were issued in 2013 against *Walter Osapiri Barasa* and in 2015 against *Paul Gicheru* and *Philip Kipkoech Bett.* The suspects have not yet been surrendered to the ICC.

261 Human Rights Watch, www.hrw.org/news/2016/04/05/icc-kenya-deputy-presidents-case-ends, 5 April 2016, quoting Elizabeth Evenson, senior international justice counsel at Human Rights Watch.

5 Conclusions

The spectacular development, since the early 1990s, of international criminal law to include systems of functional international criminal justice through a constellation of international criminal tribunals, has given rise to justified expectations that grave international crimes could, at long last, be punished and ultimately suppressed. The adoption, in 1998, of the Statute of the International Criminal Court, establishing uniform rules to be applied in all such cases, and the creation of the ICC in 2002, marked the culmination of the process which further enhanced these hopes.

However, a closer look reveals certain drawbacks which raise concerns. The most obvious among them is that international criminal justice is very slow and very expensive, the cost of international courts and tribunals being, arguably, vastly disproportionate to their performance.[1]

Furthermore, while it is true that *ex post* criminal justice such as that rendered for the first time in modern times by the IMT and the IMTFE and more recently by the ICTY and the ICTR has been short on legal justification, the ICC, which is solidly based on an *ex ante* basis and therefore finds itself on high legal and moral ground, is faced with serious challenges exactly because it is called to exercise its functions in ongoing conflicts and similar perilous situations. This obviously presents grave risks for those conducting the investigation, while it may also compromise the quality of collected information and its assessment.

Adding to these difficulties is the emerging tendency of the S.C. to refer such extremely challenging situations to the Court (Darfur, Libya) probably in order to compensate for its own lack of action where it is impeded or hesitant to act in exercise of its powers to maintain international peace and security.

Reality has shown, on the other hand, that the cooperation of states parties to the Statute – particularly as regards the execution of arrest warrants or surrender requests – is in short supply even where a state party is not directly involved in the case where its assistance is sought.[2] This has been the case with several African states which expressed in this way their frustration and disappointment at the allegedly one-sided focus of the ICC on Africa, as most of the court's cases refer to African countries and prosecutions predominantly concern African nationals, including political leaders.[3] Further complaints, which are not necessarily unfounded, have led some of these African states to

1 Thus, in the first ten years of its existence, the ICC's costs amounted to $900 million. In their respective ten first years, the ICTY cost $695 million and the ICTR about a $1 billion.

2 *See* the lengthy ICC-ASP/16/Res.2, Resolution on cooperation adopted by the ASP in December 2017.

3 Thus, currently, all 26 cases pending before the Court concern Africans, while 9 out of the 10 situations under investigation concern African countries.

express their intention to leave the ICC, an extreme step under any circumstances – which Burundi was the first to take.[4] It is of course true that the Court has been dealing overwhelmingly with African cases and African nationals. It is also true, however, that Africa is the most represented continent in the Court and its Statute and that a significant number of cases was based on self-referrals, all of which contribute to Africa being – so far – the main focus of the ICC. At this time, the crisis seems to be subsiding; however, it is far from over and will probably continue casting a shadow over the relationship between the African Continent and the ICC well into the future.[5] This of course in no way excludes the possibility of such a situation appearing elsewhere, as happened recently with the Philippines.[6]

Another matter which has been hotly debated is the allegedly antagonistic relationship between peace and justice (when, for example, peace could, supposedly, be attained by granting amnesty to the perpetrators of crimes under the jurisdiction of the ICC) and the dilemma resulting therefrom.[7]

It can firstly be observed that such 'dilemma' is in most cases yet another unfortunate consequence of the inaction of the international community as expressed by the S.C., to take up its responsibilities with regard to the maintenance of international peace and security.

As regards existing pathways to deal with this admittedly great challenge, the solutions proposed by scholars and practitioners on the matter cover the whole spectrum, ranging from those proclaiming that the ICC should participate in or even play the role of peacemaker through its judicial functions, to that maintaining that it should restrict itself solely to the latter. Intermediate solutions combine the two roles.

It is of course an undeniable truth that the ICC cannot and indeed should not isolate itself from the world around it and that it is unavoidably influenced by the realities of the human societies it operates in at each time. However, it is not its role to participate in peace efforts as such; peace is, in any event, always served by justice in the shorter or longer term. However, any direct participation or contribution of the ICC to peace efforts would risk compromising its role and credibility. Furthermore, the ICC Statute itself provides for only one possibility to take into account other (non-legal) circumstances: it

4 The withdrawal of Burundi from the Rome Statute took effect on 27 October 2017.

5 *See*, generally, Kamari M. Clarke, Abel S. Knottnerus and Eefje de Volder (eds), *Africa and the ICC, Perceptions of Justice*.

6 The withdrawal of which from the Rome Statute took effect on 17 March 2019.

7 C. Stahn, Complementarity, amnesties and alternative forms of justice: Some interpretative guidelines for the International Criminal Court, *Journal of International Criminal Justice*, Vol. 3, Issue 3, July 2005, pp. 695-720.

is Article 53(1)(c), but, again, strictly – and this is most important – 'in the interests of justice'.[8]

Mention is sometimes made of Article 16 of the Statute and the possibilities it offers to the S.C. to defer a case – even *ad infinitum*, which may be brought or is already pending before the ICC for any reason, including, presumably, in order to 'give peace a chance'.[9] Leaving aside the fact that Article 16 has been an unfortunate intrusion of politics into the Statute as has been amply proved so far,[10] it must be emphasized that it would be equally unfortunate if use was made of it to accommodate the needs of a 'peace process' conducted by the S.C. or under its aegis. Most probably, the ultimate result would be compromising the integrity of the Court and creating – justifiably – a sense of selective justice and 'double standards'. In any event, the ICC does not control the use of Article 16 and this should be made clear if and when the article is so used.

Despite all these problems and setbacks, the ICC constitutes the greatest institutional novelty which saw the light of day at the beginning of the twenty-first century after a long period of inertia in the domain of international criminal justice. As such, it can form the focal point for it, unifying and streamlining its elements and serving as a yardstick and an inspiration for national legislations and courts alike. At the same time, it will, hopefully, be a powerful deterrent against the commission of egregious crimes which are a reality in many parts of the world. Furthermore, the addition of the crime of aggression in the jurisdiction of the Statute, and its recent activation (as from 17 July 2018) gives hope and perspective that a crime which the international community has failed to face since World War II will, finally, find the punishment it deserves.

---

8 Art. 53(1)(c) provides that: "The Prosecutor shall, having evaluated the information made available to him or her, initiate an investigation unless he or she determines that there is no reasonable basis to proceed under this Statute. In deciding whether to initiate an investigation, the Prosecutor shall consider whether:... [c]Taking into account the gravity of the crime and the interests of victims, there are nonetheless substantial reasons to believe that an investigation would not serve the interests of justice."

9 Art. 16 provides that: "No investigation or prosecution may be commenced or proceeded with under this Statute for a period of twelve months after the Security Council, in a resolution adopted under Chapter VII of the Charter of the United Nations, has requested the Court to that effect; that request may be renewed by the Council under the same conditions."

10 Art. 16 was indeed used to pass the very controversial S.C. Resolution 1422 (2002) which requested the ICC to defer any prosecutions of peacekeepers from non-state parties to the Rome Statute for a period of twelve months. The deferral was renewed for another year by S.C. Resolution 1487 (2003). A further renewal attempt in 2004 did not come to fruition as it became apparent that there was no state support for it, particularly because of revelations concerning the situation in the *Abu Graib* prison in Iraq (*see* Ademola Abbas, The competence of the Security Council to terminate the jurisdiction of the International Criminal Court, *Texas International Law Journal*, 40, 2005, pp. 263-297).

Part II
Human Rights and International Humanitarian Law in the Face of Terrorism

6 Advancements and Setbacks

6.1 After World War II

Since the end of that War, the advancement of international human rights law (IHRL) has been continuous, with the adoption of a great number of international legal instruments, universal and regional, enshrining a constantly expanding spectrum of such rights, and with the establishment of several judicial organs applying IHRL. This last element differentiated this branch of law from international humanitarian law (IHL); nonetheless, although there were no special international judicial organs applying IHL, the normative progression of this law ran parallel to that of human rights, both, in fact, influencing and promoting the other.

In the same period, there has been a steady increase in terrorist incidents with an international character. The starting point was in the late 1960s and into the 1970s, when the Palestinian Liberation Organization (PLO) mounted several attacks in Europe on land, in the air and later even at sea.[1]

The terrorist phenomenon went on to appear in different forms and with variable origin, ideology and *modus operandi* over the years, reaching its culmination with the 11 September 2001 attacks by *Al Qaeda* in New York, Washington and Pennsylvania.

The grave security concerns generated by these attacks led to a flurry of counter-terrorism measures adopted by the U.N. and other organizations, among which NATO and the EU, as well as by individual countries, particularly the U.S. and European ones.

In the legal domain, the reaction of the international community was the adoption, mainly in the context of the U.N., of a series of 'sectoral' anti-terrorism agreements, which means that each one was specific to a particular type of terrorist activity.

The U.N. organs also adopted Resolutions purporting to strengthen and concretize cooperation for combating international terrorism, *inter alia* through the establishment of specific mechanisms to that effect. Specialized organizations within the U.N. system[2] also stepped up their efforts to this end.

As national and international counter-terrorism measures continuously intensified, however, so did criticism that some of them did not conform with or in some cases

---

1 Such incidents were the hijacking, in July 1968, of *El Al* Flight 426 from Rome to Tel Aviv, and the killing of 12 persons, 11 of whom were Israeli athletes and coaches, in the 1972 Munich Olympics by the Palestinian Black September Organization. In 1985 there was also the attack of Palestinian guerillas against the Italian cruise ship *Achille Lauro* in the territorial sea of Egypt (*see* Part. III, p. 99, fn. 416).

2 Such as the International Atomic Energy Agency IAEA), the International Civil Aviation Organization (ICAO), the International Maritime Organization (IMO), the United Nations Office on Drugs and Crime (UNIDC), the World Health Organization (WHO) and the International Criminal Police Organization (INTERPOL).

even violated the rules of IHRL and IHL.[3] Doubtless, the relationship between counter-terrorism and human rights can be antagonistic, complex and precarious. The same is true, although perhaps less visibly so, with regard to the relationship between counter-terrorism and humanitarian law or refugee law. Indeed, while states are under an obligation to ensure that the counter-terrorism measures they take comply with human rights standards (as well as with IHL and refugee law, where applicable), human rights abuses have never ceased to be registered while combating terrorism.

Before discussing the relationship between human rights and humanitarian law on the one hand, and counter-terrorism on the other, a few introductory notes concerning each one of these notions could be of relevance.

6.2 NOTES ON HUMAN RIGHTS LAW

As a concept, human rights, i.e. rights 'inherent to all human beings', 'without discrimination', which are 'interrelated, interdependent and indivisible' 'universal and inalienable'[4] find their origin mainly in the European Enlightenment and the philosophical ideas of *Voltaire, Diderot, Rousseau, Locke, Hutcheson* and others. Human rights were given strong impetus by the American and French Revolutions[5] while in the nineteenth century the notion of human rights was central to the issue of the abolition of slavery.[6] Since then, both the idea of and the efforts for the implementation of human rights have been constantly progressing, particularly in the second half of the twentieth century.

---

3 On this and related issues *see* OHCHR, Digest of Jurisprudence of the United Nations and Regional Organizations on the Protection of Human Rights while Countering Terrorism, 2003; OHCHR, Fact Sheet No. 32 on Human Rights, Terrorism and Counter-Terrorism, 2008; Manfred Nowak, Anne Charbord (eds) *Using Human Rights to Counter Terrorism*, Edward Elgar Publishing, 2018; Aniceto Masferrer, Clive Walker (eds), *Counter-Terrorism, Human Rights and the Rule of Law: Crossing Legal Boundaries in Defence of the State*, Edward Elgar Publishing, 2013; David J. Whittaker, *Counter-Terrorism and Human Rights*, Routledge, 2013; Alex P. Schmid, Terrorism and Human Rights: A Perspective from the United Nations, *Terrorism and Political Violence*, 17:1-2, 25-35, 2007; Giuseppe Nesi, *International Cooperation in Counter-Terrorism*, Ashgate, 2006.

4 Quotations selectively taken from the text appearing on the website of the Office of the High Commissioner for Human Rights. Full text available at: www.ohchr.org/EN/Issues/Pages/WhatareHumanRights.aspx.

5 See, e.g., the 1776 United States Declaration of Independence and its famous *dictum*, embodying the essence of human rights: "We hold these truths to be self-evident, that all men are created equal, that they are endowed by their Creator with certain unalienable Rights, that among these are Life, Liberty and the pursuit of Happiness."

6 See Jonathan Israel, Democratic Enlightenment: Philosophy, Revolution, and Human Rights 1750-1790.

6.2.1 *Indivisibility of Human Rights*

It is a basic principle underpinning the fundamental post-war human rights text, i.e. the 1948 Universal Declaration of Human Rights,[7] as well as all the important human rights instruments that followed, that these rights are indivisible, interlinked and interdependent.[8] Despite this, it remains true that the priorities of different regions, political systems or individual states differ as regards the importance they attribute to each category of rights (broadly, civil and political on the one hand, social and economic on the other).[9] Thus, civil and political rights, which are fundamentally connected with the system of democracy, are usually prioritized by western states, while developing states are inclined to place more importance to social and economic rights, which are closely connected to development.[10] Cultural rights appear to be in a class of their own or may be considered to belong to either category. It must be noted, finally, that there have also been voices which have been critical of the 'overuse' of human rights on philosophical and legal grounds.[11]

6.2.2 *Human Rights in the U.N. Context*

The trend for the formulation of human rights into legal norms started with the Charter of the United Nations elevating the protection and promotion of human rights to one of the basic goals of the Organization. The Preamble of the Charter affirms the "faith in

7 Art. 2 of the Declaration.

8 *See also* Art. 55(c) of the Charter of the United Nations and the Vienna Declaration and Programme of Action (adopted by the World Conference on Human Rights in Vienna on 25 June 1993).

9 Karel Vasak in 'A 30 year struggle,' UNESCO Courier, November 1977, p. 29, distinguished "three generations" of human rights: a) civil and political rights (such as the right to life and the right to political participation) b) economic, social and cultural rights and c) solidarity rights (such as right to peace, right to clean environment).

10 Two are the prevailing general theories with respect to the differences between western and developing states in connection with human rights, the "universalist" and the "relativist." The former maintains that human rights apply to all people regardless of culture, race, sex or religion. The latter admits that differences in culture condone practices which may run contrary to the western notion of human rights. Imposing such western notions to other countries would constitute "cultural imperialism" according to this theory.

11 From contemporary writers *see, e.g.*, Alain Pellet, *"Human rightism" and International Law*, Gilberto Amado Memorial Lecture, U.N., 2000; Alain de Benoist, *Beyond Human Rights*, Arktos Media, 2011; David W. Kennedy, The International Human Rights Regime: Still Part of the Problem? In Examining Critical Perspective on Human Rights, *by* Rob Dickinson, Elena Katselli, Colin Murray, Ole W. Pedersen (eds), 19-34, Cambridge, UK: Cambridge University Press, 2012, available at: https://dash.harvard.edu/handle/1/15749103 accessed 16 April 2018.

fundamental human rights, in the equal rights of men and women," while Article 1(3) states that one of the Organization's purposes is "promoting and encouraging respect for human rights and for fundamental freedoms for all without distinction as to race, sex, language or religion."[12] Three years later, in 1948, the Universal Declaration of Human Rights was adopted by the General Assembly of the United Nations[13, 14] marking a milestone in the general acceptance of human rights and its importance for the world at large.

A host of universal normative instruments on human rights were adopted thereafter. Most prominent among them are the two U.N. International Covenants of 1966, one on civil and political rights,[15] and the other on economic, social and cultural rights.[16] Most of the rights enshrined in the ICCPR, together with those in the 1948 Universal Declaration embody rules of customary international law which are therefore binding on all states[17] and which are formulated either as rights or as prohibitions. Some of them are considered to have attained a *jus cogens* status (peremptory norms), which means that they cannot be derogated from under any circumstances. Such, for example, is the case of the prohibition of slavery, torture and racial discrimination.[18]

Many more multilateral conventions dealing with particular aspects of human rights were adopted in the U.N. context in the last decades of the twentieth century and in the beginning of the twenty-first. Most of these global legal instruments have had spectacular success, gathering the membership of the great majority of states. Among them are the Conventions on the Elimination of All Forms of Racial Discrimination,[19] on the Rights of the Child,[20] on the Elimination of Discrimination against Women,[21] as well as the Convention against Torture,[22] the Convention for the Protection of All Persons from En-

12 Furthermore, Art. 55 of the Charter provides that: "With a view to the creation of conditions of stability and well-being which are necessary for peaceful and friendly relations among nations based on respect for the principle of equal rights and self-determination of peoples, the United Nations shall promote: ...c) universal respect for, and observance of, human rights and fundamental freedoms for all without distinction as to race, sex, language, or religion."

13 The 1945 Conference in San Francisco had, however, already inserted respect of human rights into the U.N. Charter.

14 The Declaration was drafted by the Human Rights Commission chaired by the then First Lady Eleanor Roosevelt.

15 (ICCPR), of 16 December 1966. Entry into force on 23 March 1976. Parties 169.

16 (ICESCR), of 16 December 1966. Entry into force on 3 January 1976. Parties 166.

17 *Case concerning Military and Paramilitary Activities in and against Nicaragua* (*Nicaragua v. United States of America*), Merits, Judgment of 27 June 1986, I.C.J. Reports 1986, paras. 172-201.

18 *See* Draft Articles on State Responsibility, Commentary on draft Art. 26, Compliance with Peremptory Norms.

19 (CERD), of 20 November 1963. Entry into force on 4 January 1969.

20 (CRC), of 20 November 1989. Entry into force on 2 September 1990.

21 (CEDAW), of 18 December 1979. Entry into force on 3 September 1981.

22 (CAT), of 10 December 1984. Entry into force on 26 June 1987.

forced Disappearance,[23] the Convention on the Rights of Persons with Disabilities[24] and the Convention on Migrant Workers.[25]

6.2.3 *Regional Agreements*

On a regional level, the 1950 European Convention on Human Rights and Fundamental Freedoms (ECHR)[26] adopted in the context of the Council of Europe (CoE),[27] placed Europe at the forefront of developments in human rights law. This was achieved not only by the normative recognition of human rights as a fundamental component of a legal system based on the rule of law but also by providing individuals whose human rights had allegedly been violated by a state party to the Convention with the possibility to resort to an international judicial organ, the European Court of Human Rights, seated in Strasbourg (ECtHR).[28]

The ECHR has been amended by Protocols Nos. 11, 14 and 16[29] and supplemented by six Protocols.[30]

In the EU context, securing respect and promotion for human rights is a fundamental goal which is served by multiple means, on the basis of the 'Charter of Fundamental Rights of the European Union'.[31] It is also one of the conditions which must be fulfilled for a state to join the Union.[32]

There has also been a long discussion about EU accession to the ECHR, and indeed the Treaty of Lisbon provided for a duty of the EU to do so. However, the European Court of Justice (ECJ) ruled in December 2014 that the negotiated agreement which was put before it for opinion did not safeguard the EU's underlying balance and the autonomy of its law. Although both the Parliament and the Commission strongly support EU's accession to ECHR, the matter remains unsettled and the opinions of experts on the matter continue being divided.[33]

23 (CED), of 20 December 2006. Entry into force on 23 December 2010.
24 (CRPD), of 13 December 2006. Entry into force on 3 May 2008.
25 (CMW), of 18 December 1990. Entry into force on June 2003.
26 The ECHR was adopted on 4 November 1950 and entered into force on 3 September 1953.
27 Founded in 1949 and currently counting 47 member states. All members are parties to the ECHR.
28 *Cour Européenne de droits de l'homme.*
29 Protocol 16 entered *into force on* 1 August 2018, while Protocol No. 15 has not yet entered into force.
30 Nos. 1, 4, 6, 7, 12 and 13.
31 2000/C 364/01. The Charter entered into force in 2009.
32 Among the 1993 "Copenhagen criteria" of the EU which have to be met for that purpose, are "stable institutions guaranteeing democracy, the rule of law, human rights and respect for and protection of minorities ..."
33 European Parliament Think Tank, EU accession to the European Convention on Human Rights (ECHR), 6 July 2017; Legislative Train Schedule, Area of Justice and Fundamental Rights, Completion of EU accession to the ECHR, 20 January 2019.

Legal systems of human rights protection were also developed elsewhere in the world. In America, the Convention on Human Rights was adopted in 1969[34] in the context of the Organization of American States (OAS),[35] while in Africa, the African Charter on Human and People's Rights was adopted in 1981 in *Banjul*, Gambia, by a Summit Meeting of the (then) Organization of African Union (OAU).[36]

6.3 Implementation and Application

Enshrining human rights in international legal instruments does not necessarily identify with securing their implementation and respect. To achieve this, several models have been used, the most effective for the purpose being resort to an international judicial organ which is independent from its member states, and where claims for the violation of one or more human rights of the petitioner may be adjudicated on.

6.3.1 The European Court of Human Rights (ECtHR)

Among the existing international courts on human rights, the ECtHR, already mentioned above, is the oldest and most well-known one. The Court began operating in 1959 and has been very successful, having delivered thousands of judgments concerning violations of the European Convention on Human Rights or of any of its Protocols.[37] Applications may be submitted by individuals, groups and non-governmental organizations who are directly and significantly affected by a violation or violations of the Convention or its Protocols by a state party and who need not be nationals or have any legal connection with that state.[38] In all cases, the prior exhaustion of domestic remedies is required.[39] Following a 1998 reform of the system, individuals may now submit their applications directly to the Court.[40] Appeals are decided by the Grand Chamber. Applications may

---

34 "Pact of San José, Costa Rica" (B-32) of 22 November 1969. The Treaty entered into force on 18 July 1978 and has 25 member states.

35 OAS was constituted by the Charter of the OAS (119 UNT.S. 3.), signed in Bogotà, Colombia, in 1948. The Charter entered into force on 13 December 1951, and was subsequently amended by the Protocol of Buenos Aires of 27 February 1967, by the Protocol of Cartagena de Indias of 5 December 1985, by the Protocol of Washington of 14. 12. 1992 and by the Protocol of Managua of 10 June 1993. All 35 American states are members to OAS.

36 On 27 June 1981. The Charter entered into force on 21 October 1986.

37 If the right at issue is contained in a Protocol for which ratification by all states parties is not required, then the state which has allegedly violated a right provided for in the Protocol in question must be a party thereto.

38 *See* Practical Guide on Admissibility Criteria, European Court of Human Rights, updated 31 December 2018.

39 ECHR, Art. 35(1). *See also* the Practical Guide, *supra*, fn. 38.

40 *See infra*, p. 8, fn. 43.

also be submitted by states parties to the ECHR against other such states (interstate applications).[41]

The Court has produced a vast body of jurisprudence on all the rights and issues covered by the ECHR and its Protocols,[42] as in the decades following its establishment, the jurisdictional ambit of the European Court of Human Rights has been greatly expanded, as mentioned above, by the adoption of the Protocols to the ECHR which create an extended network of protected rights everywhere in Europe and further afield.

6.3.2 *The Inter-American Court of Human Rights*

This Court is based on the American Convention on Human Rights. The Convention was adopted in the context of the OAS,[43] in *San José*, Costa Rica, on 22 November 1969. The Court, which has its seat in *San José*, began to operate in 1979, and is tasked to resolve contentious disputes and issue advisory opinions on specific questions of law. The Court may hear a case if the state involved in that case has accepted the Court's jurisdiction either in advance for all cases or on an *ad hoc* basis.[44] Individuals do not have direct access to the Inter-American Court, having to go through the Inter-American Commission on Human Rights (IACHR),[45] which was established in 1959 as a principal and autonomous organ of OAS and became functional in 1960.[46] The Commission's role is to act as the first step in the admissibility process for contentious cases and promote friendly settlements between parties. It also investigates and presents reports on human rights conditions in the American States, irrespective of whether a concrete claim has

41 ECHR, Art. 33. On inter-state applications *see* Isabella Risini, The Inter-State Application under the European Convention on Human Rights, Brill, 2018.

42 *See* https://hudoc.echr.coe.int.

43 All the American states are members of OAS.

44 Twenty-two states have accepted the jurisdiction of the Court.

45 *Comisión Interamericana de Derechos Humanos.*

46 *See* Lea Shaver, The Inter-American Human Rights System: An Effective Institution for Regional Rights Protection?, 9 *Wash. U. Global Stud. L. Rev.* 639 (2010), available at: http://openscholarship.wustl.edu/law_globalstudies/vol9/iss4/4, last accessed 26 February 2018.

been submitted.[47] The Commission is based in Washington, D.C., home of the OAS headquarters.[48]

6.3.3 *The African Court of Justice and Human Rights (AfCHPR)*

This is the successor of the African Court of Justice of the African Union and the African Court on Human and Peoples' Rights.[49] The African system on human rights comprises also the African Commission on Human and Peoples' Rights (ACHPR) which was established in 1987 to oversee and interpret the African Charter on Human and Peoples' Rights (*Banjul Charter*) with the aim of protecting and promoting human rights and fundamental freedoms in Africa. The Commission may receive complaints (communications) by states, organizations and individuals alleging violations of the Charter by a state party to it. It can subsequently make recommendations to the state party concerned and to the Assembly of the African Union (AU) but its recommendations are not legally binding.

The AfCHPR has jurisdiction over all cases and disputes submitted to it concerning the interpretation and application of the African Charter and was established in 1998 by a Protocol to the Charter in order to complement and reinforce the functions of the Commission.[50] States parties to the Protocol and African intergovernmental organizations may submit cases to the Court. Individuals from state parties which have made a declaration accepting the jurisdiction of the Court on individual petitions as well as non-governmental organizations with observer status before the Commission can also bring cases before the Court[51] which takes binding decisions, including orders of compensation or reparation. The Court delivered its first judgment in 2009.

47 This system is similar to that which applied under the ECHR until its reformation in 1999. Indeed, from 1953 to 1998, the European Convention (ECHR) provided for a system of individual applications according to which a state member had the option to accept the right of individuals to submit applications for violations of their rights under the Convention (former Art. 25). There was a further option to accept the Court's jurisdiction to hear cases reported upon by the Commission (former Art. 46). As from 1998 the options became mandatory rules for all member states. Furthermore, until 1999, an important component of the Convention system was the "European Commission on Human Rights." The Commission examined whether an application was admissible and if so, it identified the relevant facts with a view to achieve a friendly settlement between the parties. If no such settlement was reached, the Commission issued a report concerning whether there had been a violation of the ECHR and referred the matter to the Court accordingly. Today, individual applications are directly addressed to the Court.

48 The official languages of OAS organs are English, Spanish, Portuguese, and French.

49 The African Court of Justice and Human Rights was formed in 2004. The Court was established by virtue of Art. 1 of the Protocol to the Charter on Human and Peoples' Rights on the Establishment of an African Court on Human and Peoples' Rights. The Court has its seat in Arusha, Tanzania.

50 The Protocol was adopted in *Ouagadougou,* Burkina Faso, and came into force on 25 January 2004, following its ratification by 15 states.

51 Art. 34(6) of the Charter.

6.3.4 *Mechanisms Established by U.N. Human Rights Treaties*

Such Mechanisms for the control of the application and implementation of the human rights protection systems they establish have also been adopted by most of the U.N. Human Rights Conventions. Thus:

- The 1966 International Covenant on Civil and Political Rights (ICCPR) has set up the Human Rights Committee, which is a body of independent experts (this is also the case with all the committees set up in the context of other international U.N. human rights instruments), which monitors the implementation of the Covenant by its states parties. This is done by establishing a reporting system according to which such states initially submit a report within one year after the Covenant enters into force for them, and thereafter whenever the Committee so requests (as a rule every four years). The Committee examines each report, expresses any concerns it may have and formulates relevant recommendations to the state party concerned in the form of 'concluding observations'. The Covenant provides that the Committee may also examine interstate complaints,[52] while complaints by individuals for alleged violations of the Covenant may be submitted only with regard to states which are parties to the Optional Protocol to the ICCPR.[53]
- The Committee on Economic, Social and Cultural Rights monitors the implementation of the 1966 Covenant on Economic, Social and Cultural Rights (ICESCR), making general comments on the performance of the states which are party to it. There is also an Optional Protocol adopted in 2008,[54] by virtue of which the Committee is recognized to have competence to receive and consider communications by or on behalf of individuals or groups of individuals under the jurisdiction of a state party who claim to have suffered a violation by that state of any of the rights provided for in the Covenant.[55] The Committee may also receive interstate communications on the basis of the Optional Protocol.[56]
- The Committee on the Elimination of Racial Discrimination monitors the implementation of the related Convention (CERD) and reviews the performance of states parties to it by receiving reports from them, initially within a year after the entry into force of the Convention in their regard, and subsequently biannually. The Committee may also examine interstate complaints and issue relevant recommendations. A state party may, by making a declaration to this effect, recognize the Commission's competence to consider communications from individuals claiming to be victims of viola-

52 Of 16 December 1966. Entry into force on 23 March 1976. There is also a second Protocol to the Covenant (of 15 December 1989-Entry into force: 11 July 1991) which aims at the abolition of the death penalty.

53 Of 16 December 1966. Entry into force on 23 March 1976. There is also a second Protocol to the Covenant (of 15 December 1989-Entry into force: 11 July 1991) which aims at the abolition of the death penalty.

54 18 June 2008. Entry into force 5 May 2013.

55 Arts. 1-9 of the Optional Protocol.

56 *Ibid.*, Art. 10.

tion of their rights provided for in the Convention, and issue relevant recommendations. Here again, as in the case of the other U.N. Human Rights Conventions, these recommendations are not legally binding on the states to which they are addressed.

- The Committee on the Elimination of Discrimination against Women (CEDAW) monitors the implementation of the synonymous Convention, by way of commenting on reports received from states parties within one year after the entry into force of the Convention for them and every four years thereafter. It furthermore makes general recommendations while it may also consider complaints brought against states which have adhered to the 1999 Optional Protocol to CEDAW.[57]
- The Committee against Torture monitors the implementation of the related Convention by receiving reports from states parties every four years (following their first report submitted within a year after the entry into force of the Convention for them), as well as by issuing general recommendations and making inquiries. A state party may declare that it recognizes the competence of the Committee to consider communications from a state party claiming that another party is not fulfilling its obligations (interstate communication), provided that the latter has also made such a declaration. A significant development towards ensuring the protection of detainees against torture and other cruel, inhuman or degrading treatment has been the adoption of the 2002 Optional Protocol[58] to the Convention against Torture. The Protocol sets up a Subcommittee on Prevention of Torture with a mandate to visit places of detention in states parties. It also requires the latter to establish national preventive mechanisms with access to prisoners and other detainees as well as to prisons and places of detention. The monitoring system thus established by the Protocol echoes the very effective one set up by the 1987 European Convention for the Repression of Torture and Inhuman or Degrading Treatment or Punishment (CPT).[59] Indeed, the Committee established by the European Convention makes its findings 'on the ground', visiting prisons and police stations and other places where persons are detained, finding out first hand if the requirements of the Convention are being fulfilled and making practical recommendations to the state concerned.[60]
- The Committee on the Rights of the Child monitors the implementation of the related U.N. Convention (CRC) on the basis of reports submitted by states parties initially within the first two years after the entry into force of the Convention for them and subsequently every five years. The Committee may make suggestions and general recommendations concerning the information received.[61] It also receives reports

57 Of 6 December 1999. Entry into force on 22 December 2000.

58 Of 18 December 2002. Entry into force on 22 June 2006.

59 Of 26 November 1987. Entry into force on 1 February 1989.

60 Rod Morgan, The CPT Model: An examination, in Linos-Alexander Sicilianos (ed), *The Prevention of Human Rights Violations, International Studies in Human Rights, Marangopoulos Foundation for Human Rights*, Martinus Nijhoff Publishers, Ant. N. Sakkoulas Publishers, 2001, pp. 3-37.

61 Art. 45.

from member states to the two Optional Protocols to the Convention, adopted on 25 May 2000, i.e. a) on the involvement of children in armed conflict[62] and b) on the sale of children, child prostitution and child pornography,[63] thereby generally monitoring the implementation of these instruments. Although the Committee did not have the power to examine individual complaints by virtue of the Convention and its two optional protocols, a third Optional Protocol 'on a communications procedure', adopted in 2011,[64] now provides for the possibility of communications being submitted 'by or on behalf of an individual or group of individuals' under the jurisdiction of a state party, who claim that any of the rights set forth in the Convention and its first two optional protocols have been violated by that state.

- The Committee on Migrant Workers monitors the implementation of the 1990 Convention on the Rights of All Migrant Workers and Members of their Families. The Committee receives reports from states parties concerning measures they have taken to implement the Convention within one year after the entry into force of the Convention for them and subsequently every five years.
- The Committee on the Rights of Persons with Disabilities monitors the implementation of the related Convention by receiving 'comprehensive reports' on measures taken by states parties to implement their obligations under the Convention and on relevant progress they have made in this respect. Each state party submits its first report within two years after the entry into force of the Convention for it. Subsequent reports are submitted at least every four years and whenever the Committee so requests. On the basis of an Optional Protocol to the Convention,[65] the Committee is empowered to receive and consider communications from or on behalf of individuals or groups of individuals who are subject to the jurisdiction of a state party thereto, and who claim that the state in question has violated their rights under the Convention.

It may be concluded from the above brief review that the systems originally established by the U.N. conventional instruments in order to control their implementation were usually limited to setting up a reporting system, at the epicentre of which was an independent committee which examined the reports and formulated recommendations. Gradually, however, this system has been fortified with the possibility of states parties to address complaints *inter se* (interstate complaints) for non-compliance with a party's obligations under the treaty. Further on the possibility was added for individuals or groups of individuals under the jurisdiction of a state party to address complaints against that state for violation of their rights as set forth in that instrument. This is done, however, almost

62 Entry into force on 12 February 2002.

63 Entry into force on 18 January 2002.

64 On 19 December 2011. Entry into force on 14 April 2014.

65 Of 13 December 2006. Entry into force on 3 May 2008.

exclusively on an optional basis, i.e. through the adherence of states wishing to do so to an optional protocol to the treaty in question. Furthermore, the findings of the monitoring body (Committee) on such complaints do not have a legally binding character on the state party concerned, although the moral gravity of such findings cannot be ignored.

6.4 Extraterritorial Application of Human Rights Law

The most important international human rights conventions do not, in reality, address the issue of the extraterritorial application of human rights law. Indeed, they usually limit themselves to refer in a general manner to their application on persons on the territory of a state party to them and/or under that state's jurisdiction. The ICCPR and the ECHR are relevant examples.[66] However, the interpretation of the rules and the jurisprudence of international courts and tribunals on the matter have gradually clarified and extended the jurisdiction of human right instruments and, as a consequence, of the domestic legislation of states parties. An important role in this respect has been played by the Human Rights Committee of the 1966 Covenant of Civil and Political Rights.

Indeed, the Committee has confirmed, in its General Comment 31, that states parties to the Covenant must ensure the rights provided for in that instrument to all persons, including non-citizens, not only on their own territory but also on territory which, although not under their sovereignty, is within their power or effective control.

The ICJ has also found in its Wall Advisory Opinion[67] that the ICCPR is applicable to acts done by a state in the exercise of its jurisdiction outside its own territory.[68] It is also very important that in the same opinion, the ICJ confirmed the same finding in respect of the Convention on the Rights of the Child.[69]

As far as the ECHR is concerned, although its Article 1 provides that "[t]he High Contracting Parties shall secure to everyone within their jurisdiction the rights and freedoms defined in Section I of this Convention," indicating the will of the drafters to attribute extraterritorial applicability to it, the exact contours of such extraterritoriality have been left undefined.

66 Art. 2(1) of the ICCPR; Art.1 of the ECHR.

67 Legal Consequences of the Construction of a Wall in the Occupied Palestinian Territory, Advisory Opinion of 9 July 2004, I.C.J. Reports 2004, para. 111. *See* paras. 108-110.

68 Paras. 109 *et seq. See also* Case concerning *Armed Activities on the Territory of the Congo (Democratic Republic of the Congo v. Uganda),* Judgment of 19 December 2005, I.C.J. Reports 2005, paras. 216-217. For regional cases, *see* Inter-American Commission on Human Rights, *Coard et al. v. United States*, Case 10.951, Report NI 109/99, 29 September 1999, para. 37. For the deviating U.S. position on this matter, *see infra*, p. 56.

69 *Ibid.*, paras. 107-113.

The ECtHR nonetheless recognized, in the *Loizidou Case*[70] that the Convention did have extraterritorial applicability. In that case, the Court found, indeed, that as the Turkish army had effective control over the northern part of Cyprus, Turkey had jurisdiction over that territory in accordance with Article 1, and was therefore responsible for not allowing the applicant *Loizidou* to have access to her property there. In its *Banković* admissibility judgment of 2001,[71] the Court held, however, that NATO states which had conducted air raids on the radio and television station Radio *Televizije Srbije (RTS)* in Belgrade, in 1999,[72] had not violated the right to life of those killed due to the attack.[73] The ECtHR, theorized that

> the Convention is a multi-lateral treaty operating [...] in an essentially regional context and notably in the legal space (espace juridique) of the Contracting States [...] The Convention was not designed to be applied throughout the world, even in respect of the conduct of Contracting States.[74]

The Court went on to accommodate its findings in *Loizidou*, stating that extraterritorial jurisdiction had been recognized "only when the territory in question was one that, but for the specific circumstances, would normally be covered by the Convention."[75] The subsequent relevant judgments of the Court on the cases of *Al-Skeini*[76] and *Al-Jeddah*[77] did not support the finding in *Banković*, holding that the Convention may have extra-

70 *Loizidou v. Turkey*, Preliminary Objections (Application No. 15 318/89) Judgment, 23 March 1995, para. 62; *Loizidou v. Turkey*, (Merits) Judgment, 18 December 1996, para. 52.

71 *Banković, Stojanović, Stoimedovski, Joksimović and Suković v. Belgium, the Czech Republic, Denmark, France, Germany, Greece, Hungary, Iceland, Italy, Luxembourg, the Netherlands, Norway, Poland, Portugal, Spain, Turkey and the United Kingdom*, Application No. 52207/99, Grand Chamber decision (admissibility) of 12 December 2001.

72 The air raids were conducted as part of NATO operations in response to the situation in Kosovo.

73 *Bankovic, supra*, para. 82.

74 *Ibid.*, para. 80.

75 *Ibid.*

76 *Al-Skeini and others v. the United Kingdom*, application No. 55721/07, Grand Chamber judgment, 7 July 2011, paras. 106-186. The case concerned an appeal on a U.K. decision not to investigate the circumstances of the death of six Iraqi civilians killed in 2003 in the Iraqi city of *Basrah*, occupied by U.K. forces at the time. The appeal was based on the ground that the U.K. Human Rights Act 1998 had extraterritorial application where the U.K. was an occupying power.

77 *Al-Jedda v. the United Kingdom*, application No. 27021/08, Grand Chamber judgment of 7 July 2011. In that case, the U.K. argued that, since the British troops operating in Iraq formed part of a multinational force under the U.N., the U.K. could not be held accountable for the detention of the applicant. However, the Court found that the applicant was under the jurisdiction of the U.K. because he was detained in a detention facility operated by British troops. The Court also found that there had been a violation of Art. 5(1) of the Convention (para. 85) as the U.K. and the U.S. assumed and exercised in Iraq some of the public powers normally exercised by a sovereign government. The U.K. had authority and was responsible for the maintenance of security in Southeastern Iraq. The Court considered that the U.K., through its soldiers, engaged in security operations in *Basrah* during the period in question, exercised authority and control over individuals killed in the course of such security operations, and that a jurisdictional link had been established between the deceased and the U.K.

territorial application over persons under the jurisdiction of a state party thereto, although that state might not have jurisdiction over the territory itself. It accepted therefore that – as it is generally considered today – the extraterritorial application of IHRL presents a territorial and a personal aspect. From the territorial aspect, all persons found within the territory of a state are presumed to be within its territorial jurisdiction.[78] From the personal aspect, a state has personal jurisdiction where it exercises physical power, authority or control over individuals, irrespective of where they are found.[79] In *Al-Skeini*, by adopting the 'personal model' of jurisdiction, the Court concluded that the United Kingdom exercised authority and control over the individuals killed in the course of security operations conducted by its military personnel in *Basrah* in southeastern Iraq at the time, thus establishing a jurisdictional link between the victims and the U.K. for the purposes of Article 1 of the Convention. The Court upheld, however, the *Banković* principle, i.e. that the ECHR is applicable extraterritorially only on an exceptional basis and not in every case where a state exercises control over persons. Nonetheless, in the *Al-Jedda Case*, which was also related to U.K. operations in southern Iraq, the Court ruled that *Al-Jedda* was within the U.K.'s jurisdiction and that the U.K. rather than the U.N. exercised effective control over the military operations in that region. Generally, in both these cases, the Court tried to reconcile the diverging positions it had taken at different times or which it had developed elsewhere (personal model of jurisdiction, ultimate control and authority,[80] 'legal space'[81]). In so doing, it justified, in essence, the conclusion of *Martin Scheinin* that:

78 Unless it is proved that the state was not able to exercise such control.

79 *Al-Skeini, supra; Ilaşcu v. Moldova and Russia*, Application No. 48787/99, judgment of 8 July 2004, para. 392; *Al-Jedda v. the United Kingdom, supra; Al-Saadoon and Mufdhi v. United Kingdom* (Admissibility) (2009) 49 EHRR 1040; *Medvedyev v. France* [2010] ECHR 384, para. 67. In this case, (App. No. 3394/03, para. 67, the Court found that the applicants were within French jurisdiction by virtue of the exercise by French agents of *de facto* 'full and exclusive control' over a ship and its crew from the time of its interception in international waters 'in a continuous and uninterrupted manner'); *Issa v. Turkey,* 2005, 41 EHRR 567; *Ocalan v. Turkey* (2005) 41 EHRR 45. In *Al Skeini* (2011) 53 EHRR 18, it was held that: 'The Court does not consider that jurisdiction in the above cases arose solely from the control exercised by the Contracting State over the buildings, aircraft or ship in which the individuals were held. What is decisive in such cases is the exercise of physical power and control over the person in question'. It is clear that, whenever the state through its agents exercises control and authority over an individual, the state is under an obligation under Art. 1 to secure to that individual the rights and freedoms under Section 1 of the Convention that are relevant to the situation of that individual. In this sense, therefore, the Convention rights can be 'divided and tailored' (paras.136-7). *See also* Human Rights Commission: *Burgos v. Uruguay, supra,* and Inter-American Commission on Human Rights: *Armando Alejandre Jr. et al. v. Republic of Cuba, infra*, p. 78, fn. 334.

80 As in *Behrami and Behrami v. France* (Application No. 71412/01), and *Saramati v. France, Germany and Norway* (No. 78166/01), ECHR, Judgment, 2 May 2007.

81 *Bankovic, supra*, para. 80.

> Authority and control over individuals as a basis for state jurisdiction simply boils down to the proposition that a state has obligations under human rights treaties towards all individuals whose human rights it is able to violate.[82]

6.5 Humanitarian Intervention and Responsibility to Protect[83]

In the light of the importance recognized to human rights today – despite disagreements and differentiations – it would be no overstatement that respect to these rights constitutes the basic fabric that binds modern societies together. As much as it is important, however, to build a system based on the rule of law with human rights at its epicentre on a domestic level, it has always been considered very important to also have one operating on a global level, i.e. establish a system capable of preventing mass violations of human rights by authoritarian regimes or large-scale atrocities committed in cases of interethnic strife, civil wars or other similar situations. Indeed, the international community, as represented by the U.N., has repeatedly been accused of failing to avert or intervene in catastrophic situations of this kind. Such situations had emerged or are still continuing in, for example, the Darfur region in Sudan, DR Congo, Syria, Libya, Myanmar (Rohingya crisis), in Yemen and elswhere, while new ones may spring up at any time. These failures are mainly due to the political difficulties or indeed the impossibility to achieve consensus within the S.C. so as to take urgent and meaningful action concerning situations of such gravity. To overcome these difficulties, two ideas have been proposed at different times: 'humanitarian intervention' and more recently, 'responsibility to protect' (RtoP or R2P).[84] The basic idea of both is to allow the unilateral intervention of one or more states in the state or region where the humanitarian catastrophe is taking place. Calling for the prevention of and the protection of people from genocide, war crimes, ethnic cleansing and crimes against humanity, 'Responsibility to Protect' was endorsed by all U.N. member states at the 2005 World Summit[85] and further analysed by successive Reports of the Secretary General.[86] As there were strong hesitations, however, for adopting the principle without guarantees that its invocation would be sincere and would not conceal an intervening country's other interests, the adopted version of R2P provides that

82 Martin Scheinin, 'Extraterritorial Effect of the International Covenant on Civil and Political Rights', in F. Coomans & M. Kamminga (eds), *Extraterritorial Application of Human Rights Treaties* (Intersentia 2004), p. 76.

83 It is noted that the questions dealt with under this subheader could have been examined under both 'Notes on Human Rights' and 'Notes on International Humanitarian Law' as in the writer's view, they straddle both.

84 Errol P. Mendes, *Global Governance, Human Rights and International Law*, Routledge, 2014.

85 A/RES/60/1 of 24 October 2005, paras. 138-139.

86 *E.g.*, A/63/677 of 12 January 2009, A/66/874–S/2012/578 of 25 July 2012, A/72/884 -S/2018/525 of 1 June 2018.

collective action will be taken through the Security Council.[87] This certainly safe and reasonable way to proceed would seem, however, to bring any attempt of solution back to square one, since it is exactly the inaction of the S.C. that usually prevents 'collective' intervention in the case of mass violations of human rights or commission of atrocities in the first place. Although this would appear to lead to a quasi-intractable situation, it remains nonetheless true that, in the last analysis, it is indeed the S.C. that should take up such 'responsibility to protect' in the broader context of 'collective security' that the U.N. Charter purports to embrace and promote. As indeed aptly set out by the 2005 World Summit Outcome,

> [I]n this context, we are prepared to take collective action, in a timely and decisive manner, through the Security Council, in accordance with the Charter, including Chapter VII, on a case-by-case basis and in cooperation with relevant regional organizations as appropriate, should peaceful means be inadequate and national authorities are manifestly failing to protect their populations from genocide, war crimes, ethnic cleansing and crimes against humanity ...[88]

87 A/RES/60/1, *supra,* fn. 74, para. 139.

88 *Ibid.*

7 Notes on International Humanitarian Law

7.1 Scope and Sources of IHL[1]

International humanitarian law (IHL) – examined in connection with war crimes in Part I[2] – provides for the protection of persons in armed conflict and in situations of enemy occupation, while it also regulates the conduct of hostilities. The main pillars of IHL are the 1949 four Geneva Conventions[3] and their two 1977 Additional Protocols.[4] The Geneva Conventions constitute customary international law, and this is also the view of the overwhelming majority of states as regards Protocol I. Customary international law on armed conflicts also includes the 1907 Hague Regulations regarding the conduct of hostilities.[5]

According to Article 2 common to the Geneva Conventions, an international armed conflict may (only) take place between two or more states.[6] Its existence must rely on objective criteria based on the realities on the ground and not on the wishes of the states involved which may or may not declare a 'state of war' depending on their own political

---

1 For IHL generally, *see* Dieter Fleck, *The Handbook of International Humanitarian Law*, 2017; Emily Crawford, Alison Pert, *International Humanitarian Law*, Cambridge University Press, 2015; Jonathan Crowe, Kylie Weston-Scheuber, *Principles of International Humanitarian Law*, Edward Elgar, 2013; Yoram Dinstein, *Non-International Armed Conflicts in International Law*, Cambridge University Press, 2014; Orna Ben-Naftali (ed), *International Humanitarian Law and Human Rights Law*, Pas de Deux, Oxford University Press, 2011; ICRC, International Humanitarian Law

2 *Supra*, pp. 58-80.

3 Convention I for the Amelioration of the Condition of the Wounded and Sick in Armed Forces in the Field; Convention II for the Amelioration of the Condition of the Wounded, Sick and Shipwrecked of Armed Forces at Sea; Convention III relative to the Treatment of Prisoners of War; Convention IV relative to the Protection of Civilian Persons in Time of War.

4 Protocol I relating to the Protection of Victims of International Armed Conflicts; Protocol II relating to the Protection of Victims of Non-international Armed Conflicts. Both were adopted on 8 June 1977. Protocol III relating to the Adoption of an Additional Distinctive Emblem (enshrining the Red Crystal Emblem) was adopted on 8 December 2005.

5 Regulations Respecting the Laws and Customs of War on Land, annexed to The Hague Convention IV, Respecting the Laws and Customs of War on Land of 18 October 1907.

6 Common Art. 2 provides that:

1. "In addition to the provisions which shall be implemented in peace time, the present Convention shall apply to all cases of declared war or of any other armed conflict which may arise between two or more of the High Contracting Parties, even if the state of war is not recognized by one of them.
2. The Convention shall also apply to all cases of total or partial occupation of the territory of a High Contracting Party, even if the said occupation meets with no armed resistance."

or other considerations,[7] a fact which is confirmed by the Commentary to the Conventions when dealing with the meaning of 'armed conflict'.[8] If, on the basis of such objective criteria, there is indeed an international armed conflict, the applicable law is IHL.

The only provision of the Geneva Conventions which, as noted in Part I, applies in non-international conflicts is Article 3. Additional Protocol II also applies in the case of such conflicts. The fundamental principles enshrined by these instruments are those of military necessity,[9] distinction,[10] proportionality[11] and humanity.[12, 13]

7.2 Simultaneous Applicability of Human Rights Law (IHRL) and International Humanitarian Law (IHL) in Armed Conflict[14]

The applicability of both these branches of law in situations of armed conflict or occupation, a possibility not accepted until recent years, is now recognized by international jurisprudence as developed by the ICJ, the *ad hoc* tribunals and regional courts. As expected, the Human Rights Committee also vigorously supports this development.[15]

---

7 One reason for a state declaring or admitting that it is in a state of war and that, consequently, is having IHL as applicable law, could be, *inter alia,* that this would secure the immunity of its armed forces.

8 "[A]ny difference arising between two States and leading to the intervention of armed forces is an armed conflict within the meaning of Article 2, even if one of the Parties denies the existence of a state of war. It makes no difference how long the conflict lasts, or how much slaughter takes place. The respect due to human personality is not measured by the number of victims..." (Jean S. Pictet, Commentary on the Geneva Convention for the Amelioration of the Wounded and Sick in Armed Forces in the Field, p. 32, 1952).

9 There are different interpretations as to what constitutes 'military necessity'. In its 'broad' interpretation, it is taken to mean that armed forces can do whatever is necessary – if not unlawful under other IHL rules – to achieve their military objectives. In a more restrictive sense, military necessity is evaluated not according to the estimates of the armed forces concerned but according to objective military criteria.

10 The principle of distinction means that civilians may not be made the object of attack unless, and only for as long as, they take a direct part in hostilities. Where there is doubt as to whether a person is a civilian or is taking a direct part in hostilities, civilian status must be presumed (Additional Protocol I, Art. 50(1)).

11 The principle of proportionality means that an objective assessment must be made each time whether the attack would cause incidental loss of civilian life or injury to civilians which would be excessive in relation to the anticipated concrete and direct military advantage (AP I, Arts. 51(5)(b) and 57): *See* Henckaerts & Oswald-Beck, Customary International Humanitarian Law Rules, ICRC (2005) (ICRC Rules) Rule 14.

12 The principle aims at minimizing human suffering (without, however, compromising military necessity). The 1868 St. Petersburg Declaration formulates this as setting the 'technical limits at which the necessities of war ought to yield to the requirements of humanity' (St. Petersburg Declaration, Renouncing the Use, in Time of War, of Explosive Projectiles under 400 Grammes Weight, 1868, Laws of Armed Conflict, 102).

13 On the basic principles of IHL, *see also* Part I, p. 58.

14 On this topic, *see* Theodor Meron, The Humanization of Humanitarian Law, 94 *AJIL* 243, 2000; Marko Milanovic, Norm Conflicts, International Humanitarian Law and Human Rights law, http://ssrn.com/abstract=1531596, 2010; Rule of Law in Armed Conflict Project (Rulac), Interaction between humanitarian law and human rights in armed conflict, Adh Génève, 17 October 2014; Fiona E. Nairn, The relationship between International Humanitarian Law and Human Rights Law: Parallel Application or Norm Conflict? http://ssrn.com/abstract=2021839, 2012; William Schabas, Lex Specialis? Belt and Suspenders? The parallel Operation of Human Rights law and the Law of Armed Conflict, and the Conundrum of *jus ad bellum*, 2007.

15 *See* General Comment 4 and observations on various state reports.

The ICJ has confirmed the simultaneous applicability of IHRL and IHL in several judgments and advisory opinions. Thus, in its 1996 Advisory Opinion 'on the Legality of the Threat or Use of Nuclear Weapons', it found that:

> the right not arbitrarily to be deprived of one's life applies also in hostilities. The test of what is an arbitrary deprivation of life, however, then falls to be determined by the applicable lex specialis, namely the law applicable in armed conflict ...[16]

In the same case, the Court also asserted that:

> the protection of the International Covenant on Civil and Political Rights does not cease in times of war, except by operation of Article 4 of the Covenant whereby certain provisions may be derogated from in a time of national emergency.

The ICJ drew the same conclusion in its Advisory Opinion on the *Legal Consequences of the Construction of a Wall in the Occupied Palestinian Territory (Wall Opinion)*,[17] where it affirmed the applicability of IHRL also in situations of military occupation. It stated that:

> More generally, the Court considers that the protection offered by human rights conventions does not cease in case of armed conflict, save through the effect of provisions for derogation of the kind to be found in art. 4 of the International Covenant on Civil and Political Rights. As regards the relationship between international humanitarian law and human rights law, there are thus three possible situations: some rights may be exclusively matters of international humanitarian law; others may be exclusively matters of human rights law; yet others may be matters of both these branches of international law.[18]

Another affirmation is contained in the Court's judgment on the 2005 Case of the *Democratic Republic of the Congo v. Uganda*, where, after recalling previous findings on the matter, the ICJ held that:

---

16 ICJ, *Legality of the threat or use of nuclear weapons*, Advisory Opinion, 8 July 1996, para. 25.
17 ICJ, *Legal Consequences of the Construction of a wall in the occupied Palestinian territory*, Advisory Opinion, para. 106.
18 *Ibid.*

> The Court further concluded that international human rights instruments are applicable in respect of acts done by a State in the exercise of its jurisdiction outside of its own territory, particularly in occupied territories.[19, 20]

The ECtR, on its part, has found that the European Convention on Human Rights is also applicable on territories under military occupation. It did so in the abovementioned *Loizidou Case* which concerned the Turkish occupation of Northern Cyprus,[21] as well in those of *Al-Skeini* and *Al-Jedda*, also mentioned above, which related to the exercise of jurisdiction by the U.K. in southeastern Iraq during the war in that country.[22] The Court has applied the Convention even in the case of brief occupations, as in *Ilaşcu v. Moldova* and *Russia*.[23] A similar approach with regard to internal conflicts has been taken by the Inter-American Court on Human Rights in the Case of *Bámaca Velasquez v. Guatemala*,[24] relating to the civil war in Guatemala (1960-1996).

But in what ways can these two branches of law apply together? First, it is generally accepted that it is both possible and desirable that the branch of law which is more developed on a particular issue should inform the other which is less so. Thus, for instance, as regards the notion of 'torture', it is clear that IHRL can inform IHL, as the former has far more developed rules on this issue than the latter. This has been accepted by international jurisprudence, particularly by ICTY in the *Delalic* and *Furundzija* Cases.[25] In the *Wall Opinion*, the ICJ stated in a general manner that IHL was *lex specialis* to IHRL on matters of occupation, having found that:

---

19 ICJ, *Case concerning armed activities on the territory of the Congo (Democratic Republic of the Congo v. Uganda)*, 9 January 2006, paras. 216-220, 345(3), para. 216.

20 General Comment No 31 of the Human Rights Committee also states, in connection with the application of the ICCPR in armed conflict, that: "The ICCPR applies also in situations of armed conflict to which the rules of IHL are applicable. While, in respect of certain Covenant rights, more specific rules of IHL may be specially relevant for the purposes of the interpretation of Covenant rights, both spheres of law are complementary, not mutually exclusive" (para. 11).

21 *Loizidou (Preliminary Objections)* Application No. 15318/89, (1995) 20 EHRR 99; *Loizidou v. Turkey*, Judgment (Merits), Grand Chamber judgment, 18 December 1996, para. 62.

22 *Al-Skeini v. U.K. (supra*, fn. 66*)* and *Al-Jedda v. U.K. (supra*, fn. 67*)*.

23 *Ilaşcu and Others v. Moldova and Russia*, Application No. 48787/99, Judgment, 8 July 2004.

24 *Bámaca Velasquez v. Guatemala*, Judgment, 25 November 2000, para. 207, where it is stated that: "[T]he Court considers that it has been proved that, at the time of the facts of this case, an internal conflict was taking place in Guatemala (*supra* 121 b). As has previously been stated (*supra* 143 and 174), instead of exonerating the State from its obligations to respect and guarantee human rights, this fact obliged it to act in accordance with such obligations. Therefore, and as established in Article 3 common to the Geneva Conventions of August 12, 1949, confronted with an internal armed conflict, the State should grant those persons who are not participating directly in the hostilities or who have been placed hors de combat for whatever reason, humane treatment, without any unfavorable distinctions. In particular, international humanitarian law prohibits attempts against the life and personal integrity of those mentioned above, at any place and time." (Corte Interamericana de Derechos Humanos, Caso Bámaca vs. Guatemala, Sentencia de 22 de febrero de 2002, Reparaciones y Costas).

25 *Delalic*, Trial Chamber, IT-96-21-T, 16 November 1998, paras. 440-459; *Furundzija*, Trial Chamber, IT-95-17/1, 10 December 1998, para. 159.

> ... In order to answer the question put to it, the Court will have to take into consideration both these branches of international law, namely human rights law and, as lex specialis, international humanitarian law.[26]

7.3 POSSIBILITY OF CONFLICT BETWEEN IHL AND IHRL

Although the simultaneous applicability of IHL and IHRL norms is generally accepted, there has been a lengthy discussion among scholars and commentators on the method to use in order to resolve an eventual conflict between these norms where they would both be applicable. Evidently, one such method is identifying which is the applicable *lex specialis* in each particular case, as did the ICJ in its abovementioned finding in connection with a state of occupation. However, it has been seen that in many cases this method is too vague and inconclusive. Indeed, although *lex specialis* is known and used in domestic legal systems where there is a clear hierarchy of norms, it cannot be easily transposed into the international sphere. This is mostly due to the fragmented and decentralized nature of international law[27] which has been rather haphazardly developed mainly by treaties, each one negotiated and adopted in its own legal environment[28] and which, among other differentiations, may be bilateral, regional or global, therefore not allowing the *lex specialis* method to be always meaningfully applicable. Nor is jurisprudence always helpful in this respect, since the extent of coverage by either *lex generalis* or *lex specialis* in each particular case often remains unclear.

To overcome the difficulties inherent in the application of *lex specialis*[29] as a method for the resolution of conflicts arising out of the parallel application of IHL and IHRL, several alternatives have been proposed, none of which, however, seems to provide a convincing solution to the problem. Among these proposals is the application of the norms which are most favourable to the individual(s) concerned.[30] Although attractive from a humanistic point of view, this proposal remains, however, too subjective to apply in a consistent manner. The ICJ, it is to be noted, has not upheld such a solution.[31] Other proposals which support various ideas such as the 'complementary and harmonious', the 'interpretive' or even the 'creative' interpretation theories suffer, similarly, from a considerable degree of subjectivity. A factual approach on a case-by-case basis would seem,

---

26 *Wall Opinion, supra,* para. 106.

27 See Marti Koskenniemi, Fragmentation of International Law: Difficulties arising from the Diversification and expansion of International Law, *Report of the Study Group of the International Law Commission*, 2006, pp. 56-122.

28 Fiona E. Nairn, *loc. cit.,* p. 9.

29 Which seem to have been recognized by the ICJ which has refrained from referring expressly to it in the case of *DRC v. Uganda, supra,* fn. 95.

30 William Schabas, Lex Specialis? Belt and Suspenders? The parallel Operation of Human Rights law and the Law of Armed Conflict, and the Conundrum of *jus ad bellum (supra)*, fn. 90.

31 *DRC v. Uganda, supra,* paras. 218-221.

therefore, best suited to overcome the problem; nonetheless, this, in its turn, would defy predictability.

In any event, even if they could be applied, these proposals would still leave certain situations insoluble. Classically, such a situation would arise in cases of occupation where the occupier would be bound to apply by virtue of The Hague Regulations[32] and the Fourth Geneva Convention,[33] the legal regime in force in the occupied state. At the same time, the occupying power would have to apply, on the same territory now under its jurisdiction, the relevant IHRL rules which, however, could be in direct clash with the legal regime in question (example: obligation to apply the *shariah* rules applicable in the country, which would impose severe corporal punishment in the case of certain crimes, a penalty which would be prohibited under IHRL). Under such, still rather rare circumstances, a political decision seems to be the only solution capable of resolving the Gordian knot, until a permanent and secure solution can be established under international law.

32 Art. 43.
33 Art. 64.

8 Notes on International Terrorism

8.1 Past and Present of the Phenomenon[1]

Terrorism in its contemporary forms has been at the epicentre of intense international political and legal discourse for the last fifty years at least, from the 1960s and 1970s, when the PLO and other Palestinian organizations mounted various attacks, to this day which has been marked by the atrocities of ISIS committed mainly in the territories of Iraq and Syria when occupied by that organization. However, terrorism has been known and practised throughout human history, in different ideological, societal and geographical contexts, under different names, in infinite variations and with various goals.[2] Its first manifestations in archaic societies appear to have been linked with the suppression and terror exercised by despots for the purpose of perpetuating their rule. In more recent times, during the French Revolution, state terrorism (*la terreur*) had been exercised by the revolutionary government in 1793-1794. Terrorism also prevailed in the Soviet Union during the Stalinist period; Arab states, on the other hand, have characterized Israeli policies against the Palestinians as state terrorism. A variation of state terrorism is 'state-sponsored' terrorism, which was attributed particularly by the U.S. to states which instigated or assisted insurgencies in other countries. Iran, Iraq and Syria have been among the states accused of terrorism of this type at various times.

State-targeted terrorism goes in the opposite direction, being usually identified with the struggle of ethnic groups or minorities against the state they live in and which state uses or is perceived to use oppressive policies or practices against these groups or minorities. State-targeted terrorism may also be exercised by individuals or groups on ideological grounds such as nihilism and anarchism.

International and domestic terrorism, on the other hand, is a rather technical distinction with apparently clear legal contours and consequences. These, however, are often blurred by spillover and even wider effects which are usually conveyed by the term 'transnational terrorism'.

1 On the issue of terrorism generally, *see* Ben Saul (ed), *Research Handbook on International Law and Terrorism*, Edward Elgar Publishing, 2016; Martha Crenshaw (ed), *Terrorism in Context*, The Pennsylvania State University Press, 2007; For recent developments of the terrorist phenomenon, *see* Bruce Hoffman, *Inside Terrorism, Columbia Studies in Terrorism and Irregular Warfare*, 3rd edn., 2017.

2 For the History of Terrorism, *see* Gérard Chaliand and Arnaud Blin (eds), *History of Terrorism, From Antiquity to Al Quaeda*, University of California Press, 2007; Walter Laqueur, *A History of Terrorism*, 2017; Randall D. Law, *Terrorism: A History (Themes in History)*, Polity Press, 2016.

At the same time, the difficulty of drawing a clear distinction between different phenomena such as national liberation movements on the one hand and terrorism on the other reflects opposing political aims, an opposition which marked particularly the decolonization era. As regards the differentiation between 'political crime' and 'terrorist act', the former usually exonerating perpetrators of crimes committed in the context of national liberation movements and similar offences from punishment and extradition, it has lost much of its traditional justification today. As a result of this change, agreements concluded in the context of the U.N. have 'depoliticized' terrorist crimes, in the sense that the qualification of political crime cannot be used any more for the purpose of denying the extradition of the perpetrators or letting them go unpunished.[3]

8.2 COMBATTING TERRORISM IN THE U.N. CONTEXT

8.2.1 U.N. Conventions on Terrorism

The U.N. has dealt with terrorism in a number of binding normative instruments relating to particular aspects of the phenomenon. The first ones among these instruments were adopted, as already noted, in the 1960s as a legal response to the hijacking of commercial airplanes by Palestinian extremist groups mainly aiming to achieve the release of Palestinian detainees. They were followed by other instruments (Conventions, Protocols) which dealt with the taking of hostages, maritime terrorism, terrorism at airports, terrorist bombings, terrorist financing and other facets of terrorist practices. In all, nineteen

3 *See, e.g.*, Art. 11 of the 1997 U.N. Convention for the Suppression of Terrorist Bombings, which provides that "None of the offences set forth in article 2 shall be regarded, for the purposes of extradition or mutual legal assistance, as a political offence or as an offence connected with a political offence or as an offence inspired by political motives. Accordingly, a request for extradition or for mutual legal assistance based on such an offence may not be refused on the sole ground that it concerns a political offence or an offence connected with a political offence or an offence inspired by political motives."

such 'sectoral' anti-terrorism instruments,[4] either original or amending previous ones, have been adopted thus far, while an agreement dealing comprehensively with terrorism and intended to complement these instruments remains unaccomplished for many years now, having failed to garner consensus on the question of the definition of terrorism.[5]

All anti-terrorism Conventions require states parties to criminalize the conduct covered and described in each one of them, accept and apply the principle *aut dedere aut judicare* (extradite or prosecute) and provide a legal basis for cooperation on extradition and legal assistance.

8.2.2 *U.N. Resolutions on Terrorism and Related Measures*

A turning point in the way terrorism was viewed has undoubtedly been the series of terrorist attacks in New York, Washington, D.C., and Pennsylvania on 11 September, 2001. These attacks struck a terrible blow on the confidence particularly of western countries regarding their capability to confront the terrorist phenomenon. On the next day of the attack, the S.C. adopted Resolution 1368[6] under Chapter VII of the U.N. Charter, where it was stated that the S.C. "regards such acts, like any act of international terrorism,

4 Chronologically these are: 1) 1963 Convention on Offences and Certain Other Acts Committed On Board Aircraft ('Tokyo Convention'), entry into force 4 December 1969 (*see also* Protocol No. 19 herebelow); 2) 1970 Convention for the Suppression of Unlawful Seizure of Aircraft ('Hague Convention'), entry into force 14 October 1971 (*see also* Protocol No. 18, herebelow); 3) 1971 Convention for the Suppression of Unlawful Acts against the Safety of Civil Aviation ('Montreal Convention'), entry into force 26 January 1973 (*see also* Protocol No. 7 and Convention No. 17 herebelow); 4) 1973 Convention on the Prevention and Punishment of Crimes Against Internationally Protected Persons; 5) 1979 International Convention against the Taking of Hostages; 6) 1980 Convention on the Physical Protection of Nuclear Material (*see also* Amendment No. 13 herebelow); 7) 1988 Protocol for the Suppression of Unlawful Acts of Violence at Airports Serving International Civil Aviation, supplementary to the Convention for the Suppression of Unlawful Acts against the Safety of Civil Aviation, entry into force 6 August 1989; 8) 1988 Convention for the Suppression of Unlawful Acts against the Safety of Maritime Navigation, entry into force 1 March 1992 (*see also* Protocol No. 14 herebelow); 9) 1988 Protocol for the Suppression of unlawful acts against the safety of fixed platforms located on the continental shelf, entry into force 1 March 1992 (*see also* Protocol No. 15 herebelow); 10) 1991 Convention on the Marking of Plastic Explosives for the Purpose of Detection, entry into force 21 June 1998; 11) 1997 International Convention for the Suppression of Terrorist Bombings, entry into force 23 May 2001; 12) 1999 International Convention for the suppression of the financing of terrorism, entry into force 10 April 2002; 13) 2005 Amendment to the Convention on the physical protection of nuclear material, entry into force 8 May 2016; 14) 2005 Protocol to the Convention for the suppression of unlawful acts against the safety of maritime navigation, entry into force 28 July 2010; 15) 2005 Protocol to the Protocol for the suppression of unlawful acts against the safety of fixed platforms located on the continental shelf, entry into force 28 July 2010; 16) 2005 International Convention for the suppression of acts of nuclear terrorism, Atomic Energy Agency (IAEA), entry into force 7 July 2007; 17) 2010 Convention for the suppression of unlawful acts relating to international civil aviation, entry into force 1 July 2018; 18) 2010 Protocol supplementary to the Convention for the suppression of unlawful seizure of aircraft, entry into force 1 January 2018; 19) 2014 Protocol supplementary to the Convention on offences and certain other acts committed on board aircraft, not yet in force.

5 *See infra*, section 8.2.3.

6 S/RES/1368 of 12 September 2001.

as a threat to international peace and security." Furthermore, in response to the urgent need to take strong measures to avert the possibility of such an attack being repeated and to bring the perpetrators to justice, the S.C. adopted, on 28 September 2001, under Chapter VII, Resolution 1373[7] which required, *inter alia*, the criminalization of terrorist acts and terrorism financing, the penalization of acts in support or in preparation of such offences, the freezing of funds belonging to persons committing or attempting to commit terrorist acts, and the strengthening of state cooperation and information-sharing on terrorism issues.

To supervise the implementation by states of the measures it provides for, Resolution 1373 has established a monitoring body, the Counter-Terrorism Committee (CTC), later expanded by S.C. Resolution 1624 of 14 September 2005 to also cover incitement to terrorism.[8] The Committee offers assistance to states to build their counter-terrorism capacity while it also receives regular reports from them concerning their implementation of the measures required. In the performance of its tasks, the CTC is assisted by the Counter-Terrorism Committee Executive Directorate (CTED), which was established by the S.C. in 2004.

The CTC is one of three counter-terrorism bodies established by the S.C. to deal with issues of terrorism. In fact, the Council had been dealing with terrorism issues since the late 1990s in connection with Al-Qaida and the Taliban, and the regime established by the CTC was added to that of the Al-Qaida and Taliban sanctions. The latter was managed by the '1267 Committee'[9] or 'Al-Qaida Sanctions Committee' which monitored the implementation by states of sanctions (freezing of assets, travel ban, arms embargo) against the Taliban, then controlling Afghanistan, for the support they offered to *Al-Qaeda* and its leader *Usama bin Laden*.[10]

The remit of the Al-Qaida Sanctions Committee was later expanded to include sanctions against ISIS.[11]

The third U.N. CTC is called the '1540 Committee' after Resolution 1540 (2004) on the non-proliferation of weapons of mass destruction (WMD) which established it. In the following years, its mandate was reinforced and extended in time until 2021 by a series of subsequent resolutions. Resolution 1540 affirms, as subsequent resolutions also do, that

---

7 S/RES/1373 of 28 September 2001.

8 The Preamble of the Resolution refers to the serious threat which the taking of relevant measures could pose to freedom of expression. By Resolution 2129 of 17 December 2013, the S.C. encouraged the Executive Directorate to further develop its activities in the field of human rights and the rule of law in connection with the implementation of resolutions 1373 (2001) and 1624 (2005).

9 Established in 1999 on the basis of S.C. Resolution 1267 of 15 October 1999.

10 Later also against individuals and entities included in the 'Consolidated Sanctions List' – which includes all individuals and entities subject to sanctions measures imposed by the Security Council – on the basis of their association with *Al Qaeda, Usama Bin Laden* and the *Taliban*.

11 Henceforth the "Al-Qaida Sanctions Committee' has been recast as 'Security Council Committee established pursuant to resolutions 1267 (1999) 1989 (2011) and 2253 (2015) concerning ISIL (Da'Esh) Al-Qaida and Associated Individual Groups and Entities' (www.un.org/sc/suborg/en/sanctions/1267).

the proliferation of nuclear, chemical and biological weapons and their means of delivery constitutes a threat to international peace and security.[12] The resolution requires states to refrain from supporting, by any means, non-state actors to develop, acquire, manufacture, or in any way use nuclear, chemical or biological weapons and their delivery systems. It furthermore obliges states to adopt legislation to prevent the proliferation of such weapons and establish domestic controls over related materials to prevent their illicit trafficking. It also encourages enhanced international cooperation on such efforts. The resolution expresses support for multilateral treaties the aim of which is to eliminate or prevent the proliferation of WMD and emphasizes the importance for all states to fully implement them.[13]

It is, however, easily noticeable that there is a significant degree of overlap between these various bodies and organs,[14] a fact which is not conducive to a streamlined response to the many problems faced by the U.N. as well as by states and individuals in connection with counter-terrorism.[15]

8.2.3 The Question of the Definition of Terrorism

In domestic legislations, definitions of terrorism are quite common and they usually comprise various types of criminal offences sharing certain specific features, mainly a goal to spread terror to the general public. It is these especially dangerous features which attract heavier sanctions for these crimes than for common crimes.

The existence of definitions of terrorism on the domestic level, has not, however, facilitated the adoption of a definition of international terrorism, i.e. terrorism with an international dimension or operating on an international level, although there have been serious efforts to do so.

---

12 Resolutions 1673 (2006), 1810 (2008) and 1977 (2011) reaffirm that the proliferation of nuclear, chemical and biological weapons and their means of delivery constitutes a threat to international peace and security, and extends the mandate of the 1540 Committee for a period of ten years to 2021.

13 The Resolution also affirms that none of the obligations it imposes shall conflict with or alter the rights and obligations of states parties to the Treaty on the Non-Proliferation of Nuclear Weapons, the Chemical Weapons Convention, or the Biological Weapons Convention or alter the responsibilities of the IAEA and OPCW.

14 *I.e.*, the OHCHR, the Counter-Terrorism Executive Directorate, the Counter-Terrorism Implementation Task Force, the Terrorism Prevention Branch of UNODC and the mandate(s) of Special Rapporteurs on the promotion and protection of human rights and fundamental freedoms while countering terrorism.

15 To resolve such issues Resolution 71/291 of 15 June 2017 has created the Office of Counter-Terrorism to assist Member States "in implementing the Global Counter-Terrorism Strategy and enhancing coordination and coherence across the Counter-Terrorism Implementation Task Force (Coordination Compact entities)." The Office is also tasked "to ensure the balanced implementation of the four pillars of the Strategy, strengthening the delivery of United Nations counter-terrorism capacity-building assistance to Member States, improving visibility, advocacy and resource mobilization for United Nations counter-terrorism efforts…"

It is certainly far from easy to come to a common understanding of an extremely diverse, multifaceted and politically fraught phenomenon as international terrorism is, let alone encapsulate it into a single term or a definition.[16] It is therefore no surprise that despite these efforts, the notion remains elusive, meaning different things to different people and nations. Perhaps one of its most successfully graphic descriptions is contained in the phrase 'one man's terrorist is another man's freedom fighter', coined at the time of decolonization, which, however, still accurately points out the differences in the perception of political realities which prevent finding common ground on this issue.[17]

Nonetheless, the U.N. General Assembly and the Security Council have both adopted resolutions – before and after the terrorist attacks of 11 September 2001 – which have put forward fairly accurate descriptions of international terrorism. Among those preceding 9/11 is the well-known G.A. Resolution 49/60 of 1994[18] which incorporated a 'Declaration on Measures to eliminate international terrorism' where (terrorism) was qualified as 'criminal acts intended or calculated to provoke a state of terror in the general public, a group of persons or particular persons for political purposes' adding that such acts 'are in any circumstances unjustifiable, whatever the considerations of a political, philosophical, ideological, racial, ethnic, religious or other nature that may be invoked to justify them'.

Post-9/11, the Security Council described terrorism in Resolution 1566 (2004)[19] as

> criminal acts, including against civilians, committed with the intent to cause death or serious bodily injury, or taking of hostages, with the purpose to provoke a state of terror in the general public or in a group of persons or particular persons, intimidate a population or compel a Government or an international organization to do or to abstain from doing any act.

Also in 2004, the Secretary General's High-level Panel on Threats, Challenges and Change[20] identified terrorism as acts

> intended to cause death or serious bodily harm to civilians or non-combatants, when the purpose of such an act, by its nature or context, is to intimidate a population, or to compel a Government or an international organization to do or to abstain from doing any act

16 On this issue *see* Alan Greene, Defining terrorism: One size fits all? *ICLQ* vol 66, April 2017 pp. 411-440, doi: 10.1017/S0020589317000070.

17 *See infra*, fn. 116.

18 A/RES/49/60 of 9 December 1994.

19 A/RES/1566 of 8 October 2004.

20 Available at: www.un.org/en/peacebuilding/pdf/historical/hlp_more_secure_world.pdf.

referring to key elements contained in the abovementioned S.C. Resolution 1566 (2004) and the 1999 International Convention for the suppression of the financing of terrorism. The latter provides that terrorism includes any

> act intended to cause death or serious bodily injury to a civilian, or to any other person not taking an active part in the hostilities in a situation of armed conflict, when the purpose of such act, by its nature or context, is to intimidate a population, or to compel a Government or an international organization to do or to abstain from doing any act.[21]

The Draft Comprehensive Convention on International Terrorism was expected to reach a final conclusion on the issue of the definition. However, such conclusion remains pending.[22, 23]

8.2.4 *Regional Agreements on Terrorism*

The Council of Europe has produced several Conventions relating to terrorism; two of them are of a general character: one on the Prevention of Terrorism, adopted in 2005[24] and an older one on the Suppression of Terrorism adopted in 1977.[25] A Convention dealing with the financing of terrorism was also adopted in 2005,[26] while a Protocol

21 Art. 2 1(b).

22 While Member States have agreed on many provisions of the draft comprehensive convention, diverging views on whether or not national liberation movements should be excluded from its scope of application have prevented consensus on the adoption of the full text. Art. 2 of the Draft Comprehensive Convention contains a definition of terrorism which includes 'by any means, unlawfully and intentionally' causing: "(a) Death or serious bodily injury to any person; or (b) Serious damage to public or private property, including a place of public use, a State or government facility, a public transportation system, an infrastructure facility or to the environment; or (c) Damage to property, places, facilities or systems referred to in paragraph 1 (b) of the present article resulting or likely to result in major economic loss; when the purpose of the conduct, by its nature or context, is to intimidate a population, or to compel a Government or an international organization to do or to abstain from doing any act." The draft article further stipulates that an offence is committed by a person who 'participates as an accomplice', 'organizes or directs others to commit' or 'contributes to the commission' of any of offences as set forth the particular article, on certain conditions which are also set forth therein. It must be noted that many states define terrorism in their national laws in ways that draw on these elements, although to differing degrees.

23 *See* Mahmoud Hmoud, Negotiating the Draft Comprehensive Convention on International Terrorism: Major Bones of Contention, *Journal of International Criminal Justice*, Volume 4, Issue 5, 1 November 2006, pp. 1031-1043.

24 Council of Europe Convention on the Prevention of Terrorism, Warsaw, 16 May 2005.

25 European Convention on the Suppression of Terrorism, Strasbourg, 27.I.1977, amended on 15/05/2003.

26 Council of Europe Convention on Laundering, Search, Seizure and Confiscation of the Proceeds from Crime and on the Financing of Terrorism, Warsaw, 16 May 2005.

Additional to the Convention on the Prevention of Terrorism mentioned above deals with the issue of foreign terrorist fighters (FTF).[27]

Regional approaches to terrorism have similarly been developed in the context of the European Union,[28] the League of Arab States,[29] the Organization for Security and Co-operation in Europe,[30] the Organization of American States,[31] the Organization of the African Union,[32] the Organization of the Islamic Conference,[33] the South Asian Association for Regional Cooperation[34] and other international organizations.

8.3 THE ROME STATUTE AND TERRORIST CRIMES

During the elaboration of the Rome Statute of the International Criminal Court, several states argued for the inclusion of terrorism in the jurisdiction of the Court as a separate crime. The majority disagreed, however, precisely because of the inexistence of a definition – and the lack of will to find one – of terrorism. The Final Act of the 1998 Rome Conference provided, however, that the Review Conference – which took place in Kampala, Uganda, in 2010 – should consider terrorism, among other crimes, with a view to arriving at an acceptable definition and with its inclusion in the list of crimes within the jurisdiction of the Court. However, this did not happen in the Kampala Conference.

Although 'terrorism' is not as such included in the list of crimes under the jurisdiction of the International Criminal Court, its Statute contains various offences which may encompass terrorist conduct depending on the circumstances of each particular case. Thus, a terrorist act may constitute any among numerous crimes against humanity provided for in Article 7 of the Rome Statute, such as torture, sexual crimes and persecution, provided that it is "committed as part of a widespread or systematic attack directed

---

27 Additional Protocol to the Council of Europe Convention on the Prevention of Terrorism, Riga, 22 October 2015. An Action Plan addressing the fight against violent extremism and radicalization leading to terrorism was also put forward.

28 *See* The European Union's Policies on Counter-Terrorism Relevance, Coherence and Effectiveness Study, European Union, 2017, available at: www.europarl.europa.eu/supporting-analyses, last visited October 2017.

29 *See* Larissa Van Den Herik and Nico Schrijver (eds) *Counter-Terrorism Strategies in a Fragmented International Legal Order*, Cambridge University Press, 2013.

30 Anti-terrorist activities are central to OSCE's efforts to address transnational threats to security. These are guided by the 'OSCE Consolidated Framework for the Fight against Terrorism' which identifies the operational principles and strategic focus of the OSCE in this domain. Activities undertaken aim, *inter alia*, at the implementation of the international legal framework against terrorism, strengthening travel document security, countering violent extremism, radicalization, and the use of the Internet for terrorist purposes.

31 Inter-American Convention against terrorism of 3 June 2002.

32 Organization of the African Union (OAU) Convention on the Prevention and Combating of Terrorism of 1 July 1999.

33 In 1999, the Organization of Islamic Cooperation (OIC) adopted its own Convention on Combatting International Terrorism.

34 The South Asian Association for Regional Cooperation (SAARC) Regional Convention on the Suppression of Terrorism of 4 November 1987.

against any civilian population, with knowledge of the attack."[35] A terrorist act may also fall within the category of war crimes under Article 8 of the ICC Statute, e.g. as an indiscriminate attack against civilians, or as hostage-taking.

On the other hand, the jurisprudence of international criminal tribunals includes judgments on cases involving terrorist crimes. ICTY tried for the first time a case involving the commission of the war crime of terror under Article 3 of its Statute and convicted the defendant for it.[36] The Court found that the crime of terror against the civilian population consisted of elements common with other war crimes as well as of elements which it drew from the Convention for the Suppression of the Financing of Terrorism.[37]

8.4 On the Subject of ISIS[38]

The most discussed terrorist activity in recent years has been that of the so-called 'Islamic State' (IS or ISIS or ISIL).[39] The speed with which this extremist organization, which has been characterized by the Security Council as a 'splinter group of Al-Qaida' occupied over 30% of Iraqi and Syrian territory in 2014, took by surprise not only Syria, Iraq and the wider Middle East, but the world at large.

Having taken over oil wells and refineries in northern Iraq and Syria, ISIS could then engage in the production and sale of oil, thus getting hold of large amounts of money which allowed it to finance its military operations.[40] It also received funds from sympathizing states in the Middle East, while more came from the taxation and extortion of the population and the looting of banks in the areas it occupied[41] as well as from kidnap-

35 See Christopher Greenwood, "International Law and the 'War against Terrorism'", *International Affairs*, vol. 78, N° 2 (April 2002), p. 301.

36 ICTY, *Galic*, Case No. IT-98-29, Judgment, 5 December 2003. The Tribunal added the following specific elements (para. 133):

1. "Acts of violence directed against the civilian population or individual civilians not taking direct part in hostilities causing death or serious injury to body or health within the civilian population;
2. "The offender wilfully made the civilian population or individual civilians not taking part in hostilities the object of those acts of violence;
3. "The above offence was committed with the primary purpose of spreading terror among the civilian population."

37 *Ibid.*

38 Islamic State (IS) or Islamic State of Iraq and Syria (ISIS) or Islamic State of Iraq and the Levant (ISIL) or Daesh (transliteration of the acronym داعش meaning 'Islamic State of Iraq and the Levant' (Arabic: الدولة الإسلامية في العراق والشام).

39 ISIS origins are traced in the Organization *Jama'at al-Tawhid wal-Jihad* which had been formed by *Abu Musab al-Zarqawi* in Jordan in 1999 and was active in Iraq post-2003. In Iraq *Jama'at al-Tawhid wal-Jihad* was in close connection with *Al-Qaeda.*

40 CNN, Self-funded and deep-rooted: How ISIS makes its millions, by Scott Bronstein and Drew Griffin, CNN Investigations 7 October 2014.

41 *Ibid.*

pings and, last but by no means least, from the sale of plundered antiquities from archaeological sites or museums.[42, 43]

In August 2014, the U.S. and other countries, Western and Arab,[44] started attacking ISIS targets in Iraq and Syria, releasing bombs and cruise missiles. Iraq had given its consent for foreign military action against ISIS on its territory; therefore, the war against ISIS in that country remained a non-international one. By contrast, in Syria, the U.S. participated in the war without such consent (which had, however, been granted to Russia), which transformed the war into an international armed conflict. As Syria protested, claiming violation of international law, the U.S. at first invoked humanitarian intervention and, finally, collective self-defence on behalf of Iraq.[45]

At the same time, on Syrian territory there was an ongoing non-international conflict between Syrian state forces – assisted by Russian ones – and ISIS as well as against other groups.

During this time, the absence of reaction on the part of the U.N., although not surprising, was no less disheartening. Indeed, the Security Council was not in a position to decide on action and adopt measures against ISIS in Syria and Iraq, due to the use of veto by Russia and China. It took a whole year and, perhaps, a clearer realization of the danger that ISIS represented following its numerous attacks outside of Syria and Iraq, before the S.C. could finally adopt, unanimously, Resolution 2249 (2015) on this issue. The Resolution determined that ISIS constituted 'an unprecedented threat to international peace and security', and called states 'that have the capacity to do so to take all necessary measures' to prevent and suppress the terrorist acts 'on the territory under the control of ISIL… in Syria and Iraq'. It therefore lifted, specifically with regard to ISIS and related terrorist organizations, the legal impediments encountered by states already operating in Syria against these organizations due to lack of consent by Syria.

Clearly, ISIS has certain characteristic features which differentiate it crucially from other non-state actors involved in terrorism. The occupation of large swathes of territory in both, Iraq and Syria, has been the biggest of these differentiations; the relative localization of the war it conducted on these territories is another, although the ISIS attacks in other countries such as Tunisia, Belgium, France, Lebanon, Russia, Germany and Turkey demonstrated the capacity of ISIS to mount operations in other parts of the world; it must, however, be noted that the claims of many terrorist groups or individuals engaging in terrorist acts on their own, that they are affiliated with ISIS, remain largely unsubstan-

---

42 Newsweek, How does ISIS fund its reign of terror? By Janine di Giovanni, Leah McGrath Goodman and Damien Sharkov, 11 June 2014.

43 On the crimes related to the destruction of archaeological sites and cultural heritage monuments by ISIS, *see also* PART I.

44 Including Australia, France, Turkey and the United Kingdom.

45 Letter from Samantha J. Power, Representative of the U.S. to the U.N., to U.N. Secretary General Ban Ki-moon, dated 23 September 2014, available at: www.justsecurity.org/15436/war-powers-resolution-article-51-letters-force-syria-isil-khorasan-group/, last accessed 26 February 2018.

tiated, as no central direction or planning of these attacks has been proved.[46] This also distinguishes, to a certain degree, ISIS from other terrorist organizations such as *Al-Qaeda* (from which it probably originates), the main focus of which was planning and executing attacks far removed from its base in Afghanistan.

8.4.1 ISIS Crimes and the ICC

ISIS has made no effort to conceal the crimes its members and supporters have committed. On the contrary, it considered them rather as a sight to publicize. Thus, many executions, particularly beheadings of hostages, have taken place in full camera view for the obvious purpose of instilling terror and even 'attracting' new recruits. And although no crime of terrorism as such is included in the jurisdiction of the ICC,[47] the crimes committed by ISIS in Iraq and Syria certainly fall within the ambit of other crimes provided for in the ICC Statute. Indeed, there have been, *inter alia*, mass murders, abductions of civilians and using thousands as human shields, intentional shelling of civilians and civilian residences, recruitment and use of children,[48] sexual crimes, as well as persecution of Christian and other religious minorities and the destruction or severe damage of sites of major cultural importance, such as the site of *Palmyra* in Syria.[49] This open-ended list of crimes against humanity and war crimes is spearheaded by the atrocities (most probably legally constituting genocide) against the *Yazidis of Sinjar* in Iraq which was accompanied by the enslavement and other abuses of *Yazidi* women and girls and the recruitment and indoctrination of *Yazidi* boys, thousands of whom remain unaccounted for.[50]

Despite efforts to have a Resolution coming out of the S.C. which would refer the situation of mass atrocities committed in Iraq and Syria to the ICC, this has not been possible. Although this creates an untenable 'inequality of treatment' between situations referred and not referred to the ICC by the S.C. (why Darfur or Libya and not Syria and Iraq?) which, though easily answered (political reasons), it is always difficult to accept on ethical grounds. Furthermore, as neither Syria nor Iraq are parties to the ICC Statute, neither would be expected to refer these crimes to the ICC (even more so since the Syrian regime at least has allegedly committed grave crimes in the course of the conflict(s) on its territory while the allies of both may also face charges for various crimes). Similarly, a

46 It is a hallmark of ISIS tactics to claim responsibility for every attack which could share some of its own characteristics. It has however been shown that very few – if at all – of these attacks have in fact been masterminded or conducted by ISIS.

47 *See supra*, p. 114.

48 *See, e.g.*, Office of the U.N. High Commissioner for Human Rights, Report of the U.N. Assistance Mission for Iraq (UNAMI), on the Protection of Civilians in the context of the Ninewa Operations and the retaking of Mosul City, 17 October 2016 – 10 July 2017.

49 *See, e.g.*, Human Rights Watch, World Report 2016.

50 On this issue *see also supra*, PART I.

proprio motu referral by the ICC Prosecutor would equally be excluded, as he/she would be under the same jurisdictional constrictions as apply in connection with non-members to the ICC. Given the above, the possibility for prosecution is left at this stage with individual states (whether parties to the ICC Statute or not) which could do so in respect of their own nationals who have been associated with ISIS and are suspected of committing crimes under these states' own domestic legislation (on the basis of the active nationality principle) or in respect of persons who, although not being their nationals, have committed such crimes against their national(s) (on the basis of the passive nationality principle). Where neither the perpetrator or perpetrators nor the victim (or victims) of such crimes are their nationals, a state may prosecute on the basis of its universal jurisdiction over certain grave crimes as provided by either conventional or customary international law. Already a number of states have been trying such cases on the basis of the abovementioned principles.

It should also be said that the ICC Prosecutor's possibilities for prosecution remain intact as regards nationals of states parties to the Statute who have been ISIS fighters suspected for the commission of crimes under the ICC (complementary) jurisdiction in Syria and Iraq, provided that no state has exercised primary jurisdiction over them.

In 2016, the U.N. General Assembly adopted Resolution 71/248[51] establishing an 'international, impartial and independent mechanism' to assist with accountability for the perpetrators of mass atrocity crimes in the Syrian civil war since March 2011. Although the ultimate goal of this initiative is rather nebulous, the main question remains whether the political will to proceed in this fashion exists in reality, particularly as it has been conspicuously absent in the context of the S.C. which is usually the main motivator in such cases.[52] Finally, by Resolution 2379/2017,[53] the S.C. requested the Secretary General to establish an independent investigative team to support domestic efforts to hold ISIS accountable for its actions in Iraq.

On the ground, following what seems to be the final demise of ISIS in the Middle East,[54] hundreds or even thousands of its fighters with a great variety of nationalities have been captured and held in camps under Kurdish control. However, many states of the captives' nationalities are hesitant to exercise jurisdiction over them. In view of such hesitations, and a situation which tends to become unmanageable, as it is very probable that a great number of these former fighters – who may be responsible for the commission of grave crimes – will be able to escape, the Kurdish administration in Northern Syria seems to have asked for the setting up of a special tribunal for them in Northern Syria.[55] It must be admitted that the situation would indeed justify taking such a step,

51 A/RES/71/248 of 21 December 2016.
52 *See* Alex Whiting, An Investigation Mechanism for Syria, JICJ 15 (2017), pp. 231237.
53 S/RES/2379 of 21 September 2017.
54 *Baghouz*, Syria, was its last (?) stronghold which fell following the onslaught of Kurdish and Syrian forces.
55 BBC News, 26 March 2019.

much along the lines of the *ad hoc* or special tribunals set up to try the perpetrators of grave crimes committed in other international and non-international conflicts, as has been seen above.

8.5 Human Rights While Countering Terrorism

8.5.1 The Problems and the Means to Confront Them

8.5.1.1 The U.N. Efforts

Global conventions on terrorism require, just as regional ones, compliance with the provisions of human rights law while combating the phenomenon in any of its manifestations. For example, the 1997 U.N. Convention for the Suppression of Terrorist Bombings demands in its Article 14 that any accused or defendant under the Convention be afforded all rights and guarantees provided by the law of the state where that person is found, as well as those provided by international law, including international law of human rights. Furthermore, Article 12 clarifies that the Convention cannot be interpreted as imposing an obligation to extradite or to afford mutual legal assistance, if the requested state party has substantial grounds to believe that the request for extradition for the offences set forth in the Convention or for mutual legal assistance with respect to these offences has been made for discriminatory reasons, i.e. for

> the purpose of prosecuting or punishing a person on account of that person's race, religion, nationality, ethnic origin or political opinion or that compliance with the request would cause prejudice to that person's position for any of these reasons.[56]

Finally, Article 19 of the Convention contains a catch-all provision making it clear that the Convention does not affect the other rights, obligations and responsibilities of states and individuals under international law, including IHL.

The same treatment is afforded to the accused or defendants under the 1999 Convention on terrorist financing (Arts. 15, 17 and 21 respectively).

In the wake of the 9/11 attacks, however, the world-wide proliferation of security and counter-terrorism legislation and the exponential increase of the measures taken for its implementation had significant consequences on the application of human rights as well as on the way these were henceforth perceived on a national and international level. In other words, the need to uphold and respect human rights tended to lose priority, if it was not blatantly disregarded, over the urgent necessity to serve counter-terrorism efforts.

56 This clause was known as "clause française".

In spite of this development or, most probably, because of this, it has since been a mantra in all documents on terrorism emanating from U.N. organs and from other organizations alike, that any measures taken by states to combat terrorism must comply with their obligations under international human rights law, refugee law and international humanitarian law.[57] Thus, in its resolution 1456 (2003), the Security Council stated that

> States must ensure that any measure taken to combat terrorism comply with all their obligations under international law, and should adopt such measures in accordance with international law, in particular international human rights, refugee, and humanitarian law.

There was reaffirmation of this position in Security Council Resolution 1624 (2005). Similarly, in the 2006 United Nations Global Counter-Terrorism Strategy, Member States undertook to ensure respect for human rights and the rule of law as the fundamental basis of the fight against terrorism.[58]

The 2005 World Summit Outcome also concluded that international cooperation to fight terrorism must be conducted in conformity with international law, including the Charter of the United Nations and relevant international conventions and protocols.[59]

The General Assembly Resolutions on measures to eliminate international terrorism adopted since 1972 have, similarly, emphasized that states must ensure that any measures taken to combat terrorism comply with their obligations under international law, in particular international human rights, refugee and humanitarian law.[60]

In the context of an effort to identify the root causes of terrorism, the 2004 High-level Panel on Threats, Challenges and Change emphasized that "recruitment by international terrorist groups was aided by grievances nurtured by poverty, foreign occupation, and the absence of human rights and democracy ..."[61] In a similar vein, a Presidential Statement adopted by the S.C. on 27 September 2010[62] stated that:

---

57 *E.g.*, S.C. Resolutions S/RES/1456 (2003), Annex, para. 6, S/RES/1624 (2005), para. 4; G.A Resolutions: United Nations Global Counter-Terrorism Strategy contained in General Assembly Resolution /RES/60/288 of 8 September 2006 and its reviews in G.A. Resolutions A/RES/62/272 of 5 September 2008, A/RES/64/297 of 8 September 2010, A/RES/66/762 of 4 April 2012, A/RES/68/276 of 13 June 2014, A/RES/70/291 of 1 July 2016, A/RES/72/284 of 26 June 2018 (The United Nations Global Counter-Terrorism Strategy Review). *See also* the 2005 G.A. World Summit Outcome Document, A/RES/60/1 of 16 September 2005.

58 *See* in particular Part IV of the Action Plan to the Strategy (G.A. Resolution A/RES/60/288 of 8 September 2006 and its reviews by subsequent G.A. Resolutions.

59 A/RES/60/1 of 24 October 2005, para. 85.

60 *See, e.g.*, G.A. Resolution A/RES/60/158 of 28 February 2006 para. 1, and subsequent Resolutions on the 'Protection of Human Rights and Fundamental Freedoms while Countering Terrorism'.

61 A More Secure World: Our Shared Responsibility, Report of the Secretary-General's High-level Panel on Threats, Challenges and Change, A/59/565 of 2 December 2004, para. 21.

62 S/PRST/2010/19.

> The Security Council recognizes that terrorism will not be defeated by military force, law enforcement measures, and intelligence operations alone, and underlines the need to address the conditions conducive to the spread of terrorism, including, but not limited to, the need to strengthen efforts for the successful prevention and peaceful resolution of prolonged conflicts, and the need to promote the rule of law, the protection of human rights and fundamental freedoms, good governance, tolerance and inclusiveness to offer a viable alternative to those who could be susceptible to terrorist recruitment and to radicalization leading to violence.

The Council further recognized, in this regard, 'that development, peace and security, and human rights are interlinked and mutually reinforcing'.

Mention should also be made of the 2006 United Nations Secretary General's Report 'Uniting against terrorism: recommendations for a global counter-terrorism strategy'[63] which, again, emphasized that effective counter-terrorism measures and human rights protection are not conflicting, but rather complementary and mutually reinforcing goals. This is also the view held by treaty-based bodies.

On a more practical level, i.e. on that of the U.N. Counter – Terrorism Committees, several efforts have been made so as to ensure their adherence to human rights requirements in carrying out their tasks. In pursuit of this goal, the CTED has a human rights component included in its mandate, and the same is true of the Counter-Terrorism Implementation Task Force (CTITF).[64] The Global Counter-Terrorism Strategy also puts increasing emphasis on human rights.

Finally, the Terrorism Prevention Branch of the United Nations Office on Drugs and Crime (UNODC) incorporates human rights elements in its capacity-building programme and assistance projects, by including issues such as parliamentary supervision of counter-terrorism measures, extradition and mutual legal assistance, and the rights of victims of terrorism.

However, the resolve of the U.N. to secure respect of human rights while countering terrorism, as expressed at all levels – in resolutions, statements, programs, in the work of its counter-terrorism committees, as well as in the Security Council's implementation machinery – has regrettably been shown to remain to a large extent unfulfilled in practice. It is indeed noteworthy that even these latter mechanisms set up for the implementation

---

63 Resolution A/60/825 of 27 April.2006.

64 The CTITF is a coordinating mechanism which engages in a range of international capacity-building initiatives which include some human rights components, the ultimate objective being to assist states in the full implementation of the United Nations Global Counter-Terrorism Strategy. Among the ongoing initiatives of the Task Force with a human rights focus are the creation of a support portal for victims of terrorism and a campaign to improve communications strategies for such victims.

of the U.N. Resolutions have been found to be lacking in the scrupulous application of human rights while performing their tasks (see 10 below, under Conclusions).

8.5.1.2 The EU Judicial Control as a New Paradigm

A major change of paradigm was signalled by the judgment of the European Court of Justice (ECJ) in the case of *Kadi and Al Barakaat*.[65] The judgment, issued in 2013, confirmed a judgment delivered by the General Court on the same case, forming a new perception in the jurisprudence of the EU Courts and having a wider resonance in the interpretation and implementation of human rights law vis-à-vis international counter-terrorism legislation and measures. Indeed, it was the first time that the ECJ confirmed its jurisdiction to review the lawfulness of a measure implementing a Security Council Re-

65 *Yassin Abdullah Kadi and Al Barakaat International Foundation v. Council of the European Union and Commission of the European Communities.*

solution imposing sanctions. It was, furthermore, on the basis of its finding that the particular Resolution was not in conformity with human rights standards as applied in the EU that the ECJ went on for the first time to annul an EC Regulation giving effect to a UNSC Resolution.[66]

66 *Kadi,* a Saudi Arabia resident and *Al Barakaat International Foundation* were found by U.N. competent organs to be associated with *Usama bin Laden,* the *Al Qaeda* network and the *Taliban.* As a result, in 2001 their names were added to the Consolidated List maintained by the Sanctions Committee established by the UNSC under Chapter VII of the U.N. Charter, and then also transposed into the List annexed to the European Union Regulation (EC) No 881/2002 ordering the freezing of the assets of both. *Kadi* and *Al Barakaat* initiated proceedings before the Court of First Instance (CFI, General Court) and requested annulment of the Regulation on the ground that it infringed *inter alia* on their right to property, the right to be heard before a court of law and the right to effective judicial review. All claims of the applicants were rejected by the CFI judgment of 21 September 2005 (Judgments of the General Court in *Case T-306/01 Yusuf and Al Barakaat International Foundation v Council and Commission* and *Case T-315/01 Kadi v Council and Commission* – judgment known as '*Kadi I*') – which confirmed the validity of the Regulation, on the basis that the Court had no jurisdiction to review either the validity of the Regulation or that of the relevant S.C. Resolutions, except in respect of *jus cogens* norms. On appeal, however, the European Court of Justice (Grand Chamber) in its judgment of 3 September 2008 (in *Joined Cases C-402/05 P and C-415/05 P Kadi and Al Barakaat International Foundation v Council and Commission*), found that the EU Courts must ensure the review of the lawfulness of all EU acts, including those taken in implementation of U.N. Security Council Resolutions. The Court ordered the annulment of the Regulation whereby the names of the appellants had been added to the List, since that Regulation infringed on a number of fundamental rights which the appellants enjoyed under EU law (right of defence, right to effective judicial protection). As neither the evidence against *Kadi* nor the reason for his inclusion in the List had been disclosed to him, the European Commission disclosed to *Kadi* the summary of reasons for his being listed which had been provided to it by the U.N. Sanctions Committee. After obtaining *Kadi's* comments on those reasons, the Commission decided, by means of a further Commission Regulation '(Regulation (EC) No 1190/2008 of 28.11.2008 amending for the 101st time Council Regulation (EC) No 881/2002 imposing certain specific restrictive measures directed against certain persons and entities associated with Usama bin Laden, the Al-Qaeda network and the Taliban)' to keep his name on the EU List of persons subject to restrictive measures. The General Court, however, annulled this further Commission Regulation (Judgment of the General Court of 30 September 2010 on *Case T-85/09 Yassin Abdullah Kadi v Commission, known as Kadi II),* holding that a full judicial review of the lawfulness of that measure had to be ensured by the Court, which included the information and evidence substantiating the reasons for taking it. Since such information and evidence had not been disclosed and the summary of reasons provided by the Sanctions Committee appeared too vague, the General Court concluded that *Kadi's* rights of defence and his right to effective judicial protection had been infringed upon. The Commission, the Council and the U.K. appealed against the judgment. The ECJ delivered its judgment on the *Joined Cases C-584/10 P, C-593/10 P and C-595/10 P Commission, Council, United Kingdom v. Yassin Abdullah Kadi,* on 18 July 2013, dismissing the appeal.

8.5.2 *International Human Rights Instruments and the Possibility of Restrictions (Limitations) or Derogations*[67]

A classically lawful way to confront terrorism without encroaching upon fundamental human rights – as opposed to presumably 'non-fundamental ones' – is to resort to the possibility provided for by all human rights instruments to restrict the application of or even derogate from certain articles which protect such 'non-fundamental rights', which are specifically identified. This possibility is meant to provide the regime established by human rights instruments with a measure of flexibility in case that specific circumstances so warrant. Obviously, the threat of terrorist activities and the occurrence of terrorist incidents constitute, *par excellence*, instances where such restrictions or derogations may be used.

8.5.2.1 The Possibility of Restrictions (Limitations)

Under the ICCPR, restrictions may be imposed on the rights to freedom of expression, freedom of assembly and association and freedom of movement.[68] Under the ECHR, the rights provided in Articles 8-11 thereof, i.e. the right to respect for private and family life, freedom of thought, conscience and religion, freedom of expression and freedom of assembly and association may be subject to restrictions. Similarly, the American Convention on Human Rights provides that restrictions may apply, *inter alia*, to the right of assembly, freedom of association and freedom of movement and residence.[69] Restrictions may also apply to rights recognized in the African Charter of Human and Peoples' rights (*Banjul* Charter),[70] such as the freedom of assembly and the right of freedom of movement and residence.[71]

The imposition of restrictions is subject to certain conditions,[72] for example that they must be prescribed by law, or be 'necessary in a democratic society'[73] and, of course, taken in pursuance of one or more legitimate purposes, ranging from the interests of national security, public safety or the economic well-being of the country, to the preven-

67 Emilie M. Hafner-Burton, Laurence R. Helfer, and Christopher J. Fariss. Emergency and Escape: Explaining Derogations from Human Rights Treaties, International Organization 65, Fall 2011, pp. 673-707; Scott P. Sheeran Reconceptualizing States of Emergency under International Human Rights Law: Theory, Legal Doctrine, and Politics, *Michigan Journal of International Law*, Vol. 34, Issue 3, 2013; V. Pillai Aneesh, State of Emergency and Derogation of Human Rights, 2013; John Reynolds, Emergency Derogations and the International Human Rights Project, in *Empire, Emergency and International Law*, pp. 111-137, Cambridge University Press, 2017, doi: 10.1017/978136779095.007

68 Respectively Arts. 19(2), 21 and 22, 12(3). On this topic *see* Siracusa Principles on the limitation and derogation provisions in the International Covenant on Civil and Political Rights, Commission on Human Rights, E/CN.4/1985/4, Annex.

69 Respectively Arts. 15, 16(2) and 22(3).

70 Of 27 June 1981. Entry into force on 21 October 1986.

71 Arts. 11 and 12(1) respectively.

72 Human Rights Committee, General Comment No. 31, para. 6.

73 This condition is included in all the relevant Arts. 8-11 of the ECHR.

tion of disorder or crime, the protection of health or morals, or the protection of the rights and freedoms of others.[74] Restrictions must, as a rule, respect the general principles of equality and non-discrimination,[75, 76] while also being necessary for the attainment of a specific objective and proportionate to the effects they have.[77]

It derives from the above that not all human rights instruments provide that the same rights may be subject to restrictions or that such restrictions are the same, nor that the grounds for which they have been imposed are the same or even similar. For example, Article 18 of the ICCPR which provides for limitations to the right to freedom of thought, conscience, religion and belief, does not include national security as a permissible ground for limitations.

8.5.2.2 The Possibility of Derogations

According to Article 4 of the ICCPR,

> [I]n In time of public emergency which threatens the life of the nation…., the States Parties…may take measures derogating from their obligations under the present Covenant to the extent strictly required by the exigencies of the situation …

Similarly, Article 15 of the ECHR provides that

> In time of war or other public emergency threatening the life of the nation any High Contracting Party may take measures derogating from its obligations under [the] Convention to the extent strictly required by the exigencies of the situation, provided that such measures are not inconsistent with its other obligations under international law.

---

74 *See, e.g.*, Art. 8 of the ECHR on the right to respect for private and family life. The African Charter provides that the right of assembly may be subject to necessary restrictions provided for by the law, in particular 'in the interest of national security, the safety, health, ethics and rights and freedoms of others'. An individual has the right of freedom of movement and residence within the borders of a state 'if he abides by the law' (Art. 12(1)). However, the right of an individual to leave any country including his own, and to return to his country (Art. 12(2)) may be subject to restrictions which are 'provided for by law for the protection of national security, law and order, public health or morality'.

75 Art. 14 of the ECHR, Arts. 2(1) and 26 of the ICCPR.

76 As found by the ECtHR, in *Sunday Times v. United Kingdom*, N° 6538/74, Judgment, 26 April 1979, para. 49.

77 *See, e.g.*, Note of the Office of the High Commissioner for Human Rights to the Chair of the Counter-Terrorism Committee, entitled: 'A Human Rights perspective on counter-terrorism measures', E/CN.4/2002/18 and Annex thereto, para. 4 (d).

Similar terms are also used in Article 27 (Suspension of Guarantees) of the American Convention on Human Rights.[78]

On the other hand, no derogation clause is included in the African Charter. The African Commission on Human and Peoples' Rights, has held in this respect that emergencies or special circumstances cannot justify limitations on the rights and freedoms enshrined in the Charter and that

> [T]he only legitimate reasons for limiting the rights and freedoms of the African Charter are found in Article 27 (2), that is, that the rights of the Charter "shall be exercised with due regard to the rights of others, collective security, morality and common interest."[79]

The Commission goes on to find that

> The justification of limitations must be strictly proportionate with and absolutely necessary.... Most important, a limitation may not erode a right such that the right itself becomes illusory.[80]

Clearly, emergencies of the magnitude described in Article 4 of the ICCPR and in the corresponding Articles 15 of the ECHR and 27 of the American Convention on human rights create a particularly exceptional situation.[81] It is also clear that such a situation may be due to and result from terrorist acts, as has been repeatedly seen in reality. Thus, the U.K. derogated from the ECHR and the ICCPR prohibition of arbitrary arrest and detention for four years following the 9/11 terrorist attacks.[82] The U.K. had also derogated from the same rights from 1976 to 1984 as well as from 1988 to 2001, invoking widespread bombings, killings and civil disturbances in Northern Ireland.[83] Israel has invoked similar reasons for its continuous derogation from the ICCPR since 1991.[84] Following the 2016 abortive *coup d'état* in Turkey, it was announced that the country would derogate from the ECHR and the ICCPR for the duration of the state of emergency which had

78 The article requires that the emergency must threaten the 'independence or security' of the state.

79 *Constitutional Rights Project, Civil Liberties Organization and Media Rights Agenda v. Nigeria*, communications N° 140/94, N° 141/94, N° 145/95, paras. 41-42. *See also* Malcolm D. Evans, Rachel Murray (eds), The African Charter on Human and Peoples' Rights: The System in Practice, 1986-2000, Cambridge University Press, 2002; Louise Doswald-Beck, Human Rights in Times of Conflict and Terrorism, Oxford University Press, 2011.

80 Constitutional Rights Project, *supra*, fn. 764, para. 42.

81 *See* Human Rights Committee General Comment N° 29.

82 The derogation did not apply to U.K. citizens.

83 The derogations applied, however, only with regard to suspect members of the Irish Republican Army (IRA).

84 Such as continuous threats and attacks on the country's very existence, threats of war, actual armed attacks and campaigns of terrorism resulting in the murder and injury to human beings.

been proclaimed. In 2018 the state of emergency was extended for the sixth time, the derogation from both instruments therefore being also extended. The massive crackdown on those perceived responsible for the coup has also been continuing.

The ECtHR has confronted situations like the ones mentioned above several times and its jurisprudence on whether or not terrorist acts or threats may justify the imposition of a state of emergency confirms that this is a matter which must be assessed on a case-by-case basis.[85]

According to the ICCPR, the derogating state must inform, through the United Nations Secretary General, the other states parties to the Covenant of the provisions from which it has decided to derogate and of the reasons that compelled it to do so.[86]

Similarly, the ECHR demands that a state party which makes use of a derogation keep the Secretary General of the Council of Europe informed of the measures and the reasons which prompted their application, as well as of their eventual cessation.[87]

The measures taken must be only those required to face the particular situation and may stay in place only for as long as strictly required for that purpose.[88] As in the case of restrictions, all measures taken must be necessary and proportionate to the effects they cause, while the ultimate goal should remain the restoration of normality and the return of the rights which have been derogated from to full applicability at the earliest time

85 In the significant number of cases which have been brought before the ECtHR concerning the conditions for the legitimate application of Art. 15 (*see* in particular *Lawless v. Ireland (No 3)*, N° 332/57, Judgment, 1 July 1961, paras. 28, 29; *Brannigan and McBride v. United Kingdom*, N° 14553/89, N° 14554/89, Judgment of 25 May 1993; *Aksoy v. Turkey*, No. 21987/93 Judgment, 18 December 1996, para. 70), the Court has identified certain criteria, among which: a) The emergency must be actual or imminent; b) the crisis which concerns only a particular region of the state can amount to a public emergency threatening 'the life of the nation' (*see, e.g., Ireland v. the United Kingdom*, No. 5310/71, Judgment, 18 January 1978, para. 205); c) if, however, measures are taken outside the territory to which the derogation applies, the derogation will not apply and the Government concerned will not be able to rely on it to justify the measures (*see, e.g., Sakik and Others v. Turkey*, 87/1996/706/898-903, Judgment, 26 November 1997, para. 39; *Sadak v. Turkey*, nos. 25142/94 and 27099/95, 8 April 2004 para. 56); d) any measures taken should seek to protect the democratic order from the threats to it, and every effort should be made to safeguard the values of a democratic society, such as pluralism, tolerance and broadmindedness (*Mehmet Hasan Altan v. Turkey*, Judgment, No. 13237/17, 20 March 2018, para. 210; *Şahin Alpay v. Turkey*, Judgment, No. 16538/17, 20 March 2018. para. 180).

86 Art. 4(3).

87 Art. 15(3).

88 *See* in this connection, the case of *Jorge Landinelli Silva et al. v. Uruguay*, communication No. 34/1978 referring to a situation of emergency in Uruguay on the basis of which Uruguay derogated from certain ICCPR provisions, where the Human Rights Committee stated that it did "[n]ot see what ground could be adduced to support the contention that, in order to restore peace and order, it was necessary to deprive all citizens, who as members of certain political groups had been candidates in the elections of 1966 and 1971, of any political right for a period as long as 15 years. This measure applies to everyone, without distinction as to whether he sought to promote his political opinions by peaceful means or by resorting to, or advocating the use of, violent means" (Official Records of the GA, Thirty-sixth Session, Supplement No. 40 (A/36/40), annex XII, communication R.8/34, para. 8.4), cited by the Special Rapporteur on the Promotion and Protection of Human Rights and Fundamental Freedoms while Countering Terrorism (UNGA doc. (A/61/267), 16 August 2006, para. 27, fn. 22).

possible. If the situation of emergency and consequent derogations continues, the requirements must be regularly reviewed by independent organs. An assessment of the compliance of the measures taken with applicable rules of international law must also be made by these organs.

According to Article 4(1) of the ICCPR, the measures must not be inconsistent with other obligations that the state has assumed under international law, and not involve discrimination solely on the ground of race, colour, sex, language, religion or social origin. An ultimate safety valve is contained in Article 5 (1) of the ICCPR which clarifies that nothing in the Covenant (therefore including the possibility to derogate from certain articles) can be interpreted as implying any right to engage in activity aimed at the destruction of the rights and freedoms set out in it.

8.5.2.3 Non-Derogable Human Rights

Even a state of emergency does not, however, justify derogation from certain fundamental human rights. Thus, Article 4(2) of the ICCPR identifies as non-derogable the right to life, freedom from torture or cruel, inhuman or degrading treatment or punishment, the prohibition of slavery and servitude, freedom from imprisonment for failure to fulfil a contract, freedom from retrospective penalties, the right to be recognized as a person before the law, and freedom of thought, conscience and religion.[89] As already noted, Article 4(1) of the Covenant also specifies that any derogating measures must be consistent with obligations under international law. It is particularly significant that the ICCPR Human Rights Committee has vastly widened the ambit of non-derogable provisions by giving an extensive interpretation to the provisions of Article 4(2) of the Covenant. Thus, the Committee has identified, in its General Comment No. 29,[90] the following rights and prohibitions which cannot be derogated from, on the basis of fundamentally important considerations: a) the prohibition of conduct constituting the basis for individual criminal responsibility for crimes against humanity[91]; b) the right of all persons deprived of their liberty to be treated with humanity and with respect for the inherent dignity of the human person, as this is a norm of general (customary) international law[92]; c) the prohibitions against the taking of hostages, abductions or unacknowledged detention, for the same reason; d) the international protection of the rights of persons belonging to minorities, because its elements are covered by equally non-derogable provisions; e) the deportation or forcible transfer of population without grounds permitted under international law, as they constitute crimes against humanity; f) the prohibition against propaganda for war or in advocacy of national, racial or religious hatred, as such acts constitute incitement to discrimination, hostility or violence; g) the right to a fair trial, which is explicitly

89 *See also* Human Rights Committee, General Comment N° 29.
90 Of 31 August 2001.
91 General Comment 29, para. 12.
92 *Ibid.*, para. 13 (a) to (e).

guaranteed under international humanitarian law during armed conflict, and must therefore also be respected during a state of emergency;[93] h) the right to an effective remedy even in the exceptional case of derogation from certain rights, as the right to such a remedy is a treaty obligation inherent in the Covenant as a whole.[94]

Furthermore, the Committee maintains that the protection of rights recognized as non-derogable requires that certain procedural safeguards, including judicial guarantees, be available in all situations.[95] Fundamental requirements of fair trial (principles of legality and rule of law, conviction for a criminal offence by a court of law, presumption of innocence) must be respected during a state of emergency.[96] Finally, the protection of non-derogable rights requires that the right to take proceedings before a court not be diminished by the decision of the state party concerned to derogate from the Covenant.[97]

Under Article 15(2) of the ECHR, there can be no derogation from Article 2 (right to life) except as regards death resulting from lawful acts of war. Similarly, there can be no derogation from Articles 3 (prohibition of torture), 4(1) (prohibition of slavery) and 7 (application of the legality principle).

In the context of OAS, the Inter-American Court of Human Rights found, in its 1987 advisory opinion on *habeas corpus in* emergency situations,

> that writs of habeas corpus and of "amparo"[98] are among those judicial remedies that are essential for the protection of various rights whose derogation is prohibited and that serve, moreover, to preserve legality in a democratic society.... The constitutions and legal systems of the States parties that authorize, expressly or by implication, the suspension of the legal remedies of habeas corpus or of "amparo" in emergency situations cannot be deemed to be compatible with the international obligations imposed on these States by the Convention.[99]

Although the conditions which apply for the application of derogations are generally formulated and therefore allow for differing interpretations, the substantial body of ju-

93 *Ibid.*, paras. 14 and 15.
94 *Ibid.*, para. 14.
95 *Ibid.*, para. 15.
96 *Ibid.*, para. 16.
97 *Ibid.*
98 According to Gloria Orrego Hoyos "The writ of amparo, like the habeas corpus, may be invoked by any person who believes that any of his/her rights, is being violated. However, one of the great progresses of the amparo in Latin America [is] that it enables citizens to invoke the action for the violation of any right protected either explicitly or implicitly by the Constitution or by any applicable international treaties ..." (GlobaLex, available at: www.nyulawglobal.org/globalex/Amparo.html) last accessed on 18 September 2017.
99 Inter-American Court of Human Rights, Advisory Opinion OC-8/87 of 30 January 1987 on *habeas corpus* in emergency situations (Arts. 27(2), 25(1) and 7(6)), requested by the American Commission on Human Rights (paras. 42-43).

risprudence of international courts and tribunals which has been developed in their respect greatly assists in the assessment of the measures taken by states and their conformity with the relevant Conventions. Reports and other relevant documents which have been produced by treaty bodies also play a great part for this purpose,[100] as do the guidelines issued by competent international organizations.[101] The extensive doctrinal analysis which exists on these issues also contributes in this direction.[102]

8.6 INTERNATIONAL HUMANITARIAN LAW WHILE COUNTERING TERRORISM

8.6.1 Acts of Terrorism Under IHL

The Fourth Geneva Convention prohibits 'measures of terrorism'[103] stating that 'collective penalties and likewise all measures of intimidation and terrorism are prohibited'. Acts of terrorism against persons who do not take a direct part or who no longer take part in hostilities are similarly prohibited by Additional Protocol II.[104] Acts or threats of violence the primary purpose of which is to spread terror among the civilian population are prohibited by both Additional Protocols.[105] According to the ICRC, while even a lawful attack on a military objective may spread fear among civilians, these particular provisions which are related to the conduct of hostilities, aim at prohibiting "attacks that specifically aim to terrorize civilians, for example campaigns of shelling or sniping of civilians in urban areas."[106]

Furthermore, as the ICRC rightly observes, IHL prohibits many acts committed in armed conflict which would be considered terrorist if they were committed in times of peace.[107] Such acts would be for instance those which violate the basic principle of dis-

100 *See, e.g.*, Inter-American Commission on Human Rights, "Report on Terrorism and Human Rights," 22 October 2002.

101 *See, e.g.*, Council of Europe Guidelines on Human rights and the Fight against Terrorism adopted by the Committee of Ministers on 11 July 2002, Doc. H (2002)4.

102 *See, e.g.*, Alex Conte, *Human Rights in the Prevention and Punishment of Terrorism*, Springer, 2010; Mary Arden, *Human Rights in the Age of Terrorism in Human Rights and European Law*, January 2015. Manfred Nowak, Anne Charbord (eds), *Using Human Rights to Counter Terrorism*, Edward Elgar Publishing, 2018.

103 Art. 33 (2nd sentence).

104 AP II, Art. 4(2)(d).

105 AP I, Art. 51, and AP II, Art. 13(2).

106 ICRC, "International Humanitarian Law and Terrorism: Questions and Answers," *supra*, fn. 191.

107 International Committee of the Red Cross, "International Humanitarian Law and Terrorism: Questions and Answers," 1 January 2011, available at www.icrc.org.

tinction,[108] such as indiscriminate attacks against civilians and civilian objects, the use of 'human shields' and hostage-taking. However, qualifying such acts as terrorist in the context of armed conflict is, in reality, of no legal consequence, as they already constitute war crimes under international law for which those responsible must be prosecuted.

Finally, it must be stressed that acts of terrorism in the context of IHL are those undertaken by the belligerent parties in connection with either an international or a non-international armed conflict. This means that they cannot be engaged in by groups of persons who engage in terrorist activities outside an armed conflict. These latter acts would be criminalized by domestic legislation as such or in implementation of binding international instruments (bilateral or multilateral) on the matter.[109]

8.7 International Refugee Law While Countering Terrorism

The implementation of international and domestic counter-terrorism measures by states has had a negative impact on refugee protection, a fact which became particularly obvious during the unprecedented flow of refugees fleeing war in the Middle East and in other parts of the world. Indeed, restrictions on, or even lack of, access to asylum procedures have been imposed or registered in many countries and in many cases. Asylum seekers and refugees are often viewed with suspicion by the general public as possibly involved in terrorist acts before coming into the host country or as using asylum as a cover for engaging in illegal activities of this kind, therefore posing a threat to the country of asylum. This became particularly visible as ISIS was losing ground in Syria and fighters enclaved in small areas, particularly in *Idlib*, many of them *jihadis* or associated with *Al Quaeda* or other terrorist organizations, have been seeking to flee following the refugee trail into Europe.

Reflecting such concerns, S.C. Resolution 1373 (2001) referred, *inter alia*, to a potential risk that refugee status might be abused for terrorist purposes. The Resolution urged states not to grant refugee status to asylum seekers who have planned, facilitated or participated in the commission of terrorist acts[110] and to prevent the abuse of refugee status by persons involved in such acts.[111]

108 In accordance with this principle, parties to a conflict must at all times distinguish between civilians and combatants and between civilian objects and military objectives. The latter are defined as "those objects which by their nature, location, purpose or use make an effective contribution to military action and whose total or partial destruction, capture or neutralization, in the circumstances applicable at the time, offers a definite military advantage" (Art. 52(2) of Additional Protocol I and Art. 1(f) of Additional Protocol II). Attacks may be directed only against combatants and military objects. Civilians lose their protection for such time as they participate directly in the hostilities (Art. 51(3) of Additional Protocol I, and Art. 13(3) of Additional Protocol II). *See also supra*, fn. 86.

109 For multilateral Conventions dealing with terrorism, *see supra*, 8.2.1, fn. 4.

110 Para. 3(f).

111 Para. 3(g).

In fact, Resolution 1373 did not introduce new obligations into international refugee law. Article 1F of the 1951 Convention on the Status of Refugees[112] contains provisions (exclusion clauses) ensuring that refugee status is not granted to persons who, although otherwise meeting the refugee criteria of Article 1,

> there are serious reasons for considering that they have committed a war crime, a crime against humanity, a serious non-political crime outside the country of refuge prior to admission to that country as a refugee, or have been guilty of acts contrary to the purposes and principles of the U.N.

Terrorist acts, although not specifically mentioned in the Convention, will fall within the ambit of the abovementioned crimes, i.e. either in the 'non-political crimes' category[113] or, most probably, in the even broader and rather unclear category of 'acts contrary to the purposes and principles of the U.N.' If so, the refugee status will be cancelled (*ex tunc*) or revoked (*ex nunc*).[114]

The UNHCR has addressed the issue of refugees and asylum seekers who may be involved in terrorist activities in the context of Guidelines on the application of exclusion clauses under the 1951 Convention.[115] The Guidelines place particular emphasis on the need that assessments regarding the exclusion clauses be made on a case-by-case basis, and applied with caution, i.e. in a restrictive manner. By contrast, a summary rejection of a request of asylum may amount to *refoulement*, i.e. expulsion or return of a refugee 'to the frontiers of territories where his life or freedom would be threatened on account of his race, religion, nationality, membership of a particular social group or political opinion' which is prohibited by international refugee law (principle of *non-refoulement*).[116] The exceptions allowed to *non-refoulement* are contained in Article 33(2) of the 1951 Convention and concern persons who have already been determined to be refugees and for

---

112 Convention relating to the status of refugees of 28 July 1951 as amended by the Protocol Relating to the Status of Refugees of 1967.

113 All sectoral conventions on terrorism exclude the qualification of 'political crime' for any terrorist act.

114 *See also* UNHCR, "Note on the cancellation of refugee status" (22 November 2004).

115 *See* UNHCR, Guidelines on International Protection No. 5: Application of the Exclusion Clauses: Art. 1F of the 1951 Convention relating to the Status of Refugees, pp. 115-122 (in particular paras. 25-27), contained in the Handbook and Guidelines on Procedures and Criteria for Determining Refugee Status under the 1951 Convention and the Protocol of 31 January 1967 Relating to the Status of Refugees, Geneva, 2011.

116 Art. 33(1).

whom there are reasonable grounds to believe that they represent a danger to the security of the country of asylum. Such danger may also derive from the fact that the refugee has been convicted for a particularly heinous crime.

Finally, the 1951 Convention provides for the possibility of expulsion to a third country on national security or public order grounds under Article 32.[117] Procedural requirements must be complied with in all cases.[118]

According to Paragraph 12 of General Comment No. 31 of the Human Rights Committee,[119] the ICCPR also confers an obligation on States

> not to extradite, deport, expel or otherwise remove a person from their territory, where there are substantial grounds for believing that there is a real risk of irreparable harm... either in the country to which removal is to be effected or in any country to which the person may subsequently be removed.

As already mentioned above, *refoulement* is absolutely prohibited under international law if there is a risk of torture or other cruel, inhuman or degrading treatment.[120] The obligation also applies in cases involving a risk of irreparable harm and in cases of arbitrary deprivation of life (including undue imposition of the death penalty), enforced disappearance, and exposure to a manifestly unfair trial.

---

117 Which provides: "1. The Contracting States shall not expel a refugee lawfully in their territory save on grounds of national security or public order. 2. The expulsion of such a refugee shall be only in pursuance of a decision reached in accordance with due process of law. Except where compelling reasons of national security otherwise require, the refugee shall be allowed to submit evidence to clear himself, and to appeal to and be represented for the purpose before competent authority or a person or persons specially designated by the competent authority. 3. The Contracting States shall allow such a refugee a reasonable period within which to seek legal admission into another country. The Contracting States reserve the right to apply during that period such internal measures as they may deem necessary."

118 Consisting in the issuance of decisions by competent authorities in accordance with rules of due process, and the possibility of appeal (Art. 32(2), *supra*, fn. 203).

119 Adopted on 29 March 2004 and referring to Art. 2(1) of the ICCPR.

120 *See, e.g.*, ECtHR, *Saadi v. Italy*, No. 37201/06, Judgment, 28 February 2008, paras. 123, 125-142; *Chahal v. United Kingdom*, N° 70/1995/576/662, Judgment, 15 November 1996, para. 74, both confirming *Soering v. the United Kingdom* No. 14038/88, Judgment, 7 July 1989.

9 Two Cases of Clash Between IHRL and Counterterrorism Measures

There are a number of instances where the clash between respect for international human rights law, international humanitarian law, refugee law as well as international criminal law on the one hand and anti-terrorism measures and counter-terrorism in general on the other, reaches a climax which creates an acute controversy, both on a domestic and on an international level. Two examples of such instances, a) Guantanamo Detainees and b) Targeted killings, are examined below.

9.1 Guantanamo Detainees

About 800 detainees captured by the U.S. and other allied forces in the war in Afghanistan as well as in the context of the 'global war on terror' declared against terrorism by former U.S. President *George Bush* following the 'September 11' attacks, have been held in the U.S. military base on Guantanamo Bay, Cuba, where some are still being held.[1] The case of these detainees has raised a host of legal issues, both at the domestic level in the U.S. and also from the viewpoint of international law. These questions are related, *inter alia*, with the 'global war on terror' paradigm, with human rights violations and with the extraterritorial application of the ICCPR.

9.1.1 Global War on Terror

Following the 2001 terrorist attacks against the U.S. on American soil, the paradigm put forward by the Bush administration in its fight against terrorism was that of 'global war on terror'.[2] The phrase is a neologism which does not derive from or conform to any legal definition or perception of 'international armed conflict' as enshrined in relevant international texts which are universally accepted (such as the U.N. Charter or the Geneva Conventions). It would therefore seem to be a political catch-phrase rather than a legal

1 The first detainees started arriving at Guantanamo Bay detention facility on 11 January 2002. Under the Bush Administration over 500 detainees were transferred or released to other countries. The Obama Administration transferred 197. Until 2018 there were 41 detainees held there (Human Rights First, Guantanamo by the Numbers, Fact Sheet February 2018, available at: www.humanrightsfirst.org/sites/default/files/gtmo-by-the-numbers.pdf, last accessed 22 April 2018).

2 On the basis of the Authorization granted to the President to use all "necessary and appropriate force" against those whom he determined "planned, authorized, committed or aided" the September 11 attacks, or who harboured these persons or groups (AUMF).

term which could be evaluated in a legal context. However, it was not devoid of substantive meaning, which consisted in the proposition that the U.S. was engaged in an armed conflict with *Al-Qaeda*, i.e. one against non-state actors (therefore of a non-international character)[3] which could take place beyond the geographical limits of the then hot battlefield (Afghanistan or Iraq), and be fought out anywhere in the world including in countries which were not in any way involved with or were unaware of the presence of terrorists on their territory. As such, the 'global war on terror' paradigm was widely contested. The *Obama* administration expressly abandoned it, still insisting, however, on the existence of a war outside Afghanistan.[4] It claimed, in fact, that the U.S. was facing a growing threat from *Al Qaeda* affiliates all over the world, who also maintained bases in Yemen, Somalia, the Maghreb and the Sahel.

Again, this perception met with a lot of circumspection on the part of most scholars, who doubted whether the *Obama* doctrine was, in reality, substantially different from 'global war on terror'.

9.1.2 Human Rights Violations

Another issue, the most important one, is that of the long list of human rights violations registered in *Guantanamo*, among which the violation of the prohibition of torture or other cruel, inhuman or degrading treatment or punishment, arbitrary detention, discrimination, as well as numerous violations of due process rules. Although the *Obama* administration stopped torture practices and gradually transferred many prisoners abroad, it left a number of detainees indefinitely without charges.[5] The policies of the *Trump* Administration on the matter have been expressed to be the expansion of the use of Guantanamo.[6]

3 *Hamdan v. Rumsfeld*, 548 U.S. 557, 2006, para. 4. d. ii.

4 *See* The *Obama* Administration and International Law, Keynote Address by Harold Koh, Legal Adviser, Department of State, at the Annual Meeting of the American Society of International Law, 25 March 2010. *See also* Christine Gray, Targeted Killings: Recent U.S. Attempts to Create a Legal Framework, Paper No. 52/2013, November 2013, Legal Studies Research Paper Series, University of Cambridge.

5 Of the 41 detainees currently at Guantanamo, 28 "have been held as enemy combatants, but without charge, for up to 16 years" (Donald Trump vs. Guantánamo's Forever Prisoners, New York Times, Editorial Board, 16 January 2018, available at: www.nytimes.com/2018/01/16/opinion/trump-guantanamo-prisoners.html). On 10 January 2019 there were still 40 detainees at Guantanamo (Amnesty International, News, USA Penal Institutions).

6 *Ibid.* Also, New York Times, Charlie Savage and Adam Goldman, 18 August 2017, Trump Officials Renew Effort to Expand Use of – Prison at Guantánamo, available at www.nytimes.com/2017/08/18/US/politics/trump-guantanamo-executive-order.html, last accessed 1 March 2018. Also, New York Times, Aisha I. Saad and Zoe A. Y. Weinberg, Remember Guantánamo? March 15, 2018 (Opinion), last accessed 13 October 2018.

9.1.2.1 Extraterritorial Application of the ICCPR[7]

Human rights violations in Guantanamo base are closely connected to the position of the U.S. which does not accept the extraterritorial application of the 1966 U.N. Covenant on Civil and Political rights (ICCPR), maintaining that the latter's scope of application is limited within the U.S. territory. As the base lies on Cuban soil, the U.S. therefore considers that it is not bound by the obligations provided for in that instrument.[8]

9.1.3 Military Commissions

Military Commissions were authorized to try suspected terrorists since President *Bush* issued, in November 2001, a Military Order to that effect.[9] The Order provided that persons falling under its provisions would not be able to appeal a decision or to obtain any other relief before the U.S. Courts. However, in *Rasul v. Bush*,[10] the Supreme Court ruled that the U.S. had operational sovereignty over Guantanamo base.[11] As a result, the U.S. courts had jurisdiction to hear *habeas corpus* petitions of foreign nationals suspected of terrorism held at Guantanamo base who had henceforth the right to challenge their imprisonment. The Supreme Court thus invalidated, in essence, the abovementioned provision of the Military Order.[12, 13] Congress then enacted the Detainee Treatment Act of 2005. Although the Act did not authorize military commissions, it revoked all judicial jurisdiction over *habeas* claims by persons detained as 'enemy combatants'.[14, 15] Furthermore, it created jurisdiction in the Court of Appeals for the District of Columbia Circuit to hear appeals of final decisions of military commissions.

In its seminal judgment on *Hamdan v. Rumsfeld* of 2006,[16] the Supreme Court held that it could exercise jurisdiction over a case which was already pending before it. The Supreme Court also found that the Bush Presidency lacked constitutional authority to

7 On the extraterritorial application of IHRL generally, *see supra*, p. 12.

8 Marko Milanovic, Foreign Surveillance and Human Rights, Part 2, Interpreting the ICCPR, EJIL Talk, 26 November 2013; Beth Van Schaack, The United States' Position on the Extraterritorial Application of Human Rights Obligations: Now is the Time for Change, International Law Studies, Naval War College, vol. 90, 2014.

9 Detention, Treatment and Trial of Certain non-Citizens in the War Against Terrorism, 1(a), 66 Fed. Reg. 57, 833(November 16, 2001).

10 542 U.S. 466 (2004).

11 The area where Guantanamo base is located in Cuba remains Cuban territory which has been leased to the U.S.

12 The Court therefore overturned the precedent set in *Johnson v. Eisentrager* (1950).

13 In connection with U.N. citizens detained as suspected enemy combatants, the Court found, in *Hamdi v. Rumsfeld* (2004), that they had the right to *habeas corpus* challenge of their detention.

14 By amending title 28, U.S. Code.

15 According to section 1005(e) of the Act: "[N]o court, justice, or judge shall have jurisdiction to hear or consider an application for a writ of habeas corpus filed by or on behalf of an alien detained at the Department of Defence at Guantanamo Bay, Cuba."

16 *Hamdam v. Rumsfeld*, 548 U.S. 557 (2006).

create the Guantanamo military commissions as a system separate from the existing federal and military justice systems without congressional approval. Congress could authorize the use of military commissions, but they were required to follow procedural rules similar to those applicable in court martial proceedings, in accordance with the Uniform Code of Military Justice. The Supreme Court also confirmed the unlawfulness, under domestic and international law, of the use of torture and cruel and humiliating treatment by the U.S. Government.

In response, Congress passed the Military Commissions Act of 2006, which authorized military commissions and established procedural rules which followed, although with some important deviations, the Uniform Code. The 2006 Act also amended the Detainee Treatment Act, taking away from the judiciary *habeas* jurisdiction in all cases brought by detainees, including pending ones. The Act allowed, *inter alia*, trials *in absentia*, and the introduction of coerced evidence while it denied the accused full access to exculpatory evidence.

The Military Commissions restarted their functions following the issuance, by the Department of Defence, of regulations relating to the conduct of their proceedings pursuant to the Military Commissions Act 2006. In June 2007, the Supreme Court agreed to hear outstanding *habeas corpus*, opening up the possibility that they might overturn some or all of the provisions of the Military Commissions Act.

In June 2008, the Supreme Court issued an important judgment, *Boumediene v. Bush*, ruling that the Guantanamo detainees were entitled to the protection of the U.S. Constitution, and that they had the right to bring petitions for a writ of *habeas corpus* before the U.S. courts.

Upon taking office in January 2009, President *Obama* halted the functions of Military Commissions in order to review the situation. In May 2009, the Administration stated that it was considering restarting the military commissions system making certain changes to the procedural rules. Finally, a new Military Commissions Act was enacted in 28 October 2009 adopting some of the proposals submitted by the *Obama* Administration.[17] The changes concerned a limited number of points. Thus, *inter alia*, the definition of 'cruel or inhuman treatment' which under the Military Commissions Act 2006 was as provided by U.S. domestic law, was modified to refer to treatment that constitutes a grave breach of common Art. 3 of the Geneva Conventions, regardless of where the crime takes place or of the nationality of the victim. In connection with the death penalty, the 2006 Act under which an accused sentenced to death could waive but not withdraw an appeal, was modified by the 2009 Act so that the accused could neither waive nor withdraw the appeal.

17 For an analysis of the Military Commissions Act of 2009, *see* Jennifer K. Elsea, *Legislative Attorney, Congressional Research Service, The Military Commissions Act of 2009: Overview and Legal Issues*, 2010.

9.1.4 *Concluding remarks*

Eighteen years since the first detainees arrived at Guantanamo prison, successive Administrations and successive changes in legislation have not managed to correct a situation of continuing violations of the human rights of those still held there. It is, furthermore, doubtful whether this state of affairs is going to change in the near future.

9.2 Targeted Killings

9.2.1 *Introduction*

The term 'targeted killings'[18] became widely known in recent years and, lacking legal definition, is used empirically in the context of the struggle against terrorism to denote practices consisting in eliminating specific individuals who, according to those deciding the killing, represent a terrorist threat.

Targeted killings constitute an avowed or semi-avowed policy of a number of states which has significantly increased in the last decades particularly as a response to 'asymmetric warfare'. Most of the states which resort to it do not, as a rule, publicly admit

18 On this and connected topics *see* Reports by Ben Emmerson, Special Rapporteur on the Promotion and Protection of Human Rights and Fundamental Freedoms while Countering Terrorism: A/HRC/34/61, 21 February 2017 (Advance edited version) and A/HRC/25/59, 28 February.2.2014; Markus Gunneflo, Targeted killing: A Legal and Political History, New York: Cambridge University Press, 2016; Report by Philip Alston, Special Rapporteur on Extrajudicial, Summary or Arbitrary executions, Study on Targeted Killings, A/HRC/14/24, Add. 6, 28 May.5.2010; Report by Christof Heyns, Special Rapporteur on extrajudicial, summary or arbitrary executions, on issues regarding armed drones and the right to life, A/68/382, 13 September.9.2013; Report by Martin Scheinin, Special Rapporteur on the promotion and protection of human rights and fundamental freedoms while countering terrorism (*see* UNGA doc. A/61/267, 16 August.8.2006 and Human Rights Council doc. A/HRC/4/26 of 29 January.1.2007, paras. 74-78); Nils Melzer, *Targeted Killing in International Law* (2008); Gabriella Blum and Phillip Heymann, Law and Targeted Killing, *Harvard National Security Journal*, Vol. I, 27 June.6.2010; Christine Gray, *International Law and the Use of Force*, 2008; Marco Sassoli and Laura M. Olson, The Relationship Between International Humanitarian Law and Human Rights Law Where it Matters: Admissible Killing and Internment of Fighters in Non- International Armed Conflicts, 90 *Int'l Rev. Red Cross*, pp. 599-627, September 2008; Marco Sassoli, *Transnational Armed Groups and International Humanitarian Law*, HPCR Paper Series, Winter 2006; C. J. Greenwood, War, Terrorism and International Law, in *Essays on War in International Law*, Cameron May, 2006; Helen Duffy, *The War on Terror and the Framework of International Law*, Cambridge University Press, 2005; Ronald Otto, *Targeted Killings and International Law: With Special Regard to Human Rights and International Humanitarian Law*, Springer, 2012.

doing so. Thus, Israel, which had been conducting such operations since 1972 following the assassination of Israeli athletes in the Munich Olympics,[19] made public its policy of targeted killings of alleged terrorists only in 2000, invoking self-defence.[20] In the context of its armed fight against *Al-Qaeda, the Taliban* and forces associated to them, the U.S. has conducted targeted killings in Afghanistan, Pakistan,[21] Yemen, Iraq, Somalia, Libya and elsewhere,[22] the most notorious case being that of *Usama Bin Laden* in Pakistan in 2011.[23] The U.K. reportedly had conducted several targeted killings in Northern Ireland until the 1990s,[24] while similar reports have Russia carrying out such killings in Chechnya.[25] As a rule, however, these operations are shrouded in secrecy, despite some (unsuccessful) efforts to promote transparency and accountability in their regard.[26]

From a historical perspective, the practice of targeted killing is not new, the closest terms used in the past being those of 'political assassination' and 'political crime'. Today other related terms, not necessarily identical to targeted killings, are 'extrajudicial', 'summary' and 'arbitrary' executions. Generally, 'targeted killings' is a wider term which may include any of the above notions. As seen below, a targeted killing may, under certain conditions, be legal, while 'extrajudicial', 'summary' and 'arbitrary' executions are always illegal.[27]

---

19 In the Case of *Public Committee Against Torture in Israel v. The Government of Israel* (the *Targeted Killings* case), Israeli Supreme Court, Judgment, 2006, the Court held that the legality of targeted killings has to be determined on an individual basis, excluding any general pronouncement about whether targeted killings are lawful or unlawful. The Court determined that the law applicable on the matter was the customary law of international armed conflict and rejected the justification put forward by the Israeli Government that terrorists were 'unlawful combatants'. It held, instead, that under certain conditions it was lawful to kill civilians as long as they 'directly participated in hostilities'.

20 The number of such killings, usually targeting members of groups such as *Fatah, Hamas,* and *Islamic Jihad,* is in the hundreds – *see,* indicatively, Israel Counter-Terrorism, Targeted killing of terrorists (Updated May 2017) in the *Jewish Virtual Library,* accessed at www.jewishvirtuallibrary.org, on 31 October 2018; *see also* Orna Ben-Naftali and Keren R. Michaeli, We Must Not Make a Scarecrow of the Law': A Legal Analysis of the Israeli Policy of Targeted Killing, Cornell International Law Journal, Spring 2003. Also "Attacks on Gaza jihadists signal quiet Israeli revival of targeted killings," *Haaretz,* 26 July 2014.

21 Mainly in the area of *Waziristan,* the Federally Administered Tribal Areas (FATA) in the North of the country.

22 *See also infra,* section 9.2.3.6.

23 *Usama bin Laden* was killed in *Abbottabad,* in Northeastern Pakistan, in May 2011, in an operation by the code name 'Neptune Spear'. The U.S. Administration justified the killing on the basis of *bin Laden* being the leader of an enemy force and a legitimate target in their armed conflict with *Al Quaeda.* They also argued that *bin Laden* continued to pose an imminent threat to the United States. On this subject, *see* Harold Hongiu Koh, 'The Lawfulness of the U.S. Operation against Usama bin Laden,' http://opiniojuris.org/2011/05/19/the-lawfulness-of-the US-operation-against-Usama-bin laden.

24 In 2015, two British ISIS fighters, *Reyaad Khan and Ruhul Amin,* were killed by British drones in *Raqqa,* Syria (The Guardian, 7 September 2015).

25 Russia started its military operations in Chechnya in 1999 as a counter-terrorism operation. In that context it claimed killing warlord *Omar Ibn al Khattab* in 2002 (The Guardian, 26 April 2002). Russian security agents also killed, in 2006, Chechen warlord *Shamil Basayev,* who had claimed responsibility for the *Beslan* School attack in 2004, in which 331 people, half of them children, were killed (CNN, 17 July 2006).

26 *See infra.*

27 *Infra,* pp. 72 *et seq. See also* Philip Alston Report, *supra,* p. 53, fn. 212, p. 5, para. 10.

9.2.2 *Definition and Context*

In his Report to the Human Rights Council, *Philip Alston*[28] proposes the following definition of targeted killing:

> A targeted killing is the intentional, premeditated and deliberate use of lethal force by states or their agents acting under color of law, or by an organized armed group in armed conflict, against a specific individual who is not in the physical custody of the perpetrator.[29]

Targeted killings carried out by a state[30] may take place on its own territory – or on territory under its jurisdiction – or on the territory of another state. The persons targeted may be of that state's own or of a different nationality. Targeted killings can, furthermore, take place either in the context of an armed conflict or in time of peace. They may also be carried out either by the armed forces of a state[31] or by secret operations conducted by its intelligence agents.[32, 33]

Targeted killings carried out on a state's own territory will be governed by the domestic law of that state (including the relevant international law obligations which are binding on it). Generally, such killings may, depending on the circumstances, be or claimed by the state conducting them to be an act of law enforcement which, if not in compliance with human rights law, will constitute a violation of the human right to life of the targeted person(s), and a criminal act (murder) under domestic law for the persons who planned, decided on and materially perpetrated the crime (an agent or other person acting upon that state's orders).[34]

When the targeted killing or killings are committed abroad, the justifications usually put forward by the state which has carried them out are: a) that the targeted killing was

28 *Ibid.* p. 4, para. 1.

29 *See also* the definition of Nils Melzer *(op. cit., supra,* pp. 3-4*)* which describes a targeted killing as the "use of lethal force by a subject of international law that is directed against an individually selected person who is not in custody and that is intentional (rather than negligent or reckless), premeditated (rather than merely voluntary), and deliberate (meaning that 'the death of the targeted person [is] the actual aim of the operation, as opposed to deprivations of life which, although intentional and premeditated, remain the incidental result of an operation pursuing other aims)."

30 This is the most common case which involves the most serious issues of international law. Targeted killings committed by non-state actors are governed by the domestic law of the states concerned including the relevant anti-terrorism conventions. If the non-state actors involved in the killing are parties to a non-international conflict, the applicable law will be the IHL governing such conflicts.

31 Such was the case of the *Bin Laden* killing in Pakistan, which was carried out by U.S. *Navy Seals.*

32 Exemplified by the killing by Israel of *Hamas* military leader *Al-Mahbouh*, in a hotel in Dubai in 2010.

33 There are differences in the law which is applicable in each one of these cases and, consequently, in the treatment of the perpetrators of the killing(s) – *see* the Philip Alston Report, *supra.*

34 If not carried out in the context of law enforcement or if the law enforcement operation exceeds permissible limits under international law, *see infra,*.

carried out in self-defence[35] pursuant to Article 51(1) of the U.N. Charter,[36] following a terrorist attack launched from the territory of the state where the targeted killing was carried out (territorial state) and which (terrorist attack) the territorial state was either unable or unwilling to prevent; b) that it has acted with the consent of the territorial state[37]; c) that there is a state of international armed conflict between itself and the territorial state or of non-international conflict between itself and the non-state actors who performed the terrorist attack. These justifications correspond to different branches of international law, namely the law relating to interstate use of force, international humanitarian law and international human rights law. Here we shall examine the relevance and applicability of the invoked rules in connection with the justifications proposed. Connected issues will also be examined, where relevant.

9.2.3 *Targeted Killings Conducted in Self-Defence*

9.2.3.1 The Wider Issue: Self-Defence Against Non-State Actors

The question of targeted killings conducted by a state in self-defence, a matter which concerns *jus ad bellum* is, in principle, inscribed within the overarching one whether a state may exercise its right of self-defence 'against an armed attack', as provided in Article 51 of the U.N. Charter, conducted not only by another state which acts in violation of Article 2(4) of the U.N. Charter – a rule of *jus cogens* character – but also by non-state actors. Although the classical approach would be to restrict the right to self-defence to the former case only, i.e. where the aggressor is a state, legal doctrine and jurisprudence were compelled to consider, in view of the increasing number of attacks by non-state actors in recent years, the possibility that self-defence might also be exercised against an armed attack by such actors. Despite, however, the extensive study of the matter particularly following the 2001 terrorist attacks in the U.S. and some jurisprudential attempts thereon, there is still no certainty as to the recognition of such a legal possibility. Before the 2001 attacks, in the *Case Concerning Military and Paramilitary Activities in and against*

---

35 According to Art. 21 of the Draft Articles on State Responsibility "The wrongfulness of an act of a State is precluded if the act constitutes a lawful measure of self-defence taken in conformity with the Charter of the United Nations".

36 Which is as follows: "Nothing in the present Charter shall impair the inherent right of individual or collective self-defence if an armed attack occurs against a Member of the United Nations, until the Security Council has taken measures necessary to maintain international peace and security. Measures taken by Members in the exercise of this right of self-defence shall be immediately reported to the Security Council and shall not in any way affect the authority and responsibility of the Security Council under the present Charter to take at any time such action as it deems necessary in order to maintain or restore international peace and security."

37 Where a state willingly accepts the activities of non-state actors against another state to be conducted from its territory, it would be considered as endorsing such action. If that action amounted to armed attack, it would therefore justify the exercise of self-defence.

Nicaragua,[38] the ICJ, although recognizing that Article 3(g) of GA Resolution 3314 of 1974 on the Definition of Aggression, 'armed attack' also includes attacks by 'armed bands, groups, irregulars, or mercenaries', concluded that they must have been sent 'by or on behalf of a State' (which should have 'effective control' of the military or paramilitary operations for its responsibility to arise).[39, 40] In 2004, the Court seemed to endorse this position again – although not in a direct manner – in its Advisory Opinion on the *Legal Consequences of the Construction of a Wall in the Occupied Palestinian Territory* (Wall Opinion).[41] Generally, the ICJ pronouncements after 9/11 demonstrate ambiguity in this respect,[42] while the matter appears to be also evaded in the 2001 Draft Articles on State Responsibility.[43] More assertive, on the other hand – without however being entirely clear – were S.C. Resolutions 1368 and 1373 of 2001[44] which elevated the 2011 Al Qaeda terrorist attacks in the U.S. to 'a threat to international peace and security'. In any event, the conduct of states following the 9/11 attacks implicitly manifested the acceptance of the right of self-defence of the U.S. and supported *Operation 'Enduring Freedom'* against Afghanistan[45] as legitimate exercise of that right.

9.2.3.2 Theories in Relation to Self-Defence Against Non-State Actors

One of these theories claims that customary international law – which, according to its proponents, has not been superseded by Article 51 of the U.N. Charter[46] – allows action in self-defence against an armed attack by non-state actors (which would include terrorists). To strengthen their argument, they indicate that in contrast to its Article 2(4), Article 51 of the U.N. Charter does not expressly refer to a 'state' as the generator of an attack which gives rise to a right of self-defence. They also put special emphasis on the fact that the right of self-defence is qualified as 'inherent' in Article 51 which, they claim,

38 *Nicaragua v. United States of America*, Judgment, 27 June.6.1986, I.C.J. Reports 1986, p. 14.

39 *Ibid.*, para. 115.

40 *Ibid.*, para. 194.

41 *Legal Consequences of the Construction of a Wall in the Occupied Palestinian Territory*, Advisory Opinion, 9 July 2004, I. C. J. Reports 2004, p. 136, para. 139.

42 *As reflected in "Armed Activities on the Territory of the Congo" (DRC v. Uganda)*, ICJ Reports (2005) 168, para. 147. *See also* Christine Gray, *International Law and the Use of Force*, Oxford University Press, 3rd edn. 2008, pp. 133-36.

43 Art. 8 of the articles provides that: "The conduct of a person or group of persons shall be considered an act of a State under international law if the person or group of persons is in fact acting on the instructions of, or under the direction or control of that State in carrying out the conduct." (Draft Articles on Responsibility of States for Internationally Wrongful Acts, in Report of the International Law Commission on the Work of Its Fifty-third Session, U.N. GAOR, 56th Sess., Supp. No. 10, at 43, U.N. Doc. A/56/10 (2001), *available at* www.org.un/law/ilc).

44 S/RES/1368 (2001) adopted on 12 September 2001 and S/RES/1373 (2001) adopted on 28 September 2001.

45 Then ruled by the *Taliban* and accused of providing safe haven to *Al Qaeda* and *Usama bin Laden.*

46 Concerning Art. 51 itself, it is generally accepted that it deliberately uses the notion of 'armed attack' instead of the much wider term 'use of force' appearing in Art. 2(4) of the Charter, in order to restrict the possibility to exercise self-defence to serious cases. The term 'armed attack' forms part of the Definition of Aggression in UNGA Res. 3314.

proves exactly that this article has not superseded customary international law on the matter. Thus, it is argued, the exercise of self-defence against non-state actors is possible. Inevitably, these views were substantially strengthened in the wake of the 2001 *Al Qaeda* attacks in New York and Washington. They also found support in the abovementioned S.C. Resolutions 1368 and 1373, adopted right after 11 September 2001,[47] as well as in NATO's invocation of Article 5 collective self-defence provision[48] following these attacks.

Many of these ideas have been espoused, as will be seen below, by the U.S. doctrine on the matter, particularly after 9/11,[49] although with various fluctuations according to the Administrations in power at each time.

The degree of intensity of the action undertaken by non-state actors required for it to be considered an 'armed attack', against which there is a right of self-defence, is another subject of controversy. The jurisprudence of the ICJ asserts that sporadic, low-intensity attacks do not attain the level of armed attack that would justify the invocation of self-defence.[50] The same goes for assistance provided to rebels "in the form of the provision of weapons or logistical or other support."[51] However, here again there are opinions which advocate more flexibility, i.e. allowing self-defence even in cases where the armed attack is less than full-fledged. These views also support a less constraining interpretation of the principles of necessity and proportionality in connection with self-defence, in the sense of allowing self-defence to be resorted to more easily by attributing less '*gravitas*' to them.[52] In the same vein, they suggest that less deference should be paid to the principle of territorial integrity when self-defence is being exercised.[53]

According to another theory put forward by some U.S. scholars, legitimate self-defence would obviate the applicability of IHL and IHRL ('robust' self-defence).[54] The theory has met with strong criticism, the main argument being that it confuses ('conflates') *jus ad bellum* and *jus in bello*.[55] Its proponents draw their theory from the ICJ Nuclear

47 S/RES 1368(2001), of 12 September 2001, S/RES/1372 (2001) of 28 September 2001.

48 Press Release, North Atlantic Council, 12 Sept. 2001, *available at* www.nato.int/docu/pr/2001/p01-124e.htm.

49 As formulated by the Parks Memorandum and Abraham D. Sofaer (*see infra*, 9.2.3.6, fn. 91.

50 *Military and Paramilitary Activities, supra*,,1986,14; *Oil Platforms* (*Iran v. US*), 2003 ICJ 161, 6 November 2003; *Armed Activities (DRC v. Uganda)*, 2005 ICJ 116, 19 December 2005; *Wall Opinion*, 2004, ICJ 136.

51 *Military and Paramilitary Activities, supra*, 1986, 14, at 104.

52 The principles of necessity and proportionality which also apply in the case of self-defence are aimed at halting and repelling an attack and not being retaliatory or punitive (*see* Declaration on Principles of International Law concerning Friendly Relations and Co-operation among States in accordance with the Charter of the United Nations (UNGA Res. 2625(XXV)).

53 Sofaer, *supra*.

54 Kenneth Anderson, Targeted killings in U.S. Counterterrorism Strategy and law, available at: www.brookings.edu/papers/2009/0511_counterterrorism_anderson.aspx; Kenneth Anderson, Predators over Pakistan, *The Weekly Standard*, 8 March 2010; Michael Dennis, 'Non application of civil and political rights treaties extraterritorially during times of armed conflict', 2007 (40) *Israel Law Review* 453. For a response to this theory *see* Philip Alston, *supra*, fn. 226, p. 13 *et seq.*

55 Christopher Greenwood, The Relationship between *jus ad bellum* and *jus in bello, Review of International Studies*, 1983, 221, 222-23.

Weapons Advisory Opinion, according to which, while "the threat or use of nuclear weapons would generally" violate IHL, it could not conclude that such threat or use "would be lawful or unlawful in an extreme circumstance of self-defence, in which the very survival of a State would be at stake."[56]

This finding itself has been criticized as creating confusion.[57] Its critics assume that its aim is to address the most extreme of situations where a state's very survival is hanging in the balance and it is not, therefore, applicable in less crucial circumstances. In any event, this theory is unambiguously dangerous as would be any theory supporting the non-application of IHL in armed conflict or occupation. In recognition of such danger, the Draft Articles on State Responsibility make it abundantly clear that states may not invoke self-defence as justification for their violations of IHL.[58]

A view which has been expressed in connection with self-defence in response to attacks by non-state actors is that a higher degree of violence by such actors would be required to justify the exercise of self-defence than would be the case if the armed attack were conducted by another state.[59] There is no real justification, in our view, as to why it should be so.

9.2.3.3 Anticipatory and Pre-emptive Self-Defence[60]

Under Article 51 of the U.N. Charter, the right to self-defence may be exercised only after an attack has manifested itself.[61] Nevertheless, a number of arguments have promoted a more expansive perception of the matter. Among them is one which claims that customary international law allows anticipatory self-defence. Other arguments are based on pragmatic factors, primarily that if self-defence is delayed until the armed attack has taken place, it is very probable that it will be already too late for the attacked state to exercise self-defence effectively. The restrictive position replies that a wide interpretation of self-defence would allow its use as pretext for launching an armed attack, and that it

56 ICJ, *Legality of the Threat or Use of Nuclear Weapons*, Advisory Opinion, 8 July 1996, para. 25.

57 Christopher Greenwood, The Advisory Opinion on Nuclear Weapons and the Contribution of the International Court to International Humanitarian Law, *Int'l Rev. Red Cross*, No. 316, 1997, p. 65; Jasmine Moussa, Can JUS. Ad Bellum Override Jus in Bello? Reaffirming the Separation of the Two Bodies of Law, *Int'l Rev. Red Cross*, No. 872, 2008, p. 963.

58 ILC, Draft Articles on State Responsibility at 166-167.

59 *See* The Chatham House Principles of International Law on the Use of Force by States in Self-Defence (2005), principle 6; and Leiden Policy Recommendations on Counter-terrorism and International Law, Grotius Centre for International Legal Studies (2010), para. 38; Also, Klaus Kreß, Some reflections on the International Legal Framework Governing Transnational Armed Conflicts, p. 251.

60 *See* Anthony Clark Arend International Law and the Preemptive Use of Military Force, *The Washington Quarterly*, Spring 2003; Leo Van Den Hole, *Anticipatory Self-Defence under International Law*, 2003; Kinga Tibori Szabo, *Anticipatory Action in Self-Defence, Essence and Limits under International Law*, The Hague, 2011.

61 On this 'restrictive' interpretation of Art. 51 *see*, for instance, Ian Brownlie, *The Use of Force in Self-Defence*, 1961; Hans Kelsen, *Principles of International Law*, 61, 1952; Yoram Dinstein, *War, Aggression and Self-Defence*, Cambridge, 2001; Michael Glennon, The fog of Law: Self-defense, inherence and incoherence in article 51 of the United Nations Charter, 25, *Harvard J.L. & PUB. POL'Y* 539, 547, 2002.

leaves the door open to errors and mistaken interpretations of the true intentions of the potential aggressor who, despite indications to the contrary, may not, in the end, proceed to the attack. The matter is extremely delicate, which explains why both views have found significant support. It would seem, however, that the more 'expansive' one – i.e. that which recognizes a broader possibility to claim self-defence (anticipatory self-defence) – is supported by the majority of writers[62] and is reflected in most state practice. According to its terms, which follow the *Caroline Case* formula,[63] self-defence includes the right to use force against a real and imminent threat when "the necessity of that self-defence is instant, overwhelming, and leaving no choice of means, and no moment of deliberation"[64] (setting out the principles of 'necessity', 'proportionality' and 'immediacy').

A further view which has at times been reflected in U.S. policy but generally lacks substantial support is that which would allow 'pre-emptive self-defence', i.e. the use of force even when a threat is not imminent and 'uncertainty remains as to the time and place of the enemy's attack'.[65, 66]

With regard to targeted killings, undertaken in anticipatory self-defence, which is often the case, it seems that the pattern to be followed in order to assess their legitimacy under international law would be the same as in the case of self-defence against non-state actors in general. Targeted killings as pre-emptive self-defence would, on the other hand, be *ab initio* illegal.

9.2.3.4 Self-Defence (Including by Targeted Killings) in the Case of 'Unable or Unwilling' State

A targeted killing operation has been claimed to be legally possible if the territorial state is unable or unwilling to prevent a terrorist group from using its territory for launching attacks against the state carrying out the killing or is providing safe haven to that terrorist group – and could, in fact, be directed against both, the non-state actors and the unable or

62 *See*, for instance, D.W. Bowett, *Self-defence in international law*, pp. 188-192, Manchester University Press, 1958; D.P. O'Connell, International law, 1970, 317-318, Oscar Schachter, The right of states to use armed force, 82 *Mich. L. Rev.* 1984, 1620, 1633-35.

63 Letter from Mr. Webster to Lord Ashburton, 6 August 1842, in R. Y. Jennings, The Caroline and McLeod cases, *American Journal of International Law*, vol. 32, No. 1, January 1938.

64 *Ibid. See* Yoram Dinstein, War, Aggression and Self-defense, Cambridge, 2001, at 167. Also Thomas M. Franck, *Recourse to Force: State Action Against Threats and Armed Attacks*, 2002, 107.

65 "The National Strategy of the United States," Washington DC, Office of the White House, 2002, at 15. *See also* Christine Gray, The U.S. national security strategy and the new 'Bush Doctrine' on preemptive self-defence, 2002, 1 Chinese JIL 437.

66 As Leo Van Den Hole rightly observes, "Without the sine qua non of necessity, proportionality and immediacy, anticipatory self-defence becomes nothing more than a slippery slope of naked aggression" (Anticipatory Self-Defence Under International Law, *American University International Law Review*, Vol. 19, Issue I, p. 106, 2003).

unwilling state. This theory has been developed by a number of scholars[67] and by the U.S. in the broader context of justifying the element of 'necessity' in exercising self-defence against non-state actors.[68] It has not, however, been widely supported by legal theory or state practice, while even when used, the parameters invoked have been wavering.[69, 70] Indeed, an assertion of inability or unwillingness on the part of the state invoking self-defence so as to justify the necessity of its action, may of course be highly subjective and it is up to it to provide proof in support of the existence of such necessity. At the very least, that state should show that it had asked the territorial state to take action on the matter, and that its request went unheeded.

9.2.3.5 Lawfulness of Self-Defence Claim

According to Article 51 of the U.N. Charter, measures adopted by states in exercise of self-defence must be reported to the Security Council.[71] This would also cover the case where self-defence is exercised against non-state actors (including by targeted killings). The process serves the need to keep the S.C. informed on a matter which has the potential of putting international peace and security at risk. At the same time, it presumably serves the purpose of checking the lawfulness of the action taken by the reporting state. Nevertheless, as failure to report does not impinge on such lawfulness, that purpose remains unfulfilled. Article 51 goes on to provide that the right to self-defence continues until the Security Council has taken measures necessary to maintain international peace and security. The structure of this process, although containing some elements of potential legality control, does not in any way satisfy its requirements. Such control may, of course, be done by the S.C. by means of a relevant resolution, but this is only a probability. An ICJ pronouncement on the matter remains, on the other hand, the best option but it usually comes late, if at all.

9.2.3.6 The U.S. Doctrine on Self-Defence Against Non-State Actors (Including by Targeted Killings)

It has already been noted that the U.S. adopted a targeted killing program after the 9/11 attacks. Originally such killings took place in Afghanistan in the context of the war there,

---

67 Among which Paulina Starski, Right to Self-Defense, Attribution and the Non-State Actor – Birth of the "Unable or Unwilling" Standard? 2015, Max-Planck-Institut für ausländisches öffentliches Recht und Völkerrecht, available at: www.zaoerv.de/75_2015/75_2015_3_a_455_502.pdf

68 *See* letter dated 23 September 2014 from the Permanent Representative of the United States of America to the U.N. Secretary-General, U.N. Doc. S/2014/695, 23 September 2014. The letter announced the launch of an air campaign against ISIS on Syrian territory and put forward as justification the inability and lack of will of Syria to confront the 'safe havens' of ISIS in the country.

69 *See* Olivier Corten, The 'Unwilling or Unable' Test: Has it Been, and Could it be Accepted? Leiden Journal of International Law,2016, 29, pp. 777-799.

70 Daniel Bethlehem, "Self-defense against an actual or imminent armed attack by non-State actors," *American Journal of International Law*, vol. 106, No. 4 (2012), pp. 770 and 776.

71 *Nicaragua v. United States*, para. 235; *Armed Activities in the Territory of the Congo*, para. 145.

expanding in 2002 to Yemen, where the first such killing was that of the alleged *Al Qaeda* leader *Ali Qaed Senyan al-Harithi*, thought to be responsible for the USS Cole bombing, and five other men. It was also in Yemen that the first U.S. citizen, *Anwar Al-Awlaki*,[72] was killed in 2011, causing significant legal controversy in the U.S. Targeted killings operations in large numbers were also conducted in Pakistan where the 'emblematic' killing of *Usama bin Laden* took place in 2011, as well as in Somalia and Libya.

Mention has been made above of the U.S. positions concerning specific terrorism issues. In its 2016 'Report on the Legal and Policy Frameworks Guiding the United States' Use of Military Force and Related National Security Operations',[73] then President *Obama* expressed the Administration's support for the inherent right of self-defence against non-state actors in general. In this connection, the Report made specific mention of the Caroline incident[74] as proof of precedent anterior to the 9/11 attacks. It also supported that the right of self-defence may be exercised not only after the attack has occurred but also where it is imminent. To do so, it took account of a variety of factors, including

> the nature and immediacy of the threat; the probability of an attack; whether the anticipated attack is part of a concerted pattern of continuing armed activity; the likely scale of the attack and the injury, loss, or damage likely to result therefrom in the absence of mitigating action; and the likelihood that there will be other opportunities to undertake effective action in self-defence that may be expected to cause less serious collateral injury, loss, or damage

also taking account of contemporary technological possibilities. In this respect,

> the absence of specific evidence of where an attack will take place or of the precise nature of an attack does not preclude a conclusion that an armed attack is imminent

for the purposes of exercising self-defence. Such exercise is also permissible where the state against which force is to be used is unable or unwilling to face the threat located on its territory, if necessary, without its consent. It is, however, admitted that 'the unable or unwilling standard is not a license to wage war globally or to disregard the borders and territorial integrity of other States'. The U.S. does not, however, consider its use of mili-

---

72 *Anwar Al-Awlaki* was a dual U.S. and Yemeni citizen placed in the list of individuals targeted for killing. In June 2004, a Memorandum which was classified until then was made public by the U.S. Department of Justice, justifying the killing (*see* Charlie Savage, Justice Department Memo Approving Targeted Killing of *Anwar Al-Awlaki, The New York Times*, 23 June 2014).

73 December 2016, available at www.justsecurity.org/wp-content/uploads/2016/12/framework.Report_Final.pdf, last accessed on 29 October 2017.

74 The incident involved the use of force by the United Kingdom in self-defence against a non-State actor located in the United States.

tary force against a non-state actor with which it is engaged in an armed conflict to be confined to 'hot battlefields', as long as hostilities continue.

Such reasoning and justifications have, however, been put in doubt,[75] particularly in connection with targeted killings carried out in the context of self-defence against *Al-Qaeda* and its affiliates outside Afghanistan or Iraq which did not constitute 'hot battlefields' any more. Indeed, the invocation of self-defence in these cases appears to be problematic since an exceedingly long period of time has elapsed since the *Al-Qaeda* attacks and even more since the beginning of 'Operation Enduring Freedom' in Afghanistan in 2001. The notion of 'imminence' of the terrorist threat, appears, in fact, to be used as a kind of justification for the controversial idea of pre-emptive self-defence,[76] while the criteria of willingness and ability of the states involved[77] are generally vague and left to the exclusive judgment of the state acting in self-defence (including in the form of targeted killings).[78]

There has been also an effort on the part of the U.S. to uphold the argument that its operations in various countries against manifold groups are part of one and the same conflict against *Al-Qaeda* and its affiliates or co-belligerents. Apart from the fact that co-belligerence is a notion which is rather alien to non-international armed conflicts, it is generally accepted that individuals belonging to groups with different command and control structures or with different military hierarchies should not be regarded as forming part of the same group, even if there are close ties between them.[79] In reality, there is great diversity between these groups and the existence of connections between them is far from certain, while their linkage to *Al Qaeda* (or *ISIS*) may only be on an inspirational level and have very little to do with their operational planning and activity. Indeed, in the majority of cases, such groups usually establish their own independent agendas, adopting from the abovementioned organizations mainly their radical religious beliefs, ruthless behaviour[80] and, occasionally, their *modus operandi*.[81]

In fact, the efforts of the U.S. to show that every aspect of its fight against terrorism is part of its fight against *Al-Qaeda*, the Taliban and their affiliates, are likely motivated by its need to satisfy the conditions of its own domestic legislation, since the President is

75 Christine Gray, *op. cit.* pp.10-12; C.J. Greenwood, *War, Terrorism and International law in Essays on War in International Law* (Cameron May 2006), 409; Alston (n12) paras. 53-56.

76 *See* the 2004 Report of the High-level Panel on Threats, Challenges and Change addressed to the Secretary-General, which seems to suggest a connection of imminence with pre-emptive self-defence. Generally, the terms used to convey the relevant notions are rather confusing.

77 Which the U.S. doctrine did not specify, leaving it open whether the 'involved states' can be third states or only those where the theatre of war is found.

78 Georg Nolte, Preventive Use of Force and Preventive Killings, 2004, 5, Theoretical Inquiries in Law 111.

79 ICTY, *Haradinaj, supra*, p. 144.

80 *E.g.*, groups such as *Boko Haram* in Nigeria and *Al-Shabaab* in Somalia would seem to have no or limited operational connections with *Al Qaeda* or between themselves.

81 As noted by Christof Heyns in his Report, *supra*, 9.2.1, fn. 21, the idea that every group may be squeezed under the same political and operational umbrella "ignores the significant differences between the various forms of armed conflict and opens the door for an expansion of targeting without clear limits" (para. 61).

acting under the 'Authorization for Use of Military Force' (AUMF) passed by Congress after the 9/11 attacks which restricts the President's authorization only to the use of all necessary and appropriate force against those who planned, authorized, committed, or aided the terrorist attacks of 9/11, or who harboured those responsible.[82, 83]

The positions held by the U.S. over these years in connection with the legal issues, which are central to its fight against terrorism in general and targeted killings in particular, have been mentioned in various instances above. From these positions a doctrine has emerged which seems to be nuanced according to the Administration in power at each given time.

Thus, during the *George W. Bush* administration, the doctrine applied for the justification of targeted killings relied largely on the 1989 Parks Memorandum,[84] which had examined the possibility for the U.S. to carry out assassinations in various situations, including counter-terrorism operations, and whether this would be contrary to either U.S. policy – which prohibited assassinations on the basis of Executive Order 12333[85] – or international law. The Memorandum came to the conclusion that where there was a threat to U.S. citizens or national security, as determined by the President, the use of military force against legitimate targets would not constitute assassination and would not, therefore, be prohibited.[86]

---

82 "...the President is authorized to use all necessary and appropriate force against those nations, organizations, or persons he determines planned, authorized, committed, or aided the terrorist attacks that occurred on September 11, 2001, or harbored such organizations or persons, in order to prevent any future acts of international terrorism against the United States by such nations, organizations or persons" (Public Law 107–40—Sept. 18, 2001, Joint Resolution, Sec. 2 (a)).

83 Among others, *John Bellinger III,* former Legal Adviser in the State Department under President *George W. Bush,* has stated that "the AUMF needs to be updated as it provides insufficient authority for the U.S. military and intelligence personnel to conduct counter terrorism operations today...." (*The Washington Post* "A counter-terrorism law in need of updating," 26 November 2010).

84 Written by W. Hays Parks, Special Assistant for Law of War Matters to the Judge Advocate General of the Army. The memorandum examined the question of assassination from a national and international law perspective in view of the revision of a U.S. Army Law of War Manual (Memorandum reprinted at ARMY LAW., Dec. 1989, p. 4, available at: www.loc.gov/rr/frd/Military_Law/pdf/12-1989.pdf.

85 The Order, signed by President *Ronald Reagan* on 4 December 1981 (amended by Executive Orders of 2003, 2004 and 2008), was related to the United States Intelligence Activities, aimed at expanding the data collection capabilities of the National Security Agency (NSA). It also contained a provision proscribing sponsoring or engaging in assassinations.

86 According to the *Parks* Memorandum, the illegal assassinations prohibited by Executive Order 12333 should be distinguished from the targeting of groups or individuals who posed a "direct threat" to the U.S. According to the Memorandum, the prohibition covered murder for political reasons. Abraham Sofaer, then Legal Adviser to the State Department, had pointed out that the prohibition should also apply to the illegal killing of "even an ordinary citizen, so long as the act has a political purpose." However, the prohibition did not preclude the targeted killing in self-defense of specific individuals who pose a direct threat to U.S. citizens or national security in peacetime. This was permissible, according to *Parks and Sofaer,* under the principle of self-defense enshrined in Article 51 of the U.N. Charter and customary international law (Sixth Annual A. Solf lecture in International law: Terrorism, the Law, and the National Defense, 126 MIL.L.REV. 89, 119(1989)). For an analysis of the *Parks* Memorandum and the *Parks-Sofaer* doctrine *see* Gabriella Blum and Philip Heymann, *Law and Targeted Killing, loc. cit.,* (*supra,* 9.2.1, fn. 21), pp. 155-165.

In its abovementioned 2016 'Report on the Legal and Policy Frameworks Guiding the United States' Use of Military Force and Related National Security Operations', the *Obama* Administration – during which targeted killings increased dramatically – bases the legal justification of such killings on the law of armed conflict as well as on the possibility for 'direct action against terrorist targets located outside the U.S. and areas of active hostilities'.[87] The Report goes on to clarify that the determination as to whether a region constitutes an 'area of active hostilities' does not depend exclusively on whether there is an armed conflict under international law taking place in the country at issue, but also, among other things, 'on the size and scope of the terrorist threat, the scope and intensity of U.S. counter-terrorism operations and the necessity of protecting any U.S. forces in the relevant location'.[88]

In conclusion, it would seem that the U.S. doctrine on the matter has not changed substantially from administration to administration and that it is suffering from ambiguities and inconsistencies which create serious doubts as to its conformity with international law, to the extent that it condones U.S. targeted killing operations, relating to the once hot and now extinct battlefield with *Al Qaeda* and the *Taliban*. Conversely, it has found justification in connection with ISIS and other similar groups in Iraq where there has been an active battlefield since 2011.

9.2.3.7 Concluding Remarks on Self-Defence, Including by Targeted Killings, Against Non-State Actors

The legal terrain concerning self-defence of this type remains far from solid. The adoption of 'inclusive' solutions, i.e. such that would allow self-defence against a state from which an attack by non-state actors has been launched or where the perpetrators are found, entails obvious risks, because that state might have no real connection with them.[89] This is particularly so in the latter case, i.e. when the perpetrators are found in a state other than that from which they carried out the attack, taking into account the possibilities for extreme mobility across borders which exist today in most parts of the world.

Furthermore, assertions or indications of cooperation, assistance, harbouring, or tolerance afforded to terrorists by the state from the territory of which the attack of the non-state actors (terrorists) was launched or where they are found, or of that state's unwill-

87 *Ibid.*, pp. 24-25.

88 *Ibid.*, p. 25.

89 According to the Parks Memorandum, *supra*, fn. 302: "[H]istorically, the United States has resorted to the use of military force in peacetime where another nation has failed to discharge its international responsibilities in protecting U.S. citizens from acts of violence originating in or launched from its sovereign territory, or has been culpable in aiding and abetting international criminal activities" (p. 7). The Memorandum cites certain examples, among which are the assistance offered by the U.S. Army personnel to the Bolivian Army in its campaign to capture or kill *Ernesto 'Che' Guevara* in 1967 and using naval ships to force an Egypt Air airliner carrying the *Achille Lauro* hijackers, to land at the U.S. Naval Air Station at *Sigonella*, Italy, in 1985.

ingness to prevent the terrorist activities or apprehend and punish those responsible, must be substantiated by the state invoking self-defence. Absent a declaration admitting such cooperation, aiding or harbouring or other proof of the involvement of the state from where the non-state actors operate or are found, there is a danger of erroneous assessment of the actual situation and a risk of mistaken reaction on the part of the state invoking self-defence. Where the state or states involved belong to the category of failed or semi-failed states which cannot, in reality, face the challenges presented by well-organized attacks by non-state actors from their territory, the situation is even more complicated. Indeed, the exercise of self-defence based on such (genuine) inability risks punishing a state and a population which are not responsible for such acts.

Ultimately, however, it has to be accepted that a claim of self-defence would be sustainable if the urgency of the matter were such that would not allow for prior consultation, deliberation or confirmation of the actual situation by the state exercising self-defence. Such a step should, however, be taken in full cognizance of potential consequences.

Indeed, if the claim of self-defence involving a targeted killing is not substantiated, the question arises whether the targeted killing may itself be considered as an act of aggression.[90] In reality, it will be rare for a single targeted killing to constitute such an act or considered to violate the principle of non-use of force. It could not, *a fortiori*, qualify as an 'armed attack'. Where, however, air strikes by manned aircraft or by drones or other 'aggressive' means of this type are used to carry out the operation, or where collateral damage exceeds the measure required by the proportionality criterion, the violation of Article 2(4) of the U.N. Charter[91] will be established and an armed attack presumed, even if there was no engagement with the armed forces of the state where the killing took place (territorial state). The latter state would then have a legal basis to exercise its own self-defence, while, in addition, it could present claims of an economic nature, such as, *inter alia*, compensation, damages and reparations for the damage suffered, in accordance with the terms of state responsibility attributable to the state which conducted the killing.

In the light of the above, it would appear necessary to take into account certain determining factors when considering the legality of the exercise of self-defence against non-state actors, including, in particular, the case where such self-defence takes the form of targeted killings. These factors would include: the magnitude of the terrorist

90 *See* Resolution S/RES/611 of 25 April 1988 which condemned Israel for the killing, by Israeli commandos, of *Khalil al-Wazir (Abu Jihad)*, top aide to PLO leader *Yasser Arafat* in Tunisia. The Resolution qualified the violation of Tunisian territory as an act of aggression. The U.S. State Department also condemned the act as 'political assassination'. This Resolution came three years after Resolution S/RES/573 (1985) which had condemned Israel for an air raid of its air force in Tunisia against the headquarters of the PLO there.

91 Which is as follows: "All Members shall refrain in their international relations from the threat or use of force against the territorial integrity or political independence of any state, or in any other manner inconsistent with the purposes of the United Nations."

attack which should be equivalent to that of an attack by a state; the need to comply with the principles of proportionality and necessity[92]; in case the attack of the non-state actors was launched from a 'failed' state or where there are doubts as to whether a particular state or which state is responsible for the attack, a prior S.C. resolution allowing to launch a counter-attack would be the best option.[93]

9.2.4 *Consent of the Territorial State to the Targeted Killing(s) and Lack Thereof*[94]

In principle, consent of a state to action – including targeted killings – undertaken by another state in self-defence (or otherwise) against non-state actors on the former state's territory eliminates the illegality of such action[95] as regards the relationship between the states concerned. With regard to human rights, however, the consenting state is bound by the obligation to secure their respect in all circumstances, which means that it may not itself resort to killing nor allow another state to do so but in law-enforcement operations, provided that this is necessary action in order to protect life and there is no other less drastic means, such as capture or incapacitation of the suspect, to achieve this purpose.[96] The fact that another state has conducted the targeted killing does not, therefore, in any way exonerate the state where the killing is taking place (territorial state) from its own responsibility, even if it is ready to relinquish its exclusive jurisdiction to conduct law enforcement operations on its own territory.

9.2.4.1 Lack of Consent

Targeted killings committed by a state on the territory of another state (territorial state) without the latter's consent are, in principle, illegal as a matter of general international law, as they violate the sovereignty of the latter state.[97] Indeed, as already noted, a state

---

92 Necessity in self-defence requires a state to assess whether it can defend itself by means other than by the use of armed force. Proportionality in self-defence requires the state in question to use force to the extent necessary to meet defensive objectives.

93 It may be recalled – in connection with the 'failed state' scenario-, that, in the case of piracy off the coast of Somalia where non-state actors (pirates) caused severe harm to international navigation and to the interests of many states, which did not, however, reach the level of 'armed attack' against any of them in particular, the S.C. adopted Resolutions which allowed action to be taken not only in the territorial sea of Somalia but also on its territory itself (*see infra*, Part III).

94 On this topic *see* Art. 20 of the Draft Articles on the Responsibility of States for Internationally Wrongful Acts and Commentary, 2001, Yearbook of the International Law Commission 2001, vol. II, Part Two.

95 Such consent existed, it seems, on the part of Yemen, in the case of the targeted killing of *Harithi* and a group of other persons in 2002 (*see supra*, 9.2.3.6, p. 170).

96 Philip Alston, *op. cit.*, p. 11, para. 32.

97 On this issue, *see* Dapo Akande, who maintains that in case of use of force by a state against non-state actors on the territory of another state who has not consented to that action, gives rise to an international conflict between the two states. However, he does not refer specifically to the case of targeted killings (Classification of Conflicts: relevant legal concepts, in Elizabeth Wilmshurst (ed), *International Law and the Classification of Conflicts*, Oxford University Press, 2012, pp. 70 *et seq.*).

may not carry out law enforcement or other operations of a similar nature on foreign territory, as these fall under the exclusive competence of the territorial state by virtue of its sovereignty, and this is more emphatically so when done with a view to killing a person. Further consequences might arise for that state, as described above.

9.2.5 Targeted Killings in Armed Conflict

9.2.5.1 Targeted Killings in International Armed Conflict (IAC)

In such context (i.e. where there is an international armed conflict between the state conducting the targeted killing and the state where the killing took place), IHL is obviously the applicable law. As a consequence, targeted killings are not illegal provided that the targeted person (or persons) is an enemy combatant. Combatants may indeed be targeted at any time and any place. Civilians may not be targeted, unless and for as long as the targeted person is 'directly participating in hostilities'.[98] The notion of 'direct participation in hostilities'[99] has been controversial, as its inherent vagueness regarding key questions, such as what, in fact, constitutes 'direct' participation and the required length of such participation, lends itself to various and often opposing interpretations. As a contribution to the discussion on the matter, the ICRC issued, in 2009, a 'Guidance on Direct Participation in Hostilities' which sets out a number of criteria indicating that an individual is participating directly in hostilities.[100]

One of the issues dealt with by the Guidance is whether capture may be an alternative to targeted killing under IHL. The answer given by the ICRC is, as expected, in the affirmative, on the basis of considerations of humanity.[101] Generally, however, the issue has been connected with the interpretation of the principle of necessity and the superior hierarchical position attributed to it by many scholars.[102]

Undoubtedly, the 'Guidance' is a useful tool for states. However, it is a far cry from being considered reflective of state practice and, even less, customary law. Indeed, criti-

98 Additional Protocol I, Art. 51(3).

99 On this issue *see* Michael N. Schmitt, The Interpretive Guidance on the Notion of Direct Participation in Hostilities: a critical analysis, *Harvard National Security Journal*, vol. 1, 2010. Also, Michael N. Schmitt, Military Necessity and Humanity in International Humanitarian Law: Preserving the Delicate Balance, *Virginia Journal of International Law*, vol. 50, No. 4, 2010; Dapo Akande, Clearing the Fog of War? The ICRC's Interpretive Guidance on Direct Participation in Hostilities, *International and Comparative Law Quarterly*, vol. 59, No. 1 (January 2010), pp. 180 and 191.

100 According to Philip Alston, *supra*, 9.2.1, fn. 21: "..in order to protect the vast majority of civilians, direct participation may only include conduct close to that of a fighter, or conduct that directly supports combat. More attenuated acts, such as providing financial support, advocacy, or other non-combat aid, does not constitute direct participation" (para. 60).

101 ICRC, Interpretive Guidance, p. 82.

102 *See, e.g.*, Michael N. Schmitt, Military Necessity and Humanity in International Humanitarian Law, *supra*, fn. 313, pp. 795 and 835. *Contra*, in particular with regard to individual or groups considered to be terrorists in territories far removed from the theatre of operations, *see* Ryan Goodman, The Power to Kill or Capture Enemy Combatants, European Journal of International Law, vol. 24, n. 3, 2013, pp.819 *et seq*.

cism has been levelled against it from two sides with diametrically differing views,[103] i.e. those who maintain that the Guidance is too restrictive for states and at the same time too expansive for IHL purposes and those who hold the opposite view.[104]

9.2.5.2 Targeted Killings in Non-International Armed Conflict (NIAC)

Targeted killings may also be carried out in non-international conflict, i.e. a conflict in which the belligerent parties are on the one hand a state and on the other one or more non-state actors (insurgents, rebels) or one in which the parties are all non-state actors.[105] Again, the existence of this type of armed conflict is determined by the application of objective criteria,[106] which may not always coincide with the claims or the *desiderata* of the parties involved in the armed conflict.[107] 'Enemy combatants' are not recognized under the IHL applicable in NIACs. In such conflicts, 'combatants' are replaced by 'fighters' or '*de facto* combatants', i.e. civilians who 'directly participate in hostilities', and who alone may be lawfully attacked for as long as they do so.[108] In this respect, the 2009

103 A response to such criticism on certain issues is given by Nils Melzer, Keeping the Balance Between Military Necessity and Humanity: A Response to Four Critiques of the ICRC's Interpretive Guidance on the Notion of Direct Participation in Hostilities, 42 NYU J. Int'l L. and Politics, 829, 858, 2010.

104 Among the latter, *see, e.g.*, the criticism by Philip Alston, *supra*, 9.2.1, fn. 21, in connection with the category of armed group members who perform 'continuous combat function' and can therefore be targeted anywhere and at any time (ICRC Guidance at 66).

105 Non-international armed conflicts are governed only by common Art. 3 of the Geneva Conventions and possibly by Protocol II to them (if the state involved in the non-international conflict is party to it).

106 To be considered an internal armed conflict, such conflict must exceed a certain level of intensity and duration. Thus, the intensity of the violence must go beyond that of internal disturbances and tensions, such as riots, isolated and sporadic acts of violence and other acts of similar nature. An indication that this threshold has been reached can be the use by the government of military forces instead of law enforcement units. Additionally, the violence among the fighting parties must be protracted (ICTY, *Tadić,* Appeal on Jurisdiction, Case No. IT-94-I-AR72, 2 October 1995, 35 I.L.M. 32, 54, para. 70 (1996); ICTR, *Musema, supra*, para. 248. The requirement of protracted violence, however, refers more to the intensity of the armed violence than its duration (ICTY, *Haradinaj and others*, case No. IT-04-84-T, Trial Chamber judgment of 3 April 2008, para. 49; ICTY, Fatmir *Limaj, Haradin Bala, Isak Musliu,* Case No. IT-03-66-T, Trial Chamber Judgment of 30 November 2005, para. 90). Furthermore, the application of IHL presupposes that the group or groups involved in the conflict fulfil certain criteria (Lindsay Moir, The Law of Armed Conflict, 2002; ICRC Commentary, *supra*, note 97 (common Art. 3); ICTY, *Delalić,* Judgment, 16 November 1998, para. 184; ICTR, *Musema*, Judgment of 27 January 2000, para. 248. For a list of these criteria *see* Philip Alston, *supra,* 9.2.1, fn. 21, paras. 52 *et seq.*), among which *e.g.*, to have a minimal level of organization which allows the armed forces fighting them to identify an adversary (Art. 3 common to the Geneva Conventions and Additional Protocol II) and the capability to apply the Geneva Conventions, *i.e.,* adequate command structure and separation of military and political command *(Ibid).* International jurisprudence has elaborated certain further indicative criteria, which include apart from command structure, the existence of headquarters and of a group's ability to plan and carry out military operations.

107 Which they may not wish to admit. *E.g.*, the U.K. has never admitted that it was involved in an internal armed conflict with the Irish Republican Army (IRA). By contrast, the U.S. claims that it is involved in internal armed conflict with *Al Quaeda* and its affiliates.

108 Additional Protocol II, Art. 13(3).

'Interpretive Guidance on Direct Participation in Hostilities' of the ICRC[109] takes the view that in NIAC, civilians who participate directly in hostilities and are members of an armed group who have a 'continuous combat function' may be targeted at all times and in all places. For those who do not operate in such a way, the ICRC Guidance proposes that the existence of direct participation should be assessed in connection with each single act, the earliest point of which would be the concrete preparatory measures for that specific act and the terminal one when the activity ends.[110]

On the broader issue whether a non-international conflict may exist between a state and non-state actors operating from another state which is not part of that conflict (territorial state), where the former state (intervening state) uses force solely at the non-state actors, the majority view seems to be that this is indeed the case.[111] In the U.S., this view has found (indirect) support in the Supreme Court's judgment on *Hamdan v. Rumsfeld*[112] which recognized that common Article 3 of the Geneva Conventions is applicable in such cases. The view, however, has been also supported that where the territorial state has not consented to the intervening state's action, an international conflict necessarily arises between all the parties concerned. This view is also opposed to the idea of two armed conflicts running parallel, i.e. an international one between the state attacking the non-state actors and the territorial state, and a non-international one between the former state and the non-state actors in question.[113]

It has also been argued that although *Al Qaeda* and other terrorist groups, whether associated or not with *Al Qaeda*, have mounted serious attacks in many countries in Asia, Europe, North America and Africa, neither the intensity (with the exception of the 9/11 attacks) nor the duration of their operations could justify the establishment of a state of non-international conflict between these non-state actors and the state where the attacks were carried out or against the interests of which they operate. Furthermore, as noted above, the structural characteristics of these groups, with the exception of ISIS, could not qualify them as parties to such a conflict in terms of IHL.[114]

109 Nils Melzer, Interpretive Guidance on the Notion of Direct Participation in Hostilities under International Humanitarian Law, ICRC, 2009. *See also* Dapo Akande, "Clearing the fog of war?" *(supra)* International and Comparative Law Quarterly, vol. 59, No. 1 (January 2010).

110 Further requirements to be cumulatively met for a specific act to be qualified as 'direct participation in hostilities' are set by the ICRC Guidance.

111 *See, e.g.*, Noam Lubell, Extraterritorial Use of Force Against Non-State Actors, 2010, Part II; Claus Kreβ, 'Some Reflections on the International Legal Framework Governing Transnational Armed Conflicts,' 2010, 15 Journal of Conflict and Security Law 245.

112 *Hamdan v. Rumsfeld*, 548 U.S. 557 (2006).

113 Dapo Akande, Classification of armed conflicts: Relevant legal concepts, in Elizabeth Wilmshurst (ed), International Law and the Classification of Conflicts, Chapter 3, Oxford University Press, 2012, also available at http://ssrn.com/abstract=2038217.

114 Philip Alston, *supra*, 9.2.1, fn. 21, p. 18, para. 54, underlines that none of these states, with the possible exception of Pakistan, has recognized the existence of an armed conflict against *Al Qaeda* or its 'associates' in their territory.

It is also widely supported, rightly, that *Al Qaeda* and similar non-state actors would fulfil the required criteria to be considered parties in a non-international conflict only within the confines of the active battlefield(s) (theatre of war) of a specific state.[115] This denies the possibility of a non-international conflict taking place wherever in the world, as is – presumably – the U.S. position regarding its armed conflict with *Al Qaeda*. Where such NIAC is taking place within the theatre of war, the applicable law is IHL. If, however, the state where the operation is taking place, including a consenting one, is not part of that theatre, the targeted killing would be unlawful as a matter of IHRL.[116]

It must finally be underlined that the principles mentioned above with regard to international conflicts are also applicable in connection with non-international ones.[117]

9.2.5.3 Targeted Killings Outside the Context of an Armed Conflict[118]

Just like any targeted killing committed on national territory, a targeted killing on foreign territory which is not conducted as part of an ongoing armed conflict would fall into the category of criminal acts (murder, terrorist act) under the domestic law of both the territorial state and the state which carried out the killing. It would also be a violation of IHRL, i.e. a violation of the right to life, which would be attributable to the state which carried out the killing, as well as to the territorial state if it has consented to its commission.

The right to life is justifiably regarded as the supreme right, and the prohibition of arbitrarily depriving a person of it encapsulates a rule of customary international law of a *jus cogens* character.[119] Intentionally killing a person in times of peace is legally possible only where this is strictly necessary to protect against an imminent threat to life[120] and constitutes the last resort for this purpose. In the case of targeted killings, however, it is neither necessary nor even possible to identify applicable conditions, since the *ab initio* existence of a decision to kill makes, by definition, targeted killing a violation of the right to life.

As regards the latter state, however, while it would be bound by IHRL on its own territory and on the territory on which it exercises jurisdiction, the law seems to be un-

115 *E.g.*, Marko Milanovic, EJIL Talk, On Whether IHL applies to Drone Strikes Outside Areas of Active Hostilities, 5 October 1017.

116 For violation of the right to life.

117 *See The Manual on Non-International Armed Conflict (with Commentary)*, International Institute of Humanitarian Law (Drafting Committee: Michael Schmitt, Charles Garraway, Yoram Dinstein), 2006.

118 On this topic, *see* Sigrun Skogly, Beyond national borders: States' human rights obligations in international cooperation, 2006.

119 Art. 3 of the 1948 Universal Declaration of human rights; Art. 6(1) of the International Covenant on Civil and Political Rights; Art. 2 of the European Convention for the Protection of Human Rights and Fundamental Freedoms; Art. 4 of the American Convention on Human Rights and Art. 4 of the African Charter on Human and Peoples' Rights.

120 *See* ECtHR, *McCann and others v. United Kingdom of Great Britain and Northern Ireland*, application No. 18984/91, judgment of 27 September 1995 paras. 203-214.

settled as to whether it would be so bound outside these territories. A legal vacuum leaving such situations uncovered seems to persist in terms of international law, which needs to be examined in some more detail.

9.2.5.4 Extraterritorial Application of IHRL in the Case of Targeted Killings[121]

The general issue of the extraterritorial application of IHRL has already been examined, particularly in connection with the application of the European Convention on Human Rights (ECHR) where there is a constantly expanding jurisprudence on the matter. However, there is very limited jurisprudence from which to infer a basis of jurisdiction for the application of IHRL specifically regarding targeted killings carried out by a state through its agents, where such agents (e.g. a sniper) do not have physical power, authority or control over the targeted person, or where the killing is conducted by drone.[122] Such a case was *Alejandre v. Cuba* brought before the IACHR in 1999.[123] It is, however, to be expected that such rules will develop either by extending the ambit of those already existing on the general issue – which is the most probable scenario – or even by formulating new ones.

9.2.5.5 The Law Enforcement Model

Another model which has been proposed for the 'creation' of jurisdiction of the operating state in the case of targeted killings is that of law enforcement, i.e. the application of law enforcement rules to regulate the use of force by the state carrying out the killing. The international standards that such law should respect are set out in certain soft-law inter-

---

121 *See* John C. Dehn, Targeted Killing, Human Rights and Ungoverned Spaces: Considering Territorial State Human Rights Obligations, Harvard International Law Journal, December 2012; Sarah Joseph, Adam McBeth (eds), Research Handbook on International Human Rights Law, Edward Elgar, 2010.

122 *See* Christof Heyns Report, *supra,* paras. 48-51.

123 *Armando Alejandre Jr., Carlos Costa, Mario de la Peña and Pablo Morales v. Republic of Cuba,* Case 11589, Report No. 86/99, 29 September 1999, paras. 23-25, (Brothers to the Rescue). The case, which was brought before the Inter-American Commission on Human Rights, concerned the death of four individuals whose private aircraft was shot down by a Cuban military MIG-29. The aircraft was in international airspace when downed. The Commission found that Cuba had violated the right to life and to fair trial of the victims. Concerning the extraterritorial nature of the acts it stated: "The fact that events took place outside Cuban jurisdiction, does not limit the Commission's competence ratione loci because, as previously stated, when agents of a state, whether military or civilian, exercise power and authority over persons outside national territory, the state's obligation to respect human rights continues – in this case the rights enshrined in the American Declaration. The Commission finds conclusive evidence that agents of the Cuban State, although outside their territory, placed the civilian pilots of the 'Brothers to the Rescue' Organization under their authority. Consequently, the Commission is competent ratione loci to apply the American Convention extraterritorially to the Cuban State in connection with the events that took place in international airspace on February 24, 1996." *See also* Human Rights Committee, General Comment No. 31 (2004), on the Nature of the General Legal Obligation Imposed on States Parties, para. 10; Human Rights Commission: *Sergio Euben Lopez Burgos v. Uruguay,* Communication No. R.12/52, U.N. Doc. Supp. No. 40 (A/36/40) at 176, 1981; Inter-American Commission on Human Rights (IACHR): *Coard and others v. United States,* case 10.951, Report No. 109/99, 29 September 1999, para. 37.

national instruments.[124] The findings of international human rights bodies and courts do not, on their part, seem to follow the same pattern in such cases. In some of them, the possibility is not excluded for lethal force to be used after all other measures have been exhausted or in extreme situations where a population's safety is at risk.[125] Sometimes it is not clear whether the latter finding applies only to domestic targeted killings under a law enforcement model or to extraterritorial targeted killings as well. In general, the tendency of human rights bodies and international courts is rather to find the means to afford protection to the population of a state against a terrorist attack or threat than to indicate a clear legal basis for the application of human rights. In any event, the law enforcement model, whether domestically or extraterritorially applied, considers lethal use of force as the last resort while trying to capture persons for any reason, including terrorism, while what is sought in the case of targeted killings is exactly to kill and not capture the individual in question. Generally, therefore, and irrespective of the legal correctness of the basis used, the result under both, law enforcement rules and IHRL would be the same.

9.2.6 *Use of Drones (Unmanned Aerial Vehicles – UAVs)[126] in Targeted Killings[127]*

Although drones were originally developed to be used for intelligence gathering, reconnaissance and surveillance purposes, they were subsequently found useful for hitting

124 *See* Basic Principles on the Use of Force and Firearms by Law Enforcement Officials, adopted by the 9th U.S. Congress on the Prevention of Crime and Treatment of Offenders, Havana, 1990, U.N. Doc. A/CONF.144/28/Rev. 1, 1990.

125 In the case of *Isayeva*, the ECtHR found that Russia could use deadly force against Chechen rebels, even when there was no indication that the latter were posing an immediate threat to the Russian forces (*Isayeva v. Russia*, Application No. 57950/00, Judgment, 24 February 2005).

126 Also known as Unmanned Combat Aircraft Systems (UCAS).

127 *See* the 2017 Report by Ben Emmerson, *supra*, fn. 249; Report by Christof Heyns, *supra*, fn. 249; Jane Mayer, The Predator War, The New Yorker, 26 October 2009; *Stanford Law School and Global Justice Clinic*, NYU School of Law, Living under Drones, September 2012, at http://livingunderdrones.org; Melzer, Human Rights Implications of the Usage of Drones; Sascha-Dominik Bachmann, Targeted Killings: Contemporary Challenges, Risks and Opportunities, Journal of Conflict and Security Law, 2013, Vol. 18 No. 2, pp. 259-288; Christof Heyns, *Dapo Akande*, Lawrence Hill-Cawthorne and Thompson Chengeta, The International Law Framework Regulating the Use of Armed Drones, 2016, *International* and *Comparative Law Quarterly*, Vol. 65, issue 4, pp. 791-*827*, available at https://doi.org/10.1017/S0020589316000385, last accessed on 28 October 2017.

targets on the ground. The U.S. has been using drones for such operations in Afghanistan, Pakistan,[128] Iraq, Yemen, Somalia and Libya.[129] Drones use laser-guided missiles and are remotely operated by pilots who are usually thousands of miles away from the location of the target.[130] As a result, the capacity of these pilots to appreciate the actual situation on the ground can be severely limited, with grave consequences for the correct identification of the target, which often results in the killing and injury of persons unrelated to it. In fact, drones gained notoriety by the civilian casualties they have caused on the ground, particularly in Pakistan. Further grave consequences, including social, psychological and economic ones, are inevitable. Despite the outcry, the use of drones by states and non-state actors has been expanding exponentially for a variety of reasons, principally because of their strategic advantage of minimizing the time between recognition of the target and its elimination without risk to the sending state's forces. Additionally, states appreciate the avoidance of deploying 'boots on the ground' which, apart from its political advantages, also significantly reduces the costs of the sending state. However, while it was originally thought that non-deployment of troops would also avert the negative feelings of local societies, the argument entirely lost conviction following the huge negative impact of 'collateral damage' that drones have caused in reality.

Drones can be used to conduct targeted killings either in the context of an armed conflict whether international or non-international, or outside such context.

From a legal perspective, targeted killings by drone are assimilated to targeted killings by other means and the justifications put forward by the states using drones for this purpose are the same as those used for targeting killings by such other means, namely: a) that the killing is conducted in the exercise of self-defence on the territory of a state which is unable or unwilling to restrain the non-state actors (terrorists) on that territory who have launched an attack against the state sending the drone(s); b) that there is consent of the state where the drone killing is conducted; and c) that there is an armed

128 *Al Qaeda*'s deputy leader *Abu Yahya al-Libi* was killed by a drone operation, as was the local *Al Qaeda* leader in Pakistan *Badar Mansoon*. The estimate of the deaths from drone attacks differ widely according to the source used. *E.g.*, the "Bureau of Investigative Journalism" (www.thebureauinvestigates.com/category/projects/drones/) reports 2,347-3,792 deaths in Pakistan of whom 416-957 civilians between 2004-2014, and 339-494 deaths in Yemen of whom 64-83 civilians from 2002-2014. International Security (www.securitydata.newamerica.net/drones) reports that in the same periods in Pakistan out of the 2132-3496 deaths by drone strike, 258-307 were civilians, and in Yemen out of 798-1043 deaths, 81-87 were civilians.

129 The secret targeted killing program is mainly conducted by the Central Intelligence Agency (CIA) using 'Predator' or 'Reaper' drones. They are operated from the CIA headquarters in Langley, Virginia, while pilots *in situ* in secret airfields in Afghanistan and Pakistan handle take offs and landings.

130 *See* Mary Ellen O'Connell, Unlawful Killing with Combat Drones. A Case Study of Pakistan, 2004-2009, Notre Dame School Legal Studies Research Paper No. 09-43, 20 December 2009, available at http://papers.ssrn.com/so13/papers.cfm?abstract_id=1501144; Sean D. Murphy, The International Legality of U.S. Military Cross-Border Operations from Afghanistan into Pakistan, The George Washington University Law School Public Law and Legal Theory Working Paper No. 451 (9 November 2008, available at http://papers.ssrn.com/so13/papers.cfm?abstract_id=1296733.

conflict between the state carrying out the killing by drone and the state on the territory of which the killing takes place.

Philip Alston has observed that in practice, "outside the context of armed conflict, the use of drones for targeted killings is almost never likely to be legal."[131] In general agreement with this assessment, it must also be noted that the law applicable within that conflict, whether international or non-international, is both IHL and IHRL; outside the context of armed conflict of either type, killings by drone are governed, like any other killing by a state – or now also, in some cases, by non-state actors – by IHRL.

9.2.6.1 'Collateral Damage' in Targeted Killings by Drone

Where a state of armed conflict exists between the state which carries out an attack by drone and the state where the attack is taking place, IHL requires, just as in all situations of attack, taking all necessary precautions to prevent or minimize damage to civilians who, although not targeted, find themselves victims of such attack.[132] In practice, however, it has been shown that drone use would most likely violate such IHL principles and rules. The same conclusion would be reached *a fortiori* where there is no state of armed conflict between the two states in question and IHRL is the applicable law.

9.2.6.2 Signature Strikes[133]

These are strikes targeting individuals on the basis of certain criteria, mainly their location, appearance or behavioural patterns. Once again, this is a novel concept which is unknown to IHL. In most cases of targeting of this type, an accurate identification of the person or persons targeted will not be possible, and the risk of killing individuals not directly participating in hostilities will be great. Such killings would therefore be unlawful under IHL[134] and the same holds true with regard to IHRL, for violation of the right to life.

9.2.6.3 Transparency and Accountability[135]

Where human rights law is violated, those responsible must be held to account and this is even more so where the violation concerns the right to life. It has furthermore been held that not investigating and punishing, as appropriate, those responsible, is in itself a viola-

---

131 Report of the Special Rapporteur on extrajudicial, summary or arbitrary executions, Philip Alston, *supra*, 9.2.1, fn. 21, p. 25, para. 85.

132 *See* "Living under drones: death, injury, and trauma to civilians from U.S. drone practices in Pakistan" (2012), International Human Rights and Conflict Resolution Clinic at Stanford Law School and Global Justice Clinic at New York University School of Law, available from http://livingunderdrones.org/wp-content/uploads/2012/10/Stanford-NYU-LIVING-UNDERDRONES.pdf.

133 Kevin Jon Heller, "'One hell of a killing machine': signature strikes and international law," *Journal of International Criminal Justice*, vol. 11, No. 1 (2012), pp. 8-20.

134 Additional Protocol I, Art. 50(1). *See also* ICRC, Commentary on the Additional Protocols of 8 June 1977 to the Geneva Conventions, Commentary on Additional Protocol II, Art. 13 para. 3, 4787 and 4789.

135 *See* Philip Alston, *supra*, paras. 87-92;

tion of this right.[136] Accountability is dependent on public access to information which, in turn, is the cornerstone of transparency. Although transparency is a sensitive issue, as the argument of compromising the success of operations may hold true, there is no doubt that general information such as the criteria applied for targeting individuals, the approving authority and the precautions taken should be disclosed.[137] Accountability is equally of the essence in the case of armed conflict where war crimes are being committed. In such situations, the families of persons missing or killed have a right to know of the fate or the circumstances of the death of their relative. The need to abide by these standards is even more acute in the case of drone strikes where the possibility of unlawfulness and lethal consequences are both very high.

136 ECtHR, *Kaya v. Turkey*, Application No. 22729/93, judgment of 19 February 1998, paras. 86-92; Human Rights Committee, General Comment No. 31 (2004), para. 15.

137 Christof Heyns, *supra*, paras. 135 *et seq*. *See also* the Principles on the effective prevention and investigation of extra-legal, arbitrary and summary executions, E.SC res. 1989/65, annex, 1989 UNESCOR Supp. (No. 1) at 52, U.N. Doc. E/1989/89 (1989), para. 16.

10 Conclusions

The relationship between human rights and terrorism in legal terms has passed through various stages. Originally, such relationship was not even considered, as human rights were conceived, and rightly so, as a wall of protection against authoritarian state rule (civil and political rights) and as positive action taken by states to ameliorate the economic and social situation of individuals (social and economic rights), while terrorism was dealt with as criminal activity of an aggravated nature conducted by individuals, which states had to face mainly by establishing severe criminal sanctions in their domestic legislation and by enhancing their cooperation on the international level.

Finally, however, as the terrorist threat intensified, there was an urge of a political rather than legal nature[1] to identify and assert a perceived conceptual antithesis and direct conflict between human rights and terrorism, which eventually took the form of declaratory phraseology such as 'terrorism obstructing the enjoyment of human rights' or 'terrorism aiming at the destruction of human rights' which have been inserted in many U.N. Resolutions and other mainly U.N. texts since the 1990s. This however, did not, in the author's view, offer any advantage; instead, it tended to blur the issue which is that terrorist acts constitute heinous crimes which should be punished with severe penal sanctions in accordance with the applicable rules of national and international criminal law (and not in the context of IHRL).

Furthermore, in recent years, it has become clear that very often, measures taken to counter-terrorism, i.e. aiming to shield the general public against the terrorist phenomenon, may nonetheless severely affect the human rights of persons against whom there may be a – still unsubstantiated – suspicion of engaging in or aiding terrorist activities. To face this situation, it is by no means sufficient to simply remind of the need for 'respect to international humanitarian law, human rights law and refugee law while combating terrorism', as habitually reiterated in international documents. Human rights must indeed be respected at all times – any derogations can be tolerated only under the strict conditions prescribed by international law,[2] while cutting down on them is certainly not conducive to combating terrorism. On the contrary, strengthening and solidifying human rights should be the reply in facing the terrorist phenomenon. Taking the opposite course, i.e. stifling and restricting human rights discredits and corrodes the very moral basis of the fight against terrorism.

1 There was indeed a number of states which were insistent on having such an association between human rights (violations) and terrorism so as to emphasize and justify criminal charges brought against certain organizations operating on their territory by attributing to them the additional charge of violating human rights.

2 *See supra*, pp. 39-46.

This, of course, is no easy task. Even in the United Nations context, respect for human rights while combating terrorism did not, and to a large extent continues not to materialize in practice, as confirmed by a series of important Reports produced by U.N. Special Rapporteurs and Ombudspersons on the matter. Certainly, some glaring deficiencies in the process of including individuals suspected for terrorist activity in the U.N. 'sanctions list' have been corrected and in this respect much is owed to the Office of the Ombudsperson. Indeed, as the Special Rapporteur on Human Rights and Terrorism *Ben Emmerson* observed in his 2017 Report, the Office has delisted several individuals and entities since its inception while very few applications for such delisting have been refused.[3] This proves, according to the Special Rapporteur, 'the potential for error (or continuing error)' and re-emphasizes 'the need for fair and clear listing and delisting procedures that meet international standards of fairness'.[4] Some further improvements have also been brought by the adoption of relevant S.C. Resolutions.[5] However, information which is crucial to petitioners for delisting may still not be available to them, which seriously affects their possibility to present their case efficiently. Generally, the procedure remains opaque and due process requirements are not fully met. As observed by the former Ombudsperson, *Catherine Marchi-Uhel*,[6] when referring to certain practices within the U.N. on the matter: "Such practice lends support to those who consider that, short of a judicial mechanism, full fairness and transparency cannot be guaranteed."[7] This is an almost inescapable conclusion in view of an 'administrative' procedure, as listing is, which nonetheless produces sanctions essentially of a criminal character, such as the freezing of assets against individuals or legal entities, without the guarantees offered by criminal proceedings.

These shortcomings of the U.N. listing system have been lucidly addressed by the seminal judgments taken by the Grand Chamber of the European Court of Justice in the *Kadi Case*[8] and by the Grand Chamber of the European Court of Human Rights in *Al-Dulimi*.[9] Both have made it amply clear that national courts must be able, when called

3 *See* para. 18 of the Report *(supra,* fn. 249), where it is mentioned, referring to doc. S/2016/671 – Report of the Office of the Ombudsperson Catherine Marchi-Uhel (*see infra*, fn. 381) covering the period from 2 February 2016 to 31 July 2016 (para. 6) – that, in all, 45 individuals and 28 entities have been delisted, while only 12 applications have been refused.

4 *Ibid.*

5 Resolutions 2083 (2012) and 2161 (2014) which require that decisions to delist or retain be accompanied by reasons to be provided within sixty days.

6 Ombudsperson for the Security Council Committee pursuant to resolutions 1267 (1999), 1989 (2011) and 2253 (2015) concerning Islamic State in Iraq and the Levant (ISIL/Da'esh), Al-Qaida and associated individuals, groups, undertakings and entities.

7 Letter to the U.N. Secretary-General of 10 July 2017 where she refers to "an increasing intrusion of the Committee (writer's note: ISIL (Da'esh) and Al-Qaida Sanctions Committee) in a sensitive area for the fairness to petitioners of the Ombudsperson's process. I have witnessed a set-back imposed by the Committee concerning the right of petitioners to receive substantive reasons when they are retained on the sanctions list as a result of the Ombudsperson's recommendation."

8 *Supra,* 8.5.1.2.

9 *Al-Dulimi and Montana Management Inc. v. Switzerland*, Application No. 5809/08, judgment of 21 June 2016, para. 140.

to implement U.N. sanctions against listed persons, to have at their disposal all the information required to determine whether the original listing by the Sanctions Committee was based on sound legal ground. If not, "national authorities may find themselves legally unable to fully implement the sanctions at the national level."[10] It is this solemn warning that reminds everyone involved in counter-terrorism, including the U.N., that human rights must have priority, always.

Finally and most disturbingly, the gravely serious possibility that certain information or intelligence may have been obtained by torture is, as the Special Rapporteur *Ben Emmerson* points out, an unexplored issue which needs to be urgently addressed.[11]

Regarding the legislative and jurisprudential practice of states in connection with human rights while countering terrorism, it is clear that there is great disparity between the way this matter is viewed and dealt with by states across the world, as is unavoidable to happen taking into account the diversity of needs, perceptions and legal traditions in a legally decentralized world.

Thus, in the U.S., a leading country in the fight against terrorism, a variety of differences and a wavering interplay between successive Administrations, Congress and the Judiciary have led to an institutional roller coaster revealing the doubts and uncertainties of principle and practice between all these major factors on the matter. Nonetheless, the numerous cases concerning the Guantanamo detainees have given the opportunity to the courts to confirm the applicability of some basic precepts of human rights law, both domestic and international.

In the EU, states and courts are bound by the jurisprudence of the Union's judicial organs, which provide a powerful focal point for them, while the relevant jurisprudence of the ECtHR has been another guiding beacon for the legal systems of the Council of Europe states.

In conclusion, it may be observed that despite the existence of certain regional forces promoting convergence, the global picture regarding human rights in the face of terrorism is one of fragmentation and ambivalence, reflecting the difficulties the international community is experiencing in coming to grips with the problem. The guidance of the U.N., even if not flawed, is not as visible as it should be, while international law provides little more than a piecemeal approach. In such a legal environment, individual states and organizations and their legal systems are mostly left to their own devices, which will not generally be conducive to the best solutions.

---

10 Ben Emmerson, 2017 Report of the Special Rapporteur on the Promotion and Protection of Human Rights and Fundamental Freedoms while Countering Terrorism (A/HRC/34/61), *supra*, para. 20, referring to the 'Fair and Clear Procedures for a more Effective United Nations Sanctions System' proposals to the Security Council by the Group of Like-Minded States on Targeted Sanctions, 12 November 2015.

11 *Ibid.*, paras. 21-24, referring to the Feinstein Report, released by the U.S. Senate on 9 December 2014, concerning the Detention and Interrogation Program of the Central Intelligence Agency (CIA). The Feinstein Report confirms the existence of a policy emanating from the higher echelons of the *Bush* Administration, authorizing the use of torture and other methods constituting grave human rights violations on 'high-value detainees'. Some European countries were also participating in the program and there have been relevant judgments of the ECtHR against them.

Part III
Aspects of International Law of the Sea

Scope

This Part defines itself as 'Aspects of International Law of the Sea' in recognition of the fact that it can provide limited coverage of this vast subject of international law. It will therefore be confined to the examination of only some of the fundamental topics that this law encompasses. These include the maritime zones to which a coastal state is entitled (territorial sea, contiguous zone, continental shelf and exclusive economic zone), which will be examined together with questions relating to their delimitation. Further on, some specific cases of delimitation presenting particular features or difficulties (Delimitation in the Arctic Ocean, Arctic continental shelf claims beyond 200 n.m.) or where sovereignty issues are involved (East China Sea Islands, South China Sea Islands) are examined. Conversely, issues relating, *inter alia*, to the high seas, international straits, the marine environment, fisheries, the 'Area' and dispute settlement are not dealt with, while others are only partly covered (e.g. in connection with territorial waters, the question of innocent passage is not examined).

Finally, certain topics which have preoccupied international law of the sea in recent years, such as piracy and maritime terrorism, will be laid out.

11 UNCLOS and Maritime Zones

11.1 UNCLOS

Beyond any doubt, the United Nations Convention on the Law of the Sea (UNCLOS)[1] has been the single most important treaty on the law of the sea thus far. Hailed as such as from its adoption in 1982, its commanding influence on jurisprudence and legal theory, already visible at that time, only increased after its entry into force in 1994.[2] UNCLOS has codified and crystallized existing customary international law of the sea, while it has been a powerful tool for its progressive development.[3]

At the same time, UNCLOS has been the culmination of a surprisingly fast normative process which took international law of the sea from a few basic rules, primarily comprising little more than the rule of a 3 n.m. territorial sea and the freedom of the high seas to an intermediate phase consisting of the 1958 four Geneva Conventions[4] and from then on to the UNCLOS system.

Although the 1958 Geneva Convention on the Territorial Sea and the Contiguous Zone had not managed to set a concrete breadth for the territorial sea, it contained other rules which mirrored a wide consensus of the international community, such as those on delimitation, which were later taken up by UNCLOS. The 1958 Convention on the Continental Shelf, on its part, recognized the sovereign right of a coastal state to exploit the seabed and its subsoil beyond its territorial waters to a depth of 200 m (*isobath*) or to a depth allowing the exploitation of natural resources. UNCLOS modified this notion of the Continental Shelf (CS), eliminating (partially) the depth criterion and (fully) the ex-

---

1 1836 UNTS 42 (No 31364) ILM (1994) 1313.

2 16 November 1994.

3 On Law of the Sea *see* Robin R. Churchill & Alan V. Lowe, *The Law of the Sea*, 3rd edn, Manchester University Press, 2008; Donald R. Rothwell, Alex Oude Elferink, Karen N. Scott, Tim Stephens (eds), *The Oxford Handbook of the Law of the Sea*, Oxford University Press, 2015; *Ibid.*, Malcolm D. Evans, *Maritime Boundary Delimitation*, pp. 254-279; L. Caflisch, La délimitation des espaces entre Etats dont les côtes se font face ou sont adjacentes, in R. Dupuy and D. Vignes (eds), *Traité du Nouveau Droit de la Mer*, 1985, pp. 375-440; John Norton Moore, Myron H. Nordquist, Satya N. Nandan, Shabtai Rosenne (eds), *United Nations Convention on the Law of the Sea 1982: A Commentary*, 7 Vols. and Supplementary Documents, Center for Oceans Law and Policy, University of Virginia, Martinus Nijhoff/*Brill*, 1984-2014; Yoshifumi Tanaka, *Predictability and Flexibility in the Law of Maritime Delimitation*, Hart Publishing, 2006; Yoshifumi Tanaka, *The International law of the Sea*, Cambridge University Press, 2012; Alex G. Oude Elferink, Tore Henriksen, Signe Veierud Busch (eds), *Maritime Boundary Delimitation: The Case Law: Is it Consistent and Predictable?* Cambridge University Press, 2018.

4 Convention on the Territorial Sea and the Contiguous Zone, Convention on the Continental Shelf, Convention on the High Seas, Convention on Fishing and Conservation of the Living Resources of the High Seas. All opened for signature on 29 April 1958 and entered into force between 1962 and 1964.

ploitability one.[5] UNCLOS furthermore introduced the notion of the Exclusive Economic Zone (EEZ) which is now developing its full potential with the number of coastal states proclaiming one steadily increasing.

Today, many of the provisions of UNCLOS have acquired an international customary law character.[6] Such provisions are, *inter alia*, those which establish a breadth of territorial sea of up to 12 n.m.,[7] the notion of CS as defined in Article 76[8] and the right of islands to maritime zones in parity with continental territory.[9] On the other hand, the rules concerning the 200 n.m. EEZ, archipelagic waters or the Area do not have, or have not yet acquired such a character.[10]

UNCLOS defines and regulates the spectrum of powers states have in the maritime zones where they exercise sovereignty or sovereign rights, establishes the ways in which these zones are delimited between adjacent or opposite states, specifies the content of the freedom of the high seas and its exceptions, sets out rules for navigation and environmental protection and regulates a host of other questions, including those pertaining to the 'Area',[11] i.e. the sea bed, the ocean floor and their subsoil beyond the limits of national jurisdiction[12] which have been reserved for the benefit of all as 'common heritage of mankind'.

Neither the negotiation nor the adoption of the 1982 Convention has been an easy task. Even more difficult was the period that ensued. Indeed, the U.S. and other industrialized states would not become party to UNCLOS because of their objections to Chapter XI on the 'Area'.[13] Had they insisted on their refusal, the Convention would likely enter into force with almost only developing states as parties, which would not only deprive the Convention of much of its allure as a universal instrument but would also

---

5 *See infra*, at: 11.2.2.2.

6 *See, e.g., Maritime Delimitation and Territorial Questions between Qatar and Bahrain, (Qatar v. Bahrain)*, Merits, Judgment, 16 March 2001, I.C.J. Reports 2001, p. 40, para. 167.

7 As recognized in *Territorial and Maritime Dispute (Nicaragua v. Colombia)*, Judgment, 19 November 2012, I.C.J. Reports 2012, p. 624, para. 177.

8 *Case concerning the Continental Shelf (Libya v. Malta)*, Judgment, 21 March 1984, p. 13, para. 77; *Territorial and Maritime Dispute (Nicaragua v. Colombia)*, Judgment, 2012, *supra*, fn. 7, para. 139; *Ibid.*, para. 118; *Case Concerning Maritime Dispute (Peru v. Chile)*, Judgment, 27 January 2014, para. 179.

9 *Qatar v. Bahrain, supra*, fn. 6, Judgment, para.185; *Nicaragua v. Colombia, supra*, fn. 7, para. 139.

10 Tullio Treves, The High Seas as Potential Exclusive Economic Zones in the Mediterranean, (1. The Zonal Scheme of the UNCLOS), in Marcelo Kohen, Robert Kolb and Djacoba Liva Tehindrazanarivelo (eds), *Perspectives of International Law in the 21st century*, Martinus Nijhoff, 2011, pp. 175-176; *Contra*, as regards archipelagic waters (*i.e.*, accepting the relevant rules as customary law): Donald Rothwell and Tim Stephens, *The International Law of the Sea*, Hart Publishing, 2010, p. 189. On the question of which UNCLOS rules have an international customary law character, *see* Ashley Roach, Today's Customary International Law of the Sea, in *Ocean Development and International Law*, July 2014, http://dx.doi.org/10.1080/00908320.2014.929460, last accessed 30 April 2018.

11 UNCLOS, Chapter XI.

12 UNCLOS, Art. 1(1).

13 In the opinion of these states, the provisions of Chapter XI did not take their economic interests properly into account and the most important stakeholders were not adequately represented in the institutional set-up of the Convention.

burden its parties with very high costs. As a result of this situation, Chapter XI was amended by the conclusion of an Agreement in 1994 to this effect[14] before the Convention entered into force – a move unprecedented in international law[15] – which deviated from 'normal' rules of the law of treaties.[16]

Today, the near totality of the world community of states is party to UNCLOS,[17] the exceptions being few and far between. The most notable absence is that of the U.S. which signed but has not, as yet, ratified the Convention, despite the changes made to it by the 1994 Agreement. Numerous administrations have tried to pass the requisite legislation through a perennially hesitant Congress without success. Nonetheless, the U.S. remains reassuring that as most of the UNCLOS rules already constitute customary rules of international law, the U.S. considers them binding on it as well.

---

14 Agreement relating to the implementation of Part XI of UNCLOS, New York, 28 July 1994. An Annex to the Agreement, comprising nine sections, contains the amendments brought to that Part. In accordance with these amendments, some basic articles of Part XI, in particular those concerning the limitation of seabed production and mandatory technology transfer, will not be applicable. A Finance Committee has been established which takes its decisions on matters of substance by consensus, and which includes the five largest financial contributors to the administrative budget of the Authority in its membership. With the amendments brought about by Section 3 of the Annex to the 1994 Agreement, power-sharing between the Assembly and the Council in the decision-making process has been changed in favour of the Council. At the same time, the role of the group of industrialized and deep sea mining states has been greatly enhanced in many ways. These states are also favoured within the decision-making procedure of the Council by a 'chamber voting' system (Section 3, para. 9 of the Annex to the Agreement). Finally, under Section 3 para. 15 of the Annex, among the 36 members of the Council, four must be among states which are the largest consumers or importers of the commodities produced from minerals derived from the seabed, four must have made the largest investments in deep seabed mining, four must be major importers of the exploited minerals, six must be from developing states and eighteen from among states of all regions. The four largest consumers must include the one state having the largest economy at the time of the Convention's entry into force and one East European state with the largest economy in that region.

15 Anthony Aust, Amendment of Treaties, refers, however, to certain other, lesser known cases of multilateral agreements which were amended before coming into force (in Alexander Orakhelashvili and Sarah Williams (eds), *40 Years of the Vienna Convention on the Law of Treaties*), British Institute of International and Comparative Law, 2010, pp. 53-54.

16 Art. 1 of the Agreement stipulates that its parties 'undertake to implement Part XI in accordance with this Agreement'. The Annex to the Agreement, which contains the actual amendments brought about to Part XI is to be considered 'an integral part' of it. Art. 2 stipulates that the provisions of the Agreement and those of Part XI 'shall be interpreted and applied together as a single instrument', and that 'the Agreement shall prevail' in the case of inconsistency between them. Any ratification of UNCLOS subsequent to the adoption of the Agreement would entail consent to be also bound by the Agreement. No state could be party to the Agreement without being party to UNCLOS. However, the Agreement went even further by providing that those states which were already party to UNCLOS would be considered party to the Agreement provided that they had signed the Agreement and had not objected to the procedure within twelve months from its adoption ('simplified procedure'). Although this constitutes a deviation from the law of treaties, there were no objections and thus the new system proceeded as foreseen. After its adoption on 28 July 1994, the Agreement was applied provisionally as from 16 November 1994, *i.e.*, the date of entry into force of UNCLOS, and entered definitively into force in 1996.

17 168 states have ratified or acceded to the UNCLOS so far (23 June 2019) while 150 have ratified or acceded to the Agreement on Part XI.

Other countries which are not parties to UNCLOS are Libya, Israel, Turkey, Syria, Iran, Eritrea, Colombia and Venezuela.

11.2 MARITIME ZONES UNDER UNCLOS

These comprise the Territorial Sea, the Contiguous Zone, the CS and the EEZ. One fundamental distinction between them is that which places the territorial sea in a class of its own, as it is the only one where the coastal state exercises sovereignty. The other zones provide the coastal state with the right to exercise jurisdiction for particular purposes, and may therefore be qualified as 'jurisdictional zones'.

UNCLOS also refers to internal waters,[18] i.e. the waters extending landward of the baseline. Internal waters differ from the territorial sea insofar as no right of innocent passage may be exercised there and it is generally accepted that the sovereignty of the coastal state over such waters is assimilated to sovereignty over land (although there are also differing views on this).[19]

Beyond these maritime zones lie the high seas and 'the Area', the legal status of which is also regulated by UNCLOS. As already noted, however, these maritime areas remain outside the scope of this part.

11.2.1 Territorial Sea

Territorial sea is the oldest maritime zone known to international law. According to UNCLOS Article 3, its breadth may not exceed 12 n.m. measured from the baselines,[20] a rule which is now recognized to form part of international customary law.[21] The great majority of coastal states have already proclaimed a territorial sea of such breadth, usually extending their hitherto 3 or 6 n.m. zones.

A coastal state may establish the breadth of its territorial sea by unilateral act which is valid *erga omnes* as long as the applicable international law has been complied with (mainly not exceeding 12 n.m. and respecting the rules on delimitation in the case of overlapping territorial sea zones).[22]

---

18 UNCLOS Art. 8 *et al.*

19 Marcelo Cohen, Is the Internal Waters Regime Excluded from the United Nations Convention on the Law of the Sea? in Lilian Castillo (ed), *Law of the Sea, From Grotius to the International Tribunal for the Law of the Sea*, Liber Amicorum Judge Hugo Caminos, Brill, 2015, pp. 110-124.

20 According to Art. 3 "Every State has the right to establish the breadth of its territorial sea up to a limit not exceeding 12 nautical miles, measured from baselines determined in accordance with this Convention."

21 *See, e.g., Nicaragua v. Colombia,* Judgment, 2012, *supra,* fn. 7, paras. 177 *et seq. See also* Ashley Roach, Today's Customary International Law of the Sea, *supra,* fn. 10.

22 *See also infra*, section 11.2.1.2, under "Delimitation of the territorial sea."

Within its territorial waters (territorial sea) the coastal state exercises sovereignty; nonetheless, foreign ships may pass through, in exercise of their right of innocent passage, in accordance with Articles 17 *et seq.*

11.2.1.1 Territorial Sea of Islands

UNCLOS does not treat islands differently from continental land as regards their entitlement to a 12 n.m. territorial sea zone. Article 121(2) is unequivocal on this, stating that: "the territorial sea... of an island [is] determined in accordance with the provisions of this Convention applicable to other land territory." Rocks are also entitled to a territorial sea of the same breadth.[23] A specific set of rules regarding islands forming an archipelagic state is laid down in UNCLOS.[24]

11.2.1.2 Delimitation of the Territorial Sea

In connection with the delimitation of the territorial sea,[25] whether between adjacent or opposite states (in the latter case, where the distance between the states concerned is less than 24 n.m.), UNCLOS Article 15 – which reproduces Article 12(1) of the 1958 Geneva Convention on the Territorial Sea and the Contiguous Zone – sets out two options: the conclusion of an agreement between those states or, where such agreement does not exist or has not been possible, the application of the equidistance rule. Equidistance, in the terms of Article 15, is effected by drawing a line, each point of which is at an equal distance from the nearest points from which the breadth of the territorial seas of each state is measured (*median line*).[26] Article 15, the customary law character of which has been recognized by the ICJ,[27] goes on to provide that equidistance may be set aside where so required because of the existence of 'historic title' or other 'special circumstances'.[28]

Historic title must be based on long-standing practice of the coastal state, which has been accepted by other states. If so, it would justify a larger territorial sea than that resulting from the application of the 'equidistance-median line' rule. Furthermore,

---

23 Art. 121 is as follows: "1. An island is a naturally formed area of land, surrounded by water, which is above water at high tide. 2. Except as provided for in paragraph 3, the territorial sea, the contiguous zone, the exclusive economic zone and the continental shelf of an island are determined in accordance with the provisions of this Convention applicable to other land territory. 3. Rocks which cannot sustain human habitation or economic life of their own shall have no exclusive economic zone or continental shelf."

24 UNCLOS Arts. 46-54.

25 Which is considered the simplest and most standardized type of maritime delimitation.

26 As equidistance is a principle and the median line is the method of its application, they are usually referred to together as *'equidistance-median line'*.

27 *Qatar v. Bahrain, supra*, fn. 6, para. 175.

28 UNCLOS Art. 15 provides: "Where the coasts of two States are opposite or adjacent to each other, neither of the two States is entitled, failing agreement between them to the contrary, to extend its territorial sea beyond the median line every point of which is equidistant from the nearest points on the baselines from which the breadth of the territorial seas of each of the two States is measured. The above provision does not apply, however, where it is necessary by reason of historic title or other special circumstances to delimit the territorial seas of the two States in a way which is at variance therewith."

UNCLOS specifically provides for the closure of 'historic bays' which exceed the limits set by its provisions,[29] while the existence of historic fishing rights has been recognized by jurisprudence.[30]

As other 'special circumstances' are left undefined in UNCLOS, jurisprudence is the basic means for their identification. According to this jurisprudence, 'special circumstances' are mostly associated with an unusual coastal configuration,[31] navigational channels and the presence of islands or other maritime features in the area under delimitation, which require the adjustment of the median line. In any event, 'special circumstances' constitute an exception to the rule of equidistance and as such they have to be narrowly construed. This has led to the formulation of a 'two-stage approach', according to which, the delimitation of the territorial sea between two states (whether opposite or adjacent) is effected by drawing a provisional equidistance line which may then be adjusted in the light of the existence of special circumstances (corrective function of special circumstances). The two-stage approach was applied in the *Eritrea/Yemen Case*[32] in the drawing of the 'international single boundary' between the two countries, and later adopted in several other judgments, among which *Qatar v. Bahrain*[33] for the delimitation of the territorial sea under both UNCLOS Article 15 and customary international law, in the *Guyana/Suriname* Arbitration,[34] the *Bangladesh/Myanmar* ITLOS Case[35] and the *Bangladesh/India* Arbitration.[36] The ICJ has affirmed that this is the most 'logical approach' in applying Article 15.[37]

Nonetheless, there have been cases where jurisprudence has favoured the use of another method instead of equidistance. Such was the 2007 *Nicaragua v. Honduras Case*,[38] in which the ICJ adopted the angle-bisector method (i.e. the line formed by bisecting the angle created by a linear approximation of coastlines) invoking coastal instability at the

29 UNCLOS Art. 10(6).

30 *See, e.g., Qatar v. Bahrain, supra,* regarding pearling rights.

31 *North Sea Continental Shelf Case,* Judgment, I.C.J. Reports 1969, p. 3 at p. 49, para. 91; cf. pp. 48-50, paras. 88-89.

32 *Maritime Delimitation in the Red Sea, Eritrea/Yemen* (Second Stage), 17 December 1999, Reports of International Arbitral Awards, Volume XXII, pp. 335-410. In the first stage of this Case, the Tribunal decided on the sovereignty of the two countries over several groups of islands. In the second stage it decided on the delimitation of a 'single, all purpose' maritime boundary between them.

33 *Supra,* fn. 6.

34 *Arbitration regarding the delimitation of the maritime boundary between Guyana and Suriname,* Award of 17 September 2007, Reports of International Arbitral Awards, vol. XXX pp. 1-144).

35 ITLOS, *Dispute concerning Delimitation of the Maritime Boundary between Bangladesh and Myanmar in the Bay of Bengal* (Bangladesh/Myanmar), Judgment of 14 March 2012. For observations as to the method used, *see* Irini Papanicolopulu, From the North Sea to the Bay of Bengal: Maritime Delimitation at the International Tribunal for the Law of the Sea, EJIL Talk, 23 March 2012.

36 *Bay of Bengal Maritime Boundary Arbitration, Bangladesh/India,* Award of 7 July 2014.

37 *Qatar v. Bahrain,* Judgment, *supra,* fn. 6, para. 176.

38 *Case Concerning Territorial and Maritime Dispute Between Nicaragua and Honduras in the Caribbean Sea (Nicaragua v. Honduras),* Judgment, 8 October 2007, I.C.J. Reports, 2007, p. 659.

mouth of *River Coco* which did not allow the identification of suitable base points to draw an equidistance line.[39]

Despite these exceptions and certain other cases where the order of delimitation as prescribed by Article 15 has been inverted or otherwise not adhered to,[40] it is beyond doubt that equidistance-median line remains the method which is overwhelmingly adopted by states in their bilateral treaties dealing with territorial sea delimitation involving either continental land or islands, while it also retains a predominant place in jurisprudence on the same matter.[41]

11.2.1.3 Delimitation in the Presence of Islands

UNCLOS Article 15 on territorial sea delimitation, i.e. the rule of equidistance-median line and its corollary exception of special circumstances, are, as noted above, equally applicable to delimitation of the territorial sea of continental land belonging to one state and that of an island or islands belonging to another state as well as between the territorial sea zones of islands belonging to different states.

Jurisprudence has generally accorded a 12 n.m. territorial sea zone to islands, including rocks, as long as they stay above water at high tide, i.e. provided they fall within the definition of 'island'.[42] This even in the case of very small islands to which no effect was otherwise recognized (e.g. on the maritime boundary with another state or in the delimitation of maritime zones) or which were not themselves accorded any other maritime zones (CS, EEZ). Thus, in the *Eritrea/Yemen Case*,[43] the Yemeni lone island of *Jabal al-Tayr* and the island group of *Jabal al-Zubayr* (both 'barren and inhospitable') which lay in the middle of the area to be delimited (i.e. near or on the median line between the relevant coasts), although not given any effect on the median line (single, all-purpose boundary),[44] they were accorded a full territorial sea of 12 n.m. 'even on their western side'.[45]

---

39 This method was also used in the Cases of the *Gulf of Maine* (Delimitation of the Maritime Boundary in the Gulf of Maine Area, Judgment, I.C.J. Reports 1984) and *Guinea and Guinea-Bissau* (Arbitral Award, *Delimitation of the maritime boundary between Guinea and Guinea-Bissau*, 14.2.1985, RIAA, Vol. XIX, pp. 149-196).

40 For a critique of case law after 2007 on this issue, *see* Massimo Lando, Judicial Uncertainties on Territorial Sea Delimitation under article 15 of UNCLOS, *International and Comparative Law Quarterly*, Vol. 66, Issue 3, July 2017. According to Lando, the two stages of the territorial sea delimitation method have been 'inverted' which could 'entail important practical effects on future delimitation disputes'.

41 *See, e.g., Bay of Bengal Maritime Boundary Arbitration, supra*, fn. 36, paras. 246-247; also *Dispute concerning Delimitation of the Maritime between Ghana and Côte d'Ivoire in the Atlantic Ocean (Ghana/Côte d'Ivoire)*, ITLOS, Judgment No. 23, 23 September 2017, where the Tribunal applied strict equidistance for the delimitation of the single maritime boundary between the two countries involved.

42 Art. 121(1).

43 *Supra*, fn. 32.

44 *Ibid.*, paras. 147-148.

45 *Ibid.*, para. 119.

In the 2007 *Nicaragua v. Honduras Case*, the ICJ recognized a 12 n.m. territorial zone to four islands which lay in the area to be delimited[46]; it did not, however, attribute any other maritime zones to them as it seems there was consent of the parties to this effect.[47]

Other relevant cases in this context are those of *Romania v. Ukraine*,[48] *Bangladesh/Myanmar*[49] as well as the abovementioned *Nicaragua v. Colombia*,[50] which mostly concerned the delimitation of CS and EEZ. In the first one among them, where the ICJ did not otherwise recognize any jurisdictional zones to *Serpent's island*, the latter was afforded a full 12 n.m. territorial sea, albeit on the basis of a prior agreement of the parties.[51] Similarly, in *Bangladesh/Myanmar*,[52] the first delimitation case brought before ITLOS, the Tribunal accepted that *St. Martin's Island*, although totally deprived of jurisdictional zones, was entitled to a 12 n.m. territorial sea where there was no overlapping with Myanmar.[53] The Tribunal did not accept the argumentation of Myanmar that St. Martin's constituted a special circumstance for the purposes of territorial sea delimitation,[54] adding, rather unfortunately, however, that in its view there was no jurisprudence or state practice proving the existence of a general rule "concerning the effect to be given to islands in maritime delimitation. It depends on the particular circumstances of each case."[55]

In the 2012 *Nicaragua v. Colombia Case*,[56] the Court, recognizing a 12 n.m. territorial sea to all Colombian islands, confirmed that "islands, regardless of their size, enjoy the same status and generate the same maritime rights, as other land territory."[57] At the same time, finding that the marked disparity in the coastal lengths of the two countries constituted relevant circumstances which justified a significant eastwards shift of the provisional median line, the court found it necessary to clarify that: "The line cannot, however,

46 These were: *Bobel Cay, Savanna Cay, Port Royal Cay, and South Cay.*

47 Thus, the Judgment states that "as regards the islands in dispute no claim has been made by either Party for maritime areas other than the territorial sea" (para. 262).

48 ICJ, *Maritime Delimitation in the Black Sea (Romania v. Ukraine)* Judgment, 3 February 2009, I.C.J. Reports 2009, p. 61.

49 ITLOS, *Bangladesh/Myanmar, supra,* fn. 35.

50 ICJ, *Territorial and Maritime Dispute (Nicaragua v. Colombia)* Judgment, 2012, *supra,* fn. 7.

51 Para. 188 of the Judgment.

52 *Supra,* fn. 35.

53 The Tribunal observed that, "in giving St. Martin's Island full effect in the delimitation of the territorial sea, the delimitation line will reach a point where the island's territorial sea no longer overlaps with the territorial sea of Myanmar. At this point, the territorial sea around St. Martin's Island begins to meet the exclusive economic zone and the continental shelf of Myanmar. This will occur in the area defined by the 12 nm envelope of arcs of the territorial sea of St. Martin's Island beyond point 8" (Judgment, para. 168).

54 Judgment, *supra,* paras. 151, 152. Bangladesh, on its part, claimed that Myanmar had "attempted to manufacture a 'special circumstance' where none exists" (para. 138).

55 *Ibid.*, para. 147.

56 *Supra,* fn. 7. Colombia, which is not a party to UNCLOS, has a significant number of islands at a closer distance to Nicaragua than itself (they are at a distance of about 185-230 from the coast of Nicaragua and more than 300 n.m. from that of Colombia). Sovereignty over some of these islands was also disputed.

57 *Ibid.*, para. 176. In this respect the ICJ specifically referred to *Qatar v. Bahrain*, para. 185 *in fine*.

be shifted so far that it cuts across the 12-nautical-mile territorial sea around any of the Colombian islands ....”[58] In the same case, the ICJ held that:

> A case where an island was not afforded any territorial sea in delimitation by agreement, was that of an island situated in a strait of less than 24 n.m. between two coastal states and the island was ignored so that both states may be afforded proportionate territorial seas.[59]

It may be concluded, therefore, that, despite some exceptions, the jurisprudence of international judicial organs has been consistently confirming the recognition of a 12 n.m. territorial sea to all islands.

Another aspect regarding the presence of islands and its effect on delimitation, which has been clarified by jurisprudence is that when the territorial sea of an island (or, for that matter, of continental land), is competing with a sovereign rights (jurisdictional) zone, such as a CS claim, the former prevails, as sovereignty is of higher importance. Thus, in *Bangladesh/Myanmar*, the Tribunal affirmed that any conclusion to the contrary would result in more weight being given to the sovereign rights and jurisdiction of Myanmar in its EEZ and CS than to the sovereignty of Bangladesh over its territorial sea.[60] In the same vein, the Tribunal in the *Dubai/Sharjah Arbitration*[61] held that the right of the island of *Abu Musa* over its territorial sea prevailed over any existing or future claims of neighbouring states over a CS.[62]

Enclaves. An important element to take into consideration in drawing the delimitation line for the territorial sea – or the other zones – of islands, is the possibility for them to be ‘enclaved’ within foreign sovereignty or jurisdiction without connection to the sovereignty they belong to. There are cases where this consideration has been taken into account and others in which it has not. Examples of the latter type are found in the

58 *Nicaragua v. Colombia, supra,* fn. 7, para. 233.

59 *Ibid.*, para. 179. In this paragraph, the Court refers, with regard to the exception of overlapping territorial seas, to *Qatar v. Bahrain*, where *Qita't Jaradah*, a very small island (12 by 4 metres) lying within the 12 n.m. territorial seas of both Bahrain and Qatar and found to belong to Bahrain, was held by the ICJ to constitute a special circumstance, as its eastern side could generate a disproportionate effect on the maritime boundary (*Qatar v. Bahrain*, para. 219); the delimitation line of the boundary passed, therefore, exactly to the east of the island, thus according no effect to it on the territorial sea of Bahrain. By contrast, the only slightly bigger island of *Janan*, which was recognized by the Court to belong to Qatar (*Janan* is located at 2.9 miles from the Qatari coast), was not found to constitute a special circumstance and was accorded full effect on the Qatari territorial sea. It is noteworthy that in the same case of *Qatar v. Bahrain* the Court affirmed that Art. 121(2) reflects customary international law, and that “islands, regardless of their size, enjoy the same status, and therefore generate the same maritime rights as land territory” (*Qatar v. Bahrain*, para. 185. Also, *Nicaragua v. Colombia*, para. 176).

60 *Supra*, fn. 35, para. 169. *See also Nicaragua v. Colombia, supra*, fn. 7, para. 178.

61 *Dubai/Sharjah*, Border Arbitration, 19 October 1981, 91 *International Law Reports*, pp. 543, 674.

62 According to the Tribunal this right existed “ex principio...independently and separately from either the actual or potential continental shelf claims of neighbouring states.”

1977 *Anglo-French Arbitration*, where the *Channel Islands*, to which a 12 n.m. territorial sea was attributed, remained nonetheless partially enclaved. Similarly, on the basis of the 1992 *Canada-France Arbitration* concerning delimitation between *New Foundland* and the French islands of *St. Pierre and Miquelon*, the latter remained partially enclaved (mostly within 24-miles enclaves).

In *Nicaragua v. Colombia*, the ICJ opined that the formation of 'enclaves' leads to fragmentation of the maritime space with unfortunate consequences in the management of maritime resources, policing and maintenance of public order at sea. The Court observed:

> ... In the Court's view, confining Colombia to a succession of enclaves drawn around each of its islands, as Nicaragua proposes, would disregard that second requirement. Even if each island were to be given an enclave of 12 nautical miles and not 3 nautical miles as suggested by Nicaragua, the effect would be to cut off Colombia from the substantial areas to the east of the principal islands, where those islands generate an entitlement to a continental shelf and exclusive economic zone. In addition, the Nicaraguan proposal would produce a disorderly pattern of several distinct Colombian enclaves within a maritime space which otherwise pertained to Nicaragua with unfortunate consequences for the orderly management of maritime resources, policing and the public order of the oceans in general, all of which would be better served by a simpler and more coherent division of the relevant area.[63]

11.2.1.4 The Slovenia/Croatia Case (Arbitration)[64]

This case presents some interesting characteristics which are connected with or impact on territorial sea delimitation. The Arbitral Tribunal was mandated by the 2009 agreement concluded by the two countries to determine the course of the maritime and land

63 Judgment, para. 230. Nonetheless, the Court recognized enclaves in the case of two maritime features (the banks of *Quitaseño* and *Serrana*) to which it accorded only a 12 n.m. of territorial sea (Judgment, para. 238).

64 PCA Case No. 2012-04, *In the matter of an arbitration under the Arbitration Agreement between the Government of the Republic of Croatia and the Government of the Republic of Slovenia, signed on 4 November 2009,* Final Award, 29 May 2017. Leaving behind them a long history of wrangling concerning their maritime and land boundary in the Bay of Piran and other related issues, Slovenia and Croatia reached an agreement (Stockholm, 4 November 2009) to submit their dispute(s) to an Arbitral Tribunal formed under PCA, which would decide on the course of the boundary between the two countries as well as on Slovenia's access to the high seas and on 'the regime for the use of the relevant maritime areas'. The Agreement was negotiated under EU auspices and its conclusion allowed the lifting of Slovenia's reservations (Art. 9) as regards the opening and closing of negotiation chapters between Croatia and the EU 'where the obstacle is related to the dispute', a matter of great importance for Croatia's accession to the EU. Slovenia was already a member of the EU at the date of signature of the arbitration agreement, as she had acceded on 1 May 2004. Croatia was a candidate state at the time, and became an EU member state on 1 July 2013.

boundary between them by applying the "rules and principles of international law,"[65] while "international law, equity and the principle of good neighbourly relations in order to achieve a fair and equitable result"[66] would be applicable in order to determine Slovenia's 'Junction to the High Sea'[67] and the regime of the other relevant maritime areas. The fact that the Tribunal was mandated to decide on the Junction suggests that its establishment had already been agreed upon. Furthermore, the Tribunal had obviously been instructed to adjudicate on an *ex aequo et bono* basis, since reference to 'good neighbourly relations' as a principle for deciding the matter, naturally leads to this conclusion.

In connection with the Bay of Piran – which, according to the Award, constitutes an 'indentation in the Gulf of Trieste'[68] – flanked by *Cape Madona* of Slovenia to the North-East and *Cape Savudrija* of Croatia to the South-West, the Tribunal found that it remained internal waters within the limits existing prior to the dissolution of the SFRY, the effect of such dissolution being 'a question of state succession'.[69] Furthermore, as there had been no formal division of the Bay between the two Republics prior to the dissolution of Yugoslavia and in the absence of any provision on the delimitation of internal waters in 'Law of the Sea Conventions', the same principles would be applicable with regard to the Bay as for the delimitation of land territories. In the particular case, the principle would be *uti possidetis* as informed by relevant *effectivités*. On the basis of these considerations, Slovenia was awarded three quarters and Croatia one quarter of the Bay.

Concerning the determination of the respective territorial seas, which extend seaward of the Bay, the Tribunal unexpectedly revived the near-defunct principle of 'natural prolongation' which it transposed from the domain of CS to that of the territorial sea.[70] Another principle it found applicable is that "the effects of an incidental special feature from which an unjustifiable difference of treatment could result"[71] "should be abated when effecting a maritime delimitation."[72] In the instant case, the Tribunal identified the 'incidental special feature' in

> the fact that.... the coastline of Croatia turns sharply southwards around Cape Savudrija, so that the Croatian basepoints that control the equidistance line are located on a very small stretch of coast whose general (north-facing) direction

65 Final Award, *supra*, fn. 34, para. 109, referring to Art. 3(1)(a) of the Agreement on Dispute Settlement between the two countries.

66 *Ibid.*, Art. 3(1)(b).

67 *See infra*, pp. 10-11.

68 Final Award, *supra*, fn. 34, para. 8. Indeed, the Bay of Piran represents a small fraction of the Gulf of Trieste, *i.e.*, about 3.3% of its total area. The mouth of the Bay is approximately 5 km wide.

69 Final Award, para. 885. The Tribunal makes reference to the ICJ Judgment on the Land, Island and Maritime Frontier Dispute Case (El Salvador/Honduras: Nicaragua intervening) I.C.J. Reports 1992, p. 351 at pp. 589, 599-600; paras. 385, 401.

70 Final Award, para. 1008.

71 Quoted from the North Sea Continental Shelf Judgment, I.C.J. Reports 1969, p. 3, para. 91.

72 Final Award, para. 1009.

> is markedly different from the general (southwest-facing) direction of much the greater part of the Croatian coastline, and deflect the equidistance line very significantly towards the north, greatly exaggerating the "boxed-in" nature of Slovenia's maritime zone.[73]

In an effort to reconcile these two 'principles', the Tribunal furthermore stated that the latter should not encroach on the principle of natural prolongation.[74]

Based on this rationale, the Tribunal modified the provisional equidistance line so as not to disproportionately exacerbate the 'boxed-in' nature of Slovenia's maritime zone.[75]

Furthermore, the Tribunal affirmed that in the particular case there was no question of delimiting EEZs, as the parties had, in effect, instructed the Tribunal to treat the maritime areas beyond territorial seas as high seas.[76]

Finally, the Tribunal established the Junction, i.e. the maritime 'corridor' which secures Slovenia's access to and from international waters and airspace.[77] The Junction lies within the Croatian territorial sea, its external side following the maritime border with the Italian territorial waters as agreed by the *Treaty of Osimo* of 10 November 1975 between Italy and Yugoslavia. Within the Junction the Arbitral Award provides for a very broad 'freedom of communication' for all ships and aircraft of all nationalities whether civil or military, 'for the purposes of uninterrupted and uninterruptible access to and from Slovenia, including its territorial sea and its airspace'; this freedom also includes the laying of cables and pipelines.[78]

The freedom of communication thus established is not subject to any criterion of innocence and cannot be suspended under any circumstances. Submarines are not obligated to navigate on the surface and they are not subject to any coastal state controls or requirements other than those allowed under the UNCLOS EEZ legal regime.[79] It is therefore clear that the rights of Croatia over the Junction include, apart from those expressly provided for in the Award, those exercised by a coastal state over its EEZ. The Tribunal confirms this also in a negative way, by expressly *not* attributing to Slovenia the rights pertaining to EEZ in the Junction.[80]

---

73 *Ibid.*, para. 1011.
74 *Ibid.* para. 1008.
75 *Ibid.*, para. 1011.
76 *Ibid.*, para. 1015.
77 The Junction is approximately 2.5 n.m. wide and 10 n.m. long.
78 Final Award, para. 1123 and 1124.
79 *Ibid.*, para. 1127.
80 *See Ibid.*, para. 1126 which provides: "The freedom of communication shall not include the freedom to explore, exploit, conserve or manage the natural resources, whether living or non-living, of the waters or the seabed or the subsoil in the Junction Area, nor shall it include the right to establish and use artificial islands, installations or structures, or the right to engage in marine scientific research, or the right to take measures for the protection or preservation of the marine environment."

Furthermore, ships and aircraft in the Junction area 'shall not be subject to boarding, arrest, detention, diversion or any other form of interference by Croatia' while there.[81] Given the many instances where such boardings, diversions, etc. may be legally undertaken under many international conventional and other instruments, particularly related to counter terrorism and the suppression of weapons of mass destruction (WMD) transportation, the clarifications contained in the Final Award which refer to such obligations are of great importance[82] although, perhaps, not entirely sufficient.[83]

11.2.2 Jurisdictional Zones

11.2.2.1 Contiguous Zone

This maritime belt, which is contiguous to the territorial sea,[84] was established for the first time in the 1958 'Convention on the Territorial Sea and the Contiguous Zone'.[85] Its breadth together with that of the territorial sea could not, under that Convention, exceed 12 n.m.[86] measured from the baselines. Under UNCLOS, the breadth of the contiguous zone "may not extend beyond 24 nautical miles from the baselines from which the breadth of the territorial sea is measured."[87] The purpose of this zone, as described in UNCLOS, is to provide the coastal state with the possibility to prevent and punish the infringement of its customs, fiscal, immigration or sanitary laws and regulations within its territory or territorial sea.[88]

Archaeological or Historical Objects

Coastal states in the adjacent maritime areas of which (including their seabed and subsoil) are contained archaeological or historical objects have a particular interest in UNCLOS Article 303, which establishes a direct functional linkage with Article 33 on the Contiguous Zone. Indeed, Article 303(2) provides that,

> [i]n order to control traffic in such objects, the coastal State may, in applying article 33, presume that their removal from the seabed in the zone referred to in that article without its approval would result in an infringement within its territory or territorial sea of the laws and regulations referred to in that article.

---

81 *Ibid.*, para. 1129.
82 Final Award, para. 1135.
83 *E.g.*, the cases provided for in UNCLOS Art. 110 (Right of Visit) may not be covered.
84 On this subject *see* John Noyes, The Territorial Sea and Contiguous Zone in Donald Rothwell, Alex Oude Elferink, Karen Scott, and Tim Stephens (eds), *The Oxford Handbook of the Law of the Sea*, 2015.
85 Art. 24.
86 At the time this was already an indication that the breadth of the territorial sea on its own could reach but not exceed 12 n.m.
87 UNCLOS Art. 33(2).
88 UNCLOS Art. 33(1).

A parallel rule is found in UNCLOS Article 149 which belongs to Part XI of the Convention dealing with the 'Area'[89] and provides that:

> All objects of an archaeological and historical nature found in the Area shall be preserved or disposed of for the benefit of mankind as a whole, particular regard being paid to the preferential rights of the State or country of origin, or the State of cultural origin, or the State of historical and archaeological origin.

A difference between Articles 149 and 303 is that the former expressly refers to the preferential rights of the state or country of origin, whether cultural, historical or archaeological. This is not done in Article 303, presumably because in its case the state from which the objects originate and which has preferential rights on them (by virtue of its own domestic legislation) will be the coastal state to which the article specifically refers. In fact, Article 303 creates a true 'archaeological zone', the breadth of which is assimilated with that of the contiguous zone, within which the coastal state exercises jurisdiction for the protection of 'objects of an archaeological and historical nature found at sea'.[90]

A specific conventional instrument dealing with such objects is the 2001 UNESCO Convention on the Protection of the Underwater Cultural Heritage,[91] which also recognizes the jurisdiction of the coastal state over cultural objects found within its contiguous zone.[92] It also creates a complex system of protection of underwater cultural heritage in the EEZ and on the CS, through consultations among contracting parties.[93, 94]

11.2.2.2 Continental Shelf (CS)

The 1958 Convention on the Continental Shelf was the first multilateral instrument to regulate this zone, finding its inspiration in the Truman Proclamation on the Continental Shelf of 28 September 1945. The Convention defined 'continental shelf' as the seabed and subsoil of the submarine areas adjacent to the (continental and insular) coast beyond the territorial sea, "to a depth of 200 metres or, beyond that limit, to where the depth of the superjacent waters admits of the exploitation of the natural resources of the said areas."[95] UNCLOS changed this by providing for the establishment of a 200 n.m. zone measured

89 Arts. 133-149.

90 UNCLOS Art. 303(1).

91 Paris, 2 November 2001. The Convention entered into force on 2 January 2009.

92 Art. 8 of the Convention.

93 Some questions are raised, however, *inter alia*, as to the conformity of the UNESCO Convention with UNCLOS on this issue, as – despite assurances to the contrary-, the UNESCO Convention provisions as well as the Rules it provides for the protection of underwater cultural heritage in the CS and the EEZ may also be applied in the contiguous zone. In such a case, it is possible that the rights recognized by UNCLOS to the coastal state in that zone may be diluted.

94 *See* Krateros Ioannou and Anastasia Strati, Law of the Sea, 4th edn, Athens, Nomiki Vivliothiki, 2013 (in Greek), pp. 93-99.

95 Art. 1a) of the 1958 Convention on the Continental Shelf.

from the baselines in case the natural prolongation of the land territory of the coastal state does not extend to the outer edge of the continental margin. If there is such a prolongation, the shelf may extend beyond 200 n.m. but not exceed 350 n.m. (648 km) from the baselines or, alternatively, not exceed 100 n.m. (185 km) seaward of the isobath of 2,500 m, i.e. the line connecting the depth of 2,500 m. In the latter case, the CS may extend beyond 350 n.m., and the same may happen where there are some specific geomorphological circumstances (certain types of submarine elevations).[96]

Where the CS extends beyond 200 nautical miles from the baselines from which the breadth of the territorial sea is measured, the coastal state has to submit information on its limits to the 'Commission on the Limits of the Continental Shelf' provided for in UNCLOS Article 76(8).[97] The Commission makes recommendations to the coastal state as regards the establishment of the outer limits of its CS. Once established by the coastal State on the basis of these recommendations, the limits of its CS are final and binding.

The benefits offered by an extended CS will continue to be a serious incentive for coastal states with large oceanic fronts to submit such claims to the Commission on the Limits of the Continental Shelf.

The rights of a coastal state over its CS exist *ipso facto* and *ab initio*, which means that no specific claim or declaration is needed to be made by that state to ascertain its rights there. While the CS offers all possibilities of exploration and exploitation of the seabed and its subsoil, it also secures that superjacent waters retain the legal character of the high seas, thus allowing international navigation to enjoy unimpeded passage, a matter of major importance to international shipping, particularly in narrow, closed or semi-enclosed seas.

11.2.2.3 Exclusive Economic Zone (EEZ)[98]

This is the most recent addition to the jurisdictional maritime zones recognized by international law, which finds its origin in the establishment, in 1947, by Chile and Peru, of

96 The relevant paras. 1, 5 and 6 of Art. 76 provide that: "1. The continental shelf of a coastal State comprises the seabed and subsoil of the submarine areas that extend beyond its territorial sea throughout the natural prolongation of its land territory to the outer edge of the continental margin, or to a distance of 200 nautical miles from the baselines from which the breadth of the territorial sea is measured where the outer edge of the continental margin does not extend up to that distance. 5. The fixed points comprising the line of the outer limits of the continental shelf on the seabed, drawn in accordance with paragraph 4 (a)(i) and (ii), either shall not exceed 350 nautical miles from the baselines from which the breadth of the territorial sea is measured or shall not exceed 100 nautical miles from the 2,500 metre isobath, which is a line connecting the depth of 2,500 metres. 6. Notwithstanding the provisions of paragraph 5, on submarine ridges, the outer limit of the continental shelf shall not exceed 350 nautical miles from the baselines from which the breadth of the territorial sea is measured. This paragraph does not apply to submarine elevations that are natural components of the continental margin, such as its plateaux, rises, caps, banks and spurs."

97 *See infra,* at 12.4.

98 Robert Beckman and Tara Davenport, The EEZ Regime: Reflections after 30 Years, Papers from the Law of the Sea Institute, UC Berkeley–Korea Institute of Ocean Science and Technology Conference, held in Seoul, Korea, May 2012, available at: www.law.berkeley.edu/files/Beckman-Davenport-final.pdf.

maritime zones extending to 200 n.m. based on their need to acquire exclusive fishing rights in an extended area of the high seas adjacent to their territorial seas. In addition to such rights, UNCLOS has provided coastal states with further sovereign rights which they may exercise within their respective EEZs to the exclusion of other states.[99] Among these are the exploration, exploitation, conservation and management of natural resources, living or nonliving, which are found on the seabed and its subsoil and in the superjacent waters, as well as the production of energy from the water, the currents and the winds. Furthermore, UNCLOS regulates in detail the jurisdiction that a coastal state has, *inter alia*, to construct artificial islands, conduct marine scientific research, protect the marine environment[100] and impose customs, fiscal, health, safety and immigration laws in relation to these activities.

According to UNCLOS, a coastal state has to make a declaration in order to establish its EEZ. This differentiates this zone from the CS which needs no special declaration for its establishment, as it is recognized to exist *ipso facto* and *ab initio*.

In reality, the EEZ absorbs the CS, as it encompasses the sea bed and its subsoil (which constitutes the CS), adding to them their superjacent waters (the water column) up to the surface of the sea. The EEZ cannot, however, follow an eventual extension of the CS beyond 200 n.m.[101]

11.2.2.4 Delimitation of Jurisdictional Zones (CS, EEZ)

The delimitation of the CS between states with opposite coasts – where the breadth of the particular sea is less than 400 n.m., or between states with adjacent coasts[102] or where there are overlapping claims for extending the outer limit of the CS beyond 200 n.m. – is governed by the rules established in UNCLOS Article 83,[103] i.e. by agreement on the basis of international law, in order to reach an 'equitable solution', and if this is not possible, by resorting to one of the procedures prescribed by UNCLOS for dispute settlement.[104]

99 Arts. 55 to 75 (Part V).

100 UNCLOS Art. 56.

101 UNCLOS Art. 57.

102 L. Caflisch, La délimitation des espaces entre Etats dont les côtes se font face ou sont adjacentes, in R. Dupuy and D. Vignes (eds), *Traité du Nouveau Droit de la Mer*, 1985, 375-440, p. 413.

103 Art. 83 reads as follows: "1. The delimitation of the continental shelf between States with opposite or adjacent coasts shall be effected by agreement on the basis of international law, as referred to in Article 38 of the Statute of the International Court of Justice, in order to achieve an equitable solution. 2. If no agreement can be reached within a reasonable period of time, the States concerned shall resort to the procedures provided for in Part XV. 3. Pending agreement as provided for in paragraph 1, the States concerned, in a spirit of understanding and cooperation, shall make every effort to enter into provisional arrangements of a practical nature and, during this transitional period, not to jeopardize or hamper the reaching of the final agreement. Such arrangements shall be without prejudice to the final delimitation. 4. Where there is an agreement in force between the States concerned, questions relating to the delimitation of the continental shelf shall be determined in accordance with the provisions of that agreement."

104 In UNCLOS Part XV.

The delimitation of the EEZ follows the same regulatory pattern as the delimitation of the CS. Indeed, UNCLOS Article 74 which governs EEZ delimitation is identical with its Article 83 governing the delimitation of the CS.

Pre-UNCLOS, the ICJ had stated in its 1969 seminal judgment on the *Continental Shelf Case*[105] that equidistance was not a rule of customary law and that the delimitation of the CS should be 'equitable' and take into account 'relevant circumstances'.[106] During discussions in the Third Conference on the Law of the Sea,[107] there were two basic approaches as to how to delimit jurisdictional maritime zones: 'equidistance' and 'equitable principles', which was a matter of intense controversy between the negotiating states. Finally, UNCLOS, having retained equidistance in combination with special circumstances with regard to territorial sea delimitation,[108] went on to adopt agreement on the basis of international law with a view to achieving 'an equitable solution'[109] in the case of the delimitation of jurisdictional zones.

Post-UNCLOS, jurisprudence was originally inclined towards a 'result-oriented' (case-by-case) approach to delimitation, which consists in stressing the attainment of equitable results and rejecting any obligatory delimitation method. This approach – which had found its origin in the aforementioned 1969 ICJ judgment on the *North Sea Continental Shelf Cases* – was adopted, in general terms, also in the cases of *Tunisia v. Libya,*[110] *Gulf of Maine,*[111] *Guinea/Guinea Bissau,*[112] and *St. Pierre and Miquelon,*[113] and it concerned the delimitation between states with adjacent coasts. Gradually, however, jurisprudence turned towards embracing the idea of 'corrective equity', which, much along the lines used in territorial sea delimitation, consists in employing two stages (later three)[114] in the delimitation of jurisdictional zones: an 'equidistance (median) line' is drawn first, and, at a second stage, consideration is given as to whether there are circum-

105 *North Sea Continental Shelf Case, (Germany/Denmark, Germany/Netherlands),* Judgment, 20 February 1969, I.C.J. Reports 1969, p. 3.

106 "[D]elimitation [of the continental shelf] is to be effected by agreement in accordance with equitable principles, and taking account of all the relevant circumstances..." (*North Sea Continental Shelf Case,* Judgment, 1969, *supra,* fn. 31, para. 101).

107 Held between 1973 and 1982.

108 *Supra,* at 11.2.1.2.

109 According to Art. 74(1): "The delimitation of the exclusive economic zone between States with opposite or adjacent coasts shall be effected by agreement on the basis of international law, as referred to in Article 38 of the Statute of the International Court of Justice, in order to achieve an equitable solution." Art. 83(1) of UNCLOS dealing with the delimitation of the continental shelf is identical.

110 *Continental Shelf (Tunisia/Libyan Arab Jamahiriya),* Judgment, I.C.J. Reports 1982, p. 18, the Court found that: "..[e]quidistance is not, in the view of the Court, either a mandatory legal principle, or a method having some privileged status in relation to other methods" (para. 110).

111 *Delimitation of the Maritime Boundary in the Gulf of Maine Area,* Judgment, I.C.J. Reports 1984, p. 299-300, para. 112.

112 Arbitral Award, *Delimitation of the maritime boundary between Guinea and Guinea-Bissau,* 14 February 1985, RIAA, Vol. XIX, pp. 149-196.

113 Arbitral Award, *Delimitation of maritime areas between Canada and France,* 10 June 1992, RIAA, Vol. XXI pp. 265-341.

114 *See infra* at 11.2.2.9.

stances justifying its adjustment. If so, the median line is shifted as appropriate.[115] The 'corrective equity' approach has been adopted in, among others, the *Anglo-French Continental* Shelf,[116]*Jan Mayen,*[117] *Eritrea/Yemen,*[118] *Qatar v. Bahrain,*[119] *Cameroon v. Nigeria,*[120] *Bangladesh/Myanmar*[121] and *Nicaragua v. Colombia*[122] Cases.

Overall, the 'corrective equity' approach is seen by jurisprudence as representing the better option in cases involving opposite coastal states; nonetheless, it has also been employed in cases involving adjacent states (e.g. *Cameroon v. Nigeria*).[123]

In qualitative terms, despite an apparent element of flexibility, the 'result-oriented' approach to delimitation suffers from obvious unpredictability to the point of 'legal impressionism',as eloquently expressed by Yoshifumi Tanaka,[124] a factor which has been decisive in its decline. By contrast, 'corrective equity' seems to provide a higher degree of legal security, which accounts for its increasing use.[125]

11.2.2.5 Relevant Circumstances

As to the question what constitutes 'relevant circumstances', it is generally considered that these may be identified in certain geographical characteristics, such as the coastal configuration of the states involved and the presence of islands or other maritime features. Generally, however, the justifications put forward in judgments or awards as to why certain situations may or may not be considered 'relevant circumstances' vary widely, even in the context of the same case.[126]

Among the elements also suggested to constitute relevant circumstances have been geological and geomorphological circumstances, historical title, the existence of mineral, oil and other deposits, and social and economic circumstances.

---

115 See Yoshifumi Tanaka, Predictability and Flexibility in the Law of Maritime Delimitation, 2006, pp. 119 *et seq.*

116 Arbitral Award, *Delimitation of the Continental Shelf between the United Kingdom of Great Britain and Northern Ireland, and the French Republic* (U.K., France), 30 June 1977-14 March 1978, RIAA Vol. XXI pp. 265-341.

117 *Maritime Delimitation in the Area between Greenland and Jan Mayen (Denmark v. Norway),* Judgment, 14 June 1993, I.C.J. Reports 1993.

118 *Supra,* fn. 32.

119 *Supra,* fn. 6.

120 *Cameroon v. Nigeria: Equatorial Guinea intervening,* Judgment, 10 October, 2002.

121 *Supra,* fn. 35.

122 *Supra,* fn. 7.

123 Some cases, such as *Libya v. Malta (Continental Shelf (Libyan Arab Jamahiriya v. Malta)* Judgment, I. C.J. Reports 1985, p. 13) have borrowed elements from both approaches, thus being, to a certain extent at least, 'hybrid'.

124 *Op. cit.,* p. 123.

125 For an analysis of the 'corrective approach,' *see Guyana/Suriname,* Award (*supra* fn. 34), paras. 335-341.

126 *E.g.,* in the 1993 *Jan Mayen (Denmark v. Norway)* Judgment (*supra* fn. 117), although the Court found that the island of *Jan Mayen* should receive less than full equidistance effect, it did not consider the Danish argument according to which *Jan Mayen* should have been entitled to less continental shelf due to the scant number of its inhabitants and its limited economic life (paras. 79-80).

In connection with geological and geomorphological circumstances, the ICJ in its earlier judgments had considered that certain such circumstances were indeed 'relevant' for delimitation purposes.[127] Now, however, it steadily holds the position that such circumstances are not to be taken into account. Thus, in the *Libya v. Malta Case*, the Court held that:

> ... [s]ince the development of the law enables a State to claim that the continental shelf appertaining to it extends up to as far as 200 miles from its coast, there is no reason to ascribe any role to geological or geophysical factors within that distance either in verifying the legal title of the States concerned or in proceeding to a delimitation as between their claims.[128]

In the 2012 *Nicaragua v. Colombia Case* judgment, the ICJ found that geomorphological considerations were not justified in connection with the delimitation of maritime zones of islands[129] and arguments that 'the islands were sitting on foreign continental shelf' put forward so as to deprive those islands of such maritime zones were groundless. The Court held that:

> It has repeatedly been made clear that geological or geomorphological considerations are not relevant to the delimitation of overlapping entitlements within 200 nautical miles of the coasts of States .... The reality is that the Nicaraguan mainland and fringing islands, and the Colombian islands, are located on the same continental shelf. That fact cannot, in and of itself, give one State's entitlements priority over those of the other in respect of the area where their claims overlap.[130]

In connection with historical title, while such title is treated like a special circumstance justifying a change in the delimitation of the territorial sea by equidistance,[131] the success

---

127 *E.g.*, in its judgments on the *North Sea Continental Shelf*, and in the *Gulf of Maine* (*supra*, fn. 31).
128 *Continental Shelf (Libyan Arab Jamahiriya v. Malta)*, Judgment, I. C.J. Reports 1985, p. 13, para. 39.
129 *See also infra*, 11.2.2.6.
130 Para. 214 of the Judgment.
131 UNCLOS Art. 15.

of a similar claim in connection with jurisdictional zones is doubtful at best,[132] with the eventual exception of traditionally exercised fishing.[133]

Social and economic factors have rarely been taken into account for delimitation purposes. In the *Gulf of Maine Case*, the ICJ formulated a test according to which, in order to be taken into account, such factors should be 'likely to entail catastrophic repercussions for the livelihood and economic well-being of the population'; this requirement was not, however, found to be satisfied in the particular case.[134] Similarly, in *Libya v. Malta*, the Court refused to take such factors into account.[135] It did, however, do so in the *Jan Mayen Case*.[136]

Finally, the existence of oil deposits and oil wells and the connected oil concessions have not been considered to constitute relevant circumstances.[137]

11.2.2.6 Delimitation of the CS and EEZ of Islands

UNCLOS Article 121(2) which, as already noted, reflects a rule of customary international law, is also applicable with regard to the jurisdictional zones of islands, attributing to them all such zones on an equal footing with continental land territory, with the explanatory addition, in Paragraph 121(3), that "rocks which cannot sustain human habitation or economic life of their own" will not have either CS or EEZ. The obvious lack of precision of this 'clarification' leaves room for interpretations which often clash with the fundamental principle stated in Art. 121(2). Indeed, although the quest for the real meaning of 'economic life of their own' and 'sustenance' of 'human habitation' remains a constant in legal debate,[138] no interpretation should be allowed to reverse the rule contained in art. 121(2).

Jurisprudence, on its part, has confirmed that islands are entitled to jurisdictional zones on an equal footing with continental land, as, for example, in *Qatar v. Bahrain*[139]

132 So far the ICJ has not accepted such a claim. The same conclusion can be drawn from the 2016 Award of the Arbitral Tribunal on the *Philippines v. China Case* (*see infra*, at 13.3.7).

133 *Maritime Delimitation in the Area between Greenland and Jan Mayen (Denmark v. Norway), supra* fn. 126, paras. 76-78. On the other hand, the claim of Bahrain in *Qatar v. Bahrain* (*supra*, fn. 7) that it had historic title to pearling banks found on the Qatari side of the provisional equidistance line of the single maritime border between the two states was not retained by the Court, *inter alia* because pearl diving was traditionally considered to be a right common to the coastal population, rather than subject to the sovereignty of one of the two states.

134 *Gulf of Maine, supra*, fn. 111, para. 237.

135 *Supra*, fn. 128, para. 50.

136 *Supra*, fn. 117, para. 76.

137 *Land and Maritime Boundary between Cameroon and Nigeria (Equatorial Guinea intervening), supra*, fn. 120, pp. 447-448, para. 304.

138 See *The Republic of Philippines v. The People's Republic of China, PCA case No. 2013-19*, Award, 12 July 2016, paras. 473 *et seq*. See also D. Bowett, Islands, Rocks, Reefs and Low-Tide Elevations in Maritime Boundary Delimitation, in J. Charney and L. Alexander (eds), *International Maritime Boundaries* (1993) 151.

139 *See* para. 185 where the ICJ found that 'islands, regardless of their size, in this respect enjoy the same status and therefore generate the same maritime rights, as other land territory.'

and in *Nicaragua v. Colombia.* [140] Nonetheless, there are cases where it has been less assertive in this respect, by relying on a variety of often questionable conditions as 'relevant circumstances', an approach which remains largely unjustified in terms of international law of the sea. [141]

11.2.2.7 Delimitation of a Single Maritime Boundary

The possibility to delimit a single maritime boundary for the CS and the EEZ does not originate from customary or (multilateral) treaty law. It is a product of state practice, finding its *raison d'être* in the quest for 'regulatory simplicity'.[142] The *Gulf of Maine Case* was the first where a single boundary was drawn by the ICJ.[143] Since then, this type of delimitation has been applied several times[144] and it is by now an established request of states wishing to have their maritime boundary delimited by an international organ that the boundary serve the purposes of both, the CS and the EEZ.

As the delimitation rules in Articles 74(1) and 83(1) are identical, it is reasonable that 'equitable principles-relevant circumstances' should also be applicable in the delimitation of a single maritime boundary. In this context, the ICJ observed in the *Gulf of Maine Case*, that coastal geography is equally relevant to the delimitation of both the EEZ and the CS and indicated that in such cases preference must be given to criteria 'derived from

140 *See* para 176, where the Court, after repeating its finding in *Qatar v. Bahrain*, noted that 'a comparatively small island may give an entitlement to a considerable maritime area.'

141 Some of the judgments or awards which have thus curtailed or denied the right of islands to have effect on or be accorded jurisdictional zones, have already been mentioned or commented on above (e.g. the 1981 *Dubai/Sharja* arbitration, *supra*, fn. 61 ; the 1999 *Eritrea/Yemen* arbitration, *supra*, fn. 32, although this award did also accord full effect to certain islands. Other such judgments were issued in a number of cases, among which the 1982 Tunisia v. Libya (*supra* fn. 110) and the 1984 Gulf of Maine (Canada/USA, *supra* fn. 111) Cases. Similarly, in the 2009 *Romania v. Ukraine (Black Sea) Case (supra*, fn. 48), no effect was accorded to the Ukrainian Serpent's Island with regard to jurisdictional zones, while in the 2012 *Bangladesh/Myanmar Case*, ITLOS, taking an exaggerated view of the geographical position of *St. Martin's island* which belongs to Bangladesh but lies on the other side of the Bay of Bengal at a short distance from the coastline of Myanmar, decided not to recognize any effect to the island as regards both, CS and EEZ. According to the Tribunal's reasoning, *St. Martin's* could not be taken as a base point for delimitation because an unwarranted distortion of the delimitation line would be caused, which would be tantamount to '*judicial refashioning of geography*', a finding which, however, rather seems to 'refashion the law' on this matter. The reasons (relevant circumstances) put forward in judgments or awards recognizing limited or no effect to maritime features vary widely and include, *inter alia*, their size which may be qualified as 'small', 'tiny' or 'minor' or their (significant) distance from '*terra firma*' or their character of uninhabited rocks or low-tide elevations. In the recent case of *Costa Rica v. Nicaragua* (Maritime Delimitation in the Carribean Sea and the Pacific Ocean and Land Boundary in the Northern Part of Isla Portillos, General List 157 and 165, Judgment, 2 February 2018), the ICJ considered that the Nicaraguan *Corn Islands*, given their limited size and significant distance from the mainland coast, should be awarded only half effect, which was also attributed to the Nicaraguan *Santa Helena* Peninsula (Ibid, para. 198).

142 Judge Shi Jiuyong, Maritime Delimitation in the Jurisprudence of the International Court of Justice, Chinese Journal of international Law, Vol. 9, Issue 2, 1 June 2010, pp. 271-291.

143 *Supra*, fn. 111, Judgment, para. 194.

144 *See, e.g., Qatar v. Bahrain*, Merits, *supra*, fn. 6, Judgment, para. 173.

geography' which, 'because of their more neutral character, are best suited for use in a multi-purpose delimitation.'[145]

11.2.2.8 Relationship between 'Special' and 'Relevant' Circumstances and the Median Line (Equidistance) as an Equitable Solution

Regarding the nature of the relationship between 'special circumstances' constituting the corollary of equidistance as a rule for the delimitation of the territorial sea and 'relevant circumstances', which is associated with the equitable principles applicable in the case of EEZ and CS delimitation, jurisprudence has gradually come to recognize that there is similarity or *rapprochement* in the interpretation of the notions that these phrases express. Thus, in the 1993 *Jan Mayen* delimitation[146] the Court, commenting on equidistance/special circumstances as endorsed in art. 6 of the 1958 Convention on the Continental Shelf (CSC) for the delimitation of CS, observed that there is *"inevitably a tendency towards assimilation between the special circumstances of art. 6 of the Convention on the Continental Shelf (CSC) and the relevant circumstances under customary law."*[147] Further on in the same case, the Court found that "[P]rima facie, a median line delimitation between opposite coasts results in general in an equitable solution, particularly if the coasts in question are nearly parallel."[148] A similar conclusion was reached by the ICJ in *Qatar v. Bahrain*, which found a close connection between the "equidistance-special circumstances" and the "equitable principles-relevant circumstances" rules. It asserted, indeed, that the two sets of principles were "closely interrelated"[149] and that equidistance was also applicable in the delimitation of adjacent coastlines.[150] The same was found in *Cameroon v. Nigeria*[151] and *Peru v. Chile.*[152] The awards of arbitral tribunals have also recognized the value of equidistance as an equitable delimitation method, either for opposite or adjacent coastlines, as in the cases of *Guyana/Suriname,*[153] *Barbados/Trinidad and Tobago,*[154] *Eritrea/Yemen*[155] and *Bangladesh/India.*[156]

---

145 *Gulf of Maine Case,* Judgment, paras. 194-195.

146 *Supra,* fn. 117.

147 *Ibid,* para. 56.

148 *Ibid,* para 64.

149 *Supra,* fn. 6, Judgment, p. 40, para. 231. See also: *Barbados/Trinidad and Tobago,* 2006, XXVII RIAA 147, para. 305; *Cameroon v. Nigeria: Equatorial Guinea intervening, supra,* fn. 120, 2002, para. 288.

150 *Supra,* fn. 6, Judgment, para. 231.

151 *Supra,* fn. 120, Judgment, para. 306.

152 *Maritime Dispute (Peru v. Chile),* Judgment, I.C.J. Reports 2014, p. 3, paras. 189 *et seq.*

153 *Arbitration regarding the delimitation of the maritime boundary between Guyana and Suriname,* Award of 17.9.2007, *(supra),* fn. 34, para. 338 *et seq.* The Case did not involve the delimitation of the maritime zones of islands.

154 *Arbitration between Barbados and the Republic of Trinidad and Tobago, relating to the delimitation of the exclusive economic zone and the continental shelf between them,* Decision of 11.4. 2006, Reports of International Arbitral Awards, vol. XXVII pp.147-25, paras. 305-306.

155 Para. 131.

156 Paras. 345, 346.

Having found that the median line itself led to an equitable result, some judgments concluded that there were no circumstances requiring the adjustment of the provisional delimitation line either in all its length[157] or partially.[158]

11.2.2.9 Methodology of Delimitation of Jurisdictional Zones

As discussed above, the ICJ gradually developed a two-stage method to be applied in maritime delimitation. A third stage was added in the *Black Sea Case* which has been established since then and is now followed as a general rule in the delimitation of jurisdictional zones.[159]

The first two stages of the methodology are identical with those used for territorial sea delimitation. Thus, in the first stage, a provisional equidistance line has to be drawn.[160] This task requires the Court to determine the 'relevant coasts' to be taken into account, i.e. those which generate overlapping maritime claims (and which may be either continental or insular). Relevant base points will then have to be identified and, although the parties may indicate such base points, the Court must not rely solely on the choice of base points made by them. According to jurisprudence, the Court must select base points by reference to the physical geography of the relevant coasts.[161]

An island can be used as base point for maritime delimitation.[162] In *Nicaragua v. Colombia*, the Court recognized low-tide elevations[163] as points to be used for delimitation purposes if located within the 12 n.m. territorial sea limit.[164]

157 *Peru v. Chile, supra*, para. 191; *Guyana/Suriname, supra*, paras. 377, 392; *Romania v. Ukraine (Black Sea) Case, supra*, fn. 48.

158 *Qatar v. Bahrain*, Barbados/Trinidad and Tobago, Eritrea/Yemen.

159 The two-stage approach which was developed in the *Jan Mayen* Case under Art 6 of the Continental Shelf Convention (CSC) and customary international law (for the fisheries zone), was later transformed into the 'three-stage approach' in the *Black Sea Case*, by removing the proportionality test from the second stage and using it as a third stage for the delimitation of the EEZ and CS.

160 According to the ICJ in *Qatar and Bahrain*: "[T]he most logical and widely practiced approach is first to draw provisionally an equidistance line and then to consider whether that line must be adjusted in the light of the existence of special circumstances" (Merits, Judgment, *supra*, p. 94, para. 176).

161 *Romania v. Ukraine, supra*, para. 137.

162 *Qatar v. Bahrain*, para. 195. In *Nicaragua v. Colombia*, the ICJ did not take into account *Quitasueño* as a base point for delimitation because, although it is an island (as it is above water at high tide), it is too small (1 sq. m.), thus posing, according to the Court, a question of disproportionality as to its effect on the delimitation (paras. 200-202).

163 A low-tide elevation is, according to UNCLOS Art. 13(1) "a naturally formed area of land which is surrounded by and above water at low tide but submerged at high tide. Where a low-tide elevation is situated wholly or partly at a distance not exceeding the breadth of the territorial sea from the mainland or an island, the low-water line on that elevation may be used as the baseline for measuring the breadth of the territorial sea."

164 The Court notes: "Accordingly, the boundary between the continental shelf and exclusive economic zone of Nicaragua and the Colombian territorial sea around Quitasueño will follow a 12-nautical-mile envelope of arcs measured from QS 32 and from the low-tide elevations located within 12 nautical miles from QS 32" (para. 238).

The next (second) stage starts once the provisional equidistance line has been drawn, and consists in finding whether there are circumstances (it should be reminded, in this respect, that an osmosis of 'special' and 'relevant' circumstances has developed through jurisprudence) which justify an adjustment of the line in order to achieve an equitable result. Such circumstances may consist in a variety of specificities, particularly regarding the geography of the coastline. The provisional equidistance line will then have to be adjusted (shifted) accordingly, as has happened, for example, in the cases of *Greenland/Jan Mayen* and *Cameroon v. Nigeria*. Conversely, in other cases, the Court decided that there was no need to adjust the provisional equidistance line.[165]

In the third stage,

> the Court conducts a disproportionality test in which it assesses whether the effect of the line, as adjusted, is such that the Parties' respective shares of the relevant area are markedly disproportionate to the lengths of their relevant coasts.[166]

This means that the provisional equidistance line must be set against a proportionality yardstick, by the application of which a comparison is made between the length of the coastlines of the states involved in the delimitation – where there is a significant disparity between them – and the maritime areas allocated to each one by means of the provisional equidistance line.[167] Where this comparison reveals that the maritime areas allocated do not reflect, in a significant way, the ratio of the respective coastal lengths, the provisional equidistance line is adjusted to achieve a line which is more reflective of that ratio. However, in no way does this process have to result in a delimitation which is mathematically proportionate to the ratio between coastal lengths of the states involved in the delimitation.[168] Taking the example of *Nicaragua v. Colombia* in which the proportionality test was applied, the Court considered the length of the Nicaraguan coast in relation to that of the Colombian islands in order to achieve an 'equitable result' of the final delimitation line of the maritime area west of the Colombian islands, i.e. on the side facing Nicaragua. Although the geographical relation was 1:8 in favour of Nicaragua, the Court came to the recognition of a ratio of 1:3.44 in its favour; in other words, the Colombian

165 See *supra*, at 11.2.2.8.

166 *Nicaragua v. Colombia*, Judgment, *supra*, fn. 7, para. 193.

167 In the *North Sea Continental Shelf Case*, the ICJ defined proportionality as "the element of a reasonable degree of proportionality which a delimitation effected according to equitable principles ought to bring about between the extent of the continental shelf appertaining to the States concerned and the lengths of their respective coastlines, – these being measured according to their general direction …" (*North Sea Continental Shelf, Judgment*, I.C.J. Reports 1969, p. 52, para. 98.)

168 See Greenland/Jan Mayen (*Denmark v. Norway*), Judgment, I.C.J. Reports 1993, pp. 66-67, para. 64 and *Maritime Delimitation in the Black Sea (Romania v. Ukraine)*, Judgment, 3 February 2009, p. 39, para. 122.

islands received almost one third of the maritime space awarded to Nicaragua, illustrating the flexibility shown by the Court in applying proportionality.[169]

Finally, the delimitation process has to identify the starting and end points of the delimitation, taking into account the rights of third states which do not participate in the process.[170] With regard to this question, the Court observed that, as Article 59 of the Statute of the Court makes clear,

> it is axiomatic that a judgment of the Court is not binding on any State other than the parties to the case. Moreover, the Court has always taken care not to draw a boundary line which extends into areas where the rights of third States may be affected.[171]

11.2.2.10 Prior Agreements

The whole process of delimitation is usually preceded by an investigation whether there is an agreement between the parties to the dispute which may be applicable thereon. Thus, in the case of the *Land and Maritime Boundary between Cameroon and Nigeria*, a series of agreements, the validity of which was disputed by Nigeria, had to be examined.[172] The same type of examination took place in the *Greenland/Jan Mayen Case*.[173] The possibility of existence of a tacit agreement, although remote, is not altogether rejected by the ICJ[174]; its legal rationale would, however, come close to that of historical title.

---

169 Many delimitation judgments have examined whether the parameters of proportionality have been applied, either outside or within the 'proportionality test' spelled out in by the ICJ in the *Black Sea Case*. Among the first (where proportionality was examined 'outside' the proportionality test) are the cases on the *Gulf of Maine* (ICJ, *supra*, fn. 111); *Greenland/Jan Mayen* (ICJ, *supra*, fn. 117); *Libya v. Malta*, (ICJ, *supra*, fn. 8); *St. Pierre and Miquelon Maritime Boundary Arbitration: (Canada/France)*, 2 June 1992, International Legal Materials, Vol. 31, pp. 1149-1178; *Case concerning the delimitation of the exclusive economic zone and continental shelf in the Caribbean Sea, (Barbados/Trinidad and Tobago)*, Reports of International Arbitral Awards (RIAA), Vol. XXVII pp. 147-251, 2006; *Delimitation of the maritime boundary between Guinea and Guinea-Bissau*, RIAA, Vol. XIX, pp. 149-196, 14 February 1985. Among the second, (those where proportionality was applied as a test constituting the third stage of the delimitation) are, besides the *Black Sea case* (ICJ, *supra*, fn. 48), *Nicaragua v. Colombia*, (ICJ, *supra*, fn. 7); *Peru v. Chile*, (*supra*, fn. 8), 27 January 2014; *Bangladesh/Myanmar*, *supra*, fn. 35; *Bangladesh/India*, 7 July 2014, *supra*, fn. 36; *Ghana/Côte d'Ivoire*, ITLOS, *Dispute Concerning delimitation of the Maritime Boundary between Ghana and Côte d'Ivoire in the Atlantic Ocean*, Case No. 23, Judgment, 23 September 2017.

170 According to Judge Shi (*supra*, fn. 142), the jurisprudence of the ICJ reveals two approaches to take into account the rights of third states: a) the terminal point of the delimitation is left open indicating, at the same time, the direction which the delimitation line is to follow in order to reach the point of meeting with the rights of the third state and b) the line stops at the ultimate point of the third state's claim. Judge Shi favours the first approach particularly insofar as it does not prejudge the rights of the third state. He criticizes the second because it makes the Court's jurisdiction dependent on the third state's claims.

171 *Nicaragua v. Colombia* (*supra*, fn. 7), Judgment, para. 228.

172 *Cameroon v. Nigeria: Equatorial Guinea intervening*, Judgment, I.C.J. Reports 2002, p. 303, paras. 31 *et seq.*

173 *Supra*, fn. 117, Judgment, paras. 22 *et seq.*

174 *Nicaragua v. Honduras*, 2007, I.C.J, Reports 735, para. 253.

12 A Specific Case of CS Delimitation: The Arctic Ocean[1]

12.1 Introduction

The Arctic region encompasses the area around the North Pole, to the north of the Arctic Circle,[2] straddling Asia, Europe and North America. The eight states which have territories in this region (Arctic states) are Canada, Denmark, Finland, Iceland, Norway, the Russian Federation, Sweden and the U.S. Five of these, namely Canada, Denmark, Norway, Russia and the U.S., have coastal frontage in the region (coastal Arctic states)[3] and can therefore claim maritime zones in the Arctic Ocean in accordance with UNCLOS.[4]

12.2 Effects of Climate Change

Global warming has been taking a heavy toll on the Arctic where its pace is twice that observed in other parts of the world. This has caused a dramatic reduction of ice on this ocean – which, with 5,440,000 square miles is the smallest of all the oceans – in the last decades.[5] This phenomenon, combined with the melting of glaciers and permafrost on land – all of them expected to continue and most probably accelerate in the years to come – will not only irreparably change the Arctic; it will also have a devastating effect on the sea and ocean levels worldwide, causing the flooding and disappearance of low-lying continental coastal areas, low-lying islands and atolls.

Nonetheless, this new reality has also opened new economic prospects for the states coastal to the Arctic Ocean, by the opening of new navigational routes and the possibility,

1 On this issue *see* Suzanne Lalonde and Ted L. McDorman (eds), International Law and Politics of the Arctic Ocean: Essays in honor of *Donat Pharand*, 2015; D. Rothwell and Christopher Joyner, The Polar Ocean and the Law of the Sea in Alex G. Oude Elferink and Donald R. Rothwell, The Law of the Sea and Polar Maritime Delimitation and Jurisdiction, 2001; *Ibid.*, Christopher Joyner, The Status of Ice in International Law.

2 Latitude 66 degrees, 32 minutes North.

3 Iceland argues, however, that she, too, should be considered an Arctic coastal state since its EEZ falls within the Arctic and extends to the Greenland Sea adjoining the Arctic Ocean (Naja Bentzen with Marc Hall, Arctic continental shelf claims: Mapping interests in the circumpolar North, Briefing, for the European Parliament, January 2017).

4 All polar coastal states are parties to the UNCLOS (1833 U.N.T.S. 397, available at: www.un.org/Depts/los/convention_agreements/texts/unclos/unclos_e.pdf), except the U.S. However, the U.S. considers UNCLOS as reflecting, to a large extent, customary international law which is therefore binding on it.

5 2018 has in fact been recorded as the warmest year ever in the Arctic.

with the constant advancement of technology, of the exploration and exploitation of resources in the ocean.[6]

The prospective navigational routes have the potential to drastically shorten distances between the continents. Most known is the Northwest Passage, i.e. the shipping routes which may connect the Atlantic and the Pacific through the Canadian Arctic.[7, 8] The Northeast Passage (also known as the Northern Sea Route) denotes the shipping routes which may connect Europe and Asia along the northern shores of Russia,[9] while the opening of a transpolar route, running through the middle of the Arctic Ocean and connecting the Atlantic and the Pacific Oceans, is not excluded.[10]

Concerning the Arctic Ocean resources, the U.S. Geological Survey estimates that they may potentially amount to 22% of the world's undiscovered conventional oil and natural gas.[11] The prospect of their exploration and exploitation, facilitated by the melting of ice, is therefore of the greatest economic interest and has inevitably generated what the media describe as the 'Arctic Scramble', i.e. the rush of the Arctic coastal states to secure their claims over the ocean and its resources. In this context, Russia's planting of a titanium flag 4,261 m beneath the North Pole in August 2007[12] was interpreted as a 'pre-emptive strike' for this purpose. In the wake of this move, ministers from the Arctic coastal states met in *Ilulissat*, Greenland, in May 2008, to sign a Declaration where they stated their willingness to proceed to the 'orderly settlement' of any potential overlapping claims while they also affirmed that there was "no need to develop a new comprehensive international legal regime to govern the Arctic Ocean."[13]

The Declaration also placed particular emphasis on the need to protect the sensitive Arctic environment and to closely cooperate in all sectors relevant to the Arctic. Cooperation is indeed a recurring theme in official statements of Arctic states, and a target also served by the Arctic Council, a circumpolar body with an increasingly visible role in such cooperation as well as in coordination and interaction between Arctic states, Arctic indigenous communities and other Arctic inhabitants, regarding all things polar, particular attention being paid to sustainable development and environmental protection.[14]

6 The Arctic Ocean covers an area of 5,440,000 square miles.

7 Aptly called *"The Arctic Grail"*; *See* P. Berton, The Arctic Grail: The Quest for the Northwest Passage and the North Pole, 1818-1909, McClelland and Stewart, Toronto, 1988.

8 In August 2016, *Crystal Serenity* became the first cruise liner to pass through the Northwest Passage.

9 The 'Northern Route' could shorten shipping routes between northern Europe and north-east Asia by 40%.

10 *See* T. Potts, C. Schofield, Current Legal Developments, The Arctic, *The International Journal of Marine and Coastal Law* 23, 2008, pp. 151-176.

11 Available at: https://pubs.usgs.gov/fs/2008/3049/fs2008-3049.pdf According to their estimates, 90 billion barrels of oil, 1,669 trillion cubic feet of natural gas, and 44 billion barrels of natural gas liquids may remain to be found in the Arctic, of which approximately 84% in offshore areas.

12 In the course of their *Arktika* expedition.

13 Paras. 1 and 2. The *Ilulissat* Declaration is available at: www.oceanlaw.org/downloads/arctic/Ilulissat_Declaration.pdf

14 Their website: www.arctic-council.org/index.php/en/about-us.

12.3 The Legal Situation

It should be noted at the outset that, from a legal point of view, the presence of ice, ice sheet or floating ice does not bear consequences on the legal regime of the Arctic Ocean (or the Southern oceans, for that matter).[15] This is true under customary law of the sea as well as under UNCLOS. The delimitation of all maritime zones in the Arctic Ocean remains, therefore, under the same regime as all maritime spaces in other parts of the world. This means that the extent of the maritime zones in the Arctic states is measured from the normal baselines and not from those further ones which are being created by the ice present on the shoreline and beyond.[16] Neither can sovereignty be claimed on icebergs or ice islands floating on the Arctic Ocean.

The only provision of UNCLOS which is specific to Arctic coastal states is Article 234, which restricts itself to providing for the right of such states to adopt legislation aimed at protecting the marine environment in their exclusive economic zones (EEZs) from pollution from vessels. The article is careful to include provisions not allowing a discriminatory character of this legislation and requiring a fair balance between the needs of navigation, which are particularly acute in the harsh Arctic climatic conditions, and the preservation of the marine environment, using, to this end, the 'best available scientific evidence'.

As no multilateral treaty governs delimitation in the Arctic Ocean, maritime boundaries are usually negotiated bilaterally by coastal states. Some of them, particularly recent ones, are mentioned here.

12.3.1 Russia and Norway

Russia and Norway have come to an agreement 'Concerning Maritime Delimitation and Cooperation in the *Barents Sea* and the Arctic Ocean' (*Murmansk*, 15 September 2010)[17] after four decades of negotiations.[18] The *Barents Sea* forms part of the Arctic Ocean and

15 Christopher Joyner, The status of Ice in International Law, in *The Law of the Sea and Polar Maritime Delimitation and Jurisdiction, supra*, fn. 1, pp. 23-48.

16 *Ibid.*, Robin R. Churchill, "Claims to Maritime Zones in the Arctic, Law of the Sea: Normality or Polar Peculiarity?" pp. 105-124, where the author aptly notes that "...a coastal state's territorial sea and EEZ cannot expand and contract in accord with the fluctuating extent of frozen water offshore. The baseline for demarcating these jurisdictional zones remain the land's shoreline, not the seaward protrusion of the ice-margin."

17 Treaty available at: www.regjeringen.no/upload/UD/Vedlegg/Folkerett/avtale_engelsk.pdf On its content *see* Øystein Jensen, Treaty between Norway and the Russian Federation concerning Maritime Delimitation and Cooperation in the Barents Sea and the Arctic Ocean, in *The International Journal of Marine and Coastal Law*, Vol. 26, 2011, pp. 151-168.

18 Norway and the Soviet Union concluded their first maritime boundary in the Arctic in 1957. This boundary did not, however, extend into the *Barents Sea*.

extends to the north of the Norwegian and Russian mainland coastlines. It contains large fish stocks while it is also estimated to hold vast hydrocarbon resources.[19]

The Agreement establishes a legal framework for the coordinated exploration and exploitation of transboundary hydrocarbon resources[20] and provides for the continued cooperation of the parties in connection with fisheries. It defines a single maritime boundary between the parties' respective continental shelves and EEZs in the *Barents Sea* and the Arctic Ocean.

Another legal regime in the *Barents Sea* is dealing with the Arctic archipelago of *Svalbard*, which lies midway between Norway and the North Pole.[21] The archipelago, which as from the nineteenth century had been considered *terra nullius*, is now governed by the *Svalbard* (formerly *Spitsbergen*) Treaty of 9 February 1920.[22] The membership of the Treaty today counts 45 states, including all the members of the Arctic Council, China, Japan and a number of EU Member States.[23] The Treaty recognized Norwegian sovereignty over the *Svalbard* archipelago (*Spitsbergen* at the time). In exchange for this recognition, the archipelago was demilitarized and Norway has undertaken the obligation to grant every other state party unfettered access to it, i.e. these states must be admitted on an equal footing for purposes of running and exercising all maritime, industrial, mining or commercial activities and enterprises on land and in the territorial waters of the Archipelago. Norway has established a 12 n.m. territorial sea and a 200 n.m. fisheries protection zone around *Svalbard* while her continental shelf zone extends, in places, beyond 200 miles. At the same time, Norway claims that the other parties to the *Svalbard* Treaty do not have equal rights of fishing and mining in zones beyond the territorial sea of the archipelago because at the time the Agreement was concluded such jurisdictional zones were unknown to international law. Not all of the other parties agree, however, with the Norwegian views on this matter. Russia in particular strongly opposes Norway's claims, despite the conclusion of the 2010 Treaty between the two countries.

---

19 Estimated to reach 11 billion barrels of crude oil, 380 trillion cubic feet of natural gas, and two billion barrels of natural gas liquids (*see* T. R. Klett & D. L. Gautier, *Assessment of Undiscovered Petroleum Resources of the Barents Sea Shelf*: U.S. Geological Survey Fact Sheet 2009).

20 Thus ending a moratorium of thirty years on geological exploration and on the exploitation of hydrocarbons in the disputed areas.

21 To the East is the archipelago of *Novaja Zemlya*, to the north the archipelago of *Franz Josef Land*, both under Russian sovereignty, while Greenland lies to the West.

22 Treaty Concerning the Archipelago of Spitsbergen (Svalbard Treaty), 9 February 1920, 43 Stat. 1892, 2 L.N.T.S.7, available at www.sysselmannen.no/The_Svalbard_Treaty_9ssFy.pdf.file. The Treaty entered into force on 14 August 1925.

23 France, Italy, the U.K., the Netherlands, Sweden, Germany.

12.3.2 *Norway and Denmark*

Norway and Denmark also concluded an Agreement (20 February 2006) concerning the delimitation of the continental shelf and the fisheries zones between Greenland (Denmark) and *Svalbard* (Norway). However, the maritime boundary between the outer continental shelves between *Svalbard* and Greenland has not been delimited yet.

12.3.3 *U.S. and Canada*

Other Arctic states have similar conflicting claims in the area. Thus, for the last four decades, a dispute has existed between the U.S. and Canada regarding the *Beaufort Sea* (which lies between the U.S. state of *Alaska* and the Canadian territory of *Yukon*). Canada claims that the maritime boundary extends to the west up to a distance of 200 n.m. along the land border between Alaska and the Yukon, and into the Beaufort Sea along the meridian, while the U.S. contends that the boundary is vertical to the coast, which runs to a distance of 200 n.m., following a line of equidistance from the coast. As a result of this difference, a wedge-shaped maritime area of about 21,000 km^2 is claimed by both states.

The position of Canada invokes the 1825 Treaty of Saint Petersburg between Great Britain and Imperial Russia, which established the boundary between them. Canada succeeded Great Britain in the treaty which stipulates in Article III that:

> the line of demarcation shall follow the summit of the mountains situated parallel to the Coast, as far as the point of intersection of the 141st degree of West longitude [...] and, finally, from the said point of intersection, the said Meridian Line of the 141st degree, in its prolongation as far as the Frozen Ocean. (in French '...dans sa prolongation jusqu'à la Mer Glaciale')

The question which is being asked here is, as aptly put by *Donat Pharand*: "The preposition 'jusqu'à' is inclusive or exclusive of the object to which the preposition relates?"[24]

The U.S., on its part, claims that equidistance must be the method to apply for determining a maritime boundary, if equitable, which is the case in the present instance.

The Canadian side replies that equidistance does not result in an equitable boundary. It points out that the coast of *Yukon* is concave, whereas the coast of Alaska is convex, and that the application of equidistance would result in a significant extension of the U.S. entitlement. This dispute has important material underpinnings, due to the possible presence of natural reserves within the disputed wedge. Because of this, Canada argues that 'special circumstances' apply, a contention that the U.S. rejects, while, at the same time,

24 Donat Pharand and Umberto Leanza (eds), *The Continental Shelf and the EEZ-Le Plateau Continental et la Zone Economique Exclusive*, Kluwer/Nijhoff, 1993, pp. 175-176.

both states agree that they are bound by the 1958 Convention on the Continental Shelf.[25] Despite ongoing negotiating efforts, the dispute remains unresolved, although there is continuous cooperation between the two countries on environmental protection and other relevant matters.[26]

12.3.4 Canada and Denmark

On 28 November 2012, the two countries came to an *ad referendum* agreement with regard to the *Lincoln Sea* maritime boundary to complete their 1973 agreement,[27] which established the maritime boundary between Canada and Greenland. Under the latter agreement, the boundary went as far north as the *Lincoln Sea* but did not include it.[28] The *Lincoln Sea* lies in the Arctic Ocean north of the Canadian *Ellesmere Island* and Greenland. The line agreed *ad referendum* in the *Lincoln Sea* follows the principle of equidistance and extends 200 n.m. from the coast of *Ellesmere Island* and northern Greenland. An issue which has been pending since the 1970s concerning a small area in the Lincoln Sea will therefore be resolved upon ratification of the tentative treaty. However, the sovereignty dispute between the two states over *Hans Island*, which is standing midway to the Arctic Ocean, is not being resolved by the treaty.[29] In 2018, the two sides agreed, however, to renew their efforts to come to an agreement over the island.

25 Convention on the Continental Shelf Art. 6, Apr. 29, 1958, 499 U.N.T.S. 311, available at http://untreaty.un.org/ilc/texts/instruments/english/conventions/8_1_1958_continental_shelf.pdf. Art. 6(1) thereof provides: "Where the same continental shelf is adjacent to the territories of two or more States whose coasts are opposite each other, the boundary of the continental shelf appertaining to such States shall be determined by agreement between them. In the absence of agreement, and unless another boundary line is justified by special circumstances, the boundary is the median line, every point of which is equidistant from the nearest points of the baselines from which the breadth of the territorial sea of each State is measured. The same rule applies, according to Article 6(2) of the 1958 Convention, [w]here the same continental shelf is adjacent to the territories of two adjacent States."

26 *E.g.*, in December 2016 Canada's Prime Minister *Trudeau* and U.S. President *Obama* announced a freeze on new oil and gas drilling in their Arctic waters. Developments under the current *Trump* Administration remain to be seen.

27 Although the1973 Treaty concerns the continental shelf, it has in fact been used as delimitation line to define fishing zones. The delimitation is based on the equidistance principle.

28 The delimitation line goes from the Davis Strait in the south to the Nares Strait (*Robson Channel*) in the north, the latter being the strait between the northernmost part of *Ellesmere Island* and Greenland. The boundary follows a median line 200 nautical miles from the respective coasts except in the *Nares Strait* and *Kane Basin*, the northernmost part of the boundary, because of the proximity of *Ellesmere Island* to Greenland (*see* Jacques Hartmann, EJIL Talk, 10 January 2013).

29 *Hans Island* is uninhabited and has neither oil deposits nor, according to the delimitation agreed, any territorial sea. The island was not known until 2005 when the then Canadian Minister of Defence hoisted the Canadian flag there. The Danish Government issued an official protest which was followed by a rush of expeditions carried out by the national forces of the two states. Each expedition party removed the other's flag to hoist their own, presumably to demonstrate 'effective control' over the island. Still, there seems to exist little, if at all, irrefutable evidence as to title of one or the other country over the island.

12.3.5 *U.S. and Russia*

The U.S. and Russia concluded, in 1990, an agreement on their maritime (EEZ) boundary line spanning 1,600 n.m. in the *Bering Sea, Bering Strait* and *Chukchi Sea.*[30] The boundary was based on that established in the Treaty of 1867 by which the U.S. bought Alaska from Russia.[31] It is noteworthy that under the 1990 Agreement, the maritime boundary extends to the north through the Bering Strait and Chukchi Sea into the Arctic Ocean 'as far as permitted under international law'.[32]

30 Called the *"Baker-Shevardnadze Line"* after the names of the respective Secretaries of State who signed the Agreement.

31 Treaty text available at: www.loc.gov/rr/program/bib/ourdocs/Alaska.html.

32 Art. 2(1).

12.4 Arctic Continental Shelf Claims Beyond 200 n.m.[33]

Such claims may be made in accordance with the rules contained in Article 76 on the 'Definition of the continental shelf'.[34] These rules provide that a state wishing to extend its continental shelf beyond 200 n.m. has to present its claim (submission) to the Com-

33 On this issue, *see* David A. Colson, The Delimitation of the Outer Continental Shelf Between Neighboring States, *American Journal of International Law*, Vol. 97, 2003, pp. 91-107; Ron Macnab, The Outer Limits of the Continental Shelf in the Arctic Ocean in Myron Nordquist, John N. Moore & Tomas Heidar (eds), *Legal and scientific Aspects of Continental Shelf Limits*, Martinus Nijhoff, 2004, pp. 301-311; Sean Murphy, Contemporary Practice of the United States Relating to International Law: U.S. Reaction to Russian Continental Shelf Claim, *American Journal of International Law*, Vol. 96, 2002, pp. 969-970; Ted McDorman, The Outer Continental Shelf Limits in the Arctic Ocean: Legal Framework and Recent Developments, in: Davor Vidas (ed), *Law, Technology and Science for Oceans in Globalisation*, Brill/Martinus Nijhoff, 2010; Naja Bentzen with Marc Hall, Arctic continental shelf claims (*supra*, fn.).

34 Art. 76 reads as follows: "[1.]The continental shelf of a coastal State comprises the seabed and subsoil of the submarine areas that extend beyond its territorial sea throughout the natural prolongation of its land territory to the outer edge of the continental margin, or to a distance of 200 nautical miles from the baselines from which the breadth of the territorial sea is measured where the outer edge of the continental margin does not extend up to that distance. 2. The continental shelf of a coastal State shall not extend beyond the limits provided for in paragraphs 4 to 6. 3. The continental margin comprises the submerged prolongation of the land mass of the coastal State, and consists of the seabed and subsoil of the shelf, the slope and the rise. It does not include the deep ocean floor with its oceanic ridges or the subsoil thereof. 4. (a) For the purposes of this Convention, the coastal State shall establish the outer edge of the continental margin wherever the margin extends beyond 200 nautical miles from the baselines from which the breadth of the territorial sea is measured, by either: (i) a line delineated in accordance with paragraph 7 by reference to the outermost fixed points at each of which the thickness of sedimentary rocks is at least 1 per cent of the shortest distance from such point to the foot of the continental slope; or (ii) a line delineated in accordance with paragraph 7 by reference to fixed points not more than 60 nautical miles from the foot of the continental slope. (b) In the absence of evidence to the contrary, the foot of the continental slope shall be determined as the point of maximum change in the gradient at its base. 5. The fixed points comprising the line of the outer limits of the continental shelf on the seabed, drawn in accordance with paragraph 4 (a)(i) and (ii), either shall not exceed 350 nautical miles from the baselines from which the breadth of the territorial sea is measured or shall not exceed 100 nautical miles from the 2,500 metre isobath, which is a line connecting the depth of 2,500 metres. 6. Notwithstanding the provisions of paragraph 5, on submarine ridges, the outer limit of the continental shelf shall not exceed 350 nautical miles from the baselines from which the breadth of the territorial sea is measured. This paragraph does not apply to submarine elevations that are natural components of the continental margin, such as its plateaux, rises, caps, banks and spurs. 7. The coastal State shall delineate the outer limits of its continental shelf, where that shelf extends beyond 200 nautical miles from the baselines from which the breadth of the territorial sea is measured, by straight lines not exceeding 60 nautical miles in length, connecting fixed points, defined by coordinates of latitude and longitude. 8. Information on the limits of the continental shelf beyond 200 nautical miles from the baselines from which the breadth of the territorial sea is measured shall be submitted by the coastal State to the set up under Annex II on the basis of equitable geographical representation. The Commission on the Limits of the Continental Shelf shall make recommendations to coastal States on matters related to the establishment of the outer limits of their continental shelf. The limits of the shelf established by a coastal State on the basis of these recommendations shall be final and binding. 9. The coastal State shall deposit with the Secretary-General of the United Nations charts and relevant information, including geodetic data, permanently describing the outer limits of its continental shelf. The Secretary-General shall give due publicity thereto. 10. The provisions of this article are without prejudice to the question of delimitation of the continental shelf between States with opposite or adjacent coasts."

mission on the Limits of the Continental Shelf (CLCS).[35] Preparing a CLCS submission involves collecting and analysing data on the depth and geophysical characteristics of the seabed and its subsoil in the particular area. If the submission meets with the approval of the CLCS, the submitting country obtains exclusive rights to the resources on or below the seabed of that area. However, as the research required is far from an easy matter, the Arctic Ocean coastal states have undertaken extensive research for years, often carrying out joint operations for this purpose.

The time limit for a state to make a submission to the CLCS for an extended continental shelf is ten years as from the date the UNCLOS entered into force for that state.[36] However, as the process of collecting data and information is demanding and time-consuming, many submitting states prefer to make a partial or coordinated submission which has the benefit of 'stopping the clock' until a full submission may be made.[37] The Commission issues its recommendations on the submission, which are final and binding.

12.4.1 Norway Submissions

In 2006, Norway made submissions to the CLCS claiming a continental shelf extending beyond its 200 n.m. EEZ in three areas in the north-eastern Atlantic and in the Arctic: the *Loop Hole* in the Barents Sea, the Western *Nansen Basin* in the Arctic Ocean and the *Ban Banana Hole* in the Norwegian Sea. In 2009, the CLCS issued its recommendations to Norway on its 2006 submission, which advised that Norway and Russia conclude agreements on disputes in the Arctic Ocean, in the Barents Sea and in the Norwegian and Greenland Seas. As already mentioned, a Treaty on Maritime Delimitation in the *Barents Sea* was indeed concluded in 2010. The CLCS issued its final (favourable) recommendations on the 2009 Norwegian submission for asserting sovereign rights over a substantial area of extended continental shelf.

Russia made a partial revised submission to the CLCS in 2015 with reference to its prior one of 2001 for extending the limits of its continental shelf beyond 200 n.m. in the Arctic Ocean.

35 The CLCS consists of twenty-one members who are experts in the field of geology, geophysics or hydrography. For some critical observations on its functions, *see* Christopher Joyner, The Status of Ice in International Law, loc. cit., pp. 23-49.

36 Art. 4 of Annex II to the UNCLOS.

37 On the basis of a 2008 Decision of the Meeting of the Parties to the Convention that the 2009 time-limit could consist only in the submission of 'preliminary information' and description of the status of preparation and intended date for making a full submission (UN doc. SPLOS/184). *See also* Clive R. Symmons (ed), *Selected Contemporary Issues in the Law of the Sea*, Martinus Nijhoff, 2011, pp. 281

12.4.2 Russia Submissions

In its 2015 submission, Russia provided evidence to the effect that *Lomonosov* Ridge is a continental extension of the Russian landmass. In 2016, it provided additional evidence in connection with its claim concerning *Lomonosov* Ridge, the *Mendeleev* Elevation and the *Chukchi* high plain.

12.4.3 Canada Submissions

Canada presented a request to the CLCS to establish the outer limit of its continental shelf in the Atlantic Ocean in 2013. It also submitted a preliminary dossier regarding the external limits of its continental shelf in the Arctic Ocean, claiming over 1.2 million km^2. The Canadian final claim on the Arctic continental shelf, which will include the *Lomonosov*[38] and *Alpha-Mendeleev*[39] Ridges, is expected to be submitted in 2019. The claim will most probably bring Canada at odds with Russia and Denmark which also claim *Lomonosov Ridge* as part of their own continental shelf.

12.4.4 Denmark Submissions

In 2014, Denmark filed a submission with the CLCS to define the outer limits of its continental shelf beyond 200 n.m. off the coast of Greenland in the Arctic Ocean. The area comprises approximately 895,541 km^2. In 2012, Denmark had presented a partial submission for the area to the south of Greenland, and in 2013, a partial submission to the area to the north-east of Greenland.

The only Arctic coastal state which has not made submissions to the CLCS, as it is not a party to UNCLOS, is the U.S.

---

38 The *Lomonosov Ridge,* is a 1,210 miles (1,800 km) long underwater mountain range that runs through the North Pole from Siberia almost to the junction of *Ellesmere Island* and Greenland, dividing the Arctic Ocean into two major basins: the *Eurasia Basin* and the *Amerasia Basin.* According to the U.S. Geological Survey, the *Lomonosov Ridge* could hold 1.1 billion barrels of technically recoverable undiscovered oil and 7.16 trillion cubic feet of natural gas.

39 The *Mendeleev Ridge* is located in the Arctic Ocean and extends from the shelf of the East Siberian Sea to the central areas of that Ocean. It is attached to and constitutes a complex with the *Alpha Ridge* of the *Amerasia Basin.*

12.4.5 *Difficulties in Defining the Outer Limits of the Continental Shelf*[40]

The difficulty in identifying the legal status and continental shelf entitlement beyond 200 n.m. for each Arctic coastal state lies, to a large extent, in the fact that the existence of the 'natural prolongation' requirement is not easily identifiable in the case of the Arctic Ocean. Furthermore, distinguishing between submarine ridges and submarine elevations has been controversial, as is the relationship between these submarine features (to which the different kinds of 'highs' mentioned in Article 76(6) must be added) and the continental margin.[41] These difficulties are particularly prominent in the case of the most important features in the Arctic Ocean, i.e. the *Lomonosov* and the *Alpha-Mendeleev* Ridges, which are adjoining to the continental shelves of Russia, Greenland and Canada. Furthermore, whether these may be considered as belonging to one or the other state's continental shelf on the basis of their geomorphological features (probably the former to Denmark, Russia and Canada and the latter to Russia and Canada) is a matter which will have to be convincingly shown by the interested states, ideally in cooperation between themselves. Already, however, this endeavour has been causing certain negative reactions, such as that of the U.S. which has argued, in response to the 2001 submission of Russia, that the *Lomonosov* is a 'freestanding feature in the deep, oceanic part of the Arctic Ocean basin, and not a natural component of the continental margins of either Russia or any other State'.

12.4.6 *Settlement of Disputes*

In principle, the recommendations of the CLCS are 'without prejudice to the question of delimitation of the continental shelf between States with opposite or adjacent coasts', (UNCLOS, Art. 76(10)). Nevertheless, the Rules of Procedure of the CLCS,[42] although reiterating this premise in the exercise of the Commission's functions,[43] go to great lengths in order to secure that no problems will arise from any conflicting interests of another state with the Commission's review process of a submission. Thus, the Commission asks for several (alternative) 'guarantees' before engaging in the review of a submission, including joint submissions by the states between which a dispute exists concerning the matter before the Commission or, if that is not possible, the consent of the state with which the submitting state is involved in a dispute. These requirements point in the direction of a possible prior settlement of an existing dispute, which can be made by any legal means available to the states involved. Such means may be an agreement

40 *See* Michael Byers with James Baker, *International Law and the Arctic*, Cambridge University Press, 2013.

41 By contrast, 'oceanic ridges' cannot be part of the continental margin.

42 www.un.org/depts/los/clcs_new/commission_rules.htm.

43 *Ibid.*, Addendum I, para. 1, available at: https://documents-dds-ny.un.org/doc/UNDOC/GEN/N08/309/23/PDF/N0830923.pdf.

reached through negotiations or any of the procedures prescribed by UNCLOS (arbitration, resort to ITLOS or the ICJ). If such a prior settlement is not attained, however, "the submissions made before the Commission and the recommendations approved by the Commission thereon shall not prejudice the position of States which are parties to a land or maritime dispute."[44]

12.5 Concluding Remarks

Although the 'Arctic race' may be a hyperbolic media expression, it remains true that the stakes in the Arctic Ocean are too high for the Arctic coastal states not to feel compelled to act on them. Nonetheless, it is also beyond doubt that the exploitation of the Arctic has negative sides which cannot be ignored. It is, firstly, far from certain that such exploitation will not be prejudicial to the Arctic environment. Secondly – and, perhaps, equally importantly – the urge to secure national benefits may leave the Arctic Ocean with little to offer – indeed only two small seabed areas – as part of the 'Area'. It is clear that, almost four decades after the adoption of UNCLOS, the lofty idea for a 'Common Heritage of Mankind' remains without much appeal to contemporary perceptions.

44 *Ibid.*, para. 5(b).

13 Two Cases Involving Sovereignty Issues Over Islands (East China Sea and South China Sea Islands)

13.1 The Land Dominates the Sea

The delimitation processes referred to above do not deal with issues arising where sovereignty over an island is in dispute, nor is UNCLOS or customary law of the sea applicable with regard to issues of sovereignty over insular or continental land as such. However, as the maxim 'the land dominates the sea' is always applicable in law of the sea issues,[1] it is obviously of paramount importance that disputes regarding sovereignty which impact on delimitation be settled before the delimitation of maritime zones is undertaken. Several such disputes have already been submitted to the ICJ or arbitration in conjunction with delimitation cases. Among these was the *Qatar v. Bahrain Case*, where the ICJ decided on sovereignty over a significant number of islands. A similar issue was decided upon by the arbitral tribunal in *Eritrea/Yemen* as well as by the ICJ in *Nicaragua v. Colombia*. Two cases which involve questions of sovereignty over islands will be examined below. Significantly, neither of them can be based on a clear conventional legal regime, whether bilateral or regional, to determine such sovereignty issues. However, all the parties to the disputes in question are parties to UNCLOS which, therefore, is otherwise fully applicable.

1 *North Sea Continental Shelf Cases,* 1969 ICJ Rep. 51, para. 96; *Aegean Sea Continental Shelf Case,* 1978 ICJ Rep. 36, para. 86; *Qatar v. Bahrain,* 2001 ICJ Rep. 97, para. 185.

13.2 East China Sea Islands (Diaoyu or Senkaku Islands)

The dispute between China (PRC) and Japan regarding sovereignty over the eight uninhabited islands and rocks,[2] called *Diaoyu* by China and *Senkaku* by Japan, is well known.[3] Tensions over this issue have on occasion reached very high levels in recent years, some incidents having the potential to develop even into full-blown military confrontation.[4]

13.2.1 The Islands

The islands, the total surface area of which is about 7 km^2, are situated in the East China Sea, and are governed by Japan.[5] They lie east of China, southwest of Japan and northeast of Taiwan (ROC), being closer to China[6] than to Japan[7] and even closer to Taiwan.[8] It is also important that they are situated on the shipping lane between *Fuzhu* on the Chinese mainland and the Japanese *Ryukyu islands*,[9] and have always constituted a navigational landmark for ships travelling through the area.[10]

---

2 In fact five islands and three rocks. The biggest among them is *Diaoyu/Uotsuri*. Their total surface area is about 7 km^2.

3 Amid the extensive legal literature on this issue, by Chinese, Japanese and other international law or international policy scholars, *see* Zhongqi Pan, Sino-Japanese Dispute over the Diaoyu/Senkaku Islands: The Pending Controversy from the Chinese perspective, *Journal of Chinese Political Science*, vol. 12, no. 1, 2007, pp. 71-82; Hungdah Chiu, An analysis of the Sino-Japanese Dispute over the T'iaoyutai Islets (Senkaku Gunto), 15 *Chinese Taiwan Yearbook of International Law and Affairs*, 9, 9, 1996-1997; William B. Heflin, Diaoyu/Senkaku Islands Dispute: Japan and China, Oceans Apart, 18 *Asian-Pacific Law and Policy Journal* 1, 2, 2000; Jean-Marc Blanchard, The U.S. Role in the Sino-Japanese Dispute over the Diaoyu (Senkaku) Islands 1945-1971, *China Quarterly*, No. 161, March 2000, pp. 95-12; Carlos Ramos-Mrosovsky, *International Law's Unhelpful Role in the Senkaku Islands*, 2008; Erica Strecker Downs and Philip Saunders, Legitimacy and the Limits of Nationalism: China and the Diaoyu Islands, *International Security*, Vol. 23, No. 3, Winter 1998/99, pp. 114-146; Matsui Yoshiro, International Law of Territorial Acquisition and the Dispute over the Senkaku (Diaoyu) Islands, *Japanese Annual of International Law*, No. 40, 1997, pp. 3-31; Suganuma Unryu, *Sovereign Rights and Territorial Space in Sino-Japanese Relations: Irredentism and the Diaoyu/Senkaku Islands*, Honolulu, H.I.: University of Hawaii Press, 2000, pp. 120-21; Koji Taira, The China-Japan Clash over the Diaoyu/Senkaku islands, available at www.japanfocus.org/-Koji-Taira/2119.

4 One of those concerned the purchase by the Japanese government of three of the islands for $26.2 million from their private owners in 2012.

5 At least since 1972.

6 About 200 n.m. from mainland China.

7 About 240 n.m. from *Okinawa*, the largest of the Japanese *Riukiyu islands* (*see infra* at section 13.2.2).

8 120 n.m. from Taiwan.

9 Comprising *Osumi, Tokara, Amami, Okinawa* and *Sakishima* Islands (the last ones consisting of the *Miyako* and *Yaeyama* Islands). The largest is *Okinawa*.

10 The East China Sea has a maximum breadth of 360 n.m.

13.2.2 Chinese and Japanese Positions and Arguments – Relevant Treaties

Both countries claim the islands, while Taiwan has also presented its own claim.[11] Japan maintains that there is no written evidence of either contestant's sovereignty over the islands before the nineteenth century and that the islands were *terra nullius* until then. The Japanese side also mentions the exploration of the islands by a Japanese national, *Koga Tatsuhiro*, who took a concession from the Japanese authorities to carry out an investment there in 1884.[12] Japan invokes, therefore, occupation and effective exercise of sovereignty over the islands. She finally proclaimed that the islands constituted part of the Japanese territory in 1895.[13]

China, on her side, maintains that the islands are mentioned in documents issued during the Ming[14] and Qing[15] Chinese Dynasties and that they were known as being Chinese to the *Ryukyu Kingdom* which traded with China at the time.[16] China invokes historical title, namely that she exercised sovereignty over the islands since time immemorial and that Chinese fishermen used the *Diaoyu* as their operational base to fish in the waters around them.[17] The Chinese provide further elements of evidence, among which is an 1885 letter of the Japanese Foreign Minister, *Inoue Kaoru*, indirectly acknowledging Chinese title over the islands.

One of the major points of disagreement in the dispute is whether the *Diaoyu/Senkaku* islands were included in those considered to belong to *Formosa* (now Taiwan) in terms of the *Shimonoseki Treaty*, i.e. the Treaty concluded between China and Japan on 17 April 1895, after the first Sino-Japanese war (1894-1895) which ended with the victory of Japan. By that treaty, Japan forced China to cede Taiwan and its attached islands,[18] as well as the *Penghu islands* (*Pescadores*).[19]

---

11 Taiwan calls the islands '*Diaoyutai*' or '*T'iaoyutai*'.

12 To trade in guano and bird feathers.

13 Japan claims that in 1896, after incorporating the islands into *Okinawa's Yaeyama County*, the Japanese government leased four islands to the abovementioned *Koga Tatsuhiro* for thirty years.

14 1368-1644 A.D.

15 1644-1911 A.D.

16 The *Ryukyu Kingdom* was annexed by Japan in 1879 forming the *Okinawa Prefecture*.

17 China also claims that the islands were used, additionally, as a source of '*shi cong yong*', a rare herb used in Chinese traditional medicine. Thus in 1893 the *Dowager Empress* (Empress Mother) *Ci Xi* granted the islands to her doctor *Sheng Xuan-hui* who had treated her illness with the particular herb (*See* Carlos Ramos Mrosovsky, *University of Pennsylvania Journal of International Law (U Pa. J. Int'l L.)*, vol. 29:4, 2008, p. 926, citing, *inter alios*, Tao Cheng, The Sino-Japanese Dispute over the Tiao-yu-tai (Senkaku) Islands and the Law of Territorial Acquisition, *University of Virginia Journal of International Law (Va. J. Int'l L.)* vol. 14, 1974, p. 257.

18 Art. 2 of the Treaty stipulates: "China cedes to Japan in perpetuity and full sovereignty the following territories, together with all fortifications, arsenals, and public property thereon: [..] (b) The island of Formosa, together with all islands appertaining or belonging to the said island of Formosa."

19 Art. 2 of the Treaty also stipulates: "China cedes…(c) The Pescadores Group, that is to say, all islands lying between the 119th and 120th degrees of longitude east of Greenwich and the 23rd and 24th degrees of north latitude."

If these islands were indeed so included, as China asserts, it would constitute proof that the *Diaoyu/Senkaku* belonged to China, part of which was Taiwan at the time.[20] Japan contends, however, that the islands were not included in the *Shimonoseki Treaty* because they already belonged to Japan. It therefore considers it therefore consequential that the Treaty would not refer to them. To strengthen its arguments, Japan refers to various elements, among which that Japan proclaimed its sovereignty over the *Senkaku islands* before the beginning of the negotiations for the *Shimonoseki Treaty* on 20 March 1895[21] and that in the negotiations for the Treaty, China, while protesting for the cession of Taiwan with all its islands to Japan, she did not mention the *Diaoyu/Senkaku*. If, the Japanese argument goes, the Chinese side had recognized these islands as part of its territory, it would have protested against their 'cession' as well. Therefore, Japan concludes, China acquiesced to Japan's sovereignty over the islands.

With Japan's defeat in World War II in 1945, the Allies demanded, on the basis of the Declarations of Cairo of November 1943[22] and Potsdam of July 1945, the return to China of territories illegally occupied by Japan, such as Taiwan which Japan had seized from China. The territories to be returned were, however, only indicatively referred to in both Declarations. The Treaty of San Francisco of 1951 concluded between Japan and the Allies in 1945,[23] provided in its Article 3 that the U.S. would exercise all powers of administration, legislation and jurisdiction over the territory of the islands of *Nansei Shoto* south of 29 degrees north latitude (including the *Ryukyu Islands* and the *Daito Islands*[24]). It is, however, disputed whether *Nansei Shoto* (Southwestern islands) would include the *Diaoyu/Senkaku*.

In any event, in 1972, the islands were given over to Japan, by virtue of the Okinawa Reversion Agreement of 1971 between the U.S. and Japan,[25] most probably indicating U.S. new political priorities in the region.[26]

---

20 China fully agrees with Taiwan on this issue.

21 The proclamation took place on 14 January 1895.

22 In the terms of the Cairo Declaration, "all the territories Japan has stolen from the Chinese, such as Manchuria, Formosa and the Pescadores, shall be returned to the Republic of China."

23 Peace Treaty of 8 September 1951, concluded between Japan and 48 of the Allies, among which the U.S., the United Kingdom, France, the Netherlands, Canada, Australia, Indonesia, Iran, Iraq, Mexico, Greece, Turkey, Laos and Vietnam. China (PRC), Taiwan (ROC), South Korea (ROK) and North Korea (DPRK) were not invited to participate in the Peace Conference. The Soviet Union participated in the Conference but did not sign the Treaty.

24 This is a small cluster of islands, 194 n.m. east of *Okinawa*.

25 Under this Treaty, signed on 17 June 1971, the U.S. relinquished all territories, rights and interests it held under Art. III of the Treaty of San Francisco of 1951 in favour of Japan.

26 By that time the two countries had become close allies, as China was now under Communist rule after the successful campaign of *Mao Ze Dong* and his ascent to power in 1948. However, later on the U.S. tried to follow a neutral stance on the Sino-Japanese dispute over the *Dioyu/Senkaku* islands.

At about that time (1970), China and Taiwan started claiming sovereignty over the islands and in 1971 China issued a statement to that effect. In December 1971, the Chinese government officially claimed sovereignty over the islands.[27] Irrespective of the legal side of the dispute, it is perhaps no coincidence that the vivid interest of countries of the area in the particular islands started when the U.N. Economic Commission for Asia and the Far East (ECAFE) issued a report in 1969 which referred to the possibility for the existence of vast oil and gas resources around the *Diaoyu/Senkaku* islands in the East China Sea.[28]

13.2.3 Concluding Remarks

The attribution of sovereignty over the *Diaoyu/Senkaku* islands will provide jurisdiction over large swathes of continental shelf in the East China Sea[29] which would offer either China or Japan, both extremely energy-hungry,[30] with the possibility to explore and exploit the huge resources these areas contain. However, proof of legal title in terms of international law appears to be difficult. Neither of the two countries seems to have a decisive 'legal edge' over the other at first sight, legal argumentation having to move on the slippery ground of research over historical events and their legal relevance on *effectivités* over a long period of time, and on treaties which are largely inconclusive as they present gaps and ambiguities concerning the subject matter of the dispute. The solution to the issue would therefore seem to lie in third-party settlement, which should, ideally,

27 In its domestic legislation, China issued, in 1992, a law on 'The Territorial Sea and Contiguous Zone of the People's Republic of China' in which it formally declares that the *'T'iaoyutai'* islands are sovereign Chinese territory.

28 *See* Selig S. Harrison, Seabed Petroleum in Northeast Asia: Conflict or Cooperation? Woodrow Wilson International Center for Scholars, 2005, available at www.wilsoncenter.org/topics/docs/Asia_petroleum.pdf

29 Estimated to be around 20.000 sq. n.m.

30 China's demand for of oil imports is expected to rise to 500 million tons and for natural gas to over 100 billion cubic meters by 2020. For comparison, in 2009 China imported 204 million tons of oil and just about 5 billion cubic meters of natural gas.

be resorted to by common agreement. Such an agreement seems, however, to be a remote possibility, given the strong nationalistic sentiments prevalent in both countries and the inflammatory rhetoric used in public speech on the matter, which has led to the failure of negotiations for more than forty years so far.

13.3 South China Sea Islands (Spratly and Paracel Islands)[31]

13.3.1 Spratly and Paracel Islands

Parallel to the dispute concerning the *Diaoyu/Senkaku* islands in the East China Sea is the dispute concerning the *Spratlys*, the *Paracels* and other islands, islets and maritime features in the South China Sea.[32]

The *Spratlys* constitute an archipelago of at least 140 uninhabited and barren islands, atolls, low-tide elevations, rocks, reefs, etc. with a total surface of about 10 km^2 which are spread over the east side of the South China Sea.[33] The *Paracels* include about 30 islands, low-tide elevations and other similar maritime features. Their total surface is less than 8 km^2 and they are located on the west side of the South China Sea and to the northwest of

31 *See* Choon-Ho Park, *The South China Sea Disputes: Who owns the islands and the natural resources*, 1978; Lee G. Cordner, The Spratly Islands Dispute and the Law of the Sea, *Ocean Development & International Law*, Vol. 25, Iss.1, 1994; Monique Chemillier-Gendreau, *Sovereignty Over the Paracel and Spratly Islands*, Martinus Nijhoff, 2000; Shicun Wu, Solving Disputes for Regional Cooperation and Development in the South China Sea, *A Chinese Perspective*, 2013; Christopher C. Joyner, The Spratly Islands Dispute in the South China Sea: Problems, Policies, and Prospects for Diplomatic Accommodation in Ranjeet K. Singh (ed), *Investigating Confidence-Building Measures in the Asia-Pacific Region* (Washington D.C.), The Henry L. Stimson Center, 1999; Zhiguo Gao, Bing Bing Jia, The Nine-Dash Line in the South China Sea: History, Status and Implications, in Agora: The South China Sea, *AJIL*, Vol. 107, No. 1, January 2013, pp. 98-123; *Ibid.*, Florian Dupuy, Pierre-Marie Dupuy, *A Legal Analysis of China's Historic Rights in the South China Sea*, pp. 124-141; *Ibid.*, Robert Beckman, *The U.N. Convention on the Law of the Sea and the Maritime Disputes in the South China Sea*, pp. 142-163; Melissa H. Loja, A Critical Legal Approach to the South China Sea Territorial Dispute, *Brill Online*, 2018; Geneviève Bastid Burdeau, Le puzzle de la situation dans la mer de Chine meridional: un défi pour la securité régionale et mondiale, *Annuaire français de droit international*, vol. 61 (2015), pp. 75-91.

32 This Sea is called Southern Sea by China, Eastern Sea by Vietnam, West Philippines Sea by the Philippines: *See* David Scott, Conflict Irresolution in the South China Sea, *Asian Survey*, Vol. 52, No. 6, 2012, pp. 1019-1042.

33 The South China Sea covers an area of about 1,423,000 square miles (3,685,000 square km). It extends from the *Straits of Malacca* to the Southeast to the *Taiwan Strait* in the Northeast. Its width is 550-650 n.m. while its length exceeds 1,200 n.m. The countries surrounding the South China Sea are China, Vietnam, Malaysia, the Philippines, Brunei Darussalam and Indonesia.

the *Spratly islands*. Other maritime features in this sea are the *Pratas*,[34] the *Macclesfield Bank*[35] and the *Scarborough Shoal*.[36]

13.3.2 The South China Sea

The South China Sea, linking the Pacific and Indian oceans, is a major sea lane which sees the passage of over half of the world's maritime traffic (in terms of tonnage), as well as of one third of the world's crude oil and over half of the world's LNG transports to China, Taiwan, Japan and South Korea. The strategic and geostrategic importance of the South China Sea islands is therefore obvious and cannot be overestimated. Adding to their importance, these insular formations are situated within fishing grounds among the richest in the world, while large oil and natural gas reserves are known to exist in their adjacent waters.[37] It is therefore not surprising that they attract parallel and, inevitably, conflicting claims[38] by almost all the countries surrounding the South China Sea.

13.3.3 Claims Over the Spratly Islands[39, 40]

These islands are being claimed by China, Taiwan, Vietnam, Malaysia, the Philippines and Brunei Darussalam. This has generated serious controversies between these states,[41] frequently escalating into military incidents.[42] Military forces from China, Taiwan, Vietnam, Malaysia and the Philippines have occupied and are stationed on a significant

---

34 The *Pratas Islands* (*Dongsha* in Chinese) are three islands constituting an atoll in the north-eastern part of the South China Sea with a surface area of less than 2.5 km^2. The islands are governed by Taiwan while they are claimed by China. *Dongsha* Island is the largest in this insular group.

35 *Macclesfield Bank* (*Zhongsha* in Chinese) is a submerged atoll east of the *Paracel* Islands and north of the *Spratlys.*

36 *Scarborough* Shoal (*Huangyan* in Chinese) is an atoll between *Macclesfield Bank* and the Philippine island of *Luzon*. It has a lagoon surrounded by reef which is mostly submerged even at low tide. There are, however, some rocks which remain above water at high tide. *Scarborough Shoal* is now under Chinese rule.

37 The U.S. Energy Information Agency estimates that the South China Sea holds about 190 trillion cubic feet of natural gas and 11 billion barrels of oil in proved and probable reserves, as referred in 'Blueprint for Cooperation on oil and Gas Protection in the South China Sea' of the 'Asia Maritime Transparency Initiative', available at https://amti.csis.org/a-blueprint-for-cooperation-on-oil-and-gas-production-in-the-south-china-sea, of 25 July 2018, last accessed on 6 November 2018.

38 As expressed in relevant Notes-Verbales deposited with the U.N.

39 *Nansha* in Chinese, *Truang Sa* in Vietnamese.

40 Historical records do not frequently refer to the *Spratlys* which are sometimes confused with the *Paracels.* Various names have been used for the former (*e.g., Wan-li chang-sha, Shih-t'ang*). The name officially adopted by Taiwan for them is *Nansha ch'un-tao.*

41 At the same time Indonesia, although not a contestant in connection with the *Spratly islands*, is protesting about the claims of China and Taiwan as they extend into its own jurisdictional zones.

42 An important incident took place in 1988, when the Chinese and Vietnamese navies confronted each other at the Johnson Reef (a reef in the Spratly islands under the control of the PRC) causing the death of 70 sailors, and the sinking of several Vietnamese boats.

number of these maritime features, in an effort to prove sovereignty of their respective countries over them.[43] Brunei, which has established no such presence, is also claiming an exclusive economic zone (EEZ) to itself in the south-eastern part of the region. China, now a world superpower, has increased patrols in the area, thus expressing its readiness to confront the claims of the other states. It has furthermore engaged energetically for years in an 'island-building process', which is watched with great circumspection and protested against by the other countries in the region, while it has caused serious frictions with the U.S. which has increased its naval presence in the area.

13.3.4 Claims Over the Paracel Islands[44]

Following a military confrontation between China and Vietnam in 1974, all of the *Paracel islands* are now controlled by China and administered by its *Hainan Province*. They continue, nonetheless, to be claimed by Vietnam and Taiwan.

13.3.5 Positions and Arguments of the Parties to the Dispute Over the Paracel and the Spratly Islands – Historical Elements

The main contestants, Vietnam and China, insist on their historical title on both groups of islands.[45] In the case of Vietnam, the title invoked with regard to the *Paracels* dates to the early eighteenth century, when Vietnam established a government-sponsored company to exploit their resources. In the early nineteenth century, the official annexation of the Paracels took place, followed, according to the Vietnamese, by uninterrupted administration of the islands by successive Nguyen dynasties. Vietnam (*Annam*) became a French protectorate in the context of French Indochina in 1884, and the Governor-General of France issued in 1932 a Decree incorporating the *Paracels* into a Vietnamese province. Despite the fact that China gained control, as already mentioned, over the *Paracels* in 1974, Vietnam has taken various administrative steps in their respect since then, and in 2012 passed a law concerning its maritime borders which include both the *Paracel* and the *Spratly* islands.

In connection with the *Spratlys*, France, in its capacity of Protecting Power of Vietnam, sent ships on various expeditionary missions there in 1925, 1927 and 1930, and finally took possession of the islands in 1933. From 1956 to 1973, the Vietnamese government issued a number of administrative decrees in their regard. The Chinese refuted

43 Vietnam occupies 27 islands, China 7, Taiwan 1, the Philippines 8, and Malaysia 3. The biggest one among these islands *(Itu-Aba)* belongs to Taiwan.

44 *Xisha* in Chinese, *Hoang Sa* in Vietnamese.

45 *See* Hungdah Chiu & Choon-Ho Park, Legal Status of the Paracel and Spratly Islands, *Ocean Development & International Law*, 3:1, 1975, https://doi.org/10.1080/00908327509545556, retrieved on 1 January 2018.

the French claims of sovereignty, arguing that the islands had been continuously inhabited or used by Chinese nationals which, in China's view, proved existing Chinese sovereignty. To establish its title on both groups of islands, China refers to Chinese historical records dating as far back as the twelfth and thirteenth centuries, such as the well-known book *Chu-fan-Chi* by *Chau Ju-Kua*, an inspector of foreign trade in *Fukien Lu Province* at the time of the *Southern Sung Dynasty* (1127-1279).[46] More importantly, China also invokes an Agreement between China and *Tonkin* (Northern Vietnam during the French colonial period) which concerns the Delimitation of the Frontier between them, which was signed on 26 June 1887. According to Chinese writers, the geographical coordinates provided by the text of the Agreement for the boundary attribute both the *Paracels* and the *Spratlys* to China.[47] Furthermore, it appears that the *Kuangtung* provincial government had repeatedly issued permits in the 1920s and into the 1930s to Chinese nationals to exploit the resources on *Paracel* islands.

In 1931, France notified the Chinese Legation in Paris of its claim over the *Paracel islands* as it also did with regard to the *Spratlys*, on behalf of its protectorate, Vietnam. In 1933, France announced the occupation of nine islets in the South China Sea, causing the protest of China. An exchange of notes between the two countries ensued, rejecting each other's arguments on historical and legal grounds.

In 1939, Japan occupied both, the *Paracels* and the *Spratlies*, officially attributing to them the collective name of *Shinnan Gunto*. Upon their defeat by the Allied Powers, the Japanese withdrew from the islands in 1945, Taiwan occupying them almost immediately thereafter. When *Mao Zedong* prevailed in mainland China, the Chinese forces took over *Hainan Island*, as well as the *Paracel* and *Spratly* islands.

As noted above,[48] neither China nor Taiwan participated in the 1951 San Francisco Conference. China issued a statement (through its then Foreign Minister *Zhou Enlai*) affirming China's sovereignty over the *Paracels* and *Spratlys* and denying any possible effect over China of the Agreement to be concluded between the Allies and Japan. On 28 April 1952, Taiwan and Japan concluded a bilateral Peace Treaty which recognized, in Article 2, that by virtue of the San Francisco Peace Treaty, Japan had renounced all rights, title and claim to Taiwan (*Formosa*) and *Penghu islands* (the *Pescadores*) as well as over the *Spratly* and the *Paracel* islands.

In 1956, the Philippines claimed the *Spratly islands*,[49] attracting a response by China indicating, *inter alia*, that those islands lay outside the territorial confines of the Philip-

46 *Ibid.*, p. 9.

47 According to the Agreement: "Au Kouang-Tong…Les îles qui sont à l'est du méridien de Paris 105° 43' de longitude est, c'est-à-dire de la ligne nord-sud passant par la pointe orientale de l'île de Tch'a Kou ou Ouan-chan (Tra-co) et formant la frontière sont également attribuées à la Chine. Les îles Gotho et les autres îles qui sont à l'ouest du ce méridien appartiennent à l'Annam."

48 *See supra*, fn. 156.

49 In that year, the Philippines 'bought' the islands from a Philippino, *Thomas Cloma*, who had 'explored' them and called them 'Freedomland'.

pines as stipulated in the 1898 Peace Treaty between the U.S. and Spain. The dispute came to international attention in 1978 when the Philippines declared a number of the islands to be Philippine territory under the name of *Kalayaan* island group which they included into their own *Palawan Province*. The Philippines, an archipelagic state under UNCLOS, are putting forward the argument that the islands, which were *terra nullius* before they claimed them, lie within their 200 n.m. EEZ. Furthermore, the Philippines are strongly opposed to the Chinese occupation of the *Mischief Reef*[50] in 1995[51] and what appears to be the effective military control of *Scarborough Shoal* since mid-2013[52] after at least two decades of various incidents and a stand-off in 2012.

Finally, in 2013, the Philippines resorted to an arbitration procedure under ITLOS, which is examined below.[53]

13.3.6 The 'Nine-Dash Line'

To confirm its claims, China has issued the so-called 'Nine-Dash Line' (or *Nine-Dot Line* or *U-shaped line*) which appears on Chinese maps and by which it has included the largest part (over 80%) of all the South China Sea area into some undefined type of Chinese jurisdiction.[54] The 'Nine-Dash Line', issued in May 2009, came as a response to Malaysia and Vietnam's joint submission to the United Nations regarding their own claims in the South China Sea and caused, in its turn, the reaction in April 2011 of the Philippines which filed a formal protest in the United Nations concerning this 'Line'.

However, the U-shaped line is no novelty for China. In fact, it was first introduced in 1947 by the *Kuomintang* government. At the time it consisted of 11 dashes and included, originally, parts of the *Gulf of Tonkin* off the northern coast of Vietnam. The line was later modified by China to drop the two dashes in the *Gulf of Tonkin*. As already noted, however, what it includes is not clearly specified.[55] According to the prevailing view, what the 'Nine-Dash Line' purports to do is to confirm the 'historic title' of China in the South China Sea. Again, historic title remains a largely undefined term in UNCLOS (Art. 15) which leaves it up to jurisprudence and doctrinal analysis to define. The International law

---

50 This is a cluster of low tide elevations surrounded by a lagoon. PRC maintains a number of troops there.

51 China and the Philippines were embroiled in a confrontation in 1999 over the construction by the Chinese of three structures on *Mischief Reef* which was completed in that year.

52 In April 2012 the Philippine Navy apprehended eight Chinese fishing vessels in the disputed *Scarborough Shoal*, an incident which started the so-called 'Scarborough Shoal stand-off'.

53 *Infra*, pp. 39 *et seq.*

54 Li Jinming & Li Dexia, The Dotted Line on the Chinese Map of the South China Sea: A Note, Ocean Development and International Law, Vol. 34, Issue 3-4, 2003, pp. 229-277; *See also* the articles by Zhiguo Gao, Bing Bing Jia for the Chinese views and Florian Dupuy, Pierre-Marie Dupuy and Robert Beckman for the 'Western' ones, *loc. cit.*, (*supra*, fn. 257).

55 According to Jörn Dosch, *loc. cit.*, the waters covered by the contested map would include several oil, natural gas, and condensate fields of the Philippines (*Malampaya* and *Camago*), Malaysia (fields offshore *Sarawak*), Indonesia (*Natuna Islands*) and Vietnam (several blocks off the Vietnamese coast).

Commission (ILC) has expressed the view that in order to assert a claim to historic waters, three conditions must be met: a) states which claim historic right should exercise sovereignty in the waters; b) the exercise of sovereignty should have been continuous for a long time and should have become the usage; and c) it should be tolerated by other states.[56] It would appear, therefore, that historic title can only refer to sovereignty and not to jurisdictional zones, such as the EEZ and the continental shelf, which means that the 'Nine-Dash Line' should be considered to exclude jurisdictional zones (the EEZ was not, in any case, recognized as such up to the entry into force of UNCLOS). This seems to coincide with the views of certain scholars who believe that the 'Nine-Dash Line' refers only to sovereignty over the islands which are included in it and their adjacent (territorial) waters.[57] Yet others support the view that the 'Line' plays a dual role: firstly, it defines China's sovereignty over the islands of the South China Sea and secondly it indicates China's traditional maritime boundary line in that Sea.[58] The latter theory, however, leaves unexplained what is the status attributed by the 'Nine-Dash Line' to the waters which are not territorial and lie to the west of the line.

56 ILC Yearbook, Vol. II, 1962, p. 6.

57 Gao Zhiguo, the South China Sea : From Conflict to Cooperation, Ocean Development and International Law, Vol. 25, 1994; Zhao Lihai, Studies on the law of the Sea (in Chinese), Beijing University Press, 1996, 1996, both cited by L. Jinming and L. Dexia, *loc.cit.*, p. 291.

58 L. Jinming and L. Dexia, *loc.cit.*, pp. 293-294.

13.3.7 *The South China Sea Arbitration and Award*

The Philippines initiated proceedings against China in 2013 under UNCLOS Article 287[59] and Annex VII on Arbitration, and an Arbitral Tribunal was constituted under these provisions.

China never accepted the jurisdiction of the Tribunal and did not participate in the proceedings. It did, however, express her opinions on both the tribunal's jurisdiction and on the substance, mainly in a 2014 Position Paper issued by the Chinese Ministry of Foreign Affairs.[60, 61]

The main argument of China regarding the lack of jurisdiction of the Tribunal was that the claims of the Philippines disguised, in effect, a sovereignty dispute which is excluded from the Convention's scope of application.[62] China had, furthermore, submitted an opt-out clause in connection with maritime boundary (delimitation) disputes which, again, she argued, put her outside the reach of any court's jurisdiction on such issues.[63]

However, the submissions of the Philippines did not put forward either sovereignty or boundary delimitation questions, concentrating, instead, on whether the maritime fea-

---

59 The article is entitled: 'Choice of procedure' and reads as follows: "1. When signing, ratifying or acceding to this Convention or at any time thereafter, a State shall be free to choose, by means of a written declaration, one or more of the following means for the settlement of disputes concerning the interpretation or application of this Convention: (a) the International Tribunal for the Law of the Sea established in accordance with Annex VI; (b) the International Court of Justice; (c) an arbitral tribunal constituted in accordance with Annex VII; (d) a special arbitral tribunal constituted in accordance with Annex VIII for one or more of the categories of disputes specified therein. 2. A declaration made under paragraph 1 shall not affect or be affected by the obligation of a State Party to accept the jurisdiction of the Seabed Disputes Chamber of the International Tribunal for the Law of the Sea to the extent and in the manner provided for in Part XI, section 5.3. A State Party, which is a party to a dispute not covered by a declaration in force, shall be deemed to have accepted arbitration in accordance with Annex VII. 4. If the parties to a dispute have accepted the same procedure for the settlement of the dispute, it may be submitted only to that procedure, unless the parties otherwise agree. 5. If the parties to a dispute have not accepted the same procedure for the settlement of the dispute, it may be submitted only to arbitration in accordance with Annex VII, unless the parties otherwise agree. 6. A declaration made under paragraph 1 shall remain in force until three months after notice of revocation has been deposited with the Secretary-General of the United Nations. 7. A new declaration, a notice of revocation or the expiry of a declaration does not in any way affect proceedings pending before a court or tribunal having jurisdiction under this article, unless the parties otherwise agree. 8. Declarations and notices referred to in this article shall be deposited with the Secretary-General of the United Nations, who shall transmit copies thereof to the States Parties."

60 www.fmprc.gov.cn/mfa_eng/zxxx_662805/t1217147.shtml issued on 7 January 2014.

61 For an analysis of the Chinese position *see* Sienho Yee, The South China Sea Arbitration (*The Philippines v. China*): Potential Jurisdictional Obstacles or Objections' (2014) 13 *Chinese Journal of International Law*, 1 December 2014, pp. 663-739; Zhiguo Gao and Bing Bing Jia, The Nine-Dash Line in the South China Sea: History, Status, and Implications, *supra*, fn. 257; Stefan Talmon and Bing Bing Gia (eds), *The South China Sea Arbitration: A Chinese Perspective*, 2014.

62 On this issue, *see* Stefan Salmon, *op. cit.*, pp. 25-48.

63 The Declaration, which was submitted on 25 August 2006, reads as follows: "The Government of the People's Republic of China does not accept any of the procedures provided for in Section 2 of Part XV of the Convention with respect to all the categories of disputes referred to in paragraph 1 (a) (b) and (c) of Article 298 of the Convention.

tures in question were capable of generating jurisdictional zones. Furthermore, the Tribunal found in its first 2014 Award on Jurisdiction and Admissibility[64] (which settled certain jurisdictional issues while others, considered to be linked with the merits, were deferred to be settled by the final Award) that as the relationship between UNCLOS and prior legal regimes applicable in the disputed area was a question of 'interpretation and application' of UNCLOS, it fell within its jurisdiction.

In its final Award,[65] the Tribunal found that the 'historic rights' claimed by China did not constitute 'title', i.e. they did not confer sovereignty.[66] As a consequence, they could be examined by the Tribunal to ascertain whether they were compatible with UNCLOS. On the merits of the case, the Tribunal found unanimously, and "without prejudice to any questions of sovereignty or maritime boundary delimitation"[67] that a) there was no legal basis for China's claim to historic rights to resources within the sea areas falling within the 'Nine-Dash Line'; b) China's claim was incompatible with the detailed allocation of rights and maritime zones in UNCLOS, concluding that even if China did have such rights, they had, upon China's accession to the Convention and its entry into force "been superseded, as a matter of law and as between the Philippines and China, by the limits of the maritime zones provided for by the Convention"[68]; c) in connection with the legal status of maritime features in the disputed area, the Tribunal concluded that none of the *Spratly Islands* was capable of generating extended maritime zones, nor could they generate such rights 'collectively as a unit'; d) China had violated the sovereign rights of the Philippines in its EEZ by (i) its interfering with Philippine fishing and petroleum exploration, (ii) constructing artificial islands and (iii) failing to prevent Chinese fishermen from fishing in the zone; e) China's recent large-scale land reclamation and the construction of artificial islands in the *Spratly islands* had severely damaged the marine environment and breached various obligations under UNCLOS regarding its protection and preservation; f) China's conduct had aggravated the dispute; g) *Mischief Reef* was a low tide elevation within the Philippines EEZ, over which no state could claim either sovereignty or sovereign rights; and g) China had violated Article 300 of UNCLOS, i.e. the duty to act in good faith.[69]

64 The Republic of Philippines v. The People's Republic of China, PCA case No. 2013-19," Award on Jurisdiction and Admissibility, 29 October 2015.

65 *The Republic of Philippines v. The People's Republic of China, PCA case No. 2013-19,* Award, 12 July 2016.

66 In this respect, the Tribunal noted, *inter alia,* that "...In practice, to establish the exclusive historic right to living and non-living resources within the 'nine-dash line', which China now appears to claim, it would be necessary to show that China had historically sought to prohibit or restrict the exploitation of such resources by the nationals of other States and that those States had acquiesced in such restrictions. In the Tribunal's view, such a claim cannot be supported...." (para. 270 of the Award).

67 Para. 1203 of the Award.

68 Para. 262 of the Award.

69 *See* Douglas Guilfoyle, *Philippines v. China*, First Thoughts on the Award on the South China Sea Case, *EJIL Talk*, 12 July 2016.

In sum, the Award upheld the Philippine claims on almost all points. On the merits, the Award finds a solid basis on the UNCLOS provisions and applicable customary law. However, doubts have been expressed – justifiably in our view – as to the jurisdictional powers of the Tribunal over the matter, in view, in particular, of the declaration China had made under UNCLOS Article 298(1)(a)(i).[70]

---

70 On this issue, *see* Sreenavasa Rao Pemmaraju, *Chinese Journal of International Law*, Volume 15, Issue 2, 1 June 2016, pp. 265-307, available at https://doi.org/10.1093/chinesejil/jmw019.

14 Piracy[1]

14.1 Introduction

Piracy is the archetypical international crime (*crimen jure gentium*) and in all probability the first to have ever been qualified as such. Being fearful of and abhorred by piratical attacks, nations and peoples all along human history considered pirates as 'enemies of humankind' (*hostes humani generis*) and extraordinary measures were resorted to in order to suppress their activities. Despite its decline in modern times, the phenomenon of piracy has never been completely eradicated, as its recent revival in parts of Africa and elsewhere has shown. From today's legal perspective, which is based on the legal tradition of the last five centuries at least, piracy is an international crime under customary international law[2] which is subject to universal jurisdiction, i.e. any state can lawfully intercept a pirate ship and any state's courts can exercise criminal jurisdiction over pirates.[3, 4]

14.2 Historical Notes

The history of piracy dates back for millennia, in reality as far back as humans have travelled the seas. It has also been a widespread phenomenon, having affected almost all parts of the world with different degrees of intensity at different times.

Mycenaean Greece suffered piracy attacks by the 'Sea peoples' as did all the Eastern Mediterranean and the Aegean Sea, probably as early as the fourteenth century B.C. During the times of the Roman Empire, there were pirate attacks in the Mediterranean, disrupting commerce, while the Adriatic suffered the attacks of *Illyrian* and *Dalmatian* pirates. Following a piracy attack against the port of *Ostia* near Rome and its setting on

---

1 *See* Daniel Heller-Roazen, *The enemy of all: Piracy and the Law of Nations*, 31, 2009; Peter Lehr (ed), *Violence at Sea: Piracy in the Age of Global Terrorism*, Routledge, 2007; Douglas Guilfoyle, ed., *Modern Piracy: Legal Challenges and Responses*, Cheltenham, Edward Elgar Publishing, 2013; Panos Koutrakos and Achilles Skordas (eds), *The Law and Practice of Piracy at Sea: European and International Perspective*, Hart Publishing, 2014; James Kraska, *Contemporary Maritime Piracy: International Law, Strategy, and Diplomacy at Sea (Contemporary Military, Strategic, and Security Issues)*, 2011; Michael P. Scharf, Michael A. Newton, Milena Sterio (eds), *Prosecuting Maritime Piracy: Domestic Solutions to International Crimes*, Cambridge University Press, 2015; Martin N. Murphy, *Contemporary Piracy and Maritime Terrorism: The Threat to International Security*, London, International Institute for Strategic Studies, 2007.

2 Which is also embodied in UNCLOS on this question.

3 *Infra*, at 14.4.1.1.

4 Cherif Bassiouni, Universal Jurisdiction for International Crimes: Historical Perspectives and Contemporary Practice, 42 *Va. J. Int'l L.* 81, (2001).

fire, *lex Gabinia* was promulgated in 67 B.C. giving Pompey extraordinary powers to eradicate piracy, which he did very successfully.

In Byzantine times, Emperor Justinian's Digest (*Digesta*) of 533 A.D. refers to piracy,[5] a well-known phenomenon in the Empire. From the eighth to the twelfth century, the Vikings of Scandinavia plagued the Baltic Sea with their piratical attacks, venturing as far south as Spain.

The golden age of piracy was, however, the seventeenth and early eighteenth centuries. At that time, the phenomenon was particularly acute in the Caribbean Sea, where mostly French, English and Dutch pirates (buccaneers), controlling seaports among which the most important were *Port Royal* in Jamaica, *Tortuga* in Haiti and *Nassau* in the Bahamas, attacked and looted Spanish vessels, getting possession of great wealth. During the same period, pirates also engaged in the slave trade – then at its height – from West Africa to the Caribbean.

Although a pirate is typically identified as a ruthless robber acting at sea for his own and his gang's gain, it was common for pirates to be commissioned by authorities of their home country – usually a king – to attack enemy ships and share the spoils with them.[6] In the sixteenth century, the most notable such 'privateer' was *Francis Drake* who was in the service of Queen Elizabeth I of England to destroy Spanish ships, and who was later knighted by her for his exploits. Nonetheless, probably the first national law dealing with piracy was the English Act 'On offences at Sea' of 1536 on the basis of which England began to try pirates under Common Law.[7]

From the sixteenth century, *Barbary corsairs* (pirates operating from North Africa coasts, particularly from Tunis and Algiers) attacked ships and coastal towns all over the Mediterranean until the early nineteenth century, engaging mostly in the slave trade and selling slaves to the Ottoman Empire.[8] Their activities finally stopped with the occupation of Algiers by France in 1830.

The Persian Gulf was another prime location for piratical operations, usually targeting ships of the East India Company.[9] Similarly, in the eighteenth century, Hindu *Maratha* privateers attacked ships of the East India Company in the Indian Ocean between Goa

5 Book XIV, Title II (Concerning the Rhodian Law of Jettison).

6 For this purpose they were provided with 'Letters of marque', a sort of license provided by the authority who commissioned them.

7 The Act – which obviously did not cover privateers – was repealed in 1967. The English 'Piracy Act' was enacted in 1698 and repealed in 1993.

8 *Hayreddin Barbarossa* and his brother *Oruc Reis* were the most famous corsairs.

9 The ICJ judgment in *Qatar v. Bahrain* (*supra*, 11.1, fn. 6) gives a clear picture of the role piracy played in the history of these two states and of the British involvement aiming at its control.

and Mumbai, requiring that the ships pay taxes when transiting through waters under their control.

Pirates were intensely active in the waters of most of Southeast Asia and in the Yellow Sea. In the South China Sea,[10] Chinese pirates conducted piratical assaults off the southern coast of China from *Zhejiang Province* to *Hainan Island* from the eighteenth to the early nineteenth century[11] under the *Ming* and *Qing Dynasties*. Pirates also operated between Singapore and Hong Kong, particularly at the choke point of the *Malacca Straits*.

The forms piratical activities took were manifold, generally involving not only sea operations but also raids on land.[12] Extortion, slave trade and hostage-taking were also usual corollary activities.

The end of organized piracy came in the nineteenth century when national navies became strong enough to patrol the seas and fight off pirate attacks. Thus, the British navy cleared the South China Sea while the Dutch did the same in the waters around Indonesia. Privateering which had continued until the beginning of the nineteenth century was finally banned by the Declaration of Paris of 16 April 1856 signed by most maritime nations.[13]

Nonetheless, and although the danger of piracy has been drastically reduced since then, it was never, as already noted, completely extinguished. In many parts of the world, usually in waters off the coasts of developing countries, there are sporadic reappearances of the piratical phenomenon, which may occasionally take important dimensions, as will be seen below.

---

10 Zou Keyuan and Dr Shicun Wu (ed), *Maritime Security in the South China Sea*, Ashgate, 2009; Graham Gerard Ong-Webb, Introduction – Southeast Asian Piracy: Research and Developments, in *Piracy, Maritime Terrorism and Securing the Malacca Straits* in Graham Gerard Ong-Webb (ed), Singapore: Institute of Southeast Asian Studies, 2006.

11 *See* Robert Antony, Like Froth Floating on the Sea: The World of Pirates and Seafarers in Late Imperial South China, Institute for East Asian Studies, *China Research Monographs*, No. 56, Berkeley, California University Press, 2003.

12 An example is provided by the Cyclades islands in the Aegean Sea, the capital towns of which (hora-*Χώρα*) were, as a rule, built on high ground in the interior and away from the seashore in past centuries because of the fear of pirate attacks.

13 The Declaration of Paris was signed upon the conclusion of the Treaty of Paris on 30 March 1856 which ended the Crimean War (1853-1856). The Declaration provided that parties would not issue *letters of marque*. Fifty states signed the Declaration.

14.3 PIRACY AND ARMED ROBBERY IN RECENT YEARS[14]

14.3.1 *Piracy Off the Coast of Somalia*

After reaching a peak in 2011, piracy off the coast of Somalia[15] has followed a sharp downward trend with no attacks being registered against merchant vessels from 2012 to early 2017.[16] However, some serious attacks happened again during 2017, reminding the international community that piracy is still capable of a revival in the region if vigilance wanes and, most importantly, if the root causes of piracy are not vigorously addressed.

At the height of the phenomenon, the Red Sea, the Gulf of Aden, the Somali Basin and as far down as the Mozambique Channel, Madagascar and the Seychelles, as well as a vast maritime area which includes the Arabian Sea and the Indian Ocean up to the coastline of India, had been the theatre of hundreds of pirate attacks, primarily by Somali pirates. The direct cause of this situation was the extreme weakness of Somalia which practically lacked effective administration and even more so, any effective means to combat piracy. In fact, the then Transitional Federal Government of Somalia (TFG)[17] controlled only part of the Somali territory, much of the rest being dominated by the Sunni-Islamist organization *Al Shabaab* (The Youth) considered to be connected with *Al Qaeda* and later with ISIS. Although no operational or other cooperation between pirates and *Al Shabaab* – which is still active particularly in southern and central Somalia – seemed to exist,[18] the ongoing conflict between the Somali Government and *Al Shabaab* has been a major destabilizing factor in the country, which further aggravated its political and social fragility.

At the time, although the political situation appeared to be better in *Somaliland* and *Puntland* in the northwest and northeast respectively, it was *Puntland* and the region of

---

14 Ashley Roach, Countering Piracy off Somalia: International Law and International Institutions, *American Journal of International Law*, 2010, 104 (3), pp. 397-415; Tullio Treves, Piracy, Law of the Sea and Use of Force: Developments off the Coast of Somalia, *The European Journal of International Law*, 2009, 20(2), pp. 399-414.

15 The Somali coast is the second longest in Africa, extending to 3025 km.

16 Report of the Secretary-General on the situation with respect to piracy and armed robbery at sea off the coast of Somalia, 12 October 2017, p. 1.

17 The Transitional Federal Government (TFG) came to power in 2004. With the assistance of Ethiopia, it took control of most of southern Somalia, ousting the *Islamic Courts Union* (ICU) forces (which, however, were later transformed into the more radical *Al Shabaab*). Succeeding in getting hold of a large part of the territory by 2012, the Government adopted a provisional Constitution which transformed the country into a Federation, and a Federal Government (FGS) was established. As of 2016, Somalia has been officially divided into six regional states: *Puntland, Galmudug, Jubaland, South West State, Hirshabelle and Somaliland.* In 2017, elections took place and a new federal parliament was elected. *Somaliland* declared its independence in 1991 and has no relations with the Government of Somalia. However, no country has recognized it as an independent state.

18 Some cases of 'protection money' payments to *Al-Shabaab* have, however, been reported in the areas where both groups are present and active.

Galmudug which were the on-land centres for piracy activities and it was off their coasts that pirated ships and the so-called motherships[19] were usually anchored.

The root causes of the phenomenon, however, should be mainly sought, according to the Somalis, in the illegal dumping of toxic materials off its coastline and the illegal fishing by foreign fishermen and fishing fleets in Somali waters. They claimed that both these activities have had a direct impact on the livelihoods of the Somali coastal populations, leading to their impoverishment and, to a large extent, their turning to piracy as a means of supporting themselves.[20] In any event, the inability of the Somali government to confront the situation gave free reign to piracy which, making full use of the desperation of many destitute young people, managed to extract large amounts of money, mainly through the collection of ransom for the liberation of captive crew members. Money laundering was then undertaken by piracy chiefs through investments around the world.

Piracy in the Western Indian Ocean reached a point where it put at serious risk the international shipping industry and international trade while also representing a grave danger for the life of seafarers. The world community had therefore to mobilize, and it finally did so to an unprecedented degree.

Playing a pioneering role in that effort, the U.N. Security Council unanimously adopted a series of Resolutions under Chapter VII of the Charter which, spanning the years from 2008 to 2018, provided authorization to international naval forces to combat piracy and armed robbery off the Somali Coast.[21]

14.3.1.1 Deployment of Naval Forces

On the basis of these resolutions, naval forces were deployed in the context of three operations: 'Ocean Shield' by NATO, 'EU NAVFOR' ('Atalanta') by the EU and 'Combined Task Force 151' by the American-led maritime multinational coalition force. Other countries, such as India, Japan, China, Russia and Iran, with an increased interest in the protection of international shipping and the capability to do so, offered assistance to the counter-piracy efforts independently. All the countries contributing naval forces participate in the SHADE mechanism (Shared Awareness and Deconfliction) which has coordination duties.

Naval operations were successful enough in curbing piracy off the coast of Somalia, almost halving the number of attacks. Naval ships patrolled the 'International Recom-

19 Motherships are vessels hijacked by pirates for the purpose of being used for pirate attacks. High speed craft (skiffs) are launched from motherships in the final phase of the attack.

20 Catrina Stewart, "Somalia threatened by illegal fishermen after West chases away pirates," *The Guardian*, 31 October 2015. According to the SG Report of 2017, these claims may be exaggerated (*supra*, fn. 16).

21 These Resolutions are: S/RES/1816(2008), S/RES/1838(2008), S/RES/1846(2008), S/RES/1851(2008), S/RES/1897(2009), S/RES/1918(2010), S/RES/1950(2010), S/RES/1976(2011), S/RES/2015(2011), S/RES/2020(2011), S/RES/2077(2012), S/RES/2125(2013), S/RES/2184(2014), S/RES/2246 (2015), S/RES/2316 (2016), S/RES/2383 (2017), S/RES/2442 (2018).

mended Transit Corridor' (IRTC) and even escorted merchant ships from Aden to the end of the area where pirate danger was present.

However, they could not completely eradicate the phenomenon on their own, because of their limited number, the sheer size of the maritime areas to be patrolled and the very high costs involved. Resort to more flexible means was required for this purpose, as will be seen below.[22]

Already, following the long lull in piracy attacks off Somalia – despite some recent spikes – NATO terminated *Ocean Shield* after seven years of operations. By contrast, the *EU NAVFOR* Somalia Operation *Atalanta* has been extended until 31 December 2020.

14.3.1.2 The Contact Group

The Contact Group on Piracy off the Coast of Somalia (CGPCS), consisting of more than sixty states, was established by the U.N. Security Council[23] to coordinate the efforts of the international community in view of the growing impact of piracy on humanitarian aid, commercial shipping and regional trade in the Horn of Africa.

The Contact Group established five Working Groups to deal with: operational and capacity building, legal questions, self-protection within the industry, communication and awareness-raising, and piracy financial networks.

In 2010, a Trust Fund was set up by the UNSG at the request of the Contact Group in order, *inter alia*, to defray the expenses associated with prosecution of suspected pirates and other activities related to implementing the Contact Group's objectives regarding combating piracy, and support relevant legal capacity-building activities. Initially administered by the Office on Drugs and Crime (UNODC), the administration of the Trust Fund was transferred to the UNDP Multi-Partner Trust Fund Office (MPTF Office) in 2012.[24]

Furthermore, the U.N. offered assistance through the International Maritime Organization (IMO), the UNODC, the U.N. Development Programme (UNDP) and the U.N. Political Office for Somalia (UNPOS).

14.3.1.3 The International Maritime Organization (IMO)

Having undertaken a particularly active role regarding piracy off Somalia, IMO adopted and vigorously promoted 'Best Management Practices' (BMP), urging merchant ships to

22 *See infra*, at 14.9.
23 The 'Contact Group on Piracy off the Coast of Somalia (CGPCS)' was established on 14 January 2009 pursuant to UNSC Resolution 1851 (2008).
24 Upon a 2012 decision of the Contact Group.

take a series of measures for their effective self-protection against pirate attacks.[25] The BMP has been a valuable aid for ships transiting the 'High Risk Area' (HRA).[26]

The IMO also adopted the 'Djibouti Code of Conduct', a non-binding instrument, participants to which committed themselves to share and report information regarding piracy in their area through a system of national focal points and information centres, interdict ships suspected of acts of piracy or armed robbery and ensure that those committing or attempting to commit such acts against ships are arrested and prosecuted. They have also undertaken to provide care, treatment and repatriation for seafarers, fishermen, shipboard personnel, passengers and other victims of such acts. The Code differentiates between piracy on the high seas, where UNCLOS rules apply, and armed robbery in internal, archipelagic, and territorial waters where the authorization of the coastal state is necessary, including in cases of hot pursuit from the high seas ('reverse hot pursuit').

The Code, which has ensured the cooperation of most of the countries in the region, widened its material scope through the 'Jeddah amendment' adopted in 2017, which addresses additional illicit maritime activities threatening regional maritime safety and security, i.e. arms, drugs and wildlife trafficking; maritime terrorism; illegal, unreported and unregulated fishing; illegal oil bunkering; crude oil theft; human trafficking, and illegal toxic waste dumping. The ultimate purpose of the amendment is to emphasize and promote the tools for wholesome and effective maritime governance.

14.3.1.4 The Office on Drugs and Crime (UNODC)

The UNODC put in place a number of specific programmes targeting areas where its assistance was particularly needed. The Piracy Prisoners Transfer Programme supports prison-related operations – its original aim being to facilitate the transfer of convicted pirates, if consenting, back to Somalia. Major infrastructure projects were undertaken to support these programmes.[27]

In the context of its 'Global Maritime Crime Programme' for the Horn of Africa, the Office carried out several capacity-building projects along the Somali coast, involving mentoring, procurement, construction and training for police and coastguard. As a result,

---

25 As a minimum, ships' masters must receive updated information before and during sailing through the defined High Risk Area, while ships must register with the Maritime Security Centre Horn of Africa (MSCHOA) and report to United Kingdom Maritime Trade Operations (UKMTO), Dubai. They must also implement effectively all recommended preventive, evasive and defensive measures.

26 "'High Risk Area' is an area as defined in the Best Management Practices (BMP) for Protection against Somalia-based Piracy (MSC.1/Circ.1339), unless otherwise defined by the flag State. For BMP purposes, the High Risk Area is bounded by *Suez* and the *Straits of Hormuz* to the North, 10°S and 78°E" (para. 2.4).

27 Thus, the construction or improvement of prison facilities was undertaken by the UNODC in *Mandhera* and *Hargeysa*, Somaliland, and in *Bosasso* and *Garowe*, Puntland (www.unodc.org/unodc/en/piracy/piracy-prisoner-transfer-programme.html). In *Bosasso*, a Port Police Building was also built, while in Somalia, the *Mogadishu* Prison and Court Complex is under construction. The prison facility in Mogadishu will be the most advanced in Somalia, while the Court Complex will allow conducting trials of high-risk prisoners, such as pirates and terrorists.

Somali maritime institutions now have improved situational awareness and better communication with the international naval forces operating in HRAs.

14.3.1.5 Regional Action and Initiatives

The Somali-led 'Kampala Process' was a forum which succeeded in bringing together officials from all regions in Somalia to agree on the strategy to fight maritime crime. To this effect, it also secured the vital exchange of information between the Federal Somali Government, Galmudug, Puntland and Somaliland. As from 2014, the Kampala Process has been recast as 'Regional Maritime Coordination Mechanism' (RMCM) and its Secretariat functions are being performed by UNODC.

To combat Somali piracy on land, the East African 'Intergovernmental Authority on Development' (IGAD) put forward a relevant strategy while also emphasizing the need to address the root causes of piracy.[28]

14.3.1.6 The 'Legal Working Group' (l.w.g)

Of particular importance has been the work carried out by the l.w.g. established by the Contact Group on Piracy off the Coast of Somalia.[29] The Group was called to deal with the various legal problems facing the international operations to fight piracy off the coast of Somalia. Its main effort was to establish common legal standards with regard, *inter alia*, to the collection of evidence to be used for prosecution purposes as well as other issues facilitating prosecution which is pivotal for the whole anti-piracy effort. In this connection, the Report of *Jack Lang*, appointed by the UNSG as special envoy on piracy, was published in 2011.[30] The Report addressed the question of the prosecution of pirates and formulated certain recommendations which were discussed in the l.w.g. Many, if not the totality of the legal problems dealt with by the l.w.g., were relevant not only to the anti-piracy efforts off the coast of Somalia but also to any similar situation arising in any part of the world. From that perspective, the work of the group was both ground-breaking and very useful.[31]

14.3.1.7 Addressing the 'Root Causes'

In 2009, FAO adopted the Agreement entitled '2009 Port State Measures to Prevent, Deter and Eliminate Illegal, Unreported and Unregulated Fishing of the Food and Agriculture Organization of the United Nations' which entered into force in 2016. This is the

28 AMISOM (African Union Mission in Somalia), *i.e.*, the African Union's (AU) peace-keeping force operating in Somalia with U.N. approval, is not directly involved in anti-piracy efforts.

29 *See supra*, at 14.3.1.2.

30 S/2011/30 of 25 January 2011, containing a Letter dated 24 January 2011 from the Secretary-General to the President of the Security Council and Annex entitled "Report of the Special Adviser to the Secretary-General on Legal Issues Related to Piracy off the Coast of Somalia."

31 The 'legal working group' was chaired by Denmark. Some of the main problems and questions examined by the Group will be mentioned in various places below.

first international instrument to focus on these harmful practices and Somalia, at her request, has been receiving assistance with its implementation. Taking also into account that the Jeddah amendment of the Djibouti Code is also addressing this issue, there is hope that at least some of the root causes of piracy in the Gulf of Aden will begin gathering international attention, which may lead to serious efforts to suppress them.

14.3.2 Piracy in the South China Sea and in Southeast Asia[32]

'Piracy', *David Rosenberg* says, "is an ancient, persistent, and elusive phenomenon in the South China Sea."[33] The *Malacca Straits* are, indeed, recognized as being 'pirate infested', although criminal activity of this type in the area technically constitutes - in contrast to the Somalia case - armed robbery rather than piracy since it takes place overwhelmingly in the territorial sea or the internal waters of neighbouring states. The reasons for the persistence of the phenomenon are in large measure due to the geographic configuration of the region and the prevailing climatic environment: narrowness of passage, reefs, heavy rainfall, jungles and mountains all around combined with traffic so dense that passing ships are forced to reduce speed to a minimum. There is also poverty as well as a historical tradition of shipping, privateering and piracy. During the 1990s, there were still no measures in place to combat the phenomenon. This, however, changed drastically in the early years of this century following intense pressure from the international community which could not afford to ignore the situation, given the extreme importance of the Malacca Straits.[34]

---

32 Robert C. Beckman and J. Ashley Roach, eds., *Piracy and International Maritime crimes in ASEAN: Prospects for Cooperation*, Chelthenam, UK: Edward Elgar Publishing, 2012; Adam J. Young, *Contemporary Maritime Piracy in Southeast Asia: History, Causes, and Remedies* (Singapore: Institute of Southeast Asian Studies, International Institute for Asian Studies, 2007), p. 9; Eric Frécon, Pirates set the Straits on Fire, Causes and Context of the Pirate Arsons in the Malay Archipelagos since the Nineties, in Werner Vom Busch and Tobias Retting (eds), *Covering Maritime Piracy in Southeast Asia*, Kuala Lumpur, 13-15 July 2006, Conrad Adenauer Foundation, Singapore, pp. 17-41; Karen Kvashny, *Modern Maritime Piracy in Asia: A Case Study of Transnational Organized Crime* (dissertation, University of California, Irvine, 2003); Eduardo Ma R Santos, Piracy and Armed Robbery against Ships in the Philippines, in Graham Gerard Ong-Webb, ed., Piracy, *Maritime Terrorism and Securing the Malacca Straits*, Singapore, ISEAS, 2006, pp. 37-51; *Ibid.*, Stefan Eklöf, *Political Piracy and Maritime Terrorism: A Comparison between the Straits of Malacca and the Southern Philippines*, pp. 52-67; *Ibid.*, Mark Valencia, *The Politics of Anti-piracy and Anti-terrorism Responses*, pp. 84-102.

33 David Rosenberg, The Political Economy of Piracy in the South China Sea, in Bruce Elleman, Andrew Forbes, and David Rosenberg (eds), *Piracy and Maritime Crime: Historical and Modern Case Studies*, Naval War College Newport Papers, 2010, Chapter 5, p. 79.

34 Most influential in this respect was the Joint War Committee (JWC) of the Lloyd's Market Association listing of the Malacca Straits and certain areas in the southern Philippines as 'prone to hull war, strikes, terrorism and related perils'. This caused an increase of marine insurance premiums for vessels transiting these areas, which alarmed the states concerned. The listing was removed in 2006.

14.3.2.1 Response to the Problem

As a result of this pressure, countries neighbouring the Straits – Singapore, Malaysia, Indonesia – intensified patrolling of the area, while the IMO and the International Maritime Bureau (IMB) monitored the situation through their Piracy Reporting Centres. The IMO required that all ocean-going vessels over 300 gross tons be equipped with an Identification System (AIS), while the IMB endorsed similarly effective measures. At the same time, the modernization and the anti-piracy training of the Coast Guard of the region enhanced their capabilities. By 2006, the alert over the *Malacca Straits* and the adjoining areas had been lifted.

The success of the regional anti-piracy operations in the Straits of Malacca and Singapore exemplifies the importance of regional information-sharing in connection with piracy. The Regional Cooperation Agreement on Combating Piracy and Armed Robbery against ships in Asia (RECAAP),[35] concluded in 2004 by sixteen Asian countries under the auspices of the IMO, has played a central role to this effect.

Piracy incidents have not been eradicated completely, however, and this is true of the South China Sea and Southeast Asia in general. Nor is small-scale armed robbery within the territorial waters of the neighbouring states, particularly Indonesia, a thing of the past. Here again it is social factors which need to be addressed, but this, of course, is a much larger goal.

14.3.3 Piracy in the Gulf of Guinea

In recent years, the Gulf of Guinea has developed into the most active centre for piracy and armed robbery attacks worldwide, a trend which continues until today.[36] As ports around the Gulf are increasingly busy with the maritime transport of commodities such as gold and iron ore, and the whole of the Gulf area is transited by tankers to and from

35 The RECAAP includes an Information Sharing Centre (ISC) which facilitates the sharing of information regarding piracy incidents.

36 *See* the Economist, 16 January 2018, the article by *W.B.* under the title 'What is happening to Africa's pirates?' reporting that "in 2017, 33 incidents of piracy and robbery at sea, successful or otherwise, were reported within 12 nautical miles of the coastline." *See also* Alexander Holmgren, Piracy's Persistence in the Gulf of Guinea, African Defence Review, 13 January 2014. For 2018 the International Maritime Bureau (IMB) of the International Chamber of Commerce (ICC) reported that piracy attacks more than doubled in the Gulf of Guinea. According to the same source, 201 incidents of maritime piracy and armed robbery were reported worldwide in 2018, from 180 in 2017.

Nigeria and Angola, the major oil-producing countries in West Africa, poverty-stricken parts of the population are driven to join gangs preying on this new wealth.[37]

Only part of the attacks in the Gulf of Guinea constitute piracy in the legal sense[38] since, as opposed to the Somalia case, most of them take place in the territorial and internal waters of the states around the Gulf – thus constituting armed robbery – and not on the high seas. Targeting of vessels and their crews can, in fact, happen anywhere along the coast, the rivers, the estuaries, the ports and the anchorages, but also in waters far off the coast and into the high seas. More often than not, the attack is directed against fully loaded tankers, the aim being to steal the oil and sell it to other ships or on the black market on land.[39] While piracy off Somalia has been mainly directed towards kidnapping the crew with a view to get ransom for their release, the hostages being therefore viewed as trade asset,[40] this was not initially the pattern in the Gulf of Guinea, where the attacks often resulted in killing members of the crew, presumably because the latter were perceived as an obstacle to the success of the attack. Later, however, kidnappings for ransom in the Gulf of Guinea increased, accounting, in 2016-2017, for more than half of them worldwide,[41] the reason being, it is estimated, the decrease in the price of oil at the time which made kidnappings more profitable.[42]

The majority of attacks originate in Nigeria, with Benin and Togo following. Cameroon, Gabon, Benin, Equatorial Guinea and Ivory Coast have also seen many piracy and armed robbery cases in their waters or close to them.

Although the peak year in incidents in the region was 2011, and a gradual decline in such activity has been observed since, the Gulf of Guinea remains a piracy hotspot with a high degree of insecurity.[43] The UNSC has issued two Resolutions on the matter, encouraging *inter alia*, the states concerned to counter, through concerted action, piracy

---

37 Crude oil production in Nigeria reached a peak of 2.44 million bbl/d in 2005, but declined in the following years due to attacks from militant groups. In 2016 it plunged to less than 1,75 due to the same reasons; it recovered, however, in 2017 to reach 2,095 (source: https://ycharts.com/indicators/nigeria_crude_oil_productionb). A limited amount of the crude oil (less than a quarter) is processed in Nigeria. Oil can therefore be targeted by pirates or robbers either when exported from the country as crude oil or when (part of it) is re-imported as refined product for consumption in Nigeria.

38 *See infra*, at 14.4.

39 Christina Barrios, Fighting Piracy in the Gulf of Guinea, European Union Institute for Security Studies, May 2013.

40 At the height of piracy incidents off the coast of Somalia, seafarers kidnapped in the Gulf of Aden spent an average of eleven months in captivity compared to an average of four days for those kidnapped in the Gulf of Guinea (*See Alexander Holmgren, Swat Security Systems*, Pirates on the other side: Maritime piracy in the Gulf of Guinea, 31 October 2013).

41 Thirty-four seafarers were kidnapped in the Gulf of Guinea out of a total of sixty-two worldwide in 2017 (*See* Bartélemy Blédé, Institute for Security Studies (ISS) Africa, 28 February 2017).

42 *See* Alice Vervaeke, European Union Institute for Security Studies, (EUISS), June 2017.

43 According to the International Maritime Bureau's Piracy Reporting Centre, in 2018, attacks in waters between the Ivory Coast and the Democratic Republic of Congo accounted "for all six hijackings worldwide, 13 of the 18 ships fired upon, 130 of the 141 hostages taken globally, and 78 of 83 seafarers kidnapped for ransom".

and armed robbery in the Gulf by conducting bilateral or regional maritime patrols and to convene a joint Summit in order to develop a regional anti-piracy strategy.[44]

14.3.3.1 Response to the Problem

Despite the declared wish and the efforts of states in the region to have the assistance of western states in combating piracy, as the latter have done in the case of Somalia, neither NATO nor the EU which had led the western naval deployment in Somalia have expressed the same willingness to do so in the Gulf of Guinea. The EU restricted itself to expressing the intention to provide assistance in the form of advice and training with a view to strengthening the capacity of states in the region in their efforts to curb piracy. It seems that the reticence of western states to engage more actively in the anti-piracy effort in the Gulf of Guinea is their belief that the states concerned could confront it by themselves, as they have the requisite naval and police forces, which differentiates the situation in this region from that in Somalia where no such regional capabilities existed. Nigeria and Ghana are, however, the only states in the Gulf with a real capacity to do so. Coordinated patrols by coastal authorities (Nigeria, Benin)[45] have had some positive impact on the situation but it is recognized that this by no means suffices to curb the problem.[46] Generally, the law enforcement capacity of the affected countries is limited while, yet again, the root causes remain poverty, unemployment, lack of prospects for young people, endemic corruption, political and social tensions and weak governance.

Finally, the most successful model to protect ships in the Gulf of Guinea proved to be, as described by *Dirk Steffen*, one invented at the peak of the Niger Delta insurgency (2006-2009) which allowed private companies to supply and maintain patrol boats in order to serve primarily the Nigerian Navy, but also offer their services with weapons and Nigerian Navy crews on board, for the protection of commercial vessels.[47] A substantial number of private companies signed an MoU for this purpose with the Nigerian Navy in 2016.

---

44 S/RES/2018 (2011) and S/RES/2039 (2012). See also the IMO "Strategy for implementing sustainable maritime security measures in West and Central Africa" issued on 26 April 2017.

45 Benin and Nigeria have concluded an agreement on maritime safety and carry out joint patrols since 2011. Benin, which relies heavily on shipping, has lost approximately 40% of its port revenue; it is also estimated that piracy has resulted in a US$ 81 million loss in customs revenue.

46 IMB warns that pirates are very mobile in the region. As an example, they refer to the hijacking of a tanker off *Port Gentil* in Gabon in July 2013, by suspected Nigerian pirates.

47 Dirk Steffen, Gulf of Guinea Maritime Security in 2016, 11 April 2017, Center for International Maritime Security (http://cimsec.org). Article available at: http://cimsec.org/gulf-guinea-maritime-security-2016/31716, last visited 21 December 2017.

Cooperation and coordination between the states of the Gulf of Guinea remains, however, of the essence. In this respect, twenty-two Western and Central African states manifested their political will to combat the phenomenon by adopting the Yaoundé Code of Conduct in 2013.[48] The Code incorporates elements of the (original) Djibouti Code of Conduct but it is wider in scope as it addresses a range of illicit activities at sea including illegal fishing, drug smuggling and piracy.[49] The Lomé Charter (African Charter on Maritime Security and Safety and Development in Africa), adopted in Togo at the African Union Summit in 2016, goes further than the Yaoundé Code – which is a soft-law instrument – in that it is a legally binding text. The Charter renews and extends the resolve of fifty-five African states to cooperate closely in both, suppressing all forms of illicit activities in African maritime areas and developing a 'blue ocean economy'.

14.4 International and Domestic Law

14.4.1 International Law

14.4.1.1 UNCLOS

The Law of the Sea Convention deals with piracy in Articles 100-107 and 110. These articles repeat almost *verbatim* Articles 14-22 of the 1958 Geneva Convention on the High Seas and are considered to constitute international customary law.

UNCLOS gives, in Article 101, the following definition of piracy:

a. any illegal acts of violence or detention, or any act of depredation, committed for private ends by the crew or the passengers of a private ship or a private aircraft, and directed:
   i. on the high seas, against another ship or aircraft, or against persons or property on board such ship or aircraft;
   ii. against a ship, aircraft, persons or property in a place outside the jurisdiction of any State;

48 "Code of Conduct Concerning the Repression of Piracy, Armed Robbery against Ships, and Illicit Maritime Activity in West and Central Africa." The Yaoundé Code was adopted at the Summit of the Heads of State and Government of the Economic Community of West African States (ECOWAS), the Economic Community of Central African States (ECCAS) and the Gulf of Guinea Commission (GGC), in response to the S.C. Resolutions mentioned above.

49 Much in the same way as is done in the Jeddah amendment to the Djibouti Code of Conduct.

b. any act of voluntary participation in the operation of a ship or of an aircraft with knowledge of facts making it a pirate ship or aircraft;
c. any act of inciting or of intentionally facilitating an act described in subparagraph (a) or (b).[50]

To these acts are assimilated, according to Article 102, those committed

> by a warship, government ship or government aircraft whose crew has mutinied and taken control of the ship or aircraft are assimilated to acts committed by a private ship or aircraft.

Piracy may be committed, according to this definition, only on the high seas, including the EEZ a coastal state may have declared. The definition of piracy includes only action by one ship (or aircraft) against another. Acts of violence committed without the involvement of two ships[51] do not constitute piracy. This being the case, there is no piracy where, for example, the crew or passengers take control of the ship in order to demand ransom or for any other gainful purpose ('private gain'). Such acts remain under the exclusive jurisdiction of the flag state, to the exclusion of international or universal jurisdiction.

Crimes of the same nature as piracy, committed against ships in the territorial waters of a state, are considered to be, as often said above, 'armed robbery', a crime which UNCLOS, however, neither addresses nor defines. By contrast, the notion of 'armed robbery' is regularly used in the context of the IMO. In any event, acts of armed robbery in the territorial and internal waters belong to the jurisdiction of the coastal state. As a consequence, any action within these waters by ships having the nationality of another state for the purpose of repressing such acts, may be undertaken only with the consent of the coastal state or, alternatively, by a Security Council resolution, which was the case with Somali piracy.[52] It is also to be noted that UNCLOS does not allow hot pursuit in reverse, i.e. hot pursuit which begins on the high seas and continues into the territorial

50 Art. 102 provides that when these acts are committed by a warship or government ship whose crew has mutinied and taken control of the ship or aircraft, they are assimilated to acts committed by a private ship or aircraft. It is also clarified (Art. 103) that a ship or aircraft may retain its nationality although it has become a pirate ship or aircraft. The retention or loss of nationality is determined by the law of the state from which such nationality was derived (Art. 104).

51 Or, according to Art. 101 an aircraft and a ship, or two aircraft.

52 *See supra*, at 14.3.1.

waters of a coastal state.[53] This can only be done with the consent of the coastal state – as can be inferred from UNCLOS; it is, however, clearly spelled out in the Djibouti Code of Conduct.[54]

UNCLOS does not cover conspiracy or attempt to commit piracy or other inchoate offences connected with piracy. Perpetrators must therefore be caught *in flagrante delicto*, i.e. when the act is being committed. By contrast, these offences are provided for in the Djibouti Code of Conduct.

---

53 According to UNCLOS Art. 111:

1. "The hot pursuit of a foreign ship may be undertaken when the competent authorities of the coastal State have good reason to believe that the ship has violated the laws and regulations of that State. Such pursuit must be commenced when the foreign ship or one of its boats is within the internal waters, the archipelagic waters, the territorial sea or the contiguous zone of the pursuing State, and may only be continued outside the territorial sea or the contiguous zone if the pursuit has not been interrupted. It is not necessary that, at the time when the foreign ship within the territorial sea or the contiguous zone receives the order to stop, the ship giving the order should likewise be within the territorial sea or the contiguous zone. If the foreign ship is within a contiguous zone, as defined in article 33, the pursuit may only be undertaken if there has been a violation of the rights for the protection of which the zone was established.
2. The right of hot pursuit shall apply mutatis mutandis to violations in the exclusive economic zone or on the continental shelf, including safety zones around continental shelf installations, of the laws and regulations of the coastal State applicable in accordance with this Convention to the exclusive economic zone or the continental shelf, including such safety zones.
3. The right of hot pursuit ceases as soon as the ship pursued enters the territorial sea of its own State or of a third State.
4. Hot pursuit is not deemed to have begun unless the pursuing ship has satisfied itself by such practicable means as may be available that the ship pursued or one of its boats or other craft working as a team and using the ship pursued as a mother ship is within the limits of the territorial sea, or, as the case may be, within the contiguous zone or the exclusive economic zone or above the continental shelf. The pursuit may only be commenced after a visual or auditory signal to stop has been given at a distance which enables it to be seen or heard by the foreign ship.
5. The right of hot pursuit may be exercised only by warships or military aircraft, or other ships or aircraft clearly marked and identifiable as being on government service and authorized to that effect.
6. Where hot pursuit is effected by an aircraft:
   (a) the provisions of paragraphs 1 to 4 shall apply mutatis mutandis; (b) the aircraft giving the order to stop must itself actively pursue the ship until a ship or another aircraft of the coastal State, summoned by the aircraft, arrives to take over the pursuit, unless the aircraft is itself able to arrest the ship. It does not suffice to justify an arrest outside the territorial sea that the ship was merely sighted by the aircraft as an offender or suspected offender, if it was not both ordered to stop and pursued by the aircraft itself or other aircraft or ships which continue the pursuit without interruption.
7. The release of a ship arrested within the jurisdiction of a State and escorted to a port of that State for the purposes of an inquiry before the competent authorities may not be claimed solely on the ground that the ship, in the course of its voyage, was escorted across a portion of the exclusive economic zone or the high seas, if the circumstances rendered this necessary.
8. Where a ship has been stopped or arrested outside the territorial sea in circumstances which do not justify the exercise of the right of hot pursuit, it shall be compensated for any loss or damage that may have been thereby sustained."

54 *See supra*, at 14.3.1.3.

14.4.1.2 Jurisdiction Over Piracy Under UNCLOS

UNCLOS Article 100 requires cooperation to the largest extent in order to suppress the piracy phenomenon. Article 105 provides, furthermore, that any state may confiscate a pirate ship, arrest persons on board and proceed to the confiscation of property on the ship. UNCLOS establishes, therefore, universal jurisdiction in connection with piracy when the seizure (and arrest of pirates) takes place on the high seas, a solution which is in harmony with international customary law. The article goes on to provide that the courts of the state which carried out the seizure may decide upon the penalties to be imposed and may also determine the action to be taken with regard to the ships or property, subject to the rights of third parties acting in good faith. Whether an obligation arises from this provision for the seizing state to also prosecute the pirates remains uncertain.

14.4.1.3 Piracy Under S.C. Resolutions Adopted in the Case of Somalia

These Resolutions[55] provided for action which goes beyond the UNCLOS provisions, by allowing not only foreign naval operations within Somali territorial waters, but later also action against pirate bases on Somali territory, all with the consent of the Somali government (which had already been granted). Recognizing, however, that this could, potentially, constitute an unwanted precedent, the Resolution went on to assert that these provisions 'shall not be considered as establishing customary law'. Such an assertion can, of course, have only a limited effect, if at all, on the process of formation of customary law which depends on factors which cannot be dictated or foreseen by any such statement.[56]

The Resolutions having been adopted under Chapter VII of the U.N. Charter, the consent of the coastal state (Somalia) was superfluous. Nonetheless, they did provide for such consent, rather in order to expressly demonstrate deference to Somalia's sovereignty over its territorial waters.

The *raison d'être* of Resolution 1816 (2008),[57] however, was mainly to make the rules of international law concerning piracy on the high seas also applicable in Somali territo-

55 S.C. 1816(2008) and subsequent ones, especially Res. 1846(2008) and 1851(2008).

56 Thus, Tullio Treves, *loc. cit.*, rightly, although very carefully, points out that: "...[i]t cannot be ruled out that, if authorizations similar to those granted as regards the Somali situation were to be routinely granted in other situations, the possible formation of a customary rule could be at least discussed."

57 Para. 7 of the Resolution provides that: "(The S.C)... Decides that for a period of six months from the date of this resolution, States cooperating with the TFG in the fight against piracy and armed robbery at sea off the coast of Somalia, for which advance notification has been provided by the TFG to the Secretary-General, may:

a. Enter the territorial waters of Somalia for the purpose of repressing acts of piracy and armed robbery at sea, in a manner consistent with such action permitted on the high seas with respect to piracy under relevant international law; and
b. Use, within the territorial waters of Somalia, in a manner consistent with action permitted on the high seas with respect to piracy under relevant international law, all necessary means to repress acts of piracy and armed robbery..."

rial waters[58] (termed 'armed robbery' for the purpose) adding that states acting under these rules within the territorial waters of Somalia may use 'all necessary means', thus clearly alluding to use of force. Furthermore, the Resolution was careful to provide that anti-piracy and anti-armed robbery action within Somali territorial waters would only be carried out by those states which were 'cooperating with the TFG' and not by any state, as would have been the case on the high seas.

The authorization provided by Resolution 1816 was limited *ratione temporis* to six months with a possibility of extension, which has in fact been taking place ever since by the adoption of successive resolutions.[59] The resolutions clarify, furthermore, that their provisions and the authorizations they contain are not meant to adversely impact on the right of innocent passage of ships of third states, nor to affect the rights, obligations or responsibilities of member States under international law, including those under UNCLOS, with respect to any other situation. This assertion, just as the one with respect to the 'non-establishment of customary international law' mentioned above, is meant to address the concerns of developing states that the UNCLOS provisions and customary law might be put at risk and ultimately set aside[60] by the content of the resolutions on Somali piracy.

14.4.2 Piracy in Domestic Law

Domestic legislations differ as regards the definition of piracy and other issues related to it. There are, for example, differentiations in national legislations as regards the location where piracy may be committed. Most countries incorporate the UNCLOS solution, recognizing that piracy may be committed only on the high seas (U.S.,[61] Thailand, Greece[62]). Other domestic legislations do not differentiate between maritime zones, accepting its commission in territorial or even internal waters (Japan). Some are silent on the matter of location (Singapore), while other legislations do not expressly deal with piracy at all (Spain). In fact, this last category seems to be the largest, as considerably fewer than half of the countries of the world seem to have adopted relevant legislation.

58 Including those on 'reverse' hot pursuit.

59 Starting from Resolution 1846 (2008) the authorization to undertake all necessary measures 'in Somalia' is extended to twelve months (para. 10). *See also* para. 6 of Res. 1851 (2008), as renewed by para. 7 of Res.1897 (2009), para. 7 of Res. 1950 (2010), para. 9 of Res. 2020 (2011), para. 12 of Resolution 2077 (2012), para. 12 of Res. 2125 (2013), para. 13 of Res. 2184 (2014), para. 14 of Res. 2246 (2015), para. 14 of Res. 2316 (2016), para. 14 of Res. 2383 (2017) and para. 14 of Res. 2442 (2018).

60 Similar safeguards are contained in the Djibouti Code of Conduct.

61 18 USC. § 1651 (Piracy under law of nations).

62 Art. 8 of the Greek Penal Code.

14.4.2.1 Jurisdiction Over Piracy in Domestic Legislations

Again, national legislations differ as regards the question of jurisdiction over piracy. Classically, the flag state of the pirated ship will have primary jurisdiction over the perpetrators of the piracy attack. Jurisdiction may also be recognized – and this is usually the case – to a state which has a linkage with the particular incident, such as the state of the nationality of the victims or the perpetrators (international jurisdiction). Universal jurisdiction, on the other hand, which requires no linkage with the ship or the incident, is the most 'liberal' and at the same the one which is most consistent with the legal nature of piracy as a crime under customary international law and it is also the option adopted by UNCLOS.

14.5 PROSECUTION AND PROPOSED BASES OF JURISDICTION

It soon became apparent in the case of Somalia that states involved in anti-piracy operations which had proceeded to seizures and arrests were reluctant or even negative at the prospect of exercising the powers afforded to them by international law (international customary law, UNCLOS) and the relevant S.C. Resolutions, i.e. to prosecute and submit the pirates and armed robbers arrested to criminal proceedings before their own courts. Several reasons were invoked for this, such as lack of national legislation, legal difficulties in the collection of evidence in the ocean by personnel with no adequate qualifications for the task and the possibility to violate human rights,[63] especially due to delays in the transfer of the alleged perpetrator(s) to the place where criminal proceedings were to be held.[64] Some states suggested that, after having served their sentences and been released on their territory, pirates might request asylum, which would have to be granted to them as it could not be secured that their state of origin would not violate their human rights upon their return,[65] probably by prosecuting them again. Thus, in a number of cases, suspected pirates were released after being arrested.[66]

To respond to the problem of lack of national legislation to implement the prosecution obligations of arresting states deriving from the abovementioned S.C. Resolutions, several bases of jurisdiction have been proposed. Among them was using the relevant

63 S.C. Resolutions 1816(2008) and 1846(2008) specifically mention the need to respect human rights law (paras. 11 and 14 respectively).

64 The questions of collection of evidence and of human rights considerations will be examined below, pp. 90.

65 As all European countries are party to ECHR, they are prohibited from delivering suspects to states 'where they risk the death penalty or being tortured.'

66 *See, e.g.*, "Outgunned Somali pirates can hardly believe their luck," *The Guardian*, 8 May 2012, on the release of 17 captured pirates from the Danish Navy ship *Absalon*, as no state would accept exercising jurisdiction in their regard.

provisions of the 1988 Convention on the Suppression of Unlawful Acts at Sea (SUA Convention).[67, 68] SUA criminalizes a number of acts committed against or on a ship,[69] such as seizing or exercising control over it by force or threat, performing acts of violence against persons on board, placing devices or substances which are likely to destroy the ship, etc.[70] In such cases, a state party to the Convention must exercise jurisdiction if it is or was the flag state of the ship at the time the offence was committed, or if the crime was committed on its territory (including its territorial sea) or by a national of that state.[71] There are some other cases where an SUA state party also has the option to establish jurisdiction, including where a victim of any of the crimes in question is its national or – and this was an innovation of the Convention – where the crime has been committed in an attempt to compel the particular state to do or abstain from doing any act.[72] In all cases it is compulsory for the state in the territory of which the alleged offender is present to establish jurisdiction if it does not extradite him/her to a state which has established jurisdiction.[73]

The SUA Convention is not mentioned in Resolution 1816 (2008). It is nonetheless recalled in Resolution 1846 (2008) which urges states to implement the obligations deriving from it.[74]

Despite the 'technical' possibility to exercise jurisdiction under SUA, states have, however, been reluctant to do so, considering, perhaps, that SUA is, in substance, unsuitable to apply in cases of piracy crimes. This because it is a *par excellence* anti-terrorist Convention as evident from its Preamble and *travaux préparatoires*, while, furthermore, the

67 Adopted 10 March 1988. Entry into force 1 March 1992. Most of the states involved in the fight against piracy off Somalia as well as neighbouring coastal states such as Djibouti, Kenya, and Yemen (but not Somalia) are parties to SUA.

68 On the SUA Convention *see* Natalino Ronzitti (ed), The Rome Convention for the Suppression of Unlawful Acts Against the Safety of Maritime Navigation, in *Maritime Terrorism and International Law* (1990), p. 69.

69 Under Art. 4(1) of the SUA, the "Convention applies if the ship is navigating or is scheduled to navigate into, through or from waters beyond the outer limit of the territorial sea of a single State, or the lateral limits of its territorial sea with adjacent States." This means that only ships navigating between ports of the same state *(cabotage)* are excluded from the scope of the Convention. Even in this case, however, Art. 4(2) provides that the Convention is applicable if the offender or alleged offender is found in the territory of a State party other than the State referred to in para. 1.

70 Art. 3 of the Convention.

71 *Ibid.*, Art. 6(1).

72 Art. 6(2).

73 Art. 6(4).

74 According to operative para. 15 of this Resolution, the S.C. "Notes that the 1988 Convention for the Suppression of Unlawful Acts Against the Safety of Maritime Navigation ('SUA Convention') provides for parties to create criminal offences, establish jurisdiction, and accept delivery of persons responsible for or suspected of seizing or exercising control over a ship by force or threat thereof or any other form of intimidation; urges States parties to the SUA Convention to fully implement their obligations under said Convention and cooperate with the Secretary-General and the IMO to build judicial capacity for the successful prosecution of persons suspected of piracy and armed robbery at sea off the coast of Somalia;"

element of private gain, which is essential to the notion of piracy, is absent from the crimes under SUA.[75]

Other jurisdictional bases proposed in order to cover existing gaps in national legislations were the 1979 International Convention on Hostages and the 2000 Palermo Convention on Transnational Organized Crime. Both, however, would be of limited use in connection with piracy crimes. It would seem, therefore, that the best solution remains the straightforward adoption of domestic legislation specifically addressing piracy in accordance with UNCLOS and customary international law. By now, a significant number of states has adopted such legislation and can try piracy cases.[76]

14.6 Transfer

A solution to the difficulties of states to prosecute pirates and have them serve their sentences on their own territory (which was applied in the case of Somali piracy, but, presumably, could apply in any other similar case) was transferring pirates for prosecution, trial and/or serving sentences to countries of the region i.e. close to Somalia. This option was vigorously pursued and put into effect by the conclusion of bilateral or multilateral agreements. Such agreementswere concluded between the EU and Kenya,[77] Tanzania,[78] Seychelles[79] and Mauritius[80] as well as bilaterally between a number of countries and Kenya, Tanzania and the Seychelles (e.g. U.S.-Kenya, U.K.-Kenya, Denmark-Kenya,

---

75 This is also true of SUA as amended in 2005 (*see infra*, p. 36, on SUA as an anti-terrorist Convention).

76 Information available at: www.un.org/depts/los/LEGISLATIONANDTREATIES/STATEFILES/LBR.htm.

77 Annex to Exchange of Letters between the European Union and the Government of Kenya "on the conditions and modalities for the transfer of persons suspected of having committed acts of piracy and detained by the European Union-led naval force (EUNAVFOR), and seized property in the possession of EUNAVFOR, from EUNAVFOR to Kenya and for their treatment after such transfer." Detailed provisions for the protection of the human rights of pirates and armed robbers captured by the EU by naval forces and transferred to Kenya are set out in Arts. 3 and 4 of the Annex.

78 Agreement between the European Union and the United Republic of Tanzania "on the conditions of transfer of suspected pirates and associated seized property from the European Union-led Naval Force to the United Republic of Tanzania" of 1 April 2014.

79 Exchange of Letters between the European Union and the Republic of Seychelles "on the Conditions and Modalities for the Transfer of Suspected Pirates and Armed Robbers from EUNAVFOR to the Republic of Seychelles and for their Treatment after such Transfer," of 10 November 2009.

80 *Agreement* between the *European* Union and the Republic of *Mauritius* 'on the conditions of transfer of suspected pirates and associated seized property from the *European* Union-led naval force to the Republic of *Mauritius* and on the conditions of suspected pirates after transfer' of 14 July 2011.

Seychelles-Kenya).[81, 82] Efforts were made, in these agreements, to standardize requirements concerning evidence and to safeguard human rights.

However, in order to cope with their increased workload and to improve the conditions in which their tasks would be carried out, the local courts needed adequate funding. This need was indeed addressed through the concerted efforts of the U.N. and its organizations and agencies, the EU and individual states, as will be seen below.

Concerning post-trial transfers, legal and practical frameworks have been set up so that pirates can be prosecuted in one country and serve their sentences in UNODC-constructed prisons in Somalia (Mogadishu, Puntland as well as in Somaliland) or in other countries of the region.[83] Sentence serving obviously requires assurances that human rights will be respected. This is done through, among other things, independent monitoring of the prisons.

14.7 Human Rights, Law Enforcement and Collection of Evidence

14.7.1 Human Rights Issues

In many cases, the reticence of states to exercise jurisdiction for piracy is due to difficulties arising out of their obligation to safeguard the human rights of the arrested pirates during the latters' detention on board their ships (conditions of detention). The eventuality of protracted detention which would considerably exceed the maximum period prescribed by domestic legislation or international conventions has also been put forward as a main concern. Two cases which were brought before the ECtHR (*Rigopoulos v. Spain*[84] and *Medvedyev v. France*[85]) and concerned very similar circumstances shed some light on the question.[86] The question submitted to the Court was whether detention

81 James T. Gathii, Kenya's Piracy Prosecutions, AJIL, 104 (3) 416-435, 2010.

82 *See also* European Union Joint Action 2008/851/CSFP 42 on the EU military operation against piracy and armed robbery off the Somali coast, which provides that, if the competent authorities of the flag state of the ship *'which took them [the pirates] captive'* cannot or do not wish to exercise its jurisdiction, the persons arrested during the operation with a view to their prosecution shall be transferred to a 'Member State or any third State which wishes to exercise its jurisdiction over the aforementioned persons'.

83 In the context of its Global Maritime Crime Programme, the UNODC has expanded prison capacity in Somalia, so that individuals convicted of piracy outside the country can serve their sentences there (*see also supra*, p. 9). Improvements were also made regarding prison capacity in Mauritius, Kenya and Tanzania. Furthermore, the Detention and Transfer Programme has developed substantial experience in the transfer of sentenced prisoners back home to serve their sentences. If willing to do so, it is far better for prisoners to serve their sentences in the home country, which allows them to have access to their families, live in their own environment and culture and have training and education which is tailored to their needs and in their own language.

84 ECtHR, *Rigopoulos v. Spain*, 37388/97, Decision, 12 January 1999.

85 ECtHR, *Medvedyev and Others v. France*, Judgment, 29 March 2010.

86 In both these cases, the applicants were arrested following ship boarding which was carried out with the consent of the flag state, on suspicion of smuggling narcotic drugs which was confirmed thereafter.

of the suspects on the arresting naval vessel for about two weeks was compatible with Article 5(3) of the European Convention on Human Rights according to which arrested or detained persons must be brought promptly before a judge or other officer authorized by law to exercise judicial power. The Court, although affirming that in principle a detention of such duration was not compatible with the abovementioned provision, found in both cases that their circumstances were exceptional enough to justify non-violation of ECHR Article 5(3).

14.7.2 Law Enforcement and Collection of Evidence Issues – 'Shipriders'

Lack of sufficient evidence is a common occurrence in piracy cases and many detained suspects are released for this reason. The collection of evidence and the modalities to do so for purposes of prosecution is, therefore, an issue of major concern in operations against piracy. A related and often controversial issue on a national level is the law enforcement possibilities recognized to a warship by its flag state. Indeed, more often than not, naval officers on warships participating in anti-piracy operations are not endowed with or have very limited powers of law enforcement, including collection of evidence. This is due to the fact that domestic legislations do not usually envisage the possibility of law enforcement occurring away from their own territory.

To resolve these difficulties, a solution which has been consistently put forward and which is also proposed by S.C. Resolution 1846 on piracy off the coast of Somalia, is providing for the use of 'shipriders' (i.e. law enforcement officials of the state which is finally going to take custody of the pirates and where the trial is going to take place) who are allowed, following agreement to this effect, to get on board the ship where the pirates are detained, in order to collect such evidence.[87] This solution is known to certain systems,[88] but not to other, which view such possibility with some circumspection as a sort of 'transgression' of a foreign jurisdiction over the ship which is, normally, under the jurisdiction of the flag state. Nonetheless, the agreements concluded between U.K. and Kenya and U.S. and Kenya provide for such a possibility.[89]

14.8 Tribunal(s) for Piracy Cases

Prosecution and trial of pirates by national judicial systems would, undoubtedly, be the normal course to follow. However, various other possibilities were explored by the above-

87 Res. 1846(2008), para. 3.

88 The use of 'shipriders' is provided for in some bilateral agreements concluded by the U.S. regarding drug trafficking as, for instance, in the Agreement concluded with Jamaica in 1997 (Arts. 7-9);

89 Shipriders are also provided for under the name of 'Embarked Officers' in the Code of Conduct of 2009 for the West Indian ocean and the Gulf of Aden (Art. 7).

mentioned l.w.g. on piracy,[90] particularly that of the creation of special regional tribunals, or even of a global tribunal. Another, even more imaginative idea concerned the inclusion of piracy in the jurisdiction of the International Criminal Court. These ideas did not muster general support for various reasons and particularly because of the cost and the time requirements involved.[91] The Group concluded that pirates should be tried either by competent national courts or by courts of the states close to the region where the piratical events occurred, following agreements to that effect between the states concerned. It is indeed much simpler to vest national courts with the required jurisdiction to deal with piracy cases where this is not yet the case, and even more so where such jurisdiction already exists. This course of action is also in full conformity with UNCLOS and its embrace of universal jurisdiction in connection with piracy.[92] Finally, mention should be made of the idea to elaborate a special Convention on piracy,[93] so as to unify and elaborate on the rather sparse rules on this crime. Although not given any follow-up, this idea does not appear to be devoid of merit.

14.9 Defending Ships from Piracy Attacks and Related Legal Issues

As discussed above, the primary means for anti-piracy operations off the coast of Somalia has been the deployment of naval forces.[94] However, it soon became clear that despite the indisputable usefulness of such forces in combating the phenomenon, they could not cover the vast maritime expanses of the western Indian Ocean, nor could they be flexible enough to secure the avoidance of delays, a matter of crucial importance to merchant shipping. It was therefore necessary for ships to be also provided with 'individualized protection'. Such protection could be provided by the use of either 'Vessel Protection Detachments' (VPDs) or 'Privately Contracted Armed Security Personnel' (PCASP).

14.9.1 Vessel Protection Detachments

These are detachments of naval forces which step on board commercial vessels of their own or other nationality, in the latter case following permission of the flag state of the

90 *See supra,* at 14.3.1.6.

91 As a follow-up to *Jack Lang's* report, consideration had also been given to placing a Somali court on piracy outside Somalia with a view to prosecuting pirates there. However, this idea did not find substantial support, either.

92 On the basis of data until September 2012, 21 states had prosecuted 1179 cases, and 600 pirates have been convicted. Among the western states which have taken judicial action are Germany, Italy, France, Spain and the U.S.A.

93 Such a proposal had been made by Ukraine in the context of the Sixth Committee of the U.N. General Assembly.

94 *See supra,* at 14.3.1.1.

vessels. A first question which may arise in connection with the use of VPDs is one of domestic law which can only be answered by the (domestic) law either of the state which provides or which uses such VPDs. The question consists in whether such Detachments – which belong to the armed forces of the state from which they originate – may be used for purposes of law enforcement, in other words in order to carry out police duties.

Another question is whether their use has practical advantages over other solutions, such as the use of Privately Contracted Security Personnel (PCASP). The debate that emerged in this connection, particularly in the context of the l.w.g., showed clearly, at the initial phase of its work, that if VPDs could be legitimately formed or used under domestic law, most states would rather favour them over privately contracted personnel, as VPDs could be relied upon for better quality services. Similarly, shipping companies saw considerable advantages in VPDs, as the latter guaranteed, *inter alia*, adequate training and lower cost contracts compared to those for personnel contracted through Private Maritime Security Companies (PMSCs). Nonetheless, it was also recognized that the use of VPDs might give rise to several problems relating to international law, in particular concerning state responsibility (i.e. of the state of the forces to which the VPDs belong) and jurisdictional immunity (with respect to any unlawful acts VPDs might be engaged in while carrying out their duties). These concerns found justification in the 'Enrica Lexie' incident in the Indian Ocean[95] which led to a protracted dispute between Italy and India.[96]

95 On 15 February 2012, the Italian M/V *Enrica Lexie*, a privately owned tanker, was sailing, at the time of the incident, from Singapore to Djibouti with an Italian Vessel Protection Department (VPD) on board, as the maritime area along the Kerala coastline was considered high-risk for piracy. During that part of the voyage, two Italian marines fired against a fishing boat, the *St. Antony*, which they mistakenly thought to be carrying pirates, killing two Indian fishermen. The Indian Coast Guard intercepted the *Enrica Lexie* at 36 n.m. from the coast of Kerala, leading it to *Kochi Port*. The Italian marines were arrested and charged with homicide. There followed a period of high diplomatic tension with several episodes between India and Italy which only seemed to agree that the incident took place at 20.5 n.m. off the Indian coast, *i.e.*, in Indian contiguous zone and EEZ. As regards the substance of the dispute, Italy contends that within these zones, India has no sovereignty, but only some sovereign rights, *i.e.*, those recognized in Arts. 33 and 56 of UNCLOS. Italy also invokes UNCLOS Art. 97. India invokes its domestic law by virtue of which the Indian Penal Code is applicable to its EEZ as well as, *inter alia*, the fact that the offence was directed towards Indian nationals (passive personality principle) and that the death of the Indian fishermen occurred on board an Indian ship. Therefore, India maintains that it has concurrent jurisdiction over the case (objective territoriality principle). In June 2015, Italy resorted to Art. 287 and Annex VII Art. 1 of UNCLOS to have the dispute resolved by arbitration. The case is henceforth pending before an arbitral tribunal.

96 For the Italian views *see* Natalino Ronzitti, The Enrica Lexie Incident: Law of the Sea and Immunity of State Officials Issues, at: www.sidi-isil.org/wp content/uploads/2012/05/01_Ronzitti.pdf. For the Indian views *see* Manimuthu Ghandi, The Enrica Lexie Incident: Seeing Beyond the Grey Areas of International Law, Indian Journal of International Law, 53, 1, 2013.

14.9.2 Privately Contracted Armed Security Personnel (PCASP)

The use of private armed guards has, finally proved in practice, to be the most successful solution for the suppression of the piratical phenomenon off the coast of Somalia.[97] Despite the initial misgivings of both, states and the shipping industry, the use of armed civilian guards was, indeed, finally found to offer considerable advantages, among which flexibility and avoidance of delays, both of which are, by contrast, weak points in protection by other means. It was also shown that the presence alone of armed guards on board commercial vessels constituted a powerful deterrence against piracy attacks.

14.9.2.1 Applicable Law

Nevertheless, a host of questions at the national and international law level, which were connected to the use of PCASP, had to be resolved. Among them were: the adoption of national legislation establishing rules for the functioning and control of the reliability and competence of companies which recruit and train armed guards; setting out modalities and requirements for the issuance of relevant permits; regulating the use of weapons and the degree of use of force allowed. Only a limited number of states had, however, adopted such legislation despite the fact that more and more private companies became available to offer personnel for the protection of ships from piracy attacks.[98]

On an international level, there are two (non-binding) instruments which appeared to be of relevance to PCASP, i.e. a) the Montreux Document on Obligations and Good Practices of States Regarding Operations of PCASP during Armed Conflict[99] and b) the International Code of Conduct for Private Security Service Providers (ICoC).[100] None of them is, however, directly addressing the use of PCASP for vessel protection against piracy. Indeed, the former is meant to apply to private companies which are contracted by states only in situations of armed conflict. The ICoC, on the other hand, is addressing the private security industry and sets out principles and procedures for use by the provi-

97 *See* Douglas Guilfoyle, 3rd UAE Counter Piracy Conference/Briefing paper; James Kraska, "International Regulation of Private Maritime Security Companies," Naval War College Information Paper 13-4 (2013).

98 Such legislation has been adopted, *e.g.*, by the U.K. Department for Transport, as "Interim Guidance to U.K. Flagged Shipping on the Use of Armed Guards to Defend Against the Threat of Piracy in Exceptional Circumstances," Version 1.2 (May 2013); by Greece (Law No. 4058 of 22 March 2012, which regulates some basic issues in relation to the conditions for the granting of permits to companies which do business in this sector); by Liberia as "Use of Armed Security on Board Vessels," IMO Doc. MSC 89/18/6 (8 March 2011); by France (2014-742 Act authorizing private security activities on board of French vessels, and relevant decrees). *See also* Comparison of Flag State Laws on Armed Guards and Arms on Board, International Chamber of Shipping (ICS) and European Community Shipowners' Associations (ECSA) February 2017, available at: www.ics-shipping.org/docs/default-source/Piracy-Docs/comparison-of-flag-state-laws-on-armed-guards-and-arms-on-board-2017.pdf?sfvrsn=0, last visited 26 December 2017.

99 "Montreux Document on Pertinent International Legal Obligations and Good Practices for States related to Operations of Private Military and Security Companies during Armed Conflict," 2008.

100 The Code was elaborated at the initiative of Switzerland with the participation of many stakeholders. It was finalized in 2010. Available at: https://icoca.ch/en/the_icoc, last visited 10 January 2018.

ders of such services with a view to securing respect for the rule of law and human rights. It does not, however, refer to the specific case of armed guards deployed on board merchant ships to defend them against acts of piracy and armed robbery.

The IMO was, finally, the organization which dealt with the matter at hand, producing a series of non-binding documents entitled 'Interim Guidance' or 'Interim Recommendations' on the use of PCASP on board ships in the HRA, which are addressed to Flag, Port and Coastal States and to Shipowners, Ship Operators, and Shipmasters.[101] The IMO has also issued guidance to Private Maritime Security Companies (PMSCs), i.e. companies which provide PCASP).[102]

Taking into account some basic elements of national maritime laws and international law of the sea as well as the IMO recommendations and guidance on the use of PCASP, the following rules and recommendations would be applicable in connection with the use of PCASP:

a. As UNCLOS stipulates in Article 92, a ship is subject to the exclusive jurisdiction of the flag state on the high seas. The duties of the flag state are designated in Article 94.
b. **i.** It is up to the discretion of flag states to determine whether or not and on which conditions the use of PCASP on board ships flying their flag is authorized. In so doing, flag states should take into account, *inter alia*, the possibility of violence as a result of the use of firearms and of the carriage of armed personnel on board; **ii.** The carriage of such personnel, their firearms and security-related equipment is subject to flag state legislation and policies; **iii.** Flag states must make known to masters, seafarers, shipowners, operators and relevant companies the legislation and national policy on carriage of armed security of PCASP, on accountability for non-compliance, and on the relationship of PCASP with the Master while on board; **iv.** The parties concerned must know and be required to comply with all relevant rules and regulations of flag, port and coastal states.
c. **i.** If the flag state authorizes the use of PCASP, it is the shipowner who will decide whether or not to use PCASP on a particular ship or in a particular voyage; **ii.** the shipowner should undertake a rigorous examination of the reliability, capabilities and maturity of the companies considered and conduct a series of checks (criminal background, history of employment of the PMSC, its insurance cover, etc.); **iii.** He/she should do so taking into consideration that apart from the laws and regulations im-

101 IMO Revised Interim Recommendations for Flag states Regarding the Use of Privately Contracted Armed Security Personnel on Board Ships in the High Risk Area (MSC.1/Circ.1406/Rev.3 12 June 2015); IMO Interim Recommendations for Port and Coastal states regarding the use of PCASP on board Ships in the High Risk Area (IMO doc. MSC.1/Circ. 1408/Rev. 1 of 25 May 2012); IMO Revised Interim Guidance to Shipowners, Ship Operators and Shipmasters on the Use of Privately Contracted Armed Security Personnel on Board Ships in the High Risk Area (MSC.1/Circ.1405/Rev. 2 of 25 May 2012).

102 IMO Interim Guidance to Private Maritime Security Companies Providing Privately Contracted Armed Security Personnel on board Ships in the High Risk Area (MSC.1/Circ.1443, 25 May 2012).

posed by the flag state concerning the use of PMSC and PCASP, port and coastal states' laws also apply to ships;

d. the ship's master has 'overriding authority' regarding all personnel and activities aboard his/her vessel.[103]
e. The port and coastal state should have in place relevant policies and related procedures to be complied with by ships carrying PCASP which arrive in, stay at, or depart from a port[104] as well as concerning the embarkation and disembarkation of such personnel and their weapons.[105] As these rules are of crucial importance to ships carrying PCASP and to the shipping industry in general, they must be well publicized by the port state. The same is true of port state rules concerning storage, security and control of firearms.[106]
f. A wide spectrum of responsibilities and a long list of obligations is incumbent on PMSCs, i.e. the companies which employ, control, train and provide PCASP to the shipping industry.[107] **i.** PMSCs must secure the appropriate training[108] and competence, through procedures of selection and vetting of the PCASPs they provide,[109] as well as the proper management of firearms and ammunition by them;[110] **ii.** PMSCs must have awareness and knowledge of applicable legislation of flag, port and coastal states with regard, *inter alia*, to the transport, carriage, storage and use of firearms as well as regarding use of force; **iii.** In view of the complexity of applicable laws concerning these issues, PMSCs must have access to competent maritime legal advice on a 24/7 basis;[111] **iv.** Insurance cover should be held for a variety of situations and eventualities; **v.** PMSCs must have and impart to their PCASPs good knowledge regarding the use of force rules at each time and each particular location.[112]

---

103 IMO Revised Interim Guidance to Shipowners, Ship Operators and Shipmasters on the Use of Privately Contracted Armed Security Personnel on Board Ships in the High Risk Area (*supra*, fn. 101) Annex, para. 5.9.1.

104 IMO Interim Recommendations for Port and Coastal states regarding the use of PCASP on board Ships in the High Risk Area (*supra*, fn. 101), Annex, para. 4.

105 *Ibid.*, para. 7.

106 On the related issue of 'floating armouries', *i.e.*, platforms set up by PMSCs (or governments) on the high seas in order to embark and disembark PCASP and firearms, *see* "Piracy Fears over Ships Laden with Weapons in International Waters," The Guardian Africa Network, 10 January 2013; Alexis Wilpon, Floating Armories: A Legal Grey Area in Arms Trade and the Law of the Sea, available at www.law.georgetown.edu/international-law-journal/wp-content/uploads/sites/21/2018/05/48-3-Floating-Armories.pdf, 2014, last visited 15 February 2019.

107 They must also have appropriate professional certification and be able to provide documents relating to their legal status, financial standing, experience, etc. (*see* IMO Interim Guidance to Private Maritime Security Companies Providing Privately Contracted Armed Security Personnel on board Ships in the High Risk Area (*supra*, fn. 102), Annex, paras. 2.3 and 2.4, as well as paras. 3.1 and 3.2).

108 *Ibid.*, para. 4.3.

109 *Ibid.*, para. 4.2.

110 *Ibid.*, paras. 5.9 and 5.10.

111 *Ibid.*, para. 3.3.

112 *See infra*, at 14.10.2.

14.9.2.2 Passage Through the Territorial Sea

A rather vexed question is whether the passage through the territorial sea of ships carrying PCASP and their firearms is innocent or not. It would seem that the answer is in the affirmative if the ship does not proceed to enter a port of the coastal state, which means that mere carriage of such personnel and their firearms does not change passage to non-innocent. Any use of the weapons however, may give rise to a claim of non-innocent passage.[113]

14.10 USE OF FORCE IN ANTI-PIRACY OPERATIONS

Use of force is always a possibility in anti-piracy. This is clearly implied in UNCLOS and S.C. Resolutions regarding piracy off the coast of Somalia and it is spelled out in the EU Council Joint Action when defining its *Operation Atalanta*.[114] Obviously, this is not use of force in the sense of Article 2 Paragraph 4 of the U.N. Charter, where such use of force is exercised by one state against another state. It is use of force by state actors (when force is resorted to by naval ships) against non-state actors (pirates) as well use of force by non-state actors (PCASPs) against non-state actors (pirates).

14.10.1 Use of Force by State Actors

Although endorsing the use of force in anti-piracy operations, neither UNCLOS nor the abovementioned S.C. resolutions concerning piracy off the Somali coasts specify the particular law applicable in such situations, restricting themselves to referring to applicable international law in general. The question is therefore asked which the applicable international law is, bearing in mind that international humanitarian law would not be included, as no situation of armed conflict exists in the situations under examination. It can firstly be observed that warships escorting commercial ships through the HRA or patrolling there would apply the rules of engagement (ROE) applicable within the context of the operations they participate in (regional agreement). Individual states participating in the anti-piracy effort off the Somali coasts are, on the other hand, bound by their own national laws as far as use of force is concerned. Nonetheless, the application of any domestic law would remain under the condition of its compliance with international law. This brings back the question of identification of the law which is applicable with regard to anti-piracy operations where state actors are involved. Such law may be traced

113 Sally Buckley, Legal Aspects of the Use of Private Armed Guards, WG 2, 8th Meeting on Legal Issues, 20 June 2011, Compendium, WG2 Toolbox, 2012.

114 Council Joint Action 2008/851/CFSP of 10 November 2008 on a European Union military operation to contribute to the deterrence, prevention and repression of acts of piracy and armed robbery off the Somali coast, Art. 2(d).

in international jurisprudence. One case on this point is the 1999 *M/V Saiga No 2* where ITLOS found that:

> international law ... requires that the use of force must be avoided as far as possible and, where force is inevitable, it must not go beyond what is reasonable and necessary in the circumstances. Considerations of humanity must apply in the law of the sea, as they do in other areas of international law.[115]

This same case refers to earlier jurisprudence which is relevant on the matter at hand, i.e. the 1935 *I' m Alone Case* between Canada and the U.S.,[116] and the 1962 *The Red Crusader Case* (Commission of Enquiry), between Denmark and the United Kingdom.[117] It also refers to the 1995 U.N. Fish Stocks Agreement,[118] Article 22(1)(f) of which stipulates that:

> 1. The inspecting State shall ensure that its duly authorized inspectors:...(f) avoid the use of force except when and to the degree necessary to ensure the safety of the inspectors and where the inspectors are obstructed in the execution of their duties. The degree of force used shall not exceed that reasonably required in the circumstances.

14.10.2 Use of Force by Non-State Actors (PCASPs)

UNCLOS does not authorize use of force by private actors. As a consequence, private actors may only use force in self-defence, i.e. within the limits allowed by most domestic criminal legislations and by several international criminal law conventions.

On their part, the IMO Guidelines regarding the use of force by PCASPs are usefully detailed.[119] Thus, PMSCs are advised to recognize that laws governing the use of force may differ over time and according to location and ensure that the PCASP operating for them understand and comply with these laws. In particular, PCASP should act according to these applicable laws in the knowledge that their role is exclusively for the protection of life of persons on board and the ship from armed pirate attacks; All reasonable steps should be taken to avoid the use of force and, if, finally, force is used, it should be part of a graduated response plan, including, in particular, the strict implementation of BMP

115 *St. Vincent and the Grenadines v. Guinea*, 1999, ITLOS No. 2, 51 [1999] ITLOS Rep 10, para. 155. For an analysis of this and the other relevant judgments *see* Tullio Treves, *loc. cit., supra,* at 14.3.1, fn. 14.
116 U.N.R.I.A.A., Vol. III, p. 1609.
117 I.L.R. Vol. 35, p. 485.
118 Agreement for the Implementation of the Provisions of the United Nations Convention on the Law of the Sea of 10 December 1982 relating to the Conservation and Management of Straddling Fish Stocks and Highly Migratory Fish Stocks.
119 *See supra,* fn. 102, paras. 5.15-5.17.U.

(Best Management Practices) in force; The Guidelines remind, furthermore, that the use of force must not exceed what is strictly necessary and reasonable in the circumstances and that care should be taken to minimize damage and injury and to respect and preserve human life; it is finally spelled out that the PCASP should only use firearms against persons in self-defence or in defence of others. An agreed plan of gradual response for use of force, including warning procedures, must be documented and signed prior to embarkation by all relevant parties.

The Baltic and International Maritime Council (BIMCO)[120] has also produced a model contract (GUARDCON)[121] with Guidelines on this issue.[122]

14.11 Responsibility

It is also highly probable that issues of responsibility may arise during anti-piracy operations because of the death or injury of a person such as a crew member or third person, as well as because of the loss of or damage to the ship or cargo. It has been argued that such responsibility may be attributed to the (flag) state because it has authorized the use of PCASP, in accordance with the Draft Articles on State Responsibility[123] (draft Arts. 5, 7-9, 11) already reflecting customary international law. It is our view that this constitutes an extremely wide interpretation of this law, particularly since it is not the particular state which has contracted the personnel in question.[124] It is a different matter if that state has not, in a particular case, exercised or has exercised defective control over the operational worthiness of the company, a situation which may eventually give rise to its responsibility.

120 BIMCO is the world's largest international shipping association, with 2,100 members in about 120 countries. Its headquarters is in Copenhagen.

121 Guidance on Rules for the Use of Force (Annex).

122 *Inter alia,* this Guidance provides that PCASP must: (a) Be trained and qualified to relevant documented PMSC standards in the use of force in accordance with flag state law; (b) If they use force, do so in a manner consistent with applicable law; (c) If they use force, not exceed what is strictly necessary; (d) Use force proportionately and in a manner appropriate to the situation; (e) Have clear and unambiguous instructions and training on when and how force may be used; and (f) Take all reasonable steps to avoid the use of lethal force.

123 Available at: http://legal.un.org/ilc/texts/instruments/english/commentaries/9_6_2001.pdf.

124 Cf. Commentary of the ILC on the abovementioned articles.

15 Terrorism at Sea[1]

15.1 Legal Response

Terrorism hit the maritime world in 1981 with the *Achille Lauro* incident.[2] As a response, the IMO 'Convention on the suppression of unlawful acts against the safety of maritime navigation' (SUA Convention)[3] was adopted in Rome on 10 March 1988[4] and entered into force on 1 March 1992. Since then, and particularly following the 9 November 2001 terrorist attack on U.S. soil and the consequent emphasis put by IMO on states becoming parties to SUA with a view to enhancing maritime security, there has been a spectacular increase in its membership, from 52 states which it counted in early 2001, to 152 states in 2006 and 174 in 2019.

SUA does not establish universal jurisdiction for maritime terrorism offences; it does, however, considerably extend the number of states which either have to or may exercise jurisdiction over them. The principle *aut dedere aut judicare*[5](extradite or prosecute), usually adopted in the context of anti-terrorism Conventions, is endorsed by this Convention as well.[6]

---

1 *See* Natalino Ronzitti (ed), *Maritime terrorism and International Law*, Kluwer/Martinus Nijhoff Publishers, 1990; Robert Beckman, Jurisdiction over Pirates and Maritime Terrorists, in Clive H. Schofield, Seokwoo Lee, Moon-sang Kwon (eds), *The Limits of Maritime Jurisdiction*, 2014, pp. 349-372; Robert Beckman, The 1988 SUA Convention and 2005 SUA Protocol: Tools to Combat Piracy, Armed Robbery and Maritime Terrorism, in Rupert Herbert-Burns, Sam Bateman, Peter Lehr (eds), *Lloyd's MIU Handbook of Maritime Security*, 2009, pp.187-200. On the difference between Piracy and Terrorism at Sea, *see* Douglas Guilfoyle, Piracy, Terrorism and War (*Guilfoyle* does not support the distinction between piracy and terrorism), British Yearbook of International and Comparative Law, 2012, Seminar Report, available at www.biicl.org/files/6319_guilfoyle_piracy_and_terrorism_revised_11_09_2012.pdf, last accessed 29 May 2018.

2 In that incident, a group of Palestinian guerrillas hijacked, on 5 October 1985, the Italian cruise ship *Achille Lauro,* which was sailing in Egyptian territorial waters. The hijackers threatened to kill the passengers if a number of Palestinian detainees in Israeli prisons were not released. Finally, the captors of the ship killed one passenger, *Leon Klinghoffer,* a Jewish American, and later surrendered to Egyptian authorities, having been promised safe conduct out of Egypt. However, the aircraft they boarded was intercepted by U.S. fighters in international airspace and forced to land at the U.S. base of *Sigonella,* in Italy. The four Palestinians who were arrested were brought to trial in Italy.

3 On SUA, *see also supra,* at 14.5.

4 Together with SUA a Protocol on the suppression of unlawful acts against the safety of fixed platforms on the continental shelf (SUA Protocol) was adopted.

5 Such as the1963 Convention on Offences and Certain Other Acts Committed On Board Aircraft ('Tokyo Convention') and the 1971 Convention for the Suppression of Unlawful Acts against the Safety of Civil Aviation ('Montreal Convention').

6 Art. 6, para. 4 of the Convention.

The adoption of two Protocols significantly amending SUA in 2005[7] – an initiative which was energetically pursued by the U.S. following the 9/11 attacks – added new acts as reprehensible offences under the Convention. These fall into three categories: a) new acts of maritime terrorism, such as using the ship as a weapon or as a means to carry out a terrorist attack, which (acts), apart from requiring specific knowledge and intent, also require the existence of a 'terrorist motive', i.e. their purpose must be to "intimidate a population" or "compel a government to do or abstain from doing any act ..."[8]; b) transporting weapons of mass destruction (WMD), their delivery systems and related materials on commercial vessels, acts which, although also requiring specific knowledge and intent, do not require a 'terrorist motive', because, their proponents argued, even without it or with some other motive (e.g. the prospect of profit) their criminalization under SUA would be justified[9]; and c) transporting any person who has committed an offence not only under SUA but also under any other international anti-terrorist Convention, provided that there is, again, specific knowledge and intent of any person (e.g. the shipmaster or a member of the crew) to assist that person to evade criminal prosecution.[10]

The amendments were the object of severe criticism during the time of their negotiation, as they (those under (b) and (c) above) were rightly considered to go far beyond the scope of SUA which is an instrument dealing with maritime terrorism. Indeed, the amendments under (a) are the only ones remaining squarely within the same objective, while those under (b) deal with the altogether different matter of non-proliferation of WMD. Even more extraordinary is the creation of a special jurisdiction under (c), based on the transportation of the perpetrator not only of any of the offences provided for in SUA as amended but also of the offences of any one of the multitude of anti-terrorist conventions in force which are, obviously, completely unrelated to the specific issue of maritime security. If not anything else, these amendments create a conceptual blur which is not to the benefit of the goals pursued either by them or by the Conventions they become 'artificially' related to. There were also other objections, such as those concerning the possibility of boarding at sea,[11] which would entail delays and additional costs for the shipping industry. These questions are hardly addressed by the amendments, despite an otherwise serious attempt to provide certain safeguards with regard to boarding.[12]

7 a) 2005 Protocol to the Convention for the Suppression of Unlawful Acts against the Safety of Maritime Navigation b) *2005 Protocol to the Protocol* for the Suppression of Unlawful Acts against the Safety of Fixed Platforms Located on the Continental Shelf. Both Protocols were adopted in London on 14 October 2005 and both entered into force on 28 July 2010.

8 Art. 3*bis* 1(a) of the Convention as amended by the 2005 Protocol.

9 Art. 3*bis* 1(b) of the Convention as amended by the 2005 Protocol.

10 Art. 3*ter* of the Convention as amended by the 2005 Protocol. On this categorization *see also* Robert Beckman, *loc. cit.*, pp. 190-193.

11 Art. 8*bis* 5 of the Convention as amended by the 2005 Protocol.

12 Art. 8*bis* 10 of the Convention as amended by the 2005 Protocol.

15.1.1 Operational Initiatives

Among them was 'Active Endeavour', a NATO maritime operation in the Mediterranean initiated in the context of Article 5 of the North Atlantic Treaty. 'Active Endeavour' pursued its operations from 2001 (post 9/11) until 2016, providing maritime security by carrying out anti-terrorism patrols and boardings. It was replaced in 2016 by Operation 'Sea Guardian' which is active outside Article 5.

In connection with the fight against the proliferation of WMD which, as noted above, has been linked mainly with maritime terrorism, mention should also be made of the 'Proliferation Security Initiative' (PSI), set out by the U.S. under the Bush Administration in 2003 and consisting in a political (non-legal) commitment among endorsing nations to prevent the spread of such weapons and of their delivery systems. This is done by preemptive interdiction, which includes detaining and searching ships and aircraft when entering the territorial waters or the airspace of states participating in the PSI where there are suspicions that these ships or aircraft engage in such activities. The PSI has continued operating under the *Obama* and *Trump* Administrations, the initially eleven nations which endorsed the 'PSI Statement of Interdiction Principles' having reached 105.[13]

---

13 *See Joanna M. Gabryszewski,* The Proliferation Security Initiative in 2017: U.S. Interagency Perspectives July 2017, available at: http://wmdcenter.ndu.edu/Portals/97/Documents/Publications/Proceedings/CSWMD%20Proceedings%20July%202017.pdf?ver=2017-07-10-155453-910, last accessed on 3 January 2018.

16 Conclusions

Contemporary international law of the sea has been shaped by the landmark adoption of the Montego Bay Convention of 1982. Indeed, UNCLOS is a true 'Constitution of the Oceans and Seas' which has provided the basis for all subsequent instruments in this domain, whether of regional or global, normative or soft-law character which have emerged since then and which deal with a host of older or contemporary issues and phenomena, among which the protection of the marine environment, the exploitation of marine resources, the suppression of maritime terrorism, of piracy, of the transport of WMD by sea, etc.

The realities affecting the 'domain of the sea' have also seen important changes and developments in the decades that followed the adoption and entry into force of UNCLOS. Climate change is one of them; another one is the dramatic increase in focus on resources at sea. These resources include fish stocks, the overexploitation of which combined with the pollution of the marine environment and climate change have caused their serious decline. And, of course, resources beneath the seabed, i.e. hydrocarbons and natural gas; the prospect for their exploitation has led to an unprecedented rush for their discovery and exploration as well as to a flurry of construction of offshore pipelines to transport them, often across many countries, to a world which is ever more energy-hungry.

As a consequence, the importance of jurisdictional zones – continental shelf and exclusive economic zone – which provide access to these resources has substantially increased. In many cases, this creates a necessity for the delimitation of these jurisdictional zones between neighbouring states, which, in its turn, promotes resort to mechanisms which may undertake this task and resolve any related dispute on the matter. In reality this means resort to an international judicial organ (the ICJ or ITLOS) or to an arbitral tribunal.[1] These courts and tribunals have already issued important judgments on delimitation of maritime zones, solidifying a corpus of jurisprudence which interprets the provisions of UNCLOS and standardizes their application. The ICJ continues to be the main generator of such jurisprudence, having produced a significant number of judgments dealing with delimitation and related questions, among which are, for example, to name two relatively recent ones, the 2018 *Case concerning the Maritime Delimitation in the Caribbean Sea and the Pacific Ocean* between Costa Rica and Nicaragua[2] and the 2012 *Case on the Territorial and Maritime Dispute between Nicaragua and Colombia.*[3] ITLOS is also gradually entering this particular arena, having issued its first case on maritime

1 For parties to UNCLOS, resort to a resolution mechanism will be compulsory through the application of the relevant provisions of the Convention and in accordance with their terms.

2 Of 2 February 2018.

3 *See supra*, at 11.1, fn. 7.

delimitation in 2012 on the *Maritime Boundary between Bangladesh and Myanmar in the Bay of Bengal*,[4] and the second in 2017 (*Ghana/Côte d'Ivoire*).[5]

Arbitral Tribunals have also been making significant contribution to the evolution of this crucial aspect of international law of the sea and relevant questions. A relatively recent example is the 2016 *South China Sea Arbitration Award* (the *Philippines v. China*)[6] which, despite the non-participation of China, has dealt with important questions relating to one of the most contentious issues the world has been faced with in recent decades.[7]

At the same time, and for the same reasons as mentioned above, there is a marked tendency of ocean-front states to expand their continental shelves beyond 200 n.m. One of the main consequences of this expansion will, however, be to deprive 'the Area' – which should be constituting the 'Common Heritage of Mankind' – of much of its significance, and nowhere is this more obvious than in the Arctic Ocean, only a small part of which will, most probably, be left as such 'common heritage'.

On a different note, new, renewed and unexpected dangers have appeared in the vast expanses of the world's oceans and seas in the last decades. Such is the case of the ancient phenomenon of piracy in its contemporary metamorphosis, which, often using modern means, presents risks similar to its ancient prototype insofar as its destructive and disruptive power is concerned. Although receding in some places, as in the case of piracy off Somalia, having been successfully dealt with due to an unprecedented show of firmness in political will by the international community, it continues unabated elsewhere. It should furthermore not be forgotten that, as aptly observed by the UNSG, (good) 'results are reversible'.[8]

Another phenomenon which had caused justifiable concern mostly in the 1980s, maritime terrorism, has not yet, thankfully, lived up to the fears it generated at the time,[9] thanks again, in large measure, to the concerted efforts of states and international organizations.

Other unlawful acts which often take place at sea (mainly the illicit transport of narcotic drugs and weapons) have made it imperative for the international community to react by imposing restrictions and controls on voyaging vessels by way of an increasing number of conventions and other instruments. Among these are the 1988 U.N. Vienna Convention against Illicit Traffic in Narcotic Drugs and Psychotropic Substances,[10] the

4 *See supra*, at 11.2.1.2, fn. 35.
5 *Delimitation of the Maritime Boundary between Ghana* and *Côte d'Ivoire in the Atlantic Ocean*, 23 September 2017.
6 *See supra*, at 13.3.7, fn. 65.
7 *See supra*, at 13.3.5.
8 SG Report (S/2013/623) pursuant to S.C. Res. 2077 (2012).
9 An exception was the attack, on 12 October 2000, of Al-Qaeda militants against the U.S. naval destroyer, the USS Cole, in the Yemeni port of Aden.
10 The Convention entered into force on 11 November 1990.

1988 Convention on the Suppression of Unlawful Acts at Sea (SUA), as amended by the 2005 Protocol which allows boarding at sea in search for weapons of mass destruction (WMD), and the Proliferation Security Initiative (PSI), on account of which the notion of the High Seas and its Freedom, is very different from what it was once perceived to be.

All in all, more regulation of the seas has been achieved, and this is a welcome development. There is, indeed, a need for intervention on the high seas wherever and whenever illegal acts are taking or may take place there so as to prevent those vast maritime areas from turning into lawless terrain; at the same time, there should be caution and care so as to avoid, to the extent possible, a disruptive and harmful effect on lawful international shipping and on maritime routes which secure the fast and efficient flows of international trade and communication, a major achievement of modern times.

Part IV
Water in International Law

17 The Element and the Data

17.1 Water Is Life

No other natural substance, with the exception of air, is so essential and irreplaceable for human, animal and plant life, as water. Water is also of crucial importance for a great variety of human activities ranging from agriculture to industry. Only a very small portion of water in the hydrosphere[1] can, however, be used to satisfy human needs, as 97.5% thereof, which is the water of oceans and seas,[2] is saline.[3] But even the remaining 2.5% which is fresh water, can only in small part be used to serve the needs of human life, since 68.9% of it is frozen in polar ice caps, ice sheets and glaciers. Liquid fresh water which can be used for these purposes is found either in rivers and lakes (surface waters) and amounts to 0.3% thereof, or underground (groundwater) constituting the overwhelmingly larger quantity of liquid fresh water, amounting to 29.9% thereof (if glaciers and other frozen water are excluded, groundwater represents more than 97% of freshwater in liquid form that is potentially available for human use). Finally, the remaining 0.9% includes soil moisture, swamp waters, permafrost, water in the atmosphere and water which is present in living organisms and vegetation.[4]

17.1.1 Hydrological Cycle

Water is subject to the hydrological cycle, i.e. it is perpetually changing from one form to the other (ice, liquid, vapour) and from one 'reservoir' to the other (underground, earth surface, ocean, ice caps, etc.).[5] In all its transformations and the different courses it takes, the amount of water in the hydrosphere has remained the same for an estimated three billion years and is immune, as such, to any human activity and to any natural event. This means, at the same time, that the quantity of water in the hydrosphere is finite and amounts, according to scientific estimates, to approximately 1,385,990,800 km^3.

---

1 "Hydrosphere includes all the free water existing in liquid, solid or gaseous state, on the Earth's surface and in the crust down to a depth of 2,000 metres." (Definition given in the1998 UNESCO Report containing a summary of the monograph 'World Water Resources' by Igor Shiklomanov, prepared in the framework of the International Hydrological Programme).

2 Oceans and seas constitute 71 %, *i.e.*, more than two thirds of the Earth's surface.

3 For water to be fresh, its salt content must be lower than 3 grams per litre.

4 Most of the data (in percentages) cited have been taken from the 1998 UNESCO Report by Shiklomanov, *supra*, fn. 1 (data provided in other studies or sources do not differ in a significant way).

5 The processes involved include evaporation, evapotranspiration (the combination of evaporation and transpiration) precipitation, runoff and infiltration among other. For a description of how these processes develop *see* Laurence Boisson de Chazournes, Fresh Water in International Law, 2013, pp. 3-4, fn. 13.

17.1.2 Increasing Demand

While the quantity of water is finite, global demand for it increased dramatically in the past century and has been continuing to do so ever since. Thus, total annual water withdrawal which was less than 580 km^3 in 1900 has risen to more than 3,900 km^3 in 2010. The reasons are primarily the exponential growth of the earth's population which has increased six-fold since 1900 reaching 7.7 billion in 2017 and is expected to rise to between 9.4 and 10.2 billion by 2050.[6] This will lead to the increase of the demand for water as well as for food, energy and industrial products which prompt water use increase in their turn. Moreover, the growth of income and rising living standards of a considerable segment of world population have led to a change in consumption patterns promoting an even stronger demand for water. All this, together with urbanization[7] and trade globalization, has caused contemporary global water demand to rise to an all-time high in human history, standing, today, at about 4,600 km^3 per year and projected to increase to between 5,500 and 6,000 km^3 per year by 2050,[8, 9] although there are great differences between developed and developing countries in this respect.[10]

In terms of allocation of its uses, 70% of available fresh water is used for land irrigation. It is an exceedingly high percentage which is due, to a considerable extent, to the inadequate or antiquated agricultural methods used in many parts of the world.[11] Industrial production accounts for 22% of the use of fresh water resources (15% of which is used for the production of energy) while domestic uses take up 8% of such resources. All these uses are estimated to grow, inescapably imposing yet further strain on the availability of fresh water. Moreover, there is competition between the various uses of water (e.g. for domestic purposes as against industrial ones) just as between various users (e.g. residents in one location as against those in another) either on a national level (e.g. between provinces of the same state) or on an international one (between states sharing the same watercourse). National or international disputes may and do arise due to such competition, while efforts to resolve them often trespass on other wider and equally very

6 From 1,6 billion in 1900, 2,525,149 billion in 1955, 7 billion in 2011 and 7,349 billion in 2015. The global population is currently growing at a rate of 83 million per year.

7 Already, more than 50% of the world population lives in urban settlements.

8 Source: The United Nations World Water Development Report 2018, Nature-Based Solutions for Water, (Published by UNESCO) p. 11, referring to Burek *et al.*, 2016.

9 The U.N. World Water Development Report 2015 observes that the relationship between population growth and the increase in water consumption is not linear, however, as in the last decades the demand increase rate for water was double that of population growth (citing Shiklomanov, 1999; USCB, 2012).

10 Indeed, *per capita* withdrawals differ sharply, ranging (in cubic metres per year-cm^3) from about 39 in Sierra Leone to about 1590 in the USA (source: FAO AQUASTAT website (www.fao.org/nr/water/aquastat/main/index.stm).

11 In least developed states, the percentage of water used for irrigation exceeds 90% of the total available fresh water.

important interests, such as the protection of the ecosystems which are dependent on the same water resources.

17.1.3 Contamination and Overexploitation

Another factor with a negative impact on the availability of water for consumption is the contamination of surface and underground water bodies with chemicals used as fertilizers in the cultivation of agricultural produce. The disposal of waste water from domestic and industrial uses without any or without adequate treatment also causes the contamination of water bodies. Finally, the overexploitation of the existing fresh water resources very often leads to progressive salinization of groundwater and drainage basins, which makes their water inadequate for human consumption and for the ecosystems which depend on it.

17.1.4 Climate Change and Global Warming

This is a threat which has been extensively discussed in recent years. It is estimated – although there is still a degree of uncertainty and speculation due to the complexity of the issue – that climate change and global warming resulting from it could aggravate the world water resources situation (natural water balance and water availability).[12] Water resources may be seriously affected in a variety of ways by spatial and temporal changes induced by climate change.[13] For example, temperature increase may cause higher evapotranspiration,[14] thus reducing water availability. There is also the risk that sea level rise may allow the intrusion of seawater into coastal aquifers causing their salinization. Particularly vulnerable are obviously those in low-lying lands, such as the coastal aquifers of Bangladesh and other countries in Southeast Asia. A host of other consequences may affect biodiversity and the ecosystems. At the same time, an increase in fresh water availability may be expected on high latitudes. However, as extreme weather on a greater frequency rate is another occurrence linked to climate change, rainfall is very likely to be part of storms that lead to floods and damage to water quality.[15] Furthermore, in the most arid regions of the planet, the situation will worsen as droughts will intensify.[16]

12 The 5th Assessment Report of the Intergovernmental Panel on Climate Change (IPCC) estimates that for each degree of global warming, approximately 7% of the global population will face an almost 20 % decrease in renewable water resources.

13 The U.N. World Water Development Report 2015, Water for a Sustainable World, UNESCO 2015, pp. 65-67.

14 *Supra*, fn. 5.

15 Climate Change 2014 Synthesis Report, pp. 67-68.

16 *Ibid.*

In response to the risks owed to climate change, the world community has adopted a number of conventional or soft law instruments of a wider nature, primarily the 1992 United Nations Framework Convention on Climate Change (UNFCCC), the 1997 Kyoto Protocol and the 2015 Paris Agreement which, however, do not specifically address water issues. On a regional level, significant efforts for a better legal response to water problems have been made, in Europe, by the European Union, and by the United Nations Economic Commission for Europe (UNECE). Many other regional organizations and fora operate in other regions of the world, such as those established by ECOSOC, including the Economic Commission for Africa (UNECA), the Economic and Social Commission for Western Asia (ESCWA), the Economic Commission for Asia and the Far East (ECAFE) and the Economic Commission for Latin America and the Caribbean (UNECLAC).

17.1.5 Differences in Water Availability

Water availability varies greatly in different parts of the world,[17] creating drastically different natural, human and societal environments. The most arid regions are obviously the most disadvantaged. Water-rich regions, on the other hand, are normally those in high altitudes which do not attract large concentrations of population due to the scarcity of arable land. The most heavily populated regions are usually those within watercourse basins, as the proximity of water and the availability of arable land allows for the cultivation of crops, provides work, creates wealth and supports livelihoods; this, as a natural consequence, has attracted large numbers of people to settle there since the dawn of history.[18] Nonetheless, these regions may suffer from the occasional excess of water, mainly in the form of floods which may destroy crops, housing and infrastructure.

17.1.5.1 Response to Water Shortages

The usual response of humanity to water shortages has been to transfer water from water-rich regions to those which are less fortunate in that respect.[19] Examples span the earth and the millennia, from the Sumerian canals in Mesopotamia[20] and the *Eupalinian Aque-*

17 Estimates for the minimum *per capita* water requirement for domestic human uses vary widely from 15 litres per person per day (Sphere Humanitarian Charter and Minimum Standards in Humanitarian Response, 2018) to 50 litres per person per day (Gleik, Basic water requirements for human activities: meeting basic needs, Water International, 1996), although parameters taken into account a vary. *See also* World Health Organization, How much water is needed in emergencies? (updated 2013).

18 Known as 'fluvial civilizations'.

19 Stephen C. McCaffrey, The Law of International Watercourses, Oxford monographs in international law, 2001, pp. 8-15.

20 Which are estimated to have irrigated agricultural land and supplied Mesopotamian cities such as Nineveh and Babylon with water from the Tigris and Euphrates Rivers from about 3500 B.C. to 1500 B.C.

duct on the island of *Samos* in ancient Greece[21] to modern era colossal works such as the *Hoover Dam* on the Colorado River[22] providing water and electricity to California, and the 'Great Man-Made River' of Libya which brings water from aquifers in the south of the country to the northern coast for domestic and irrigation purposes.[23]

Such transfers have made urbanization possible in all historical periods. It is beyond any doubt, however, that the sheer magnitude of several such pharaonic projects of the modern era has generated problems which often outweigh the benefits they purport to offer.

Today, further methods or processes which have been successfully used to supply fresh water include the desalination of sea water and waste water treatment and recycling.

Desalination, i.e. the removal of salts and minerals from water so that it may be used for consumption, has been employed particularly in Saudi Arabia, the U.A.E., Israel and the U.S. (mostly in California).[24] Desalination is, however, the most energy-intensive technology for water treatment, which makes it costly and therefore available only to those countries which can afford to invest in it[25]; nevertheless, it appears that an increasing number of states are resorting to it or have expressed their intention to do so.

Waste water treatment, which is also employed mostly in developed countries, uses different types of technology which, like desalination, may raise financial and environmental issues.

21 The aqueduct was constructed in the sixth century B.C. and ran under *Mount Kastro* to provide fresh water to *Pythagoreion*, then capital of the island of *Samos*. It was used for a millennium and is mentioned by the Greek historian *Herodotus*.

22 The Dam is situated on the Nevada-Arizona border and was inaugurated in 1935. Providing water and hydroelectric power which was then transferred to California and the Southwest of the U.S., it generated unprecedented growth in those regions.

23 The project was inaugurated by *Muammar Gaddafi* in 1984 and was planned to be executed in five stages, three of which have been completed. The water withdrawals planned were, however, so massive that fears had been expressed that the water supply of neighbouring countries such as Egypt and Chad could be put in jeopardy. As a result of the NATO attack on Libya in July 2011 and the bombardment of part of the pipeline, water transfer has been cut down to less than half. The future of the project thus remains doubtful, a prospect further enhanced by the current state of civil war prevalent in the country.

24 There are more than 16,000 desalination plants worldwide. Their operating capacity totals about 70 million m^3 per day.

25 Desalination processes used worldwide absorb about 0.4% of global electricity consumption.

18 Transboundary Watercourses and Transboundary Basins

18.1 Rivers and Lakes

The greatest natural sources of fresh water, which are at present readily available to humanity for the satisfaction of its needs – both basic and non-basic – are rivers and lakes. From an international law perspective, our interest focuses, however, only on those water bodies which are international or transboundary (there is no difference between these terms), i.e. those which cross or mark the frontier (boundary-ies) between two or more states.

There are about 276 transboundary watercourses in the world.[1] Among these, 180 cross or mark the boundaries of two states, the rest of more. The transboundary drainage basins[2, 3] of these watercourses cover almost half of the Earth's surface.[4] Two-thirds of these basins are shared by two countries, the rest by more.[5]

1 The number of international basins or of the states these watercourses cross or demarcate, may change due to political changes in the respective territories. Thus, the break-up of the Soviet Union and of Yugoslavia in the 1990s internationalized the basins of the *Dnieper,* the *Don,* and the *Volga Rivers* and changed the political composition of some basins which were already international, such as those of the *Danube* and the *Aral Sea*. Conversely, the unification of two or more states may have the opposite result, *i.e.,* the nationalization of a basin which was international until then. Such was the case of Germany, where the *Weser River* basin became national after the unification of Western and Eastern Germany in 1990.

2 'Drainage basin' is defined to be "an area of land from which the rain *flows into a particular river* or *lake*, etc." (Cambridge English Dictionary). 'Catchment area' or 'river basin' is another term which conveys the same meaning.

3 68 in Europe, 64 in Africa, 60 in Asia, 46 in North America and 38 in South America

4 The territory of 148 countries includes parts of one or more transboundary river basins. The territory of 39 countries is included by 90% or more within one or more transboundary river basins, while 21 lie entirely within one or more of these transboundary basins.

5 Thus, the *Nile Basin* is shared by 11 states, the *Congo* and the *Amazon* by 9 states. The *Mekong* and the *Rhine* basins are shared by 6 states. The *Danube River* has a basin shared by a record number of 19 states (the river itself crosses 10 riparian states). The basin of *Lake Chad* traverses 7 states, while the *Aral Sea*, before its current state of near extinction, was neighbouring 6 states. The *Congo Basin* is shared by 7 states and that of *Zambezi* by 8. The basin of the *Ganges Brahmaputra-Meghna*, is distributed between 5 countries.

18.2 GROUNDWATER

As mentioned above, about 97% of the world's fresh water resources is groundwater and humans have used it as much as they could since antiquity to satisfy their needs.[6] Springs, the manifestation of the existence of underground water, were of vital importance for this purpose, as were wells that were excavated to reach water which could not be found on the ground, especially in arid or semi-arid regions. Until the middle of the past century, however, the capability to abstract underground water was minimal. This has changed dramatically from the 1950s onwards. Major improvements in drilling and pumping technology and the advancement of hydrogeology and geological mapping have led to groundwater becoming 'the world's most extracted raw material'.[7] As a result, groundwater today covers the needs of more than 50% of the world's population. It is indicative that 70% of the piped drinking water supply in the European Union area comes from groundwater and that groundwater is almost the sole source of water supply across large swathes of Northern Africa.

However, the continuous increase in the world's population and the consequential increase in the demand for food, energy and industrial production is expected to lead to further increase in the use of, and reliance on, groundwater. It is therefore of great importance that the already existing phenomena of excessive abstraction and pollution of groundwater be urgently addressed in order to secure the sustainability of this most valuable resource.

18.2.1 Aquifers

Aquifers are the 'reservoirs' of groundwater. There are a great number of aquifers practically in all regions of the world, the exception being very small or remote islands. According to the International Law Association's Seoul Rules of 1986, the term 'aquifer'

> ... [c]omprehends all underground waters bearing strata capable of yielding water on a practical basis, whether these are in other instruments or context called by another name such as "groundwater reservoir," "groundwater catch-

6 On the history of the legal regimes on groundwater under various ancient and modern systems, *see* Dante A. Caponera and Dominique Alhéritière, Principles for International Groundwater Law, first published in the *Natural Resources Journal*, the University of New Mexico School of Law, Vol.18, July 1978, pp. 589-619.

7 Among other, see UNESCO, Igor S. Zektser and Lorne G. Everett (eds), *Groundwater resources of the world and their use*, IHP-VI, Series on Groundwater No. 6, 2004, p. 24.

> ment area," etc., including the waters in fissured or fractured rock formations and the structures containing deep, so-called "fossil waters."[8, 9]

There are two types of aquifer, confined and unconfined (free). A confined aquifer is "a water-bearing stratum that is confined or overlain by a rock layer that does not transmit water in any appreciable amount or that is impermeable."[10] An aquifer is unconfined

> when its upper surface (water table) is open to the atmosphere through permeable material. As opposed to a confined aquifer, the water table in an unconfined aquifer system has no overlying impervious rock layer to separate it from the atmosphere.[11]

Confined aquifers may be of impressive dimensions, some of the biggest being found, rather paradoxically, in some of the most arid regions of the world, like North Africa and the Arabian Peninsula.[12, 13] A confined aquifer may contain 'fossil water' or 'paleowater' meaning water that has been geologically sealed in the aquifer for thousands of years or even longer.[14] Although such groundwater bodies may not interact with surface waters, i.e. they may not be rechargeable, there is, as a rule, interaction between surface and groundwater. It is, in fact, estimated that about 30% of the flow of surface waters comes from groundwater and, conversely, that seepage from surface waters is the principal way by which most aquifers are recharged.

---

8 Art. 1, fn. 1. (Text contained in the Report of the Sixty-Second Conference, Seoul Conference Report, 1986, Committee on International Water Resources, pp. 251-274.

9 See also *infra*, at 18.6.3.

10 Encyclopaedia Britannica: www.britannica.com.

11 *Ibid.*

12 Such aquifers are the *Nubian Sandstone Aquifer System* (NSAS) shared by Chad, Egypt, Libya and Sudan, covering a subterranean area of 2,892,867 km^2; the *Lake Chad Basin* shared by Chad, Niger, Nigeria, Cameroon, Central African Republic and Algeria extending to 2,271,303 km^2; the *Taoudeni Basin* between Algeria, Mali, Mauritania covering 1,260,940 km^2, the *Umm er Radhuma-Dammam Aquifer System (Centre)*: Gulf, between Saudi Arabia, United Arab Emirates, Bahrain and Qatar covering 345,213 km^2; the *Umm er Radhuma-Dammam Aquifer System (South)*: *Rub' al Khali Aquifer* between Oman, Saudi Arabia, United Arab Emirates and Yemen covering 791,877 km^2 (Source: Transboundary Aquifers of the World, Special Edition for the 7th World Water Forum 1915 (maps), igrac – International Groundwater Resources Assessment Centre-, available at: isarm.org/download/file/fid/10, last accessed 2 November 2018).

13 An aquifer with a mixed degree of confinement (it is mostly unconfined, but in some parts confined) is the gigantic *Amazonas Aquifer* in South America, the largest in the world, which is shared by Bolivia, Brazil, Colombia, Ecuador, Peru and Venezuela and extends to 4,056,605 km^2.

14 An aquifer containing 'fossil water' is the *Nubian Sandstone Aquifer* in North Africa (*see supra*, fn. 12). The water in that aquifer is estimated to have percolated into the sandstone between 10,000 and 1,000,000 years ago. Another well-known aquifer containing fossil water is the *Ogallala Aquifer*, also known as the *High Plains* Aquifer, which is located under the *Great Plains* of the United States.

As noted by *McCaffrey*, there are two points regarding the physical aspect of groundwater that must be particularly noted. One is that most groundwater is in constant motion, its speed ranging from extremely slow to very fast, and the second that although it may be present in areas where there is no surface water, it is 'normally closely associated with rivers and lakes'.[15] These two features of groundwater prove that actions of one state with respect to groundwater, such as pumping or pollution, may affect groundwater or surface water in another state. The same may happen to the groundwater of a state when similar activities are undertaken with respect to surface waters in another state.[16] This leads to the conclusion that surface water and groundwater cannot and should not be treated separately either in legal terms or in terms of planning and management; they must, instead, be dealt with in an integrated and holistic manner which would secure their best use and sustainability as has already been recognized in various international texts, instances, fora and by many organizations.[17]

18.3 Water Disputes

Sharing watercourses and their basins, which means sharing a precious natural resource, may, and more often than not does give rise to friction and disputes between sharing states, usually depending on their upstream or downstream location with regard to it. Downstream countries are, as a rule, disadvantaged vis-à-vis the upstream ones with which they share the watercourse, as the upstream location allows a freer hand as to the use of the waters, be it unlimited withdrawals for irrigation or the building of hydropower dams and reservoirs. Where that happens, it is to be expected that it will meet with the consternation of the downstream country/-ies and very probably lead to friction between the states involved. On the other hand, a downstream location is not entirely devoid of the possibility to cause damage to an upstream riparian, as is the case, for example, of a downstream country dam which may cause flooding to an upper riparian (as, for instance, between Germany and the Netherlands). Generally, as technology allows building ever bigger constructions – which are therefore more invasive to human societies and the environment – in order to harness the waters of transboundary watercourses, the poten-

15 *Op. cit.*, p. 29.
16 *Ibid.*, p. 30.
17 Such as the 1986 ILA Seoul Rules on international groundwaters.

tial for new disputes, whether national or international, and the exacerbation of existing ones increases.[18]

Upstream countries may also cause the pollution of transboundary waters by their acts or omissions in connection with the use they make of these waters. The consequences are often far-reaching and not confined to waters alone. It is also a usual occurrence that the state where the watercourse exits into the ocean/sea takes little or no precaution to avoid the risk of polluting the adjacent sea waters, to the eventual detriment of other coastal states.

18.4 International Water Law

International water law is the branch of international law which deals with transboundary or international watercourses, which may be rivers, lakes or groundwater. International water law finds its sources in existing international agreements, on the practice of states, on important soft law instruments and on an increasing number of international judicial decisions and arbitral awards issued in connection with water-related disputes. The writings of publicists as well as domestic legislations and national jurisprudence may also take part in the formation of this law, just as in that of any other branch of international law. Furthermore, a number of theories put forward by jurists, usually reflecting the status of international relations at a given time or place, have underpinned the tendencies of international water law in its evolutional course over the past century and until today. We will refer to some of these factors in brief.

18.4.1 Bilateral, Multilateral and Basin Agreements

Agreements governing transboundary watercourses are no novelty of modern times. Indeed, such agreements appear to have existed since 2,500 B.C. The oldest known are those

18 A recent example of such a huge construction is the *Three-Gorges Dam* on the Yangtze River in *Hubei Province*, China, which was completed in 2009 and has been fully functional since 2015. It is the largest hydropower station in the world and has caused major concerns and controversy due to its massive invasion in the natural, cultural and social environment of the region in its proximity and beyond. It has caused the flooding of archaeological sites, led to ecological disruption and greatly increased the risk of landslides. About 1,300,000 people had to be displaced to allow for its construction. An example of an international dispute over a similarly huge dam construction – which, however, appears to have subsided) – is that caused by the construction of the *Rogun Dam*, a hydropower plant on the *River Vahkish*, between Tajikistan and Uzbekistan. The *Rogun Dam* is planned to be the highest in the world. The project originated in the Soviet era, but building has been stalled by economic difficulties. It has met with the strong opposition of neighbouring Uzbekistan, as the *Vakhsh* is a tributary of the *Amu Darya River*, the volume of which is bound to be impacted by the Dam. The waters of the *Amu Darya* are of crucial importance to the cultivation of cotton, a major produce of Uzbekistan. Other well-known examples of international disputes concerning water sharing and dam building on international rivers are those regarding the *Nile* and the *Euphrates and Tigris Rivers* which are examined below (at 22.1 and 22.2).

which bound the Sumerian city-states of *Lagash* and *Umma* in relation to the waters of the *River Tigris*. The Food and Agricultural Organization of the United Nations (FAO) has identified more than 3,600 international treaties on water issues, dating from 805 to 1984 A.D.[19] The great majority of them are concerned with navigation and, to a lesser extent, boundary demarcation and fisheries, but there is a considerable number which also deal with water use *per se*, such as, primarily, water sharing and flood control.[20] The past century has seen a gradual increase in agreements of the latter type (water use) between states sharing the same transboundary watercourse. It is indicative of this tendency that 300 water agreements have been concluded since 1947 on various issues relating to water (among other, water sharing, irrigation, hydropower, flood control, pollution prevention), which is a sign of growing awareness that such issues need to be addressed in cooperation between states rather than by each one in isolation. Over ninety international water agreements to manage shared water basins have been concluded in Africa alone.[21] It is therefore now better understood that agreements concluded at the basin level (basin specific), i.e. those in which all basin states participate, are preferable by far, because of the very nature of the watercourse which defies any piecemeal approach, requiring, instead, a comprehensive, integrated and holistic management.

Despite the impressive increase in water agreements, there is still an equally impressive number of about 160 international basins in the world for which there is no such normative framework. But even from those basins which do have one, only a small percentage (less than 20%) involves all the basin countries, which, as already noted, drastically reduces their effectiveness. Furthermore, most of the existing agreements do not deal with some very important aspects of watercourse management, such as water quality monitoring and dispute settlement procedures.

18.4.2 Regional Agreements

In the last decades, several regional organizations, realizing the importance of water issues in their respective regions, undertook to produce regional conventions on these issues and have done so with remarkable success. Thus, at the initiative of the United Nations Economic Commission for Europe, two Conventions were elaborated in the 1990s, namely the Convention on Environmental Impact Assessment in a Transboundary Context (1991) and the Convention on the Protection and Use of Transboundary

19 UN Water, International Decade for Action "Water for Life" 2005-2015.

20 *See also* Meredith A. Giordano and Aaron T. Wolf, Atlas of International Freshwater Agreements, UNEP, 2002, which refers to more than 400 water agreements concluded since 1820.

21 www.unesco.org/new/fileadmin/MULTIMEDIA/HQ/SC/pdf/IYWC_pressKit_EN.pdf.

Watercourses and International Lakes (1992).[22] There followed the Protocol on Water and Health[23] and the Aarhus Convention on Public Participation.[24]

The European Union has also been very active on these questions by issuing a number of relevant Directives, among which the most important is the Water Framework Directive 2000/60.[25]

In Africa, the Southern African Development Community (SADC) has formulated several instruments supporting collaborative initiatives concerning international waters. Furthermore, the SADC member states,[26] drawing their inspiration from the 1997 Watercourses Convention (see below under 'Universal Agreements'), have concluded the 2000 Revised Protocol on Shared Watercourses in the SADC region.

18.4.3 Universal Agreements

In contrast to the plethora of agreements of the types referred to above, i.e. bilateral and regional, there was, until recently, a paucity of universal agreements dealing with transboundary waters. This gap has now been filled with two such conventional texts. One is the '1997 U.N. Convention on the Law of the Non-Navigational Uses of International Watercourses', adopted in New York, which entered into force on 17 August 2014 (hereinafter 1997 Watercourses Convention or New York Convention), and the other the abovementioned '1992 Convention on the Protection and Use of Transboundary Watercourses and International Lakes' adopted in Helsinki (hereinafter 1992 Water Convention or Helsinki Convention). The latter, originally conceived and adopted as a regional Convention for the Economic Commission for Europe states (UNECE)[27] where it proved to be very successful, was amended in 2003 to allow accession by any U.N. member state.[28] The idea was to promote the successful transboundary cooperation scheme offered by the Convention to all countries, so that they might also benefit from it. It was on

22 This Convention has been transformed from regional to universal (*see infra*, at 18.4.3).

23 Protocol on Water and Health to the 1992 Convention on the Protection and Use of Transboundary Watercourses and International Lakes, 1999.

24 Convention on Access to Information, Public Participation in Decision-making and Access to Justice in Environmental Matters, Aarhus, Denmark, 1998.

25 Directive 2000/60/EC of the European Parliament and of the Council of 23 October 2000 establishing a framework for Community action in the field of water policy, as amended in 2014. Other Directives which deal with related issues are Directive 2006/118/EC on the protection of groundwater against pollution and deterioration, as amended; Directive 2008/105/EC on Environmental Quality Standards; and Directive 2007/60/EC on the assessment and management of flood risks.

26 Angola, Botswana, DRC Congo, Lesotho, Madagascar, Malawi, Mauritius, Mozambique, Namibia, Seychelles, South Africa, Swaziland, Tanzania, Zambia, Zimbabwe.

27 It entered into force for that region in 1996.

28 For this purpose Arts. 25 and 26 of the Helsinki Convention were amended in 2003, to allow accession by countries outside the UNECE region. The amendments entered into force on 6 February 2013. As of 1 March 2016, all United Nations Member States can accede to the Helsinki Convention.

the basis of this rationale that the 1992 Water Convention was turned, as from 1 March 2016, into a universal normative text.

18.4.3.1 The New York and Helsinki Conventions: Similarities, Differences and Complementarity

As regards their respective origins, the 1997 New York Watercourses Convention was elaborated by the International Law Commission (ILC) with a view to becoming a global legal instrument concerning transboundary waters. As representative of all major legal systems of the world as well as of a great variety of legal, political and geopolitical considerations, the ILC embarked on a difficult process to negotiate the text – also involving the Sixth (Legal) Committee of the U.N. – which spanned twenty years. The Draft produced by this painstaking work was then submitted to a special U.N. Working Group convened in New York in 1997, in the context of the U.N. General Assembly, in order to consider the text, negotiate its terms and possibly adopt it. Indeed, following a thorough legal and political scrutiny by the participating states and intense negotiations between them, a political compromise was struck – mainly between upstream and downstream countries – which made the adoption of the Convention possible.

By contrast, the 1992 Helsinki Water Convention was elaborated in the context of the UNECE and therefore negotiated by states most of which had already had a vast experience of cooperation on transboundary water issues. There was therefore a much more uniform understanding of the problems involved and a consensual climate which contributed to the convergence of positions, while the participation of experts in the field provided the possibility to adopt bolder solutions in dealing with practical and operational questions.

The above differences in the origin, negotiation process and the way of adoption of the two Conventions explain the differences in their corresponding approaches. Thus, a characteristic feature of the New York Convention is that it places particular emphasis on elaborating on the general principles of international water law, i.e. the principle of equitable and reasonable utilization and participation, and the principle of not causing significant harm ('no significant harm' rule), between which it tries to find an equilibrium.[29] This was indeed a major issue in the New York negotiation process, although one of symbolic and theoretical character rather than of practical significance. Conversely, the 1992 Water Convention has adopted a more nuanced approach, primarily referring to the 'no significant harm' rule and requiring the taking of appropriate measures in order to prevent, mitigate and control any 'transboundary impact', the latter being a notion to which the Convention attributes a broad meaning.[30] The 1992 Convention also refers to the principle of reasonable and equitable utilization in the context of harm prevention,

29 An analysis of these fundamental principles is made in the relevant Chapter 20 on General Principles of International Water Law.

30 Helsinki Convention, art. 1(2).

without, however establishing any priority between this principle and that enshrined in the 'no significant harm' rule.[31]

More generally, the Helsinki Convention focuses primarily on practical measures for the prevention of pollution and for the protection of the environment.

From another viewpoint, the New York Convention deals extensively with the procedural aspects of cooperation (planned measures) which have to be communicated to the other riparians likely to be affected by them. Indeed, it provides for a considerable number of procedural obligations – which are far more developed and detailed than those contained in the Helsinki Convention – referring to consultations and negotiations for the realization of such planned measures.[32] In the case of the Helsinki Convention, these obligations are less analysed as it is expected that this task will be performed mainly by the joint bodies to be established by the riparian states.

On the issue of joint bodies, it must be observed that the Helsinki Convention imposes a specific obligation on riparian states to conclude agreements between them in order to establish such joint bodies which are specified in detail. In sequence to their establishment, these bodies undertake to perform a multitude of tasks in the context of riparian state cooperation. In fact, joint bodies are used by the Helsinki Convention as a real tool not only for the management of a transboundary watercourse but also (and this is, perhaps, their most important function) in order to resolve any problem arising between the riparians while still at its initial stage, thus averting its eventual development into a full-fledged inter-riparian dispute.[33] By contrast, the New York Convention adopts a facultative provision on this matter leaving to riparian states the option to set up such bodies or not.[34]

From yet another angle, it is clear that there is a much more 'forward-looking' element in the Helsinki Convention, insofar as it provides for a periodically convened Meeting of the Parties which may take decisions tailored to the needs arising out of its implementation. The 1992 Convention has also been endowed with a permanent Secretariat which, *inter alia*, assists states parties in their implementation of the Convention, thus being a valuable instrument for states which are experiencing problems in that regard. A new organ that has been established by the Meeting of the Parties of the Convention is the Implementation Committee which will also offer assistance in such cases. There is also the Legal Board, a long-standing body which has made a major contribution to resolving and clarifying legal issues concerning the interpretation of the Convention. The Legal Board has also drawn up several soft law instruments which analyse and shed light on

31 Art. 2(2)(c).

32 *Ibid.*, Arts. 17-19.

33 In case of a dispute which it has not been possible to resolve, the Convention provides that it has to be submitted either to the ICJ or to arbitration (art. 22).

34 Arts. 8(2) and 24 of the New York Convention. Unresolved disputes can be (unilaterally) submitted to (compulsory) fact-finding, as well as, facultatively, to either the ICJ or to arbitration (art. 33). See also *infra*, at 21.1.

the provisions of the Convention, thus promoting and facilitating its implementation. At the same time, the Legal Board has studied various related issues, taking the Convention into new legal ground and putting forward new ideas which may constitute a forerunner for developments in international water law.

It may be said, generally, that the New York Convention constitutes mainly an instrument of codification of applicable rules of international law which represent, in large measure, 'minimum standards', while the Helsinki Convention is an instrument of environmental character which aims at the progressive development of international law in the domain of transboundary waters.[35]

It must, finally, be emphatically stressed that, irrespective of any differences between them, both Conventions share the same goal and serve the same purpose, which is the promotion of cooperation between riparian states with regard to the utilization, protection and management of international waters to the benefit of both, present and future generations.[36]

It is also certain that the two Conventions can successfully complement each other as there is no incompatibility between them. [37] It is noticeable, in this connection, that several states have become party to both, while more have expressed their intention to do so.

18.4.4 Other Instruments and Documents

Among the many soft-law instruments forming part of the sources of international water law, most important are the Rules elaborated by the International Law Association (ILA) in 1966[38] (Helsinki Rules), in 1986 (Seoul Rules)[39] and in 2004 (Berlin Rules) on Water Resources.[40, 41] A number of texts dealing with environmental issues are also relevant, among which the 1972 Stockholm Declaration on the Human Environment is a very important one. Furthermore, the OECD Council has issued a series of recommendations concerning the management and protection of transboundary resources relevant to inter-

35 Further elements of similarity and divergence between the Helsinki and the New York Conventions can be found in Chapter 20 on General Principles of International Water Law.

36 Stephen McCaffrey, The 1997 Convention: Compatibility and Complementarity in A. Tanzi, O. McIntyre, A. Kolliopoulos, A. Rieu-Clarke, R. Kinna (eds) *The UNECE Convention on the Protection and Use of Transboundary Watercourses and International Lakes*, p. 58

37 *See* Attila Tanzi, Comparing the 1992 UNECE Helsinki Water Convention with the 1997 U.N. New York Convention on international water-course: harmonization over conflict, 15 October 2014.

38 Helsinki Rules on the Uses of the Waters of International Rivers. International Law Association, Report of the Fifty-Second Conference, Helsinki, August, 1966.

39 Seoul Rules on International Groundwaters, International Law Association, Report of the Sixty-Second Conference, Seoul, 1986.

40 Berlin Rules on Water Resources, International Law Association, Report of the 71st Conference, Berlin, 2004.

41 On all three sets of Rules see also infra, 18.6. 2 on Groundwater in International Law

national rivers. Apart from its leading normative role with regard to transboundary waters, the U.N. is naturally involved in a great number of other activities in connection with them, either as such or as part of the U.N. environmental agenda.[42] It was in the latter context that an early, important document, the 1972 Stockholm Declaration on the Human Environment – which also referred to water –, was adopted by the United Nations Conference on the Human Environment. The U.N. has also consistently taken action on the issue of transboundary waters through UNESCO and FAO. Thus, UNESCO has also issued a significant number of reports registering the status and prospects of international watercourses, promoting transboundary cooperation and raising awareness on a variety of relevant issues, such as transboundary groundwaters and aquifers. FAO has also dealt with transboundary waters in various documents it has issued.

18.5 Doctrinal Bases of International Water Law

A number of doctrines or theories have been supported and/or applied as bases for the international law which is applicable with regard to the use of an international watercourse on the territory of a state, a use which obviously directly impacts upon other states which share the same watercourse.[43] These are: a) the doctrine of absolute territorial sovereignty; b) the doctrine of absolute territorial integrity; c) the doctrine of limited territorial sovereignty; and d) the theory of the community of interests.

The first of these theories, purporting to be based on the principle of the territorial sovereignty of states, claims that no limit may be set to the possibility of a country to use the waters of an international watercourse on its territory as it pleases, or, in other words, that it is not obligated to have regard to the possible adverse effects on the interests of any other state(s) sharing the watercourse. This idea, which serves the interests of upstream countries in a maximalist way, is exemplified by the *Harmon Doctrine* formulated in 1895 in an Opinion by Attorney General Harmon of the U.S. as a response to the complaints of Mexico concerning the excessive withdrawals of water from the Rio Grande by U.S. farmers.[44] However, as shown by *McCaffrey*, the doctrine has not been upheld by the U.S. administration, which finally took a different position in this as well as in all similar cases.[45] In any event, this doctrine is so conspicuously oblivious of the interests of other states sharing a transboundary watercourse that it is not being – and in reality could not

42 The related activities of the U.N. Economic Commission for Europe (UNECE) are examined separately, as appropriate.

43 For an analysis of these theories, *see* McCaffrey, *op. cit.*, pp. 112-174.

44 For a full account of the facts relating to the Opinion of Attorney General *Judson Harmon* and a legal analysis thereof *see* McCaffrey, *op. cit.*, pp. 78 *et seq.*

45 *Op. cit.*, pp. 109-111.

be – supported today. As aptly observed by *McCaffrey*, this theory "is at best an anachronism that has no place in today's interdependent, water-scarce world."[46]

The second theory of 'absolute territorial integrity' or of 'natural water flow' is the exact opposite of the first, maintaining that upper riparians may not proceed to any action beyond reasonable use of the waters within their own territories which would modify the natural flow of the waters in lower riparians. Clearly, this theory is fully protective of the interests of downstream countries.[47]

The theory of limited territorial sovereignty, insofar as it may refer to inter-riparian relations, stands in the middle of the first two, recognizing that a state cannot make such use of the part of an international watercourse which is on its territory as to cause significant harm to other riparians.[48] It would seem that this theory is the prevailing one in state practice, national legislations and international agreements on water issues today.

Finally, the theory of the community of interests sees an international watercourse as a natural *unicum*. It therefore emphasizes the fact that all riparian states have a common interest in the use and protection of the watercourse which secures their own interests as well. Without doubt, this theory is the most positive and forward-looking one, as it promotes collaboration and the softening of antagonistic attitudes between riparian states. Although it has also found support in international jurisprudence,[49] it has not acquired universal acceptance as yet.

18.6 Groundwater in International Law

Despite the huge quantity of groundwater underneath the earth's surface and its importance for human life in itself as well as for the social and economic development of humankind, it is surprising that, until recently, there were very few international agreements referring to shared groundwater, in sharp contrast with the abundance and early appearance of international legal instruments dealing with surface water. The scarcity of agreements on groundwater was, furthermore, combined with the relative paucity of their regulatory content, which in most cases duplicated that concerning surface waters. It is indicative of the limited attention paid to groundwater that there are very few cases brought before international instances on disputes involving groundwater. Indeed, in the last decades only two cases involving some groundwater questions have been brought

46 *Ibid.* p. 114.
47 *See, e.g.*, the position of Egypt vis-à-vis its upstream co-riparians to the Nile (*infra*, pp. 50 *et seq.*).
48 McCaffrey, *op. cit.*, p. 137.
49 *Case concerning the Gabčikovo-Nagymaros Project (Hungary/Slovakia)*, ICJ Rep. 7, 1997 (for the facts of the case *see infra*, at 21.2.1.1 and fn. 3 there.).

before the ICJ, namely the *Gabčikovo-Nagymaros*[50] and the *Pulp Mills Cases*,[51] the Court having, however, paid rather cursory attention to them in its related judgments.

18.6.1 Agreements Concerning Groundwater

Older such agreements (whether bilateral, multilateral or regional)[52] tend to be part of frontier demarcation agreements, such as the 1888 Agreement between the United Kingdom (on behalf of Somaliland) and France (on behalf of Djibouti), providing for the common use by both parties of the *Hadou* wells,[53] and the 1923 border agreement between Britain (on behalf of Palestine) and France (on behalf of Syria) which refers to spring waters for demarcation purposes.[54] Some bilateral water agreements may refer, apart from surface waters, also to groundwater. Thus, the former Yugoslavia had concluded a number of agreements with its neighbours which covered both surface and groundwater, such as the 1958 Agreement concerning Water Economy Questions with Bulgaria. One of several regional agreements dealing with both, surface and groundwater, is the 2000 Windhoek Revised Protocol on Shared Watercourses in the SADC.[55]

The basin approach taken by some agreements should be noted as more prone to address all water-related issues in the particular basin, including groundwater, in a more effective way. Among these few agreements are the 1994 Sofia Convention on Co-operation for the Protection and Sustainable Use of the River Danube[56] and the 1999 Bern Convention on the Protection of the Rhine.[57]

Other water agreements, although not directly referring to groundwater, have developed into dealing with issues related to it, such as the 1944 Treaty between the U.S. and Mexico 'relating to the Utilization of the Waters of the Colorado and Tijuana rivers and

50 *Supra*, fn. 43.

51 *Pulp Mills on the River Uruguay (Argentina/Uruguay)*, Judgment of 20 April 2010, I.C.J. Rep. 2010, p. 14.

52 For older treaties and interstate compacts (the latter for federal states) referring to or containing provisions on groundwater *see* Dante A. Caponera and Dominique Alhéritière, *op. cit.*, pp. 593-594 and L.A. Teclaff and A. E. Utton, International Groundwater Law, N.Y., Oceana Publications, 1981.

53 Treaty of 2-9 February 1889, B.F.S.P. 672 (Caponera, *loc. cit.*, fn. 22).

54 Agreement respecting the boundary line between Syria and Palestine from the Mediterranean to *El Hammé (Newcombe/Paulet* Agreement), 7 March 1923, available at: https://treaties.fco.gov.uk/responsive/app/consolidatedSearch/, last accessed 1 January 2017.

55 Text available at: www.internationalwaterlaw.org/documents/regionaldocs/Revised-SADC-SharedWatercourse-Protocol-2000.pdf, last accessed 1 January 2017.

56 Text available at: www.icpdr.org/main/icpdr/danube-river-protection-convention, last accessed 18 March 2018.

57 Text available at: www.iksr.org/fileadmin/user_upload/Dokumente_en/convention_ on_tthe_protection_of__the_rhine.pdf, last accessed 18 March 2018.

of the Rio Grande'.[58, 59] Finally, mention of groundwater may be made, usually together with surface waters, in agreements which, although not specific to waters at all, consider water issues an important element within their particular context. An example of such a case is the Treaty of Peace between Jordan and Israel,[60] which also distributes surface and groundwater between the two countries.

Agreements dealing exclusively with a specific groundwater source (aquifer) are more recent and still rather rare. One example is the 2007 Convention on the Protection, Utilization, Recharge and Monitoring of the Franco-Swiss Genevese Aquifer[61] between the Community of the 'Annemassienne' region, the Community of the 'Génèvois' Rural Districts, and the Rural District of *Viry*, on one part and the Republic and Canton of Geneva, on the other.[62] Other such recent agreements are the 2010 *Guaraní Aquifer* Agreement, concluded between Argentina, Brazil, Paraguay and Uruguay[63] and the 2015 Agreement between Jordan and Saudi Arabia for the Management and Utilization of the Groundwaters in the *Al-Sag/Al-Disi* Layer.[64]

In the same category are two agreements which were concluded between Chad, Egypt, Libya, Sudan and Egypt in connection with the *Nubian Sandstone Aquifer System* (NSAS) in 2000,[65] while in 2002 Algeria, Libya and Tunisia signed a procès verbal on the estab-

58 Text available at: www.ibwc.gov/Files/1944Treaty.pdf, last accessed 18 March 2018.

59 This became necessary by the growing dependence on groundwater of the urban centres developed along the Rio Grande (Bravo) where the river constitutes the frontier between the U.S. and Mexico. To address the situation which was not covered by the Treaty, use was made of the Minutes, the conclusion of which is provided by the Treaty. Thus, by virtue of Minute 242 of 1973, an agreement was reached limiting the pumping of groundwater within five miles from either side of the boundary between Arizona and Sonora. At the same time, common scientific research on aquifers straddling the border continues to be conducted.

60 Signed on 26 October 1994 at the *Wadi Araba crossing* point between Israel and Jordan. Text available at: FAO Legislative Study 86, www.fao.org/docrep/008/y5739e/y5739e00.htm, no. 22.

61 *Convention relative à la protection, à l' utilization et à la réalimentation de la nappe souterraine franco-suisse du Génèvois.* Text available at: www.internationalwaterlaw.org/documents/regionaldocs/2008Franko-Swiss-Aquifer-English.pdf last accessed 18 March 2018.

62 This agreement replaced the 1977 Arrangement on the Protection, Utilization, and Recharge of the Franco-Swiss Genevese Aquifer between The State Council of the Republic and Canton of Genevaand the Prefect of Haute-Savoie (*Arrangement relatif à la protection, à l' utilization et à la réalimentation de la nappe souterraine franco-suisse du Génèvois*).

63 Text in English translation (unofficial) available at: www.internationalwaterlaw.org/documents/regionaldocs/Guarani_Aquifer_Agreement English.pdf, last accessed on 18 March 2018

64 Text available at: www.internationalwaterlaw.org/documents/.../Disi_Aquifer_Agreement-English2015 last accessed 18 March 2018.

65 Programme for the Development of a Regional Strategy for the Utilization of the Nubian Sandstone Aquifer System (NSAS) – Agreement No. 1 – *Terms of Reference for the Monitoring and Exchange of Groundwater Information of the Nubian Sandstone Aquifer System. Agreement No 2 – Terms of Reference for Monitoring and Data Sharing, Tripoli, 5 October 2000 (FAO Legislative Study 86);* Stefano Burchi and Kerstin Mechlem, *Groundwater in international law, Compilation of treaties and other legal instruments, 2005, last revised 2009, pp. 4-6), available at:* www.fao.org/3/a-y5739e.pdf, *last accessed 9 March 2018; Text also available at:* http://iwlearn.net/publications/legal-frameworks/nubian-sandstone-aquifer-system-nsas)

lishment of a Consultation Mechanism for the *Northwestern Sahara Aquifer System* (SASS).[66]

As far as universal agreements on transboundary waters are concerned, the 1992 Helsinki Water Convention, although expressly including groundwater in the matters that it governs, does not treat such water as a distinct issue which needs to be addressed in a specific way. Thus, it simply includes groundwater in its definition of transboundary waters.[67, 68] Under the U.N. Watercourses Convention (New York Convention), its provisions would apply to groundwater only if an aquifer were connected hydrologically to surface waters straddling different States.[69] Confined aquifers are not therefore included in the scope of the Convention. Conscious of this gap, the ILC started work on transboundary groundwater in 2003 and the 'Draft Articles on the Law of Transboundary Aquifers' which it produced were adopted by the U.N. General Assembly in 2008,[70] never acquiring, however, the form of a binding document.

18.6.2 Other Legal Texts

A substantial number of international organizations, whether interstate or non-governmental, have dealt with groundwater and produced relevant legal texts, usually non-binding, such as studies, recommendations, guidelines, etc. which have undoubtedly promoted cooperation of states on issues concerning groundwater and helped their better understanding of such issues. Prominent in this respect is the work of the ILA which drew up a series of Rules in 1966, 1986 and 2004, referred to earlier, that greatly influenced relevant work undertaken in various *fora*, among which the work of the ILC when the latter was preparing its Draft Articles on Groundwater, issued in 2008 – as, of course, the Commission's previous work on what became the 1997 U.N. Convention on the Non-Navigational Uses of International Watercourses.

The 1966 ILA Helsinki Rules on the Use of Waters of International Rivers[71] refer to groundwater in Article II and ascertain that they apply to such waters as well. The 1986 ILA Seoul Rules on International Groundwater deal, as their name indicates, specifically

66 *Ibid.*, pp. 6-8.

67 Art. 1(1).

68 *See*, however, *infra*, at 18.6.2.

69 According to Art. 2(a) of the Convention: "'Watercourse' means a system of surface waters and groundwaters constituting by virtue of their physical relationship a unitary whole and normally flowing into a common terminus." According to Art. 2(b): "'International watercourse' means a watercourse, parts of which are situated in different States."

70 According to the Draft Articles: "'aquifer' means a permeable water-bearing geological formation underlain by a less permeable layer and the water contained in the saturated zone of the formation" while 'aquifer system' means a series of two or more aquifers that are hydraulically connected" (draft Arts. 1(a) and 2(a)).

71 Text available at: www.internationalwaterlaw.org/.../intldocs/Helsinki_Rules_with_comments.pdf, last accessed 18 March 2018.

and exclusively with such water,[72] while the 2004 voluminous Berlin Rules on Water Resources dedicate a special section (Section VIII) to groundwater, Article 42 of which deals with transboundary aquifers.[73]

Finally, the 1989 Bellagio Model Agreement concerning the Use of Transboundary Groundwaters,[74] drawn up by an expert Conference, is a forward-looking text based on the experience of the groundwater situation between the U.S. and Mexico.[75]

Among organizations which have dealt with groundwater, mention should be made of the Asian-African Legal Consultative Committee (now Organization-AALCO) as one of the first regional organizations to have done so.[76] The OECD has also conducted studies on groundwater in the context of its research on water and has established country profiles with regard to their use.[77]

The EU, having already issued two Directives dealing indirectly with groundwater,[78] adopted, in 2006, a Directive specifically addressing the protection of groundwater against pollution and deterioration (amended in 2014).[79]

The UNECE, on its part, has been particularly active on groundwater issues,[80] its efforts culminating in the adoption of a set of 'Model Provisions on Transboundary Groundwaters with Commentaries',[81] which effectively complement the 1992 Helsinki Convention with regard to groundwater. The Model Provisions adopt an integrated basin approach with regard to the management of both, surface and groundwater (Art. 2), and confirm the applicability of the principles enshrined in the Convention to groundwater, taking, however, into account the specific condition of such water, i.e. its particular vulnerability to pollution and the risks of excessive abstractions. The precautionary principle and the ecosystemic principle are of paramount importance in this context.[82]

---

72 *Supra,* section 18.4.4.

73 Text available at: www.internationalwaterlaw.org/documents/intldocs/ILA_Berlin_Rules-2004, last accessed 13 March 2018.

74 Text available at: Stefano Burchi and Kerstin Mechlem, *op. cit.*, pp. 536 *et seq.*

75 *See* Robert D. Hayton, Albert E. Utton, Bellagio Model Agreement concerning the Use of Transboundary Groundwater, Natural Resources Journal, Summer 1989.

76 Report of the Fourteenth Session held at New Delhi (proposition II-1), 7-14 (Jan. 1973).

77 *See* OECD (2015), Drying wells, rising stakes: Towards sustainable agricultural groundwater use, OECD studies on water, OECD publishing, Paris.

78 Council Directive 91/676/EEC concerning the protection of waters against pollution caused by nitrates from agricultural sources, 12 December 1991 and Directive 2000/60/EC of the European Parliament and of the Council Establishing a Framework for Community Action in the Field of Water Policy, 23 October 2000.

79 *See supra,* section 18.4.3 fn. 25.

80 United Nations Economic Commission for Europe – Guidelines on Monitoring and Assessment of Transboundary Groundwaters, 2000. *See also* the UNECE 2003 Guide to implementing the Water Convention.

81 Text available at: www.unece.org/fileadmin/DAM/...model_provisions/ece_mp.wat_40_eng.pdf, last accessed 1 January 2017.

82 *See* Attila Tanzi and Alexandros Kolliopoulos, The international water law process and transboundary groundwater: Supplementing the Water Convention with the 2012 Model Provisions, in Attila Tanzi, Owen McIntyre, Alexandros Kolliopoulos, Alistair Rieu-Clarke and Remy Kinna (eds), *op. cit.*, pp. 408-420.

18.6.3 Some Further Observations on Groundwater

The elements provided in abundance by scientific research, the views of publicists and international organizations and the developing practice of states with regard to transboundary groundwater, all converge towards the realization that no effective legal treatment and management of such water is possible without taking into account both surface and groundwater bodies and all other elements forming part of the particular drainage basin in an all-inclusive manner. It appears indeed, no separation between surface and groundwater coexisting in the same basin is in fact possible, the two constituting a whole, one feeding and impacting on the other. As a consequence, a workable institutional framework for transboundary waters has to include both. Although such a conclusion may seem natural today, it has been late to emerge due to the relative 'invisibility' of groundwater. Now, however, our knowledge of this element, as well as of the enormity of its dimensions and its importance to humanity and life on earth in general, does not allow for further delay. At the same time, account must be taken of the particular vulnerability of groundwater and of its natural differentiations (e.g. confined, unconfined, fossil) which define its limitations and dictate a sensitive and differentiated approach in each case. As with all matters dealing with transboundary waters, however, this is not a politically uncomplicated matter. Nonetheless, as has been shown by the progress achieved thus far in connection with transboundary surface water, the inclusion of related groundwater in holistic, integrated and sustainable management plans at the basin level is well within the reach of the international community and of its individual member states.

19 (Access to) Water as a Human Right

There has been much discussion in recent years about the recognition of the existence of such a human right. Although this discussion is not over yet, there are clear indications that a 'right to water' is indeed emerging. A milestone in this process has been General Comment 15 on the right to water which was adopted by the Committee on Economic, Social and Cultural Rights on 20 January 2003, which monitors the implementation of the International Covenant on Economic, Social and Cultural Rights (ICESCR) by its states parties. The General Comment defines the Right to (access to) Water as the right of everyone to sufficient, safe, acceptable and physically accessible and affordable water for personal and domestic uses, while it emphasizes its relationship with other rights by stating that "...[it] is indispensable for leading a life in human dignity. It is a prerequisite for the realisation of other human rights."[1]

In 2010, the United Nations General Assembly (UNGA) expressly recognized, by its Resolution 64/292,[2] the human right to water and sanitation and acknowledged that clean drinking water and sanitation are essential to the realization of all human rights. The Resolution requests states and international organizations to provide developing countries with the necessary means (financial resources, capacity-building, technology transfer), so that the latter may be able to provide safe, clean, accessible and affordable drinking water and sanitation to everyone.

To the above texts was added, also in 2010, a Resolution by the Human Rights Council which also upholds the same objective of providing human rights status to access to water and sanitation.[3]

The 2003 General Comment 15 states that the legal basis of the right to water is found in Articles 11 and 12 of the ICESCR, which deal with the rights to an adequate standard of living and to the highest attainable standard of health. This raises the question of the nature of the legal relationship between the right to water and these rights. Here it has to be observed that, although the interpretative value of the abovementioned resolutions is beyond doubt, the fact remains that they constitute soft law instruments which cannot impose legal obligations on states as such.[4] The ensuing unclear legal situation has to be added to the more general one surrounding the so-called 'welfare rights', and the prob-

1 Art. I.1
2 A/RES/64/292 of 28 July 2010.
3 A/HRC/RES/15/9 of 30 September 2010.
4 *See* McCaffrey, The Human Right to Water in E. Brown Weiss, L. Boisson de Chazournes and N. Bernasconi-Osterwalder, Fresh water and International Economic Law, 2005, Oxford University Press.

lems in connection with their justiciability and, ultimately, their enforceability.[5] These difficulties have not however, created obstacles to the tendency to recognize 'normative value' to the right to water, which has continued to gain momentum in a variety of fora and bodies.

On the other hand, the closest parallel to a human right to water which can be identified in a conventional text is the notion of 'vital human needs', which was adopted in Article 10(2) of the 1997 New York Convention. The latter, however, is a legal instrument dealing with water resources and not with human rights. Nonetheless, it has been suggested[6] that it would be preferable for 'access to water' to be connected with normative (conventional) instruments relating to the law of water resources rather than with human rights such as the economic social and cultural ones, the justiciability of which is, as already mentioned, rather doubtful. If so, a more direct connection with the right to water could be offered by the 1999 Protocol on Water and Health.[7] Although not recognizing a human right to water as such, the Protocol requires its states parties to ensure access to drinking water to everyone.[8] This is a clear 'hard law' obligation which, as rightly suggested by *Attila Tanzi*,[9] could adequately correspond to the requirements of General Comment 15 and support a justiciability claim of the right to water before national and international courts.[10]

5 On these questions *see* Owen McIntyre, The UNECE Water Convention and the Human Right to Access to Water: The Protocol on Water and Health, in The UNECE Convention on the Protection and Use of Transboundary Watercourses and International Lakes, *op. cit.*, pp. 345-366.

6 *Ibid.*, p. 359.

7 *Supra*, section 18.4.2, fn. 23.

8 Art. 6(1)(a).

9 *See* Attila Tanzi, Reducing the Gap between International Water law and Human Rights Law in The UNECE Protocol on Water and Health, 2010, 12 International Community Law Review, pp. 267-285, at 272.

10 *Ibid.*, at 276. This argumentation is supported by McIntyre, *supra*, pp. 363-364.

20 General Principles of International Water Law

20.1 Three Fundamental Principles

There are three fundamental principles in international water law with respect to transboundary waters: the principle of equitable and reasonable utilization, the principle (obligation) not to cause significant harm (no-harm rule) and the principle of cooperation. All three constitute central elements – with some differences in emphasis – in the two universal conventions which deal with transboundary waters, i.e. the 1992 Helsinki Water Convention and the 1997 New York Watercourses Convention, forming the basis of their respective legal frameworks. They also form part of international customary law and have been endorsed by the jurisprudence of the International Court of Justice.[1]

The principle of equitable and reasonable utilization and the principle not to cause significant harm (no-harm rule) are, furthermore, closely linked, none of them having priority over the other. On the contrary, they are complementary and mutually reinforcing.[2]

In fact, these two principles constitute two sides of the same coin, reflecting together the community of interests of riparian countries in the use of transboundary waters. In this context, the principle of equitable and reasonable utilization is generally viewed as a safeguard for the right of upper riparian states to develop the water resources on their territory, while the no-harm rule is seen as a means to protect lower riparians against damage caused by possible excesses of the upstream states in the use of transboundary waters. Although this 'interest-based' perception may not always correspond to the realities on the ground, it is not devoid of a large measure of truth. In a wider context, the complementary application of these two principles in a spirit of mutual confidence and cooperation, as required by the third principle of cooperation, is the foundation for a beneficial use of transboundary waters by all riparians. More particularly on each one of the three following principles.

---

1 They have also been taken up by the 2008 ILC Draft Articles on Transboundary Aquifers.

2 This is, *inter alia*, shown by the actual wording of the relevant articles of both the aforementioned conventions. Thus, Art. 2(2)(c) of the Helsinki Convention which deals with the principle of equitable and reasonable utilization, provides that the principle is applicable '*in the case of activities which cause or are likely to cause transboundary impact*'. This wording refers directly to Art. 2(1), which enshrines the no-harm rule. Similarly, Art. 7 of the New York Convention which enshrines the principle of no-harm provides, *inter alia*, that riparian states must take, when harm is caused, all the necessary measures to eliminate or reduce it 'taking into account, as appropriate, the provisions of articles 5 and 6' which refer exactly to the principle of reasonable and equitable utilization.

20.1.1 The Principle of Reasonable and Equitable Utilization

The principle has been recognized as a rule of international customary law by the ICJ. Indeed, the Court has referred to the 'basic right' of a riparian state "to an equitable and reasonable sharing of the resources of an international watercourse."[3]

Both universal Conventions on transboundary waters recognize the fundamental significance of the principle of equitable and reasonable utilization of transboundary waters.[4] There is, however, a noticeable difference between them in how each one of them expresses this fact. Thus, the 1992 Water Convention restricts itself to enunciating that "The parties shall, in particular, take all appropriate measures: ...[t]o ensure that transboundary waters are used in an equitable and reasonable manner taking into particular account their transboundary character...."[5] The principle is more explicitly expressed in the 1997 Watercourses Convention which provides that riparian states must

> participate in the use, development and protection of an international watercourse in an equitable and reasonable manner ... taking also into account the interests of the other riparian states, as well as the protection of the watercourse.[6]

Furthermore, the New York Watercourses Convention provides a list of factors of direct relevance to what constitutes equitable and reasonable utilization.[7] The Helsinki Convention, on the other hand, tends to concentrate more on the notion of 'transboundary impact' and on the protection of watercourses from pollution. However, these differences between the two instruments relate to focus and emphasis rather than to substantive divergence and are mostly due to the different circumstances in which they were negotiated and adopted.

Although originally meant to apply only to the allocation (apportionment) of transboundary waters,[8] the principle of equitable and reasonable utilization is now accepted to apply, just as in the case of the no-harm rule, to water quantity and water quality issues alike. This is because of the growing realization that these two issues cannot be separated in reality, because, *inter alia*, a lower quantity adversely affects the depuration capacity of waters and therefore makes them more prone to pollution. Thus, the 1992 Water Con-

3 *Gabčikovo-Nagymaros*, 1997 (*supra,*) para. 78.
4 On this issue generally and in connection with the 1992 Water Convention in particular, *see* Owen McIntyre "The Principle of Reasonable and Equitable Utilization" in The UNECE Convention on the Protection and Use of Transboundary Watercourses and International Lakes, *op. cit.*, pp. 146-159.
5 Art. 2(2)(c).
6 Art. 5(2).
7 Art. 6(1).
8 McCaffrey, *op. cit.*, p. 325.

vention links, in Article 2(2)(c), the equitable and reasonable use of transboundary waters with the avoidance of transboundary impact, which may also refer to water quantity.

However, the emergence of conflict between proposed uses of transboundary waters by different riparians cannot be excluded. In search of adequate solutions to such situations, the riparian states must make an assessment of a wide range of factors which may apply in a given case. A number of such factors are listed in the aforementioned Article 6 of the 1997 Watercourses Convention including, *inter alia*, geographical and hydrographic factors, the economic and social needs of riparian states, the population which depends on the watercourse, the effects of the utilization of a riparian state on other riparian states, etc. As the circumstances of the watercourse and of the riparian states may differ widely, the list of factors contained in Article 6 is indicative and none of them is given predominance, i.e. no utilization has inherent priority over the others. As rightly observed by *McCaffrey*, equitable utilization is not 'abstract and static' but an 'ongoing process' for which a multitude of data and information must be provided by co-riparians and regularly updated.[9] However, there is one category of needs which has to be given priority, and that category is identified by the 1997 New York Convention in its Article 10(2) to be that of 'vital human needs'. Indeed, according to this provision:

> In the event of a conflict between uses of an international watercourse, it shall be resolved with reference to articles 5 to 7, with special regard being given to the requirements of vital human needs.[10]

Particularly with regard to the issue of water allocation, as there is no precise formula of a scientific nature which is applicable, a fair solution will have to be assessed individually for each particular watercourse, taking into account all the relevant factors, including those mentioned in Article 6 of the 1997 Watercourses Convention. Cooperation between riparian states in order to make all such assessments is, no doubt, of the essence.[11]

Finally, the principle of equitable and reasonable utilization has, apart from a substantive, also a procedural component consisting in proceeding to a variety of acts, such as actively participating in cooperative activities (sharing information and data, consultations for any number of questions arising from the use of the watercourse and its basin) and giving notification of planned measures.[12] Without this constellation of activities, it

9 *Op. cit.*, p. 342 *et seq.*

10 Further explanation of the phrase is contained in the 'statement of understanding', based on the ILC commentary which accompanies the text of the Convention and which reads as follows: "In determining 'vital human need,' special attention is to be paid to providing sufficient water to sustain human life, including both drinking water and water required for production of food in order to prevent starvation" (Available at: http://legal.un.org/ilc/texts/8_3.shtml, last accessed 2 November 2018).

11 *See* Arts. 11 and 13 of the 1992 Helsinki Convention.

12 The judgment on the *Pulp Mills Case (Argentina v. Uruguay)* (*supra*) recognizes that the elaboration of an EIA constitutes a rule of customary international law and is therefore obligatory.

would indeed be difficult to perceive any use of transboundary waters as equitable and reasonable.

20.1.2 The Obligation Not to Cause Significant Harm (No-Harm Rule)

Both universal conventions refer to this obligation[13] which exemplifies, in essence, the very core of the principle of equitable and reasonable utilization. Their relevant provisions stem from a general principle of international law, recognized as such by the ICJ's 1996 advisory opinion on the 'Legality of the threat or the use of nuclear weapons'. In that opinion, the Court stated that

> the environment is not an abstraction but represents the living space, the quality of life and the very health of human beings, including generations unborn. The existence of the general obligation of States to ensure that activities within their jurisdiction and control respect the environment of other States or of areas beyond national control is now part of the corpus of international law relating to the environment.[14]

The 1997 Watercourses Convention requires riparian states to take all appropriate measures to prevent causing significant harm to other riparian states. Where harm nonetheless happens, they are obliged to eliminate or mitigate the harm done[15] and even 'discuss' the question of compensation.

Under the 1992 Water Convention, 'significant harm' is replaced by the notion of 'transboundary impact' which is defined so as to encompass

> any significant adverse effect on the environment resulting from a change in the conditions of transboundary waters and includes, inter alia, effects on human health and safety, flora, fauna, soil, air, water, climate, landscape or historical monuments or cultural heritage or socio-economic conditions in another state.[16]

---

13 On this issue generally and in connection with 1992 Water Convention in particular, *see* Attila Tanzi and Alexandros Kolliopoulos, 'The No-Harm Rule' in The UNECE Convention on the Protection and Use of Transboundary Watercourses and International Lakes, *op. cit.*, pp.133-145.

14 ICJ Rep. 1996, p. 2, para. 29.

15 Art. 7.

16 *See* Art. 1(2) of the 1992 Water Convention.

It is noteworthy, even striking, that the definition is so broad as to cover not only the effects of transboundary impact on the waters themselves and on human health and safety but also on elements which go far beyond the parameters of the 'natural environment'.[17] It also upholds and promotes the 'ecosystemic approach' (which views the drainage basin in ecosystemic terms) which is further enhanced in other provisions of the Convention.[18]

The source of impact, which must always be a human activity, can be located anywhere in the country where it originates from and not necessarily in or near the border area.

The 1992 Water Convention requires that all necessary measures be taken to prevent transboundary impact. Their objective is to ensure, in particular, a rational water management, the conservation of water resources, combating pollution and the protection of the ecosystems.[19] Where impact has, however, already occurred, the aim of the measures shifts to its control and reduction.[20]

Like all the other principles relating to transboundary waters, the no-harm rule reflects the community of interests of riparian states in the use of these waters, and as such it is applicable not only on upstream but also on downstream states. The latter are not, therefore, free to treat the watercourses on their territory without consideration for the consequences that their behaviour might have on other states. Moreover, given that the principles enshrined by the two Conventions intend to cover all aspects relevant to transboundary waters, the application of the no-harm rule is not restricted to pollution problems which may affect such waters, but may also apply to issues affecting their quantity.

In both Conventions, the application of the rule requires harm (transboundary impact in the case of the 1992 Water Convention) to be 'significant', which means that minor incidents do not reach the required level of harm for responsibility to arise.[21] Obviously, the identification of what constitutes significant harm in each case depends on the particular features of the case in question. Thus, a polluting event with transboundary effect which could have caused significant harm in the case of a small river may not do so in the case of a bigger one which has a higher depurifying capacity.

The no-harm rule does not impose an absolute obligation on riparian states. Thus, parties to either the 1992 Water Convention or the 1997 Watercourses Convention (or to both) must take 'all appropriate measures' in order to prevent, control and reduce trans-

17 An example of impact on historical monuments, is that caused by the building of the *Aswan Dam* in Egypt. As a result of the building of the Dam, a part of *Nubia,* was flooded and the *Abu Simbel* ancient temples and statues had to be relocated, with the help of UNESCO, so that they might be saved. A similar situation has arisen today in Southeastern Turkey with the construction of the *Ilisu Dam* and the planned flooding of the *Hansakeyf* town and district which will cause the destruction of very important archaeological monuments.

18 Particularly in Art. 2(2)(d) of the Water Convention.

19 Art. 2(2) of the Water Convention.

20 *Ibid.*, Art. 2(1).

21 Art. 1(2) of the 1992 Water Convention and Art. 7 of the 1997 Watercourses Convention.

boundary impact[22] or to prevent, eliminate or mitigate such significant harm.[23] The no-harm rule is, therefore, an obligation of a due diligence character, i.e. one of conduct, not of result, which means that the state in question will not have committed a violation of the rule if it is shown that it has indeed made adequate efforts to prevent or reduce the harm caused, irrespective of whether these efforts were successful or not. In assessing the efforts made by the state where the harmful event originated, the degree of economic and administrative development of that state will also be taken into account, so that the more developed a state is, the higher the applicable standards will be. Indeed, the in-built flexibility of a 'due diligence' obligation requires an evaluation of both state policy and state capabilities on a case-by-case basis. In this context, the degree of economic and administrative development of the state where the activity in question originates is an important factor. This, conversely, does not mean that a state can simply invoke its (presumably low) economic or social level as an excuse for not respecting the conventional provisions which are binding on it.

The riparian state's compliance with the minimum standards set by the applicable convention(s) will also be assessed in the light of that state's attitude with regard to the tools which these Conventions provide for, by examining, for example, if the state in question had fixed, prior to the incident, water quality objectives or emission limits as required by the 1992 Water Convention.[24]

20.1.3 Connected Principles

The no-harm rule and the principle of 'equitable and reasonable utilization' are connected with a number of other environmental principles, namely 1) the precautionary principle, 2) the polluter pays principle and 3) the principle of sustainable development (or sustainability principle).[25]

1. The precautionary principle aims to ensure that state action to prevent potential transboundary impact from the release of hazardous substances into the transboundary waters must proceed even if scientific research has not fully proved a causal link between those substances and transboundary impact.[26]

---

22 Art. 2(1) of the1992 Water Convention.
23 Art. 7 of the 1997 Watercourses Convention.
24 Art. 3(3).
25 The 1992 Water Convention provides in Art. 2(5) that parties to the Convention 'shall be guided' by these principles.
26 On this issue generally and in connection with 1992 Water Convention in particular, *see* Nicolas de Sadeleer and Mehdy Abbas Khayli, "The role of the Precautionary Principle in the Convention on the Protection and Use of Transboundary Watercourses and International Lakes" in The UNECE Convention on the Protection and Use of Transboundary Watercourses and International Lakes, *op. cit.*, pp. 160-175.

2. The purpose of the 'polluter pays principle' is to internalize the costs of pollution borne by public authorities and is related either to the costs of pollution prevention or to those incurred for remedial action (preventive and curative function).[27]
3. Finally, the 'sustainability principle', enshrined already in the Rio Conference of 1992, purports to secure that water resources will be available not only for the present but also for future generations.[28] Thus, the 1992 Water Convention requires that water resources "...be managed so that the needs of the present generation are met without compromising the ability of future generations to meet their own needs."[29]
   The association of the principle of 'equitable and reasonable utilization' with that of 'sustainable development' adds to the former a projection into the future, not only with regard to an equitable relationship between riparians but also between generations (intergenerational equity). It is therefore clear that in any assessment of whether a specific utilization of transboundary waters is equitable, riparian states must take into account considerations regarding the conservation, environmental protection and future availability of water.
   The same attitude towards sustainability is also endorsed by the 1997 Watercourses Convention,[30] which treats this principle as an integral part of the principle of equitable and reasonable utilization[31] and includes it in the management planning of the watercourse.[32] It should be noted, however, that the 1997 Convention makes no express mention of either the 'precautionary' or the 'polluter pays' principle.

20.1.4 Obligation of Cooperation

This is a most important principle because it is the one which makes possible the realization of all the other. Indeed, in order to attain the appropriate balance between the uses of transboundary waters and reconcile any opposing interests of riparian states, the latter must cooperate on the basis of 'legality and reciprocity'. The two universal Conventions naturally place particular importance on the interdependence of riparian states and promote cooperation in an emphatic way. Thus, the 1992 Water Convention contains a series of provisions[33] which indicate specific forms of cooperation between riparians,

27 On this issue generally and in connection with 1992 Water Convention in particular, *see* Leslie-Anne Duvic-Paoli and Pierre-Marie Dupuy, "The polluter pays principle in the1992 UNECE Convention on the Protection and Use of Transboundary Watercourses and International Lakes" in The UNECE Convention on the Protection and Use of Transboundary Watercourses and International Lakes, *op. cit.,* pp. 176-194.

28 On this issue generally and in connection with 1992 Water Convention in particular, *see* Alistair Rieu-Clarke, "The Sustainability Principle" in The UNECE Convention on the Protection and Use of Transboundary Watercourses and International Lakes, *op. cit.*, pp. 195-208.

29 Art. 2(5) (c).

30 Fifth Preambular paragraph.

31 Art. 5.

32 Art. 24(2)(a).

33 Arts. 9-15.

such as consultations, the formation of joint bodies, common surveillance and assessments, etc.

The 1997 Watercourses Convention provides for that obligation in its Article 8.[34] It does so in much more general terms, however, which indicates, once more, the markedly political character of the context in which the 1997 Watercourses Convention was adopted.

Cooperation must be implemented in good faith,[35] i.e. it should not be limited to a purely formal exchange of views. It can furthermore extend to a vast array of actions and synergies, such as the conclusion of agreements, the setting out of plans, including plans of joint management (which is a possibility provided for by the EU Water Framework Directive), and the undertaking of coordinated action. In order to agree on water utilization which is sustainable and mutually beneficial, it is by far better for riparian states to consult in the context of a joint body, so that they may make common assessments of all the relevant factors and circumstances and thus arrive at solutions acceptable to all.

In sum, the fact that the necessarily general character of the two fundamental principles of international water law has to be concretized in each particular case where they have to apply makes cooperation an indispensable tool to use in this process which must not stop operating even under strained political conditions.[36]

34 Which provides in its para.1 that "Watercourse States shall cooperate on the basis of sovereign equality, territorial integrity, mutual benefit and good faith in order to attain optimal utilization and adequate protection of an international watercourse."

35 As provided in the arbitral award of *Lake Lanoux* of 1957 between Spain and France (*Lake Lanoux Arbitration (France v. Spain) (1957)* 12 R.I.A.A. 281; 24 I.L.R. 101 Arbitral Tribunal, 16 November 1957.

36 *See* Art. 30 of the 1997 Watercourses Convention.

21 Settlement of Water Disputes

21.1 The Means for Settlement

Bilateral or basin agreements as well as regional water agreements may adopt consultations or negotiations as a means for dispute resolution or opt for third-party settlement. Both universal Conventions, i.e. the 1997 Watercourses Convention and the 1992 Water Convention, put forward a choice of either arbitration or judicial settlement (resort to the ICJ), if all other methods of dispute resolution have been to no avail. To these, the 1997 Watercourses Convention adds a fact-finding committee to which any of the parties to a dispute may compel the other party (-ies) to participate if any other method of dispute settlement has failed (compulsory fact-finding). A specific procedure is provided for by the Convention to this effect.[1] As is the case with fact-finding in general, however, the outcome of this procedure is not compulsory for the parties to the dispute.[2]

21.2 Jurisprudence

A number of international (interstate) disputes over water issues have been brought before international courts such as the PCIJ under the League of Nations Covenant and the ICJ under the U.N. Charter. Others have been submitted to international arbitral tribunals. Some of these cases for which judgments were issued after 1990, are mentioned below. Moreover, in the context of the EU, a number of cases involving water issues have been referred to the European Court of Justice (ECJ, CJEU). Other cases have been brought before courts and instances which deal mostly with petitions by individuals.

1 Art. 33 (Settlement of disputes).

2 Although resort to it is.

21.2.1 *International Court of Justice Judgments*

21.2.1.1 Gabčikovo-Nagymaros (Slovakia/Hungary, 1997)[3]

In its seminal judgment on this case, the ICJ interpreted and clarified the notion of 'fundamental change of circumstances' and the question of succession of states in respect of treaties. It also found that unilaterally taking control of a shared resource constitutes a violation of international law. The Court concluded that the condition of 'grave and imminent peril' for the establishment of necessity as a ground for precluding wrongfulness had not been satisfied by Hungary which was therefore not entitled to suspend and then abandon the Project. The ICJ went on to find that because Slovakia had taken a unilateral measure to put *Gabčíkovo* into operation in its 'Variant C', she had also violated its obligations under the 1977 Treaty between Hungary and Czechoslovakia.

The Court also pronounced for the first time on sustainable development, giving an indication of what this concept consists in.

21.2.1.2 The Pulp Mills Case (Argentina v. Uruguay, 2010)[4]

In its judgment, the Court found that Uruguay had breached its notification obligations deriving from the 1975 Statute of the *Uruguay River* agreed upon by the two countries. However, the violations of the Statute, the Court stated, were only of a procedural nature,

3 *Supra*, 18.6.1, fn. 43. The facts of the case are summarily as follows: A 1977 treaty between Hungary and Czechoslovakia provided for their cooperation in the construction of series of dams and locks along the Danube where the river formed the border between the two states. Although construction started in 1978 and went on at a slow pace until 1989, Hungary then abandoned the project invoking fundamental change of circumstances and impossibility to proceed with it. Czechoslovakia put forward 'Variant C', an alternative plan for the project. After the split of Czechoslovakia into Czech Republic and Slovakia in 1993, the latter undertook the role of former Czechoslovakia, since the project was now included entirely in the part of the Danube belonging to Slovakia. Following the failure of negotiations, Slovakia adopted 'Variant C', in execution of which she dammed the Danube and appropriated 80-90% of the water. The dispute was finally referred to the ICJ in 1994 which decided on the case in 1997. The Court rejected the claim of Hungary on fundamental change of circumstances, and found that by implementing Variant C and unilaterally taking control of the water, Slovakia had violated international law and the 1977 Treaty. Finally, it ordered the parties to cooperate in the implementation of the remaining project.

4 *Supra*, 18.6.1, fn. 45. The dispute arose from the authorization by Uruguay and the subsequent construction of a pulp mill on the banks of the Uruguay River which forms the boundary between Argentina and Uruguay. Argentina instituted proceedings against Uruguay for violating relevant provisions of the1975 Statute of the River Uruguay.

as the paper mill was found to work in accordance with the appropriate technical requirements. The ICJ also found that a rule of customary international law had developed according to which an EIA is obligatory, especially in the case of shared resources.

21.2.1.3 Certain Activities Carried Out by Nicaragua in the Border Area (Costa Rica v. Nicaragua) – Question of Compensation[5]

The *Costa Rica v. Nicaragua Case*, although not referring specifically to a water issue, may certainly impact on water-related issues and, as such, it constitutes an important precedent with regard to them. Indeed, this is the first ICJ case assessing damages for environmental damage caused by unlawful acts (in the instant case breach of the sovereignty of Costa Rica by Nicaragua). Although asserting the non-existence of a single accepted methodology for assessing environmental damage for compensation purposes, the Court went on to discount the proposals of the parties on this issue, making, instead, an overall assessment of the cost for the restoration of the environment which had been damaged, as well of the cost of the impairment or loss of environmental goods and services prior to recovery. As regards the estimated period required for the recovery of the particular environment, which would allow to determine the period of time for which damages should be paid, the Court took a restrictive approach, admitting that it lacked the required evidence for this purpose.[6]

There are other cases which have been tried by the ICJ and are related to international watercourses; however, as they are connected to delimitation, navigational rights and other issues rather than water issues *per se*, they are not examined here.[7] A case which

---

5 *Certain Activities carried by Nicaragua in the Border Area (Costa Rica v. Nicaragua), Compensation owed by the Republic of Nicaragua to the Republic of Costa Rica, 2 February 2018, General List 150.* The case finds its origins in a territorial dispute between Costa Rica and Nicaragua concerning a wetland area between *Isla Portillos* and the right bank of the *San Juan River* up to its mouth at the Caribbean Sea and the *Harbor Head Lagoon.* The dispute was submitted to the ICJ by Costa Rica in 2010. In 2011 Nicaragua responded by also instituting proceedings against Costa Rica before the ICJ. The two cases were joined by the Court. In 2010, Nicaragua had started doing constructions and other works in the disputed area. In its Judgment of 16 December 2015, the Court found that sovereignty over the particular territory belonged to Costa Rica and that, as a result, Nicaragua's activities there were in breach of the sovereignty of Costa Rica. The ICJ judgment of 2 February 2018 decided on the amounts owed to Costa Rica for reparations and compensation.

6 Judgment, paras. 29-30 and 41.

7 These are: a) *The Land, Island, and Maritime Frontier Dispute (El Salvador v. Honduras, Nicaragua intervening),* 11 September 1992 and 13 September 1990, I.C.J. Reports 1992, p. 351; b) *Kasikili/Sedudu Island (Botswana v. Namibia),* Judgment, I.C.J. Reports 1999 (II), p. 1045; c) *Dispute regarding navigational and related rights (Costa Rica v. Nicaragua),* Judgment, I.C.J. Reports 2009, p. 213; *Frontier Dispute (Benin v. Niger, 2005),* Judgment, I.C.J. Judgment, I.C.J. Reports 2005, p. 90; Obligation to Negotiate Access to the Pacific Ocean *(Bolivia v. Chile),* Judgment, 1 October 2018,General List No. 153.

does concern such water issues is the *Dispute over the status and use of the waters of the Silala (Chile v. Bolivia)*, which is actually pending before the Court.[8]

21.2.2 Arbitral Awards

A relatively recent example of such awards[9] is The Indus Waters Kishenganga Arbitration (*Pakistan v. India*, 2013).[10] The case concerned a dispute between Pakistan and India over the construction by India of the *Kishenganga Hydro-Electric Project-KHEP*.[11] In its Partial Award on the case, issued in February 2013,[12] the Court held that while India could divert water from the *Kishenganga/Neelum River* in order to generate hydroelectric power, there were limitations to her right to do so, set by the provisions of the 1960 Indus Waters Treaty and by customary international law. The Court found that India was required to ensure a minimum flow of water downstream of the KHEP at all times (at a rate to be determined by the Final Award) to secure the satisfaction of the agricultural

8 Chile instituted proceedings against Bolivia before the ICJ on 6 June 2016. The Court has been requested by Chile, which is downstream on the *Silala River* to decide on a number of issues, among which whether the *Silala* river system, together with its 'subterranean portions', is an international watercourse, the use of which is governed by customary international law, as well as to be recognized the right of equitable and reasonable use of the waters of the river. Chile also requests that its 'current use' of the *Silala* river waters be recognized to her. The proceedings have been instituted on the basis of the 1948 American Treaty on Pacific Settlement (Pact of Bogotá) by virtue of which both states have accepted the compulsory jurisdiction of the ICJ.

9 Among older international awards or decisions are the *Lac Lanoux* Arbitration Award (24 rInt'l L. Rep. 101 (1957) (*Spain v. France*) and the Decision on the *Gut Dam Case* (*Canada v. U.S.*, Decisions of 15 January 1968, 12 February 1968, and 27 September 1968, issued by the Lake Ontario Claims Tribunal).

10 Final Award, 20 December 2013, available at: www.pcacases.com/web/sendAttach/48, Partial Award, 18 February 2013, www.pcacases.com/web/sendAttach/1681,

11 Arbitral proceedings were instituted by Pakistan against India under the 1960 Indus Waters Treaty between the two countries (brokered by the World Bank). The facts of the case are as follows: The Kishenganga River starts in Kashmir (*Lake Vishansar*), and then merges with the Jhelum River. According to the Indus Waters Treaty, India has the right of unrestricted use of the Eastern Rivers of the Indus Basin (*Sutlej, Ravi, and Beas*) and Pakistan of the Western Rivers of the Basin (*Chenab, Jhelum, and Indus*). However, India is allowed to use the Western Rivers in upstream areas for the generation of hydro-electric power under certain conditions. The KHEP involved the diversion of water from the *Kishenganga* (called *Neelum* in Pakistan) at a point in the *Gurez Valley*, through a network of tunnels to the powerhouse before emptying into another tributary of the *Jhelum* at a lower elevation. Pakistan raised two questions: whether the planned diversion of water and other technical features of the KHEP were in conformity with the provisions of the Treaty, and whether India was permitted under the Treaty to use the technique of drawdown flushing to control sediment in Run-of-River Plants such as the KHEP in circumstances other than unforeseen emergency. Following a request by Pakistan, the Tribunal ordered interim measures, prohibiting India to construct any permanent structures which might permanently inhibit the river's full flow. The interim measures nonetheless allowed India to undertake works which would temporarily divert the waters (sub-surface foundation of the dam). In its Partial Award the Tribunal held, *inter alia* (*see* main text), that the Waters Treaty barred India from periodically depleting the reservoirs at the KHEP below the dead-storage level (*i.e.*, the portion of storage not used for operational purposes) for drawdown flushing for purposes of sediment control. The Partial Award also lifted the Order on Interim Measures.

12 *See supra*, fn. 11.

and hydroelectrical needs of Pakistan and to take account of environmental considerations. Significantly, the Tribunal noted that the KHEP must be 'planned, built and operated with environmental sustainability in mind'.

In its Final Award issued in December 2013,[13] the Court held that India must maintain a minimum flow of 9 m^3/s into the *Kishenganga/Neelum* River below the KHEP at all times. In reaching this conclusion, the Court took into consideration both the downstream environment and the effective operation of the KHEP. The Tribunal also decided that either country could seek reconsideration of the minimum flow requirement after seven years from the diversion of water from the *Kishenganga/Neelum River* for power generation by the KHEP.

21.2.3 Other Courts, Instances and Bodies

The Court of Justice of the EU (CJEU), the European Court of Human Rights (CtHR), the Inter-American Court of Human Rights, the African Commission on Human and Peoples' Rights have delivered judgments on cases concerning water issues.[14]

It is worth noting that while the European Convention on Human Rights does not contain a right relating specifically to (access to) water or other similar right, the jurisprudence of the European Court of Human Rights has extended the ambit of other rights so as to affirm a violation of Article 8 of the Convention (right to respect for private and family life), in the case of an environmental catastrophe impacting on water (*Tătar v. Romania*).[15] In the same case, it has also confirmed the application of the precautionary and the sustainability principles. The ECtHR has also found that the limited availability or non-availability of (clean/hot) water to an inmate may amount to a breach of Article 3 of the ECHR (prohibition of torture and of inhuman or degrading treatment).[16]

13 *Ibid.*

14 Decisions issued by tribunals or other instances dealing with investor complaints (such as those issued by ICSID) are not covered.

15 Application No. 67021/01, Judgment, 27 January 2009. The case referred to the environmental disaster caused to the Danube in 2000 by an industrial accident in *Baia Mare,* Romania, where 50-100 tons of total cyanide were released into the river due to a leak from a gold mining installation. As a result of the leak, the fish produce in Hungary and Serbia was destroyed while there were consequences on the health of individuals.

16 *Iacov Stanciu v. Romania* Application No 35972/05, Judgment, of 24 July 2012, para. 179.

Several judgments relating to the right to water have also been issued by the Inter-American Court of Human Rights,[17] particularly the right to water of certain indigenous communities.[18]

As is the case with other regional Human Rights Conventions, the African Charter on Human Rights does not contain any specific mention to the right to water,[19] which has put pressure on the African Commission on Human and Peoples' Rights[20] to find a legal basis to accommodate this gap within the ambit of other rights which are covered by the African Charter.[21] The Commission has indeed identified such basis in the right to dignity (Art. 5), the right to health (Art. 16) and the right to a healthy environment (Art. 24) of the Charter.

17 *Supra*, Part II, p. 7.

18 *Indigenous Community Yakye Axa v. Paraguay*, Judgment, 17 June 2005; *Indigenous Community Sawhoyamaxa v. Paraguay*, Judgment, 29 March 2006; *Indigenous Community Xákmok Kásek v. Paraguay*, Judgment, 24 August 2010; *Saramaka People v. Suriname, Preliminary Objections, Merits, Reparations and Costs*, Judgment, 28 November 2007. On the jurisprudence of the Inter-American Court of Human Rights on water issues, *see* generally Inter-American Commission on Human Rights (IACHR), Annual Report 2015, Chapter IV.A, Access to Water in the Americas, an Introduction to the Human Right to Water in the Inter-American System.

19 Takele Soboka Bulto, African Human Rights Law Journal (AHRLJ) Vol. 11 No 2, 2011, pp.341-367.

20 *Supra*, Part II, p. 8.

21 *Sudan Human Rights Organization & Another v. Sudan* (2009) AHRLR 153 (ACHPR 2009) (Sudan) para. 207; *Institute for Human Rights and Development in Africa v. Angola* (2008) AHRLR 43 (ACHPR 2008) para. 51; *The African Commission on Human and Peoples' Rights on Centre for Minority Rights Development (Kenya) and Minority Rights Group (on behalf of Endorois Welfare Council) v. Kenya*, No 276/03, (2009); *Free Legal Assistance Group and Others v. Zaire* (2000) AHRLR 74 (ACHPR 1995) para. 47.

22 Two Cases of Unresolved Disputes

22.1 The Nile

22.1.1 The River and Its Basin

The Nile is one of the great rivers of the world,[1] and certainly the most illustrious in human history.[2] With a length of 6,695 km, it is also the world's longest river. It rises from Lake Victoria in Uganda,[3] but its more distant source is the *Kagera River* which originates in Burundi and receives its waters from tributaries rising in Burundi and Rwanda. The *Kagera*, in its turn, is the main feeder of Lake Victoria. The Nile flows in a general northerly direction through an enormous drainage basin of 2,870,000 km^2 shared by eleven countries[4] with extremely varied environmental and climatic conditions, which range from tropical to arid and hyper arid.

22.1.1.1 Trajectory of the Nile and Related Data

The headwaters of the Nile in Lake Victoria are joined by those in *Lake Kyoga* in Uganda and *Lake Albert* between Uganda and the DRC. They continue under the name of *Mountain Nile*, passing through the *Al-Sudd* wetlands in South Sudan[5] and forming the White

---

1 Physiographical data concerning the Nile are taken from various sources, including Encyclopaedia Britannica: www.britannica.com/place/Nile-River For an historical overview *see* Encyclopaedia Britannica or Dictionary of Arts, sciences and General Literature, 7th Edition, vol. XVI, Edinburgh, M.DCCC.XLIL, (1889), pp. 225-229. *See also* James R. Penn, Rivers of the World, A Social, Geographical and Environmental Sourcebook, 2001.

2 The name Nile (Arabic: النيل, transliterated as An Nil) originates from the Greek Νεῖλος although this, again, probably derives from the Semitic Nahal, meaning 'river'. Herodotus (Ηρόδοτος) travelled the Nile as far as the First Cataract at Aswan around 450 B.C., famously describing Egypt as 'the gift of the Nile' and Eratosthenes (Ερατοσθένης, 276-194 B.C.), chief librarian at the Library of Alexandria under Ptolemy III Euergetes, (Πτολεμαίος Γ' Ευεργέτης) produced a remarkably accurate map of the river.

3 Lake Victoria is shared between Uganda, Kenya and Tanzania. The Nile rises in the North of the lake, near *Jinja* in Uganda.

4 Namely Uganda, Burundi, Rwanda, the Democratic Republic of Congo (DRC), Kenya, Tanzania, Ethiopia, Eritrea, South Sudan, Sudan, and Egypt. The drainage basin of the Nile covers a huge area of about 3.3 million square kilometres (one tenth of the African Continent) which encompasses 35 degrees of latitude.

5 The *Al-Sudd* or *As-Sudd* wetlands of South Sudan is a collective term which includes the *Bahr al Jabal* and the *Bahr al Ghazal swamps*, the *Baro-Pibor-Akobo confluence wetlands* and the *Machar marshes*. The *Al-Sudd* which means 'barrier' in Arabic are among the largest wetlands in the world and include swamps, lagoons, channels and lakes, extending to an area of 320 by 400 km. The Mountain Nile passes through these wetlands moving extremely slowly due to the flatness of the ground and the masses of tall papyrus and other aquatic plants growing in the shallow waters. The huge evaporation absorbs more than half of the Mountain Nile's volume during its passage through the *Al-Sudd*.

Nile when joined by the *River Sobat* above the city of *Malakal* in that country.[6] In Sudan, the White Nile[7] merges with the Blue Nile[8] at *Khartum* to form the Nile proper, which then joins the *Atbara River*.[9] The Blue Nile, the *Atbara* as well as the *Sobat* and other smaller tributaries rise in the Ethiopian highlands and contribute the largest part of the Nile's waters. On average, about 85% of the water which reaches Lake Nasser in Egypt[10] originates in the Ethiopian Plateau, while the rest comes from the Equatorial (East African) Lake Plateau system. The Nile finally traverses Egypt to discharge, in a large delta, into the Mediterranean Sea.[11] Due to the effect of the Aswan Dam, the irrigation of agricultural regions in Egypt, as well as to the fact that in the last part of its trajectory the river crosses the desert which contributes no run-off, the volume of the Nile is greatly reduced by the time it reaches the Delta.[12] In any case, the average discharge of the Nile which is 2,830 m^3/s[13] is very small compared to that of other big rivers of the world.[14]

22.1.1.2 Historical and Environmental Notes

From a historical perspective, the Nile has always been a force of vital importance for the region and one which allowed the great ancient Egyptian civilization and the Nubian kingdoms to flourish since about 3000 B.C.[15] and 1600 B.C.[16] respectively. From an environmental perspective, the Nile has also been playing a crucial role in the formation and preservation of the great environmental diversity of its immense basin which includes

6 The confluence of the *rivers Baro and Pibor* form the *Sobat River* on the Ethiopian-South-Sudanese border.

7 The length of the White Nile (*An-Nil Al-Abyad* in Arabic) is 800 km. If the length of its principal tributary, the Mountain Nile, is added, it reaches 2,084 km. The White Nile contributes about 16% of the Nile waters on a yearly basis.

8 The length of the Blue Nile (*An-Nīl Al-Azraq* in Arabic, *Abay* in Amharic) is 1,460 km and it flows from *Lake Tana* in Ethiopia through a deep gorge to Khartoum where it joins the White Nile. The flow of the Blue Nile is highly variable, its maximum volume reached from June to September. Its main tributaries are the *Dinder* and the *Rahad*.

9 The *Atbara River* joins the Nile 320 km north of Khartoum. Like the Blue Nile, the flow of *Atbara* is highly variable, reaching maximum volume from June to September and being reduced to a series of ponds for most of the rest of the year. The main tributary of *Atbara* is *Tekeze River*, which rises near *Lalibela* in Ethiopia, marks the westernmost frontier between Eritrea and Ethiopia and running, like the Blue Nile, through a deep gorge – in fact the deepest in the world at 2,000 metres from its rim – joins *Atbara* in Sudan. The *River Tekeze*, which is longer than *Atbara*, is among those which drain the highlands of Eritrea.

10 Lake Nasser is the reservoir of the Aswan Dam. The gross capacity of Lake Nasser is 169 billion m^3.

11 The archetypical Nile Dam fans out in Lower Egypt from Alexandria in the West to Port Said in the East, measuring 240 km on the Mediterranean coastline.

12 Before the operation of the Aswan High Dam, nearly 30 billion m^3 of water reached the Mediterranean from the Nile Delta per year. With the operation of the Dam, the annual flow of the river to the sea dropped to less than 2 billion m^3.

13 Cubic metres per second.

14 For comparison, the average discharge of the Amazon – the largest in the world – is 209,000 m^3/s, *i.e.*, nearly 74 times that of the Nile. The average discharge of the Congo is 41,200 m^3/s, of the Yangtze 30,166 m^3/s, and the Mekong 14,800 m^3/s.

15 3,150 B.C. is considered to be the date of the unification of Upper and Lower Egypt under the *Pharaoh Menes*. Irrigation from the Nile has been practiced since 5,500 B.C.

16 The Nubian kingdom of *Kush* is estimated to appear at about that time.

rainforest, lakes, many major tributaries, wetlands, floodplains and deserts and is home to some of the most important ecosystems in the world. However, nowadays the river is facing serious environmental challenges. To mention but a few, there is severe land degradation and soil loss in the upper catchment areas, while the intrusion of the sea and consequent salinization of the soil is a constant threat to the river's Delta. The intensification of agriculture everywhere contributes to further depletion of the river's waters and often causes their contamination with chemicals used as fertilizers and pesticides. Finally, the construction or planned construction of projects in the region of the *Al-Sudd wetlands* is threatening their unique endemic flora and fauna.[17]

Today, over 450 million people live in the Nile basin countries and it is estimated that more than half of them are dependent on the river for their food and water security. However, expected high population growth rates in the region in the next twenty to twenty-five years will probably double that number. Expected economic development will also put more strain on the river by strengthening the demand for water to satisfy increased agricultural, industrial and domestic uses. To this picture must be added probable further pressures from the consequences of climate change.[18]

22.1.2 Legal Regime

The corpus of agreements concluded with regard to the Nile waters[19] form a legal regime which has been largely created by the colonial powers which ruled in the region, i.e. primarily the British. The main objective of this regime was therefore to serve and promote their own strategic goals and interests.[20]

In 1929, Egypt and the U.K. (on behalf of Sudan)[21] concluded the Nile Water Agreement[22] which, purporting to ensure the carrying out of irrigation projects in Sudan,

17 The most important of these is the *Jonglei Canal* project which purports to divert the waters of the Mountain Nile *(Bahr Al-Jabal)* river which now passes through the wetlands, to a canal bypassing them so as to carry the waters directly into the White Nile. The project was conceived in the beginning of the past century. Although its construction started in 1978, it has not been finalized due to war and political instability in Sudan. However, discussion on it is continuing.

18 *See supra,* at 17.1.4.

19 Only the most significant of these agreements are mentioned.

20 Securing Egyptian cooperation – and, therefore, taking primarily into account Egyptian interests when concluding agreements concerning the Nile waters – was of paramount importance to the British, given the strategic position of Egypt which controlled the Suez Canal and therefore British access to India.

21 *See infra,* fn. 23.

22 Exchange of Notes between the U.K. and Egypt in regard of the use of the River Nile for irrigation purposes, Cairo, 7 May 1929, Treaty Series No. 17 (1929).

recognized the 'natural and historic rights' of Egypt on the Nile waters. Furthermore, the agreement granted Egypt the right to inspect any upstream Nile-related water projects which could adversely affect the river's flow.[23] The conclusion of the agreement was made possible by the fact that, at the time, all the Nile basin countries were under British administration except Ethiopia and the Congo (the latter under Belgian rule). The justification for the benefits provided to Egypt was the recognition of its greater dependency on the Nile in comparison to upstream countries which had alternative solutions to ensure their water security.[24] Prior to that agreement, the U.K. had concluded another one with Ethiopia in 1902 by which the border between Ethiopia[25] and Sudan was established and any construction on the shores of *Lake Tana* (where rises the Blue Nile) as well as on the Blue Nile and the *Sobat* Rivers in Ethiopia, which could affect the flow of the Nile into Sudan, was prohibited. Similarly, an agreement between the U.K. and the Independent State of Congo,[26] concluded in 1906, provided for the prohibition of the construction of works on or near the *Semliki* or *Isango River* (rising in the DRC) which would diminish the volume of water entering Lake Albert, except in agreement with the Sudanese Government.

In 1959, Egypt and Sudan (which had recently become independent) concluded a new Nile Water Agreement,[27] after a protracted period of wrangling due to Egypt's plans to construct the Aswan High Dam (the reservoir of which extended into Sudan). In accordance with its terms, the water volumes used by the parties at the time of the conclusion of the Agreement, i.e. 48 billion m^3 (BCM) for Egypt and 4 billion m^3 for Sudan, on a yearly basis, measured at Aswan, constituted 'established rights'. The agreement then proceeded to apportion the amounts of Nile waters which had not been allocated under the 1929 Agreement, giving three quarters of the total water volume (55.5 billion m^3) to Egypt – thus allowing the construction of the Aswan High Dam in 1970[28] – the remaining one quarter (18.5 billion m^3) being allocated to Sudan.

23 According to Art. 4 (ii) "Save with the previous agreement of the Egyptian Government, no irrigation or power works or measures are to be constructed or taken on the River Nile and its branches, or on the lakes from which it flows, so far as all these are in the Sudan or in countries under British administration, which would, in such a manner as to entail any prejudice to the interests of Egypt, either reduce the quantity of water arriving in Egypt, or modify the date of its arrival, or lower its level."

24 Egypt relies on the Nile for 97% of its water needs. There are fears that with population growth and eventual reallocation of waters, Egypt could face severe water scarcity in the foreseeable future.

25 Then under *King Menelik II*.

26 Colony under the Belgian *King Leopold II* established in 1885. Belgian Congo was established in 1908 and existed until 1960.

27 Agreement between the United Arab Republic and the Republic of Sudan for the full utilization of the Nile waters, Cairo, 8 November 1959, 453 UNTS 51.

28 The Aswan High Dam has a height of 111 metres and a volume of 44,300,000 m^3.

These agreements have been criticized by the other Nile basin countries, mainly on the basis of the argument that, as they were under colonial rule at the various times the agreements were concluded,[29] they had been prevented from defending their rights on the waters of the river. With regard to the present and future, they emphasize their need to develop and take their peoples out of poverty by securing the satisfaction of their food and energy requirements through the construction of various projects which take advantage of the Nile waters. Furthermore, they reject the idea of having to subject these projects to prior control by downstream countries.

Conversely, the basis of the Egyptian and the Sudanese argumentation is that they both have historic or acquired or prior rights on the waters of the Nile, enshrined in agreements which are in force and binding on other Nile basin states.

22.1.3 The Nile Basin Initiative

Efforts to have the issues concerning the allocation and use of the Nile waters resolved having practically failed until then, an important step was taken in 1999, when ten Nile basin states (Egypt, Sudan, South Sudan, Ethiopia, Uganda, Kenya, Tanzania, Burundi, Rwanda, DRC)[30] founded the Nile Basin Initiative (NBI). Supported by the World Bank and other partners, the stated goal of the NBI was to achieve sustainable development for all the Nile Basin states through the equitable utilization of the river's water resources. A permanent commission was set up to work on these matters and to administer a multi-donor Nile Basin Trust Fund.[31]

Following ten years of work, the NBI Commission produced the Cooperative Framework Agreement (CFA or Entebbe Agreement) in 2010. Six Nile Basin states signed: Ethiopia, Rwanda, Uganda, Kenya, Tanzania and Burundi. Egypt and Sudan rejected it, mainly because they objected to Article 14(b) which did not maintain the water quotas agreed between them in their 1959 agreement, thus allowing the reallocation of the waters. The CFA was ratified by Ethiopia and Rwanda in 2013 and by Tanzania in 2015.[32]

The Agreement takes up many elements from the 1997 Convention on the Law on the Non-navigational Uses of International Watercourses (1997 U.N. Watercourses Convention) which entered into force in 2014, such as the principles of reasonable and equitable utilization and the no-harm rule, the list of factors to be take into account in order for utilization to be reasonable and equitable, etc. Although adopting the most modern

29 Ethiopia, however, was not under colonial rule at the time. The British colonies then included Kenya, Uganda, Tanganyika, and the Anglo-Egyptian Sudan (a condominium under the control of Britain from 1899 to 1956 when Sudan became independent).

30 South Sudan applied for membership to the NBI right after its independence in 2011 and became full member in 2012, while Eritrea is participating in an observer capacity.

31 The Commission has a Secretariat in Uganda.

32 Six ratifications are required for entry into force of the Agreement.

trends in international law regarding the management and use of transboundary watercourses (e.g. extensive cooperation, environmental impact assessment, exchange of information and audit requirements), it opts for a heavy mechanism for the oversight of various activities and for a dispute settlement procedure which does not, however, provide for compulsory third-party settlement with binding result.

22.1.4 Ethiopia's GERD Project

In 2011, Ethiopia began construction of the 'Grand Ethiopian Renaissance Dam' (GERD) project for the production of hydropower on the Blue Nile, in the *Benishangul-Gumuz* region in the western part of the country, near Sudan, the completion of which was originally envisaged for 2017. The huge reservoir of the Dam will have a storage capacity of 74 billion m^3, a size that is considered by experts as excessive.[33] The project caused a strong reaction on the part of Egypt and Sudan, with Egypt appearing to threaten hostilities at a certain point.[34] In 2013, Ethiopia diverted the flow of the Blue Nile so that construction of the dam could proceed.[35]

An eventual rapprochement between Egypt and Ethiopia allowed the signing, in March 2015, of a Declaration of Principles by both as well as by Sudan.[36] The signatories promised to reach an agreement on Guidelines on the operation of the Dam within a time frame of fifteen months from the preparation of the required studies. A Tripartite Committee composed of Egyptian, Sudanese and Ethiopian experts was set up to assess the impact of the operation of GERD on Egypt and Sudan.

Ethiopia undertook not to cause significant harm to Egypt and Sudan, to mitigate harm in case it happens and eventually discuss compensation. The factors that will be taken into account for an equitable and reasonable use of the river are reproducing almost *verbatim* those enumerated in Article 6 of the 1997 U.N. Watercourses Convention.[37] The Declaration, like the CFA, adds, however, the factor of the contribution of each basin country to the Nile water and the percentage of the basin belonging to each

33 GERD will be the biggest hydropower dam with an installed hydropower capacity of 6,000MW, *i.e.,* almost triple that of the Aswan High Dam (2,100 MW), and a height of 145m, that of Aswan High Dam in Egypt being 110m. The estimates for its cost differ, ranging from 4.6 billion to 7 billion U.S. dollars or even higher. The GERD will turn Ethiopia into a net exporter of electricity to states in the region.

34 In June 2013 the now deposed president of Egypt *Mohammed Morsi* stated that 'all options are open' because Egypt's water security could not be violated at all.

35 Other Nile riparian countries also plan or have already realized other projects, although none of the magnitude of GERD. Thus, the newly created South Sudan seems to have already pinpointed 16 sites along the Nile for the construction of dams. Egypt, on its side, has put into operation projects such as the desert reclamation project in the *Toshka Depression* in the Western Desert and the *Al-Salam Canal* project to reclaim land in the *Sinai Desert.*

36 Ahram online, 23 March 2015.

37 *See infra*, fn. 58.

one of them. The Declaration makes no specific reference to Egypt's prior agreements or acquired rights over the Nile waters.

Despite the significant evolution in the positions of the counties involved, as they now seem to recognize the importance of finding a common solution and that unilateral action leads to a dead end harmful to all, in reality difficulties persist.[38] Time is, of course, of the essence, as, at the moment the GERD Project's completion level stands at over a 60%.[39]

22.1.5 International Law and the Way Forward

The existing situation concerning the Nile waters, as broadly outlined above, reflects a well-known imbalance or asymmetry often observed in transboundary rivers, whereby the downstream countries, enjoying proximity to the sea/ocean and therefore having usually been developed politically, economically, culturally and technically at an earlier stage than upstream countries, also possess the means to develop the institutional and technical infrastructure required to exploit the river. In the case of Egypt, the process of its development through contact with and ample use of the Nile and the Mediterranean has a historical depth which is counted in millennia. It is therefore natural for her to invoke 'prior appropriation' and 'acquired' or 'historical rights' to maintain the *status quo* on the Nile. It is assisted in that assertion by the fact that such acquired rights were recognized to her by a series of agreements concluded during the past century regarding the Nile regime. However, some of these agreements suffer from defects which have been already pointed out by other Nile Basin countries as, for example, that some of these instruments constitute *res inter alios acta* for them. Such is the case of the 1959 agreement between Egypt and Sudan. Conversely, such would not, in principle, be the case of the 1902 agreement between Britain and Ethiopia, which would appear to be binding on the latter, as Ethiopia cannot claim that the agreement was concluded *inter alios* for her. Furthermore, the arguments she has opted to put forward to support the non-opposability (i.e. non-enforceability) of the agreement in her regard are technical rather than substantive in nature,[40] which make them appear less convincing. Nonetheless, the opposite view has been expressed as well.[41]

---

38 Ahram online, Wednesday 14 March 2018, Thursday 4 January 2018, Thursday 1 February 2018 and previous ones.

39 Africa News, 21 February 2019.

40 *E.g.*, that the 1902 Treaty was not ratified by Ethiopia and that, in any case, the wording of the relevant article of the treaty differs in the English and Amharic language versions.

41 McCaffrey, *op. cit.*, pp. 244-245, according to whom the Note-Verbale sent by Ethiopia to Cairo is tantamount to repudiation of the 1902 Agreement (still, the sender refers only indirectly to it and does not offer a specific justification).

Among the arguments put forward by other upstream Nile Basin countries against the agreements regarding the Nile regime, the *Nyerere doctrine*[42] is often mentioned. In the terms of this doctrine, a 'clean slate' approach as regards colonial agreements is justified (i.e. successor states are not bound to take up the obligations deriving from treaties concluded on their behalf by the colonial powers controlling them at the time).[43] This doctrine has been adopted by the U.N. 1978 Convention on Succession of States in respect of Treaties[44] with regard to 'newly independent states' (i.e. former colonies), by virtue of its Article 16.[45] Treaties establishing boundaries are, however, excluded from the purview of this rule (in accordance with the principle of *uti possidetis juris*), for obvious reasons of stability and maintenance of peace, an exception which has been generally respected by the states which succeeded in the colonial powers. Excluded from the rule are also 'other territorial regimes' (i.e. generally, treaty obligations relating to or imposing restrictions on the use of territory, for the benefit of any territory of a foreign state).[46] The International Law Commission (ILC) accepts that treaties governing water rights over a watercourse are included in such 'territorial regimes' thus also escaping from the purview of the general rule, i.e. the clean slate doctrine, under applicable conditions.[47]

---

42 *Julius Nyerere* (1922-1999) was the first President of Tanganyika, later renamed Tanzania after its unification with Zanzibar.

43 Tanganyika (subsequently Tanzania) (*see* fn. 204) as well as Kenya and Uganda made use of this doctrine to repudiate the 1929 Agreement.

44 The Convention entered into force on 6 November 1996. Egypt and Ethiopia are the only ones among the Nile Basin countries to have become parties to it.

45 The text of which is as follows: "*Position in respect of the treaties of the predecessor State.* A newly independent State is not bound to maintain in force, or to become a party to, any treaty by reason only of the fact that at the date of the succession of States the treaty was in force in respect of the territory to which the succession of States relates."

46 The text of the relevant Arts. 11 and 12 (which are contained in the 'General Provisions' of the Convention, are as follows:
"Article 11. *Boundary regimes* A succession of States does not as such affect: (a) a boundary established by a treaty; or (b) obligations and rights established by a treaty and relating to the regime of a boundary.
Article 12: *Other territorial regimes* 1. A succession of States does not as such affect: (a) obligations relating to the use of any territory, or to restrictions upon its use, established by a treaty for the benefit of any territory of a foreign State and considered as attaching to the territories in question; (b) rights established by a treaty for the benefit of any territory and relating to the use, or to restrictions upon the use, of any territory of a foreign State and considered as attaching to the territories in question. 2. A succession of States does not as such affect: (a) obligations relating to the use of any territory, or to restrictions upon its use, established by a treaty for the benefit of a group of States or of all States and considered as attaching to that territory; (b) rights established by a treaty for the benefit of a group of States or of all States and relating to the use of any territory, or to restrictions upon its use, and considered as attaching to that territory. 3. The provisions of the present article do not apply to treaty obligations of the predecessor State providing for the establishment of foreign military bases on the territory to which the succession of States relates."

47 Report of the International Law Commission to the U.N. General Assembly, on the work of its twenty-sixth session, 1974, Official Records of the General Assembly, Twenty-ninth session, Supplement No. 10, *YBILC*, 1974, vol. II (1), pp. 203 *et seq.*

A similar but not identical solution has been adopted by the 1969 Convention on the Law of Treaties.[48] The Convention enshrines, in its Article 62, a version of the *rebus sic stantibus* doctrine (i.e. the non-enforceability of an international agreement due to fundamentally changed circumstances).[49] From its application are, again, excluded boundary-establishing agreements.[50]

Although the 1969 Convention has not finally retained a specific article dealing with 'objective regimes'[51] nor referred to watercourses as such, there is room to consider that for the very same reasons, an exception to the *rebus sic stantibus* doctrine would also be applicable in similar cases by virtue of Article 37(2) of the Convention.[52]

On the other hand, in the context of modern international law as expressed primarily by the U.N. 1997 Watercourses Convention, 'prior rights' or 'acquired rights' or 'historical rights' are not recognized as such.[53] What is recognized is 'existing uses' of the transboundary watercourse by a state, which must be taken into account among other factors and circumstances when deciding whether the use of the watercourse is equitable and reasonable (art. 6).

What ultimately becomes apparent from the above is that neither the existing agreements entered into by the Nile Basin states, nor the principles that are being put forward by them, whether downstream or upstream, can provide a single and sustainable solution to the pressing problems of the region which often come dangerously close to a threat to its peace and security. Thus, although Egypt is not deprived of arguments to support her claims, these cannot afford her an absolute or unconditional priority over the Nile waters vis-à-vis the other Nile Basin states. In other words, it is doubtful whether Egypt could

48 Although this Convention has a very extensive membership, only two countries from those of the Nile Basin are parties thereto (Egypt, DRC).

49 *See* Elihu Lauterpacht, International Law: Disputes, War and Neutrality, pts. IX-XIV, at 14-15 Cambridge, 2004.

50 The text of the relevant paragraph is as follows: "2. A fundamental change of circumstances may not be invoked as a ground for terminating or withdrawing from a treaty: (a) if the treaty establishes a boundary; or (b) if the fundamental change is the result of a breach by the party invoking it either of an obligation under the treaty or of any other international obligation owed to any other party to the treaty."

51 *See* Sir Humphrey Waldock, Special Rapporteur, Second Report on the Law of Treaties, 1963 YBILC, vol. II, pp. 64 *et seq.* (draft Art. 17). According to Waldock, a treaty 'shall continue in force indefinitely' "if it: (a) is one establishing a boundary between two States, or effecting a cession of territory or a grant of rights in or over territory; (b) is one establishing a special international regime for a particular area, territory, river, waterway, or airspace;" (*Ibid.*, draft Art. 17(4)). *See also* Waldock, Special Rapporteur, Third Report on the Law of Treaties, 1964, *YBILC*, vol. II, pp. 26, 27 *et seq.*, Art. 63 and Commentary thereon (Treaties providing for objective regimes). The article was not, however, retained as such.

52 Which is as follows: "2. When a right has arisen for a third State in conformity with article 36, the right may not be revoked or modified by the parties if it is established that the right was intended not to be revocable or subject to modification without the consent of the third State."

53 By contrast, the plentiful jurisprudence of U.S. courts judging on interstate cases within the U.S., although older, appears to be more forthcoming in the recognition of 'prior rights'. *See, e.g., Kansas v. Colorado,* 206 U.S.(1907), *Colorado v. Kansas*, 320 U.S. 383 (1943), *Colorado v. Wyoming*, 259 U.S. 419 (1922). For an analysis of these and other cases between federal states in the U.S., *see* McCaffrey, *op. cit.*, pp. 221-228. For cases in other countries, *Ibid.*, pp. 228-231.

rely exclusively on these claims to ascertain, under international law, its prior rights on the Nile waters over the upstream, less developed, Nile Basin countries. Neither, on the other hand, is the opposite true, i.e. there cannot be a complete rejection of the right of downstream countries (Egypt's or Sudan's) to the existing uses of the waters of the Nile. Instead, their continuation has to be respected and secured in accordance with the applicable principles of international law. In that context, the construction of GERD by Ethiopia, a huge project which undoubtedly will have adverse consequences for downstream countries, needed to have been undertaken in consultation with those countries. The fact that it did not makes it even more urgent to consult now, so as to ensure that such adverse consequences may be averted or remedied to the extent possible.

The matter could, of course, be investigated and resolved in an authoritative way by resorting to a third-party settlement of the dispute(s) (with binding effect), but this has never seemed to be within the intentions of the states involved.

Taking into account all of the above, how could the content of a new understanding between the states involved be envisaged on the basis of international customary law?

The first texts to consider are existing global conventions on international watercourses, despite the fact that none of the Nile Basin countries is party to them as yet. The first one among these is the U.N. 1997 Watercourses Convention, many of the provisions of which are taken to be reflective of international customary law. A strong indication that this instrument would constitute a useful compass to use on this matter and one which would be acceptable to the Nile Basin countries is that the 2015 Declaration of Egypt, Sudan and Ethiopia refers *verbatim* to these factors – as indeed to other fundamental elements of the Watercourses Convention – despite the fact that, as already mentioned, none of the Nile Basin countries has officially adhered to it so far.

The Watercourses Convention adopts the fundamental principles of equitable and reasonable utilization of the waters of a watercourse (Art. 5)[54] and the principle of not

54 The text of Art. 5 is as follows: "1. Watercourse States shall in their respective territories utilize an international watercourse in an equitable and reasonable manner. In particular, an international watercourse shall be used and developed by watercourse States with a view to attaining optimal and sustainable utilization thereof and benefits therefrom, taking into account the interests of the watercourse States concerned, consistent with adequate protection of the watercourse. 2. Watercourse States shall participate in the use, development and protection of an international watercourse in an equitable and reasonable manner. Such participation includes both the right to utilize the watercourse and the duty to cooperate in the protection and development thereof, as provided in the present Convention."

causing significant harm to other states sharing the watercourse (Art. 7).[55] Although it is generally believed, as already noted above, that these principles are antagonistic between themselves, the principle of equitable utilization reflecting the interests of upstream states, and the 'no harm' rule[56] – viewed as a limit to the principle to equitable utilization – those of downstream countries, they have, in fact, to be seen and used as complementary to each other, aiming at the creation of a coherent system with regard to international watercourses. Nonetheless, the Convention does not define equitable utilization and the same is true of the no-harm rule.[57] It does, however, provide, repeating, on this issue, the 1966 Helsinki Rules on the Uses of the Waters of International Rivers, a series of (indicative) factors and circumstances which have to be taken into account when deciding whether the use of a watercourse is reasonable and equitable (Art. 6).[58]

The Convention expressly denies establishing any priority between these factors and circumstances, which have to be assessed in an interdependent manner.[59] Among these factors is the 'existing uses' of the waters.[60] This certainly provides an argument in favour of the Egyptian position. Other factors also 'fit in' the Egyptian situation, such as the dependency of the Egyptian population on the waters of the Nile or the existence of alternatives for the other Nile Basin countries; on the other hand, there are also other factors which would support the latters' positions, such as, primarily, development needs. A balancing exercise is unavoidable with consequent curtailing of the claims of all sides.

---

55 The text of Art. 7 is as follows: "1. Watercourse States shall, in utilizing an international watercourse in their territories, take all appropriate measures to prevent the causing of significant harm to other watercourse States. 2. Where significant harm nevertheless is caused to another watercourse State, the States whose use causes such harm shall, in the absence of agreement to such use, take all appropriate measures, having due regard for the provisions of articles 5 and 6, in consultation with the affected State, to eliminate or mitigate such harm and, where appropriate, to discuss the question of compensation." For a critical approach to Art. 7 *see* Lucius Caflisch, Regulation of the Uses of International Watercourses, in Boisson De Chazournes, Laurence; Salman, Salman M. A. (ed), *International Watercourses, Enhancing Cooperation and Managing Conflict*, Proceedings of a World Bank Seminar, 1998, pp. 13-16.

56 Which is considered to reflect the maxim *sic utere tuo ut alienum non laedas.*

57 Which is generally accepted to be a due diligence obligation and not one of result.

58 The text of Art. 6 is as follows: "Factors relevant to equitable and reasonable utilization 1. Utilization of an international watercourse in an equitable and reasonable manner within the meaning of article 5 requires taking into account all relevant factors and circumstances, including: (a) Geographic, hydrographic, hydrological, climatic, ecological and other factors of a natural character; (b) The social and economic needs of the watercourse States concerned; (c) The population dependent on the watercourse in each watercourse State; (d) The effects of the use or uses of the watercourses in one watercourse State on other watercourse States; (e) Existing and potential uses of the watercourse; (f) Conservation, protection, development and economy of use of the water resources of the watercourse and the costs of measures taken to that effect; (g) The availability of alternatives, of comparable value, to a particular planned or existing use. 2. In the application of article 5 or paragraph 1 of this article, watercourse States concerned shall, when the need arises, enter into consultations in a spirit of cooperation. 3. The weight to be given to each factor is to be determined by its importance in comparison with that of other relevant factors. In determining what is a reasonable and equitable use, all relevant factors are to be considered together and a conclusion reached on the basis of the whole."

59 *Ibid., in fine.*

60 *Ibid.*, 6(e). *See also* Chapter 2, Art. V(II)(4) of the 1966 Helsinki Rules, *supra*, fn. 86.

Another international instrument to take into account, as it expresses the most advanced trends in international water law, is the recently globalized 1992 Helsinki Convention on the Protection and Use of Transboundary Watercourses and International Lakes, drawn up in the context of the U.N. Economic Commission for Europe (UNECE Convention).[61] Its provisions on bilateral and multilateral cooperation, on the establishment of joint bodies, on monitoring and assessment, etc. would be very useful once a basic scheme for cooperation has been established.

Other guiding benchmarks must be the existing jurisprudence on relevant issues, particularly the ICJ judgment in the *Gabčikovo-Nagymaros Case*,[62] and its balanced interpretation of the principles applicable in the use of transboundary watercourses.

Of course, all the elements mentioned above already exist, to a great extent, in the CFA and, if a solution is to be found along the lines of the 2015 Declaration, it remains a question why that agreement is not being accepted by the signatories of the Declaration. The answer has to be sought, most probably, in political reasons.

The final, and rather inescapable, conclusion is that, no matter how difficult, cooperation between the Nile Basin states is the only way forward and it is most urgently needed. Developments since 2015 show that, despite recurring setbacks, finding a common understanding is not impossible, and this is already a big stride towards a solution to a hitherto seemingly intractable problem. Hopefully, it would also lead towards a better future for the entire region.

61 *See supra*, pp. 13 *et seq.*
62 *Supra*, fn. 67.

22.2 EUPHRATES AND TIGRIS[63]

22.2.1 *The Rivers and Their Basins*[64]

The Euphrates[65] and the Tigris,[66] the two major watercourses of the Middle East, are well known since antiquity and usually referred to together due to their geographical proximity, common terminus[67] and common connection with the millennial history of the region. The length of Euphrates is 2,786 km,[68] which makes it the longest river in the Middle East.[69] With a length of 1,800 km,[70] Tigris is the second longest river in the same region.[71] The countries riparian to the Euphrates are Turkey, Syria and Iraq. The River and its tributaries drain a basin of about 440,000 km^2, which is shared by Turkey, Syria, Iraq, Jordan and Saudi Arabia.[72]

---

63 Nicolas Bremer, The Regulation of the Non-Navigational Use of the Euphrates and Tigris River System, International Law Regulating the Distribution and Utilisation of the Water of Euphrates and Tigris Illustrated by the Atatürk and Ilisu Dams, Eleven International Publishing, 2017; Aysegul Kibaroglu, Adele Kirschner, Sigrid Mehring, Rüdiger Wolfrum (eds), *Water Law and Cooperation in the Euphrates-Tigris Region: A Comparative and Interdisciplinary Approach*, Martinus Nijhoff, 2013.

64 A contested point between Turkey and the other riparians is whether the Euphrates and Tigris form a single water basin, as Turkey claims, or two separate ones, as claimed by Iraq and Syria. Both positions reflect perceived advantages for their proponents – *i.e.*, in the case of a single basin, Turkey will have more possibilities to develop its projects while, in the opposite case, Syria and Iraq will enjoy more water availability.

65 Arabic: الفرات transliterated as al-Furat; Turkish: Firat. In the West the name 'Euphrates' derives from the Greek «Ευφράτης», which is a Hellenized transliteration of the ancient Persian name Ufratu, which is linked with the Akkadian name Purattu and with other names given to the river by the ancient peoples living in the region.

66 Arabic transliteration: *Dijlah*, meaning 'arrow', a reference to the river's speed. Turkish: *Dicle.* In the West, the name *Tigris* was taken from the Greek *Tίγρης* (coincidentally meaning 'Tiger') itself originating from the ancient Persian word *Tigra* which, again, finds its distant origin in the Sumerian *Idigna*, meaning 'running water'.

67 *See infra*, p. 64.

68 Inventory of Shared Water Resources in Western Asia: UN-ESCWA and BGR (United Nations Economic and Social Commission for Western Asia; Bundesanstalt für Geowissenschaften und Rohstoffe), Chapter I, Beirut, 2013, p. 55.

69 'Middle East' is understood to comprise the countries of Southwestern Asia, including Iran.

70 Inventory of Shared Water Resources in Western Asia (*supra*, fn. 68), Chapter 3, p. 107.

71 The Euphrates flows for 1,230 km in Turkey, 710 km in Syria and 1,060 km in Iraq, while Tigris flows for 400 km in Turkey and, after forming part of the Turkish-Syrian and of the Syrian-Iraqi border, flows for 1,418 km into Iraq (FAO AQUASTAT, 2009).

72 Turkey (28%), Syria 22%, Iraq (47%), Jordan (0,03%) and Saudi Arabia (2,97%) The tributary originating in Saudi Arabia dries up in summer. It is estimated that of the surface water flowing into the Euphrates, 89% is contributed by Turkey and 11% by Syria.

Turkey, Syria, Iraq and Iran are the countries riparian to the Tigris which drains, together with its tributaries, a basin of 221,000 km^2, the largest parts of which lie in Iraq, Turkey and Iran.[73]

22.2.1.1 Trajectories of the Euphrates and the Tigris

Both rivers rise from the mountains of Eastern Anatolia (the Taurus and the Anti-Taurus respectively) in Turkey, between Lake Van and the Black Sea,[74] their sources at a distance of 30 km from each other.[75] Thereafter they diverge, Euphrates following a general southwesterly direction, Tigris flowing directly to the southeast, reaching a distance of 400 km between them at the Turkey-Syria border. In Syria, Euphrates receives its only two tributaries.[76] Now following a southeast direction, it flows through the Syrian plateaus and then enters Iraq.

Tigris forms part of the Turkish-Syrian border for 32 km – without flowing into Syria – and enters Iraq at the tripoint between Iraq, Turkey and Syria.[77] In Iraq, it receives the waters of four main tributaries[78] which mostly drain the Iranian *Zagros mountains*, while in the southwest of Iraq Euphrates flows through the desert.

The land extending between Euphrates to the west and Tigris to the East, and as far South as the Persian Gulf, was called *Mesopotamia* (land between rivers) by the ancient Greeks,[79] a term which today is understood to encompass a much wider area, i.e. most of Iraq, part of southeastern Turkey, eastern Syria and part of western Iran.[80]

The two rivers start converging after their entry into Iraq, gradually almost closing a triangle, the *Al-Jazeera* (the island in Arabic) near Baghdad. At this point, the distance between the two rivers is about 50 km, which had allowed connecting them by five navigable canals already in the *Sassanid* period (third century A.D.).[81]

---

73 56,1% lies in Iraq, 24,5% in Turkey, 19% in Iran and 0,4% in Syria. Turkey contributes 51% of the Tigris water flow, Iraq 39% and Iran 10% (Inventory of Shared Water Resources in Western Asia, op. cit., Chapter I on the Euphrates, p. 49, and Chapter 3 on the Tigris, p. 101).

74 The *Murat* and the *Karasu Rivers* which rise in the Armenian highlands of Eastern Anatolia are the headwaters of the Euphrates. Tigris rises from *Lake Hazar*, a rift lake in the Anti-Taurus Mountains and receives the water of many small tributaries in Turkey.

75 Aysegul Kibaroglu and Waltina Scheumann, Euphrates-Tigris Rivers System: Political Rapprochement and Transboundary Water Cooperation (online version), 2013, p. 278.

76 The *Balikh* and the *Khabur* rivers, both rising in Turkey.

77 Tigris also defines the Iraqi-Syrian border for 5 km.

78 The *Greater Zab* originating in Turkey, the *Lesser Zab* originating in Iran, the *Uzaym* originating in Iraq, and the *Diyala* originating in Iran.

79 Μεσοποταμία in Greek.

80 Reference to the historical importance of this area is made in the 'Historical Notes', *infra*, pp. 59-60.

81 There is still an ancient waterway, Gharraf Canal, also known as Shaṭṭ al-Ghar or the Hai River, which links the Tigris at Al-Kut with the Euphrates east of Nasiriya.

Arriving at the southern alluvial plain[82] of Iraq, both rivers form numerous channels creating an extensive marshland, which used to cover 15,000-20,000 km^2 and to which we will specifically refer below.[83]

Euphrates and Tigris finally join at the town of *Al-Qurnah*, north of *Basra*, forming the *Shatt al-Arab*[84] waterway in the southeastern corner of Iraq, marking part of the border with Iran. However, most of *Shatt al-Arab's* flow derives neither from Euphrates nor from Tigris which by now have been depleted by irrigation and evaporation, but from the *Karun*, the longest river in Iran, which enters *Shatt al-Arab* at *Khorramshahr*. The *Shatt al-Arab* flows for 190 km before it empties into the Persian Gulf. A Tigris-Euphrates confluence channel also defines a part of the Kuwaiti-Iraqi border.[85]

22.2.1.2 Historical and Environmental Notes

Mesopotamia, the region which was geographically and historically defined by the Euphrates and the Tigris Rivers, has been the birthplace of the Akkadians, Sumerians, Babylonians and Assyrians. The cultures of these peoples shaped the world civilization from the beginning of recorded history (circa the thirtieth century B.C.)[86] until the fall of Babylon in 539 B.C. to the Persian *King Cyrus* and the establishment of the *Achaemenid* empire. Vestiges of the ancient settlements, cities and cultures which flourished in the region are found all over the alluvial plain together with the remnants of abandoned ancient canal systems, as irrigation was practiced in Mesopotamia since 7000 B.C.

Alexander the Great defeated the *Achaemenids* in 333 B.C. and established his own empire. After his death at Babylon in 323 B.C., Mesopotamia became part of the Hellenistic Seleucid Kingdom, i.e. one of the kingdoms formed after the death of Alexander in the whole of today's Middle East and beyond.

The energetic damming of both rivers – which will be examined in more detail below – by all riparian countries and particularly by the first upper riparian, Turkey, has greatly affected the water quantity of both rivers. It is indicative in this respect that the mean annual discharge of the Euphrates before such damming was 30 BCM, while after dam-

82 The alluvial plain begins north of Baghdad and extends to the Persian Gulf.

83 Page 60.

84 Arabic: شطّ العرب, meaning 'Stream of the Arabs'.

85 *Khorr Abdullah*, which has been a long-standing source of friction between the two countries. The matter was finally settled by agreement in 2013.

86 Suffice it to mention the *Code of Hammurabi* of 1790 BC, which was the first legal text in history to regulate irrigation rights.

ming it has dropped to 25 BCM.[87, 88] Climate change and repeated droughts have further exacerbated the negative effect of upstream dam construction on the river's water quantity.[89]

Tigris has suffered an even more dramatic decrease in discharge in the last decades, due to the same reasons as in the case of Euphrates, its mean flow level standing at 13.9 BCM at *Kut* in southern Iraq for the period 1985-2005 down from 32 BCM for the period 1931-1973.[90]

The 'Mesopotamian Marshes'

These marshes (*Al-Ahwar*) are a major feature in the flow of the Tigris and Euphrates which are the natural creators of these wetlands, the largest in the Middle East. The Marshes constitute a valuable aquatic ecosystem which provides habitat to a rich wildlife and is home to thousands of 'Marsh Arabs'[91] (*the Ma'adan*).[92] It is also the place of historical monuments dating 5,000 years.[93] Since the 1970s, however, the Marshes have suffered extensive damage due to dam construction upstream, oil exploration, drainage for agriculture and repeated droughts. The 'coup de grâce' was, however, delivered in 1994 during the Iran-Iraq war, when the *Saddam Hussein* regime organized their drainage to facilitate the conduct of his military activities and secure control over the native Shi'a Marsh Arabs. This was done mainly by building canals and dams to reroute the waters of Tigris and Euphrates so that they would go around the marshes instead of

87 *Inventory of Shared Water Resources in Western Asia, op. cit.,* Chapter I, p. 49. As an example, the mean annual flow volume of Euphrates at *Jarablus,* on the Syrian side of the Syrian-Turkish border, has been approximately 22.8 BCM between 1990 and 2010. This represents a sharp decrease since the period 1938-1973, when the mean annual flow at the same location was 30 BCM *(Ibid.,* p. 58).

88 According to M. Nouar Shamout with Glada Lahn, The Euphrates in Crisis: Channels of Cooperation for a Threatened River; Energy, Environment and Resources, Research Paper, April 2015, Chatham House (www.chatamhouse.org), "since Turkish and Syrian dams came into operation in the 1970s... the flow into Iraq has dropped from 700 m^3/s to the current level of 260 m^3/s" (p. 19);

89 *Inventory of Shared Water Resources in Western Asia, op. cit.,* pp. 55-59. On climate change effects in particular, *see* E. Bou-Zeid and M. El-Fadel, Climate Change and Water Resources in Lebanon and the Middle East, Journal of water resources planning and management, September/October 2002/355.

90 *Ibid.,* Chapter 3, p. 110. According to *Encyclopaedia Britannica,* the mean annual discharge of the Tigris, before the construction of modern dams, was estimated at 1,240m^3/s, this estimate being double that calculated for the Euphrates.

91 On the traditional way of life of the Marsh Arabs, *see* Wilfred Thesiger, The Marsh Arabs, 1964.

92 Arabic: معدان. The population of the Marsh Arabs counted half a million in the 1950s but shrank to about 20,000 after the draining of the marshes in the 1980s and 1990s. Part of the population has been, however, returning since 2003.

93 On 17 July 2016 UNESCO declared the Marshes a world heritage site. The site consists of four natural and three cultural components, namely the *Huwaizah, East and West Hammar* and *Central Marshes,* together with the archaeological sites of *Ur, Uruk* and *Eridu.* According to UNESCO, the cities of *Uruk* and *Ur* and the *Tell Eridu* archaeological site form part of the remains of the Sumerian cities and settlements that developed in southern between the 4th and the 3rd millennium BC. UNESCO also observes that the *Ahwar* of southern Iraq – also known as the Iraqi marshlands – are unique, as one of the world's largest inland delta systems, in an extremely hot and arid environment.

entering them. Burning the reeds which grew in abundance in the marshlands was another method used to dry them up. Since 2003, the drainage has stopped and, with action taken by Iraqi authorities, UNEP, UNESCO and other actors, the situation in the marshes of Mesopotamia has been reversed to a considerable degree but not entirely so, due to the negative effect of upstream dams, an effect which can only, it seems, intensify in the future.

Damming the Rivers

Iraq was the first country to construct works relating to the waters of the two rivers.[94] The earliest was the *Al Hindiya Dam* on the Euphrates which was constructed in 1914 for flood control and irrigation purposes. The *Ramadi-Habbaniya Dam*, also on the Euphrates, was constructed in 1951 and served the same purposes. In the 1960s, Iraq began constructing the *Third (or Saddam) River*, a 565km long canal to irrigate the land between the Euphrates and the Tigris,[95] which was completed in 1992. Other canals had also been built in the late 1970s, mainly to control the floods of the Tigris through diverting excess water to artificial *Lake Tharthar* to be discharged into Euphrates in dry season. However, the largest dam in Iraq is the *Mosul Dam*, near the city of Mosul, which impounds the Tigris.[96] The Dam with its reservoir was completed in 1986 and provides hydroelectricity and irrigation to the region of Mosul in Northern Iraq.[97] The second largest Iraqi dam is the *Haditha Dam* or *Qadisiya Dam*, built on the Euphrates and completed, with its reservoir, *Qadisiya Lake*, in 1985. The Dam provides hydropower, flow control and irrigation to the region near the city of *Haditha*. In Syria, the *Tabqa or Euphrates Dam* with its reservoir, *Lake Assad*, was completed in 1973 and is used for irrigation. The *Ba'ath Dam*, of lesser capacity than the *Tabqa Dam*, was completed in 1986. The *Tishreen* Dam, which was completed in 1999, is the third Syrian dam on the Euphrates and was mainly designed for hydropower production. On its part, Turkey completed the *Keban Dam*, its first dam on the Euphrates, in 1973. The *Keban Dam* was designed for purposes of irrigation and the production of hydropower and was followed by the construction of the hydropower-producing *Karakaya Dam*, which was completed in 1987. The latter has been included in Turkey's very ambitious Southeastern

---

94 In a pattern similar to that of the Nile whereby downstream countries are usually the first to develop infrastructure to exploit or regulate the waters of transboundary rivers on their territory (*see supra*, pp. 49-50).

95 The canal was designed to reclaim saline water, as salinization represents a major problem in the lower Euphrates basin. The salinization of *Shatt al-Arab* in particular is due to its weakened flow which allows seawater from the Gulf to enter the river at high tide.

96 The *Mosul Dam* on the Tigris has a height of 113 m, its length is 3,400 m and the capacity of its reservoir is of 12,500 BCM.

97 There had been reports, confirmed by engineers involved in the *Mosul Dam* construction, that the Dam was in danger of collapsing due to structural problems and damage suffered during its takeover by ISIS forces. If so, one million people might have been killed (*The Guardian*, "Mosul Dam engineers warn it could fail at any time, killing 1m people," 2 March 2016, www.theguardian.com › World › Iraq).

Anatolia Project (GAP),[98] the purpose of which is to construct twenty-two dams and nineteen hydropower plants on the Tigris and Euphrates rivers and their tributaries for purposes of irrigation and production of hydroelectric energy.[99] The centrepiece of GAP is the *Atatürk Dam*, which is impounding the Euphrates and is among the biggest dams in the world.[100]

Another Turkish dam within the GAP project is the *Ilisu Dam* on the Tigris, planned to become operational in 2019.[101] The dam will be used for irrigation, power production and flood control.

Most of the Turkish dams have caused considerable controversy between Turkey and the lower riparians, Syria and Iraq, particularly those of *Keban, Atatürk* and *Ilisu.*[102] The same is true of the dams built by Syria, which often provoked the strong reaction of Iraq.

Iran also constructed dams on tributaries of Tigris originating on Iranian territory, such as the *Karun* and the *Karkeh* rivers which enter Iraq.

In all, more than thirty dams and barrages have been built on the Euphrates and about half as many on the Tigris in the last decades, while more are planned to be built, although the military conflict in Syria and Iraq has postponed the realization of many among them.

The construction of these projects, invariably undertaken without prior consultations and any coordination between riparians, promoted intensive agricultural irrigation and had grave repercussions on the available water quantity. The quality of the waters has also suffered from the use of pesticides, waste discharge and industrial uses.

22.2.2 Legal Situation

The earliest attempt to regulate transboundary waters in the Euphrates and Tigris Basin dates back to 1920 when the then colonial powers in the region, France (on behalf of Syria) and Britain (on behalf of Iraq), concluded an Agreement[103] which, *inter alia*, established a coordination committee to examine the utilization of the Euphrates and Tigris waters.

98 Acronym for 'Güneydoğu Anadolu Projesi'.

99 The cost is estimated at 21 billion dollars. The intention was for GAP to have been completed by 2023 but the completion date has been postponed to 2047 due to financial and other reasons.

100 The *Atatürk Dam* is 169m high, 1,819m long and with a capacity of 48,700 BCM.

101 The *Ilisu Dam* will be 135m high, 1,820m long and will have a capacity of 43,8000 BCM.

102 Apart from reactions of the lower riparians there have also been domestic complaints because the Dam would flood, among dozens of villages, also the ancient city of *Hasankeyf*, which is of particular importance to the Kurdish people who live in this part of Turkey.

103 Franco-British Convention on Certain Points connected with the Mandates for Syria, the Lebanon, Palestine and Mesopotamia, 1920, LNTS Vol. 22 No 564.

In 1921, France and Turkey concluded the Ankara Treaty[104] (*Traité d' Ankara*) in which there was provision for the rights of riparian states to use transboundary waters, and for the right of the city of Aleppo to use water from the Euphrates.

The 1923 Lausanne Peace Treaty (*Traité de Paix de Lausanne*) which was concluded between the Allies in World War I and Turkey and which fixed the borders of modern Turkey after the collapse of the Ottoman Empire, set out in its Article 109 the rule that, in the case of rivers which became transboundary thereafter, riparian states constructing works and engaging in other activities on their waters, shall respect, by way of agreement, the interests and acquired rights of the other states. If an agreement on these matters would not be possible, an arbitration procedure would ('shall') be resorted to.[105] The mandatory language used in the text leaves no doubt that its intention is to secure the application of these provisions.

In 1926, France (on behalf of Syria) and Turkey concluded the Convention of Friendship and Good Neighbourly Relations, imposing on the parties the obligation to coordinate their plans regarding the use of the Euphrates waters.

In 1930, a Final Protocol, between Turkey and France, established by the Commission on the delimitation of the Turkish-Syrian Frontier, provides in connection with the Tigris that the *thalweg* principle is applicable and that all issues concerning that river should be determined on the basis of complete equality.

In 1946, Turkey and Iraq concluded an 'Agreement of Friendship and Neighbourly Relations', with an annexed Protocol 'Relative to the Regulation of the Waters of the Tigris and Euphrates and their Tributaries'. The two countries agreed to have experts collaborate, share related data and consult with each other for the selection of sites to build dams or observation stations, mainly in order to regulate the flow of the rivers and avoid the risk of floods. Irrigation and electricity production were additional goals. Furthermore, Turkey undertook to notify Iraq of any plans to construct works on the rivers or their tributaries which might impact on Iraq, so that the plans might be adapted after agreement. However, none of this seems to have been applied in practice.

In the course of the 1960s and the 1970s several meetings were held, and a number of instruments agreed on either bilaterally or trilaterally between the countries sharing the two rivers. However, they mostly either came to no tangible result, or were simply not applied.

---

104 Also known as Angora Treaty or Franklin-Bouillon Agreement (Angora was an older name for Ankara). It was signed on 20 October 1921 between France and the Grand National Assembly of Turkey and ended the war between France and Turkey.

105 The article reads as follows: "In default of any provisions to the contrary, when as the result of the fixing of a new frontier the hydraulic system (canalization, inundation, irrigation, drainage or similar matters) in a State is dependent on works executed within the territory of another State, or when use is made on the territory of a State, in virtue of pre-war usage, of water or hydraulic power, the source of which is on the territory of another State, an agreement shall be made between the States concerned to safeguard the interests and rights acquired by each of them. Failing an agreement, the matter shall be regulated by arbitration."

In 1980, Turkey and Iraq signed a Protocol establishing a Joint Technical Committee (JTC) on Regional Waters, joined by Syria in 1983. This group stopped its functions after 1993 without any progress mainly because of disagreement over Turkey's GAP and the filling of the Atatürk Dam.

In 1987, after various proposals which did not come to fruition, Turkey pledged in a Protocol on Economic Cooperation with Syria (interim agreement) that she would release an average of 500 m^3/s through the Euphrates into Syria.

In 1989, Syria and Iraq came to an agreement in Joint Minutes to share the waters of the Euphrates, according to which Syria would keep 42% of the Euphrates waters inflowing from Turkey, while Iraq would have the remaining 58%.

During the 1990s, numerous meetings and talks, both bilateral and trilateral, were held, but they invariably failed to produce results.[106]

In 2001, a Joint Communiqué was issued by the Syrian General Organization for Land Development (GOLD) – part of the Syrian Ministry of Irrigation – and the Turkish GAP RDA (Regional Development Administration) to support training and technology exchange on water issues.

In 2002, following a bilateral agreement between Syria and Iraq, a Syrian pump station was installed on the Tigris River for irrigation purposes. The agreement specified the area of the project and the volume of withdrawal.

In 2007, Turkey, Syria and Iraq decided that the periodic meetings of the JTC, which had been suspended in 1993, would be resumed. A series of such meetings were held in 2007, 2008 and 2009. In that context, it was decided that data would be shared concerning meteorological patterns and the water quality of both rivers.

In 2008, Turkey, Syria and Iraq decided to cooperate on water issues by establishing a water institute consisting of water experts from each country.[107]

Also in 2008, Turkey and Iraq signed a Joint Political Declaration on the Establishment of the High-Level Strategic Cooperation Council which provided for meetings between relevant ministries to discuss transboundary water issues.

In 2009, Turkey and Syria agreed to set up a similar mechanism of strategic cooperation.

In the same year, one MoU, among forty-eight signed between Turkey and Iraq, focused on the sharing of hydrological and meteorological information and the exchange of knowledge on related issues.

In 2009 also, Turkey and Syria signed, at the first meeting of the High-Level Strategic Cooperation Council, fifty MoUs, four of which concerned regional waters: They dealt

106 As observed by writers on this issue, there is scarcity of information concerning meetings and their results or about instruments produced in all the time-periods referred to here. For this reason there are sometimes variations in dates and data given in different writings.

107 Each riparian has appointed fifteen water engineers to conduct studies on water use efficiency and better water management, to map water resources in the region, exchange information and know-how and produce related studies and reports (A. Kibaroglu and W. Scheumann, *op. cit.*, p. 294).

with cooperation on shared waters, water quality, the development of shared water-pumping stations[108] and dams, and on joint water policy.

In the same year 2009, Turkey, Syria and Iraq decided to cooperate on water training programs and to monitor and exchange information related to climate change and drought conditions in the three countries. They also decided to modernize existing water flow gauging stations and build new ones.[109]

Since then, the onset of the civil war in Syria and the occupation of large swathes of Syrian and Iraqi territory by ISIS put an end to attempts to discuss or resolve transboundary water issues, although some information regarding such talks between Iraq and Turkey has emerged recently (in 2019).

22.2.3 Problems and Disputes

Most of the regions Tigris and Euphrates are crossing downstream of Turkey are hot, semi-arid and arid, while vast areas are plain desert. The importance of water for all uses, i.e. household use, food production and industrial use including electricity generation, cannot therefore be overestimated. Iraq, as the lowest riparian to both rivers, is particularly vulnerable, and constantly in fear that the upper riparians might exhaust most of the water before it reaches Iraqi territory. Syria finds itself in a similar position with regard to Turkey. Moreover, population increase, although not as steep as in other parts of the world, is certain to put further pressure on the need for freshwater resources. Indeed, Iraq's population is expected to almost double by 2030[110] and the same was expected for Syria, but the negative effect of the war on its population in the last years will certainly change predictions for the country.[111]

Under these circumstances, water apportionment and use has been a *par excellence* point of friction between Iraq, Turkey and Syria since the 1970s when Turkey started implementing its GAP project. It was indeed estimated that the completed project would result in Syria losing up to 40% of the water it receives from Euphrates, and Iraq up to 90%.

---

108 Thus, one MoU concerned the establishment of a pumping station on Syrian territory for water withdrawal from the Tigris.

109 A. Kibaroglu and W. Scheumann, *op. cit.* p. 295.

110 According to U.N. statistics, it will increase from 36,423 in 2015 to 54,071 in 2030. Syria will go from 18,502 million to 28, 647 million. Turkey's population is expected to increase considerably less, *i.e.*, from today's 78, 666 million 241 to 87,717 million (UN Department of Economic and Social Affairs, Population Division – 2015). World Population Prospects: The 2015 Revision, Key Findings and Advance Tables, Working Paper No. ESA/P/WP., pp. 20, 22).

111 According to UNHCR data (updated up to 15 March 2018), over 6,500,000 Syrians had fled their country since 2011 (statistics available at: https://data2.unhcr.org/en/situations/syria#_ga=2.84436633.1647787810.1521481331-1729987425.1519756184, last accessed 19 March 2018).

The construction of the Atatürk Dam in particular has been seen as a hostile act by the downstream countries, especially because Turkey shut off without notification the river's flow for a month when filling the dam. Syria and Iraq accused Turkey of causing them serious harm and Iraq even threatened to bomb the Turkish dams on the Euphrates. The situation returned to normality after the dam became operational, but the mistrust remained.

In such a situation, it would be natural to expect that efforts would be made to resolve the problems primarily between Turkey and its lower riparians as well as between the lower riparians themselves. There have, indeed, been many such efforts over the years; however, they either failed to produce results or, in the rare cases that they did, those results were either not applied or left to wither away. As has already been observed by many writers, an overarching explanation is the deep mistrust which has set in in the relations between these three countries.[112] This, in turn, is due to a number of factors, most important among which are:

a. The political relations between these countries have not been conducive to a settlement during the whole or most of the period in which the above-mentioned efforts were unfolding. This, for instance, was the case in the 1960s and 1970s when various initiatives and negotiations between Syria and Iraq on water issues failed due to the strained political climate created by the severe antagonism between the two branches of the *Ba'ath Party* which was ruling in both countries, despite periods of attempted rapprochement. As a result, it was only in 1983 that it became possible for all three countries to agree on the establishment of a technical committee for cooperation on water issues. The committee existed until the breakdown of relations with Turkey over the Atatürk Dam filling in 1990.
b. Accusations and threats have been usual, as has been the upholding of theories and positions which are widely apart. Thus, Turkey has on many occasions expressed her support for the theory of 'absolute territorial sovereignty', while the theory of 'acquired rights' has occasionally been upheld by Iraq. Both positions caused the strong reaction of the other two countries. Such diametrically opposing views are obviously not conducive to a meaningful dialogue and tend to generate even more mistrust within a wider climate which is already laden with mutual grievances and suspicions.
c. The construction of dams and their filling in particular, as already seen in the case of the *Atatürk Dam*, has been a major reason for friction. In the 1970s, there had been severe tensions between Iraq and Syria due to the construction of dams by Syria, i.e. the *Tabqa Dam* and its reservoir, *Lake Assad*, completed in 1973 and filled in 1975. The filling of *Lake Assad* caused a decrease of 25% in the quantity of the water flowing into Iraq, causing great anxiety there. The two countries found themselves on the

112 *See, e.g.*, Ali Akanda, Sarah Freeman, and Maria Placht, The Tigris-Euphrates River Basin: Mediating a Path Towards Regional Water Stability in *Al-Nakhlah, The Fletcher School Journal for issues related to Southwest Asia and Islamic Civilization*, Spring 2007, pp. 1-4.

brink of war, which was finally averted with the mediation of the then Soviet Union and Saudi Arabia. In the end, Syria agreed to release more water from the dam to Iraq. Although the terms of the agreement have not been made public, it has been unofficially known that Syria agreed to keep 40% of the river's water, leaving the remainder for Iraq. In recent years, a new crisis broke out with the construction of another GAP project, the *Ilisu Dam* on the Tigris which, again, causes major concerns to Iraq, adding another source of friction with Turkey.

d. Unilateral initiatives regarding water quantities were undertaken by Turkey several times, mostly in response to tense situations, in an effort of appeasement. Some bilateral agreements were also entered into, but, as a rule, did not take into account the third country concerned. Indeed, trilateral agreements on these issues constitute a rarity, a fact which reveals again the lack of confidence to one of the co-riparians each time – and the consequent weakness of the bilateral agreement(s) concluded.
e. Disputes became particularly acute in times of drought (e.g. in the last decade in 2008 and in 2015-2016). Thus, the already tense situation between Turkey and Syria became even more so during the 2008 drought which hit all the countries in the region. Iraq was also severely affected, Turkey conceding, following negotiations, to supply Iraq with more water at different times. Finally, in 2009, it became possible to reach some understanding between all three countries concerning the strengthening of communication between them and the development of joint stations to monitor the water flow.
f. Water has been often used as a political tool, inevitably creating another reason for mistrust. Thus, it has been suggested that Turkey used water as a political tool in 1991, when water flow in the Euphrates dropped from 500 m^3/s to 150–180 m^3/s. This was interpreted as the contribution of Turkey to the international political pressure on Iraq following the latter's invasion in and occupation of Kuwait. The Turkish government subsequently increased the flow, but its move had already been registered as an intrusion of politics in transboundary water management. Furthermore, in many cases Turkish 'concessions' in river flows to either Iraq or Syria were made in exchange for political moves by them, requiring them, in particular, to curb the Kurdish militant activity in their respective Kurdish border regions with Turkey.

Finally, there are some 'legal' points of friction between Turkey and Syria/Iraq. One of them concerns the question whether there is a single basin for both, Euphrates and Tigris (Turkish position) or two separate ones (Syrian and Iraqi position) each one believing its own position to be more advantageous to them as regards water usage and development.[113] Another point relates to whether the rivers are transboundary (Turkish position) or international (Syrian and Iraqi position). Turkey treats as 'international' rivers

113 *See supra*, 22.2.4, fn. 64.

only those which constitute international boundaries – an interpretation which does not find support either in international customary or in treaty law.[114] In essence, Turkey is claiming that Euphrates and Tigris on its territory are purely national watercourses and therefore subject to Turkish jurisdiction alone, an untenable position under contemporary international law.

22.2.4 *Armed Conflicts and Their Effects*

Successive wars in Iraq, i.e. the Iran-Iraq War in the 1980s, the Gulf War (1990-1991) and the subsequent trade embargo imposed on the country during the 1990s as well as the Iraq war (2003-2011), took a severe toll on its water infrastructure while major projects of irrigation, drainage and desalination were postponed.

Finally, the ISIS[115] occupation of important segments of Northern and Central Iraq has exacerbated the water situation in the country to an unprecedented degree. In 2013 and 2014, ISIS took control of many of the water structures (used for storage, flood control and flow regulation) on the Euphrates in both Syria and Iraq. In 2014, it captured the biggest dam in Iraq, the *Mosul Dam*. The dam was, however, recaptured a few days later by the U.S. and Kurdish forces, thus averting the possibility of ISIS releasing the waters of the dam to catastrophic result. ISIS also held the *Falluja regulator* since 2014. During the period of their control, the river flow was stopped, depriving southern Iraqi regions of water, while upstream areas were flooded. Falluja was recaptured by Iraqi forces in 2016. ISIS also held the *Haditha Dam* in Iraq until late 2014 and parts of its western side until 2016.

A worse – and much more complicated – situation prevails now (at the time of writing) in Syria, as the war goes on despite the (almost complete) defeat of ISIS. Although there cannot be an accurate assessment of the situation at this stage, it seems that a large part of the country's water infrastructure has been destroyed or damaged. ISIS controlled the *Tabqa Dam*, the largest in Syria, from early 2013 to mid-2017. During that time, the water flow behind the dam suffered a dramatic reduction, as a result of which five million Syrians were left with no access to safe water in the areas of Aleppo and partly Raqqa.[116] There were also threats from ISIS that, if under attack, they would destroy the dam by explosives, which would release a flood wave of 11 million m^3 of water, causing the

114 This means that for Turkey, Tigris and Euphrates are mere transboundary rivers under unrestricted Turkish sovereignty while on its territory, a thesis which reflects the '*Harmon doctrine*' (*supra*, p. 18). *See* Ali Akanda, Sarah Freeman, and Maria Placht, *supra, loc. cit.*, p. 2.

115 Islamic State (IS) or Islamic State of Iraq and Syria (ISIS) or Islamic State of Iraq and the Levant (ISIL) or Daesh (transliteration of the acronym داعش meaning 'Islamic State of Iraq and the Levant' (Arabic: الدولة الإسلامية في العراق والشام).

116 M. Nouar Shamout with Glada Lahn, *op. cit.*, p. 24.

destruction of the cities in its course, and putting the lives of three million people in Syria and Iraq in jeopardy. Already there are efforts under way to repair the dam.

22.2.5 International Law and the Way Forward

It is clear that so far Turkey has taken full advantage of her dominant geographical position in the region to exploit the water resources rising on her territory to the maximum degree. The lower riparians can, in essence, only hope that Turkey, which in recent years had also enjoyed spectacular economic development, will not deprive them of or further restrict their water security.

Furthermore, in sharp contrast to Turkey, they both have been the theatre of bloody international armed conflicts and relentless civil strife, while parts of their territory and water infrastructure has fallen in the hands of ISIS, all circumstances with consequences of catastrophic proportions on water availability and quality.

However, even before the onset of this extreme situation in Syria and Iraq, there was never any coordination and any particular attention paid to sustainability of the water practices of all these countries in connection with their transboundary waters, for various reasons which were briefly explored above.

At the same time, the legal situation on a regional level, with the exception of the 1923 Lausanne Peace Treaty and, perhaps, some more recent instruments or understandings (2009), consists of little more than a few agreements of declaratory rather than substantive character, which do not give rise to legally binding obligations. Even so, however, they seem to have been only erratically, if at all, taken into account. Turkey, which is the key player in water-related matters in the region, has consistently preferred to act unilaterally in providing certain assurances and benefits to the lower riparians rather than be legally bound by agreements imposing specific, long-lasting obligations. Furthermore, the political character of exchanges, which are known to have been sought by Turkey so that she might proceed to a relaxation of the limitations to water quantities provided to lower riparians, has not contributed to the creation of a better climate between the riparian countries.

Concerning participation in universal water Conventions, Turkey is not a party to the 1997 Watercourses Convention[117] nor to the 1992 Water Convention, which means that any legal obligations in its regard cannot derive but from customary international law. As far as the latter is concerned, it is true that such law has made big strides in the last years as it has already been recognized to include certain basic principles applicable to transboundary watercourses. These are the principle of equitable and reasonable utilization,

117 The Convention entered into force on 17 August 2014. Turkey was one of the three countries which voted against the adoption of the Convention at the Conference in 1997 (G.A. Res. 51/229, at 1, U.N. Doc. AJRES/51/206 (21 May 1997).

the no-harm rule and the overarching principle of cooperation. The strict application of these principles would certainly provide a viable and balanced framework for cooperation. As disagreements, would, however, be very likely to arise, given the bitter experiences of the past, a third-party settlement procedure could prove very useful. It is at this point that the – always applicable – Lausanne Peace Treaty can provide a solution, by establishing the obligation, in its Article 109, to resort to arbitration in the case of dispute. Yet again, there should, however, be a minimum degree of political will – which has not existed up to now – to make use of this procedure, as required by the Treaty, which would produce a legally binding outcome for all.

If this has been an unfortunate state of affairs in the past, the present circumstances of war and extreme violence dictate other priorities, therefore not allowing for much optimism that a sustainable solution on this matter, which remains of vital importance for the peoples of the region, could be found along the lines referred to above or in any other way in the near future. In view of this situation, a short-term solution may be sought in small-scale and step-by-step confidence-building measures and arrangements, as suggested by experts,[118] when of course, the drums of war have been silenced and a degree of normality has been restored.

118 M. Nouar Shamout with Glada Lahn, *op. cit.*, pp. 29-30.

23 Other Water Issues

23.1 Floods

Flooding is the commonest of hazards connected with rivers, the relevance of which under international water law appears where such hazard has a transboundary effect.[1] Floods may be caused by natural phenomena such as heavy or torrential rainfall in the river basin or snowmelts or other natural events.[2] Man-made floods, on the other hand, may, for instance, be caused by dam failure which is due to the poor quality of the construction or the maintenance of the dam. A combination of these factors may also cause or aggravate a flood.

In spite of its common occurrence and the fact that a number of bilateral and basin agreements contain relevant rules,[3] until recently and apart from the seminal codification work of the International Law Association (ILA) embodied in the New York Rules on Flood Control of 1972, as updated by the ILA 2004 Berlin Rules on water resources – both soft law instruments – the matter had not attracted the attention of the international legal community as much as it should have, in either a regional, subregional or – even less so – global context.[4]

This despite the fact that the appearances of the flood phenomenon have multiplied in the last decades and its consequences have become more and more catastrophic due to climate change and the urbanization of floodplains.

Indeed, most multilateral treaties on transboundary waters, including the two universal ones, although considering floods as one of the instances where prevention, control and mitigation should be exercised and cooperation of the riparians must be activated, fail to refer to any specific action needed to confront them.[5]

---

1 On the issue of floods under international water law *see* Alexandros Kolliopoulos, The UNECE Model Provisions on transboundary flood management in The UNECE Convention on the Protection and Use of Transboundary Watercourses and International Lakes, by Attila Tanzi, Owen McIntyre, Alexandros Kolliopoulos, Alistair Rieu-Klarke and Remy Kinna (eds), Brill/Nijhoff, 2015, pp. 367-378.

2 According to the ECE Guidelines (*see infra*, p. 74) "floods are climatological phenomena influenced by the geology, geomorphology, relief, soil, and vegetation conditions. Meteorological and hydrological processes can be fast or slow and can produce flash floods or more predictable slow-developing floods, also called riverine floods." According to the relevant EU Directive (*see infra* p. 75), "'flood' means the temporary covering by water of land not normally covered by water. This shall include floods from rivers, mountain torrents, Mediterranean ephemeral water courses, and floods from the sea in coastal areas, and may exclude floods from sewerage systems."

3 Alexandros Kolliopoulos, *loc. cit.*, p. 368, fn. 7.

4 Alistair Rieu-Clarke, A Survey of International Law relating to Flood Management: Existing practices and future prospects (2008) 48 Natural Resources Journal 649, 671 fn. 110.

5 In the 1997 Watercourses Convention *see* Arts. 27 (Prevention and Mitigation of Harmful Conditions) and 28 (Emergency situations) and in the 1992 Water Convention Art. 11 (Joint Monitoring and Assessment).

Considerable progress was, however, achieved in 2000 with the adoption, by the UNECE, of a set of non-binding 'Guidelines on Sustainable Flood Prevention'. Building on these Guidelines, the ECE adopted in 2006 a number of Model Provisions on Sustainable Flood Management,[6] accompanied by very useful Commentaries. Since 2007, there is also Directive 2007/60 'on the Assessment and Management of Flood Risks' which is binding on EU member states.[7] The legal status of these two instruments is obviously different, and there is also a degree of differentiation in focus between them to the extent that the Directive puts emphasis on long-term rather than short-term flood management and emergency response, which, by contrast, is the focus of the Model Provisions.[8] There is, however, no substantive incompatibility between them.

The Model Provisions cover both, natural and man-made floods, and embody all the basic principles of international water law, as expressed particularly by the Helsinki Convention to which the Model Provisions are 'attached', i.e. the no-harm rule, the principle of reasonable and equitable utilization and the principle of cooperation.[9] Thus, to comply with the no-harm rule, a state must not only prevent, control and mitigate the transboundary impact of a flood event[10] but also avoid taking measures which might transfer the risk of flood[11] to another state.[12] This is in conformity with the principle of reasonable and equitable utilization, since it would certainly be inequitable if, by alleviating the flood on its own territory, a riparian state caused flooding to another riparian, a situation which is nonetheless far from uncommon.

Flood action plans are being put forward as long-term strategy by the Model Provisions[13] and by the EU Directive 2007/60.[14] The Directive refers to joint or coordinated flood management risk plans in association with the river basin management plans provided for by EU Water Framework Directive 2000/60. Whether under the Directive or the

6 According to its drafters, the Model Provisions "are meant to help States in developing either a general bilateral or multilateral normative instrument on transboundary water issues or a flood specific one among Riparian States, in order to address transboundary flood prevention, protection and mitigation and enhance preparedness thereto. The Model Provisions may need to be adapted by the Riparian States according to their specific needs. On the other hand, States may adopt further provisions dealing with these matters in more detail, or opt for more stringent measures such as those contained in Part III of the United Nations Convention on the Law of the Non-Navigational Uses of International Watercourses... and in the UNECE 1992 Convention on the Protection and Use of Transboundary Watercourses and International Lakes...."

7 Directive 2007/60/EC of the European Parliament and of the Council of 23 October 2007 on the assessment and management of flood risks [2007] OJ L 288/27.

8 Alexandros Kolliopoulos, *loc. cit.*, p. 369.

9 Model Provision 5.

10 Model Provision 1 (1).

11 According to Model Provision 1(1), second sentence: "Flood risks are the probability of flood occurrence combined with its possible adverse impact." According to Directive 2007/60, Art. 2(2) "'Flood risk' means the combination of the probability of a flood event and of the potential adverse consequences for human health, the environment, cultural heritage and economic activity associated with a flood event."

12 Model Provision 1(2).

13 Model Provision 2, point c.

14 Art. 9.

Model Provisions, there is no doubt that transboundary cooperation, which is of paramount importance on flood issues, would be best implemented at the basin level.

For emergencies, an early warning system is envisaged in Article 7(3) of the EU Directive 2007/60 as part of a flood risk management plan, while under UNECE Model Provision 3, each riparian is obliged to provide information about any critical situation which is likely to cause flooding in the territory of another riparian state.

Finally, consultations must be held between riparians for every project which might cause either on its own or when accumulated with other existing projects or activities, a significant change in the flow or other characteristics of the watercourse or of the alluvial areas, which is likely to increase flood risk.[15]

It is clear that in connection with floods, just as with all issues of transboundary waters, cooperation between riparians is of paramount importance, a principle which forms the basis of the majority of measures envisaged in relevant texts, such as the ECE Model Provisions,[16] the EU Directive,[17] the 1997 Watercourses Convention,[18] the UNECE Guidelines on Sustainable Flood Prevention, the 1972 ILA New York Flood Control Rules and in the ILA 2004 Berlin Rules on Water Resources.[19] Such cooperation is also provided in several bilateral and regional agreements.[20]

Finally, the environmental dimension of the policies and action plans regarding floods is put forward in a number of legal texts, such as the 1999 Convention on the Protection of the Rhine and in the 2004 Action Programme for Sustainable Flood Protection in the Danube River Basin. It is also referred to, in a comprehensive manner, in the ECE Model Provisions.[21] According to them, any policy, strategy or action plan referring to floods should include measures for the protection and restoration of the natural status of a watercourse as wells as for ecosystems related to it. Action should also be undertaken to maintain and encourage the water retention capacity of the soil so that erosion might be prevented, which mainly requires adopting a policy against deforestation.

23.2 Transboundary Waters and Civil Liability in the Case of Industrial Accidents

The question of civil liability for damage caused to transboundary waters by an industrial accident in the course of a hazardous activity can be dealt with in the context of either an

15 *See* Model Provision 5.
16 In particular Arts. 2 and 3.
17 Art. 7.
18 Art. 9.
19 Art. 34(4).
20 Such as the 1999 Agreement between Kazakhstan, Kyrgyzstan, Tajikistan and Uzbekistan on cooperation on hydrometeorology, the 2002 Framework Agreement on the Sava River Basin and the 1998 Convention between Portugal and Spain.
21 Provision 4 and its Commentary.

international agreement concerning international environmental liability in general[22] or one which is specific to the particular type of damage caused by pollution transported through transboundary waters. When, in the wake of the Baia Mare accident in Romania in 2002,[23] the matter of how to deal with the question of civil liability in such cases came up in the ECE, it was decided that the second option was best and that, therefore, a legal instrument (Protocol) should be agreed upon, which would be specific to the abovementioned situation. In consequence of this decision, the 'Protocol on Civil Liability and Compensation for Damage Caused by the Transboundary Effects of Industrial Accidents on Transboundary Waters' was elaborated in the context of an Intergovernmental Working Group set up for this purpose. The Protocol was adopted in Kiev in 2003,[24] and its main features are the following:

a. Liability is channelled to the operator.
b. A strict liability regime is adopted, i.e. no fault is required to be proven for liability to arise once the harmful event occurs. The operator is liable even if it is proven that he has shown due diligence on the matter.
c. The strict liability of the operator is limited to certain amounts (caps) which are specified in Annex II of the Protocol.
d. In addition to strict liability, the Protocol also provides for a fault-based liability regime.[25] No financial limit applies to this type of liability.
e. To secure against an eventual inability to cover compensation claims pursuant to the Protocol, the operator is obliged to be insured[26] for amounts not less than the minimum limits for financial securities specified in of the Protocol.[27]

---

22 Such as the Council of Europe Lugano Convention on Civil Liability for Damage Resulting from Activities Dangerous to the Environment, 21 April 1993, available at: https://rm.coe.int/CoERMPublicCommonSearchServices/DisplayDCTMContent?documentId=090000168007c079, last accessed 12 January 2017.

23 The accident was due to a spill of cyanide-contaminated water from a gold mining installation in Romania. The contaminated water reached the Danube through the Tisza River, destroying the fish produce in Hungary and Serbia. With regard to the responsibility of Romania for the consequences of the accident on the health of individuals, *see* *Tătar v. Romania* App no 67021/01 (ECtHR, 27 January 2009).

24 The Protocol is connected with the ECE 1992 Convention on the Protection and Use of Transboundary Watercourses and International Lakes and on the ECE 1992 Convention on the Transboundary Effects of Industrial Accidents. It was adopted on 21 May 2003 and is not yet in force. It is available at: www.unece.org/fileadmin/DAM/env/civil-liability/documents/protocol_e.pdf, last accessed on 19 March 2018.

25 Art. 5 of the Protocol.

26 *Ibid.*, Art. 11.

27 Annex II, Part two. For a detailed analysis of the regime established by the Kiev Protocol *see* Phani Dascalopoulou-Livada and Alexandros Kolliopoulos, The 2003 Kiev Protocol on Civil Liability and Compensation for Damage Caused by the Transboundary Effects of Industrial Accidents on Transboundary Waters, in Attila Tanzi, Owen McIntyre, Alexandros Kolliopoulos, Alistair Rieu-Clarke, Rémy Kinna (eds), The UNECE Convention on the Protection and Use of Transboundary Watercourses and International Lakes, Brill 2015, pp. 330-344. Also, Phani Dascalopoulou-Livada and Alexandros Kolliopoulos, The Kiev Civil Liability Protocol and the Interaction between Civil and Administrative Liability Regimes, International Community Law Review, Brill/Nijhoff, 19 (2017) pp. 518-550.

Despite its considerable innovations and substantial advantages, the Kiev Protocol did not escape the fate of several other instruments on civil liability arising from transboundary damage, which have not entered into force long after their adoption.[28] However, it is far from certain that this should have necessarily been the case with the Kiev Protocol as well.[29] Indeed, it seems that the main reason for the abstention of EU states from ratifying the Protocol (with the notable exception of Hungary) is to be found in the objections of the European Commission which at the time was preparing the EU Directive on the same matter, which was eventually issued in 2004 (EU Directive 2004/35).[30] Indeed, the Commission's perception appears to have been that there would be inconsistencies and difficulties if the two instruments were to be applied in parallel.[31] However, well-founded studies on the matter[32] confirm that there is no real incompatibility or clash between them. On the contrary, it has been shown that an eventual parallel application of the Kiev Protocol and the EU Directive would give states the possibility to offer more and more effective possibilities for compensation to those who have suffered damage from transboundary water pollution.

---

28 Such as, *e.g.*, the 1993 Lugano Convention on Civil Liability for Damage Resulting from Activities Dangerous to the Environment which has not yet entered into force. On this problem, *see* Noah Sachs, Beyond the Liability Wall: Strengthening tort remedies in international environmental law, 55 UCLA Law Review, 2008, pp. 837-904.

29 At the Kiev Conference the Protocol was signed by 24 states. It was later ratified by Hungary.

30 Directive 2004/35/EC of the European Parliament and of the Council of 21 April 2004 on environmental liability with regard to the prevention and remedying of environmental damage (ELD).

31 Thus, in the 'Commission Staff Working Document, REFIT Evaluation of the Environmental Liability Directive', p. 59, it is stated that "the issues addressed in the Directive continue therefore to require action at EU level because in particular transboundary damage needs to be addressed……. also for other categories of transboundary environmental damage, such as transboundary water damage where the ELD was a relevant justification for the EU and its Member States not to accede to the Kiev Protocol."

32 *See* Marc Pallemaerts, Study on national legislation needed to implement the Protocol on Civil Liability and Compensation for Damage Caused by the Transboundary Effects of Industrial Accidents on Transboundary Waters, Institute for European Environmental Policy (IEEP), undated. Also, Bernard Dubuisson – Christophe Thiebaut, Entre responsabilité civile et mesures de police administrative, in La responsabilité environnementale, transposition de la directive 2004/35 et implications en droit interne, (Anthemis 2009) pp. 137, 150.

24 Conclusions

From a legal perspective, the situation regarding transboundary waters presents a rather optimistic picture at this stage. Indeed, in recent decades, there has been a flurry of normative developments in this field, most prominent and promising among them the entry into force of the two universal conventions adopted in the 1990s, the 1997 Convention on the Law of Non-navigational Uses of International Watercourses and the 1992 Convention on the Protection and Use of Transboundary Watercourses and International Lakes. At the same time, other binding instruments of a bilateral, regional and multilateral character continue to appear at a dynamic pace, averting to a considerable degree, although not completely eliminating, the chances of conflict due to water disputes.

At the same time, a plethora of soft-law instruments, such as those relating to the recognition of a human rights status to the right to water, may pave the way for shorter or longer term advancements of the law.

Furthermore, legal fields which until recently had not attracted particular attention are being explored. Thus, public participation in water issues is a development with a promising forward-looking character while there is a growing awareness of the interconnection between the legal study of water and that on other issues, such as health, culture and armed conflict, which is going to move international water law into the future.

On the other side, however, i.e. as regards the factual situation of transboundary waters, there is no doubt that in the last few decades there has been significant worsening, due to a multitude of factors having a cumulative negative effect on these vital resources. Population increase, climate change and pollution, are the most important among them.

We are therefore confronted with a broad picture dominated by a seemingly hard-to-bridge dichotomy, with legal advances making headway at an unprecedentedly fast pace, and realities on the ground lagging behind, while the possibility for major crises is far from extinct.

Narrowing down the focus, however, there is a fundamental conclusion to draw from the situation as described above, which is that dealing with the many problems related to shared waters from the perspective of each single country sharing the same transboundary watercourse, international lake or, in more general terms, the same watercourse basin, is both unworkable and unsustainable. Said in a positive way, it is far more efficient to address all issues relating to a basin (water, land, ecosystems) in a holistic, coordinated and integrated manner. This will allow an equitable, reasonable and sustainable management and development of water resources, while at the same time leading to the amelioration of the physical condition of transboundary waters. This is of course happening in different degrees in many parts of the world through the operation of international agreements of various types and forms, mainly regional, bilateral, and – most importantly – basin specific. On the basis of these instruments, joint bodies and other forms of institutional mechanisms endowed with wider ranging and at the same time more specifically identified powers, collaborate on an ever-increasing number of issues relating to particular watercourses, finding solutions and averting possible conflicts. Having said that, we are still a far cry from a situation where there would be legal coverage of all or the near-totality of transboundary watercourses in the world. Indeed, although the number of joint bodies and other institutional mechanisms has increased considerably, they still concern less than half of the world's watercourses, while the cases of watercourse agreements which include all the states of a transboundary river basin continue to be the exception rather than the rule.[1]

It is clear therefore that there is no other option than to continue on the path which is going forward, building on the solid legal basis and guidance offered by the two universal conventions, which need to be as widely accepted as possible and as fast as possible. The next step for states is to accelerate the pace of transposing the principles enshrined in these instruments into the bilateral or multilateral agreements or other arrangements they enter into. Finally, the most important element of all is, of course, to achieve the full implementation of the conventional obligations they undertake, so that the river basins and transboundary waters may take advantage of the positive effects envisaged by these instruments, in as many regions of the world as possible. This would be beneficial not only for the quality – and quantity – of waters and, as a result, for the lives of the people dependent on them, but also for the maintenance of international peace and security.

1 World Water Development Report, 2015, Water for a sustainable world, p. 12: "158 of the world's 263 transboundary water basins lack any type of cooperative management framework. Of the 105 water basins with water institutions, approximately two thirds include three or more riparian states (adjacent to rivers and streams); yet, less than 20% of the accompanying agreements are multilateral."

9 789462 369474

Printed by Libri Plureos GmbH in Hamburg,
Germany